UNIVERSITY OF WASHINGTON PUBLICATIONS
IN
LANGUAGE AND LITERATURE

Volume 9

November, 1935

A REFERENCE GUIDE TO THE LITERATURE OF TRAVEL

Including Voyages, Geographical Descriptions, Adventures, Shipwrecks and Expeditions

BY

EDWARD GODFREY COX

VOLUME ONE

THE OLD WORLD

GREENWOOD PRESS, PUBLISHERS
NEW YORK

Originally published in 1935 and reprinted
with the permission of the University of Washington Press

First Greenwood Reprinting 1969

Library of Congress Catalogue Card Number 70-90492

SBN 8371-2161-2

PRINTED IN UNITED STATES OF AMERICA

PREFACE

Old men and travellers lie by authority."—Ray's Proverbs.

When Imlac was about to bubble over with vain eloquence on the high function of a poet, Rasselas interrupted with: "Enough! thou hast convinced me that no man can ever be a poet!" When I read of the exacting minutia demanded of a bibliographer, the lofty pretensions ruling the indexing of even a single book—identifying first editions, first issues, succeeding editions, dates and places of publication, describing imprints, formats, variants, errors and corrections—then I hold with Rasselas and declare: "Enough! I am convinced that no man can ever be a bibliographer!" But what I mean to say is that the present work is no such bibliography. Rather, it is better described by the more modest and therefore the more honest title of "A Reference Guide to the Literature of Travel," as being more truly descriptive of its nature and material.

What I have endeavored to do in these two volumes is to list in chronological order, from the earliest date ascertainable down to and including the year 1800, all the books on foreign travels, voyages, and descriptions printed in Great Britain, together with translations from foreign tongues and Continental renderings of English works—that is to say, so far as they have come to my notice. Many titles must of necessity have escaped my net. In fact new ones have cropped up since this work has gone to press. But I can well believe that what is missing will be found to have little renown. Small fry, such as tracts and pamphlets, were allowed to slip through, save such as turned up with the more substantial catch. Despite my vigilance a sufficient number of these have crept into the company of more legitimate titles as to endanger the integrity of my original purpose and give a tinge of *ana* to the collection. I resisted, however, the temptation to admit the numerous contributions to the Royal Society volumes, as well as the individual voyages printed in Hakluyt and Purchas. Inclusion of the latter would make these volumes altogether too bulky; besides, the indexes to those works are bibliographies in themselves. No consistent attempt has been made to exhaust the list of modern reprints; what is given of these is to be looked upon as an overflow of generosity on my part. The Addenda takes care of first printings of earlier works done in the nineteenth and twentieth centuries. The notes, which are of a varied assortment, are, like the titles, the cullings from many sources, and are duly accredited to their rightful owners. The geographical sections under which works are listed are not and cannot be sharply dividing. It will be evident sometimes that a given title could just as well have been placed elsewhere. The dates standing in the outermost margin are presumably those of the first printings unless otherwise stated in the text.

Accuracy and finality are the eternal worries of a bibliographer. But when that "Corrector of Public Morals" and impeccable corrector of proofs, Alexander Cruden, could feel misgivings over the perfection of his Concordance to the Bible, what right has a mere bibliographer to hope for unqualified acquittal? "Though it be called on the title page *A Complete Concordance,* poor sinful man can do nothing absolutely perfect and complete," is his acknowledgment of frailty. And with head bowed still lower I murmur, *Mé Quoque.*

Finally, let it be noted that even if this compilation were "perfect and complete," it represents but a small portion of the record of man's restlessness, for the same lure of gold, the same drive for power, the same urge of travel, adventure, and to see the sights drove Frenchmen and Germans, Spaniards and Italians, Scandinavians and Slavs, Turk, Christian, heathen, Jew, to say goodby to family and fireside and sail out into the unknown towards the clouded glories of the West and tramp the dust of caravan routes to the ancient East. And a reading of the narratives themselves leaves one puzzled over which is more a matter of wonder—man's indomitable spirit, his power to endure and his willingness to repeat, or his capacity for cruelty, his insatiate greed, and his readiness to deny the claims of justice, pity, and peace. However that may be, this work is commended to all fireside travellers.

EDWARD GODFREY COX
University of Washington

Seattle, Washington
November 4, 1935

Contents of Volume One

A REFERENCE GUIDE TO THE
LITERATURE OF TRAVEL

I

Collections

1553 EDEN, RICHARD. A Treatyse of the Newe India, with other New
Founde Landes and Ilandes, as well eastwarde as westwarde, as they
are knowen and found in these oure Dayes, after the Descripcion of
Sebastian Munster in his Boke of vniuersall Cosmographie: where the
diligent Reader may see the good Successe and Rewarde of noble and
honeste Enterpryses, by the which not only worldly Ryches are ob-
tayned, but also God is glorified, & the Christian Fayth enlarged.
Translated out of Latin into Englishe. By Richard Eden . . . Thus end-
eth the Fyfth Boke of Sebastian Munster, of the Landes of Asia the
Greater, and of the newe founde Landes, and Ilandes. Woodcut.
London.

> Eden was reprinted by Edward Arber in his *The First Three English Books
> on America*, Birmingham, 1885. The original was the *Cosmographia Universalis* of
> Sebastian Munster published in Basel, 1544.
> Munster occupies a peculiar position as a cartographer; he far surpasses most
> of the map-drawers of his time in his exertions to get access to the latest informa-
> tion regarding the history, ethnology, and geography of the countries he describes.
> His bulky cosmography will therefore always remain an important source for the
> history of the civilization of the period in which he lived.—Nordenskiöld, quoted
> by Maggs, No. 519. The original of this book (Eden's) was a popular universal
> cosmography of small modern value or interest, and merely served to introduce
> Eden's name to the British public.—Waldman. Though this work is more of a
> cosmography than a collection of travels, it is listed here because it contains an
> account of voyages from Columbus to Magellan.

1555 EDEN, RICHARD. The Decades of the Newe Worlde or West India,
Conteyning the Nauigation and Conquestes of the Spanyeardes, with
the particular Description of the moste ryche and large landes and
Ilandes lately founde in the west Ocean perteyning to the Inheritance
of the Kinges of Spayne. In the which the diligent Reader may not
only consider what Commoditie may hereby chaunce to the hole Christian World in Tyme to come, but also learne many Secreates touchynge
the Lande, the Sea, and the Starres, very necessarie to be knowne to
al such as shal attempte any Nauigations, or otherwise haue delite to
beholde the strange and wonderfull woorkes of God and Nature.
Wrytten in the Latine Tounge by Peter Martyr of Angleria, and
translated into Englysshe by Rycharde Eden. 4to. London.

> Republished by Willes, with additions, London, 1577. See below. Reprinted
> by Arber in his *The First Three English Books on America*, 1885. Latin
> original of Martyr's *Decades* (first complete edition), Alcala de Henares, 1530.
> See below. For a translation by Lok see below under 1612.
> This is the earliest Collection of Voyages in the English language—and the
> third English book relating to America. It is of great historical importance. Be-
> sides the first Three Decades of Peter Martyr, it contains a translation of that
> author's writings on the recently discovered islands "De nuper sub D. Carolo re-
> pertis Insulis," first printed in 1521. It also contains the Bull of Pope Alexander
> VI, in Latin and English, by which the world was divided between Spain and

Portugal, as well as translations of the most important parts of the works of Oviedo, Maximilian of Transylvania, Vespuccius, Gomara, and others, pertaining to the maritime discovery of the New World.—Quoted by Maggs, No. 585. Pietro Martire Anguiera, better known by his Latinized name of Petrus Martyr, was the first historian of America. He is believed to have been the first writer to notice in his works the discovery of America by Columbus, as he is the first to publish a treatise descriptive of the natives of the new world. He was the friend and contemporary of Columbus, Vasco da Gama, Cortes, Magellan, Cabot, and Vespuccius.—Robinson, No. 26. From personal contact with these discoverers as well as from his official position as a member of the Council for the Indies, which afforded him free inspection of documents of undoubted authenticity, he was enabled to gain at first hand much valuable information regarding the discoveries of the early navigators.—Maggs, No. 465. Eden's *Decades* is a direct forerunner of Hakluyt's *Voyages* and did much to stimulate English maritime effort.—Waldman.

1530 MARTYR, PETER. De Orbe Novo Petri Martyris ab Angleria Mediolanensis Protonotarii Cesaris Senatoris Decades. Alcala de Henares.

> This is the first complete edition of the eight Decades. Numerous subsequent editions appeared in Europe. The second complete edition in Latin was that published by Hakluyt in Paris, 1587.

1577 DEE, JOHN. The Great Volume of Famous and Rich Discoveries, wherein also is the History of King Salomon every three years; his Ophirian Voyage; the Originals of Presbyter Joannes; and of the first great Cham and his Successors for many years following; the description of divers Wonderful Isles in the Northern Scythian, Tartarian and other Northern Seas, and near under the North Pole, by Record written 1200 years since with divers other rarities. London.

> Reprinted London, 1580.
> Dee was a famous character in Elizabethan days. He was versed in mathematics but was especially associated with astrology and the search for the philosopher's stone. He was a much travelled man, even going as far as St. Helena. On one occasion he made a trip to Germany to consult physicians regarding the Queen's health. At Elizabeth's request he wrote a description of the newly discovered portions of the world.

EDEN, RICHARD. The History of Travayle in the West and East Indies, and other Countreys Lying either way, towardes the fruitfull and ryche Moluccaes. As Moscouia, Persia, Arabia, Syria, Aegypte, Ethiopia, Guinea, China in Cathayo, and Giapan. With a Discourse of the Northwest Passage. Gathered in parte, and done into Englyshe by Richarde Eden. Newly set in order, augmented and finished by Richard Willes. Woodcuts. 4to. London.

> This work is not exactly a reprint of the edition of 1555, though, like that, the larger portion is taken up with Peter Martyr's *Decades of the Newe Worlde* and Oviedo's *History of the West Indies*. In this edition are included for the first time: Fourth Decade of Peter Martyr; Instructions by Willes for Frobisher, then starting on his voyage for the discovery of the Northwest Passage; Reports on China and Japan (chiefly drawn from the Jesuit Letters); Accounts of Persia (chiefly from information supplied by English merchants in 1561-68); Varthema's Navigation and Voyages, translated by Eden in 1576; A brief rehearsal of the contents of Peter Martyr's Decades 1-3; An abridgement by Willes of the Decades 5, 6, 7 and 8; Otherwise the contents of the work agree with those of the

1555 edition, save that some extracts from Corsali, Cadamasto, and Biringuccio were omitted as well as a translation of Vespucci's Latin letter.—Robinson, No. 41.

1885 EDEN, RICHARD. The First Three English Books on America, . . . being chiefly Translations, Compilations, etc., by Richard Eden, from the Writings of, Maps, etc., of Pietro Martire, Sebastian Munster, and Sebastian Cabbot. Edited by Edward Arber. 4to. Birmingham.

1580 DEE, JOHN. Navigationis ad Cathayam . . . delineatio hydrographica. London.

This may be the 2nd edition of Dee's work listed under 1577 above.

1582 HAKLUYT, RICHARD. Divers Voyages touching the Discouerie of America, and the Ilands adiacent vnto the same, made first of all by our Englishmen, and afterward by the Frenchmen and Britons: And certaine Notes of Aduertisements for Obseruations, necessarie for such as shall heereafter make the like Attempt. With two mappes annexed heereunto for the plainer vnderstanding of the whole Matter. 16mo. London.

This work was reprinted by the Hakluyt Society, London, 1850. See below.
This small collection was Hakluyt's first book. In it appears for the first time the Patent granted by Henry VII to John Cabot and his sons, and the Verrazano voyage, thereby becoming the first book in English to refer to any part of what is now the United States. It is the rarest of all Hakluyt items.—Waldman. All the items of the *Divers Voyages*, except the last—the list of American commodities—were reprinted separately in the final Voyages. This last item was incorporated in the *Discourse on the Western Planting*, 1584.—Parks.

1850 HAKLUYT, RICHARD. Divers Voyages touching the Discovery of America, And the Islands adjacent, collected and published by Richard Hakluyt, Prebendary of Bristol, in the year 1582. Edited with Notes and an Introduction by John Winter Jones, Principal Librarian of the British Museum. 2 maps and 1 illus. Hak. Soc., ser. I, vol. 7. London.

1589 HAKLUYT, RICHARD. The Principall Navigations, Voiages and Discoveries of the English Nation, made by Sea or ouer Land, to the most remote and farthest distant Quarters of the earth at any time within the compasse of these 1500 yeeres: Deuided into three seuerall parts . . . The first . . . vnto Iudea, Syria, Arabia . . . India . . . Africa . . . Promontorie of Buona Esperanza. The second . . . towards the North and Northeast by Sea . . . The Third and last . . . The Vaste and New World of America . . . Whereunto is added the last most renowned English Nauigation round about the whole Globe of the Earth. By Richard Hakluyt, Master of Artes . . . Fol. London.

2nd edit. revised and enlarged by Hakluyt, 3 vols., London, 1598-1600. See the next item.
For an analysis of the contents of this volume see Parks. Six leaves of Drake's Voyage round the World were suppressed and do not appear in all copies, as is also true of Sir Jerome Bowes' Relation of Russia. Concerning the former Hakluyt says in his preface that he had taken more than ordinary pains, and he was

therefore grieved to be obliged to omit it because someone else was preparing the narrative for publication. He must, however, have put it into type for some copies. Concerning the first issue of the latter item, it is to be noted that the narrative is written in the first person as if by Bowes himself, while in the second issue it is given entirely in the third person as if written by a member .of his suite.—Quaritch. It has been pointed out by Parks how far Ramusio's Collection (published in the 1550's) served as a model and the extent that Hakluyt went beyond this work, particularly in the matter of getting first hand narratives and in including documents of various kinds. Beazley considers this edition of 1589 to be constantly superior in clearness of arrangement and judgment of selection to any later stage of this memorable work.

1598-1600 HAKLUYT, RICHARD. The Principal Navigations, Voyages, Traffiques and Discoveries of the English Nation, made by Sea or ouerland to the Remote and Farthest Distant Quarters of the Earth at any time within the compasse of these 1600 yeres; Diuided into three seueral volumes . . . The first Volume containeth the worthy Discoueries . . . of the English towards the North and Northeast by Sea . . . the second Volume comprehendeth the principall Nauigations . . . to the South and Southeast parts of the World . . . the Third and last Volume of the Voyages . . . TO ALL PARTS OF THE NEW-FOUND WORLD OF AMERICA . . . together with the two renowned and prosperous voyages of Sir Francis Drake and M. Thomas Candish round about the Circumference of the whole earth . . . By Richard Hakluyt, Preacher, and sometime student of Christ-Church in Oxford. 3 vols. Fol. London.

Vol. 1 appeared in 1598, vol. 2 in 1599, and vol. 3 in 1600. A number of reprints and selections have been issued in the 19th and 20th centuries: In 5 vols., 4to, London, 1809-1812; selected portions edited by Goldsmid, 4 vols., 8vo, Edinburgh, 1884-86; again, with a 5th vol. added, Edinburgh, 1890; 12 vols., Glasgow, 1903-05; in Everyman's Library, 8 vols., London, 1907; 1 vol., edited with an Introduction by Masefield, London, 1927. For some of these see below.
In the ten years between 1588 and 1598 Hakluyt tapped every source available to him—witness the story of his two-hundred-mile ride to seek out the only living survivor of a Labrador expedition of 1536; he studied his material as no man had done before him, and achieved a masterpiece which, despite many criticisms leveled at various parts, puts the name of Richard Hakluyt beyond those of all other men who had written of voyages and discoveries.—Waldman. Froude described it as "the prose epic of the modern English nation." How much labor entered into the collecting of his material is confessed in his Dedication to the Lord High Admiral: "For the bringing of which into this homely and rough-hewen shape which here thou seest; what restless nights, what painefull dayes, what heat, what cold I have endured; how many long and chargeable journeys I have travailed; how many famous libraries have I searched into; what varietie of ancient and modern writers I have perused; what a number of old records, patents, privileges, letters, etc., I have redeemed from obscuritie and perishing; into how many manifold acquaintance I have entered, what expences I have not spared; and yet what faire opportunities of private gaine, preferment, and ease I have neglected."—At the time of the publication of this work, the Earl of Essex had been disgraced by Queen Elizabeth and by desire of the Queen and of his friends, the record of Essex's expedition to Cadiz was suppressed. Hakluyt, however, reprinted a number of copies a short time later for those of his friends who wished to include it.—Maggs, No. 549. Most of the original copies of the book are found with these leaves cut out. When the second issue was published in 1599, a new title was inserted in vol. 1. without mention of the Cadiz voyage. As is well known, Hakluyt's work was completed by Purchas. See below under 1613 and 1625.

1809-1812 HAKLUYT, RICHARD. The Principal Voyages, etc. Reprinted from the edition of 1598, with Additions, selected and edited by G. Woodfall. 5 vols. 4to. London.

A scarce and valuable set.

1903-05 HAKLUYT, RICHARD. The Principal Navigations, Voyages, Traffiques, and Discoveries of the English Nation, Made by Sea or Overland to the remote and farthest Quarters of the Earth at any Time within the Compasse of these 1600 yeeres. . . . With an Essay on the English Voyages of the Sixteenth Century, by Walter Raleigh, Professor of the English Language in the University of Oxford. Index by Madame Marie Michon and Miss Elizabeth Carmont. 12 vols. Hak. Soc., extra ser., 1-12. Numerous maps and plates. Glasgow.

This reprint, also known as the MacLehose edition, is the best edition of modern times.

1601 GALVANO, ANTONIO. The Discoveries of the World from their first Original vnto the Yeere of our Lord 1555. Briefly written in the Portugall tongue by Antonio Galvano, Gouernour of Ternate and chiefe Island of the Malucas: Corrected, quoted, and now published in English by Richard Hakluyt, sometime student of Christchurch in Oxford. 16mo. London.

Reprinted by Hakluyt Society, London, 1862. Portuguese original, Lisbon, 1563. See below. In Osborne II, 352-402.

According to Parks this work was translated by an unknown hand from the Portuguese. Hakluyt never saw the original text. Galvano was Governor of Ternate in the Moluccas. Hakluyt, in his dedication to Sir Robert Cecil (dated Oct. 29, 1601), gives high praise to Galvano both for his intrinsic worth and for his "restoring and settling the decayed state of the Isles of Moluccas." He also states that the above work had been translated by some unknown person many years back and that he had had it by him for twelve years, but he had been unable to obtain the original of it. The book gives a good summary of the geographical explorations of the Portuguese.

1563 GALVANO, ANTONIO. Tratado que compos o nobre notauel capitano Antonio Galvano, dos diversos e desuayrados caminhos por onde nos tempos passados a pimenta e especaria veto da India . . . 8vo. Lisbon.

1862 GALVANO, ANTONIO. The Discoveries of the World From their first Original unto the Year of our Lord 1555. By Antonio Galvano, Governor of Ternate. (Edited by F. de Sousa Tavares.) Corrected, quoted, and published by Richard Hakluyt, 1601. Now reprinted, with the original Portuguese text (1563), and edited by Admiral Charles Ramsay Drinkwater Bethune, C.B. Hak. Soc., ser. I, vol. 30. London.

1612 MARTYR, PETER. De Nouo Orbe, or the Historie of the west Indies, Contayning the actes and aduentures of the Spanyeardes, which haue conquered and peopled those Countries, inriched with varietie of pleasant relation of the Manners, Ceremonies, Lawes, Gouernments, and Warres of the Indians. Comprised in eight Decades Written by Peter Martyr a Millanoise of Angleria, Cheife Secretary to the Emperour Charles the fifth, . . . whereof three haue beene formerly translated into English by R. Eden, whereunto the other fiue, are newly added by the Industrie, and painefull Trauaile of M. Lok. Gent.   4to.   London.

Another edition of the 1612 edition was issued identical with it except that the Dedication was suppressed and a new title supplied.—Quaritch. A 2nd edit. was published in London, 1628. Parks gives a tentative date of 1625 to another edition. It was reprinted in vol. V of the 1809 edition of Hakluyt's *Principal Navigations;* and a retranslation published by F. A. McNutt, 2 vols., 1912.
This is the first complete edition of Peter Martyr in English. These Decades were the first, and, for many years, the only history of the New World. Hence its important position in American literature; this being in many respects the sole source of information concerning the discovery and conquest of America.—Robinson, No. 22. It was translated at the suggestion of Hakluyt from his Paris edition. Michael Lok or Lock travelled through almost all the lands of Christendom. He was governor of the Cathay Company and consul for the Levant Company at Aleppo. He had been treasurer of the Frobisher undertaking, "from which he reaped enormous debts."—Parks. See Eden under 1555 above.

1613   PURCHAS, SAMUEL. Purchas His Pilgrimage, or Relations of the World and the Religions observed in all Ages and Places discovered, from the Creation unto this Present. . . . a Theologicall and Geographicall Historie of Asia, Africa and America, with the Ilands adiacent; declaring the Ancient Religions before the Floud, the Heathenish, Jewish, and Saracenicall in all Ages since.   Fol.   London.

2nd edit., fol., much enlarged with Additions, London, 1614; 3rd edit., much enlarged, fol., London, 1617; 4th edit., London, 1626.
This work is not to be confused with the *Pilgrimes* of 1625. As Parks points out, it is a sort of religious geography. It draws largely upon Ramusio and Hakluyt, and the historians and political geographers of all ages. It is included here that it may be distinguished from the later Collection of Voyages. For Purchas's relations with Hakluyt see Parks.

1625   PURCHAS, SAMUEL. Purchas His Pilgrimes. In Five Bookes. The first, Contayning the Voyages and Peregrinations made by Ancient Kings, Patriarkes, Apostles, Philosophers, and others. . . . The second, A Description of all the Circum-Nauigations of the Globe. The Third, Nauigations and Voyages of English-men, alongst the Coasts of Africa, . . . The fourth, English Voyages beyond the East Indies, to the Ilands of Iapan, China, Cauchinchina, the Philippinae with others . . . The fifth, Nauigations, Voyages, Traffiques, Discoueries of the English Nation in the Easterne parts of the World . . . 4 vols.   Fol.   London.

No reprint of this work until 1905-07, when the Hakluyt Society edition appeared published by MacLehose at Glasgow. See below.
This great geographical collection (known also as *Hakluytus Posthumus,* from the engraved title in vol. I) is a continuation and enlargement of Hakluyt's *Principall Navigations.* At the death of Hakluyt there was left a large collection of voyages in manuscript which came into the hands of Purchas (as a sort of legacy), who added to them many more voyages and travels of Dutch, Spanish, and Portuguese explorers as well as of English travellers. He also incorporated many translations from early books of travel which were becoming scarce even in his day.—Quaritch. Purchas followed the general plan of Hakluyt, but he frequently put the accounts into his own words, instead of allowing the narrator to speak for himself, thereby incurring much adverse criticism from later editors of collections. The main divisions of the work fall into two parts—the first cover-

ing the world known to Ptolemy, the second coming down to his own day. Thus he brought Hakluyt up to date. Purchas died in 1628, at the age of 51, much distressed in circumstances in consequence of the losses sustained by him in the publication of this work, for which he consulted, he stated, "above thirteen hundred authors of one or another kind." On Purchas, whose name by the way seems to have been pronounced as if spelled Purkas, see Sir William Foster, "Purchas and his Pilgrimes," in *Geographical Journal*, vol. 68, pp. 193-200.

1905-07 PURCHAS, SAMUEL. Hakluytus Posthumus or Purchas His Pilgrimes. Contayning a History of the World in Sea Voyages and Lande Travells by Englishmen and others. By Samuel Purchas, B. D. Maps and illus. With an Index by Madame Marie Michon. 20 vols. Hak. Soc., extra ser., vols. 14-33. Glasgow.

> This is also known as the MacLehose edition. It is an exact reprint of the 1625 edition with the original maps and plates.

1653 DRAKE, SIR FRANCIS. Sir Francis Drake Revived. Who is or may be a Pattern to stirre up all Heroicke and active Spirits of these Times to benefit their Countrey and eternize their Names by like Noble Attempts. Being a Summary and true Relation of foure severall Voyages made by the said Sir Francis Drake to the West-Indies, viz., His dangerous adventuring for Gold and Silver with the gaining thereof . . . His Encompassing the World. His Voyage made with Christopher Varleill, Martin Frobusher, Francis Knollis and others . . . His last Voyage (in which he dyed) being accompanied with Sir John Hawkins, Sir Thomas Baskerfield, with others . . . Collected out of the Notes of the said Sir Francis Drake . . . With Notes of divers other Gentlemen (who went in the said Voyages) carefully compared together. Portrait of Sir Francis Drake. 4to. London.

> This is the first collected and the most complete edition of Drake's voyages. It comprises, with separate title pages, *Sir Francis Drake Revived* (the voyage of 1572-73) ; *The World Encompassed* (the voyage of 1577-1580) ; *A Summarie and True Discourse of his West Indian Voyage* (1585-86) ; and *A Full Relation of Another Voyage into the West Indies* (the voyage of 1595-96, during which he died). These voyages are listed elsewhere individually under their proper headings with more detail.

1674 EVELYN, JOHN. Navigation and Commerce, Their Original and Progress. Containing A succinct Account of Traffick in General ; its Benefits and Improvements : Of Discoveries, Wars and Conflicts at Sea, from the Original of Navigation to this Day ; with Special Regard to the English Nation ; Their several Voyages and Expeditions, to the Beginning of our late Differences with Holland ; In which His Majesties Title to the Dominion of the Sea is asserted, against the Novel, and later Pretenders. . . . 8vo. London.

> This book was suppressed at the demand of the Dutch Ambassador, as it contained malicious statements concerning Holland. Evelyn, in his *Diary* under 19 Aug., 1674, writes: "His Majesty told me how exceedingly the Dutch were displeased at my treatise of the 'History of Commerce'; that the Holland Ambassador had complained to him, etc., and desired that the book be called in; whilst, on the other side, he assured me that he was exceedingly pleased with

what I had done, etc. The noise of this book's suppression made it presently to be bought up. It was no other than the preface prepared to be fixed to my History of the Whole War; which I now pursued no further."—From Robinson, No. 19. Evelyn gives an interesting account of the discovery of America by Columbus, and of subsequent voyages by Vesputius, John Cabot, etc., and treats also of the exploits of Drake, Hawkins, Cavendish, Frobisher, Hudson, Raleigh, etc.—From Maggs, No. 594.

1693 LAS CASAS, BARTHOLOMEW DE. Account of the first Voyages and Discoveries in America. London.

> So cited by Pinkerton XVII. See Las Casas under date 1583, WEST INDIES.

RAY, JOHN. A Collection of Curious Travels and Voyages, in Two Tomes. The First containing Dr. Leonhart Rauwolff's Itinerary into the Eastern Countries, as Syria, Palestine, Armenia, Mesopotamia, Assyria, Chaldea, etc., translated by Nicholas Staphorst; the Second taking in many parts of Greece, Asia Minor, Egypt, Ethiopia, the Red Sea, Arabia, etc., from the Observations of Mr. Belon, Mr. Vernon, Dr. Spon, Dr. Smith, Dr. Huntingdon, Mr. Greaves, Alpinus, Vestingius, Thevenot's Collections and others: to which are added Three Catalogues of such Trees, Scrubs, and Herbs, as grow in the Levant, by John Ray. 2 vols. 8vo. London.

> Another edition, 8vo, London, 1705; again in 2 vols., 8vo, London, 1738.
> This volume was printed at the request of Sir Hans Sloane. Its importance lies chiefly in Ray's catalogue of eastern plants "Stirpium Orientalium Rariorum Catalogi III." See Ray under 1673, WEST EUROPE.

1694 ROBINSON, TANCRED. An Account of the Several Late Voyages and Discoveries to the South and North. Towards the Streights of Magellan, the South Seas, the vast Tracts of Land beyond Hollandia Nova, . . . also toward Nova Zembla, Greenland or Spitsberg, Groynland or Engrondland, . . . By Sir John Narborough, Captain Jasmen Tasman, Captain John Wood, and Frederick Marten of Hamburgh. To which are Annexed, a Large Introduction and Supplements, giving an Account of other Navigations to those Regions of the Globe. 18 copperplates (some folding) of natural history, etc., and large folding map of the Arctics. 8vo. London.

> 2nd edit., 2 vols. in 1, 8vo, London, 1711. See below.
> This collection, which sometimes goes under the name of Narborough, was dedicated to Samuel Pepys. According to Churchill *(Introduction)*, it had generally a good reputation and seemed very well to deserve it. Narborough's charts were used by Bulkeley and Cummins in their remarkable navigation from the coast of Chile through the Straits of Magellan to the east coast of South America. See Narborough and Bulkeley under dates 1694 and 1743 respectively, SOUTH AMERICA. The work contains a full description of the fauna and flora as well as of the whaling industry of the Arctic.

1711 NARBROUGH, SIR JOHN. An Account of several late Voyages and Discoveries: I. Sir John Narbrough's Voyage to the South-Sea, by

Command of King Charles the Second. . . . II. Capt. J. Tasman's Discoveries on the Coast of the South Terra Incognita (Australia). III. Capt. J. Wood's Attempt to Discover a North East Passage to China. IV. Frederick Marten's Observations made in Greenland, and other Northern Countries. To which are Added, . . . Supplement, containing short Abstracts of other Voyages into those Parts . . . 3 folding maps and 18 plates. 2 vols. in 1. 8vo. London.

1698 ACUNHA (and others). For a collection of voyages in South America see this date under SOUTH AMERICA.

1699 HACKE, WILLIAM (Captain). A Collection of Original Voyages; containing: I. Capt. Cowley's Voyage round the Globe. II. Capt. Sharp's Journey over the Isthmus of Darien and Expedition into the South Seas, written by himself. III. Capt. Wood's Voyage through the Streights of Magellan. IV. Mr. Roberts' Adventures among the Corsairs of the Levant; his Account of their way of Living; Description of the Archipelago Islands, Taking of Scio, . . . with several maps and Draughts. 8vo. London.

> Cowley's voyage is the same as that printed in Dampier, Wood's is that given in Robinson, Sharp's was written by himself, and the last piece is not regarded very highly. The collection can therefore lay little claim to originality or importance.

1703 COMMELIN, ISAAK. A Collection of Voyages undertaken by the Dutch East India Company, for the Improvement of Trade and Navigation, containing an Account of several Attempts to find out the North East Passage, and their Discoveries in the East Indies and South Seas. Together with an Historical Introduction, giving an Account of the Rise, Establishment and Progress of that Great Body. Maps. 8vo.. London.

> This collection was translated from the Dutch into French by Renneville and thence into English. It includes Pontanus'."Dissertation on a North-West Passage," a short account of Hudson's first attempt to find the North West Passage, and an "Account of the Five Rotterdam Ships which sailed June 27, 1598, to the Streight of Magellan," and accounts of various voyages to the East Indies, notably to Java and Sumatra.—Maggs, No. 479. Little can be said in behalf of this work, being no more than what is to be seen in several other collections.—Churchill, *Introduction*. It is sometimes found listed under the name of Renneville. Dutch original, Amsterdam, 1646. See below.

> 1646 COMMELIN, ISAAK. Begin ende Voortgangh van de Vereenighde Nederlandtsche Geoctroyeerde Oost-Indische Compagnie. Vervatend de voornaemste Reysen, by de Inwoonderen der selver Provintien derwaerts gedaen. Alles nevens de Beschryvingen der Rycken, Eylanden, Havenen, Revieren, Stroomen, Reeden, Winden, Diepten en Ondiepten; mitsgaders Religien, Manieren, Aerdt, Politie, en Regeeringe der Volkeren; oock mede haerder speceryen, Droogen, Geld en andere Koopmanschappen met vele Discoursen verrijckt: Nevens eenige Kopere Platen verciert, Nut en dienstigh alle curieuse, en andere Zeevarende Liebhebbers. Met drie besondere Tafels ofte Registers in twee Deelen verdeelt: Vaer van 't eerste begrijpt Veethien Voyagien den meeren-deelen voor desen noyt in 't licht geweest. 2 Deelen in 21 pts. Obl. 4to. Amsterdam.

1704 CHURCHILL, AWNSHAM, and JOHN. A Collection of Voyages and Travels some now first Printed from Original Manuscripts, others Translated out of Foreign Languages, and now first Publish'd in English. To which are added some few that have formerly appear'd in English, but do now for their Excellency and Scarceness deserve to be Re-printed. Including Nieuhoff, Smith, La Peyrere, Thomas James, Backhoff, Columbus, Del Techo, Ten Rhyne, Pelham, Gemelli Careri, etc. With a general Preface; giving an Account of the Progress of Navigation, from its first beginning to the Perfection it is now in, . . . Numerous maps and illus. 4 vols. Fol. London.

    Reprinted 6 vols., fol., London, 1732 (the edition always cited in this bibliography), with two more added in 1745, known as the Oxford Collection or after the name of its editor Osborne (so cited in this bibliography). The six volumes republished, London, 1744-46; again the whole in 8 vols., London, 1752. According to Arber the Preface is by John Locke. This is a very valuable collection, both for its range and for the fact that it gives the original accounts. It well lives up to the claims made for it by its editors.

1705 HARRIS, JOHN. Navigantium atque Itinerantium Bibliotheca: A Complete Collection of Voyages and Travels, consisting of above 400 of the most authentick Writers. Frontispieces, numerous plates, and folding maps. 2 vols. Fol. London.

    Revised and enlarged editions in 1744-48, 2 vols., fol., London (the one always cited in this bibliography); again 2 vols., fol., London, 1764.

    This great collection appears to have been got up in competition with Churchill's, but it differs from that work in being a history of all the known voyages and travels, whereas Churchill's is a collection of particular relations.— Maggs, No. 442. The first edition is valuable for the original impressions of the fine series of maps by Herman Moll, including a very good one of America, a current chart of the Channel from observations by Edmund Halley, and a map of the West Indies on Mercator's projection.—Sotheran. Among the maps there is a new one of the world according to Mercator's projection, with improvements by John Seller and Charles Price, showing the northern coast line and part of the west and south coasts of Australia, together with parts of Van Dieman's Land and New Zealand. In the second volume is given a "Retrospective View" of his whole collection in which its particular advantages are explained and an account of the uses its contents could be put to. Harris "edits" these voyages by pruning, rearranging, "digesting" in his own words with quotations interspersed taken from the originals. He adds some valuable and useful historical accounts of the growth of trade, habits of commerce, growth of Companies with exclusive rights, etc. As is usual with editors of collections, he has little good to say of his rivals.

    1764 HARRIS, JOHN. A Complete Collection of Voyages and Travels. Consisting of above 600 of the most authentic Writers, beginning with Hakluyt, Purchas, Ramusio, Thevenot, De Brye, Herrera, Oviedo, and the voyages under the Direction of the East-India Company in Holland. With others, whether published in English, Latin, French, Dutch, . . . Containing whatever has been observed in Europe, Asia, Africa, and America in respect to the Situation, Soil, Produce, Manners of the Inhabitants, their Arts, Buildings, . . . With an Introduction comprehending the Rise and Progress of the Art of Navigation. Revised with large additions and Continuations, including particular Accounts of the Manufactures and Commerce. 2 vols. Fol. London.

1708 MISCELLANEA CURIOSA. A Collection of Some of the Principal Phaenomena in Nature . . . being Discourses (eleven by Halley, by Collins, Craig, Gregory, De Moivre, Wallis, and many others) read to the Royal Society. 2nd edit. 19 folding plates. 3 vols. 8vo. London.

> 3rd edit., 3 vols., 8vo, London, 1726.
> This is a small collection of exceedingly miscellaneous tracts, vol. III of which is made up of a collection of "Curious Travels, Voyages," etc. It includes John Clayton's (the botanist) Account of Virginia, and Dr. Wallace's Journal kept on his voyage from Scotland to New Caledonia in Darien, with an Account of that Country.

A New Collection of Voyages and Travels, with historical Accounts of Discoveries and Conquests in all Parts of the World, for the Month of December, 1708. Containing the Discovery and Conquest of the Spice Islands. 4to. London.

> See under 1709 below for a Continuation.

PERIER, M. DU. A General History of all Voyages and Travels throughout the Old and New World. Copperplates. 8vo. London.

> Republished with a new title, London, 1711. French original, Paris, 1707.
> This work promises much more than it fulfills. The title page says it is going to give a Catalogue of all authors that have ever described any part of the world and a criticism of their works. But all that has appeared is apparently the above volume, which relates almost wholly to America and the West Indies. In the 1711 edition the name of Bellegarde was substituted for that of Du Perier.

> 1711 (PERIER, M. DU.). A Complete Collection of Voyages made into North and South America, in due order as they happen'd, beginning from Christopher Columbus and Americus Vespucius and descending to this present Time. Accurately describing each Country; its Natural History and product; the Religion, Customs, Manners, Trade, . . . of the Inhabitants, with whatsoever else is curious and remarkable in any kind. . . . The whole extracted from the Works of considerable Travellers. By M. L'Abbe Bellegarde. Translated from the French version printed at Paris. Cuts and 5 plates. 8vo. London.

> 1707 PERIER, M. DU. Histoire universelle des voyages faits par Mer et par Terre dans l'Ancien et dans le Nouveau Monde; pour éclarir la Géographie ancienne et moderne. Par M. Du Perier. 12mo. Paris.

1709 A New Collection of Voyages and Travels; with Historical Accounts of Discoveries and Conquests in all Parts of the World. None of them ever printed before in English. Being now first translated from the Spanish, Italian, French, Dutch, Portuguese, and other Languages. Continued monthly from December. Cuts. London.

> See also next item.

1709-1710   A Collection of Voyages and Travels. 2 vols. 4to. London.

> This was probably collected from the monthly issues cited above, and was perhaps published in opposition to Churchill.

1710   A View of the Universe; or, A New Collection of Voyages and Travels into all Parts of the World. None of them ever before printed in English. Maps. 2 vols. 4to. London.

> This work has been attributed to John Stevens, who may have been its editor. It seems to have some connection with the item listed under 1709 above. Its titles include: Molucca and the Philippines; A New Voyage to Carolina; The Travels of P. de Cieza; The Travels of the Jesuits in Ethiopia digested by Balthazar Tellez; The Travels of the Sieur Mouette in Fez and Morocco; The Travels of Peter Teixeira from India to Italy by Land; A Voyage to Madagascar by Francis Cauche.

1714   The Travels of several Learned Missioners of the Society of Jesus into divers Parts of the Archipelago, India, China, and America. Translated from the French. Index and plates. 8vo. London.

> French original. Paris, 1713.
> For a full account of these Annual Letters forwarded by the Jesuit missionaries to the central Bureau, see below under 1554-1586, ADDENDA II. See also Lockman, 1743 below.

1715   CAMPBELL, JOHN. A Collection of Voyages, originally published by John Harris, much enlarged. 2 vols. London.

> Another edition, 2 vols., London, 1744. See below. For Harris's Collection see under 1705 above.

> **1744** CAMPBELL, JOHN. Voyages and Travels containing all the Circumnavigations from the time of Columbus to Lord Anson; a complete History of the East Indies, Historical Details of the several Attempts made for the Discovery of the North-East and North-West Passage; the commercial History of Chorea and Japan; the Russian Discoveries by Land and by Sea; a distinct Account of America. 2 vols. London.

1729   DAMPIER, WILLIAM (Captain). A Collection of Voyages, containing: I. Captain William Dampier's Voyage round the World. II. The Voyages of Lionel Wafer, giving an Account of his being left on the Isthmus of America, amongst the Indians, and of their treatment of him, with a particular Description of the Country, . . . also the Natural History of those Parts, by a Fellow of the Royal Society; and Davis's Expedition to the Golden Mines. III. A Voyage round the World, containing an Account of Capt. Dampier's Expedition into the South-Seas in the Ship St. George, by W. Funnell, Mate to Capt. Dampier. IV. Capt. Cowley's Voyage round the Globe. V. Capt. Sharp's Journey over the Isthmus of Darien, and Expedition into the South-Seas. VI. Capt. Wood's Voyage through the Streights of Magellan. VII. Mr. Roberts' Adventures and Sufferings amongst the Corsairs of the Levant; his Description of the Archipelago Islands, . . . Numerous maps and plates. 4 vols. 8vo. London.

Another edition chronologically arranged was published in 27 Nos. to form 2 vols., 8vo, London, 1776.
This is generally considered the best edition of Dampier's Voyages, although it contains much that Dampier not only had no hand in writing but also much against which he protested.—Quoted by Maggs, No. 465. Dampier seems to have been at the mercy of his publisher, Knapton, who used the author's saleable volumes as mules for carrying off his unsaleable stock. . . . Vols. I and II of this edition are reprints of the earlier editions, page for page, with the same plates and maps, except that in the first volume the publisher has suppressed Dampier's Dedication to Charles Mountague, President of the Royal Society, to make room for a second title, "A New Voyage round the World," etc. The "Seventh Edition, Corrected," which takes up vol. II, is a reprint of Dampier's third volume (London, 1703) but in a broader page and paged continuously. . . . The plates are the same as those used in the previous editions. The latter half of the third volume consists of a reprint of Wafer's Voyage which is here called the third edition (for Wafer see under date 1699, CENTRAL AMERICA). . . . Vol. IV contains Funnell's Voyage (see under date 1707, CIRCUMNAVIGATIONS) exactly as described in that work, which was the occasion of a protest from Dampier. To this are added reprints of the voyages of Cowley, Sharp, Wood, and Roberts (see Hacke above, 1699). . . In some copies, however, Funnell's Voyage is reprinted with the same plates and maps but in a closer type. With these facts in view it seems better to have Dampier undefiled, and therefore the best editions of Dampier are his three volumes as originally published.—From Puttock & Simpson. See Dampier under 1697, CIRCUMNAVIGATIONS.

1730 Stories of popular Voyages and Travels; with Illustrations. Containing abridged Narratives of Travels in South America. New edition. Maps and 3 plates. 12mo. London.

1735 BARCLAY, PATRICK. The Universal Traveller: or, a Complete Account of the most Remarkable Voyages and Travels of the Eminent Men of our own and other Nations to the present Time. Containing a Relation of the Successes or Misfortunes that attended them in their various Attempts and many entertaining Descriptions of the Curiosities in Art and Nature, the Manners, Customs, . . . observable in the Countries they visited. Collected from the best Authorities, Printed or Manuscript. Fol. London.

Issued also at Dublin, 1735.
This work contains copious accounts of the Spanish colonies in North America, planting of Virginia, New England, etc., the travels of Columbus, Cortez, Pizarro, etc.—Sabin.

1741 COXE, DANIEL. A Collection of Voyages and Travels, in Three Parts. Part I. The Dangerous Voyage of Capt. Thomas James, in attempting to discover a North-west Passage to the South-Sea; with an Account of their passing the Winter in an uninhabited Island, . . . With a map. Part II. The Sieur Pontis's Voyage to America; Also an Account of the taking of Carthagena by the French in 1697. Also an Account of the several Engagements they had with the English in their return to Brest. To which is added, a new and accurate map. Part III. A Description of the English Province of Carolina; by the Spaniards call'd Florida, and by the French La Louisiane, viz., A Description of the People, Animals, Vegetables, Metals, Minerals and other rich and valuable Commodities this Province naturally produces. With a Large and Judicious Preface, proving the Right of the English to that Country; the Manner of the French usurping great Part of it; and the great Danger our Colonies will be exposed to, if not timely prevented; With many useful Remarks regarding our Plantations in general. Collected from authentick Journals, Travels, etc., of the English in that Country; the Originals of which are now in the Possession of Dr. Coxe. . . . By Daniel Coxe, Esq. . . . Map of Carolina. 3 parts. London.

> This is, in fact, a collection of three separate pieces, with a new general title. —Sabin.

1742   The Curious Traveller. Being a choice Collection of remarkable Histories, Voyages, Travels, . . . designed into Familiar Letters and Conversations. Copperplates. 8vo. London.

> This includes Spanish Cruelties in the West Indies; The Commonwealth of Bees; Mock Sea Fight on the River Thames, and such like.

1743   LOCKMAN, JOHN. Travels of the Jesuits, into Various Parts of the World: compiled from their Letters. Now first attempted in English. Intermix'd with an Account of the Manners, Government, Religion, . . . of the several Nations visited by those Fathers. 6 folding maps and plates, including a map of California. 2 vols. 8vo. London.

> 2nd edit. corrected, 2 vols., 8vo. London, 1762. (This edition includes an Account of the Spanish Settlements in America.)
> A work so entertaining and curious, that it has been translated into most of the languages of Europe. In the Letter from Father le Gobien is described "the Manner how our Missionaries discovered very lately that California Joins to the Continent of America; and is not an Island, as our modern Geographers had always imagined."—From Maggs, No. 442. For a full account of these Annual Letters see below under 1580-1661, ADDENDA II, and 1819-1854, ADDENDA II.

1745   OSBORNE, THOMAS. A Collection of Voyages and Travels, consisting of Authentic Writers in our own Tongue, which have not been before collected in English, or have only been abridged in other Collections and continued with others of Note that have published Histories, Voyages, Travels, Journals or Discoveries in other Nations and Languages, relating to any part of Asia, Africa, America, Europe, of the Islands thereof, from the earliest account to the present Time. Many cuts, maps, etc. Compiled from the curious and valuable Library of the late Earl of Oxford. 2 vols. Fol. London.

> This valuable collection is sometimes called the Harleian Collection as well as the Oxford Collection. It forms the Supplement to Churchill's Collection of Voyages. The Introduction is of the usual omnibus type designed to give universalized information. The work includes the Instructions for Travellers gathered from Robert, Earl of Essex, Sir Philip Sidney, and Secretary Davison, and a Geographical Description of Europe.

1745-47 ASTLEY, THOMAS. A New General Collection of Voyages and Travels, consisting of the most Esteemed Relations which have been hitherto published in any Language; comprehending every thing remarkable in its kind, in Europe, Asia, Africa, and America. Numerous maps and plates. 4 vols. 4to. London.

> The contents of these volumes have been translated three times, twice into French and once into Dutch.—Maggs, No. 502. Astley, whose name usually appears with this work, was but the publisher, whereas Thomas Green was the real editor. The work originally appeared in weekly numbers. Its matter was largely appropriated by the Abbé Prévost and was published by him in French as the *Histoire générale des voyages* (18 vols., Paris, 1746-1768; see Prevost below under this date, FOREIGN COLLECTIONS). In his Preface, Astley scores Purchas for his omissions, compressions, and mutilations, and Churchill for publishing what he thought was nothing but an assemblage of about fifty particular authors, whose journies took in but a few parts of the world, and therefore was not entitled to be called a General Collection. He takes Harris to task for giving only the shadows of a general collection and the skeletons of authors instead of the substance. He then states his own virtues to be: That he inserts the Relations from Hakluyt and Purchas omitted by Harris as well as those taken from them; that he restores all the authors "castrated" by Harris as well as those "maimed" by Purchas, so far as he has been able to come at the originals; that he includes some travellers left out of Purchas and some published since his day and neglected by Harris; that he has added the travellers of note which have appeared in English since 1705; that he has enriched the collection with a considerable number of foreign itineraries, which were never published before. His own method (which sins as greatly as that of any of his predecessors) is to substitute for the plan of giving each author entire the plan of separating the Journals and Adventures from the Remarks on the various countries. The former he lets stand by themselves, and the latter he incorporates with the Remarks of other travellers to the same regions. His aim is to make his Collection a System of Modern Geography and History, as well as a body of Voyages and Travels, exhibiting the Present State of all Nations. After all Churchill and Harris are much to be preferred.

1752 OSORIUS, JEROME. The History of the Portuguese, during the reign of Emmanuel: containing all their Discoveries, from the Coast of Africk to the farthest Parts of China; their Battle by Sea and Land, their Sieges, and other memorable Exploits. Including also their Discovery of the Brazils, . . . 2 vols. 8vo. London.

> Latin original, Lisbon, 1571. See below.
> In this important classical history the author has inserted a most valuable account of the discoveries of the Portuguese navigators, such as Cabral, Cortereal, Magellan, Vasco da Gama and Gaspar de Lemos. . . . The work of Osorius belongs to the classics of Portuguese Colonial history in Africa and India. It details the events under the rule of King Manuel (1495-1521). He also occupies himyourself with the history of the Missions.—From Maggs, No. 519. Osorius is called by some the Cicero of Portugal. His library was taken by Lord Essex

at the siege or plunder of Cadiz in.1596, and by him given to the Bodleian Library, then only recently founded.—From Lowndes. He was Councillor in India just after the Conquest.

1571 OSORIO DA FONSECA, JERONIMO. De rebus Emmanuelis regis Lusitaniae gestis libri duodecim. 4to. Lisbon.

1754 A New Universal History of Voyages and Travels collected from the most authentic Authors, everything worthy of Observation in the Four Quarters of the Globe, and Lives and Exploits of the most Eminent Admirals, Captains and Seamen of all Nations. 8 maps and plates. 3 vols. 8vo. London.

1755 BARROW, JOHN. A Collection of Authentic, Useful and Entertaining Voyages and Discoveries . . . by the following celebrated Commanders, viz., Christopher Columbus, Vasco da Gama, Sir Francis Drake, the Sufferings of eight Seamen, George Spitbergen (and many others). Digested in a chronological Series. Folding map of the world, plans of Louisbourg, Cartagena, Havana, and Portobello. 2 vols. 8vo. London.

> Another edition in 3 vols., 8vo, London, 1765. Translated into French, Paris, 1766; into German, Leipzig, 1767. For the French version see below.
> In addition to many other voyages related, this work also includes the story of Alexander Selkirk. Sabin gives this work as of the date 1756 with the title: A Chronological Abridgement or History of Discoveries made by Europeans in different parts of the World. 3 vols. 12mo. It was republished with the title listed above.

> 1766 (In French.) Abrégé de la collection des voyages ou histoire des découvertes faites par les Européens dans le différentes parties du monde. Extrait des relations les plus exactes et des voyageurs les plus véridiques. Traduit de l'anglois par M. Targe. 12 vols. 12mo. Paris.

1756 SMOLLETT, TOBIAS. A Compendium of Authentic and Entertaining Voyages digested in a chronological Series, the whole exhibiting a clear View of the Customs, Manners, Government, Commerce and Natural History of most Nations in the known World. . . . Charts, maps, plans, heads, etc., engraved. 7 vols. 8vo. London.

> 2nd edit., in 7 vols., 8vo, London, 1766; with addition of 2 more volumes, London, 1784.

1760 The Naval Chronicle: or, Voyages, Travels, Exploits of English Navigators and Commanders to 1759. 15 portraits and maps. 8vo. London.

> This includes the Conquest of Quebec, Siege of Louisbourg, Anson's Voyage, the taking of Guadaloupe, etc.

A New and Complete Collection of Voyages and Travels, comprising whatever is valuable of this kind in the most celebrated English, Dutch,
French, Spanish, Italian, German, Swedish and Danish Writers, . . .
exhibiting the Commerce, Produce, Manufactures, . . . of the Inhabitants. 52 engraved plates, maps, etc. 4to. London.

1760-61 NEWBERY, JOHN. The World Displayed: or, a Curious Collection
of Voyages and Travels, selected from the Writers of All Nations.
Folding maps and plates. London.

> This doubtless appeared in several volumes. 2nd edit., London, 1767; 3rd edit.,
> 20 vols. in 10, London, 1774-78; 4th edit., 16mo. London, 1790. Translated into
> German, Stuttgart, 1764. See below.
> This Newbery was the well known publisher and originator of books designed
> especially for children. He also published some of Johnson's and Goldsmith's
> works.

> 1764 (In German.) Schauplatz der Welt, oder merkwürdige Sammlung von
> See- und Landreisen. Aus dem Englischen übersetzt. Stuttgart.

1761 MÜLLER, SAMUEL. For voyages between Asia and North America
see this date under NORTH PACIFIC.

1763 DERRICK, SAMUEL. A Collection of Voyages. 2 vols. Dublin.

> Pinkerton XVII cites an edition of 2 vols., London, 1779.
> The editor is probably the Samuel Derrick who got out an edition of Dryden's
> works.

1766-68 CALLANDER, JOHN. Terra Australis Cognita; or, Voyages to the
Terra Australis, or Southern Hemisphere, during the Sixteenth, Seventeenth and Eighteenth Centuries. Containing an Account of the
Manners of the People, and the Productions of the Countries, hitherto
found in the Southern Latitudes; the Advantages that may result from
further Discoveries on this great Continent, and the Methods of establishing Colonies there, to the Advantage of Great Britain. 3 engraved folding maps. 3 vols. 8vo. Edinburgh.

> The source of this work is the French collection of voyages by President de
> Brosses, Paris, 1756. See below.
> As De Brosses had proposed that France settle Australia with her unwanted
> inhabitants, so Callander advises that the foundation of a colony be made in the
> island of New Britain as a suitable spot for the further exploration and settle-
> ment of the vast continent of New Holland. . . . He claimed that Australasia must
> fall to Great Britain because of her possession of sea power. . . . Some of the
> forty-one relations appear for the first time in English.—From Maggs, No. 491.
> Callander's manner of handling his material is as follows: He prefaces each ar-
> ticle with a short introduction containing a description of the material of which
> it is composed and an account of the writer He omits many things that do not
> pertain to what immediately concerns Australia, as well as nautical observations,
> anchorages, declinations of the needle, except when he can relegate them to short
> tables. But important journals, such as Magellan's, Drake's, Tasman's, and some

others he gives entire. The first book treats of geography, natural history, and commerce as is closely related to the subject. The three following comprehend the history of the Antarctic world during the 16th, 17th and 18th centuries, from the first discovery of Terra Australis in its Magellanic quarter by Vespucci in 1502 down to the middle of the 18th century, with an account, in each separate narrative, of the advances made in this discovery by each successive navigator. The work is valuable both for its narratives and for its editorial comments.

1756 BROSSES, PRESIDENT CHARLES DE. Histoire des navigations aux Terres Australes, contenant ce que l'on scait des moeurs et des productions des contrées découvertes jusqu'à ce jour, et où il est traité de l'utilité d'y faire de plus amples découvertes, et des moyens d'y former un établissement. 7 maps. 2 vols. 4to. Paris.

This collection contains an account of all the voyages, beginning with the second expedition of Vespucci and ending with 1747, in which navigators touched upon the supposed southern continent of Magellanica, which is now represented by Australia and some scattered islands in the Antarctic regions. This work is dated 1754 by Sabin.

1767 DALRYMPLE, ALEXANDER. An Account of the Discoveries made in the South Pacific Ocean Previous to 1764. Part I. Containing, I. A Geographical Description of Places. II. The Examination of the Conduct of the Discoverers in the Tracks they pursued. III. Investigation of what may be further expected. 7 folding plates. 8vo. London.

In his "Historical Collections," printed in 1770, Dalrymple states that only a few copies of this work were printed, and that it was not published until some time after, when it was reported that the French had discovered the Southern Continent, the great object of all his researches.—From Sabin.

KNOX, JOHN. A New Collection of Voyages, Discoveries and Travels, containing whatever is worthy of Notice, in Europe, Asia, Africa and America, in respect to the Situation and Extent of Empires, Kingdoms and Provinces, their Churches, Soil, Produce, . . . consisting of such Foreign Authors as are in most Esteem, including the Descriptions and Remarks of some late celebrated Travellers, not to be found in any other Collection. Maps, plans, and engravings. 7 vols. 8vo. London.

A capital collection, containing well-digested narratives of the voyages and discoveries of Columbus, Ulloa, Dampier, Kolbe, Rogers, Drake, Pocock, Nieuhoff, etc.—Quoted by Maggs, No. 502. Vol. III includes an account of the country and constitution of Great Britain in general and England in particular, together with a short general description of London and of the kingdom of Scotland and its laws.

1768 DRAKE, EDWARD CAVENDISH. A New Universal Collection of Authentic and Entertaining Voyages and Travels from the earliest Accounts to the present Time. . . . The whole forming a History of whatever is most worthy of notice in Europe, Asia, Africa and America. . . . Maps and plates. Fol. London.

Republished, London, 1770 and 1771.
Held in little estimation.—Lowndes.

1770-71 DALRYMPLE, ALEXANDER. An Historical Collection of Several Voyages and Discoveries in the South Pacific Ocean. Being chiefly a Literal Translation from the Spanish Writers. 18 engraved plates and folding maps. 2 vols. in 1. 4to. London.

> Another edition, 4to, London, 1775. Translated into French, Paris, 1774. See below. Into German, Hamburg, 1786. Noticed in the *Journal des Scavans*, 1775, II, 112.
> This is an important collection of voyages, relating entirely to the discoveries made between South America and New Guinea, the narratives being literal translations from the original Spanish authors. Vol. II contains the early Dutch voyages.—Maggs, No 491. Among the voyages included are those of Magellan, Mendana, Juan Fernandez, Quiros, Le Maire, Schouten, Tasman, Roggewein, etc. This collection was published to bolster up the editor's claim to the advantages accruing from securing the trade to the South Sea islands. Dalrymple is also to be remembered for some unpleasant associations with Cook's first voyage to the South Seas in 1768. This voyage was undertaken upon the recommendation of the Royal Society to George III for the purpose of observing the transit of Venus, and, as Dalrymple was a member of that Society and well versed in hydrography and astronomy, he was at first selected to head the expedition. But the Admiralty preferred to place a naval man in charge and offered it to James Cook, then a lieutenant. Dalrymple refused to serve in a subordinate capacity and so remained at home. He was a strong believer in the existence of the fabulous Southern Continent and located it a short distance west of South America. Cook, however, relegated it to the limbo of dreams by his failure to discover it on his second circumnavigation.

> 1774 (In French.) Voyages dans le mer du Sud, par les Espagnols et les Hollandois. Ouvrage traduit de l'Anglois de M. Dalrymple, par M. de Fréville. 3 folding maps. 8vo Paris.

1772-79 BONWICK, JAMES. Bonwick's Transcripts. A Collection of Extracts from the Monthly Review, dealing with works on Cook and Accounts of Botany Bay, 1772-79. London.

1773 HAWKESWORTH, JOHN. An Account of the Voyages undertaken by the order of his present Majesty for making Discoveries in the Southern Hemisphere, and successfully performed by Commodore Byron, Captain Wallis, Captain Carteret, and Captain Cook (1764-1771). Drawn up from the Journals which were kept by the several Commanders and from the Papers of Joseph Banks, Esq. By John Hawkesworth. 29 charts, maps, and views of islands, etc., and 23 plates of general views, incidents, and objects, etc., 3 vols. 4to. London.

> Another issue of the 1st edit. appeared in 3 vols., the same year, London. It is distinguished from the 1st issue by the fact that in the latter the paging beginning with vol. II runs on continuously to the end of vol. III. Another edition, 2 vols., 8vo, Dublin, 1775; again 4 vols., London, 1785; 4 vols. in 2, Perth, 1789. Translated into French, 4 vols., Paris, Lausanne, Amsterdam, 1774; again into French, including the later voyages of Cook's, together with those of Byron, Carteret, and Wallis, 14 vols., with numerous maps and plates, Paris, 1774-1789; into Dutch, Rotterdam, 1774; into German, Berlin, 1774; into Italian, with Cook's later voyages, 13 vols., Naples, 1784. Practically all later collections contain Cook's voyages. See below for titles of translations.
> Hawkesworth wrote the official account of only Cook's first voyage, for which he received 6,000 pounds from the Government. How he came to be selected by Lord Sandwich as editor of this work is related by Fanny Burney in

her *Early Diary,* September 15, 1771. In his hands were placed all the journals of Byron, Wallis, Carteret, Cook, and Banks; he received some personal contributions from Dr. Solander and had access to the Admiralty records. Being a litterateur he was expected to grace the narratives with sentiments and remarks of his own appropriate to the moment. He was probably stirred to emulate the style of the account by Chaplain Walter of Anson's voyage. He wrote the journals in the first person and so put sentiments into the mouths of the captains suited to the refinements of the age of the Noble Savage. Consequently the unique personal element of each commander is totally wanting. However, the work was one of the literary triumphs of the day. But it aroused envy and calumny. One of the charges against it was that it exhibited Free Thought, as when he omitted to regard a fortunate escape from danger as a special interposition of Providence. He shocked the delicacy of the age by failing to throw a veil over certain incidents. Garrick quarrelled with him because he did not give the bookseller Beckett the option of publishing the work Cambridge men pointed out errors in his astronomy and mathematics; and even Cook refused to affirm the accuracy of the work. "Dr. Hawkesworth dined here the same day; . . . he has had very bad health lately. Indeed I believe that the abuse so illiberally cast on him, since he obtained 6,000 pounds by writing the Voyages round the World, has really affected his health, by preying upon his mind. It is a terrible alternative, that an author must either starve and be esteemed, or be villified and get money." . . . "The world has lost one of its best ornaments—a man of letters who was worthy and honest."— From the *Early Diary* of Fanny Burney. Hawkesworth died Nov. 17, 1773. See also Smith's *Life of Sir Joseph Banks.* For remarks on the individual voyages see under CIRCUMNAVIGATIONS, 1773.

1774   (In Dutch.)   Reizen rondom de wereld van Byron, Wallis, Carteret en Cook. Uit het Engl. vert. Rotterdam.

1774   (In French.)   Relations des Voyages entrepris par ordre de S. M. Britannique, pour faire des découvertes dans l'hémisphère méridional, et successivement exécutés par le Commodore Byron, le Capitaine Carteret, le Capitaine Wallis et le Capitaine Cooke dans les vaisseaux le Dauphin, le Swallow, et l'Endeavour. Traduit de l'anglais par J. B. A. Suard. 4 vols. Paris; Lausanne; Amsterdam.

1774-1789   (In French.)   Trois Voyages traduites de l'anglais, par Suard et Demeunier. Avec la vie de Cook par Kippis traduite par Castéra. 207 maps, plates, and portraits. 14 vols. 4to. Paris.

This collection contains the two later voyages of Cook as well as those of Byron, Carteret and Wallis.

1774   (In German.)   Geschichte der See-Reisen und Entdeckungen im Süd-Meer, unternommen von Byron, Wallis, Carteret und Cook. Aus dem Englischen des Hawkesworth von J. Fr. Schiller. 66 plates and maps. 3 vols. 4to. Berlin.

1784   (In Italian.)   Storia de' Viaggi intrapresi per ordine di S. M. Brittannica dal Capitano Giacomo Cook. Ricavata dalle autentiche relazioni del medesimo, e osservazioni, con una Introduzione Generale, . . . Portrait and atlas containing 52 engraved plates and charts. 13 vols. 8vo. Naples.

1773-75   HENRY, DAVID.   An Historical Account of all the Voyages round the World, performed by English Navigators; the whole faithfully Extracted from the Journals of the Voyagers. 5 vols. 8vo. London.

The contents include the voyages of Drake, Cavendish, Cowley, Dampier, Cooke, Rogers, Clipperton and Shelvocke, Anson, Byron, Wallis, Carteret, Cook, Parkinson, Bougainville, Phipps, and Lutwidge. There is an account of Henry in the *Gentleman's Magazine,* vol. 62, stating that he compiled only the first two volumes of the four, to which he added in 1775 a fifth volume containing the Journal of Cook's voyage in the *Resolution*, 1772-75, and that of the *Adventure*, 1772-74. In 1786, a sixth volume was printed making complete the record of Cook's three voyages. It was translated into German, Leipzig, 1775-1780. See below.

> 1775-1780 (In German.) Historischer Bericht von Sämmtlichen durch die Engländer geschehenen Reisen um die Welt, in einem getreuen Auszuge aus dem See-fahrer-tagebüchern. Aus dem Englischen. 6 vols. Leipzig.

1774-78 The World Displayed: or, A Collection of Voyages and Travels, selected from the Writers of all Nations. In which the Conjectures and Interpolations of several vain Editors and Translators are expunged: . . . Numerous engravings. 20 vols. 12mo. London.

1775 DALRYMPLE, ALEXANDER. A Collection of Voyages, chiefly in the Southern Atlantic Ocean. Published from Original MSS. 4 maps. 4to. London.

> This contains Dr. Edmund Halley's two voyages in 1698 and 1700; Voyage fait aux terres Australes par M. der Loziere Bouvet en 1738-39; Journal de navigation pour un voyage de la Mer du Sud fait par S. Ducloz Guyot, en 1753-56; Journal of winds, weather, etc., at the Falkland Islands, in 1767-77, by Captain Macbride.—Sabin.

1776-77 LOWNDES, ——. Lowndes' Modern Traveller, a Collection of Useful and Entertaining Travels, exhibiting a view of the Manners, Religion, Arts, Manufactures, and Commerce of the Known World, abridged from Maundrel, Keysler, Norden, Hasselquist, Thicknesse, Johnson, Anson, and other famous Travellers. 5 maps and 16 copperplates. 6 vols. 8vo. London.

1777 The Modern Traveller. 6 vols. London.
> So cited in Pinkerton XVII. See also. 1800 below.

1778 New Discoveries concerning the World and its Inhabitants, comprehending all the Discoveries made in the several Voyages of Commodore Byron, Captains Wallis, Carteret, and Cook, together with those of Bougainville, . . . also the Voyage of Constantine John Phipps. 2 maps and 3 plates. 8vo. London.

1780 MOORE, JOHN. A New and Complete Collection of Voyages and Travels. Fol. London.

> Another edition, 2 vols., fol., London, 1785.

1782 PICKERSGILL, RICHARD. A Concise Account of the Voyages for the Discovery of a North-west Passage undertaken for finding a way to the East Indies. London.

1784 ANDERSON, GEORGE WILLIAM. A New, Authentic and Complete Collection of Voyages round the World by Capt. Cook, 1st, 2nd and 3rd Voyages, together with Drake's, Byron's, Carteret's, Wallis's and other Voyages. . . . The Whole now publishing under the immediate direction of George William Anderson, assisted by a principal Officer, who sailed in the Resolution Sloop, and by many other Gentlemen. Numerous maps and plates. Fol. London.

> Another edition in 6 vols., London 1790, has been listed, but in view of the fact that the original edition and one of 1798 are in 1 vol. fol., the correctness of the citation may be doubtful.
> Anderson gives rehashes instead of the original accounts.

1786 FORSTER, JOHN REINHOLD. The History of the Voyages and Discoveries made in the North, translated from the German of John Reinhold Forster. New and Original maps. 4to. London.

> A learned account of the various expeditions for discovering the North-West and North-East Passages.—Maggs, No. 502. This work contains a good deal of useful information, much hypothesis and conjecture, as well as some mistakes, and many peevish and ill-natured reflections, particularly on the English.—Lowndes. Forster had some grievances hanging over from his connections with Cook's voyages.

The Voyages and Travels of Columbus, Magellan, Drake, Cavendish, Dampier, Cowley, Cook, Clipperton, and Shelvocke. With an Account of the Discovery of Easter Island and Davis' Land. 8vo. Edinburgh.

1788 ADAMS, JOHN. The Flower of Modern Travels, being elegant, entertaining, and instructive Extracts, selected from the Works of the most celebrated Travellers. 12mo. London.

> Reprinted, 12mo, Boston, 1797; and 3 vols., 12mo, London. This is so cited in Sabin. See also Adams under 1790 below.

1789 BANKES, T. (Rev.). For a Collection of Travels see his *Modern Authentic and Complete System of Universal Geography,* under GEOGRAPHY.

RICHARDSON, W. A General Collection of Voyages and Discoveries made by the Portuguese and Spaniards during the Fifteenth and Sixteenth Centuries, containing the interesting and entertaining Voyages of the celebrated Gonzalez and Vas, Gonzalez Zarco, Lanzerota, Diego Gell, Cada Mosto, Pedro di Sintra, Diego d'Azambuza, Bartholomew Diaz, Vasco da Gama, Voyages to the Canary Islands, Voyages of Columbus, Nino and Guierra, Ojeda and Vespusius Cortereal, Alvarez Cabral, Francis Almeed, Albuquerque, Andrea Corsali, Voyage to St. Thomas, Voyage of de Solis, Pinzon, . . . Voyage of John Ponce, Gri-

jalva, Nieuessa, Cortes, Ojeda and Ocampo, Magellan, the West Indies, Round the World, . . . Plates and maps. 4to. London.

Richardson was the publisher of this work.

1790 ADAMS, JOHN. Modern Voyages: containing a variety of useful and
entertaining Facts, respecting the Expeditions and the principal Discoveries of Cavendish, Dampier, Anson, Byron, . . . 2 vols. 8vo.
Dublin.

Translated into French, Paris, 1800. See below.

1800 (In French.) Choix de Voyages Modernes pour l'Instruction et l'Amuse-
ment des Deux Sexes. Traduit de l'Anglais par J. F. André. Folding
map. 2 vols. 8vo. Paris. (An VIII.)

COOK, JAMES. Voyages round the World, for Making Discoveries in
the Northern and Southern Hemispheres. The First performed in the
Years 1768-1771. The Second in 1772-75. The Third and Last in
1776-1780. Containing a Relation of all the interesting Transactions
which occurred in the course of the Voyages. Including Captain Furneaux's Journal of his Proceedings during the Separation of the Ships.
Portrait and numerous engraved maps and plates. 3 vols. Newcastle.
8vo.

Included in vol. II are Phipps' and Lutwidge's Voyage towards the North
Pole: To which is prefixed an Account of the several Voyages undertaken for
the Discovery of a Northeast Passage by Forster. A Description of a Man-of-
War, tracing the Art of Shipbuilding from its Commencement to its present de-
gree of perfection. (Governor) Phil(l)ips' Voyage to Botany Bay, etc.—From
Maggs, No. 442. The narrative is written partly in the first person, following
Cook's Journal, and partly in the third, paraphrased from the official account.—
Cook *Bibliography*.

Curious and Entertaining Voyages undertaken either for Discovery, Conquest, or the Benefit of Trade; commencing with the Earliest Discoveries promoted by Prince Henry of Portugal, and 58 different Portuguese and Spanish Voyages, exhibiting various Scenes of Cruelties,
Hardships, Misfortunes and Discoveries, particularly on Columbus's
Conquest of Mexico, etc., with Magellan's Voyage round the World.
4to. London.

HOGG, (Captain). A Collection of Voyages round the World: performed by Royal Authority. Containing a complete Historical Account
of Captain Cook's First, Second, Third and Last Voyages, undertaken
for making new Discoveries. To which are added those of Byron,
Wallis, Carteret, Mulgrave, Anson, Parkinson, Lutwidge, Ives, Middleton, Smith, . . . Portrait and numerous engraved plates and maps.
6 vols. 8vo. London.

A curious and uncommon edition of Cook's voyages, originally issued in 80 weekly parts.—Maggs, No. 491. Captain Hogg was the editor of the collection. The title asserts that this is the most elegant and perfect work of its kind. In Sabin it is listed as appearing in five volumes in 1785.

An Interesting Account of the Early Voyages made by the Portuguese and Spaniards, . . . to Africa, East and West Indies, the Discovery of numerous Islands, with Particulars of the Lives of those Eminent Navigators, including the Life of Columbus; to which is added the Life of Captain Cook (extracted from Kippis). 7 plates and maps. 4to. London.

1791   Discoveries of the French in 1768-69 to the South-east of New Guinea with the subsequent visits to the same Lands by English Navigators who gave them new names, with an historical Abridgement of the Voyages and Discoveries of the Spaniards in the same seas by M. ———— (formerly a captain in the French Army). 12 charts. 4to. London.

Among its contents are the discoveries of Mendana in 1567 and 1595, de Quiros in 1606, Carteret in 1767, de Bougainville in 1768, de Surville in 17ᶠ Lieut. Shortland in 1788, etc.—Bookseller's Note.

1791-92   HERON, ROBERT. The New Universal Traveller: Travels in Africa and Asia (Vaillant, Sparrman, Niebuhr, etc.). Map and numerous engraved plates. 2 vols. 8vo. London.

The title of this item suggests that it includes more than two volumes; but the above listing is all that has come to the notice of the editor.

1796-1802   MAVOR, WILLIAM. An Historical Account of Voyages, Travels, and Discoveries from the Time of Columbus to the Present Period Portrait, plates, and maps. 26 vols. 12mo. London.

2nd edit., 28 vols., London, 1810; 3rd edit., 28 vols., London, 1813-15. This work is but a compilation, which gives the substance and "the most interesting parts of the most popular books of travel."

1800   The Modern Traveller, containing compressed Travels of Mungo Park and others in Africa. 4 vols. 12mo. London.

ADDENDA I.

1806 PHILLIPS, SIR RICHARD. A Collection of Modern and Contemporary Voyages and Travels. 6 vols. 8vo. London.

> Another edition, 11 vols., London, 1820-23.
> This contains Peron's Voyage to the Southern Hemisphere; Keith's Voyage to South America and the Cape; Bolinbroke's Voyage to Demerara; Ashe's Travels in America; Sarytschew's Voyage to North East Siberia; Voyage to India and China in H. M. S. *Caroline;* and many European travels.

1808-1814 PINKERTON, JOHN. A General Collection of the best and most interesting Voyages and Travels in all Parts of the World. Numerous plates and maps. 17 vols. 4to. London.

> Vol. XVII contains a Bibliography of Voyages (255 pp.) and a general Index (472 pp.). The bibliography has to be used with much caution, as it turns out to be full of errors in dates and names, and is often unsatisfactory because of the brevity of the wording of titles and the lack of information needed to place a given work. The collection is of great value for its texts, which it sometimes gives entire and sometimes abridged and digested, with as much use as possible of the traveller's own language.

1811-1824 KERR, ROBERT. A General History and Collection of Voyages and Travels, arranged in Systematic Order, forming a Complete History of the Origin and Progress of Navigation, Discovery and Commerce, by Sea and Land, from the Earliest Ages to the Present Time. Maps and charts. 18 vols. 8vo. Edinburgh.

> Vol. XVIII of this work contains, besides Stevenson's "Historical Sketch of the Progress and Discovery, Navigation and Commerce, from the earliest records to the beginning of the Nineteenth Century," a biographical Catalogue of Voyages and Travels. The work contains a great variety of very curious and interesting early voyages of rare occurrence only to be found otherwise in expensive and voluminous collections.—Bookseller's Note.

1813 A General Collection of Voyages and Travels including the most interesting Records of Navigators and Travellers, from the Discovery of America, by Columbus in 1492, to the Travels of Lord Valencia. Maps and engravings. 28 vols. 12mo. London.

1817 MURRAY, HUGH. An Historical Account of Discoveries and Travels in Africa, by the late John Leyden, Enlarged and completed to the present Time. 9 maps. 2 vols. 8vo. Edinburgh.

1831 The Lives and Voyages of Drake, Cavendish, and Dampier, including an Introductory View of the earlier Discoveries in the South Sea, and the History of the Buccaneers. Portraits. 8vo. Edinburgh.

1848 WRIGHT, THOMAS. Early Travels in Palestine, comprising the Narratives of Arculf, Willibald, Bernard, Saewulf, Sigurd, Benjamin of Tudela, Sir John Maundeville, de la Broquiere, and Maundrell. 8vo. London.

In Bohn's Library.

1849 Narratives of Voyages towards the North-West, In search of a Passage to Cathay and India, 1496 to 1631. With selections from the early Records of . . . the East India Company and from MSS. in the British Museum. Edited by Thomas Rundall. 2 maps. Hak. Soc., ser. I, vol. 5. London.

1856 A Collection of Documents on Spitzbergen and Greenland, Comprising a Translation from F. Martens' Voyage to Spitzbergen, 1671; a Translation from Isaac la Peyrère's *Histoire du Groenland, 1663*, and *God's Power and Providence in the Preservation of Eight Men in Greenland Nine Moneths and Twelve Dayes*, 1630. Edited by Adam White. 2 maps. Hak. Soc., ser. I, vol. 18. London.

1858 India in the Fifteenth Century, Being a Collection of Narratives of Voyages to India in the century preceding the Portuguese discovery of the Cape of Good Hope; from Latin, Persian, Russian, and Italian Sources. Translated into English and edited by Richard Henry Major, F.S.A. Hak. Soc., ser. I, vol. 22. London.

1859 Early Voyages to Terra Australis, Now called Australia. A Collection of documents, and extracts from early MS. Maps, illustrative of the history of the discovery of Australia from the beginning of the sixteenth century to the time of Captain Cook. Edited by Richard Henry Major, F.S.A. 5 maps. Hak. Soc., ser. I, vol. 25. London.

1902 BEAZLEY, C. RAYMOND. Voyages and Travels, mainly during the 16th and 17th Centuries. 2 vols. 8vo. London.

This was reprinted with very slight alterations from the *English Garner,* 8 vols., 1877-1890, London, by Edward Arber. The texts are in the main reprinted, with occasional compression, from Hakluyt's *Principal Navigations,* either of the edition of 1589 or that of 1598-1600.

1902-06 CAMDEN MISCELLANY. Vols. 10 to 14; containing Hoby's Book of Travaile, 1547-66; Journal of Sir R. Wilbraham, Solicitor General in Ireland, 1593-1616; Spanish Narratives of Santo Domingo, 1655; English Conquest of Jamaica, 1655-56; Life of Sir John Digby, 1605-1645, etc. Edited by S. R. Gardiner, W. Cunningham, C. L. Kingsford, etc. 5 vols. 4to. London.

1904-07　THWAITES, R. G. For a collection of early western travels in North America from 1748-1846, see under NORTH AMERICA.

1923　NEVINS, ALLAN. American Social History as Recorded by British Travellers. 8vo. New York.

> This work illustrates the American scene by selections from the diaries and journals of British travellers in the eastern United States of the early 19th century. Each selection is prefaced by an interesting introduction.

1924　Colonising Expeditions to the West Indies and Guiana, 1623-1667. Edited by Vincent T. Harlow, B.A., B. Litt., F.R. Hist. Soc. 6 maps and 2 plates. Hak. Soc., ser. II, vol. 56. London.

> These narratives hitherto unpublished, record the early efforts of English Adventurers to explore and occupy regions in the New World, made famous by the buccaneers of the 16th century. They thus form a vital link between the voyages of Hawkins and Raleigh and subsequent colonial history.—Hakluyt Society.

HARLEIAN MISCELLANY. Among the selections is Travels in the East. 8vo. London.

1929　KOMROFF, MANUEL. Contemporaries of Marco Polo. Consisting of the Travel Records to the Eastern World of William of Rubruck (1253-1255); The Journey of John of Pian de Carpini (1245-1247); the Journal of Friar Odoric (1318-1330); and the Oriental Travels of Rabbi Benjamin of Tudela (1160-1173). Edited by Manuel Komroff. 8vo. London.

1930　ADLER, ELKAN. Jewish Travellers, from the Ninth to the Eighteenth Century. Edited and translated with an Introduction, by Elkan Adler. Plates and map. 8vo. Broadway Travellers series. London.

> The literature of medieval travel has been greatly enriched by this latest addition to the Broadway Travellers. The Jew was from the earliest times a wanderer, and when his wanderings were due not to persecution but to the spirit of adventure and scientific enquiry, they yielded narratives full of interesting and curious information.—From the Manchester Guardian.

1931　LAWRENCE, A. W. and YOUNG, JEAN. Narratives of the Discovery of America. Edited by A. W. Lawrence and Jean Young. 8vo. London (?).

> This volume contains translations of the principal documents of both periods of America's discovery, the Sagas, which describe the Viking expeditions to Greenland, and the coasts of North America, as well as accounts of the better known voyages of Columbus and Cabot. New and complete translations have been made from the Icelandic and Spanish originals, except in the case of Columbus' Journal, where an early American version has been thoroughly revised.—Bookseller's Note.

ADDENDA II

On account of their importance in the history of travel literature some foreign collections are here listed and described. Most of these items have not been turned into English, at least in their entirety.

1507 VESPUCCI, AMERIGO. Paesi novamente retrovati e Novo Mondo. 4to. Milan (?).

> 2nd edit., Milan, 1508. Translated into Latin, Milan, 1508.
> This work is the first collection of voyages ever compiled. It contains the Italian version based on Giocondo's rendering of Vespucci's famous third voyage (the first under the Portuguese flag) . . . This voyage lasted from May 10, 1501, to September 7, 1502.—Maggs, No. 479. In notes to the Latin version Maggs goes on to say: After the letters of Columbus, it is the most important contribution to the early history of American discovery. It commences with the navigations of Alovise de Cadamosto in Ethiopia, etc., which appeared for the first time in this work, followed by the voyages of de Cintra in 1462, of Vasco da Gama in 1497-1500, of Cabral in 1500-1501, of Columbus 1492-1498, of Alonso Negro and the Pinzons, of Vespucci's Third Voyage, 1501-1502, of Cortereal, 1500-1501, etc. It also contains the narrative of Joseph, the converted Indian, brought to Portugal by Cabral, and letters relating to the Portuguese Voyages. Its chief value consists in its containing the voyages of Columbus and Vespucci. The actual author of the compilation is not definitely known.

1532 GRYNAEUS, SIMON. Novus Orbis Regionum ac Insularum veteribus incognitarum, una cum tabula cosmographica, & aliquot aliis consimilis argumenti libellis. Fol. Paris.

> This work, which may be considered as the first General History of Travels, was the compilation of John Huttich. Grynaeus only wrote the preface.—Maggs, No. 429. Its chief articles are the Voyages of Cadamosto, Columbus, the four Voyages of Vespucci, Vincente Yanez Pinzon, Marco Polo, Haiton, etc.

1554-1586 RAMUSIO, GIOVANNI BATTISTA. Delle Navigationi et Viaggi, raccolte da M. Gio. Batt. Ramusio, in tre volumi divisi. Maps. 3 vols. Fol. Venice.

> This work, which served as a model to Hakluyt, was the first great systematic collection of voyages that had so far appeared. For its contents see Sabin, Dictionary of *Books relating to America*. Vol. III is given over entirely to America.—It contains translations from works that had been published in Spanish, French, and Latin, and some from manuscripts that had never yet been published. It was compiled during the latter part of Ramusio's life and is carefully and intelligently done, as he had devoted his mature years to historical and geographical study, in which he gave instruction in a school which he carried on in his own house. He left material for a fourth volume, but the manuscript was destroyed in a fire which burned the printing-house of the publisher not long after his death in 1557. John Locke, the English philosopher, held the highest opinion of the work, asserting that it was free from that "great mass of useless matter which swells our English Hakluyt and Purchas, much more complete and full than the Latin De Bry, and in fine is the noblest work of this nature."—Maggs, No. 519.

1580-1661 ANNUAE LITTERAE SOCIETATIS JESU. Annual Letters from Brazil, Philippines, Cochin-China, Tibet, Japan, China, East Indies, South America, Canada, etc. Printed in various cities and towns and under various editors.

Under the above dates Maggs, No. 429, lists a collection of 40 vols., printed in 18 and 12mo. Quaritch, No. 415, lists 24 vols. out of 33, of the dates 1583-1658. Then there were the *Jesuit Relations,* as the phrase is generally used, sent in from Canada, which comprise the Cramoisy series, as published annually by Sebastien Cramoisy in Paris. Just how many make up this series is probably not known. In 1858, the Canadian Government had this series reprinted at Quebec in 25 vols., under the editorship of John G. Shea. For this edition and the later one issued in a greatly enlarged form by the Burrows Brothers, Cleveland, in some 73 vols., see under date 1858-1868, NORTH AMERICA. See Lockman under 1743 above; also under 1819-1854 below.

These annual reports from Jesuit missionaries stationed all over the world constitute a most vital source of historical, geographical, political, and social information. Whether there is a complete set in existence anywhere on earth is commonly doubted. Their regular appearance dates from the accession of Rudolfo Acquaviva to the generalship of the order. The system as worked out is thus described by Maggs, No. 429. Those laboring in the outposts sent in reports to their superiors on all matters relating to the Society; the Superiors and Rectors of all houses and colleges in Europe had to make a weekly report to their Provincial; the Provincial in his turn made a monthly report to the General of the Society. According to Quaritch, there was no report in 1615, the year that Acquaviva died, nor for several years afterwards. Shortly after 1650, by the same authority, reports ceased altogether.

1590-1634 DE BRY, THEODORE. Collectiones Peregrinationum in Indian orientalem et occidentalem XXV partibus comprehensae; opus illustratum figuris Fratrum de Bry et Meriani; Americae partes 13, Indiae orientalis 12. Frankfort.

These are better known as the *Grands et Petits Voyages.* Originally the design was to publish them in English, Latin, French, and German, but after the appearance of the first volume the plan was abandoned and the remainder were issued in Latin and German. De Bry died in 1598, leaving his work to be carried on by his widow and two sons-in-law. The intermittent character of the publishing and the overlapping of new parts with reissues of old ones make the problem of arranging the editions in their proper order most baffling, and in consequence these voyages have been made the subject of a large number of bibliographical studies, without an agreement being reached on the right contents of a complete set. The titles of the various lists and comparisons are given in the Bulletin of the New York Public Library, VIII, 230, introductory to a "Catalogue of the De Bry Collection of Voyages in the New York Public Library," a collection made by James Lenox and held to be the finest in existence. There is an account of the De Bry Collection in the Library of E. Dwight Church, printed in the Church Catalogue. The most complete comparative study of the Voyages is that of the Earl of Crawford, published in 1894. See *Bibliotheca Lindensiana, Collations and Notes,* No. 3, London, 1884. The series in the John Carter Brown Library, which fills sixty-one pages of the Catalogue, ranks among the first in extent, condition, and completeness. The Catalogue of this last named Library makes mention also of a study of the contents of the various parts and the sources from which they are derived, viz., the *Memoir sur la Collection des Grands et Petits Voyages* by Armand Gaston Camus, published in 1802. The *Grands Voyages* deal with America and the *Petits Voyages* with Africa and Asia. An analysis of the contents of the American voyages is to be found in Maggs, No. 442, and of the whole collection in Robinson, No. 41. De Bry undoubtedly had the assistance of Hakluyt in the publication and arrangement of some of the material for the first volume. A brief account of De Bry's work is given in Waldman, 97-100.

1598-1660 HULSIUS, LEVINUS. Sammlung von 26 Schifffahrten in verschiedene fremde Länder durch Leo Hulsium und einige andere aus
dem Holländischen ins Deutsch übersetzt und mit allerhand Anmerkungen versehen. 25 Thiele. Nurnberg, Francfurt und Hanover.

> For a description of this series in its various editions see the John Carter
> Brown Catalogues and Wilberforce Eames' *Contributions to a Catalogue of the
> Lenox Library*. Hulsius was born in Ghent, but in 1594 he settled at Frankfort
> on the Main as a publishing bookseller. Before his death in 1606 eight parts of
> his Voyages had appeared. His widow and successors continued to publish parts,
> some in connection with the De Brys, until the 26th part was issued in 1663. Less
> ambitious than the DeBrys, Hulsius contented himself with translations into Ger-
> man, only Parts IV and V appearing in Latin, in 1599, and with doubtful success,
> as the experiment was, not continued. Hardly two sets will agree in detail.—
> From John Carter Brown.

1612 Descriptio ac delineatio Geographica Detectionis Freti, sive, Transitus ad
Oceanum, supra terra Americanos, in Chinam atque Japonem ducturi,
Recens investigati ab M. Henrico Hudsono Anglo. Narratio . . . super
tractum, in quinta Orbis terrarum parte, cui Australiae Incognitae no-
men est, recens detecto, Per Capitanum Petrum Ferdinandez de Quir.
4to. Amsterdam.

> This is a hitherto unrecorded variant of the first edition of the most remark-
> able Collection of Voyages of Discovery of this period. The editor has collected
> together in this book a relation of the three most marvellous discoveries of the
> previous years in the most unknown parts of the world, viz., the Discovery of the
> Northwest Passage to America, by Henry Hudson, including the Hudson River
> and Hudson's Bay, etc. The Discovery of the Northern Coasts of Australia by
> Fernandez de Quiros. The Voyage of Isaac Massa to Siberia. For Hudson this is
> the first news printed concerning the voyage to the northern parts of America.
> For De Quiros it is the first edition in Latin of his report to the King of Spain.
> And for Isaac Massa it is also the first edition of his Relation of Siberia.—Maggs,
> No. 479.

1648 HARTGERTS, JOOST. Oost-Indische Voyagien door dien Begin en
Voortgangh, van de Vereenighde Nederlandsche Geoctroyeerde Oost-
Indische Compagnie. Vervatende de voornaemste Reysen, be de In-
woonderen der selver Provintien derwaerts ghedaen, . . . Engraved
plates and shipping vignettes. 16 parts in 1 vol. 4to. Amsterdam.

> This extraordinary Collection of Voyages is sometimes called the "Dutch De
> Bry" or the "Dutch Hulsius"; for in beauty of execution and intrinsic interest it
> rivals both of those famous collections. In point of rarity there is no comparison;
> this being scarcely known to bibliographers. How many parts Hartgerts published
> is even now uncertain, although the most active research has been made by col-
> lectors of voyages and travels for many years. The parts were probably issued
> and sold separately, and their collection into sets, with a collective title, preface,
> etc., was an afterthought. This collection has an advantage over De Brys' and
> Hulsius', in that many of the voyages are in the language in which they were
> originally written, while most of those by De Bry and Hulsius are translations.—
> Quoted by Maggs, No. 479. Maggs also lists the contents of the Collection.

1666-1672 THEVENOT, MELCHISEDEC. Relations de divers Voyages curieux, qui n'ont point esté publiées, ou qui esté traduites . . . et de
quelques Persans, Arabes et autres . . . Plates and maps. 4 vols. Fol.
Paris.

> The importance of Thevenot's Collection needs no comment. When complete
> its scope is universal, as it includes accounts from nearly all parts of the world—
> Japan, China, Philippines, Siam, Tartary, Mongolia, India, Egypt, Abyssinia, Per-
> sia, Arabia, Asia Minor, and Russia. Of American interest are the Voyage du
> Sieur Acarete à Buenos Aires, Voyage dans la rivière de la Plate, Histoire de
> l'empire mexicain. To Australia relates the Voyage de Bontehoe with a large
> map of Australia and the Expedition of Alvara de Mendano to the Solomon Is-
> lands.—From Hiersemann. It also contains the first account of the discovery of
> the River Mississippi by Father Marquette in 1673, and its folding map of that
> river, which is believed to be the first extant; a map, with explanations, of the
> discovery of the countries near the North Pole, by the Dutch; a Description of an
> overland Journey from Russia to China in 1653; and the most important, and one
> of the very earliest, maps (Tasman's) of Australia, Tasmania, and New Zeal-
> and.—Maggs, No. 502. Thevenot was born about 1629, and as a young man trav-
> elled about Europe considerably, although he left no narratives of his journeys.
> He later settled down in Paris, and devoted himself to scientific studies. He
> made the acquaintance of all who had travelled in distant lands and published the
> accounts of their travels in the above Collection.—Maggs.

1674 JUSTEL, HENRI. Recueil de Divers Voyages Faits en Afrique et en
l'Amérique. (Including) Histoire des Barbades, par R. Ligon; Extrait de l'histoire d'Ethiopie de Telles; Relation des Caraibes, par de
Laborde; Description de l'empire de Prêtre-Jean; Jamaique, Colonies
Anglaises, . . . 8 folding maps and plans and 8 plates. Fol. Paris.

> Ligon was translated from the English. See under date 1657, WEST IN-
> DIES. Some of the voyages herein contained had not been published before.

1691-93 ANZI, CONTE A. DEGLI. Il Genio Vagante Biblioteca Curiosa di
cento e piu Relazioni di Viaggi Stranieri de'nostri tempi Raccolta dal
Conte Aurelio degli Anzi. 4 folding maps and 7 plates. 4 vols.
12mo. Parma.

> This work is composed of extracts, private letters, etc., from Italian, French,
> English, and Spanish travellers.

1702 Recueil des Voyages qui ont servi à l'Establissement et aux Progres de la
Compagnie des Indes Orientales formée dans les Provinces Unies des
Pays-bas. 11 folding maps and plate. 12mo. Amsterdam.

1706-08 AA, PIETER VAN DER. Naaukeurige Versamling der Gedenk-
waardigste Zee en Land-Reyen na Ooost en West-Indien. Hundreds
of engraved plates and maps. 127 vols., bound in 29. 8vo. Amsterdam.

> Good complete sets of these Voyages are very uncommon. All of them were
> issued as separate works.—Maggs, No. 502. In this catalogue Maggs lists sep-
> arately the contents of each volume.

1715 BERNARD, J. F. Recueil de Voyages au Nord, contenant divers Mémoires très-utiles au Commerce et à la Navigation. 4 vols. 12mo. Amsterdam.

> Another edition in 10 vols., Amsterdam.
> The contents of this work go beyond the title; it is rather a universal collection, containing the voyages of a number of English explorers. Noticed in the *Journal des Scavans*, 1716, I, 278; 1718, II, 302; 1720, I, 614.

1717 Mémoires des Missions dans le Levant. 9 vols. Paris.

1729 Recueil de divers Voyages curieux en Tartarie, . . . 2 vols. Leyden.

Sammlung von Reisen in Europa. 2 vols. Hamburg.

1734 LAFITAU, J. F. Histoire des Découvertes et Conquestes des Portugais dans le Nouveau Monde. 10 plates. 3 vols. Paris.

> This is a general work on the history of Portuguese navigations in both hemispheres.—Bookseller's Note.

1735 Bergeron, P. Voyages faits principalement en Asie dans les XII, XIII, XIV, et XV siècles, par Benjamin de Tudele, Jean du Plan-Carpin, N. Ascelin, Guillaume de Rubruquis, Marc Paul Venitien, Haiton, Jean de Mandeville et Ambroise Contarini, accompagné de l'Histoire des Sarasins et des Tartares, et précédéz d'une Introduction concernant les voyages et les nouvelles découvertes des principaux voyageurs. 4to. The Hague.

1746-1768 PREVOST, A. F. (Abbé). Histoire générale des voyages, ou nouvelle collection de toutes les relations de voyages par mer et par terre, qui ont été publiées jusqu'à present dans les différentes langues de toutes les nations connues. Folding plates and charts. 18 vols. 4to. Paris.

> Vol. 17 forms the Supplement and vol. 18 is the first volume of the Continuation, of which two more volumes were published. This work is much indebted to Astley's *Collection*. See above under date 1745-47.

1747-1774 Allgemeine Historie der Reisen zu Wasser und zu Lände, oder Sammlung aller Reisebeschreibungen, welche bis jetze in verschiedenen Sprachen von aller Völkern herausgegeben worden, . . . Aus dem Englischen übersetzt. 2 Maps and plates. 21 vols. 4to. Amsterdam (some copies bear the imprint Leipzig.)

> This valuable repository contains translations of many of the early voyages and travels in America, and some Indian vocabularies, etc., mostly by J. J. Schwabe. A detailed list of the contents is given in the supplement to the index of Books in the Bates Hall of the Public Library, Boston.—Sabin.

1749-1770 DIDOT, ——. Histoire Générale des Voyages ou Nouvelle Collection de toutes les Relations de Voyages par mer et par terre. Numerous maps and views. 76 vols. 12mo. Paris.

> See Prévost under 1746-1768 above.

1750 Almindelig Histoire over Reiser til Lands og Vande, eller Samlung af alle Reisebeskrivelser oversat af Engelsk. 5 vols. Copenhagen.

> This Danish collection is likewise probably based on Astley.

1750-1764 Sammlung neuer und merkwürdiger Reisen zu Wasser und zu Lände. 11 Theile. Göttingen.

1756 BROSSES, PRESIDENT CHARLES DE. For his *Histoire des navigations* see above under Callander, 1766-68.

1768 ADELUNG, J. C. Geschichte der Schifffahrten und Versuchen zur Entdeckung des nord-östlichen wegs nach Japan und China. Halle.

1769-1771 DELAPORTE, (Abbé). Le Voyageur Francois, ou la connoissance de l'ancien et du nouveau monde, mis au jour par M. l'Abbé Delaporte. 22 vols. 8vo. Paris.

1780-06 LA HARPE, JEAN FRANCOIS DE. Abrégé de l'Histoire Générale des Voyages. Numerous engravings of views, curiosities, manners and customs, costumes, etc. 32 vols. 8vo. Paris.

1784 FORSTER, JOHANN REINHOLD. Allgemeine Geschichte der Entdeckungen und Schifffahrten im Norden. Mit neuen Original-Karten. Frankfurt a. O.

1785-86 TRASSLER, J. G. Sammlung der besten Reise-Beschreibungen. (Vols. ?.) Troppau.

1786 FABRI, JOHANN ERNST. Sammlung von Stadt-, Land- und Reisebeschreibungen. Karten. 2 Theile. Halle.

Nouveau Recueil des Voyages au Nord de l'Europe et de l'Asie. Paris (?).

> Among the references to English travellers is Dr. Johnson's Account of the Journey through Scotland and the Hebrides. Noticed in the *Journal des Scavans*, 1786, II 387.

1787-1794 PONZ, ANTONIO. Viage de Espana. Tercera Edicion, corregeda, y augmentada. 18 vols. Madrid (?).

1788 Voyages intéressantes dans différentes colonies francaise, espagnoles et anglaises. Observations importantes, relative à ces contrées, avec un mémoire sur les maladies les plus communes à Saint-Domingue avec une explication des remédes, Mémoires diverses sur Curacao, l'Ile de la Grenade dans les Antilles anglaises, la Martinique, Puorto-Rico, . . . Paris.

1788-89 PERTHES, J. L. HUB. SIMON DE. Histoire des Naufrages, ou recueil des relations les plus intéressantes des naufrages, hiverniments, delaissement, . . . sur mer depuis le 15. siècle jusqu'à présent, par M. Duromesnil. 3 vols. Paris.

1789 KREBEL, G. F. Die vornehmsten Reisen durch Italien. Hamburgh.

1791 FORSTER, J. G. A. Geschichte der Reisen, die seit Cook an der Nordwest und Nordost-Küste von Amerika und in dem Nördlichsten Amerika selbst von Meares, Dixon, Portlock, Coxe, Long, u.a.m. unternommen worden sind. Aus dem Englischen mit Zuziehung aller anderweitigen Hülfsquellen ausgearbeitet von Georg Forster. 4 maps and 27 plates. 3 vols. 4to. Berlin.

1795 BERENGER, J. P. Collection de toutes les voyages faits autour du monde. 9 vols. Paris.

1795-96 GRASSET, SAINT-SAUVER, J. Encyclopédie des voyages, contenant l'Abrégé historique des moeurs, usages, habitudes domestiques, religions, . . . 432 colored plates. 5 vols. Paris.

1796 COOK, JAMES. Premier, second et troisième voyage autour du monde fait en 1768-1780, précédé des relations de Byron, Carteret, Wallis, . . . Traduit nouvellement par Breton. 2 atlases containing 50 maps. 12 vols. Paris.

1797 GRASSET, SAINT-SAUVER. J. Histoire abrégé des découvertes des Capitaines Cook, Wilson, La Perouse, . . . Paris.

1800-1835 SPRENGEL, M. C. Bibliothek der neuesten und wichtigsten Reisebeschreibungen zur Erweiterung der Erd- und Völkerkunde, herausgegeben von M. C. Sprengel und fortgesetzt von T. F. Ehrmann. 115 Theile. Weimar.

1808 RICHARDERIE, G. BOUCHER DE LA. Bibliothèque universelle des Voyages, ou Notice complète et raisonnée de tous les voyages anciens et modernes dans les différentes parties du monde classés par ordre des pays dans leur série chronologique, . . . 6 vols. 8vo. Paris.

1819-1854 Lettres édifiantes et curieuses, écrites des missiones étrangères, avec les Annales de la Propogation de la foi. 40 vols. Lyons.

> These celebrated letters cover the activities of the Jesuit missions in various parts of the world from 1702-1776. Several editions of them, ranging from 1702-1776 to 1875-77, have appeared in various lands and various languages. For some of these see below. The collection relating to French Canada in particular is known as the "Jesuit Relations" (see under 1858-1868, NORTH AMERICA) ; for the "Annual Letters" see under 1580-1661, this Addenda. In addition there are other collections, especially those concerning the eastern part of the world. Lockman's Collection under 1743 above is a translation from the *Lettres édifiantes.*

> 1753 Cartas Edificantes, y Curiosas, escritas de las Missiones Estrangeras, por algunos Missioneros de la Compañia de Jesus: traducidas del Idioma Francès por el Padre Diego Davin, de la Compañia de Jesus. Plates and Maps. 16 vols. 4to. Madrid.

> 1753 Lettres édifiantes. 34 vols. 12mo. Venice.

1829 NAVARRETE, DON MARTIN FERNANDEZ DE. Coleccion de los Viajes y Descubrimientos que hiceron por mar los Españoles desde fines del Siglo XV. Madrid.

> 2nd edit., in 5 vols., Madrid, 1837, and later.

1837-1841 TERNAUX-COMPANS, H. Voyages, relations et mémoires originaux pour servir à l'histoire de la découverte de l'Amérique. 8vo. 20 vols. Paris.

1854-1857 CHARTON, EDOUARD. Voyageurs anciens et modernes, ou choix des relations de voyages les plus intéressantes et les plus instructives depuis le cinquième siècle avant Jésus-Christ jusqu'au dix-neuvième siècle, avec biographies, notes et indications iconographiques. 4 vols. 8vo. Paris.

1904 BÖHME, M. Die Grossen Reisesammlung des 16 Jahrhunderts und ihre Bedeutung. Strassburg.

II.

Circumnavigation

1510-1520 RASTELL, JOHN. New Interlude and a Merry of the Nature of the Four Elements.

> Rastell was the publisher of this play. It has an account of how men could sail "plain eastwards and come to England again." See under GENERAL TRAVELS.

1555 PIGAFETTA, FRANCISCO ANTONIO. A Briefe Declaratiorí of the Voyage of Nauigation made abowte the Worlde. In Eden's *The Decades of the Newe Worlde or West India.* See under COLLECTIONS.

> An English translation was made by Richard Wren (probably from the Italian), London, 1525. Reprinted in Harris I, 6-14; in Callander (drawn out of several authors) I, 73-109; in Pinkerton XI, 288-420; Hakluyt Society, 1874; Arber, *The First Three English Books on America,* Birmingham, 1885; a modern edition, Cleveland, 1906. For these and the Italian edition of 1536 see below. A bibliography is appended to the 1906 edition.
> There are two distinct accounts of Magellan's famous voyage, the first circumnavigation of the globe—this, the best and longest by Pigafetta, who accompanied Magellan on the expedition, and the second one contained in a letter by Maximilianus Transylvanus, which was translated into Italian from the Latin. This last is also found in the 1542 edition of Boemus's *Omnium Gentium Mores,* etc. (See Boemus under date 1611, GENERAL TRAVELS.) According to Callander, the first history of this epoch-marking voyage by Peter Martyr was lost in the sack of Rome by the Constable Bourbon. And the original Italian version of Pigafetta's is likewise lost but a French abridgement of it was made by Fabre and published by him in Paris, 1525. From this translation another Italian version was made and published at Venice, 1536. A fairly long detailed account of this voyage is contained in Herrera's *Historia General* of 1601 (see Herrera under date 1725-26, WEST INDIES). See also Argensola's *Discovery and Conquest of the Moluccas* under date of 1708, SOUTH SEAS.
> Magellan's voyage was the first circumnavigation of the globe, and on it was based the Portuguese claim to the discovery of Australia in 1521. (The voyage lasted from Sept. 20, 1519, to Sept. 6, 1522). Magellan himself was killed by the natives of the Philippine Islands, and his vessel arrived home under the command of Sebastian del Cano. The voyage resulted in the discovery of a route to the Pacific Ocean around South America. Various small islands in the South Seas, including the Island of Amsterdam, were discovered, and the expedition visited the Philippines, Molucca Islands, and the Ladrones, etc.—Maggs, No. 491. Magellan succeeded where Columbus failed. He had proved that the world was round; he had also demonstrated the possibility of its circumnavigation. As a sailor, a geographer, an explorer, Magellan was a great man, greater perhaps than either Columbus or Da Gama, perhaps even, as has been suggested, "the greatest of ancient and modern navigators."—Baker, *A History of Geographical Discovery and Exploration.*

1744-48 MAGELLAN, FERDINAND. The Voyage of Ferdinand Maglianes or Magellan, from the South Seas to the East-Indies. In Harris I, 6-14.

1808-1814 PIGAFETTA, FRANCISCO ANTONIO. Voyage round the World. Effected in the Years 1519-1522, with the Squadron of Magellan. With an Extract from the Treatise on Navigation by the same Author; Some Observations on the Chevalier Behaim, and a Description of his Terrestrial Globe (Paris, 1800). With an historical Introduction by the French Editor. In Pinkerton XI, 288-420.

1874 The First Voyage round the World by Magellan (1518-1521). Translated from the Accounts of Pigafetta and other contemporary writers. Accompanied by original Documents, with Notes and an Introduction, by Lord Stanley of Alderley. 2 maps and 5 illus. Hak. Soc., ser. I, vol. 52.

1906 PIGAFETTA, ANTONIO. Magellan's Voyage round the World, by Antonio Pigafetta. The original text of the Ambrosian MS. with English Translation, Notes and Bibliography. Edited by James Alexander Robertson. Portraits and facsimiles of charts and plates. 3 vols. 8vo. Cleveland.

1536 MAXIMILLIANUS TRANSYLVANUS and PIGAFETTA, F. A. Il Viaggi Fatto da gli Spagniuoli Atorno al Mondo. 4to. Venice.

> The first Italian edition. It was doubtless intended as a continuation or fourth part of the collection of voyages printed at Venice in 1534. . . . The preface of five pages is a noteworthy review of all the latest advances in geography.—From Maggs, No. 479.

1588 IGNACIO, FRIAR. For his voyage round the world see Mendoza, *The History of the great and mighty Kingdome of China,* under FAR EAST.

1598 CAVENDISH, THOMAS. The admirable and prosperous Voyage of the Worshipful Master Thomas Candish of Trimley in the Countie of Suffolke Esquire, into the South Sea, and from thence round about the Circumference of the whole earth, begun in the Yeere of our Lord 1586, and finished 1588. Written by Master Francis Pretty, lately of Ey in Suffolke, a gentleman employed in the same Action. In Hakluyt, vol. III. Fol. London.

> This relation was added to an account of Drake's Voyage in an edition of the latter of 1741. It is printed in Harris I, 23-31; in Callander I, 424-494; in Beazley I. This voyage is mentioned in Linschoten (see under 1598, EAST INDIES). There is a Dutch account, Amsterdam, 1598 and 1617. See below. According to Callander, the journal of this voyage by Francis Pretty, who was one of Cavendish's companions, was first printed in Latin, Frankfort, and next in English in Hakluyt, vol. III, whence Callander gives it verbatim.
>   Cavendish was the first, and for many years the only, Englishman to follow Drake in circumnavigating the globe. His voyage, which ran from 1586 to 1588, was, however, comparatively barren in geographical results, being largely a series of raids on Spanish colonies and shipping. The mere duplication of the feat was no small thing and his account of the disastrous attempt of Sarmiento to found a colony in the Straits of Magellan is not without interest. For his unfortunate second voyage, which had to turn back at the Straits of Magellan, see in Hakluyt, vol. III.

1617 CAVENDISH, THOMAS. Beschrijvinge vande overtreffelijcke ende wydtvermaerde zee-vaerdt vanden Edelen Heer ende Meester Thomas Candisch met drie Schepen nytghewaren end 21 Julij, 1586, ende met 1 schip wederom ghekeert in Pleymouth, den 9 Sept., 1588. . . . Hier noch by ghevoecht die Voyagie van Siere Francoys Draeck, en Siere Ian Haukens, naar West-India, anno 1595. Fol. Amsterdam.

1600-08 DRAKE, SIR FRANCIS. The famous Sir Francis Drake's Voyage into the South Sea and there hence about the whole Globe of the Earth in the years 1577, 1578, 1579, 1580. London.

> This is the version by Francis Pretty, which Hakluyt printed privately for some copies of his 1589 edition of the *Principal Navigations.* It was reprinted in 1618. It is not regarded as highly as is the version by Francis Fletcher (see below). French versions are reported for 1613, 1627, and 1641. See below.
> When Drake broke into the South Seas, he utterly wrecked the complacent security with which the Spaniards had regarded the Pacific Ocean as a Mare Nostrum. His exploits, the terror he created among the Spanish colonists, the wealth he brought back, and. the favors he received from Queen Elizabeth are all too well known to call for detail.

> 1613 (In French.) Le Voyage de l'illustre seigneur et chevalier Francois Drake, admiral d'angleterre, à l'entour du monde. Publiée par F. de Louvencourt, sieur de Vauchelles. 12mo. Paris.

>> A French version with the same title as that above is cited by Chavanne for Paris, 1627, and a second edition of this for 1641, with an English translation, London, 1761. See below for the 1641 edition. This last is referred to by Wagner *(The Spanish Southwest),* who says: "The translator's, or perhaps merely editor's, name was F. de Louvencourt, as we find it subscribed to the Dedication to St. Simon Baron de Courtomer. He had received the narrative from the Baron, one of whose tenants had been among Drake's crew in this voyage, and his own labor may not have been a translation, but merely an improvement of the French sailor's text. The narrative is certainly not identical with the English *The World Encompassed,* although it goes over the same details, yet the navigator is always styled 'nostre General,' just as he is 'our general' in the English account."—Quoted by Maggs, No. 491. "The map, however, is the most curious feature of the book, and is extremely rare. It was by a Dutchman, 'Nich Sype,' and exhibits *Nova Albion,* that is, the coast of California, and nearly all the interior of North America."—Quoted from Wagner by Maggs, No. 479. Possibly this work is a translation of Pretty's volume.

> 1641 DRAKE, FRANCIS. Le Voyage curieux faict autour du monde par Francois Drack, admiral d'Angleterre, traduit en francois par le Sieur de Louvencourt. 12mo. Paris.

1626 DRAKE, SIR FRANCIS. Sir Francis Drake Revived. Calling upon this Dull or Effeminate Age to follow his Noble Steps for Gold and Silver. By this Memorable Relation of the Rare Occurrences . . . in a third Voyage made by him into the West Indies, in the Yeares 72 and 73 . . . Faithfully taken out of the Report of M. Christopher Ceely, Ellis, Hixom, and others . . . by Philip Nichols. Reviewed by Sir Francis Drake himself. . . . Set forth by Sir Francis Drake, baronet. 4to. London.

> 2nd edit., London, 1628; again in the collected edition of 1653; with the title of "The English Hero; or Sir Francis Drake Revived," 1687, 1695, 1719, 1726, 1739, 1757, 1762. Some of these together with some other accounts are noted below.
> The version of the voyage of 1577-1580 was published by the nephew of the navigator and, according to Lowndes, is the best and earliest. It contains the intended dedication of Sir Francis Drake to Elizabeth, which is not found in the subsequent edition of 1653. It also has the dedication to Charles I not printed in that of 1653. It was stated by Callander that the original journal of this voyage was written in English by a native of Picardy, published at London in 1600 (perhaps the one listed under Francis Pretty's name). But in 1599 De Bry had pub-

lished an account in Latin at Frankfort. The original journal was translated into French, and published at Paris in 1627. A Portuguese pilot, Nuno da Silva, who was taken prisoner by Drake at the Isles of Cape Verd, wrote an account, which was included in Hakluyt. Hakluyt also inserted in his collection the journal of Cliffe, who was aboard the ship of Captain Winter, which became separated from the squadron after it passed the Straits of Magellan. It is also to be found in the Latin collection of Barlaeus, John de Late's *America*, lib. xiii, cap. 5; in Sir William Monson's collection of Naval Tracts; in Argensola's *Discovery and Conquest of the Moluccas*, and in the piece called *Drake Redevivus*. See also Purchas *His Pilgrimes*, I, lib. 2, cap. 3, and IV, lib. vi., cap. 5. There is an account in Harris I, 16-22, and in Callander I, 283-362, besides other write-ups of a more or less floating nature, which are noted below. For scholarly work on the subject one needs to consult the volumes put out by the Hakluyt Society, 1855 and 1914, the edition of the Argonaut Press, 1926, and the monumental edition of Henry R. Wagner, 1926. A companion work to *Sir Francis Drake Revived* is *The World Encompassed*, of 1628 and later. See below.

1652 (?) DRAKE, SIR FRANCIS. The Voyages and Travels of that Renowned Captain, Sir Francis Drake, into the West Indies, and Round about the World: Giving a perfect Relation of his strange Adventures, and many wonderful Discoveries, his Fight with the Spaniard, and many barbarous Nations; his taking St. Jago, St. Domingo, Carthagena, St. Augusta, and many other Places in the Golden Country of America, and other Parts of the World; His Description of Monsters, and Monstrous People. With many other remarkable Passages not before Extant: Contained in the History of His Life and Death; both pleasant and profitable for the Reader. Woodcut. London.

This work is listed without date but is put under 1652 by John Carter Brown.

1653 DRAKE, SIR FRANCIS. Sir Francis Drake Revived. Who is or may be a Patterne to stirre up all Heroicke and active Spirits of these Times to benefit their Countrey and eternize their Names by like Noble Attempts. Being a Summary and true Relation of foure severall Voyages made by the said Sir Francis Drake to the West Indies, . . 4to. London.

This is the collected edition. See under COLLECTIONS.

1671 DRAKE, SIR FRANCIS. The Life and Death of the valiant and renowned Sir Francis Drake; his Voyages and discoveries in the West Indies and about the World with his noble and valiant Action. By Samuel Clarke, late Minister of Bennet, Finck, London. 12mo. London.

1683 DRAKE, SIR FRANCIS. The Voyages of the ever renowned Sir Francis Drake to the West Indies, viz., his Great Adventures for Gold and Silver, the surprising of Nombre de Dios, his encompassing the World, and taking the Towns of St. Jago, S. Domingo, Carthagena. His last Voyage, in which he died. To which is added, His Exploits in the Spanish Invasion. 8vo. London.

1687 DRAKE, SIR FRANCIS. The English Hero: or, Sir Francis Drake Reviv'd. Being a full Account of the dangerous Voyages, Admirable Adventures, Notable Discoveries and Magnanimous atchievements of that Valiant and Renowned Commander. Engraved portrait. 12mo. London.
This work is by Richard Burton (Robert in Sabin). It was frequently reprinted, to as late at least as 1762.

1708 The Life and Glorious Reign of Queen Elizabeth. Likewise An Account of Sir Francis Drake's Voyage round the World. Also An Account of the Destruction of the great Fleet, call'd the Spanish Armada. . . (16 pp.) 8vo. London.

1741 DRAKE, SIR FRANCIS. The famous Voyage of Sir Francis Drake, with a particular Account of his Expedition in the West Indies against the Spaniards, being the first Commander that sailed round the Globe; to which is added, The Prosperous Voyage of Thomas Candish round the World. 8vo. London.

1766-68 DRAKE, SIR FRANCIS. Voyage to Magellanica and Polynesia. Abstracts from several accounts, in Callander I, 283-362. London.

1628 DRAKE, SIR FRANCIS. The World Encompassed by Sir Francis Drake. Being His next Voyage to that to Nombre de Dios; Carefully collected out of the Notes of Master Francis Fletcher, Preacher in this imployment, and divers others his followers in the same . . . 4to. London.

> 2nd edit., London, 1735; included in *Sir Francis Drake Revived,* of 1653; reprinted in Osborne II, 434-478; Hakluyt Society, 1855; Argonaut Press, London, 1926; see also Hakluyt Society, *New Light on Drake,* 1914, and Wagner's *Drake's Voyage round the World,* San Francisco, 1926, cited below.
> This work was based on the notes of Francis Fletcher, chaplain to Drake, who, according to Waldman, has given an authoritative presentation of a great adventure.

1745 DRAKE, SIR FRANCIS. The World Encompassed by Sir Francis Drake. Offered now at last to publick View, both for the Honour of the Actor, but especially for the stirring up of heroick Spirits, to benefit their Country, and eternize their Names by Like Noble Attempts. Collected out of the Notes of Mr. Francis Fletcher, Preacher in this Employment, and compared with divers others Notes that went in the same Voyage. In Osborne II, 434-478.

1855 DRAKE, SIR FRANCIS. The World Encompassed by Sir Francis Drake, Being his next Voyage to that of Nombre de Dios (by Sir Francis Drake the Younger). Collated with an unpublished Manuscript of Francis Fletcher, Chaplain to the Expedition. With Appendices illustrative of the same Voyage and Introduction, by William Sandys Wright Vaux, F. R. S., Keeper of Coins, Brit. Mus. Map. Hak. Soc., ser. I, vol. 16. London.

1914 DRAKE, SIR FRANCIS. New Light on Drake. Spanish and Portuguese Documents relating to the Circumnavigation Voyage. Discovered, translated, and annotated by Mrs. Zelia Nuttall. 3 maps and 14 illus. Hak. Soc., ser. II, vol. 34. London.

1926 DRAKE, SIR FRANCIS. The World Encompassed and Analogous Contemporary Documents concerning Sir Francis Drake's Circumnavigation of the World, with an Appreciation of the Achievement by Sir Richard Carnac Temple, edited by N. M. Penzer. Maps and illus. 4to. Argonaut Press. London.

WAGNER, HENRY R. Sir Francis Drake's Voyage round the World: Its Aims and Achievements. 73 portraits, facsimiles of maps, and other illus. 4to. San Francisco.

> The main object of this work is to bring together in one book the principal narratives and documents bearing on the expedition, and with the aid of these, to rewrite the account of the voyage. Particular attention has been paid to the identification of such places as he visited. An extended examination has been made of some recent theories about the object of the voyage, and it is believed that a correct solution has been found to this much discussed problem. . . It has seemed advisable for readier reference to reproduce the English contemporary accounts of the voyage and such of those of Spanish origin as contain anything of real value. An analysis of the cartographical documents illustrating the course of the voyage is included.—From Bookseller's Notes.

1619 SCHOUTEN, WILLIAM CORNELISON. The Relation of a Wonderfull Voiage made by William Cornelison Schovten of Horne. Shewing how South from the Streights of Magellan in Terra Del-fuego: he found and discouered a newe passage through the great South Sea, and that way sayled round the World. Describing what Islands, Countries, People, and strange Aduentures·he found in his saide Passage. (Translated from the Dutch by William Philip.) 8 maps and plates. 4to. London.

The maps and plates have French legends, with page numbering taken from the Paris issue by Gobert. The Dutch original appeared at Amsterdam, 1618. It was translated into Latin by De Bry, Frankfort, 1619. It also appeared in Purchas II, 1625. A second narrative of the voyage was published in French at Amsterdam, 1622. Other relations were printed, the most noteworthy being "Navigation Australe par Jacques le Mair et par Corn. Schouten," said to have been compiled from the Journal of Adrian Claesz, and published in the *Recueil des Voyages à Etablissement de la Compagnie des Indes Orientales,* (1702). There is also a Latin edition, Amsterdam, 1619. The account was reprinted in abstract in Harris I, 51-63; and that of Claesz in abstract in Callander II, 217-269; in Dalrymple II, 1-64; in Moore I, 49-53. See also Burney's *Chronological Historical Discoveries* II, 360.

This was one of the most remarkable voyages ever undertaken and contributed much to the science of cartography, while the numerous versions in other languages attest its popularity, indicating how much the new passage into the South Seas was appreciated. The voyage was designed to open up the way for trading expeditions into those lands thought to lie south of those monopolised by the Dutch East India Company, which had been granted exclusive rights to the region east of the Cape of Good Hope and west of the Straits of Magellan. Merchants and other interested persons, of the town of Hoorn, fitted out the expedition under the planning of Isaac Le Maire, whose son Jacob sailed in command of one of the ships. William Cornelius Schouten, who had made several trips to the East Indies, was commander-in-chief. The Straits of Le Maire, which were traversed for the first time, received its name from the patron of the expedition, and Cape Horn its name from the town of Hoorn. The discovery of this passage through the Straits of Le Maire and around Cape Horn, though entered in the log, were branded as infamous forgery by the Dutch officials at Ternate, and the ship's goods and the ship itself confiscated. Le Maire died at Mauritius on the way home. Later his rights and those of his companions to their discovery were recognized and the East India Company was ordered to return the confiscated vessel and its cargoes to its owners, and to pay àll costs and interest from the day of the illegal seizure. See the Introduction to Hakluyt Society edition of Speilbergen, *The East and West Indian Mirrour,* under date 1906 below. Schouten sailed from the Texel June 24, 1615, and returned home July 1, 1617.

1618 SCHOUTEN, WILLIAM CORNELISON. Jounal ofte Beschryvinghe van de wonderlike reyse, ghedaen door Willem Corneliez Schouten van Hoorn, inde Jaren 1615, 1616, en 1617. Hoe hy Bezuyden de Strate van Magellanes een nieuwe Passagie tot inde groote Zuyz Zee ondeckt, en voort den gheheelen Aerdkloot omgheseylt, heeft. Wat Eylanden, vreemde volvken en wonderlicke avontueren hem ontmoet zijn. 4to. Amsterdam.

1622 HERRERA, ANTONIO DE. Novvs Orbis, sive Descriptio Indiae Occidentalis . . . metaphraste C. Barlaeo, Accesserunt . . . aliorum Indiae Occidentalis Descriptiones & Navigationis omnium per Fretum Magellanicum succincta narratio. With Mexican figures and maps of America, etc. Amsterdam.

This volume is highly valuable as containing the first edition of the genuine Voyage of Le Maire (also issued in Latin and Dutch the same year) as distinguished from that which had been, through the Dutch East India Company's jealousy of Le Maire, published by Blaeu under the name of Cornelius Schouten, the Commander of one of Le Maire's vessels.—Quoted by Robinson, No. 20.

1690 CROW, FRANCIS. A Voyage round the World, or, A Pocket Library divided into several volumes, in such a method never made by any Traveller before; the work intermix'd with Essays historical, Moral and Divine; and other kinds of Learning. London.

> The author, a non-conformist divine, lived a while in Jamaica. This work is probably not his own voyage but a compilation.

1697 DAMPIER, WILLIAM. A New Voyage round the World, describing particularly the Isthmus of America, several Coasts and Islands in the West Indies, the Isles of Cape Verde, the Passage by Terra del Fuego, the South Sea Coasts of Chili, Peru, and Mexico, the Isle Guam, one of the Ladrones, Mindanao, and the Philippine and East India Islands, near Cambodia, China, Formosa, Laconia, Celebes, . . ; New Holland, Sumatra, Nicobar Isles; the Cape of Good Hope and Santa Helena. Their Soil, Rivers, Harbours, Plants, Fruits, Animals, and Inhabitants; their Customs, Religion, Government, Trade, . . . Maps and plates. 8vo. London.

> This is called vol. I. The other two follow immediately.

1699 DAMPIER, WILLIAM. Captain Dampier's Voyages and Descriptions. Vol. II in Three Parts. I. A Supplement of a Voyage round the World, describing the Countries of Tonquin, Achin, the Malacca, . . . their Products, Inhabitants, Manners, Trade, Policy, . . . 2. Two Voyages to Campeachy; with a Description of the Coasts, Products and Inhabitants; Logwood-Cutting, Trade, . . . Of Yucatan, Campeachy, New Spain, . . . 3. A Discourse of Trade-Winds, Breezes, Storms, Tides, and Currents, of the Torrid Zone throughout the World; with an Account of Natal in Africa, its Product, Negroes, . . . To which is added, An Index to both Volumes. Maps. 8vo. London.

1703 DAMPIER, WILLIAM. A Voyage to New Holland, . . in 1699, wherein is described the Canary Islands, the Isles of Mayo and St. Jago, the Bay of All Saints, with the Forts and Town of Bahia in Brasil, Cape Salvadore, . . their Inhabitants, Manners, Customs, Trade, Soil and Natural History. Maps and Plates. 8vo. London.

> This makes up vol. III.

1709 DAMPIER, WILLIAM. A Continuation of a Voyage to New Holland, . . in the Year 1699; wherein are described the Islands of Timor, Rotes, and Anabao. A Passage between the Islands Timor and Anabao; Copang and Lephao Bays. The Islands Omba, Fetter, Bande and Bird. A Description of the Coast of New Guinea. The Islands Pulo Sabuda,

Cockle, King William, Providence, Garret, Dennu, Ant, Laves, and St. John's; also a New Passage between New Guinea and Nova Britania. The Islands Ceram Bonao, Bouro, and several Islands before unknown. The Coast of Java and Streights of Sunda. Author's Arrival at Batavia. The Cape of Good Hope, St. Helena, Ascension, . . Their Inhabitants, Customs, Trade, ∴. Harbours, Soil, Birds, Fish, . . Trees, Plants, Fruits, . . Also Rivers, Birds, Fishes, . . not found in this part of the World. Maps, draughts, plates. 8vo. London.

This makes up Part II of vol. III. The chronology of the various issues of these separate volumes is not easy to keep straight. For bibliographical information concerning Dampier's works, see Sabin, *Bibliotheca Americana*, V, 188-195. Vol. I had the following issues: 2nd edit., 1697; 3rd, 1698; 4th, 1699; 5th, 1703. Vol. II, 2nd edit., 1700; 3rd, 1705. Vol. III, part 1, 2nd edit., 1709. The three volumes came out together in 12mo, London, 1717. They were published in 4 vols., London, 1729, with the addition of the Voyages by Wafer, Sharp, Funnell, etc., but over Dampier's protests. See Dampier, 1729, under COLLECTIONS. His first voyage was reprinted in Harris I, 84-130, and again, London, 1776. A number of modern reprints testify to the interest of the present day in the performances of this indefatigable navigator, as well as the numerous translations into various European languages. For some of these see below. Of the several translations into French the following may be noted: Vol. I, Amsterdam, 1698; vols. I and II, Amsterdam, 1701; the three volumes, Amsterdam, 1701-05; the same, with the inclusion of those of Wafer, Wood, Cowley, Roberts, and Sharp, in 5 vols., 1711-12. And into Dutch, with that of Woodes Rogers, Amsterdam, 1715.

Of the famous group of buccaneers that tormented the Spaniards in the "South Sea" from 1680 to 1720, Dampier was the best known and probably the most intelligent. His industry in taking careful notes of everything he saw was equalled by his assiduous pains in preserving them from destruction. His first voyage in the *Cygnet* started from Virginia, August 23, 1683, and ended Sept. 16, 1691, when he reached England. It was on this voyage that the first English landing was made on Australian shores, at the entrance of King Sound. His published report, which was anything but favorable, stirred Lord Orford and Lord Pembroke, of the Admiralty, to consider the possible advantages of a settlement in Australia. His next voyage in 1698 makes the second expedition of the English to Australia.—From Maggs, No. 491. Concerning the problem of Australia's being a continent, Dampier says that "It is not yet determined whether it is an Island or a Main Continent; but I am certain that it joyns neither to Asia, Africa, nor America." It is evident that on his first visit he knew nothing of what Tasman had discovered; but on his second expedition he used one of Tasman's charts. He furnished accurate information on the various islands in the Pacific, but he really added little to geographical discovery. Nevertheless his books are very readable. His remaining voyages were rather of the nature of buccaneering adventures.

1776 DAMPIER, WILLIAM. The Voyages and Adventures of Captain William Dampier. 2 vols. 8vo. London.

This edition contains only the three volumes written by Dampier himself and is without maps and plates. In the Preface the editor says: "The first edition of Dampier's voyages was published by himself, but not in the same order they were performed, which has a little perplexed the narrative; the language has now become partly obsolete, which renders the perusal more difficult to common readers; and the edition is now also extremely scarce. To remedy these inconveniences, the chronological order wherein the series of events happened is observed in this Edition; all old phrases and expressions are modernized; (names of things are also changed in keeping with modern usage)."— Quoted by Puttock & Simpson.

1906 DAMPIER, WILLIAM. Voyages: consisting of a New Voyage round the World, Two Voyages to Campeachy, Discourse of Winds, a Voyage to New Holland, and a Vindication in Answer to the Chimerical Relation of William Funnell. Edited by John Masefield. Portrait, 5 maps, and 18 illus. 2 vols. 8vo. London.

1927 DAMPIER, WILLIAM. A New Voyage Round the World. With an Introduction by Sir Albert Gray. Portrait, 2 facsimiles, and 4 maps. 4to. Argonaut Press. London.

1931 DAMPIER, WILLIAM. Voyages and Discoveries; with an Introduction by Blennell Wilkinson, and a Note on the Discourse of Winds by A. C. Bell. Folding maps. 4to. Argonaut Press. London.

This is the second volume of Dampier's Voyages and includes his Voyage to Tonquin; his voyages to Campeachy, in which he describes in detail his early adventures among the logwood cutters and buccaneers of the West Indies.

1698 (In French.) Nouveau voyage autour du monde où l'on décrit en particulier l'isthme de l'Amérique, plusieurs côtes et isles des Indes Occidentales, . . l'isle de Guam, Mindanao, et des autres Philippines. . . Enrichi de cartes et de figures, et traduit de l'Anglois. 2 vols. in 1. 16mo. Amsterdam.

1701 (In French.) Nouveau Voyage autour du Monde; Suite du Voyage autour du Monde, avec Traité des Vents; Supplement du Voyage autour du Monde. Maps and plates. 3 vols. 8vo. Amsterdam.

1715 (In Dutch.) Nieuwe Reize naa de Zuidzee van daar naa Oost Indien en verder rondom de Waereld begonnon in 1708 en goeyndigd in 1711. Folding maps. 4to. Amsterdam.

1699 COWLEY, AMBROSE. Voyage round the Globe in 1683. In Hacke's *Collection.* See under COLLECTIONS this date.

Reprinted in Harris I, 77-84. Given in abstract in Callander II, 528-556.
Cowley did his own publishing without the aid of any assistant. Its deficiencies are therefore excusable. But it has the merit of honesty and freedom; it openly avows his intentions of taking the ships of any nation he can master. His account of the Galapagos are considered to be very accurate, and his remarks on the designs of the Dutch at this period were pertinent to the situation at the time. He sailed from Virginia, August 23, 1683, and returned home October 12, 1686. He was one of the buccaneers, who with John Cooke did most damage to the Spaniards in the West Indies. After plundering the west coast of South America, they sailed back by way of the East Indies. From Batavia they went home in a Dutch ship. Strange to say, they were hospitably entertained by the Spaniards at Guam.

1707 FUNNELL, WILLIAM. A Voyage round the World: Containing an Account of Captain Dampier's Expedition into the South Seas, in the Ship St. George, in the Years 1703 and 1704. With his various Adventures, Engagements, . . and a particular and exact Description of several Islands in the Atlantick Ocean, the Brazilian Coasts, the Passage round Cape Horn, and the Coast of Chili, Peru, and Mexico. Together with the Author's Voyage from Anapalla on the West Coast of Mexico, to the East India. His passing by Three unknown Islands; and through a new discovered Streight, near the Coast of New Guinea. His Arrival at Amboyna; with a large Description of that and other Spice Islands; also of Batavia, the Cape of Good Hope, . . Their Rivers,

Harbours, Plants, Animals, Inhabitants, . . with divers Maps, Draughts, Figures of Plants and Animals. 8vo. London.

This work is generally taken as the fourth volume of Dampier's Collection, although there is no indication of its having been so intended at the time of publication.—Puttock & Simpson. Reprinted in Harris I, 131-150, and in Callander III, 145-227.

Funnell sailed as mate to Captain Dampier, and it was he, not Dampier, who really circumnavigated the globe on this voyage, as Dampier proceeded only as far as the South Seas. The purpose of the expedition was to harass the Spaniards and take plunder from vessels and towns of South America. Its failure was due to differences that arose between them. "Funnell arrived in England before Dampier and seized the opportunity to compose a relation of his voyage, a task for which he was ill-qualified, and which he performed with disadvantage to the public. His narrative contained much that was disapproved by Dampier, who immediately after published a 'Vindication of his Voyage' (see Dampier under date 1709, above), pointing out the misrepresentations of Funnell. This brought out 'An Answer' from John Welbe, a midshipman on board Dampier's ship, in which he charged the Captain with barbarous treatment of his crew."—Quoted by Maggs, No. 491.

1712 **COOKE, EDWARD.** A Voyage to the South Sea and Round the World, Perform'd in the Years 1708, 1709, 1710, and 1711. . . . Wherein an Account is given of Mr. Alexander Selkirk, his Manner of living and taming wild Beasts during the four Years and four Months he liv'd upon the uninhabited Island of Juan Fernandes. Cuts and maps. London.

The actual first edition of Cooke's Voyage was this one volume edition. . . Apparently there was considerable rivalry between the publishers of Cooke's account of this voyage and the publishers of Woodes Rogers' account to be the first to get their edition on the market. Cooke's work came out first, but only in this single volume, the latter part of the voyage being related in a few compressed pages at the end. The publishers almost immediately reprinted the work and extended it to two volumes, the latter part of the voyage (after leaving California) occupying the whole of Vol. II.—From Maggs, Nos. 491 and 549. The introduction to vol. II gives further information regarding Alexander Selkirk. Cooke was second captain on board the *Dutchess* on the privateering expedition of Woodes Rogers. His journal and charts are said to be inferior to those published by Rogers.—Maggs, No. 491. See below for the two volume edition.

> 1712 **COOKE, EDWARD.** A Voyage to the South Sea and Round the World, 1708-1711. Containing (vol. I) a Journal of memorable Transactions during the said Voyage; the Winds, Currents, and Variation of the Compass, the Taking of the Towns of Puna and Guayaquil, and several Prizes, one of which a rich Acapulco Ship. A Description of the American Coasts, from Tierra del Fuego to California. . . An Historical Account of all those Countries from the best Authors. With a new Map and Description of the mighty River of the Amazons. Wherein an Account is given of Mr. Alexander Selkirk, his Manner of Living and taming Wild Beasts during the four Years and four Months he liv'd upon the uninhabited Island of Juan Fernandez; and (vol. II) a Continuation of the Voyage from California, through India, North about into England. The Description of all the American Coasts along the South Sea, . . with a Table of Latitudes and Longitudes, and an Introduction, wherein, besides other material Particulars, is an Account of the Cargo of the Acapulco Prize. 20 copperplates of natural history, views, etc., 5 folding maps, and 3 folding tables. 2 vols. 8vo. London.

1712 ROGERS, WOODES. A Cruising Voyage Round the World: First to the South-Seas, thence to the East Indies, and homewards by the Cape of Good Hope. Begun in 1708 and finished in 1711. Containing a Journal of all the Remarkable Transactions; particularly, Of the Taking of Puna and Guayaquil, of the Acapulco ship, and other Prizes; An Account of Alexander Selkirk's Living alone four Years and four Months in an Island; and a brief Description of several Countries in our Course noted for Trade, especially in the South Sea. . . And an Introduction relating to the South-Sea Trade. Maps of all the Coast from the best Spanish Manuscript Draughts. 8vo. London.

> 2nd edit., corrected, 8vo, London, 1718. Another edition, London, 1722; again London, 1726. In Harris I, 150-184; in Callander III, 231-379. A modern edition, with a different title, London, 1889 and 1894; again in the Seafarers' Library, London, 1928. Translated into French, Amsterdam, 1716. See below.
> This book has been called a "buccaneering classic." It is a work of great interest and possesses a quaint humor that renders it delightful reading. In many respects the voyage was a notable one, but in none more than this, that with a mongrel crew, and with officers often mutinous, good order and discipline were maintained throughout. The original edition is extremely rare.—D. N. B. It has interest for students of literature in that from Rogers' and Cooke's accounts of Selkirk, Defoe found material for his Robinson Crusoe, who in the person of Selkirk had been left on the Island of Juan Fernandez by Captain Stradling some four years before. It is interesting to note that the Island of Guam, which treated Captain Cowley so handsomely, did likewise with Rogers. Although a Spanish colony, it was sufficiently distant from Asia and America to consider itself neutral in the disputes affecting other parts of the Spanish Empire. Rogers was one of the few fortunate adventurers to make a prize haul of the plate ship which sailed annually from Manila to Acapulco, Mexico.

> 1894 ROGERS, WOODES. Life Aboard a British Privateer in the Time of Queen Anne: being the Journal of Captain Woodes Rogers, with Notes. Illustrations and maps by Robert C. Leslie. 4to. London.

> 1928 ROGERS, WOODES. A Cruising Voyage Round the World. Edited by G. E. Manwaring, F. R. Hist. Soc. With Introduction and Notes. 8 plates. 8vo. Seafarers's Library. London.

> 1716 (In French.) Voyage autour du Monde, commencé en 1708 et fini en 1711. Où l'on a joint quelque pièces curicuses touchant la Rivière des Amazones et la Guiane. 7 folding maps, a very large one of South America, and 16 engraved plates. 3 vols. 12mo. Amsterdam.

> > The 3rd volume contains as additional matter (not in the English original) Acuna's Account of the Amazon, translated by Gomberville. —Maggs, No. 546.

1725 DEFOE, DANIEL. A New Voyage round the World by a Course never Sailed before: being a voyage undertaken by some Merchants, who afterwards proposed the setting up of an East-India Company in Flanders. Plates. 8vo. London.

> Another edition, London, 1787. See below.
> This rare book is doubtless one of Defoe's clever deceits, as much so as his *Captain Singleton*, and is probably based on Dampier.

> 1787 DEFOE, DANIEL. A Voyage Round the World, by a Course never sailed before, to which is prefixed the Life of the Author, by William Shields. 3 vols. 12mo. London.

1726 SHELVOCKE, GEORGE. A Voyage round the World by the way of the great South Sea, Perform'd in the Years 1719, 20, 21, 22, in the Speedwell, of London, of 24 Guns and 100 Men (under His Majesty's Commission to cruize on the Spaniards in the late War with the Spanish Crown) till she was cast away on the Island of Juan Fernandez, in May, 1720; and afterwards continued in the Recovery, the Jesus Maria and Sacra Familia, . . . Folding map of the world and engraved plates. 8vo. London.

Republished by Shelvocke's son, George, somewhat purged and refined, London, 1757. Reprinted in Harris I, 198-240; with a supplement from Betagh's account in Callander III, 502-583. A modern edition, London, 1928. Translated into German, Bremen, 1787. See below. See also for the general circumstances of this voyage Clipperton under date 1766-69 below.

Shelvocke sailed under a privateer's commission, but his activities were more those of a pirate; he was afterwards charged with piracy but got off on technical grounds and fled the country.—Gosse. His account is an apology for his conduct in consequence of a lawsuit started against him by the proprietors. The issue of this voyage gave the public a bad idea of all expeditions to the South Sea. Against the ill success of this voyage may be set the good fortune of Rogers' expedition. "Two histories were published of this voyage. . . The other was written by one of his officers, William Betagh (see below under 1728), who was roughly treated in Shelvocke's narrative, and who wrote his account with the design of exposing Shelvocke. Both narratives were written with plenty of spirit."—Quoted by Maggs, No. 502. The connection of this Voyage with Coleridge's "Ancient Mariner" is well known. On getting round Cape Horn, Shelvocke caused an albatross to be shot. Wordsworth, who had been reading Shelvocke, suggested to Coleridge to use this incident with expiatory consequences. It has also been pointed out that in this work is the first printed intimation of gold in California.

1757 SHELVOCKE, GEORGE. A Voyage round the world by Way of the Great South Sea: Performed in a Private Expedition during the War, which broke out with Spain in the year 1718. . . Maps and 4 plates. 8vo. London.

1787 (In German.) Reise um die Welt. 8vo. Bremen.

1728 BETAGH, WILLIAM. Voyage round the World: Being an Account of a remarkable Enterprize begun in 1719, chiefly to cruise on the Spaniards in the Great South Ocean. Relating the True historical Facts of the whole Affair; Testifyed by many imployed therein; and confirmed by Authorities from the Owners. Folding map of the world in planisphere. 8vo. London.

The author was captain of the marines in Shelvocke's voyage. His book is an attack on Captain Shelvocke, "written chiefly to undeceive mankind in the spurious account of a voyage round the world published by Captain George Shelvocke, which account is not only injurious to me, but is intirely the most absurd and false narrative that was ever deliver'd to the publick."—Quoted by Sotheran. Betagh tells his own story very differently and his lively manner gives to his narrative much beauty and spirit. This was about the last of the buccaneering expeditions. —Maggs, No. 429.

1732 CARERI, JÓHN FRANCESCO GEMELLI. A Voyage Round the
World: of Turkey, Persia, India, China, Philippine Islands, and New
Spain, translated from the Italian. Maps and plates. In Churchill
IV, 1-572. London.

> In Pinkerton XVII there is listed an Italian edition in 7 vols., 8vo, Naples,
> 1699, under the title *Giro del Mundo*. Another Italian edition, 9 vols., Venice,
> 1719. See below.
> This author's account of his travels is very voluminous. He started out on
> his journies June 13, 1693.

> 1719 CARERI, GIOVANNI FRANCESCO GEMELLI. Giro del Mondo.
> Nuova edizione accresciuta, ricorretta, e divisa in novo volumi. Con
> un indice de' viaggiatori, e loro opere. 9 vols. 16mo. Venice.

1744 ANSON, GEORGE (Commodore). An Authentic Journal of the last
Expedition under the Command of Commodore Anson. Containing a
Regular and Exact Account of the whole Proceedings and several
Transactions thereof: particularly at Madeira, St. Catherine's, St. Jul-
ian's, St. Juan Fernandez; their Manner of Living there upon Sea-
Lions, Sea-Dogs, . . . their taking the rich Spanish Galleon, . . . their go-
ing to Canton in China, . . To which is added, A Narrative of the ex-
traordinary Hardships suffered by the Adventurers in this Voyage.
London.

> Reprinted, 8vo, London, 1767.
> This rare account of Anson's voyage was done by John Philips, a midshipman
> on the *Centurion.* It antedates the official account by four years.

ANSON, GEORGE. An Authentic Account of Commodore Anson's
Expedition: containing all that was remarkable, curious and entertain-
ing, during that long and dangerous Voyage. . . Taken from a Private
Journal. London.

> Another edition, Dublin, 1745. Another surreptitious work.

ANSON, GEORGE. A Voyage to the South Seas, and to many other
Parts of the World, 1740-44, by Commodore Anson in his Majesty's
Ship the Centurion. . . The Second Part of a Voyage to the South-
Seas. . . By an Officer of the Fleet. 2 vols. 8vo. London.

> The Second Part is undated. This is a curious and very rare chap-book edi-
> tion, with crude woodcut portraits and other woodcuts.—Bookseller's Note.

1745 ANSON, GEORGE (Commodore). A True and Impartial Journal of
a Voyage to the South Seas, and round the Globe, in His Majesty's
Ship the Centurion, under the Command of Commodore George Anson.
By Pascoe Thomas, Teacher of the Mathematics on board the Centurion. Together with some historical Accounts of Chili, Peru, Mexico,

and the Empire of China, . . and lastly, several curious Observations
on a Comet seen in the South-Seas on the Coast of Mexico. 8vo.
London.

The abstracts and extracts in Harris I, 337-368, and Astley must be derived
from some of the above acounts, since these Collections antedate the official volume of 1748.

1748 ANSON, GEORGE (Commodore). A Voyage Round the World in the
Years 1740, 1, 2, 3, 4; compiled from Papers and other Materials of
the Right Honourable George Lord Anson, and published under his
Direction by Richard Walter, M.A., Chaplain of His Majesty's Ship
the Centurion in that Expedition. 42 plates. 4to. London.

Of this important work there were many subsequent editions and translations.
Four came out the same year as the original, and by 1781 there were 16. Dublin,
as usual, was not far behind with editions, which were probably for the most part
pirated ones. Of the two first issues published in 1748, one was for the author
himself, which is the genuine first, and the other, often called the first, was for
the publishers. The first French translation appeared in Amsterdam and Leipzig,
1749; a Dutch translation at Amsterdam, 1749; a German, Leipzig and Göttingen,
1749; an Italian, Livorno, 1756. Modern reprints are the ones in Everyman's Library, with an Introduction by John Masefield, London, 1911, and another, London,
1928. Some of the later editions are listed by title below.
The account by Chaplain Walter, which is written in an admirable style, is
the official one. This work was sometimes attributed to Benjamin Robins, F. R. S.,
author of *Mathematical Tracts,* London, 1761, but there appears to be no decisive
evidence for Robins' claims. For the question see James Wilson, Preface to the
Mathematical Tracts; Nichols, *Literary Anecdotes of the Eighteenth Century* II,
206; and the *Biographia Britannica,* under Anson, and the Corrigenda and Addenda to that article in vol. IV of that work.—Edinb. Cab. For a list of the
original writers on the subject of this voyage, see *Gent. Mag., 1780,* vol. L, 322.
It was noticed in the *Journal des Scavans,* 1750, I, 76; II, 158.
This famous and unfortunate expedition, consisting at the start of eight ships,
was sent under the command of George Anson at the beginning of the war with
Spain, to harass the Spaniards on the western coast of South America. Seven
ships were lost around Cape Horn and on the coast of Chili and out of 900 men
who left England on board more than 600 perished. As usual scurvy took an ap-
palling toll. The primary object of the expedition was not attained, but by the
capture of the Manila Galleon near China, Anson and the surviving members of
his crew reached England much the richer. As with many a ship before and
after, the island of Juan Fernandez proved a blessing in restoring scurvy-stricken
men to health. Among the ships wrecked was the *Wager,* whose story is told by
Lieutenant Byron and Bulkeley and Cummins (see under dates 1743 and 1768,
SOUTH AMERICA). Walter's account of the voyage is a model of what such
literature should be. The mournful beauty of the passage describing their approach
to Cape Horn compares well with that of Masefield's in his poem *Dauber.* Anson
left St. Helens Sept. 9, 1740, and got back June 15, 1744.

1751 ANSON, GEORGE. An affecting Narrative of the Unfortunate Voyage
and Catastrophe of His Majesty's Ship Wager, one of Commodore Anson's Squadron in the South Sea Expedition. Containing a full account
of its being cast away on a desolate Island, . . Compiled from Authentic Journals . . . from an Eye-Witness. London.

For the loss of the *Wager* and the divided action of the crew see
the accounts by Bulkeley and Lieut. Byron, under dates 1743 and 1768
respectively, SOUTH AMERICA.

1752 COYER, GABRIEL FRANCOIS (Abbé). A Supplement to Lord Anson's Voyage round the World. Containing a discovery and descrip-

tion of the Island of Frivola. By the Abbé Coyer. To which is prefixed an introductory Preface by the Translator. 8vo. London.

2nd edit., London, 1752; Dublin, 1752.
This is a very clever skit on Anson's famous voyage, written as a satirical romance on the French nation. "A burlesque publication, . . . it has met with universal applause, not only in France, but in almost every country upon the Continent where it has followed the book upon which it is founded."—Quoted by Maggs, No. 502.

1766-68 ANSON, GEORGE. Voyage round the World. Extract in Callander III, 644-654. London.

As a supplement to this voyage is given a letter from Captain Murray, Commander of H. M. S. *Pearl,* which got separated from Anson during the voyage.

1785 ANSON, GEORGE. Voyage Round the World, 1740-44, compiled from his Papers and Materials By Richard Walter. 2 vols. in I. 8vo. Kilmarnock.

This edition has claim to fame because it was printed at the same press as the first volume of Burns's poetry.

1928 ANSON, GEORGE. Anson's Voyage round the World. New edition with Prefatory Notes by G. S. Laird Clowes. Original plates and charts and numerous additional illus., etc. 8vo. London.

1749 (In French.) Voyage autour du monde fait dans les années 1740 à 1744 par Lord Anson envoyé par sa Majesté Britanique dans la Mer du Sud; tiré des journaux et autres papiers de ce seigneur, et publié par Richard Walter, Maitre des arts et Chapelain du Centurion dans cette expédition. Traduit de l'anglais. Maps and plates. 4to. Amsterdam and Leipzig.

1749 (In Dutch.) Reize rondom de Werreld, 1740-1744, Opgesteld uit Journalen en andere Papier en van . . . G. Anson . . . door Richard Walter. Tweede Druk. Portrait, maps and plates. 4to. Amsterdam.

1749 (In German.) Reise um die Welt Zusammengetragen von Richard Walter. Aus dem Englischen übersetzt von Eobald Toze. Maps. Leipzig and Göttingen.

1749-51 (In French.) Voyage autour du monde, fait dans les années 1740 et 1744 (redigé par Benjamin Robins) publié par Richard Walter; traduit de l'anglais par Ellie de Joncourt. 2 vols. Amsterdam.

For claims of Robins see under 1748 edition above.

1756 (In Italian.) Viaggio ottorno el mondo, fatte negli anni 1740-44. Livorno.

1772 (In German.) Reisen in das Südmeer, als Beytrag zu Anson's Reisen nebst dessen Lebensbeschreibung. Aus dem Englischen. Nürnberg.

1744-48 CLIPPERTON, JOHN. The Voyage of Captain John Clipperton round the World, from an authentic Journal. In Harris I, 184-198. London.

Also in Callander III, 444-502. See below.
Clipperton was one of the buccaneers associated with the exploits of Shelvocke and Woodes Rogers in the early part of the eighteenth century. Foreseeing

a break with Spain and hoping to duplicate, the success of Woodes Rogers, some merchants resolved to fit out two ships for the South Seas and the coasts of South America. At first Shelvocke was selected for commander, but he was replaced by Clipperton. The plan of using Flemish soldiers was abandoned when it was discovered that such a procedure would soon make for trouble aboard the vessels. The two ships had to lie at anchor at Plymouth for three months awaiting the right winds. Factions which developed during the delay increased in severity during the voyage. The start was finally made in February, 1719. There exists no separate and distinct relation of Clipperton's voyage. But there are two histories extant—one by Shelvocke and the other by Betagh (see above 1726 and 1728 respectively). As has been noted above, Shelvocke's account is an apology for his conduct; the other an acrimonious attack on Shelvocke. Clipperton certainly showed great inclination to do justice to his proprietors and to maintain the honor of his country under the circumstances.

1766-68 CLIPPERTON, JOHN. Voyage to Magellanica and round the World. In Callander III, 444-502. London.

LE HERMITE, JACQUES. Voyage of the Nassau Fleet round the Globe, under the Command of Jacques Le Hermite. In Harris I, 66-77. London.

Le Hermite, or L'Heremite, sailed from Goree April 29, 1623, and returned home January 21, 1626. This voyage did little to increase geographical knowledge. Some futile attacks were made on Spanish possessions of the west coast of South America.

ROGGEWEIN, JACOB. Commodore Roggewein's Expedition with three Ships, for the Discovery of Southern Lands under the Direction of the Dutch West India Company. From an original Journal. In Harris I, 256-320. London.

In Callander III, 584-641; in Dalrymple, 1770-71. A Dutch account, Dort, 1728. See below. Another account in German, Leipzig, 1738; in French by Charles Frederick Behrens, who was sergeant and commander of troops in Roggewein's fleet, printed at the Hague, 1739. Both accounts were translated by Dalrymple.

Roggewein sailed from the Texel, August 21, 1721, and returned home August 11, 1723. The father of the navigator proposed to the Dutch West India Company a project for discovering something of the vast continent and its islands supposed to be lying in the southern portion of the globe. Dying before it could be executed, he entrusted the expedition to his son Jacob, who performed the voyage. In their return they touched at Batavia, where their ships were seized by the Dutch East India Company. However, the States General ordered the latter to make restitution with two new ships fully rigged, pay the full value of the cargo, and pay the crew their wages and all costs. Roggewein's is the first certified account of contact with Easter Island and its great stone images, as well as the last of the great Dutch circumnavigations.

1766-68 ROGGEWEIN, JACOB. Voyage to Polynesia and Australasia. In Callander III, 584-641. London.

1728 ROGGEWEIN, JACOB. Twee Jaarige Reyze rondom de Wereld. Dort.

This work appeared without the author's name and is therefore of doubtful worth. The original journal came to light in the early part of the nineteenth century and was reprinted at Middleburg, 1838.— Quoted.

SPILBERGEN, JORIS. The Voyage of George Spilbergen in quality of Admiral of Six Dutch Ships, round the World. In Harris I, 44-50 London.

The first version of this voyage in English appeared in Purchas, 1625 (gathered out of the "Latine Journall"). An account in Callander II, 191-217. The original Dutch version edited by the Hakluyt Society, 1906. Dutch original and a Latin edition, Leyden, 1619. See below.
Spilbergen sailed from the Texel Aug. 8, 1614, and returned home July 1, 1617. He wrote two journals. The first is an account of an expedition to the East Indies equipped by Balthazar de Moucheron, who was one of the first to send out ships both east and west (before the establishment of the Chartered East India Company of Holland) to direct a fleet to the East. This expedition set out in May, 1601. The second relates his adventures, trading and exploring activities as a servant of the East India Company. He included in his second journal the account (also published under the name of Cornelisz Schouten in English, 1619) of the voyage of Jacob Le Maire, who discovered a new strait south of the Straits of Magellan. According to Callander, the original journal of this voyage was written by John Cornelitz de Maye, in Dutch, whence it was translated and published in Latin by Theodore de Bry. Purchas inserted it in his *Pilgrimes,* vol. I. It is also found in the *Collection of Dutch East India Voyages,* Amsterdam, 1716. For the confusions clinging to the question of its authorship and to various editions, see the Introduction to the Hakluyt Society edition. It was one of the most successful voyages ever undertaken by the Dutch. It resulted in the conquest of the Moluccas by the Dutch and greatly increased the power and the reputation of the Dutch East India Company.

1906 SPEILBERGEN, JORIS VAN. East and West Indian Mirror. By Joris van Speilbergen. An Account of his Voyage Round the World in the years 1614 to 1617, including the Australian Navigations of Jacob Le Maire. Translated from the Dutch edition, "Oost ende West Indische Spiegel, &c," *Nicolaes van Geelkercken:* Leyden, 1619, with Notes and an Introduction, by John A. J. de Villiers, of the Brit. Mus. With a Bibliography and Index by Basil H. Soulsby, F. S. A. 26 illus. and maps. Hak. Soc., ser. II, vol. 18. London.

1619 SPEILBERGEN, JORIS VAN. Oost ende West-Indische Spiegel der nieuwe Navigatien, Daer in vertoont werdt de leste reysen ghedaen door Joris van Speilbergen, Admirael van dese Vloote; in wat manieren hy de Wereldt rontsom gheseylt heeft. 25 plates. *By Nicolaes Geelkercken: tot Leyden, Anno* 1619. obl. 4to. Leyden.

SPEILBERGEN, JORIS VAN. Oost ende West-Indische Spiegel Der 2 lest Navigatien, ghedaen in den Jaeren 1614, 15, 16, 17, ende 18, daer in vertoont wort, in wat gestalt Joris van Speilbergen door de Magellanes de werelt rontom geseylt heeft, met eenighe Battalien so te water als te lant, ende 2 Historien de een van Oost ende de ander West-Indien, het ghetal der forten, soldaten, schepen, ende gheschut. Met de Australische Navigatien, van Jacob le Maire, die int suyden door een nieuwe Straet ghepasseert is, met veel wonders so Landen, Volcken, ende Natien, haer ontmoet zijn, in 26 coperen platen afghebeelt. *By Nicolaes van Geelkercken: tot Leyden.* obl. 4to. Leyden.

SPILBERGEN, GEORGE. Speculum Orientalis Occidentalisque Indiae Novigationum; Quarum una Georgij à Spilbergen classis cum potestate Praefecti, altera Jacobi le Maire auspicijs imperioque directa, Annis 1614, 15, 16, 17, 18. Exhibens Novi in mare Australe transitus, incognitarumque hactenus terrarum ac gentium inventionem; praelia aliquot terra marique commissa expugnationesq; urbium: una cum duabus novis utriusque Indiae Historijs, Catalogo munitionum Hollandicarum ducum et reliqui bellici appararus, Fretisque quatuor: quaeque figuris ac imaginibus illustrata. *Apud Nicolaum à Geelkercken.* 26 plates. obl. 4to. Leyden.

VAN NOORT, OLIVIER. The Voyage of Oliver Van Noort round the World. In Harris I, 31-36.

> The first version of this voyage in English appeared in Purchas's *Pilgrimes,* 1625; it purports to have been extracted out of the "Latine Diarie." Dutch original at Rotterdam, 1602. See below.
> Van Noort was the first Dutch navigator to sail round the world, and the fourth in all. He started from Goree Sept. 13, 1598, and returned home Aug. 26, 1601. His voyage made little addition to general geographical discovery, but it opened up the way to the establishment of the Dutch in the East Indies.

> 1602 VAN NOORT, OLIVIER. Beschrijving van de Voyagie om den geheelen Wereldt Cloot, ghedaen door Olivier van Noort, . . to zeylen door de Strate Magellanes. 4to. Rotterdam.

1766-68 NODAL, GARCIA DE. Voyage to Magellanica. Abstract in Callander II, 269-273. London.

> A Spanish edition, Madrid, 1621. See below.
> This is the first account of the voyage in English. It is taken from De Brosses, *Voyages aux Terre Australes,* tom. 1. De Brosses is of the opinion that there were two accounts of this expedition, one by a Spaniard, and one by a Dutchman, in the two languages respectively. An imperfect extract from the Dutch account is found in Barlaeus and the Spanish account in Laet's *America.* (The references here are probably to Barlaeus's *Rerum in Brasilia et alibi nuper Gestarum Historia,* Amsterdam, 1647, and Laet's book on America, which appeared sometime before 1642). The King of Spain, hearing of Schouten's exploit of the new passage of the Straits of Le Maire determined to explore this passage to see if it could be fortified against use by other navigators. The ships sailed on this errand from Lisbon Sept. 27, 1618, under the command of Nodal. They reached the Straits in question and sailed through and round by Cape Horn and back to Spain, taking in all but little over nine months. The King was so pleased with the celerity of the passage that he ordered the fleet of eight ships about to sail for the Philippines to use this route.—From Callander.

> 1621 NODAL, BARTH. GARCIA Y GONCALO DE. Relacion del viage, . . 8vo. Madrid.

1767 BYRON, JOHN (Commodore). Voyage round the World, in the years 1764-66, in his Majesty's Sloop the Dolphin, commanded by the Honourable Commodore Byron, containing a minute and exact Description of the Straits of Magellan and the gigantic People called the Patagonians. Together with an accurate Account of Seven Islands lately discovered in the South Seas. By an Officer on Board the said Ship. 8vo. London.

> In Callander III, 673-714, London; the official account in Hawkesworth, 1773 (see under COLLECTIONS this date), and in most later collections. Translated into French, Paris, 1767; into Italian, Florence, 1768; into German, Frankfort and Leipzig, 1769; into Spanish, Madrid, 1769. See below.
> Early in 1764 the Hon. John Byron ("Foul-Weather Jack"), was appointed in command of the *Dolphin* Frigate, the first English vessel to be sheathed with copper, and ordered to proceed to the East Indies, with secret instructions, however, to sail to the Pacific Ocean on an exploring expedition. The vessel sailed westward across the Pacific from the Straits of Magellan and managed, almost miraculously, to avoid discovering any islands except in the northern part of the Low Archipelago, where seven islands were discovered. . . He completed the circumnavigation of the globe in twenty-two months, an easy record up to that time, but a record which should not have been made on a voyage intended for dis-

covery.—From Maggs, No. 491. For Byron's association with the loss of the *Wager* on the coast of Chili, see Bulkeley, 1743, and Byron, 1768, under SOUTH AMERICA.

1767 (In French.) Voyage autour du monde fait en 1764 et 1765, sur le vaisseau de guerre anglois Le Dauphin, commandé par le chef d'escadre Byron; dans lequel on trouve une description exacte du détroit de Magellan et géans appelés Patagons, ainsi que de sept Isles nouvellement découvertes dans la Mer du Sud. Par un officier qui était au bord de ce même vaisseau. Traduit de l'anglois par Suard. 12mo. Paris.

1768 (In Italian.) Viaggio intorno al mondo, fatto dalla nave inglese il Delfino, con descrizione di varii luoghi, nazioni, plante, animali, dello Stretto Magellanico e della gigantesca nazione de'Patagoni. Con un ragguaglio de sette isole ultimamente scoperte nel Mar del Sud. Tradotto dal Inglese. Frontispiece. 4to. Florence.

1769 (In German.) Reise um die Welt in den Jahren 1764 und 1765 nebst einer genauen Beschreibung der magellanischen Strasse, der Patagonischen Riesen und der gans neu entdeckten sieben Inseln in der Südsee. Mit Anhange (des Übersetzers) worinnen eine Beschreibung der patagonischen Küste; übersetzt von Christ. Heinrich Korn. Maps. Frankfort and Leipzig.

1769 (In Spanish.) Viage del comandante Byron alrededor del Mundo, hecho ultimamente de orden del almirantazgo de Inglaterra; . . traducido del Ingles, e illustrado con notas . . . por Casimori de Ortega. 2nd edit. en que se anade el Resumen historico del viage emprendido por Magellanes y concluido por al capitan espanol Juan Sebastian del Cano (su autor C. de Ortega). Folded map. 2 vols in 1. 12mo. Madrid.

1767 JOHNSON, SAMUEL. Life of Sir Francis Drake. 12mo. London.

Probably Johnson did no more than write the preface to this work, if he had anything at all to do with it.

1771 A Journal of a Voyage Round the World, in His Majesty's Ship Endeavour, in the years 1768-1771; undertaken in Pursuit of Natural Knowledge, at the Desire of the Royal Society: containing all the various Occurrences of the Voyage, with Descriptions of several new discovered Countries in the Southern Hemisphere; and Accounts of their Soil and Productions; and of many Singularities in the Structure, Apparel, Customs, Manners, Policy, Manufactures of their Inhabitants. To which is added, A Concise Vocabulary of the Language of Otaheite. 4to. London.

Translated into French, Paris, 1772; into German, Berlin, 1772. See below. This volume, which is the earliest printed account of Cook's voyage, is an extremely important work, published anonymously and surreptitiously two months after the return of the navigator, and nearly two years before Hawkesworth's eagerly awaited *Account.* Robt. Watt, in his Bibliotheca Brittanica, 1819-1824, ascribed it to Sir Joseph Banks, but neither he nor Hawkesworth nor Solander could have been its author. It was probably the journal of one of the civilians who died at Batavia. Wood, in his *Discovery of Australia,* ascribes it to James Magra or Matra, the American midshipman, who made the voyage. It is a short but interesting narrative of Cook's first voyage.—From Maggs, No. 491. It was probably written by B. Lauragais or Dr. John Hawkesworth. Though purporting to be the actual journal of one who made the voyage, it is a compilation; the first half indeed is mostly a paraphŕase of parts of Sydney Parkinson's journal, which was not printed in full until 1773. Parkinson's name, however, is not mentioned at all.—Quaritch. This work was published by Thomas Beckett, bookseller in the Strand, who was also its editor. . . . Whoever the author was, he did not comply with Cook's request that all journals kept of the voyage be handed over to him. Of these ten were delivered. Perhaps the writer of this journal was B. Lauragais, who wrote to Sir Joseph Banks in the spring of 1772 to the effect that he was expecting reproaches for giving publication to the French Galanteries at Otaheite. Of the ten journals turned in, seven have been reprinted in the *Historical Records of New South Wales*, vol. I. Lauragais' book appeared in French by A. F. J. de Fréville: *Supplement au Voyage de Bougainville*, Paris, 1772.— From Edward Smith: *Life of Sir Joseph Banks.*

1772 (In French.) Journal d'un voyage autour du monde en 1768, 1769, 1770, 1771, . . traduit de l'anglois par M. de Fréville. 8vo. Paris.

> The same entitled, Supplement au voyage de M. de Bougainville; ou, Journal d'un voyage autour du monde, fait par MM. Banks & Solander, en 1768, 1769, 1770, 1771. Traduit de l'anglois par M. de Fréville. 8vo. Paris.

> (In German.) Nachrichten von den neuesten Entdeckungen der Engländer in der Süd-See: oder Auszug dem Tagebuch des Königlichen Schiffs The Endeavour, welches in den Jahren 1768 bis 1771, eine Reise um die Welt gethan, und auf derselben verschiedene bisher unbekannte Länder in der Südlichen Hemisphere entdeckt hat, nebst einer kurzen Beschreibung dieser Länder, deren verzüglichen Seltenheiten, Beschaffenheit der Einwohner, und einer Kleinen Probe von der Sprache die in jenes Theil der Welt üblich ist. 12mo. Berlin.

1772 BOUGAINVILLE, LOUIS ANTOINE DE. A Voyage Round the World, performed by Order of His Most Christian Majesty, in the Years 1766-69. By Lewis de Bougainville, Colonel of Foot, and Commodore of the Expedition, in the Frigate La Boudeuse, and the Store Ship l'Etoile. Translated from the French by John Reinhold Forster. 5 engraved folding charts and 1 plate. 4to. London.

> Another edition, Dublin, 8vo, 1772. 2nd edit., London, 1773. French original, Paris, 1772. See below.
> The expedition here described had to do with the delivery of the Falkland Islands to Spain (see Bougainville under·date of 1771, SOUTH AMERICA). After having performed this duty he was ordered to proceed across the Pacific Ocean to the East Indies and thence back home. This was the first French expedition to sail around the world. . . The expedition visited the Island of Tahiti, which was annexed for France and called La Nouvelle Cythere. . . Several other South Sea islands were also visited. It is most remarkable that Bougainville lost only seven men out of a crew of 200. (Compare this with Anson's loss of over 600 men out of 900.) His account is written with simplicity and some humor.— From Maggs, No. 491. Among the objectives of the voyage was the collecting of all kinds of natural history curiosities, etc.

1772 BOUGAINVILLE, LE COMPTE LOUIS ANTOINE DE. Voyage autour du monde par la frégate du roi la Boudeuse et la flute l'Etoile de 1766 à 1769. Maps. 3 vols. 4to. Paris.

> There appeared another edition, with the addition of the Voyage round the World, by Banks and Solander, translated from the English by de Fréville, in 3 vols., Paris, 1773. The Banks and Solander Voyage here referred to is probably the item listed under 1771 above.

1773 BYRON, JOHN (Commodore).   For his Voyage round the World, 1764-
      66, in the *Dolphin,* see under Hawkesworth, 1773, below, which con-
      tains the official account.   For an unofficial account see Byron, 1767,
      above.

      CARTERET, PHILIP (Captain).   For his Voyage round the World,
      1767-69, in the *Swallow,* see under Hawkesworth, 1773, below.

      Carteret sailed as lieutenant in Byron's voyage noted above. His own expe-
      dition was the most interesting as well as the most hazardous of the three here
      grouped together. Possessed of the spirit of the real adventurer, he cruised about
      looking for places which were dubious in their reported positions. He found for
      instance that Davis Land did not exist, at least where it had been located. He
      discovered Pitcairn Island, later to become famous as the refuge of the survivors
      of the *Bounty* mutiny. He visited the Society Islands, Queen Charlotte Islands,
      New Britain, New Ireland, and Mindanao. Instead of following the well travelled
      courses to the Ladrones in crossing the Pacific, he steered west south of the
      Equator. Like other navigators of the period he suffered much from scurvy. He
      retired as Rear-Admiral in 1794.

      WALLIS, SAMUEL (Captain).   For his Voyage round the World, 1766-
      68, see under Hawkesworth, 1773, below.

      Wallis spent four months in getting through the Straits of Magellan. He
      discovered the Society Islands, among them the famous Tahiti. Then he made for
      the Ladrones and so missed discovering other groups. Like most sailors he pre-
      ferred the known routes.

      DALRYMPLE, ALEXANDER.   A Letter from Mr. Dalrymple to Dr.
      Hawkesworth, occasioned by some *groundless* and *illiberal* Imputa-
      tions in his Account of the late Voyages to the South. 2 parts. 4to.
      London.

      This is Dalrymple's Observations on Dr. Hawkesworth's Preface to the Sec-
      ond Edition of the Voyages. For other criticisms of Hawkesworth see the latter
      under this date, COLLECTIONS.

      HAWKESWORTH, JOHN (Dr.)   An Account of the Voyages under-
      taken by the order of his present Majesty for making Discoveries in
      the Southern Hemisphere, and successfully performed by Commodore
      Byron, Captain Wallis, Captain Carteret, and Captain Cook (1764-
      1771). Drawn up from the Journals which were kept by the several
      Commanders and from the Papers of Joseph Banks, Esq. By John
      Hawkesworth. 20 charts, maps, and views of islands, etc., and 23
      plates of general views, incidents, and objects, etc. 3 vols. 4to.
      London.

      This official account of these four voyages has already been described under
      COLLECTIONS. The bibliography of Cook is very lengthy and decidedly con-
      fusing. The interested reader should consult the admirable *Bibliography of Captain
      James Cook,* put out by the Public Library of New South Wales, Sydney, 1928.
      Cook's own log was not printed until recent times: see below under 1893. A com-

plete and definitive edition of his three voyages taken from his own MSS. appeared in London, 1931. Banks's journal was published at London, 1896. Both of these are listed below. Translations or versions in French and German are found published in 1774 and later. See below.

Captain James Cook was the most intrepid and resourceful navigator of the century, if not of all time. Thoughtful of the health of his men, just in his dealings with the natives, and strict in his discipline, he most amply justified the Admiralty in their choice of him as commander of the three voyages that go under his name. This, his first voyage to the South Seas, had for its immediate objective the observation of the transit of Venus across the sun. For this purpose the island of Tahiti had been chosen upon the advice of Captain Wallis. An able body of scientists accompanied the expedition, among whom were Banks the botanist, afterwards President of the Royal Society, Dr. Solander, his assistant, Green the astronomer, and Parkinson the draughtsman. After completing their astronomical duties, they took up in earnest the problem of settling questions long waiting solution of what lands and land connections existed in the great southwest area of the Pacific. The chief results were these: No large land mass occupied that area; New Zealand was circumnavigated for the first time and found to consist of two large islands; the greater portion of eastern Australia was explored; no connection existed between New Holland and New Guinea; and the Great Barrier Reef was successfully navigated. In addition cattle and vegetables indigenous to Europe were introduced to many islands. The success of this voyage determined the Government to send Cook out again on further voyages of pure exploration. Probably the return of no voyager was more eagerly awaited by the British public than this one of Cook's. Naturally the book publishers were all agog to get out the first account of the voyage. Despite Cook's efforts to preserve all accounts for the use of the Admiralty, some few private journals found their way to the press.

1774 (In French.)   Relation d'un voyage autour du monde, dans les années 1769, 1770, 1771, par le lieutenant Jacques Cook, commandant le vaisseau l'Endeavour. 2 vols. Paris (?).

(In German.)   Des Lieutenant Cook's Reise um die Welt in den Jahren 1768, 1769, 1770, und 1771. In vols. 2 and 3 of *Geschichte de See-Reisen.* Berlin (?).

See also Trassler, Sammlung der besten Reisebeschreibungen, Troppau, 1785-86.

1891 KING, PHILIP G. (Hon.). Comments on Cook's Log (H. M. S. *Endeavour,* 1770). Charts and Sketches. 4to. Sydney.

1893 COOK, JAMES. Extract from the Log-book of Lieutenant James Cook, during part of his first Voyage round the World. New South Wales— Government Printed Historical Records, vol. I, pt. 1, pp. 1-174.

This consists of the private and official log-book. The private log-book is in Cook's own handwriting, and is not a complete account of the whole voyage. It begins on Feb. 12, 1770, and ends on Sept. 23, 1770. In the official log-book, extending from May, 1768, to July, 1770, the transactions of the entire voyage are recorded, probably by the Chief Officer. Both copies are in the British Mus.—*Cook Bibliography.*

COOK, JAMES (Captain). Captain Cook's Journal during his first Voyage round the World made in H. M. Bark *Endeavour,* 1768-1771: a literal transcription of the original MSS., with Notes and Introduction. Edited by W. J. L. Wharton. Facsimiles, maps, and portrait. 8vo. London.

The preface gives the history of the original triplicate journals, of which this volume is edited from the Corner copy, with additions from the Admiralty copy. None of these journals are in Cook's own handwriting.—*Cook Bibliography.*

1896 BANKS, SIR JOSEPH. Journal . . . during Captain Cook's first Voyage in H. M. S. *Endeavour*, in 1768-71, to Terra del Fuego, Otaheite, New Zealand, Australia, the Dutch East Indies, . . Edited by Sir J. D. Hooker. Portrait and charts. 8vo. London.

Banks contributed largely to the scientific findings of the expedition. He seems to have been a favorite with the natives of Tahiti. There were numerous poems and skits published on him and Queen Oberea in England. "That wild man Banks, who is poaching in every ocean for the fry of little islands that escaped the drag-net of science," is a characteristic sneer of Horace Walpole at the man of science. Dr. Johnson confessed he had some desire to go on the trip with Banks and Solander in the *Resolution* and the *Adventure* (of the second voyage) but that he soon laid it aside, saying, "there is very little of intellectual entertainment in the course. Besides I see but a small distance. So it was not worth while to go to see birds fly which I should not have seen fly; and fishes swim which I should not have seen swim."—Boswell.

PARKINSON, SYDNEY. A Journal of a Voyage to the South Sea in His Majesty's Ship the Endeavour. Faithfully transcribed from the Papers of the late Sydney Parkinson, draughtsman to Joseph Banks, Esq. . . embellished with views and designs delineated by the Author. Fol. London.

Another edition, with added matter, London, 1784. Reprinted in David Henry, vol. III, 165-470, and vol. IV, 1-222, London. Abstract in Pinkerton XI, 498-563, London. Translated into French, Paris, 1795. See below.
Parkinson was the draughtsman for the collection of natural history under the direction of Banks. He died at Batavia of dysentery on Jan. 26, 1771, on the homeward voyage. His brother Stanwick, to anticipate Hawkesworth's account, hurriedly published this journal. After a few copies had appeared, the further issue was stopped by an injunction in Chancery, on the ground of infringement of Hawkesworth's rights and of material belonging to Banks. Dr. Fothergill, a friend of the Parkinsons, afterwards bought the remainder, which appeared in 1784 as the reissue, with an Appendix.—*Cook Bibliography*.

1784 PARKINSON, SYDNEY. A Journal of a Voyage to the South Sea in His Majesty's Ship the *Endeavour* . . . To which is now added, Remarks on the Preface, by the late John Fothergill, and an appendix containing an account of the Voyages of Commodore Byron, Captain Wallis, Captain Carteret, Monsieur Bougainville, Captain Cook, and Captain Clerke. 4to. London.

1795 (In French.) Voyage autour du monde attaché à M. Banks; précédé d'un discour en forme d'Introduction par les principaux navigateurs anglais et francais qui ont précédé l'Endeavour. Traduit de l'anglais par P. F. Henri. 2 vols. Paris.

1775 COOK, JAMES. Journal of the Resolution's Voyage in 1772, 1773, 1774 and 1775, on Discovery to the Southern Hemisphere, by which the non-existence of an undiscovered Continent between the Equator and the 50th Degree of southern Latitude is demonstratively proved; also a Journal of the Adventure's Voyage in the years 1772, 1773, 1774, with an Account of the Separation of the two Ships, and the most remarkable Incidents that befel each, interspersed with historical and geographical Descriptions of the Islands and Countries discovered in the course of their respective Voyages. Folding chart with the tracts of both vessels accurately laid down, and 5 engraved plates. 8vo. London.

Another edition, 8vo., Dublin, 1776.
Hocken states: "This is the very rare account of Cook's second voyage, published surreptitiously and anonymously about eighteen months before Cook's own account. Probably John Marra or Mara, one of the gunner's mates, supplied material from his private journal, which was put into shape by some literary person in the pay of the publisher Newbery." On page 325 it is stated: "Some who had kept memorials by way of exercise, reserved their labours to gratify their friends. Of this kind is the journal now submitted to the public." The preface discloses considerable knowledge of private matters connected with the voyage and gives an account of the causes which led Mr. Banks and his staff to withdraw from the expedition at the last moment.—*Cook Bibliography.*

1776 COOK, JAMES. A Second Voyage Round the World, in the years MDCCLXXII, LXXIII, LXXIV, LXXV; by James Cook, Esq., Commander of His Majesty's Bark, the Resolution, undertaken by the order of the King, and encouraged by a Parliamentary Grant of Four Thousand Pounds. Drawn up from authentic Papers. 4to. London.

A surreptitious account of Cook's second voyage, from the journal of one of the officers, published a year before the official account. Towards the end of this volume the writer states that, after Captain Cook had announced the Admiralty's orders that all journals, etc., should be sent to the Admiralty Office, "a search was immediately made, and all the journals and papers that *could be found* were put into a box to be sent to the Admiralty Office by the first opportunity that offered." The italics here used, considered in conjunction with some satirical remarks that follow on the probable manner of publication of the official account, are a fair indication that this one is written up from a journal that could not be found.—*Cook Bibliography.* Another edition signed "by an Officer on Board," London, 1781.

1777 COOK, JAMES. A Voyage towards the South Pole and round the World, performed in his Majesty's Ships, the Resolution and Adventure, in the Years 1772-75, written by James Cook, Commander of the Resolution. In which is included Captain Furneaux's Narrative of his Proceedings in the Adventure during the Separation of the Ships. Maps, charts, portraits and views. 2 vols. 4to. London.

This is the official account of the second voyage. 2nd edit., London, 1778; 3rd, London, 1779; 4th, London, 1784; abstract in Pinkerton XI, 564-638. Translated into French at Amsterdam and Paris, 1777; again with added matter, Paris, 1778; and later. Into Dutch, Rotterdam, 1778. See below.
This voyage of 1772-75 settled the age-long question of the existence of another continent, the Terra Australis Incognita, in the negative. It was also the first scientific exploration of the South Polar Regions.—Maggs, No. 491. Banks gave up the idea of accompanying this voyage and in his place was selected a naturalist of prodigious energy, of German extraction, John Reinhold Forster. The most meticulous pains were taken to insure scientific success of the voyage. This was the first time in history that the Antarctic Circle was crossed by white men, as well as the latitude 70 degrees south. The two ships were separated in a fog but were rejoined in New Zealand. This voyage brought to light many islands and island groups, and besides circumnavigated the globe in sufficiently high latitudes as to bring to an end the dreams of philosophers of an early day. Owing to dietary precautions, only one man died during the voyage.

1778   COOK, JAMES. New Discoveries concerning the World, and its Inhabitants. In two parts. Part I. Containing a circumstantial Account of
all the Islands in the South-Sea, that have been lately discovered or
explored; . . Part II. Containing a Summary Account of Captain
Cook's attempt to discover a Southern Continent, in 1773-75. 2 folding
maps and 2 folding plates. 8vo. London.

1777   (In French.) Journal du second voyage du Capitaine Cook, sur les vais-
seaux "la Resolution" et "l'Adventure"; entrepris par ordre des S. M.
Britannique, dans les années 1774 et 1775. Traduit de l'anglais par A.
F. L. de Fréville. 1 map. 8vo. Amsterdam and Paris.

1778   (In French.) Voyage second dans l'hémisphère austral et autour du monde,
fait sur les vaisseaux du roi, "l'Adventure" et "la Resolution" en 1772-
75, écrit par Jacques Cook, dans lequel on a inseré la relation du Capitaine Furneaux et celle de M. Forster. Traduit de l'anglais par J. B.
Antoine Suard. Ouvrage enrichi de plans, de cartes, de planches, de portraits et de vues de pays dessinés pendant l'expédition par M. Hodges.
65 plates. 5 vols. Paris.
       The translator Suard explains in his introduction that he has used,
as well as Cook's account, the account in two volumes, 4to, published
by the younger Forster. He has drawn from the latter material that
is not included in Cook, and has indicated the Forster extracts by in-
verted commas. These dovetailed accounts occupy four volumes, The
fifth volume has a separate title page as follows: "Observations faites,
pendant le second voyage de M. Cook, dans l'hémisphère austral . . .
par M. Forster, père." His introduction to this volume states that it
serves as an appendix to the four preceding ones, that it forms, in English, a separate work from the account of the voyage published by the
Captain and also from that by the younger Forster, and that he has
omitted from it the material already given in those two accounts, save
for a very few repetitions.—*Cook Bibliography.*

1778   (In Dutch.) Reis naar de Zuidpool en rondom de weereld, gedaan op bevel
van Zijne Brittannische Majesteit met de schepen, de "Resolution" en
de "Adventure" in 1772, 1773, 1774, en 1775, waarbij gevoegd is, Furneaux's verslag van de "Resolution" was af geraakt. Uit het Engelsch
vertaalt. Rotterdam.

FORSTER, JOHANN GEORG ADAM. Voyage round the World in
His Britannic Majesty's Sloop Resolution, commanded by Captain
James Cook, during the Years 1772, 3, 4, and 5. Map. 2 vols. 4to.
London.

        An edition in Dublin, 2 vols., 8vo, 1777. An edition in German, Berlin, 1779-
1780. See below.
        Forster's account contained numerous and offensive attacks upon the conduct
of the officers and the crew of the *Resolution,* which produced replies from Wales
and counter replies from Forster. For these see below. Forster was but seventeen
years old when the voyage started. His account is written in "a pompous and in-
flated style and the reflections are for the most part in a very false taste." Boswell liked the work, but Dr. Johnson remarked that "there is great affectation of
fine writing in it, . . he makes me turn over many leaves at a time."—Boswell.
This is a very important work and a necessary adjunct to Cook's Voyages, which
it anticipated by several months. Humboldt said that he was indebted to it more
than to any other work for his early love of nature and tropical beauty. . . It was
originally intended that Forster senior should write the official record. However,
on his return, he had a dispute with the Admiralty over his emoluments, etc., and
he was forbidden to publish an account. He then got his son, George, to issue it,
and in consequence was dismissed by the Admiralty. He returned to Germany,
where he published the volume "Observations made during a Voyage, etc.," following the publication of the official account.—From Maggs, No. 491. For this
work see Forster, 1778, below.

1779-1780 (In German.) Reise um die Welt. Aus dem Englischen übersetzt vom Verfasser, mit Zusätzen für den deutschen Leser vermehrt. 12 Tafeln. Berlin.

1778 WALES, WILLIAM. Remarks on Mr. Forster's Account of Captain Cook's Last Voyage round the World in the years 1772-75. 8vo. London.

FORSTER, GEORGE. Reply to Mr. Wales' Remarks on Mr. Forster's Account of Captain Cook's last Voyage round the World. 8vo. London.

1778 FORSTER, GEORGE. A Letter to the Right Honourable the Earl of Sandwich, first Lord Commissioner of the Board of Admiralty, . . . from George Forster, F. R. S. 4to. London. (25 pp.)

In this the writer complains of the bad treatment he and his father had received after their return from their voyage round the world.—Sabin.

WALES, WILLIAM, and BAYLY, WILLIAM. Original Astronomical Observations made in the Course of a Voyage of Captain Cook and King towards the South Pole and round the World in his Majesty's Ship the Resolution and Adventure in 1772-75. With plates; published by order of the Commissioners. 4to. London.

2nd edit., London, 1784. Translated into French, Paris, 1778. See below.

1778 (In French.) Extrait de l'ouvrage intitulé: Observations astronomiques recueillies pendant le voyage dans l'hémisphère austral, en 1772-1775, par M. Wales et M. Bayly. (In the French translation, Paris, 1778, of Cook's second Voyage.)

Wales and Bayly were the astronomers on this expedition.

1778 FORSTER, JOHN REINHOLD. Observations made during a Voyage round the World on Physical Geography, Natural History and Ethical Philosophy, especially on 1. The Earth and its Strata; 2. Water and the Ocean; 3. The Atmosphere; 4. The Changes of the Globe; 5. Organic Bodies; 6. The Human Species. 4to. London.

Translated into French, Paris, 1778; into Italian, Venice, 1784-85. See below. For the most part this work concerns the South Sea Islands, but there are numerous remarks and observations on America, more especially Tierra del Fuego, New Georgia, and parts of South America.—Maggs, No. 442. It also contains a folding comparative table of South Sea languages, chiefly Polynesian. This account was published shortly after the appearance of the official account. Forster and his son were employed as naturalists on this voyage. His fiery temper continually involved him in broils with his shipmates. For further details concerning him see remarks under the 1777 account of the younger Forster.

1778 (In French.) Observations faites dans un voyage autour du monde, sur le géographie physique, l'histoire naturelle et la philosophie morale; traduit de l'Anglais par Pingeron. Impr. à la suite du cinquième vol. de l'édit. francaise du second voyage de Cook. Paris.

1784-85 (In Italian.) Osservazioni naturali fatte da Renaldo Forster nell' emisfero Australe. In the Italian edition of Cook's Voyages: Storia de' viaggi, tomo 9-10. Venice.

(Listed below are some other accounts of Cook's second voyage, none of them of any importance.)

1778 COOK, JAMES. Captain Cook's Attempts to discover a Southern Continent in 1772-75. In *New Discoveries Concerning the World*. See under COLLECTIONS.

1779 COOK, JAMES. An account of this second voyage in Campbell, J.: *Lives of the British Admirals*, vol. IV. London.

1784 COOK, JAMES. A Compendious History of Captain Cook's first and second Voyages, the first . . . in 1768, 1769, 1770 and 1771 in the Endeavour; the second in 1772, 1773, 1774 and 1775 in the Resolution and Adventure, including an abridgement of Captain Furneaux's Narrative . . . to which is added, A Narrative of Commodore Phipps' (now Lord Mulgrave) Voyage to the North Pole; also an Extract from Forster's Introduction to his History of Northern Discoveries on the Progress of Navigation. 12mo. London.

> This was edited by G. Kearsley. It was adapted and abridged from the quarto edition published by the Admiralty of the first and second voyages of Cook.

1785 SPARRMAN, ANDRE. For an account of a portion of this voyage see his *Voyage to the Cape of Good Hope and round the World*, under AFRICA.

> Sparrman joined the expedition, at Forster's request, at the Cape of Good Hope. He was to assist in the work of natural history. He soon returned to the Cape to pursue his own interests.

1781 COOK, JAMES. Journal of Captain Cook's last Voyage to the Pacific Ocean on Discovery, performed in the Years 1776, 1777, 1778, 1779. Cuts and charts showing the tracts of the Ships employed in this Expedition. Faithfully narrated from the original MS. 8vo. London.

> A new edition, compared with, and corrected from, the voyage published by authority, London, 1784. An edition was also published by Ledyard at Hartford, 1783, on his return to his native country, America. Translated into French, Paris, 1782. See below.
> This is a surreptitious and anonymous publication, anticipating the authorized account by more than two years. Probably it was written by John Ledyard, a sergeant of marines on the Resolution.—*Cook Bibliography*. For Ledyard see under 1785, NORTH PACIFIC.

1782 (In French.) Troisième voyage de Cook; ou Journal d'une expédition faite dans la Mer Pacifique du Sud et du Nord, en 1776, 1777, 1778, 1779, et 1780. Traduit de l'Anglois. 2nd edit. Map and frontispiece. 8vo. Paris.

FORSTER, JOHANN REINHOLD. Tagebuch einer Entdeckungsreise nach der Südsee in den Jahren 1776 bis 1780 unter Anführung der Captains Cook, Clerke, Gore and King. Mit einer verbesserten Karte und Küpfer nach der originellen Handschrift getreulich beschrieben. Eine Überschauung nebst Anmerkungen. Map and plate. 8vo. Berlin.

> This seems to be an independent German account, antedating the official publication.

1781 RICKMAN, —— (Lieutenant). Journal of Captain Cook's last Voyage to the Pacific Ocean, on Discovery; performed in the Years 1776-79. Folding map and 5 engraved plates. 8vo. Dublin.

1782 ELLIS, WILLIAM (Surgeon). For his account of Cook's last voyage see his *An Authentic Narrative of a Voyage performed by Captains Cook and Clerke,* under NORTH PACIFIC.

1784 COOK, JAMES, and KING, JAMES. Voyage to the Pacific Ocean, undertaken by the Command of His Majesty, for making Discoveries in the Northern Hemisphere, to determine the Position and Extent of the West Side of North America, its Distance from Asia, and the Practicability of a Northern Passage to Europe, performed under the Direction of Captains Cook, Clerke, and Gore, in His Majesty's Ships, the Resolution and Discovery, in the years 1776, 1777, 1778, 1779 and 1780. 3 vols: vols. I and II written by Captain J. Cook, vol. III by Captain J. King. . . Published by order of the Lords Commissioners of the Admiralty. 87 plates, of which 26 are charts, etc. 4to. London.

This, the official account, was edited by Dr. Douglas, Bishop of Salisbury. 2nd edit., London, 1785, and the 3rd the same year. In vol. III of this last are the arguments advanced by Wm. Wales against the existence of Cape Circumcision. An abridgement in 4 vols., London, 1784; a Compendious History, edited by G. Kearsley, 2 vols., London, 1785; a compilation, 4 vols., Perth, 1785; another abridgement in 4 vols., London, 1793; abstract in Pinkerton XI, 639-738, London. Translations of the official account into French, Paris, 1785; the same abridged in Italian, 1794-95; in Dutch, Rotterdam, 1787; in German, 1787-88; in Russian, St. Petersburg, 1788. An independent German account, 1781, Mannheim. Sets of the three voyages with and without the Life by Kippis are found. A set of the three in French, 14 vols. 8vo, and 3 vols. atlas 4to, Paris, 1785-1796. Some of the above described editions are listed below. Numerous articles and sections of books dealing with this voyage are to be found in *Cook Bibliography.* See also under NORTH PACIFIC under corresponding dates.

This third voyage differed from the other two in that the scene of discovery shifted from the South Seas to the North Pacific and the west coast of North America, and had as one of the objectives the attempt at a Northwest Passage to Europe. On the way to the North Pacific the voyagers touched at the Sandwich Islands, so named after Lord Sandwich but later called the Hawaiian Islands, where Cook met his death on his return from the North. This group was undoubtedly visited by the Spaniards in the sixteenth century but they had become lost to European view. Despite the hostilities between America, England, and France, the scientific nature of the expedition caused the various governments to exempt these vessels from capture. For further details of this voyage see under NORTH PACIFIC.

1784 COOK, JAMES. A Compendious History of Captain Cook's last Voyage . . . in which all the interesting transactions are recorded, particularly those relative to his unfortunate Death, (with) Abridgement of Captain Cook's last Voyage . . . his Life, by . . . King. 2 vols. 12mo. London.

This work is a new edition. An Account of the last Voyage, adapted and abridged from the quarto edition published by the Admiralty in 1784.—From *Cook Bibliography.*

1785 COOK, JAMES. Voyage to the Pacific Ocean, undertaken by Command of His Majesty, for making Discoveries in the Northern Hemisphere . . . Compiled from the various Accounts of that Voyage hitherto published. Illus. and maps. 18mo. London.

COOK, JAMES. Beauties of Captain Cook's Voyages: or, A Selection of interesting Narratives. London.

1786 SAMWELL, DAVID. A Narrative of the Death of Captain Cook; to which are added, Some Particulars concerning his Life and Character; with Observations respecting the Introduction of Venereal Diseases into the Sandwich Islands. 4to. London.

1787 COOK, JAMES. A New authentic Collection of Captain Cook's Voyages round the World, undertaken by order of His Majesty, for making new Discoveries; the first undertaken and performed in the Endeavour, 1768-1771, for observing the transit of Venus, and making Discoveries in the Southern Hemisphere; the second in the Resolution and Adventure, 1772-75, for making further Discoveries toward the South Pole, and round the World; the third and last, in the Resolution and Discovery, to the Pacific Ocean, in 1776-1780, for making new Discoveries in the Northern Hemisphere, . . comprehending the Life and Death of Captain Cook. Together with Captain Furneaux's Narrative in the Adventure, during the *Separation of the Ships in the Second Voyage, during which period several of his people were destroyed by the Natives of Queen Charlotte Sound. Written by the principal Officers who sailed in the various Ships. 8vo. London.

1788 (In Russian.) Poslednee putesestwie kapitana Cook'a okolo sweta s obstojatelstwami ego zizni i smerti. 8vo. St. Petersburg.

KIPPIS, ANDREW. The Life of Captain James Cook. Portrait. 4to. London.

> This was printed uniform with the quarto editions of the voyages. Another edition, 8vo, Dublin, 1788; again, London, 1791. Translated into French, Paris, 1789; into German, Hamburg, 1789. See below.
> This work contains an admirable précis of the three voyages, with valuable information from the original sources. It introduces most of Samwell's *Narative of Captain Cook's Death,* and also gives accounts of the various tributes to Cook's memory, . . it also includes the biographies of Green the astronomer, Ledyard, the American seaman, and Captain Clerke; as well as a notice of the various medals which were struck.—Maggs, No. 491.

1789 (In French.) Vie du Capitaine James Cook pour servir de suite à ses trois voyages. Traduit de l'anglais par J. Castéra. 2 vols. Paris.

(In German.) Leben des Capitan James Cook. Engraved portrait. 2 vols. in 1. Hamburg.

1799 COOK, JAMES. Cook's Voyages Round the World for Making Discoveries towards the North and South Poles, with an Appendix (on the settlements at Port Jackson and Norfolk Island). Portrait. 8vo. Manchester.

1931 COOK, JAMES. The First and Complete (and Definitive) Edition of the Three Voyages of James Cook in 8 volumes. Edited by Lieutenant-Commander R. T. Gould. 4to. Argonaut Press. London.

> The text is taken from Cook's original MS. journals, supplemented where necessary by those of his companions. With the original illustrations, maps, and charts, and in addition . . . many unique items, hitherto unpublished. This edition also includes a new Life of Cook and a Selection of his Letters.—From Bookseller's Announcement.

1781 ZIMMERMANN, HEINRICH. Reise um die Welt mit Captain Cook. 8vo. Mannheim.

> This seems to be an independent account. Translated into English, Wellington, 1926. See below.

1926 ZIMMERMANN, HEINRICH. Account of the third Voyage of Captain Cook, 1776-1780; translated by U. Tewsley, under the Direction of J. C. Anderson, with a few explanatory Notes. With facsimile of the title-page of the Mannheim, 1781, edition, from which the translation is made. Illus. 8vo. Wellington.

1785 (In French.). Troisième Voyage de Cook; ou, Voyage à l'Océan Pacifique, ordonné par le Roi d'Angleterre, pour faire des Découvertes dans l' hémisphère nord, pour determiner la position & l'étendue de la côte ouest de l'Amérique septentrionale . . . & resoudre la question du passage au nord. Executé sous la direction des Capitaines Cook, Clerke & Gore, sur les vaisseaux la *Resolution* & la *Découverte,* en 1776, 1777, 1778, 1779 & 1780. Traduit de l'Anglois par M. D(emeunier). Ouvrage enrichi de cartes & de plans, d'après les relevemens par le Lieutenant Henry Roberts, sous l'inspection de Capitaine Cook, & d'une multitude de planches . . . dessinés . . . par M. Webber . . . 4 vols. 4to. Paris.

1784-85 (In Italian.) Storia de' Viaggi intrapresi dal Capitano Giacomo Cook. 13 vols. 8vo., and 1 vol. 4to. Naples.

> Besides the three voyages of Cook, this contains those of Byron, Carteret, Wallis, and Bougainville.

1786 (In German.) Neueste Reisebeschreibungen, oder Jakob Cook's dritte und letzte Reise, . . in den Jahren 1776 bis 1780. Illus. and maps. 2 vols. Nürnberg.

1787 (In Dutch.) Reis naar den Stillen Oceaan, ondernomen op bevel van zyne Brittannische Majesteit, George de Derde, tot het doen van ontdekkingen in het noorder halfrond, ter uitvoer gebragt onder't bestuur van de Bevelhebbers Cook, Clerke en Gore in de Jaaren 1776, 1777, 1778, 1779 en 1780, met de schepen de *Resolution* en *Discovery* en beschreven door den Commandeur J. Cook, en door Kapitein J. King. Uit het Engelsch vertaald. 4to. Rotterdam.

1794-95 (In Italian.) Terzo Viaggio. In Berenger, J. P.: Raccolta di tutti i viaggi, tomo 6, 293-359; tomo 7. Venice (?).

1795-1809 (In Dutch.) Reizen rondom de waereld; vertaald door J. D. Pasteur. Maps and plates. 13 vols. Leyden.

1789 PORTLOCK, NATHANIEL, and DIXON, GEORGE. For their voyages around the world see under NORTH PACIFIC.

1792-93 PAGES, PIERRE MARIE FRANCOIS DE. Travels round the World in the Years 1767-1771. Together with the Supplementary Volume III, relating the Author's Voyages toward the South and North Poles. From the French. 3 vols. 8vo. London.

> 2nd edit. of vols. I and II, corrected and enlarged, London, 1793. An edition, Dublin, 1791. French original, Paris, 1782. See below.
> Volume III contains an account of two voyages; the first in 1773-74 towards

the South Pole; the second in 1776 towards the North Pole.—Lowndes. The first voyage contains an account of de Pagès journey from France to New Orleans, and a long relation of his journey through Louisiana up the Mississippi, along the Red River, and up to Nachitiches, with his stay in that place. His journey across Texas . . . to San Antonio. His visit to the Adaisse Indians . . . on to Acapulco. From here the author sails to Guam, the Philippines, and back to France via Bombay, Mesapotamia and Palestine.—From Maggs, No. 442. Pinkerton XVII regards this as a forged account of a voyage never performed. At least de Pagès did not circumnavigate the globe by water.

1782 PAGES, PIERRE MARIE FRANCOIS DE. Voyage autour du monde et vers le deux Pôles, par terre et par mer, pendant les années 1767, 1768, 1769, 1770, 1771, 1773, 1774 et 1776. 3 vols. in I. 8vo. Paris.

1793 HAMILTON, GEORGE (Surgeon). A Voyage round the World, in his Majesty's Frigate Pandora. Performed under the Direction of Captain Edwards, 1790-92. With the Discoveries made in the South-Sea; and the many Distresses experienced by the Crew from Shipwreck in a Voyage of 1100 miles in open Boats. Portrait. Berwick.

    This is the rare first edition. It was reprinted with an Introduction and Notes by Sir Basil Thomson in 1915.—Robinson, No. 20. Translated into German, Berlin, 1794. See below.
    The *Pandora* was sent out under command of Captain Edwards in search of the mutineers of the *Bounty,* the majority of whom were long since gone from Tahiti. But several were captured and taken to England, where they were tried by court martial, except the four who perished in the wreck of the *Pandora* on the Great Barrier Reef.

1794 (In German.) Reise um die Welt in der Fregatte Pandora unter Kapitain Edwards 1790-92. Nebst Entdeckungen in der Südsee. Aus dem Englischen. Mit Anmerkungen von J. R. Forster. Berlin.

1795 PARKER, JOHN. A Voyage Round the World, in the Gorgon Man of War. Performed and written by Captain John Parker, his Widow, for the Advantage of a numerous Family. London.

    "It is a rare circumstance to see a female in the list of Circumnavigators; and when we consider that it is a disconsolate Widow who details the particulars, we are sorry for the immediate occasion. In the spring of the year 1791, Mrs. Parker, at the pressing request of an affectionate husband, embarked with him on a voyage, . . for the new Colony at Port Jackson, erroneously called Botany Bay. Of the occurrences which principally attracted her notice during the voyage, both outward and homeward, she has given a plain, unvarnished, but not unentertaining recital."—Quoted by Nichols, *Literary Anecdotes,* IX, 158, from the *Monthly Review,* N. S. XX, 112. This account was published after Captain Parker's death.

1798 LA PEROUSE, JOHN FRANCIS GALAUP. A Voyage round the World in the years 1785, 1786, 1787, and 1788, with the Nautical Tables, arranged by M. L. A. Milet-Mureau; to which is prefixed a Narrative of an Interesting Voyage from Manilla to St. Blaise, and annexed travels over the Continent, with the dispatches of La Pérouse, by M. de Lesseps, translated from the French. Portrait, numerous folding maps and plates. 2 vols. 8vo. London.

This is the edition printed for John Stockdale; a second one came out in 1799. Two other translations were issued in 1798 and 1799 by two different publishers— J. Johnson, whose first appeared in 1798, and second in 1799; and J. Robinson, whose first appeared in 1799. There is also an edition printed at Edinburgh, 1798, with added matter. Original French edition, Paris, 1797. See below.

On the unexpected publication of this famous voyage at Paris in the previous year (1797), there was considerable competition among English publishers to bring out the English translation. Three different translations were made and published during 1798-99, and different engravers were employed for making the plates. Stockdale's (the one listed above) edition appeared first, in June, 1798. . . Robinson's edition of 1799 is the most esteemed edition in English, later editions being usually based on it. "The narrative of the enterprising but ill-fated La Pérouse is full of interest in all portions, but his relations of the peculiarities he observed in the natives of the North West Coast of America are especially valuable. . . The above account was transmitted from Botany Bay. After leaving this place for the South Sea Islands, the expedition was never heard of again." The expedition visited and gave accounts of Easter Island, Sandwich Islands, Navigator's or Samoan Islands, the Friendly or Tonga Islands, Norfolk Island, and Botany Bay. In December, 1787, twelve members of the expedition were murdered in the Samoan Islands. It was not until 1825 that Captain Dillon discovered what was evidently the wreckage of La Pérouse's vessels, the Astrolabe and the Boussole, on the reefs of Vanikoro, an island to the north of the New Hebrides.—Maggs, No. 491. In 1791 the French Government sent out an expedition in search of him. See under Labilliardière, 1799, below. For his discoveries on the Northwest coast of North America, see under NORTH PACIFIC this date.

1798 LA PEROUSE, J. F. G. DE. A Voyage round the World, in 1785, 1786, 1787 and 1788, published conformably to the Decree of the National Assembly, on the 22nd of April, 1791, and edited by M. L. A. Milet-Mureau. Translated from the French. Portrait, nautical tables, and the full series of 41 folding charts, maps and engraved plates. 3 vols. 8vo. London.

> This is the edition published by J. Johnson. Claims have been made for its priority over its rivals.

1798 LA PEROUSE, J. F. G. DE. Voyage Round the World, 1785-88, to which are added, A Voyage from Manilla to California, by Don. A. Maurelle, and an abstract of the Voyage and Discoveries of Capt. G. Vancouver. Map and View of Easter Island. Edinburgh.

1799 LA PEROUSE, J. F. G. DE. A Voyage round the World, performed in the Years 1785-88, by the Boussole and Astrolabe. Engraved portrait and folio atlas of 69 engraved plates and charts. 2 vols. 4to, and 1 fol. London.

> This is the edition published by J. Robinson. The Atlas bears the date 1798 in the imprint.—Maggs, No. 491.

1797 LA PEROUSE, JEAN FRANCOIS DE GALOUP, COMTE DE. Voyage autour du monde (pendant les années 1785-88), publié conformément au décret du 22 avril 1791 et rédigé par M. L. A. Milet-Mureau. 4 vols. 8vo. Paris.

> The 4th vol. is an atlas fol. containing 69 plates, of views, costume, objects of natural history, maps, etc. Other French editions soon followed, of which one was printed in London, 1799. There is also a modern French edition based on all the MSS. of the author, in 4to, 1931.

1800 LABILLARDIERE, J. J. H. DE. Voyage in Search of La Pérouse, performed by order of the Constituent Assembly, during 1791-94. Folding map and 45 plates. 4to. London.

French original, Paris, 1799-1800. See below.

After three years had passed by without any news of the ill-fated expedition under La Pérouse, the French Government sent out to the South Seas two vessels under the command of D'Entrecasteaux and Kermadee to search for him. Among the scientists on board was the naturalist Labilliardière. Although entirely unsuccessful in its search, the voyage was of considerable importance. Labilliardière gives the first scientific description of the New Zealand flax, and brought back several New Zealand plants. He describes the visits paid by the expedition to Tasmania, New Caledonia, the Solomon Islands, New Guinea, etc.—Maggs, No. 491.

1799-1800 LABILLIARDIERE, J. J. H. DE. Relation du voyage à la recherche de la Pérouse, fait par ordre de l'Assemblée Constituante, pendant les années 1791, 1792, et pendant la Première et la seconde année de la République Francoise. Par le citoyen Labillardière . . . l'un des naturalistes de l'expédition. 2 vols. 4to, atlas fol. An VIII. Paris.

1798 VANCOUVER, GEORGE. For his circumnavigation see his *Voyage of Discovery to the North Pacific Ocean,* etc., under NORTH PACIFIC.

ADDENDA

1801 MARCHAND, ETIENNE. A Voyage Round the World, 1790-92. Preceded by an historical Introduction and illustrated by charts, etc. Translated from the French of C. P. Claret Fleurieu. 2 vols. 4to. London.

French original, Paris, 1798-1800. See below.
The narrative here recorded was drawn up by Fleurieu from the journal by Captain Chanal, the second in command of the expedition. Marchand's voyage has never been published in full.

1798-1800 MARCHAND, ETIENNE. Voyage autour du monde, pendant les années 1790, 1791 et 1792, par Etienne Marchand. Précédé d'une introduction historique, auquel on a joint des recherches sur les Terres Australes de Drake, et un Examen Critique du Voyage de Roggeween. Avec cartes et figures. Par C. P. Claret Fleurieu. 4 tom. 4to. Paris.

1834 FANNING, EDMUND. Voyages round the World to the South Seas, North and South Pacific Oceans, China, . . 1792-1832. Plates. 8vo. London.

This work contains the report of the Commander of the first American exploring expedition sponsored by the U. S. Government.

III.

General Travels and Descriptions

1480 GOUSSOUIN OF METZ (?). The Mirrour of the world or thymage of the same. Translated and printed by William Caxton from the French prose version of the French rhymed Image du Monde. London.

> Reprinted 1490 and 1527.—Parks. Edited by O. H. Prior in E.E.T.S., extra ser., 110, 1913. The original version is supposed to have been written at Metz in 1245, and has been ascribed to Vincent of Beauvais. The date 1480 above is the date of the translation; that of the printing is uncertain. The original of this work is a poem consisting of 6594 rhymed couplets, and is evidently a compilation from various sources. Its most interesting feature is its descriptions of strange countries, peoples, and animals, which are frequently mentioned in medieval literature.—From Prior's Introduction.

1499 MANDEVILLE, SIR JOHN. For his travels through various countries of the East, see under FAR EAST this date.

1503 Arnold, ——. The Copy of a Carete Cumposynge the Circuit of the Worlde and the Cumpace of every Yland. (In the so-called "Arnold's Chronicle"). Printed by John of Doesborowe. Antwerp (?).

> Reprinted London, 1521. Modern edition, London, 1811.—Parks. According to the same authority, the date 1503 is dubious.

1510-1520 RASTELL, JOHN. New Interlude and a Merry of the Nature of the Four Elements.

> Edited by James Halwell, Percy Society, vol. 22, London, 1858. Reprinted by J. S. Farmer in his *Six Anonymous Plays,* London, 1905.
> Rastell was only the publisher of this work. In this play Experyence discourses at large with Studyous Desire on strange lands and marvels.

1511 Of the Newe Landes. Printed by John of Doesborowe. Antwerp (?).

> Reprinted by Arber in his *The First Three Books on America,* Birmingham, 1885.
> This work is not really concerned with the new lands. It deals mainly with Prester John and other medieval items. It may be the "printed sheet of paper" which stirred Eden to his work of translation.—From Parks.

1555 BOEMUS, JOANNES. The Fardle of Facions. Conteining the auncient maners, customes, and Lawes, of the peoples enhabiting the two partes of the earth, called Affricke and Asie. (Translated by William Watreman). 12mo. London.

> Latin original, Antwerp (?), 1520. For the title of the Latin edition of 1542 see below. Another translation, London, 1611. Reprinted in Hakluyt, vol. V of 1812 edition.

This is the first scientific approach to ethnology, portraying a "pleasant variety of things and yet more profit in the pith."—Parks. Watreman, in his dedicatory preface to the Earl of Arundel, tells how he had come across the work of Boemus and had decided to translate it, and how on finishing the first two parts published it forthwith.—Maggs, No. 519. It is only in the edition of 1542 that the exceedingly important letter of Maximilianus Transylvanus which describes Magellan's Voyage is found.—Maggs, No. 491.

1611 BOEMUS, JOANNES. The Manners, Lawes, and Customes of all Nations. Collected out of the best Writers by Joannes Boemus Aubanus, a Dutchman. . . With many other things of the same Argument, gathered out of the Historie of Nicholas Damascen. The like also out of the History of America, or Brasil, Written by John Lerius. The faith, religion and manners of the Aethiopians, and the deploration of the people of Lappia, compiled by Damianus a Goes. With a short Discourse of the Aethiopians, taken out of Jospeh Scaliger. Written in Latin and now newly translated into English. By Ed. Ashton. 4to. London.

For Latin original of this version, Lyons, 1611, see below.

1542 BOEMUS, JOANNES. Omnium Gentium Mores, Leges, & Ritus. Accessit libellus de Regionibus Septentrionalibus, carumque. Praeterea, Epistola Maximiliani Transsylvani lectu perquam iucunda, ad R. Card. Saltzburgen, De Moluccis Insulis, & aliis pluribus mirandis. 8vo. Antwerp.

1611 BOEMUS, JOANNES. Mores, Leges, et Ritvs omnivm Gentivm, Per. I. Boemum Aubanum, Teutonicum, ex multis clarissimis rerum scriptoribus collecti. Ex Nicol. Damasceni historia excerpta quaedam ejusdem argumenti. Itidem & ex Brasiliana I. Lerij historia. Fides, religio, & mores Aethiopum, ac deploratio Lappiamae gentis, Daminao a Goes auctore. De Aethiopibus etiam nonnulla ex Ios. Scaligeri lib. VII de Emendatione temporum. Cum Indice locupletissimo. Lyons.

1566 PLINY. A Summarie of the Antiquities and wonders of the Worlde, out of the sixtene first bookes. Translated out of the French of P. de Changy by I. A. London.

Reprinted 1585 and 1587 as "The Secrets and Wonders of the Worlde." The complete Pliny was translated by Philemon Holland in 1601.—Parks.

1595 DAVIS, JOHN. For his *The World's Hydrographical Description* see under GEOGRAPHY this date.

1599 ABBOT, GEORGE. A Briefe Description of the whole Worlde. London.

New editions in 1600, 1605, 1608, 1617, 1620, 1624, 1634, 1636.—Parks. The title of the 1608 edition is printed below.
This author, who was also Archbishop of Canterbury, wrote this work from the comfortable seclusion of one of his many palaces, wherein he enunciates some curious conclusions about America, as, for instance, that "the Indians had amongst them no good or wholesome food, for even that *Maiz,* whereof they make their bread, had in the root thereof *a most venomous kind of liquor,* which is no better than deadly Poyson."—From Waldman.

1608 ABBOT, GEORGE. A Briefe Description of the Whole World, wherein are particularly described all the Monarchies, Empires, and Kingdomes of the same, with their Academies, newly augmented and enlarged, with their severall Titles and situation thereunto adioyning. 4to. London.

This work, which, according to Anthony à Wood, was known as "Abbot's Geography," contains a curious account of the Discovery of America by the Welsh.—Maggs, No. 429. Its chapters include: Of America, or the New World; Of those parts of America toward the North; Of Peru and Brasile; Of those Countries that lie about the two Poles. This work as well as many other general histories and descriptions of the day could also be listed under GEOGRAPHY.

1601 BOTERO, GIOVANNI. The Travellers Breviat, or an historicall Description of the most famous Kingdomes and Common-weales therein. Relating their Scituations, Manners, Customs, ciuill Gouernment, and other memorable Matters. Translated into English (by Robert Johnson) and inlarged. 4to. London.

Other editions in 1603, 1610, 1611, 1630.—Pollard. An edition in 1616 is cited by John Carter Brown. An Italian version, Venice, 1600. See below.
This is probably the work entered in the Stationers' Registers, April 20, 1601, under the title, "The Travaylers Breviate. Or the Description of the world."— Arber, quoted by J. C. B. The titles of the issues of 1610, 1611, and 1616 are altered but the paging remains the same.—J. C. B.. Such works as this were intended for the entertainment of those who stayed at home and the instruction of those who desired to widen their experience by travel.—Cam. Hist. IV, v. The countries described are Poland, Turkey, Spain, Netherlands, England, France, Japan, China, etc. In the edition of 1616, Book VI deals with "America, commonly called, West-India," and Book VII with "America Magellanica, or Peruana."—John Carter Brown.

1611 BOTERO, GIOVANNI. Relations of the Most Famovs Kingdoms and Common-Weales thorovgh the World. Discoursing of their Scituations, Manners, Customes, Strengthes and Policies. Translated into English and enlarged with an Addition of the Estates of Venice, Saxony, Geneva, Hungary, and the East-Indies, in any language never before imprinted. 4to. London.

1630 BOTERO, GIOVANNI. Relations of the most famovs Kingdomes and Common-wealthe thorowout the World; . . Translated out of the best Italian Impression of Boterus. And since the last Edition by R. I. (Robert Johnson). Now once againe inlarged according to moderne Observation; With Addition of new Estates and Countries. Wherein many of the oversights both of the Author and Translator, are amended. And unto which a Mappe of the whole World, with a Table of the Countries, are newly added. London.

The map, engraved by Robert Vaughan, is that used in Drake, *The World Encompassed,* 1628.—John Carter Brown.

1600 BOTERO, GIOVANNI. Le Relationi Universali. 4 engraved folding maps. 4to. Venice.

1603 ORTELIUS, ABRAHAM. For his *Epitome of the Theater of the Worlde,* see under GEOGRAPHY this date.

1614   LITHGOW, WILLIAM.   The Totall Discourse of the Rare Adventures and Paineful Peregrinations of the long nineteen Yeares Travayles from Scotland to the most Famous Kingdomes in Europe, Asia, and Africa.   4to.   London.

> A 2nd impression, London, 1616. The 1st collected edition, London, 1632; later 1640; in 8vo, London, 1682; the 10th edition, with a slightly changed title, 8vo, London; Edinburgh, 1692. MacLehose edition, Glasgow, 1906. Translated into Dutch, Amsterdam, 1653. See below.
>
> Lithgow claimed that his "paynefull feet traced over (besides my passage of Seas and Rivers) 36,000 odde miles, which draweth neare to twice the circumference of the whole Earth." He set out on the first of his three journies March 7, 1609. On the third of these he was imprisoned in Spain on the charge of being a spy and tortured by the Inquisition, of which he gives an account that makes painful reading. His attempts to get redress from James I on his return were only feebly rewarded. After his exhibition of his "martyred anatomy" to the whole court, "from the King to the Kitchin," he was sent, at Royal expense, to Bath. Here his health was restored but his crushed bones were incurable. According to Maggs, No. 521, his book is probably one of the earliest authorities for coffee-drinking in Europe, Turkish baths, a pigeon-post between Aleppo and Bagdad, the long Turkish tobacco pipes, artificial incubation, and the importation of currants from Zante to England, "where some liquorous lips forsooth can now hardly digest bread, pastries, broth, and bag-puddings, without these currants."

> 1692   LITHGOW, WILLIAM.   Travels through the most Eminent Places in the Habitable World, containing an Account of the Tortures he suffered under the Spanish Inquisition by Racking and other Inhumane Usages for his owning the Protestant Religion.   8vo.   London.

> 1655   (In Dutch.)   Willwm Lithgouws 19 Jaarige Lant-Reyse, uyt Schotlant nae de vermaerde deelen des Werelts Europa, Asia en Africa.   4to.   Amsterdam.

1615   AVITY, PIERRE D'.   The Estates, Empires, and Principallities of the World, represented by ye Description of Countries, Maners of Inhabitants, Riches of Prouinces, Forces, Gouernment, Religion and the Princes that haue gouerned in euery Estate, with the beginning of all Militarie and Religious Orders, translated out of French by Edw. Grimstone, Sargeant at Armes. . . . Fol.   London.

1620   Description of the World.   London.

1621   HEYLYN, PETER.   For his *Microcosmus, or a Little Description of the Great World,* see under GEOGRAPHY this date.

1630   SMITH, JOHN (Captain).   John Smith's Travels in Europe, Asia, and Africa, and America; with a Continuation of the History of Virginia.   London.

> A 2nd edit., with slightly changed title, London, 1664; a portion in Churchill II, 328-366. A modern reprint, Edinburgh, 1910. See below.
>
> This biography of Captain John Smith was not written by Smith himself; the substance of it had appeared in Purchas in 1625. It is a highly imaginative account of his life, not improbably influenced by Shakespeare's Othello. . . Smith

died a year after its appearance, and for nearly three hundred years successive biographers have gone on trying to prove what every one knew in 1631—that he could not possibly have done all the things his first biographer said he did.—Waldman.

1664 SMITH, JOHN. The true Travels, Adventures, and Observations of John Smith, in Europe, Asia, Africa, and America, from the year 1593 to 1629; the accidents which happened to him in the Straits of Gibraltar; his services and Strategems in Hungary, . . ; how he was made Prisoner by the Turks, sold as a Slave and sent to Tartary; his Descriptions of the Tartars, and of their strange Customs and religious Creeds. London.

1910 SMITH, John (Captain). Travels and Complete Works. 12 facsimile maps and plates. 2 vols. 8vo. Edinburgh.

> A Complete and Definitive Edition of Capt. John Smith's Travels and Adventures, comprising all the illustrative and contemporary documents, introduction, and notes contributed by Prof. Edward Arber to his edition, with a new Critical and Biographical Introduction by A. G. Bradley, a Bibliography by Thomas Seccombe, and a detailed index. Reprinted verbatim from the original editions.—Maggs, No. 442.

1631 SPEED, JOHN. For his *Prospect of the Most Famous Parts of the World,* see under GEOGRAPHY this date.

1636 RALEIGH, SIR WALTER. Tvbvs Historicvs: an Historicall Perspective, discovering all the Empires and Kingdomes of the World, as they flourished respectively under the foure Imperial Monarchies. 4to. London.

1654 CAMPANELLA, THOMAS. A Discourse touching the Spanish Monarchy, wherein also we have a Political Glasse, representing each Particular Country, Province, Kingdom and Empire of the World, with Wayes of Government, . . Newly translated (by Edmund Chilmead). 4to. London.

FLECKNOE, RICHARD. A Relation of Ten Years Travells in Europe, Asia, Affrique and America. All by way of Letters occasionally written to diverse noble Personages, from place to place; And continued to this present year, with divers other Historical, Moral and Poetical Pieces of the same Author. 8vo. London.

> The date of the 1st edit. is given as 1654 by Maggs, No. 465. D.N.B. gives it as 1656.
> This is the most interesting and most scarce of all the author's productions. . . . From his own account of his travels, it appears that he went abroad in 1640 and spent three or four years in the Low Countries, . . . was at Rome in 1645. . . . From Rome he went to Constantinople about 1647, and afterwards to Portugal, and from there paid a visit to Brazil in 1648. At Rome he was visited by the famous poet Andrew Marvell, who describes him as "Fleckno, an English Priest at Rome," (he was said to have been an Irishman), and gives a quaint description of his extreme leaness, his narrow lodgings, . . . and his appetite for reciting his own poetry. He is the subject of Dryden's satire "MacFlecknoe." Flecknoe's own works were printed for private circulation, and are therefore very rare.—Maggs, No. 465.

1660 LE BLANC, VINCENT. The World Surveyed: or, the Famous Voyages and Travailes of Vincent Le Blanc or White, of Marseilles: who from the Age of Fourteen years, to Threescore and Eighteen, Travelled through most parts of the World. Viz.: the East and West Indies, Persia, Pegu, the Kingdom of Fez and Morocco, Guinny, and through all Africa. From the Cape of Good Hope into Alexandria, by the Territories of Monomotapa, of Preste John and Aegypt, into the Mediterranean Isles, and through the principal Provinces of Europe. Containing a more exact Description of several parts of the World, than hath hitherto been done by any other author. Enriched with many authentick Histories. Originally written in French, and faithfully rendered into English by F(rancis) B(rooks), Gent. With the engraved portrait of Le Blanc. Fol. London.

> French original, Paris, 1648. See below.

> 1648 LE BLANC, VINCENTE. Les voyages fameux qu'il a faits depuis l'âge de douze ans jusques à soixante aux quatres parties du monde: A scavoir aux Indes Orientales et Occidentales, en Perse et Pegur, et dans les royaumes de Fez, de Maroc et de Guinée et dans toute l'Afrique intérieure, depuis le cap de Bonne Espérance, en Alexandrie, par les terres de Monomotapa, du grand Caire et de l'Egypte, aux Isles de la mediterranée et aux prouinces de l'Europe, . . . Rédigez fidellement sur les Mémoires et registres tiréz de la Bibliothèque de Monsieur de Peiresc, par Pierre Bergeron. 4to. Paris.
>
> > Part III has some interesting accounts of Brazil, Mexico, Canada, West Indies, etc.—Quoted.

1670 HUSSEY, G. Memorabilia Mundi; or, Choice Memoirs of the History and Description of the World. 12mo. London.

1671 MERITON, GEORGE. A Geographical Description of the World. With a brief Account of the several Empires, Dominions, and Parts thereof; As also the Natures of the Peoples and Customs, Manners and Commodities, of the several Countries: with a description of the Principal Cities in each Dominion. Together with a short Direction for Travellers. 12mo. London.

> 2nd edit., 1673; 3rd edit., 12mo, London, 1679.

1679 Narrative and Deduction of the several Remarkable Cases of Sir William Courten, Sir Paul Pyndar, William Courten, and others, Adventures to the East-Indies, China and Japan, and divers other parts of Asia, Europe, Africa, and America: Recollected out of the Original Writings and Records. Fol. London.

1681 MELTON, EDWARD. Zee en Land Reisen door Egypten, West-Indien, Persien, Turkien, Oost-Indien, . . Translated from English into Dutch. Plates. Amsterdam.

> Cited by Pinkerton XVII with the English title in parenthesis: Travels by Sea and Land in Egypt, the West Indies, Persia, Turkey, the East Indies, etc.

1684 STRUYS, JANS. The Voiages and Travels of John Struys through Italy, Greece, Muscovy, Tartary, Media, Persia, East-India, Japan, and other Countries in Europe, Africa and Asia; containing Remarks and Observations upon the Manners, Religion, Polities, Customs and Laws of the Inhabitants; and a Description of their several Cities, Towns, Forts and Places of Strength, together with an Account of the Authors many Dangers by Shipwreck, Robbery, Slavery, Hunger, Torture, and the like, and Two Narratives of the Taking of Astracan by the Cossacks, sent from Capt. D. Butler. Illustrated with copperplates designed and taken from Life by the Author. Done out of the Dutch by John Morrison. 4to. London.

> Dutch original, Amsterdam, 1670. See below.
> Struys, whose real name was Jans Janszoon Strauss, made his voyages between 1647 and 1672. He recounts in full the revolt of Stenko Radzin, chief of' the Cossacks, against the Czar of Russia. He asserts that he saw in Formosa a race of men with tails.

> 1670 STRUYS, JANS. Gedenkwaerdige Reisen door Italie, Griekenland, Livland, Moscovien, Tartarie, Medien, Persien, Turkien, Japan, en Oostindien. 4to. Amsterdam.

1689 A New Description of the World, or, A Compendious Treatise of the Empires, Kingdomes, States, Provinces, Countries, Islands, Cities, . . of Europe, Asia, Africa, and America, in their Scituation, Products, Manufactures and Commodities, Geographical and Historical; and an Account of the Natures of the People, their Habits, Customs, Wars, Religion, Policies, . . as also of the Wonders and Rarities of Fishes, Beasts, Birds, Rivers, Mountains, Plants, . . . 12mo. London.

1690 PERISTOT, A. Itinera Mundi sic dicta, nempe Cosmographia, autore A. Peristot, cum Notis per Th. Hyde. Oxford.

> This interesting work will also be found in the first volume of Hyde's Syntagma.—Lowndes. Hyde was an orientalist, librarian of Bodley, 1665-1701, and Laudian Professor of Arabic in 1691, and Regius Professor of Hebrew in 1698, at Oxford. He was also the government interpreter of oriental languages and assisted in editing the Persian and Syriac versions of the Polyglot Bible.—D.N.B.

1693 AVRIL, PHILIPPE (S. J.). Travels into divers Parts of Europe and Asia, undertaken, by the French King's Order, to discover a new way by Land into China; containing many curious Remarks in Natural Philosophy, Geography, Hydrography and History: together with a description of Great Tartary, and of the different peoples who inhabit there. . . Done out of French. To which is added, A Supplement extracted from Hakluyt and Purchas; giving an Account of several Journeys over Land from Russia, Persia, and the Mogul's Country to China; together with the Roads and Distances of the Places. 12mo. London.

French original, Paris, 1692. See below.
Consisting of travels in Armenia, Tartary, China, Russia, and Moldavia (Rumania).—Sotheran.

1692 AVRIL, PHILIPPE (S. J.). Voyage en divers états d'Europe et d'Asie, entrepris pour découvrir un nouveau chemin à la Chine, contenant plusieurs remarques curieuses de physique, de géographie et d'histoire. Avec une description de la grande Tartarie et des différens peuples qui l'habitent. Illus. 4to. Paris.

1695 CARR, WILLIAM. The Travellour's Guide, and Historian's faithful Companion; giving an Account of the most remarkable matters relating to the Religion, Government, Customs, Manners, Laws, Policies, Trades, . . in all the principal Kingdoms, States, and Provinces, not only in Europe but (in) other parts of the world: more particularly England, Holland, Flanders, Denmark, Sweden, the Principal Cities of Germany, Italy, . . ; as to their Rivers, Cities, Pallaces, Fortifications, Churches, Antiquities, with Remarks on many of them. Instructions for Travelling, Prices of Land and Water Carriages, Provisions, . . A Catalogue of the Cities, with the Number of Houses in them; with many other things worthy of Note. Being the sixteen years Travels of William Carr, sometime Consul at Amsterdam. 12mo. London.

4th edit., 12mo, London, 1697.

A Description of the Four Parts of the World. . . How America was First Discovered by the Europeans, and what Purchases they have made therein. Collected from the Writings of the best Historians. (23 pp.) 8vo. Edinburgh.

Reprinted, 1695.

1696 MOCQUET, JOHN. Travels and Voyages into Africa, Asia, and America, the East and West-Indies; Syria, Jerusalem, and the Holy-Land. Performed by Mr. John Mocquet, Keeper of the Cabinet of Rarities, to the King of France, in the Thuilleries. Divided into Six Books, and Enriched with Sculptures. Translated from the French, by Nathaniel Pullen, Gent. 8vo. London.

French original, Paris, 1617 (1616 according to Hiersemann). See below.
For so many travels the relation is too short, however, there are things in it worth observing.—Churchill, *Introduction.* Mocquet is one of the earliest French travellers. He started on his journies in 1611.

1617 MOCQUET, JEAN. Voyages en Afrique, Indes orientales & occidentales. Faits par Jean Mocquet, Garde du Cabinet des singularitéz du Roy, aux Tuilleries. Diviséz en six livres & enrichiz de Figures. Dediéz av Roy. 8vo. Paris.

1699 The New Atlas, Or Travels or Voyages in Europe, Asia, Africa, and America, through the most renown'd parts of the World, viz., from England to the Dardanelles, thence to Constantinople, Aegypt, Palestine, Syria, Mesopotamia, Chaldea, Persia, East India, China, Tartary, Muscovy, and Poland; the Roman Empire, Flanders and Holland, to Spain and the West Indies; with a brief Account of Ethiopia, and the Pilgrimages to Mecca and Medina in Arabia: containing what is worthy of Remark in those vast Countries, relating to Building, Antiquities, Religion, Manners, Customs, Princes' Courts, Affairs military and civil, .. performed by an English Gentleman (with Preface signed by T. C.). 8vo. London.

> A little volume that seems to be made out of some collections of books and travels rather than any real voyage.—Churchill, *Introduction.*

1701 COLLIER, J. The Great Historical, Geographical, Genealogical Dictionary, being a curious Miscellany of Sacred and Prophane History, containing the Lives and Remarkable Actions (of famous Men of all Countries and Ages), the descriptions of Empires, . . . collected out of the best Historians, Chronologers, and Lexicographers, . . . 3 vols. Fol. London.

> The author is probably Jeremy Collier, who wrote the well-known "Short View of the Immorality and Profaneness of the English Stage." D. N. B. puts the date of the publication of the *Great Historical Dictionary* in the years 1705-1721, and states that it was an adaptation from Louis Moreri.

1702 The Present State of the Universe; or, and Account of the . . . Present Chief Princes of the World, their Coats of Arms, . . . Chief Towns, Revenues, Power and Strength, . . . 12 copperplate portraits and 70 engravings of the ensigns, colors or flags of ships at sea, belonging to the several Princes and States of the World. 12mo. London.

1705 PUFFENDORF, SAMUEL. An Introduction to the History of the Kingdoms and States of Asia, Africa, and America both ancient and modern, according to the Method of Samuel Puffendorf, Counsellor of State to the late King of Sweden. 3 parts in 1. 8vo. London.

> Noticed in the *Journal des Scavans,* 1708, IV, 240.

1723 MOTRAYE, AUBRY DE LA. Travels through Europe, Asia and into Part of Africa: containing a Great Variety of Geographical, Topographical, and Political Observations on those Parts of the World, especially on Italy, Turkey, Greece, Crim and Noghaian Tartaries, Circassia, Sweden, and Lapland. Remains of ancient Cities and Colonies, Inscriptions, Idols, Medals, Minerals, . . Revised by the Author. Translated from the French. Maps and copperplates. 2 vols. Fol. London.

> This translation was made from the author's manuscript and appeared four years ahead of the French version. See below. Another edition in 3 vols., London and the Hague, 1730-33. See below.
> Veracity and exactness, particularly so far as regards the copying of inscriptions, characterise these travels. They are valuable also for information respecting the mines of northern Europe.—Lowndes. Some of the cuts were engraved by Hogarth.

1730-33. MOTRAYE, AUBRY DE LA. Travels through Europe, Asia, and into Part of Africa. Plates and maps. 3 vols. Fol. London and the Hague.

> Vols. I and II were printed and published at London, and vol. III printed for the author at the Hague. The text is in English and French in parallel columns.

1727 MOTRAYE, AUBRY DE LA. Voyages du Sieur A. de la Motraye, en Europe, Asie & Afrique. Où l'on trouve une grande variété de Recherches géographiques, historiques, & politiques, sur l'Italie, la Grèce, . . . Maps and illus. 2 vols. The Hague.

1726 URING, NATHANIEL, (Captain). The History of the Voyages and Travels of Captain Nathaniel Uring. 8vo. London.

> 2nd edit., London, 1727; 3rd edit., 1749. Except for the insertion of sixteen errata, which appeared in the first edition, these texts are identical. Reissued verbatim from the first edition in the "Seafarer's Library," edited by Captain Alfred Dewar, with 8 half tone plates, London, 1928.
> Captain Uring was a merchant skipper in the time of Queen Anne. "A stirring life enough too, for he had known the slave trade, had been at the battle of Copenhagen, had landed to help the soldiers at Cadiz, had seen the *Torbay* crash through the boom at Vigo had carried mails from Falmouth to the West Indies, had been a prisoner in France, had been wrecked on the Mosquito Coast, had cut logwood up the Belsize, had walked the streets of Boston and spoken with Governor Dudley, and had finally been a Governor himself."—From the Introduction to the 1928 edition.

1727 SALMON, THOMAS. The Modern History, or the Present State of all the Nations (Asia and Europe). Maps and plates. 3 vols. 4to. Dublin.

1735 ATKINS, JOHN (Surgeon R. N.). A Voyage to Guinea, Brasil, and the West-Indies, in His Majesty's Ships the *Swallow* and *Weymouth*. Describing the several Islands and Settlements, viz., Madeira, the Canaries, Cape de Verde, Sierra Leon, Sesthos, Cape Apollonia, Cabo Corso, and others on the Guinea Coast; Barbadoes, Jamaica, . . in the West-Indies. The Colour, Diet, Languages, Habits, Manners, and

Religions of the Natives and Inhabitants, with Remarks on the Gold, Ivory and Slave Trade; and on the Winds, Tides and Currents of the several Coasts. 8vo. London.

> Abstract in Astley, II, 445-457.
> This volume, which chiefly consists of the personal adventures of the author, will, however, afford some insight into the manners and habits of the people.—Lowndes. This describes the voyage of the *Swallow* and the *Weymouth,* and is full of interesting information about the slave trade, and the natural history of the Gold Coast. He describes the manatee accurately, and tells much about fetish worship. He shows that there was no evidence of a general cannibalism in any negro tribe, but mentions how an English captain made one slave eat the liver of another as a punishment. He gives full accounts of the winds and currents, and leaves the impression that he was intelligent and truthful.—Sir Norman Moore, quoted by Bookseller. The author published "The Navy Surgeon" in 1732.

1739 CAMPBELL, JOHN. The Travels and Adventures of Edward Brown, Esq.; formerly a Merchant in London. Containing his Observations on France and Italy; his Voyage to the Levant; his Account of the Isle of Malta . . . his Journies thro' Egypt; together with a brief Description of the Abyssinian Empire. . . 8vo. London.

> Another edition in 2 vols., London, 1753.
> Edward Bevan is sometimes given as the name of this fictitious traveller.

1740 FRANSHAM, JOHN (of Norwich). The World in Miniature: or, the Entertaining Traveller. Containing America, and the Isles thereof, etc., in the Second Volume. Large folding plate, containing 18 engravings depicting various people of the World, etc. 2 vols. London.

> 2nd edit., 12mo, London, 1741; again, London, 1745, 1752, and 1767.

1744 LADE, ROBERT (Captain). Voyages en différentes parties de l'Afrique, de l'Asie et de l'Amérique contenant l'histoire de sa fortune et ses observations sur les colonies et le commerce des espagnols, des Anglois, des hollandois, . . Ouvrage traduit de l'Anglois. 2 maps. 2 vols. Paris.

> No English original is listed.—Hiersemann. The French translator was Prévost.

THOMPSON, CHARLES. The Travels of the Late Charles Thompson, containing his Observations on France, Italy, Turkey in Europe, the Holy Land, Arabia, Egypt, and many other parts of the World, giving a particular and faithful Account of what is most remarkable in the Manners, Religion, Polity, Antiquities and Natural History of those Countries, with a curious Description of Jerusalem, as it now appears, and other Places mentioned in the Holy Scriptures: the whole forming a complete View of the ancient and modern State of great Part of Europe, Asia, and Africa. Published from the Author's original Manuscript, interspersed with the Remarks of several other Travellers, and illustrated with Historical, Geographical, and Miscellaneous Notes by the Editor. 13 copperplates (mostly folding) by Hulett, etc., of views and plans, and 7 colored folding maps. 3 vols. 8vo. Reading.

> Another edition in 4 vols., Dublin, 1744; later editions: 3 vols., London, 1748; 2 vols., 12mo, London, 1754; 2 vols., 8vo, London, 1767.
> This is a rare work, and was unknown to Watt, Lowndes, and Allibone. In his preface the editor states that "as soon as the Proposals for printing it were published, great enquiry was made concerning its Author, as is usual on such Occasions; and some Persons not meeting with the information they expected, were pleased to insinuate, that this Name was fictitious, and that no such Gentleman ever travell'd or existed. . . . For my part, I would willingly give the inquisitive Reader all the Satisfaction in my Power concerning the Author; but I am restrain'd from doing it by his own dying Injunction." The supposed author is not in D.N.B., and the likelihood is—despite the editor's protestations—that he never existed. Of special interest are the folding views of Paris, Rome, and Jerusalem. —Sotheran. Not being listed in the D.N.B. is sometimes a proof of negligence on the part of the editors of that work, as has been too frequently experienced by the editor of this Bibliography.

1744-48 BENJAMIN OF TUDELA. The Travels of Rabbi Benjamin of Tudela through Europe, Asia, and Africa from Spain to China in the Year of Our Lord 1160-1177. From the Latin Version of Benedict Ariaz Montanus, and Constantin l'Emperour, compared with other Translations into different Languages. In Harris I, 546-555.

> This is a much abridged version. Its earliest appearance in English is to be found in Purchas, where it is also abridged. Another version, London, 1784. An abridgement in Pinkerton VII, 1-21. Later editions, 2 vols., London, 1840; in Thomas Wright's *Early Travellers in Palestine,* Bohn Library, London, 1848; in Komroff's *Contemporaries of Marco Polo,* London, 1928. See below. Hebrew original published in 1178. A Latin translation, Antwerp, 1575. It was also included in various French collections. See below.
> This famous traveller set forth in 1159/60 from Tudela in Spain to traverse the great part of the world then known, and returned home in 1177. In addition to accounts of such cities as he visited in Europe, Greece, Asia Minor, Upper Asia, Egypt, and other African lands, he gives observations on the manners and commerce of the various nations he came in contact with. But the chief object of his inquiries was the political situation of his fellow Jews. It has been charged that he only collected reports from the latter and that his work was full of absurdities and falsehoods. But according to Komroff, his descriptions are quite accurate while his love of the marvellous invests his relation with color and romance. He named the principal Jews of the congregation in each city that he visited, and made notes of commerce and trade. The information he collected agrees in the main with the writings of contemporary Arabian geographers. His travel narrative, unlike many of the early period, is one of medieval peace and culture rather than of primitive force and ignorance. He may be said to be the first of medieval travellers, for he journied farther into the eastern world than any of his predecessors. —From Komroff's Introduction to *The Contemporaries of Marco Polo.*

> 1784 BENJAMIN OF TUDELA. The Travels of Benjamin, Son of Jonas of Tudela, through Europe, Asia, and Africa, from the ancient Kingdom of Navarre to the ancient Frontiers of China; faithfully translated from the original Hebrew, and illustrated with a Dissertation, and Notes Critical, Historical, and Geographical, in which the true Character of the Author and his Intentions are impartially considered, by the Rev. B. Gerrans. 8vo. London.
>
> > This translation is rather indebted to the French version of Baratier (Amsterdam, 1784), whose mistakes it reproduces.—Delbosc-Foulché.

1840 BENJAMIN OF TUDELA. The Itinerary of Rabbi Benjamin of Tudela, translated and edited by A. Asher: Text, Bibliography, Translation, Notes, and Essays. 2 vols. 8vo. London.

1746 SIMPSON, SAMUEL. The Agreeable Historian, or Complete English Traveller. 3 vols. 8vo. London.

1748 BICKHAM, GEORGE. The British Monarchy, or A New Chorographical Description of all the Dominions Subject to the King of Great Britain, comprehending the British Isles, the American Colonies, the Electoral States, the African and Indian Settlements, and enlarging more particularly on the respective counties of England and Wales; to which are added Alphabets in all the hands made use of in this book. Maps and tables and other embellishments. Fol. London.

1751 LAMBERT, (Abbé). Curious Observations upon the Manners, Customs, Usages, Languages, Government, Mythology, Chronology, Antient and Modern Geography, Ceremonies, Religion, Astronomy, Medicine, Natural History, Commerce, Arts, and Sciences, of the Nations of Asia, Africa, and America. Translated from the French (by John Dunn). 2 vols. 8vo. London.

> Reprinted, London, 1755, and 1760. French original, Paris, 1749.
> A somewhat scarce and very interesting privately printed book, chiefly relating to the aboriginal inhabitants of America.—Sabin.

1752 An Entertaining Account of all the Countries of the known World, describing the different Habits, Customs, . . . of their Inhabitants. 15 plates, depicting the first landing of Columbus, costumes of the Chinese and Tartars, etc. 8vo. London.

> 2nd edit., London, 1752.
> Included in this work are the discovery of the West Indies by Columbus, a voyage to Virginia by Col. Norwood, A voyage round the world by Anson in 1740-44, etc.

SALMON, THOMAS. The Universal Traveller, or a Complete Description of the Several Nations of the World, . . illustrated with Charts and Maps, Prospects of the Sea Coast, Harbours and Towns. Cuts of the Habits of the several Peoples, and of the most Remarkable Animals and Vegetables. Numerous folding and other copperplates. 2 vols. Fol. London.

1753 HOUSTON, James (M. D.). The Works of James Houston, M. D., containing Memoirs of his Life and Travels in Asia, Africa, America, and most parts of Europe, . . giving a particular Account of the Scottish Expedition to Darien in America, . . the Rise, Progress, and Fall of the Two great Trading African and South-Sea Companies; the late Expedition to the Spanish West-Indies; the Taking and Restitution of Cape-Breton. . . 8vo. London.

1759-1764   MARTIN, BENJAMIN. For a Geographical and Natural History Description of America, Asia, etc., see the author's *Miscellaneous Correspondence,* under NORTH AMERICA this date.

1763-64   The Beauties of Nature and Art displayed in a Tour through the World. Many engravings. 14 vols. 12mo. London.

1766   THOMPSON, EDWARD (Lieutenant). Sailor's Letters Written to his Select Friends in England during his Voyages in Europe, Asia, Africa, and America, in 1754-59. 2 vols. in 1. 8vo. London.

> Another edition in 2 vols., 12mo, London, 1767.

1768   GOLDSMITH, OLIVER. The Present State of the British Empire in Europe, America, Africa, and Asia, containing a Concise Account of our Possessions in every Part of the Globe. 8vo. London.

1769   POIVRE, M. LE. The Travels of a Philosopher, or, Observations on the Manners and Arts of various Nations in Africa and Asia. Translated from the French. 8vo. London.

> Reprinted, 12mo, London, 1769; 12mo, Glasgow, 1770; Dublin, 1770.
> A curious and interesting little work, containing remarks on the arts and people of Asia, Africa, and America.—Lowndes.

1772   BRUCE, PETER HENRY. Memoirs of a Military Officer in the Services of Prussia, Russia, and Great Britain, with an Account of his Travels and several very interesting private Anecdotes of the Czar Peter I, of Russia. 8vo. London.

> Another edition, Dublin, 1783.

1774   ENTICK, JOHN. The Present State of the British Empire in Europe, Asia, Africa, and America. Maps. 4 vols. 4to. London.

1777   KINDERSLEY, (Mrs.). Letters from the Island of Teneriffe, Brazil, the Cape of Good Hope, and the East Indies. 8vo. London.

1779 CARVER, JONATHAN. The New Universal Traveller, containing a full and distinct Account of all the Empires, Kingdoms, and States in the known world, delineating their Situation, Climate, Soil and Produce, the whole intended to convey a clear Idea of the Present State of Europe, Asia, Africa, and America. Numerous maps, plates, views, etc. Fol. London.

> This compilation the widow of Captain Carver denied to be the work of her husband.—Lowndes. It is not probable that Capt. Jonathan Carver, the early patriot of Stillwater, Conn., had any share in this compilation. His name appears at large on the title-page, as above; there are separate headings to each district and State of North America, but no very special knowledge is exhibited by the writer, nor reference to Carver's adventures and travels. . . . The costume plates are interesting.—Bookseller's Note. For his *Travels through the Interior Parts of North America,* see under 1778, NORTH AMERICA.

1782 MACKINTOSH, WILLIAM. Travels in Europe, Asia, and Africa, describing Characters, Customs, Manners, Laws and Productions of Nature and Art, containing various Remarks on . . . Great Britain and delineating a new System for the Government and Improvement of the British Settlements in the East Indies. Begun in the year 1777, and finished in 1781. 2 vols. 8vo. London.

> For remarks on this work see Joseph Price this date below. Translated into French, London and Paris, 1786. See below. The original was published anonymously.

> 1786 (In French.) Voyages en Europe, en Asie et en Afrique, contenant la description des moeurs, coûtumes, loix, productions, manufactures de ces contrées, et l'état actuel des possessions angloises dans l'Inde. Commencés en 1777, et finis en 1781. Suivis des voyages du colonel Capper; dans les Indes, au travers de l'Egypte et du grand désert, par Bassora, en 1779. Traduit de l'anglois et accompagnés de notes sur l'original. 2 vols. 8vo. London and Paris.

PRICE, JOSEPH. Some Observations and Remarks on a late Publication entitled Travels in Europe, Asia, and Africa; in which the real Author of this new and curious Asiatic Atlantis, his Character and Abilities, are fully made known to the Public. 8vo. London.

1784 SULLIVAN, SIR RICHARD JOSEPH. Philosophical Rhapsodies, or Fragments, containing Observations on the Laws, Manners, Customs, Religion of sundry Asiatic, African, and European Nations. 3 vols. London.

1788-1797 TRUSLER, JOHN. The Habitable World Described; or, the Present State of the People in all Parts of the Globe, shewing the Extent, Climate, Productions, Animals, Religion, . . of the different Kingdoms and States, . . including all the new Discoveries. Numerous plates. 20 vols. 8vo. London.

According to the D.N.B. the author was an eccentric divine, literary compiler, and medical empiric. He was better known for his moral interpretations of Hogarth's works.

1790 MACDONALD, JOHN. Travels in various Parts of Europe, Asia, and Africa, during a Series of thirty Years and upwards. London.

> Reissued in the Broadway Travellers' Series, London, 1927. See below.
> The author was a cadet of the family of Keppoch. His adventures have to do in the main with his services as footman to various masters until his marriage with a Spanish woman. They are extremely interesting for the backstairs comment on individuals and affairs. His well-turned leg seemed to exercise its' traditional fascination upon the ladies.

> 1927 MACDONALD, JOHN. Travels (1745-1779). Memoirs of an 18th Century Footman. Edited by John Beresford. 8 plates from photographs. Broadway Travellers' Series. London.

1791 Lettres sur divers endroits de l'Europe, de l'Asie, et de l'Afrique, parcourus en 1788-89. 8vo. London.

1792 STEWART, JOHN. Travels over the most interesting Parts of the Globe, to discover the Source of Moral Motion, in the year of Man's retrospective knowledge, by astronomical calculation 5000 (1792?). 8vo. London.

> The works of this eccentric philosophical visionary ("Walking Stewart") were mostly printed for private circulation. De Quincy says, "he was a man of extraordinary genius. He has been generally treated by those who have spoken of him in print as a madman. But this is a mistake . . ." Thomas Taylor, the Platonist, attended Stewart's philosophical soirees.—Bookseller's Note. Stewart had a varied career, being at one time prime minister of the Nabob of Arcot. On his return trip from India to England he walked a good part of the way through Spain and France. His longest jaunt on foot was from Calais to Vienna in 1784.

1793 BISANI, ALEXANDER. A Picturesque Tour through Part of Europe, Asia, and Africa, containing many New Remarks on the Present State of Society, Remains of Ancient Edifices, . . Plates after "Athenian" Stuart's designs. 4to. London.

1794 THUNBERG, CARL P. Travels in Europe, Africa, and Asia. Performed between the years 1770 and 1779. 2 vols. 8vo. London.

> An edition including Journies into Caffraria, in 4 vols., 8vo. London, 1795. See under FAR EAST.

1798 THOMSON, ALEXANDER (M. D.). Letters of a Traveller on the various Countries of Europe, Asia, and Africa, containing Sketches of their Manners and Customs, . . 8vo. London.

1800 MACPHERSON, CHARLES. Memoirs of his Life and Travels in Asia, Africa, and America; written by Himself, chiefly between 1773 and 1790. London.

MOORE, MORDAUNT. Sketches of Life, Characters and Manners in various Countries. 3 vols. 8vo. London.

ADDENDA

1810-1823 CLARKE, EDWARD DANIEL. Travels in various Countries of Europe, Asia, and Africa, 1790-1800. Maps and many plates. 6 vols. 4to. London.

1829 IBN BATTUTAH. The Travels of Ibn Battutah, translated from the abridged MS. copies preserved in the Public Library of Cambridge, with Notes illustrative of the History, Geography, Botany, Antiquities, etc., occurring throughout the work. By S. Lee. Published by the Oriental Translation Fund. 4to. London.

A modern edition, London, 1929. See also Hak. Soc., ser. I, vols. 36-37, 1866.
This traveller, who was contemporary with Sir John Mandeville, began his travels in 1325 at the age of 21. He returned to Fez in 1353 at the command of the sultan then reigning. He lived until 1377-78. The history of his travels were committed to writing under the Sultan's orders but not by his own hand. As he told his story his amanuensis wrote it down adding some embellishments of his own. The work was finished in 1355 and was entitled "A Gift for the Observing wherein are set forth the Curiosities of Cities and the Wonders of Travel." —From the Hak. Soc., ser. I, vols. 36-37. This is a lively narrative and often entertaining. Battuta is guilty of inaccuracies at times and his account of China is so confusing that some of his critics have doubted whether he ever reached that region. But others have strongly upheld his veracity. He started from Tangiers, visited Egypt and other Moslem countries, such as Palestine, Syria, Arabia, Persia, proceeded down the coast of Africa to Quilos, then north to the Crimea and up the Volga, to Constantinople, back to the Crimea, and then east through the intervening countries of central Asia to India, where he remained eight years, to Ceylon, the Malay Archipelago to China. He then returned home in 1349, only to set out again, this time to Spain and to Central Africa, to the Niger and Timbuctoo and through the Sahara Desert back to Fez.
His travels and adventures reveal an interesting characteristic of Moslem society during the Middle Ages, viz., the enterprise shown by merchants and travellers in going such enormous distances and the facilities which their co-religionists provided for those who braved the perils of such arduous journies. Commerce enjoyed a high respect among the Moslems, due in part to the injunctions of the Koran, for Mohamet had been a merchant himself. Under these circumstances it is not surprising to find a very considerable mass of geographical literature in the Arabic languages. The elaborate system of posts prevailing in the territories controlled by the Caliphs and the obligation to go on pilgrimages furthered such a performance as this of Battuta's.—From *Travels in the Middle Ages,* ch. V, "Arab Travellers," by Sir T. W. Arnold, edited by A. P. Newton. See also this chapter and ch. VI, "Routes to Cathay," by Eileen Power, for descriptions of other eastern travellers, Moslem and Christian.

1866 Cathay and the Way Thither, Being a Collection of medieval notices of China, previous to the Sixteenth Century. Translated and edited by Colonel Henry Yule, R.E., C.B. With a preliminary Essay on the intercourse between China and the Western Nations previous to the discovery of the Cape Route. Maps. 2 vols. Hak. Soc., ser. I, vols. 36-37. London.

1929 IBN BATTUTA. Travels in Asia and Africa, 1325-1354. Translated and selected by H. A. R. Gibb. With an Introduction and Notes. Maps and plates. Broadway Travellers. London.

1878 SCHILTBERGER, JOHANN. The Bondage and Travels of Johann Schiltberger, a Native of Bavaria, in Europe, Asia, and Africa, from his capture at the battle of Nicopolis in 1396 to his escape and return to Europe in 1427. Translated by Commander John Buchan Telfer, R.N., F.S.A. With Notes by Professor P. Bruun, and a Preface, Introduction and Notes. Map. Hak. Soc., ser. I, vol. 58. London.

1905-1924 MUNDY, PETER. The Travels of Peter Mundy in Europe and Asia, 1608-1667. Edited by Lieut.-Col. Sir Richard Carnac Temple, Bart., C.I.E. 4 vols. Hak. Soc., ser. II, vol. 17, 1905; vol. 35, 1914; vols. 45-46, 1919; vol. 55, 1924. London.

IV.

Continental Europe

1576 ROWLANDS, RICHARD. The Post of the World. Wherein is contained the Antiquities and Originall of the most famous Cities in Europe, with their Trade. London.

1617 MORYSON, FYNES. An Itinerary VVritten By Fynes Moryson, Gent. . . . Containing His Ten Yeeres Trauell Through the Twelve Dominions of Germany, Bohmerland, Sweitzerland, Netherland, Denmarke, Poland, Italy, Turky, France, England, Scotland, and Ireland . . . Woodcut maps and plans. Fol. London.

> Reprinted by MacLehose, 4 vols., 8vo., Glasgow, 1907-08. Unpublished chapters have appeared under the title, *Shakespeare's Europe*, London, 1903. See below. The whole work was written originally in Latin and was made English by Moryson himself.
> The first part supplies a journal of his travels through Europe, Scotland, and Ireland, with plans of the chief cities and full descriptions of their monuments, "as also the rates of hiring coaches and horses from place to place with each day's expenses for diet, horse-meat and the like." The second part is a history of Tyrone's rebellion, . . . The third part consists of essays on the advantages of travel, on the geography of the various countries of Europe, and on the differences in national costume, character, religion and constitutional practice. Moryson is a sober and truthful writer. He delights in statistics respecting the mileage of his daily journeys, and the varieties in the value of coins he encountered. His descriptions of the inns in which he lodged, of the costume and the food of the countries he visited, render his work invaluable to the social historian.—Maggs, No. 505.

> > **1903** MORYSON, FYNES. Shakespeare's Europe. Unpublished Chapters of Fynes Moryson's Itinerary. Being a Survey of the Condition of Europe at the end of the 16th Century. With an Introduction and an Account of Fynes Moryson's Career by Charles Hughes. 2 facsimiles. 4to. London.

> > **1907-08** MORYSON, FYNES. An Itinerary, containing his Ten Yeeres Travell through the Twelve Dominions of Germany, Bohmerland, Sweitzerland, Netherland, Denmarke, Poland, Italy, Turkey, France, England, Scotland and Ireland, now reprinted in full for the first time since its publication in 1617. 17 facsimiles and illustrations. 4 vols. 8vo. Glasgow.

1632 LITHGOW, WILLIAM. For travels over Europe generally see his *The Totall Discourse of the Rare Adventures and Paineful Peregrinations,* under GENERAL TRAVELS AND DESCRIPTIONS.

1638 MAYERES, RANDULPH. His Travels, containing a true Recapitulation of all the remarkable Passages which befell in the Author's Peregrinations and Voyages, in severall employments in the space of Forty Years. Woodcuts. 16mo. London.

> The author's "employments" were a voyage to Ireland for Queen Elizabeth, to Breda, to Cales, to the Isle of Rhe, etc.; the details are given in verse and prose.—Lowndes.

1670   A Review of the Characters of the principal Nations of Europe. 2 vols. London.

1673   BROWNE, EDWARD (M. D.).   A Brief Account of Travels in Hungaria, Servia, Bulgaria, Macedonia, Thessaly, Austria, Styria, Carinthia, Carniola, and Friuli, through a great part of Germany and the Low-Countries, through Marca Trevisana, and Lombardy, on both sides of the Po; with some Observations on the Gold, Silver, Copper, Quicksilver Mines, and the Baths and Mineral Waters in those Parts. Copperplates. 4to. London.

> Reprinted, 4to, London, 1679; collected edition with title, *Travels in divers Parts of Europe,* fol., London, 1685; sections in Harris II, 741-759, 759-764. See also Browne under 1676, 1836, and 1923, WEST EUROPE. Translated into French, Paris, 1674. See below.
> These travels extended from 1668 to 1673. The author was the son of the distinguished physician, Sir Thomas Browne, and like his father was also a physician. As he had recommendations to people of the highest rank and learning, he had opportunities for observation superior to those of the ordinary traveller, who was generally in a hurry. He gives details of the manner of travelling usually omitted by the average man; he describes the sights to be seen in the light of their historical background. The workings of the Hungarian and Austrian mines were then practically unknown to England, as were also some of the countries themselves he visited.

> 1674   (In French.)   Relation de plusieurs voyages faits en Hongrie, Serbie, Bulgarie, Macédoine, Thessalie, Austriche, Styrie, Carinthie, Carniole, et Friuli. Enrichie de plusieurs observations tant sur les mines d'or et d'argent, de cuivre et de vif argent que des bains et eaux minérales qui sont dans ces païs. Traduit de l'anglois. 4to. Paris.

1680   PITT, MOSES.   The English Atlas; containing the Description of Muscovy, Poland, Sweden, Denmark, and the Netherlands. 4 vols. Oxford.

> Another edition, Oxford, 1683.

1693   Travels through Flanders, Holland, Germany, Sweden, Denmark, containing an Account of what is most remarkable in those Countries . . . with necessary instructions for Travellers, and a List of Common Passage Boats in Holland, with the Hours of their going out, written by an English Gentleman who resided many Years in Holland in a Publick Capacity. Folding plates. 12mo. London.

> This work was unknown to Watt and Lowndes. At the end is a list of the number of houses in each of the cities described.—Bookseller's Note.

1693-94   FERR, —— DE LA.   Voyages and Travels over all Europe, from the French (of M. de la Ferr). 3 vols. 8vo. London.

1702 NORTHLEIGH, JOHN. Topographical Descriptions; with Historico-political and medico-physical Observations, made in two several Voyages through most parts of Europe. 1 plate. 8vo. London.

> The portion dealing with France reprinted in Harris II, 727-740. See under WEST EUROPE.

Several Years' Travels through Portugal, Spain, Italy, Germany, Prussia, Sweden, Denmark, and the United Provinces. By a Gentleman. 8vo. London.

1705 The Present State of Europe, or a Genealogical, Political Description of all the Kingdoms, States, and Principalities thereof, the Ministers, Archbishops, Bishops, Civil and Military Great Officers; the various Revolutions, . . . Published in High Dutch, 1704; and now Englished. To which is added, Guicciardin's Account by what means the Pope usurp'd the Temporal Power: which is expung'd out of all the Editions . . . printed in Roman Catholic Countries; except the one translated out of Italian. London.

> Reprinted, London, 1706.

1707 A Description of all the Seats of the Present Wars of Europe, in the Netherlands, Piedmont, Lombardy, Germany, Hungary, Poland, Spain, and Portugal; being a particular Survey of all those Countries, setting forth the Situation and Distances of their Provinces, Cities, Towns, . . . with Historical Remarks upon the Places of Note, . . . With an exact Delineation of the March of the Germans from Lower Lombardy to Piedmont; . . . The whole illustrated with 9 new and exact maps, done by Mr. Moll; . . . With a large Alphabetical Table. Very useful for all that read the publick Transactions. 2nd edit. London.

> 3rd edit., London, 1707.

1714 CHANCEL, A. D. A New Journey over Europe, with Observations. 8vo. London.

> Another edition, London, 1717.
> Human nature interested him exceedingly, especially the Women. Of the Spanish ones he writes: "They are handsome and well-shaped, witty and much given to gallantry."—Bookseller's Note.

1737 PÖLLNITZ, CHARLES-LEWIS, BARON DE. The Memoirs of Charles-Lewis, Baron de Pöllnitz. Being the Observations he made in his late Travels from Prussia through Germany, Italy, France, Flanders, Holland, England, . . . In Letters to his Friend. Discovering not only the present State of the Chief Cities and Towns, but the Characters of the Principal Persons of the Several Courts. 4 vols. 8vo. London.

> The same in 2 vols., London, 1737; 2nd edit., 4 vols., London, 1739; 3rd edit., 5 vols., London, 1745. A French version, Amsterdam, 1737. See below.
> The English translator was S. Whatley. The work is mainly concerned with political matters and includes the principal German and Italian courts as well as those of France, Holland, and Poland.

1737 POELLNITZ, CHARLES-LEWIS, BARON DE. Lettres et Mémoires du Pöllnitz, contenant les Observations qu'il a faites dans ses Voyages, et le caractère des Personnes qui composent les principales Cours de l'-Europe. 3rd edit., Augmentée de deux Volumes, et d'une Table des Matiéres. 5 vols. Amsterdam.

1743-45 POCOCKE, RICHARD. For his travels over parts of Europe see his *Description of the East,* under NEAR EAST.

1752 CAMPBELL, JOHN. The Present State of Europe, explaining the Interests, Connections, Political, and Commercial View of its Several Powers. 8vo. London.

> 5th edit., revised, London, 1757.

1753 Letters from several Parts of Europe and the East, 1750, . . . In these are contained, the Writer's Observations on the Productions of Nature, Monuments of Art, and Manners of the Inhabitants. 2 vols. 8vo. London.

> Another edition, 3 vols., London, 1788.

1763 MONTAGUE, LADY MARY WORTLEY. For descriptions of her travels in Europe see her *Letters written during her Travels in Europe, Asia, and Africa,* under NEAR EAST.

1770 TOTZE, M. E. The Present State of Europe, translated from the German by Thomas Nugent. 3 vols. 8vo. London.

1772 MARSHALL, JOSEPH. Travels through Holland, Flanders, Germany, Denmark, Sweden, Lapland, Russia, the Ukraine and Poland, in the years 1768, 1769, and 1770. In which is particularly mentioned the present State of these Countries, respecting their Agriculture, Population, Manufactures, Commerce, the Arts, and Useful Undertakings. 3 vols. London.

> A 4th volume was published in 1776 dealing with travels in France and Spain. See this date under WEST EUROPE. Another edition, London, 1792.

1777 WILLIAMS, J. The Rise, Progress, and Present State of the Northern Governments, viz., United Provinces, Denmark, Sweden, Russia, and Poland, or Observations on the Nature, Constitution, Religion, Laws, Policy, Customs, and Commerce of each Government, . . . and on the Circumstances and Conjunctions which have Contributed to Produce the Various Revolutions which have happened to them. 2 vols. 4to. London.

1779 DUTENS, M. L. Itinèraire des Routes les plus fréquentées, ou Journal d'un Voyage aux Villes principales de l'Europe, En 1768, 1769, 1770, et 1771. 8vo. London.

> Distances are given in English miles. The work has to do with produce, population, interesting features en route, etc.

1783 The American Wanderer through various parts of Europe, in a Series of Letters to a Lady; interspersed with a Variety of interesting Anecdotes on Virginia. 12mo. London.

> Another edition, 12mo, Dublin, 1783 (signed by a Virginian).

1784 RANDOLPH, ——. Observations on the Present State of Denmark, Russia, and Switzerland. London.

1787 ZIMMERMAN, E. A. W. A Political Survey of the Present State of Europe in Sixteen Tables. Commerce, Government, Finance, . . . 8vo. London.

1788 BORUWLASKI, JOSEPH. Memoirs of the celebrated Dwarf, Joseph Boruwlaski, a Polish Gentleman, containing a faithful and curious Account of his Birth, Education, Marriage, Travels and Voyages, written by himself, translated from the French by Mr. des Carrieres. 8vo. London.

> A modern edition, London, 1902. See below.
> This Polish dwarf created a great stir in England (where he finally settled) and on the Continent of Europe because of his unusually small height of three feet and three inches, which was offset by wit and perfect manners. He lived from the proceeds of his concerts, but his pride led him to keep up the fiction that he did not exhibit himself for hire—people merely paid a shilling to his valet to open the door.—From D.N.B. The text is in English and French on opposite pages. The book closes with the pathetic statement: "My stature has irrevocably excluded me from the common circle of society: Nay, but few people only seem to take notice of my being a man, an honest man, a man of feeling." Parson Woodforde mentions in his *Diary* having seen him at Norwich.

> 1902 BORUWLASKI, JOSEPH. The Life and Love Letters of a Dwarf: being the Memoirs of the celebrated Dwarf, Joseph Boruwlaski, a Polish Gentleman, written by himself. Edited by R. H. Heatley. Illus. 8vo. London.

1792 ANDREWS, ——. Plans of the most celebrated Capital Cities of Europe, and some remarkable Cities in the other three parts of the World; with a Description of their most remarkable Buildings. . . . 42 folding colored plans. 4to. London.

WATKINS, THOMAS. Travels in 1787-89, through Switzerland, Italy, Sicily, the Greek Islands, to Constantinople; through part of Greece, Ragusa and the Dalmatian Isles. 2 vols. 8vo. London.

> 2nd edit., 2 vols., 8vo, London, 1794.

1798 HUNTER, WILLIAM. Travels in 1792, through France, Turkey, and Hungary, to Vienna; concluding with an Account of that City. 2nd edit., corrected and enlarged. Map and portrait of Selim III. 2 vols. London.

1800 KARAMSIN, ——. Briefe eines reisenden Russen. Translated by Richter (into German). 6 vols. Riga.

> An English translation of these letters has appeared; they are disfigured with a false sentimentality little to be expected from a Russian.—Pinkerton XVII. Pinkerton gives no date for the English version. Hence 1800 as a date is problematical.

ADDENDA

1926 TAFUR, PERO. Travels and Adventures, 1435 to 1439, translated from the Spanish, and edited with an Introduction, by Malcolm Letts. Broadway Travellers. London. See under NEAR EAST.

V.

West Europe

1522 LANGTON, ROBERT. The Pylgrimage of M. R. Langton clerke to Saynt James in Compostell. London.

> Cited by Parks. Langton was a divine and a traveller.

1549 THOMAS, WILLIAM. The Historie of Italie, a Boke excedyng profitable to be redde: because it intreateth of the Astate of many and diuers Common Weales, how thei haue ben, and now be gouerned. 4to. London.

> There is an edition listed without indication whether the first or second, in 4to, London, 1561.
> This book was suppressed and publicly burnt.—Lowndes. It was "formerly held in the highest esteem for its comprehensive account of the chief Italian states. All his works are remarkable for their methodical arrangement, his style is always lucid, and his English shows much better orthography than that current at a later period."—Quoted by Bookseller. The author was an Italian scholar and clerk of the council to Edward VI; he lived much abroad, returning to England in 1549, where he received ecclesiastical preferments during Edward's reign only to lose them all as well as his life when Mary came to the throne. In 1551 he issued a translation of Barbaro's *Voyages to the East.* See under 1873 CENTRAL ASIA.

1552 ASCHAM, ROGER. A Report and Discourse of the affaires and state of Germany, and the Emperor Charles, his Court, duryng certaine yeares (1550-52), while the said Roger was there. 4to. London.

> There are two other editions, one of 1570, and the other without date.
> This account is stated by Dr. Campbell to be one of the most delicate pieces of history that ever was penned in our language, evincing its author to have been a man as capable of shining in the cabinet as in the closet.—Lowndes.

1566 The Great Wonders that are chaunced in the Realme of Naples. Translated out of Frenche by J. A. 8vo. London.

1575 TURLER, JEROME. For his description of the realm of Naples see his *The Traveiler of Jerome Turler,* under DIRECTIONS FOR ⟶ TRAVELLERS.

1579 A Discourse of ye Lowe Cuntries since Don Jhons Deathe with ye estate and particularities of ye last yere there. With A briefe Declaration of ye commynge of Duke Casimyr thither, and his honourable enterteynment in England. London.

> So entered in the *Stationers' Register.*

1586 The Historie of the Citie of Antwerpe since the Departure of Phillip King of Spain out of Netherland, till 1586. 4to. London.

1588 HURAULT, MICHEL. A Discourse upon the present Estate of France. Translated by E. A(ggas). 4to. London.

"A more correct translation," London, 1588; again London, 1592.

1589 A Comparison of the English and Spanish Nation, composed by a French Gentleman. Translated by R(obert) A(shley). 4to. London.

DEVIREUX, ROBERT (Second Earl of Essex). A True Copie of a Discourse written by a Gentleman employed in the late Voyage of Spaine and Portugale. 4to. London.

1591 B., G., and F., A. A Discourse of the great Subtilitie and wonderful Wisdome of the Italians, whereby they beare Sway ouer the most Part of Christendome, and cunninglie behaue themselues to fetch the Quintessence out of the People's Purses. By G. B. and A. F. 4to. London.

1592 ELIOT, JOHN. The Survey or Topographical Description of France; with a new Mappe. . . . Collected out of sundry approved Authors; very amply, truly and historically digested for the pleasure of those who desire to be thoroughly acquainted in the State of the Kingdome and Dominion of France. London.

Eliot lived a rambling life on the Continent until the assassination of Henry III in 1589. He then returned to England and took up literary hack work.

FIGUEIRO, VASCO. The Spaniards Monarchie. Englished by H. O. 4to. London.

1593 GUICCIARDINI, LODOVICO. The Description of the Low Countreys, . . . gathered into an Epitome (by Thomas Danett). 16mo. London.

Reprinted, London, 1596.

1594 The Present State of Spaine, translated out of French (by Richard Sergier). 4to. London.

So cited in the *Short Title Catalogue*. Lowndes gives the translator's name as Sir Lewis Lewkenor, and adds that this was a surreptitious edition, against which the author (in another work) warns the public. Possibly there were two editions the same year. The book is very rare.

1595 FISTON, WILLIAM. The Estate of the Germaine Empire. 4to. London.

HASLETON, RICHARD. The Strange and Wonderful Things happened to Richard Hasleton, borne at Braintree·in Essex, in his ten yeares Trauailes in many Forraine Countries. Penned as he delivered it from his own Mouth. Woodcuts. 4to. London.

> Reprinted in Beazley II, *Voyages and Travels.*

1597 The Discription or Explanacon of the Plott (map or plan) of Cadiz. London.

> So entered in the *Stationers' Register.*

1599 A brief Discourse of the Voiage and Entrance of the Quene of Spayne into Italy, with the Triumphes and Pompes shewed as well in the Cities of Ostia, Ferrara, Mantua, Cremona, Milan, as in other Boroughes and Townes of Italye. Also the Report of the Voiage of the Archduke Albert into Almany (i. e., Germany). London.

> So entered in the *Stationers' Register.*

1600 CONESTAGGIO, GIROLAMO. The Historie of the uniting of the Kingdom of Portugall to the Crowne of Castill. . . . The Description of Portugall, their principall Townes, . . . Translated by Edward Blunt. London.

A True Description and Direction of what is most worthy to be seen in all Italy. London.

> In *Harl. Misc.* XII, 73-130.—Parks. The date 1600, with a question mark, is given by Parks; but in Vol. 57, ser. I, of the Hakluyt Society Series, it is stated that this work is undated but is later than 1584, and from internal evidence, it seems to have been written shortly after 1610.

1602 SHERLEY, SIR THOMAS (the Younger). A True Journall of the late Voyage made by the Right worshipfull Sir Thomas Sherley the younger knight on the Coaste of Spaine. London.

> So entered in the *Stationers' Register.*

1604 DALLINGTON, SIR ROBERT. A View of Fraunce. London.

> There was a second issue of the first edition, with a slightly different title, London (before 1610). See below.

1605 (?) DALLINGTON, SIR ROBERT. A Method For Trauell. Shewed By Taking The view of France. As it stoode in the yeare of our Lord 1598. 2 folding plates. 4to. London.

> This very early and interesting guide-book was originally printed in 1604 . . . and was entered in the *Stationers' Register* under the date of 27 March 1603 (i. e. 1604, new style). The sheets of the text were later republished with the title transcribed above and the addition of a preface and six leaves of directions for travellers. On a fly-leaf at the end of the volume (i. e., of Quaritch's copy) are some notes by a contemporary date "The thyrd of July 1610." Though it is extremely unlikely that this issue was produced later than 1605, this note affords direct evidence that it appeared before the year 1610. There is no copy of this issue in the British Museum.—Quaritch.

DALLINGTON, SIR ROBERT. A Survey of the great Dukes State in Tuscany, in 1596. 4to. London.

TACITUS. The Annales, The Description of Germanie, translated by R. Grenewey and Henry Savile. Fol. London.

TRESSWELL, ROBERT. A Relation of such Things as were observed to happen in the Journey of Charles Earle of Nottingham. Ambassadour to the King of Spain. 4to. London.

> Reprinted in *Harl. Misc.* III, and in Somers' *Collection of Tracts.* II.—Lowndes.

1607 PETIT, JOHNE FRAUNCIS LE. The History of the Lowe Cuntries conteininge first a Description of Holland, Zealand and west frezeland with ye discentes, genealogies, and memorable actes of ye Erles and princes . . . With a narracon of ye warres and troubles in ye 17 Prouinces for 40 yeres and still contynuinge. Doune in French by Johne Frauncis Le Petit and Englished by Edward Grymston. London.

> So cited in the *Stationers' Register*. See Grimston under 1609 below.

1608 HERBERT, EDWARD, LORD (of Cherbury). Of Travellers: From Paris. London.

> This satiric picture of English travellers in France is in verse and is addressed to Ben Jonson:
> > "Ben Jonson, travel is a second birth
> > Unto the Children of another earth."
> Lord Herbert eventually became English Ambassador at Paris. He was fond of travelling and soldiering, and proficient in learning and the fashionable accomplishments.

1609 GRIMSTON, EDWARD. A Generall Historie of the Netherlands, with the Genealogie and Memorable Acts of the Earls of Holland, Zeeland and West Friesland, from Thierry of Aquitaine the first Earle, successively unto Philip III, King of Spaine, continued unto this present year of 1608. Numerous engraved copperplate portraits. Fol. London.

This is apparently the same item that is entered under Petit, 1607, above. See also the following item.

GRIMSTON, EDWARD. The Low Countrey Commonwealth, conteyninge an Exact Description of the Eight United Provinces. Now made free. Translated out of French. 4to. London.

1611 CORYAT, THOMAS. Coryats Crudities. Hastily gobled vp in five Moneths trauells in France, Sauoy, Italy, Rhetia commonly called the Grisons country, Heluetia alias Switzerland, some parts of high Germany, and the Netherlands; Newly digested in the hungry aire of Odcombe in the County of Somerset, and now dispersed to the nourishment of the trauelling Members of this Kingdome. Portraits and copperplates. 4to. London.

The two following titles are also connected with this work:

Three Crvde Veines as presented in this Booke following (besides the aforesaid Crvdities) no lesse flowing in the body Booke, then the Crvdities themselves, two of Rhetoricke and one of Poesie, first written in the Latine tongue by H. Kirchnervs . . . then in the posterne of them looke and thou shalt find the posthume Poems of the Author's Father (Posthvma Fragmenta Poematvm Georgii Conjatii).

Coryats Cramb, or his colwort twise sodden, and now served with other Macaronicke dishes as the second course to his Crudities.

Another edition, London, 1776, (with added matter); a modern reprint (the MacLehose edition), 2 vols., Glasgow, 1905. See also Coryat under 1616, EAST INDIA.

Notwithstanding the novelty of this strange expedition and the very large amount of valuable information which he had gathered in his travels, Coryat found it hard to get a bookseller who would undertake the publication of his Journal. . . . He applied therefore to every person of eminence he knew, and many whom he can scarcely have known at all, to write commendatory verses upon himself, his book, and his travels, and by his unwearied pertinacity and unblushing importunity contrived to get together the most extraordinary collection of testimonial which have ever been gathered in a single sheaf. More than sixty of the most brilliant and illustrious *litterati* of the time were among the contributors to this strange farrago, the wits vying with one another in their attempts to produce mock heroic verses, turning Coryate to solemn ridicule. Ben Jonson undertook to edit these amusing panegyrics, which actually fill 108 quarto pages. . . . The book seems to have had a large sale. In fact it was the first, and for long remained the only, handbook for continental travel. . . . Perhaps of no (other) book in the English language of the same size and of the same age is it possible to say there are not two perfect copies in existence.—Canon Jessopp, in D.N.B.; quoted by Sotheran. The European travels chronicled above ended in 1608; in 1612 he resumed his roaming, largely again on foot, and finally reached India, where he died of a "flux."

1776 CORYAT, THOMAS. Crudities; reprinted from the edition of 1611. To which are now added, his Letters from India, . . . and Extracts relating to him, from various Authors: being a more particular Account of his Travels (mostly on foot) in different Parts of the Globe, than any hitherto published. Together with his Orations, Character, Death, . . . Plates. 3 vols. 8vo. London.

1612 FOUGASSE, THOMAS DE. The Generall Historie of the Magnificent State of Venice. From the First Foundation thereof untill this Present, collected out of all Authors, both Ancient and Moderne, that have written of that subject, Englished by W. Shute. Portraits. Fol. London.

A Short Reporte of the honorable Journey in Brabant by his excellency Graue Maarice lord generall of the United Netherlandishe provinces from the 26th of June, 1602, to the 19th of July followinge. Together with the takinge of Helmont and of his marchinge to the town of Graue. London.

So entered in the *Stationers' Register.*

1615 A Discourse of the Prosperitie of the United Provinces. 4to. London.

SANDYS, GEORGE. For a description of Italy and the islands adjoining see his *A Relation of a Journey begun An. Dom. 1610,* under NEAR EAST.

1617 TAYLOR, JOHN (the Water Poet). Taylor's Travels in Germanie, or Three Weekes, three Daies and three Houres Observations, and Travel from London to Hamburgh. 4to. London.

In prose, with a ludicrous dedication to Thomas Coryat.—Lowndes.

1621 Observations concerning the present Affaires of Holland. 8vo. London.

2nd edit., augmented, London, 1622. See below.

1622 More excellent Observations of the Estate and Affaires of Holland. Translated out of the Dutch Copie. 4to. London.

This is sometimes attributed to W. Usselincx.—*Short Title Catalogue.*

1623 A Journal of the Voyage of Prince Frederick Henry (of Orange) from Prague to Luerden. 4to. London.

A Trve Relation and Iornall, of the Manner of the Arrivall, and Magnificent Entertainment, giuen to the High and Mighty Prince Charles (afterwards Charles I), Prince of Great Britaine, by the King of Spaine in his Court at Madrid. London.

A Continvation of a former Relation concerning the Entertainment giuen to the Prince His Highnesse by the King of Spaine in his Court at Madrid. London.

The Ioyfull Returne, of the Most illustrious Prince, Charles Prince of Great Britaine, from the Court of Spaine. Together with a Relation of his Magnificent Entertainment in Madrid, and on his way to St. Anderas, by the King of Spaine. The Royall and Princely Gifts interchangebly giuen. Translated out of the Spanishe Copie. His most wonderfull dangers on the Seas, after his parting from thence; Miracvlovs deliuery, and most happy-safe Landing at Portsmovth on the 5. of October. . . . London.

> The purpose of Charles' visit to Spain was to attempt to arrange a marriage between himself and the Infanta Maria, but, owing to religious difficulties, the plan miscarried.—Quaritch.

1626 HYNDE, S. Iter Lusitanicum, or the Portugal Voyage, with what memorable Passages interven'd at the Shipping and in the Transporting of her most Sacred Majesty Katherine Queen of Great Britain, from Lisbon to England. Exactly observed by him that was Eye-witness of the same, Who though he published this, conceals his name. 4to. London.

> Reprinted, Edinburgh, 1626 (?).

OVERBURY, SIR THOMAS. His Observations in his Travailes vpon the State of the XVII. Provinces as they stood, A.D. 1609, the Treatie of Peace being then on foote. 4to. London. (15 leaves.)

> This curious tract was licensed ten years before it was published. Reprinted, with the addition of the State of France, 12mo, London, 1651. Reprinted in Osborne I, 251-261; in *Harl. Misc.*, vol. VII.
> The author was an accomplished gentleman, who fell a victim to the resentment of Frances, the wife of Robert, Earl of Essex, for interfering with her amour with Robert Viscount Rochester. He was committed to the Tower and died there by poison, Sept. 15, 1613. His observations display much political penetration and varied knowledge of the countries he describes.

OWEN, LEWIS. The Running Register Recording a True Relation of the State of the English Colledges, Seminaries and Cloysters in all forraine Parts. London.

1627 SINCERI, JODOCI. Itinerarium Galliae . . . cum appendices de Burdigala. 12mo. London (?).

1628 DIGBY, ——. Voyage to the Mediterranean. London.

> No other reference to this work has come to the notice of the editor.

1629 WADSWORTH, JAMES. The English Spanish Pilgrime, Or,° a New Discoverie of Spanish Popery, and Iesviticall Stratagems. With the Estate of the English Pentioners and Fugitiues vnder the King of Spaines Dominions, and else where at this present. Also laying open the new Order of the Iesuitrices and preaching Nunnes. Composed by James Wadsworth Gentleman, newly conuerted into his true mothers bosome, the Church of England, with the motiues why he left the Sea of Rome; a late Pentioner to his Maiesty of Spaine, and nominated his Captaine in Flanders: Sonne to Mr. James Wadsworth, Bachelor of Divinity, sometime of Emanuell Colledge in the Vniversity of Cambridge, who was peruerted in the yeere 1604, and late Tutor to Donia Maria Infanta of Spaine. Published by Authority. 4to. London.

> 2nd edit., corrected and amended, 4to, London, 1630; another edition, London, 1650. Reprinted as *Memoirs and Travels of Mr. James Wadsworth*, 8vo, London, 1674, and 1684. See below.
> Wadsworth made two visits to Spain, the first in 1609-1618 to Madrid and Seville; the second in 1622 to Madrid. He had a variegated career, being educated in Spain, taken prisoner to Algiers in 1623, becoming a government spy in England in 1625, and in Brussels and Paris, 1626, and a common informer against Romanists from 1630 on.—From D.N.B.

> 1630 WADSWORTH, JAMES. Further Observations of the English Spanish Pilgrime concerning Spain. 4to. London.

1636 CROWNE, WILLIAM. A True Relation of all the Remarkable Places and Passages Observed in the Travels of the right honourable Thomas, Lord Howard, Earle of Arundell and Surrey, Primer Earle, and Earle Marshall of England, Ambassadour Extraordinary to his sacred Majesty Ferdinando the second, Emperour of Germanie, Anno Domini 1636. 4to. London.

> This book is of some importance to the medical historian, as it gives an account of a journey in which William Harvey (who discovered the circulation of the blood) took part. "In the course of this journey Harvey had an opportunity of visiting several of the principal cities of Germany, and of making the acquaintance of many of the leading medical men of the time."—Robinson. A work full of imperfections and errors.—Oldys, quoted by Lowndes. The Earl of Arundel is he who formed at Arundel House the first considerable art collection in England, later presented to Oxford University.

1637 The Particular State of the Government of the Emperour Ferdinand the Second, as it was at his decease in the yeere 1636, translated out of Latin by R. W. Part II: The State of the Imperial-Court of the Emperour Ferdinand the Second: wherein is treated of all the higher and lower Officers; and principally of the several Jurisdictions of the foure Chiefe Court Officers: of Ambassadours, Residents, and Agents,

Artificers, Tradesmen, and Musicians of the Court. Translated out of Latin by R. W. The 2 parts. 4to. London.

> Specially interesting for its description of Vienna (with an estimated population of 60,000), and the manners and customs of the court.—Sotheran.

1640   CARVE, THOMAS. Itinerarium ex Hibernia per Poloniam, Germaniam, et Bohemiam. Mentz.

> The modern edition, in 3 parts, London, 1859, is the only complete one. See below. The date 1640 and place given above are taken from Pinkerton XVII.
> The author's name was really Carue, i. e., Carew. He was an army chaplain in the imperial service in Germany from before 1626 to 1643. His book was published abroad.

> 1859   CARVE, THOMAS. Itinerarium, mainly in Germany, but also the Low Countries, England, and Ireland, during the Thirty Years' War. London.

HARSDING, S. Sicily and Naples. London.

> So cited in the *Short Title Catalogue*.

1645-1655   HOWELL, JAMES. Epistolae Ho-Elianae: Familiar Letters, Domestic and Forren, divided into sundry Sections, partly Historicall, Politicall, Philosophicall. 3rd edit., with . . . New Letters never published before. 8vo. London.

> The 1st vol. of these letters came out in 1645; the 2nd in 1647; the 3rd in 1650; and the collected edition in 1655. The work was frequently reprinted, the 10th edition, which is said to be the best, appearing in 1737, and the 11th in 1754. A modern reprint of the 10th was published in 1892. See below.
> These letters relate to the reigns of James I and Charles I. They were written for the most part in the Fleet prison, where Howell was imprisoned as a Royalist from 1642 to 1651, and were generally addressed to imaginary correspondents. Some of the subjects were the political conditions and historical developments of particular countries or communities; others were general matters of interest. Howell was a great traveller; he made visits to Holland, France, and Italy, and was twice in Spain. He was an intimate friend of Ben Jonson's and was the first to hold the post of royal historiographer.

> 1892   HOWELL, JAMES. The Familiar Letters of James Howell. Reprinted from the 10th edition of 1737. Edited by Joseph Jacobs. Numerous portraits inserted. London.

1648   FELTHAM, OWEN. A Brief Character of the Low Countries under the States, being Three Weeks Observations of the Vices and Virtues of the Inhabitants. London (?).

> This is said to be a pirated edition. That of 1652 is listed by D.N.B. as though it were the first published. Reprinted 1659, 1660, 1661, 1662, 1675, and 1832. See below.
> Feltham is better known as the author of a series of moral essays called "Resolves."

1675 FELTHAM, OWEN. Batavia: or, the Hollander Displayed. Being Three Weeks Observations of the Low Countries, especially Holland. In Brief, Characters and Observations of the People and Country, the Government of their State and private Families, their Virtues and Vices. Also a Perfect Description of the People and Country of Scotland. Amsterdam.

RAYMOND, JOSEPH. An Itinerary contayning a Voyage made through Italy in the Years 1646 and 1647. Illustrated with divers figures of Antiquities never before published. 12mo. London.

In Hak. Soc., ser. II, vol. 57, this work has the following title and date.

1647 RAYMOND, JOSEPH. Il Mercurio Italico, communicating a Voyage made through Italy in the years 1646 and 1647. London.

1649 What Will You Have? A Calf with a White Face; or, a Relation of his Travailes from England into Ireland, Scotland, Poland, Holland, Amsterdam, and other places, and is now newly arrived in the Citie of London, where he means to abide. Curious woodcut on title of a Cavalier, a calf with a white face, and three Puritans. 4to. London.

1651 HOWELL, JAMES. A Survey of the Signorie of Venice, of her admired Policy, and Method of Government, with a Cohortation to all Christian Princes to resent her dangerous Condition at present. Portrait and frontispiece. Fol. London.

1652 EVELYN, JOHN. The State of France as it stood in the ninth Year of this present Monarch, Louis XIIII. written to a Friend by J. E. 8vo. London.

Evelyn was a student and a virtuoso, rich, intelligent, and an enlightened lover of books. During the Civil War he sided with King Charles; then he travelled abroad with the poet Waller, and studied anatomy at Padua. He made several visits to France, where he was much charmed with the attractions of the country. He is well known as the author of *Sylva* and his still more famous *Diary*, which, however, was not published until 1818-19. See below for the edition of 1879.

1879 EVELYN, JOHN. Diary. Edited by H. B. Wheatley. 4 vols. London.

The Globe edition, London, 1908.

1654 CAMPANELLA, THOMAS. A Discourse touching the Spanish Monarchy, laying down Directions and Practices whereby the King of Spain may attain to an Universal Monarchy, wherein also we have a Political Glasse, representing each particular Country, Province, Kingdom, and Empire of the World, newly translated into English. 4to. London.

Tomaso Campanella aimed like his contemporary, Lord Bacon, at a reform of philosophy. He was charged with conspiracy against the Spanish Government of Naples.—Bookseller's Note.

HOWELL, JAMES. Parthenopoeia; or, the History of the Most Notable and Renowned Kingdom of Naples. Portraits and cuts. Fol. London.

1655 Topographia Galliae, sive Descriptio et Delineatio Famosissimorum locorum in potentissimo Regno Galliae; partim ex usu et optimis Scriptoribus diversarum Linguarum, partim ex Relationibus fide dignis per aliquot annos Collectis, in ordinem redacta et publico data, per Martinum Zeillerum. Numerous folding plates. 4 vols. Fol. London (?).

This contains a fine old folding map of Paris, large folding view of Paris in Shakespeare's day, large folding view showing the principal churches, street views, Notre Dame, La Sorbonne, Bastile, Gardens, Louvre, the Seine, Chateaux, St. Cloud, Fontainebleau, Rennes, Bordeaux, Soissons, Troye, Dijon, etc.

1656 HEYLYN, PETER. A Survey of the Estate of France and of some of the adjoyning Ilands: taken in the Description of the Principal Cities and Chief Provinces, with the Temper, Humor and Affections of the People Generally, and an exact Accompt of the public Government in reference to the Court, the Church, and the Civill State. 4to. London.

The 6th book consists of the second journey, containing a survey of the Estate of the islands Guernsey and Jersey. Another issue of his work, under a different title, London, 1656; 2nd edit. of this latter, London, 1657; editions with still other titles, London, 1673 and 1679. See below.

His journey to France was written in a satirical vein to show that he had no French leanings. But the manuscript, which had been circulating from hand to hand, was published without his consent. He thereupon issued the work himself under the title given above. Heylyn was an ecclesiastical writer who was always engaged in the religious controversies of the day. He helped in the prosecution of Prynne for the publication of the "Histriomastrix." He also wrote works on geography. See under 1621, GEOGRAPHY.

1656 HEYLYN, PETER. France painted to the Life. 8vo. London.

This is the work that was published surreptitiously.

1673 HEYLYN, PETER. A Full Relation of Two Journeys; the one into the Mainland of France. The other into some of the Adjacent Islands (Guernsey and Jersey). Performed and digested into Six Books. London.

1679 HEYLYN, PETER. The Voyage of France, or a complete Journal of France, with the Character of the People, and the Description of the principal Cities, Fortresses, Churches, Monasteries, Universities, Palaces, and Antiquities. London.

A Relation of the Life of Christina Queen of Sweden: with Her Resignation of the Crown, Voyage to Bruxels, and Journey to Rome. Whereunto is added, Her Genius. Translated out of French, by I. H. London.

"Her Genius" was written by Urbain Chevreau, and the translation is attribute to John Howell.—From John Carter Brown Catalogue.

1660　The Character of Italie; or the Italian anatomiz'd. 12mo. London.

　　A Relation in Form of a Journal, of the Voiage and Residence which the most Excellent and most Mighty Prince Charles the II. hath made in Holland, from the 25th of May to the 2 of June, 1660, rendered into English out of the original French, by Sir William Lower, Knight. Seven folding plates, including portrait of Charles II. Fol. London.

　　　　French original, the Hague, 1660. See below.

　　　　1660　Relation en forme de Journal du Voyage et Séjour que le serenissime et très-puissant Prince Charles II, Roy de la Grand Bretagne, . . . a fait en Hollande depuis le 25 May, jusques à 2 Juin, 1660. Portrait of Charles II in armor and 3 plates. Fol. The Hague.

　　　　　　A handsomely printed work, containing many curious particulars, drawn up from public documents with great care.—Lowndes.

WARCUPP, EDMUND. Italy in its Original Glory, Ruin, and Revival: being an Exact Survey of the whole Geography and History of that Famous Country, with the Adjacent Islands of Sicily, Malta, . . . and whatever is Remarkable in Rome (the Mistress of the World). Frontispiece and folding plates. Fol. London.

1662　HOWELL, JAMES. La perambulacion de España y de Portugàl; En ub Discurso entre Carlos y Felipe. The perambulation of Spain and Portugal; In a Discourse 'twixt Charles and Philip: Which may serve for a Director How to Travel through those Countreys. London (?).

1664　Rome exactly described as to the Present State of it, under Pope Alexander the Seventh in Two curious Discourses written originally in Italian and translated into English, i. e., A Relation of the State of the Court of Rome, made in 1661 by Angelo Corraro translated by J. B. Gent., and A New Relation of Rome as to the government of the City, . . . taken out of one of the Choicest Cabinets of Rome. Frontispiece. 12mo. London.

　　　　Elsewhere the initials of the translator are given as J. T.

1668　GAILHARD, J. The Present State of the Princes and Republicks of Italy; with Observations on them, and useful Directions for those that travel thorow that Countrey. 12mo. London.

　　　　2nd edit., corrected and enlarged, with a Character of Spain, 8vo. London, 1671. See also Gailhard under 1669 below.

1669 AGLINSBY, WILLIAM. The Present State of the United Provinces of the Low Countries, as to the Government, Laws, Forces, Riches, Revenue, . . . of the Dutch. 12mo. London.

> 2nd edit., 12mo, London, 1676.

FINCH, HENEAGE (2nd Earl of Winchelsea). A True and Exact Relation of the late Prodigious Earthquake and Eruption of Mount Aetna, or Monte-Gibello; as it came in a Letter written to His Majesty from Naples by the Right Hon. the Earle of Winchelsea, His Majestie's late Ambassador to Constantinople, who in his Return from thence, visiting Catania in the Island of Sicily, was an Ey-Witness of that Dreadfull Spectacle. Together with a more particular Narrative of the same, as it is collected out of severall Relations sent from Catania. Folding copperplate. 4to. London.

> Reprinted, 8vo, London, 1775.
> This is the first English account of the eruption and is said to be remarkable for the vivid description it gives of the event.—Sotheran.

GAILHARD, J. The Present State of the Republick of Venice, as to the Government, Laws, Forces, Riches, Manners, Customes, Revenue and Territory, of that Commonwealth; with a Relation of the present War in Candia. 12mo. London.

1670 BRUNEL, ANTOINE DE, and AERSSEN, FRANCOIS VAN. A Journey into Spain. 8vo. London.

> A free and abridgd translation. French original, Paris, 1665. See below.

> 1665 BRUNEL, ANTOINE DE, and AERSSEN, FRANCOIS VAN. Voyage d'Espagne cvrieux, Historiqve et politiqve. Fait en l'année 1655. Paris.
>
> > For a fuller title see the edition of 1666 below.

> 1666 BRUNEL, ANTOINE DE, and AERSSEN, FRANCOIS VAN. Voyage d'Espagne, contenant entre plusieurs particularitéz de ce Royaume, Trois Discours Politiques sur les affaires du Protecteur d'Angleterre, la Reine de Suède, et duc de Lorraine. Revue Corrigé et Augmenté sur le MS. Avec Une Relation de l'éstat et Gouvernment de cette Monarchie; une Relation particulière de Madrid. Cologne.

LASSELS, RICHARD. The Voyage of Italy; or, a Compleat Journey through Italy. With the Characters of the People, and the Description of the Chief Towns, Churches, Monasteries, Tombs, Libraries, Pallaces, Villas, Gardens, Pictures, Statues and Antiquities. As also, of the Interest, Government, Riches, Force, . . . of all the Princes, with Instructions concerning Travel. 2 parts in 1 vol. Frontispiece. 16mo. London.

Another edition, 8vo, London, 1686; and 8vo, London, 1698. The work was translated into French.

The author was a Roman Catholic priest, professor of classics at Douay, "who travelled through Italy five times as Tutor to several of the English Nobility and Gentry." "The celebrated John Wilkes made me a present of this book, assuring me, at the time, that it is one of the best accounts of the curious things of Italy ever delivered to the world in any book of travels."—Edward Harewood, quoted by Sotheran.

The Present State of France; containing the Orders, Dignities, and Charges, of that Kingdom. Written in French; and faithfully Englished. 12mo. London.

1671 SANTOS, FRANCISCO DE LOS (O. H. S.). The Escurial, or a Description of that Wonder of the World, built by Philip II., and lately consumed by Fire, translated by a Servant of the Earl of Sandwich. 4to. London.

An edition (perhaps another translation), London, 1760. See below.

The Escurial burned in 1671. The Earl of Sandwich referred to was Edward Montagu, who perished with his ship when it was blown up in a surprise attack by the Dutch in Solebay, 1672. Pepys, of Diary fame, was his secretary.

1760 SANTOS, FRANCISCO DE LOS (Frey). A Description of the Royal Palace and Monastery of St. Laurence, called the Escurial, and of the Chapel Royal of the Pantheon, translated from the Spanish of Frey Francisco de los Santos, by George Thompson. Folding plates. 4to. London.

1672 CLARKE, SAMUEL. A Description of the Seventeen Provinces, commonly call'd the Low Countries. London.

W., T. An Exact Survey of the United Provinces of the Netherlands, of their Cities, Castles, Fortresses, and other of their Dominions there; with some Remarques of their Government, Antiquities, and memorable Actions: with an exact Map of the seventeen Provinces. Collected by T. W. 8vo. London.

1673 RAY, JOHN (F.R.S.). Observations (Topographical, Moral, and Physiological) made in a Journey through Part of the Low Countries, Germany, Italy and France, with a Catalogue of Plants not natives of England found spontaneously growing in those Parts; with a brief Account of Francis Willoughby, Esq., his Voyage through a great Part of Spain. Portrait and 3 plates. 8vo. London.

Another edition, improved, 2 vols., 8vo, London, 1738. Reprinted in Harris II, 641-693. See below. Vol. II of the 1738 edition contains Rauwolf's *Travels in the Eastern Countries,* with Extracts from those of other Travellers, and Catalogue of Plants. See also Ray under 1718 below.

Ray gives a brief yet ingenious description of everything that he saw, and curiously lays before us anything that is rare.—Locke, quoted by Sotheran. The author was the famous naturalist, known to the world of botanists for his *Flora* (1660), which is the first really systematic catalogue of the plants of a given locality. He also made a complete Flora of the British Isles (1697), which became the pocket companion of every botanist of Great Britain for generations. With Linnaeus, he was the chief founder of the science of systematic botany. He commenced his botanical tours in 1658 in company with Philip Skippon and Francis Willoughby, undertaking as his share of the enterprise the attempt to fit into a comprehensive whole the entire organic world. Wherever he went he made copious notes on things usually passed over by other travellers. His researches and publications have caused him to be regarded as the father of natural history in Great Britain.

1744-48 RAY, JOHN. Travels through the Low Countries, and Germany towards Italy. Interspersed with curious Observations, Natural, Topographical, Physiological, Philological. In Harris II, 641-658.

RAY, JOHN. The Travels of the Reverend John Ray through the Dominions of the State of Venice, Lombardy, Tuscany, Kingdom of Naples, Islands of Sicilly and Malta, the Ecclesiastical States, Bishoprick of Trent, the Country of the Grisons, Switzerland, . . . Interspersed throughout with Historical, Political, Philosophical, Physical, and Moral Reflections, together with an Account of the Abundance of Curiosities seen and examined in the Course of the Author's Voyages and Travels, and many other entertaining and instructive Particulars. In Harris II, 658-693.

TEMPLE, SIR WILLIAM. Observations of the United Provinces of the Netherlands. London.

Many subsequent editions, the 7th appearing in 12mo, corrected and enlarged, London, 1705. In his *Works,* 2 vols., fol., 1720; and *Works,* 4 vols., 8vo, London, 1770.
The author was the well known statesman who brought about the marriage of William of Orange and Mary, the instigator of the quarrel in England over Ancient and Modern Learning, and the patron of Swift, who wrote his "Battle of the Books" in behalf of the Ancients.

WILLOUGHBY, FRANCIS. A Brief Account of Francis Willoughby, Esq., through the Kingdom of Spain. See Ray above, in whose work this account is extant.

Reprinted in the 2nd edit. of Ray, 1738; abridged in Harris II, 694-705; 705-714. See below.

1744-48 WILLOUGHBY, FRANCIS. The Travels of Francis Willoughby, Esq., through the Kingdom of Spain; with Observations on the Climate and Soil, as well as Produce of the Country; Accounts of Natural Curiosities, remarkable Inscriptions, principal Commodities and Manufactures, and of the Temper, Genius and Customs of the Spanish Nation. Interspersed with Remarks by another Hand. In Harris II, 694-705.

WILLOUGHBY, FRANCIS. Travels through Portugal and Spain, with a distinct Description of the principal Cities in both Kingdoms; particularly Lisbon, Coimbra, Porto, and Braga, in the former; Madrid, Valentia, Alicant, . . . in the latter: with a curious and correct Detail of the Curiosities in the Escurial, and a succinct Description of the other Royal Palaces of their Catholick Majesties. By an English Gentleman. In Harris II, 705-714.

Willoughby parted from Ray to make this visit to Spain. Up to this time there were not many accounts of this country. But the discourses of Charles II on his travels in Spain excited the desire of Englishmen to see for themselves the land and people of the Spanish peninsula, and thus gradually the prevailing dislike and contempt for things Spanish were dissolved.

WILSON, ELIAS.   Strange and Wonderful News from Italy, or a True and impartial Relation of the Travels, Adventures, and Martyrdome of four eminent Quakers of York-shire, who in 1672 travelled through France, Italy, and Turkey to propagate their Religion, also of their Voyage to Constantinople, and of their most barbarous, cruel and bloody death, related by Elias Wilson.   4to.   London.

W., F.   News from the Channel: or, the Discovery and perfect Description of the Isle of Serke.   4to.   London.

> Reprinted in *Harl. Misc.* III.

1674   BOCCO, PAULUS.   Icones et Descriptiones rariorum Plantarum Siciliae, Malitae, Galliae et Italiae.   4to.   Oxford.

A Discourse of the Dukedom of Modena; containing the Origins, Antiquity, Government, Manners, and Qualities, of the People: As also the temperature of the Climate, with the Nature and fertility of the Soil.   4to.   London.

1676   BROWNE, EDWARD (M.D.).   An Account of several Travels through a great Part of Germany.   In four Journeys.   I. From Norwich to Colen.   II. Colen to Vienna, with a particular Description of that Imperial City.   III. From Vienna to Hamburg.   IV. From Colan to London.   Wherein the Mines, Baths, and Other Curiosities of those Parts are treated of.   Illustrated with Sculptures.   (Being a Continuation of a former Book of Travels.).   4to.   London.

> See Browne under 1673, CONTINENTAL EUROPE.

CLENCHE, JOHN.   A Tour in France and Italy made by an English Gentleman (J. C.), 1675-76.   London.

> Reprinted in Osborne I, 408-474.
> This work aims to inform the traveller what he may expect to see on his way from Dieppe to Venice, in the way of buildings, religion, revenue, trade, and other various matters of interest. The author gives especial attention to Rome, with its churches, relics, monuments of antiquity, palaces, villas, etc.

DU-MAY, L.   The Estate of the Empire, or, An Abridgement of the Laws and Government of Germany, now faithfully rendered into English.   8vo.   London.

SAMBER, ROBERT. Roma Illustrata, or a Description of the most beautiful Pieces of Painting, Sculpture, and Architecture at and near Rome. Fol. London.

1678 The Painter's Voyage of Italy. In which, all the famous Paintings of the most eminent Masters are particularised, as they are preserved in the several Cities of Italy; chiefly relating to their Altar-pieces, and such other Paintings as are ornamental in their Churches. And also many choice Pictures, kept as Jewels, in the Palaces of particular Persons. Whereunto is added, That exact Collection of Signior Septale, in his Closet at Milan. Illustrated with the Heads of some of the most renowned Painters. (Translated from the Italian) By William Lodge. 8vo. London.

1679 Popery and Tyranny, or, The Present State of France, in relation to its Government, Trade, Manner of the People, and Nature of the Country. In a Letter from an English Gentleman abroad to his Friend in London. 4to. London.

1681 The Present State of Geneva; with a brief Description of that City, and several Changes and Alterations it hath been subject to, from the first Foundation thereof until this present year 1681. 8vo. London.

1683 A Description of the City of Vienna, in its ancient and present State; with an exact and compleat Account of the Siege thereof. (In one sheet.) London.

PONTIER, G. A new Survey of the present State of Europe; containing Remarks upon several Sovereign and Republican States, as Italy, France, Lorrain, Germany, Spain, . . . With Memoirs Historical, Chronological, Topographical, Hydrographical, Political, . . . brought down to the Year 1683, by R. Pontier, chief Prothonitor of Rome. Translated by W. Beaumont. 8vo. London.

The Present State of the German and Turkish Empires, with Remarks thereupon; as also some Reflections on the Interest of the Christian Princes; with Memoirs of the Siege of Vienna, by an eminent Officer in that City. With a true Account of the great success of the Christian Forces in taking Barkan, Gran, . . . Also an historical preface of the Rise and Growth of the Turkish Empire. London.

For other accounts of the siege of Vienna see from 1683 on, under MILITARY EXPEDITIONS.

SALGADO, JAMES. A Description of the Plaza, or Market-Place of Madrid, and the Bull-baiting there. 4to. London.

> Reprinted in *Harl. Misc.* VII.
> The author was a Spanish priest who had turned Protestant.

1684 SALGADO, JAMES. The Manners and Customs of the principal Nations of Europe (in Latin and English). Fol. London.

> This tract, consisting of 14 pages, displays great discrimination of character in the various manners and peculiarities of the German, Englishman, Frenchman, Italian and Spaniard.—Lowndes.

1686 BURNET, GILBERT. Some Letters, containing an Account of what seemed most remarkable in travelling through Switzerland, Italy and Parts of Germany, . . . 1685-86. Written by G. Burnet, D.D., to the Honble. R(obert) B(oyle). 8vo. Rotterdam.

> 2nd edit., corrected and altered, 8vo, Rotterdam, 1687; a Supplement to the same, 8vo, Rotterdam, 1688; 12mo, London, 1689; London, 1708; 8vo, with an Appendix, London, 1724; in Harris II, 590-640; London, 1750 and 1758. Translated into French, Rotterdam, 1687. See below.
> The author was the 51st bishop of Sarum, probably better known for his *History of his Own Times* (1723-1734). He met with many ups and downs in his ecclesiastical career, being in and out of favor with Charles II, James II, and William III.

> 1687 BURNET, GILBERT. Some Letters, Containing an Account of what seemed most Remarkable in Travelling through Switzerland, Some Parts of Germany, . . . in the years 1685 and 1686. Written by G. Burnet, D.D., to the Hon. R(obert) B(oyle). The 2nd edition, Corrected and Altered in some places by the Author. To which is added, an Appendix, containing some Remarks on Switzerland and Italy, writ by a Person of Quality, and communicated to the Author. Together with a Table of Contents of each Letter. 8vo. Rotterdam.

>> At the close of the preliminary matter of this edition is the following note: "The Printing of the First Edition . . . falling into the hands of such workmen, as did not understand the English, and the Author, living at distance from the Press, there Hap'ned so many and great Faults in it, as marr'd the sence in divers places; which are all well corrected in this Edition, by the Care of an Englishman. . . ." Quoted by Quaritch. Concerning the work as a whole Lowndes remarks: "This curious and entertaining narrative surpasses everything in its kind extant, in the style, sentiments, matter, and method. The observations upon the corruptions and impostures of popery will afford pleasure to every consistent Protestant."

> 1688 BURNET, GILBERT. Three Letters concerning the Present State of Italy, written in the year 1687 (by Gilbert Burnet). I. Relating to the Affair of Molinos, and the Quietists. II. Relating to the Inquisition, and the State of Religion. III. Relating to the Policy and Interests of . . . the State of Italy. Being a Supplement to Dr. Burnet's Letters. 8vo. Rotterdam.

> 1689 BURNET, GILBERT. Travels in Two Volumes. I. Containing his Travels into Switzerland, Italy, and Germany, with an Appendix; Animadversions on the "Reflections" upon the Travels; three Letters of the Quietists, Inquisition, and State of Italy. II. His Translation of Lanctantius, . . . 2 vols. 12mo. London.

1687 (In French.) Voyage de Suisse, d'Italie, et de quelques endroits d'Allemagne et de France en 1685-86. Rotterdam.

A New Description of Paris; Containing a particular Account of all the
Churches, Palaces, Monasteries, Colledges, Hospitals, Libraries, Cab-
inets of Rarities, Academies, Paintings, Medals, Statues and other
Sculptures, Monuments, and publick Inscriptions. With all other re-
markable matters of that great and famous City. Translated out of
French. 12mo. London.

2nd edit., with map added, 12mo, London, 1688; reprinted, London, 1698.

The Present State of Hungary, or, A Geographical and Historical Description of that Kingdom: giving an Account of the Nature of the Country, Inhabitants, Governments, Policy, Religion, and Laws; its Division
of its Towns, Castles, Rivers, Lakes, Mountains, Product, Mines, Minerals, and other Rarities; with the memorable Battels and Sieges. To
which is added, A Short Account of Transylvania. 12mo. London.

1687 SPON, ISAAC. The History of the State and City of Geneva, from its
first Foundation to this present Time. Faithfully collected from several
Manuscripts of Jacobus, Gothofredus, Monsieur Chorier, and others.
Fol. London.

For other works of Spon see Wheler and Spon under 1682, NEAR EAST.

WOLLEY, R. The Present State of France, containing a General Description of that Kingdom, translated from the latest Edition of the
French, with Additional Observations and Remarks of the New Compiler and Digested into a Method Conformable to that of the State of
England. 8vo. London.

Wolley was a hack writer for John Dunton the bookseller, and seemingly has
done here a typical piece of hack work.

1688 CARR, WILLIAM. Remarks of the Government of several Parts of
Germany, Denmark, Switzerland, Hambourg, Lubeck, and Hanseatic
Towns; but more particularly of the United Provinces; with some few
Directions how to travel in the States' Dominions. Together
with a List of the most considerable Cities in Europe; with the num-
ber of Houses in each City. 8vo. Amsterdam and London.

Another edition, London, 1690.
Carr was the "Late Consul for the English Nation at Amsterdam."—From the
title.

A True and Exact Relation of the most dreadful Earthquake which happened in the City of Naples, . . . June 5th, 1688. Whereby about forty Cities and Villages were either wholly ruin'd or extreamly damnified; Eight thousand Persons destroyed, . . . Translated (by J. P.) from the Italian Copy, by an Eye-witness of those miserable Ruins. 4to. London. (27 pp.)

1689 A Modern View of such parts of Europe that have lately been, and still are, the places of great Transactions, viz., Italy, with all its particulars; France, with all Provinces and Bishopricks; Germany, with the Dukedom of Lorraine, and all the Electorates and Lordships of the Empire; Spain, with all its Dominions, . . . wherein is shewed the present State of all those Countries; with curious Remarks of Antiquity interwoven. 8vo. London.

WHITTIE, J. An Exact Diary of the late Expedition of the Prince of Orange from his Palace at the Hague to his landing at Torbay, and from thence to Whitehall. Folding map. 4to. London.

1690 The Present State of Germany, or, An Account of the Extent, Rise, Form, Wealth, Strength, Weaknesses and Interests, of that Empire. The Prerogatives of the Emperour; and the Privileges of the Electors, Princes, and free Cities. Adapted to the present Circumstances of that Nation. By a Person of Quality. 4to. London.

STRUTTON, RICHARD. A True Relation of the Cruelties and Barbarities of the French upon the English Prisoners of War; being a Journal of their Travels from Dinan in Britany to Thoulon, and back again. With a Description of the Situation and Fortifications of all the eminent Towns on the road; of their Prisons and Hospitals; the numbers and names of them that died; with the Charity and Sufferings of the Protestants (by "an Eye-witness"). 4to. London.

1691 An Accurate Description of the United Netherlands; and of the most considerable parts of Germany, Sweden, and Denmark. Containing a succinct Account of what is most remarkable in those Countries, and necessary Instructions for Travellers; together with, An exact Relation of the Entertainment of his most Sacred Majesty, King William, at the Hague. Illus. with figures. 8vo. London.

See 1725 below, *Travels through Flanders.*

ACTON, WILLIAM. A New Journal of Italy; containing what is most remarkable of the Antiquities of Rome, Savoy, Naples: with Observations on the Strengths, Beauty, and Scituation, of the other Towns and Forts in Italy, and the Distances; together with the best Painting, Carving, Limning, and other both natural and artificial Curiosities, taken notice of by William Acton. 12mo. London.

1691 D'AULNOY, MARIE-CATHERINE (Countess of). The Ingenious and Diverting Letters of the Lady ———'s Travels into Spain; describing the Devotions, Nunneries, Humours, Customs, Law, Militia, Trade, Diet, and Recreations, of that People, in several Letters. Intermixt with Great Variety of Modern Adventures, and surprising Accidents: Being the Truest and Best Remarks Extant, on that Court and Country. 8vo. London.

> Frequently reissued. Foulché-Delbosc lists some 16 editions before 1800. 2nd edit., 3 parts in 1 vol., 12mo, London, 1692; 4th edit., complete in 3 parts, 8vo, 1697; 7th edit., with an Additional Letter concerning the State of Spain in 1700, by an English Gentleman, 8vo, 1708; 12th edit., 2 vols., with additional matter, 12mo, 1774; modern reprint edited by Foulché-Delbosc, London, 1930. The French original, Paris, 1691. See below.
> The name is variously spelled, viz., D'Aulnoy, D'Aunoy, Dunois, and Danois. In Arber, *Term Catalogues,* III, Nov. 1698, there is an item purporting to be the Life of Countess Dunois. See below.

> 1698 The Life of the Countess Dunois, Author of the Ladies Travels into Spain. Written by herself, by way of Answer to Mon. Saint Evremond; containing withal a Modest Vindication of the Female Sex, . . . Made English from the Original. 8vo. London.
>
> > This was really written by the Countess Henriette J. de Murat.— Arber.

> 1701 D'AULNOY, MARIE-CATHERINE JUMELLE DE BERNEVILLE, COMTESSE. Memoirs of the present State of the Court and Council of Spain . . . done into English by T. Brown. 8vo. London.

> 1740 D'AULNOY, MARIE-CATHERINE. A Brief Account of Spain: with a general View of the Nature and Manners of the Spaniards. Being a Collection of several Curious Particulars relating to that People. In Four Letters. 8vo. London.

> 1774 D'AULNOY, MARIE-CATHERINE. The Lady's Travels into Spain, or, A Genuine Relation of the Religion, Laws, Commerce, Customs, and Manners of that Country. Written by the Countess of Danois, in a Series of Letters to a Friend at Paris. A new Edition, Improved. To which is added, A Description of the present King of Spain, his Manner of Living; the Characters of his Ministers, and other Officers of the Court of Spain, . . . With Instructions how to travel in Spain, and an Accurate Account of the Roads of that Country. 2 vols. 12mo. London.
>
> > The three appendices in vol. II consists of extracts from Baretti's Travels.—Foulché-Delbosc.

1930 D'AULNOY, MADAME. Travels into Spain, being the Ingenious and Diverting Letters of the Lady. Translated in the year of its publication
1691, and now published with an Introduction and Notes by R. Foulché-
Delbosc. Broadway Travellers. 8vo. London.

1691 D'AULNOY, MARIE-CATHERINE. Relation du Voyage d'Espagne,
3 vols. 12mo. Paris.

> Many subsequent editions in French and translations into other lan-
guages.

EACHARD, LAURENCE. The Duke of Savoy's Dominions most accurately described; with some adjacent parts, shewing the Bounds, Dimensions, Rivers, Riches, Strength, Religions there practiced, Languages, Dioceses, Universities; the Scituation of the principal Towns,
their Distances; also a Table of all the Towns here mentioned. Necessary for understanding these Wars. London.

EACHARD, LAURENCE. Flanders, or the Spanish Netherlands described; shewing the several Provinces, their Bounds, Dimensions,
Rivers, Riches, Strength, Traffick, Religion, Languages, Dioceses, Universities, and a large Description of the Cities; with a useful Index
of all the Cities, Towns, Ports, Rivers, . . . so as it may serve for a
Geographical Dictionary. 8vo. London.

> Reprinted, with a map of the ten provinces, London, 1692; 12mo, London, 1693.

EMILIANE, GABRIEL D'. Observations on a Journey to Naples;
wherein the Frauds of Romish Monks and Priests are further discovered. By the Author of a late Book entituled, "The Frauds of Romish Monks and Priests." 8vo. London.

> Reprinted, London, 1692; in 2 vols., London, 1704. A French version, 2 vols.,
Rotterdam, 1727. See below.
> The real name of the author was Antonio Gavin. He studied in Spain, but
having become a Protestant, he fled to England. His *Master-Key to Popery*, full
of "mendacious revelations," apeared in Ireland, 1724.

1727 (In French.) Voyage en Italie. 2 vols. Rotterdam.
Augmented to 3 vols., London, 1727.

A Late Voyage to Holland, with brief Relations of the Transactions at
the Hague: also Remarks on the Manners and Customs, Nature and
Comical Humours of the People . . . Written by an English Gentleman,
attending the Court of the King of Great Britain. In *Harl. Misc.* II.
London.

1692 BROMLEY, WILLIAM. Remarks made in Travels through France and Italy. With many Publick Inscriptions. Lately taken by a Person of Quality. 8vo. London.

> 2nd edit., London, 1705.
> The first edition was bought up by Bromley's political opponents and reissued in 1705, with the addition of a burlesque table of contents.—Lowndes. Bromley was then a candidate for the office of Speaker of the House of Commons. He won to this position in 1710, and in 1713-14 he became Secretary of State. See Hearne's *Reliquiae Hearnianae* I, 46-47. For further tours see under 1702 below.

Relation of a Journey to Spain. London.

> So cited in Pinkerton XVII.

S., J. A Description of France in its several Governments; together with the most Considerable Cities, Sea-ports, and Rivers of that Kingdom; as also the Distances, with the Longitudes and Latitudes of each Place, . . . by J. S. Folding map. 12mo. London.

1693 The Second Volume of Historical Voyages and Travels over Europe; containing all that is most curious in Spain and Portugal. Done out of French. London.

> It is stated that the first volume deals with France but the title has not come to the notice of the editor.

1694 LA CROZE, JEAN CORNANN DE. An Historical and Geographical Description of France; shewing its Government both in Church and State, Policy, Strength, Riches and Revenues, both in its Prosperity and during the War; Power of the Parliaments, State of the Nobility, . . . The Description of its Climate, Rivers, Lakes, Mountains, Sea-Ports, and other Towns and places; with their distances from each other. Necessary for the right Understanding of the present Affairs of that Kingdom. 12mo. London.

The Third Volume of Historical Travels over Europe; containing the most select Curiosities of Italy; the various Constitutions of Government under several Sovereign Princes and States; their Strength, Riches and Revenues; the Customs, Manners, Coyns, and Trade of the People. Together with a particular Description of the City of Rome, the Conclave, the Election of the Pope and Promotion of the Cardinal; accompanyed with a great number of Remarks never before imparted to the World. Done out of French. 12mo. London.

1695 LE VASSOR, MICHEL. Letters written by a French Gentleman, giving a Faithful and Particular Account of the Transactions of the Court of France relating to the Publick Interest of Europe: with Historical and Political Reflections on the Ancient and Present State of that Kingdom. London.

MISSON, MAXIMILIAN. A New Voyage to Italy, with a Description of the Chief Towns, Churches, Tombs, Libraries, Palaces, Statues, and Antiquities of that Country, together with useful Instructions for those who shall travel thither. Done into English. Numerous folding and other plates of views, costume figures, etc. 2 vols. 8vo. London.

> 2nd edit., enlarged above one-third, 2 vols., London, 1699 (the succeeding issues contained the additions) ; 4th edit., 4 vols., 8vo, London, 1714 ; in 8vo, London, 1739 ; in Harris II, 521-590. French original, the Hague, 1691, with many subsequent reprintings. See below.
> This work was highly praised by Addison. It was the first general account of Italy that had appeared of its kind, but it has been charged with errors and prejudices. Pinkerton (XVII) says, "At the time these travels appeared, they were in great request, . . . They are, however, out of date at present, besides being replete with the grossest misrepresentations of the religious state of Italy." These travels were made in 1687 and 1688. Misson was tutor to the Earl of Arran and travelled as well with several other noblemen and gentlemen. He is better known for his account of England as he saw it in Queen Anne's day.

> 1699 MISSON, MAXIMILIAN. A New Voyage to Italy, with Curious Observations on several other Countries as Germany, Switzerland, Savoy, Geneva, Flanders and Holland. Together with useful Instructions for those that shall travel thither. Done out of French. 2 vols. London.

> 1744-48 MISSON, MAXIMILIAN. The Travels of Mr. Maximilian Misson through Part of Holland, the Spanish Low Countries, Germany, Tyrol, and the Bishoprick of Trent, on his Way to Italy, containing a distinct Account of whatever appeared to him remarkable in the Places through which he passed, together with Political, Historical, and Critical Remarks upon Persons and Things, as he has Occasion to mention them. The Greater Part of Italy to his Departure out of Italy. In Harris II, 521-590.

> 1691 MISSON, MAXIMILIAN. Nouveau Voyage en Italie ; avec une Mémoire, contenant des avis utiles à ceux qui voudront faire le même Voyage. Avec figures. The Hague.

PENN, WILLIAM. An Account of William Penn's Travails in Holland and Germany, Anno MDCLXXVI. For the Service of the Gospel of Christ, by way of Journal. London.

> A 2nd impression, London, 1695, Corrected by the Author's own Copy, with Answers to some of the Letters, not before Printed.—Maggs, No. 580.

1696 DU MONT, SIEUR JEAN. For an account of some things in Germany, France, Italy, and Malta see his A New Voyage to the Levant, under NEAR EAST.

The Fourth Volume of Historical Travels over Europe; containing a Description of Holland and the rest of the United Provinces; the Grounds of their Union, and altering their Religion; also their Growth under the House of Orange; their Government, Laws, Religion, Policy, Strength, Trade, Fishing, and Bank; with a particular Account of Amsterdam, Rotterdam, Hague, . . . Done out of French. London.

KENNETT, BASIL. Romae Antiquae Notitia: or the Antiquities of Rome, I: Rise, Progress, and Decay of the Commonwealth, II: Description of the City. London.

> 2nd edit., with large additions, London, 1699; 13th edit., 8vo, London, 1763; 15th, 8vo, London, 1776. See below.
> The author was the first chaplain of the English Factory at Leghorn, where he was bothered by the Inquisition.—Sotheran. Later he became president of Corpus Christi College, Oxford. He did considerable miscellaneous writing and translating.

> 1763 KENNETT, BASIL. Romae Antiquae Notitia, or the Antiquities of Rome: Short History of the Rise, Progress, and Decay of the Commonwealth; Description of the City, Account of Religion, Government, War, Customs, . . . with Essays on Learning and Education. Views of principal buildings, etc. 8vo. London.

MOUNTAGUE, WILLIAM. The Delights of Holland, or a Three Months Travel about that and the other Provinces, with Observations and Reflections on their Trade, Wealth, Strength, Beauty, Policy, . . . together with a Catalogue of the Rarities in the Anatomical School at Leyden. ·8vo. London.

PATIN, CHARLES (M. D.). Travels through Germany, Bohemia, Swisserland, Holland, and other parts of Europe, . . . Made English and illustrated with copper cuts and a map. Portrait by Van der Gucht. London.

> Reprinted, London, 1697. French original, Paris (?), 1673.
> For those who are curious in medals this piece will be most acceptable; yet this does not lessen the value of the descriptions and other relations.—Churchill, *Introduction.* Patin was a French physician and numismatic. He was more famous for his work in the latter profession than in the former.

1698 FARIA Y SOUSA, MANUAL. The History of Portugal from the first Ages of the World to the Year 1640. Continued down to the Year 1698 by Capt. John Stevens. 8vo. London.

> Faria is considered one of the most celebrated historians and poets of Portugal.—Lowndes. See also Faria under 1695, EAST INDIES.

A Trip to Holland; being a Description of the Country, People, and Manners; as also some select Observations on Amsterdam. London.

An Answer to a late ill-natured Libel, call'd A Trip to Holland; being a
real Description of the Country; the Bravery, Wisdom, and Industry,
of its Inhabitants; and the several Vertues which have their Growth
and Encouragement in the Seven United Provinces. By a Dutch Merchant. London.

1699 DORINGTON, C. Observations concerning the present State of Religion in the Romish Church, with some Reflections upon it; made in a
Journey through some Provinces of Germany. London.

HARRIS, W. (Dr.). A Description of the King's Palace and Gardens
at Loo; with a Short Account of Holland; in which are some Observations relating to their Diseases. London.

> Harris was physician-in-ordinary to William III.

LISTER, MARTIN, (Dr.). A Journey to Paris in 1690. 6 plates. 8vo.
London.

> Reprinted in Pinkerton IV, 1-76; another edition, edited by G. Henning, Lon-
> don, 1823. Translated into French by E. de Sermizelles, Paris, 1873. A satire upon
> the book appeared at London, 1699, bound up with the original. See this date below
> under *A Succinct Description, etc.*
> This work contains learned observations on Science, Art, and Natural History,
> with interesting descriptions of the houses and people the author visited, their
> libraries, gardens, collections, etc., besides the manners and conditions of the
> French people.—Sotheran. Lister, who was a physician, passed six months in
> Paris in 1696. Being an acute and interested observer, he took particular notice
> of the way people lived. He met many famous men, among them Le Notre the
> architect of Versailles. Readers who remember Moliere's strictures on the med-
> ical profession of Paris will find here a defense of the apothecaries and doctors,
> besides a good word for the hygienic conditions of the French capital.

MARIANO, JOHN DE. The General History of Spain, from the first
peopling of it by Tubal till the Death of King Philipp III. To which
are added Two Supplements . . . the whole translated from the Spanish
by Capt. John Stevens. Fol. London.

> Spanish original, Toledo, 1601. See below.
> Another notice of the book has "translated from the Spanish of Ferdinand
> y Salcedo." The work is of considerable American interest, as it contains: The
> Discoveries and Conquests of the Spaniards in the West Indies; Controversies be-
> twixt the Crowns of Spain and Portugal concerning their Discoveries; the Sending
> of Vasco da Gama to Discover the India Sea; Death of Christopher Columbus,
> etc.—Bookseller's Note.

1601 MARIANO, JUAN DE. Historia general de España. Toledo.

A Succinct Description of France; wherein is a Character of the People;
their Religion, Customs, . . . of that Kingdom. Writ by a Gentleman
now Travelling there, to his Friend in England. Dedicated to that Eminent and Learn'd Physitian, Dr. Martin Lister; and may serve as a
Supplement to his Journey to Paris. 8vo. London.

1700   A Pilgrimage to the Grand Jubilee at Rome in the Year 1700, by an English
        Gentleman lately return'd from thence. As also, The English Nun,
        or a Comical Description of a Nunnery; . . . London.

>   The first part was reprinted, London, 1701.

1701   A Short Account of and Character of Spain: in a Letter from an Eng-
        lish Gentleman now residing at Madrid to his Friend in London.

>   The letter is signed C. T.—Foulché-Delbosc.

VERYARD, ELLIS (M.D.). For a journey through the Low Countries,
        France, Italy and Part of Spain see his *An Account of divers Choice
        Remarks, Geographical,* etc., under NEAR EAST.

A View of Paris and Places adjoining, with an Account of the Court of
        France and of the late King James, to which is added, the Present
        Posture of Affairs in that Kingdom, . . . written by a Gentleman lately
        residing at the English Ambassador's at Paris. 8vo. London.

>   Reprinted, London, 1706.

1702   BROMLEY, WILLIAM. Several Years Travels through Portugal,
        Spain, Italy, Germany, Prussia, Sweden, Denmark, and the United
        Provinces. Performed by a Gentleman. 8vo. London.

>   Reprinted in the 1705 edition of Harris II, 762-783; an abridged version of
>   the travels in the Spanish and Portuguese regions in Harris II, 706-714, 1744-48
>   edition.

A Curious Survey of France; describing their Government, Laws, Religion,
        Policy, and Strength; their Customs, Manners, Riches, . . . with a
        particular Description of Provence, Dauphine, Languedoc, Gascoigne,
        Lions, Burgundy, Berry, Anjou, Britain, Normandy, . . . Map of the
        whole country. 12mo. London.

FANSHAW, SIR RICHARD. Original Letters of his Excellency Sir
        Richard Fanshaw, during his Embassies in Spain and Portugal: which,
        together with divers Letters and Answers from the Chief Ministers
        of State of England, Spain and Portugal, contain the whole Negocia-
        tions of the Treaty of Peace between those Three Crowns. 8vo. Lon-
        don.

>   Reprinted, 2 vols., London, 1724.

DE WITT, JOHN (and other Great Men of Holland). The True Interest and Political Maxims of the Republick of Holland and West Friesland . . . treating of Liberty in General, of Manufactures, Fisheries, Traffick, Navigation, . . . Portrait. 8vo. London.

> Another edition, London, 1743.

A New Description of Spain and Portugal; containing an Account of their Government, Laws, Religion, Policy, and Strength; their Customs, Manners, and Riches; their Trade: with a Description of the City of Madrid, the Palaces of Aranjoux and the Escurial; the Kingdoms of Leon, Galicia, and Austria (Asturias?); likewise of the Kingdoms of Arragon, Catalognia, and Valentia; as also of the City of Lisbon and other places remarkable in Portugal. 12mo. London.

NORTHLEIGH, JOHN. For France see his *Topographical Descriptions* under CONTINENTAL EUROPE. The portion dealing with France reprinted in Harris II, 727-740. See below.

> 1744-48 NORTHLEIGH, JOHN. Travels through France interspersed with historical, political, and medical Observations, made with great Care and Circumspection, in two different Journeys through that Kingdom, the last of which was compleated in the Year 1702, and the Whole revised by the Author a little before his Death. In Harris II, 727-740.
>
> > In this description occurs the remark: "We are come now to Paris the Metropolis of France, that would compare with ours in England for extent and Dimension, for its Buildings and Inhabitants, but fails in all."—Bookseller's Note. The author was a physician of the Royal College of Physicians. He travelled through a good part of Europe for the sake of improvement and information.

SAVAGE, JOHN. The Antient and Present State of the Empire of Germany, containing the Respective Histories of the Electorates, Principalities, . . . and an Account of the Empire and all its Dependencies. Map. 8vo. London.

1703 A Compleat History of the Cevennes, giving a Particular Account of the Scituation, Strength, and Antiquity of the People and Country: together with several Treaties and Stipulations made since Charles IX. to this Present King Lewis XIV.; wherein the Cevennois have obtain'd many Large Privileges, both Civil and Religious, by a Doctor of the Civil Laws. 8vo. London.

1704 The Frenchman and Spaniard display'd in lively Characters: Being a brief Description of the Customs and Manners of those two Nations; shewing the great Antipathy that is between them, and the consequences that may ensue on the Arrival of Charles III. 4to. London.

A Trip to Portugal, or a View of their Strength by Sea and Land, an Exact List of their Forces; with the Names of their Regimental Officers, the Situation of their Frontier Towns, and the Prospect of their Fortifications. To which is added, A Catalogue of their Kings, . . . In a Letter from a Volunteer at Lisbon to his Friend in London. 8vo. London.

1704-05 A Trip to Spain, or, a True Description of the Comical Humors, Ridiculous Customs and foolish Laws of that lazy improvident People the Spaniards, in a Letter to a Person of Quality, from an Officer in the Royal Navy. Fol. London.

> This is a general sketch of Spain, but is principally concerned with Madrid. —Foulché-Delbosc.

1705 ADDISON, JOSEPH. Remarks on several Parts of Italy, in the years 1701, 1702, 1703. 8vo. London.

> 3rd edit., London, 1726; another, London, 1761; reprinted in Moore's Collection, London, 1785. Translated into French, Paris, 1722. See below and also Le Clerc under 1715 below.
> Thomas Hearne, the Jacobite antiquarian of Oxford, says of this book, under date of Nov. 28, 1705: "Mr. Addison's Travells is a book very trite, being made up of nothing but scraps of verses, and things which have been observed over and over, without any addition of things not discovered before; . . . though it must be acknowledged, that the book is written in a clean style, and for that reason will please novices and superficial readers." Later under Jan. 12, 1705-06, he says that Mr. Thwaites told him, "Mr. Addison's Book of Travells, which he has read all over, is not so contemptible as most would make it, being (he says) writ not only in a very clean handsome style, but with good skill, and contains several curiosities, which are not so clearly told by other authors."—*Reliquiae Hearnianae* I, pp. 73, 88. It should be noted, however, that Addison the Whig could not expect warm commendation from this uncompromising Tory. Boswell quotes Johnson as saying, "It is a tedious book, and if it were not attached to Addison's previous reputation, one would not think much of it."

> 1722 (In French.) Remarques sur divers endroits d'Italie par Mr. Addison, pour servír au voyage de Mr. Minou. 12mo. Paris.

> Noticed in the *Journal des Scavans*, 1725, I, 56.

TOLAND, JOHN. An Account of the Courts of Prussia and Hannover sent to a Minister of State. London.

> Another edition, London, 1714. See below, and also under 1723 below.
> The author is chiefly remembered for his pamphlet *Christianity Not Mysterious* (1696), which opened up the Deist controversy.

> 1714 TOLAND, JOHN. An Account of the Courts of Prussia and Hanover sent to a Minister of State, (with) the Ordinances, . . . of the Royal Academy of Berlin, and the Declaration of the Elector Palatine in favour of his Protestant Subjects. 8vo. London.

1706 The Ancient and Present State of Portugal; containing the Description of that Kingdom, its former and present Division, the manner of the Cortes or Parliament, its several Names, Forts, Rivers, Lakes, Baths, Plants, Minerals, and other Products; Religious and Military Orders, Prelates, . . . Also a Curious Account of the Inquisition; and of all the Towns and Rivers in the Kingdom; besides some of the Chiefest on the Frontiers of Spain; with an Index and a map of Portugal and Spain. 8vo. London.

A Geographical and Historical Account of the Principality of Catalonia and Earldom of Barcelona; containing the Description of that Country and City, and all other places of Note; its principal Rivers; Succession of its Princes; and all notable Revolutions . . . 4to. London.

The Travels of an English Gentleman to Rome. London.

So cited by Pinkerton XVII.

1708 The History of the Government of Venice: Wherein the Policies, Councils, Magistrates and Laws of that State are fully related; and the Use of the Balloting Box exactly described. 8vo. London.

1709 Letters to a Nobleman, from a Gentleman Travelling through Holland, Flanders, and France; with a Description of Ghent, Lisle, . . . and the Courts of Versailles and St. Germain. 8vo. London.

MONTAGUE, RALPH (Duke of). Life, containing his Travels abroad; his Marriages, Children, and other Actions at Home, with his Death, . . . 8vo. London.

1711 BAUDRIER, SIEUR DU. A New Journey to Paris: Together with some Secret Transactions between the Fr***h K**g, and an Eng**** Gentleman (Matthew Prior). By the Lieut. du Baudrier (pseudonym for Jonathan Swift). Translated from the French. 8vo. London.

HOTOMAN, FRANCIS. Franco-Galliae; or an Account of the Ancient Free State of France and Most other Parts of Europe, before the Loss of their Liberties, written originally in 1574; and translated into English (by Robert Molesworth). 8vo. London.

The translator was the Molesworth who incurred the displeasure of the Danish King for his *Account of Denmark*. See under 1694, NORTH EUROPE.

LEONHARDI, JOHN. An Account of the Grisons; or a Description of the Free and Independent Common-Wealth of the three Rhaetish Leagues. 8vo. London.

> An interesting and scarce tract on Communities.—Bookseller's Note.

1712 BROME, JAMES. Travels through Portugal, Spain, and Italy. 8vo. London.

> These travels took place in about 1708.

MONTFAUCON, BERNARD DE (Father). The Travels of the Learned Father Montfaucon from Paris thro' Italy, containing an Account of many Antiquities at Vienne, Arles, Nismes, and Marseilles, the Delights of Italy and Rome—viz., Libraries, Statues, Paintings, Temples, Churches, . . . Illus. Translated from the Latin original. 8vo. London.

> 2nd edit., with a slightly different title, revised, fol., London, 1725. Latin original, Paris, 1702. See below.

> 1725 MONTFAUCON, BERNARD DE. The Antiquities of Italy, being his Travels from Paris through Italy in 1698-99, Translated from the Latin Original, revised by J. Henley. Fol. London.

> 1702 MONTFAUCON, BERNARD DE. Diarum italicum sive monumentorum veterum bibliothecarum notitiae singulares itinerario italico collectae. 4to. Paris.

A Particular Description of the Famous Town and Cittadel of Dunkirk, with all its Fortifications, viz., Rice-Bank, Forts, Harbour, Peere, the Bason, Number of the Ships, . . . (also) Churches, Nunneries, . . . 4to. In *Harl. Misc.*, II, 329-337. London.

1714 STANYAN, ABRAHAM. An Account of Switzerland, written in the Year 1714. Vignette of Shakespeare on title. 8vo. London.

> Reprinted, Edinburgh, 1756. Translated into French, 1756.
> The author was educated at Christ Church, Oxford. He became Under Secretary of State 1715-16, and Clerk to the Privy Council in 1719. The book was "destined to enlighten the profound darkness which he found prevailing as to the constitution, religion, and manners of the Federated Cantons . . . It was used by William Coxe in his Sketches . . . of Swisserland (see under 1779 below). It was commended by Lord Chesterfield to his son."—D.N.B., quoted by Sotheran. "I have often wondered that a Country situated almost in the Middle of Europe, as Switzerland is, should be so little known, that not only the Generality of People have scarce any idea of it, but that even some Men bred up to Foreign Affairs hardly know the Names of the several Cantons, or what Religion they are."—Preface, quoted by Sotheran. "The Swiss," said Dr. Johnson in 1778, "admit that there is but one error in Stanyan."

1715 LE CLERC, J. Observations on Mr. Addison's Travels through Italy. London.

> See Addison under 1705 above.

A New Journey to France; with an exact Description of the Sea-Coast from London, to Calais, . . . London.

The Present State of His Majesty's Dominions in Germany, containing an exact Description of the same. Map and folding genealogy of the Brunswick line traced from Woden. 8vo. London.

1716 The Antient and Modern History of the Balearick Islands, or of the Kingdom of Majorca, which comprehends the Islands of Majorca, Minorca, Yvica, Formentera, and others, with their natural and geographical Description. Translated from the original Spanish, by Colin Campbell. Maps. 8vo. London.

DRYDEN, JOHN. A Voyage to Sicily and Malta, written when he accompanied Mr. Cecill in that Expedition in the Years 1700 and 1701. 8vo. London.

> The author was the second son of John Dryden the poet and dramatist. He translated Juvenal's Fourteenth Satire for his father's version, and wrote one mediocre comedy.—D.N.B.

1717 CHANCEL, A. D. A New Journey over Europe. London.

Relation d'un Voyage nouvellement fait par la France. London.

1718 RAY, JOHN, and WILLOUGHBY, FRANCIS. Philosophical Letters between the late Learned Mr. Ray and . . . Correspondents, Natives, and Foreigners; to which are added those of Francis Willoughby, Esq., consisting of Curious Discoveries in the History of Birds, Insects, Plants, Fossils, . . . edited by W. Derham. 8vo. London.

> See Ray under 1673 above.

Travels from London to Rome on Foot. 8vo. London.

> Such a mode of travelling, which is equivalent to our modern hiking, was rare in this century. So must Goldsmith have travelled, as did Wordsworth and Jones in 1790.

1721   A Letter from an English Traveller at Rome to his Father, of the 6th May
       (8 pp.).   4to.   London.

1722   RICHARDSON, JONATHAN.   An Account of the Statues and
       Bas-reliefs, Drawings and Pictures in Italy, France, . . . with Remarks,
       . . . London.

> This is probably the elder Richardson, the painter, who won some distinction
> for his treatise, *Theory of Painting* (1715). He succeeded Kneller in public favor
> as a portrait painter.

1723   TOLAND, JOHN.   An Historical Account of the Life and Writings of
       the late Eminently Famous Mr. John Toland, containing a faithful ac-
       count of his travels in Germany, Holland, . . . An Account of the Con-
       troversies wherein he was engaged . . . an exact Catalogue of his
       Writings, by one of his most intimate Friends.   8vo.   London.

> See Toland under 1705 above.

       Vertot's Miscellanies: Consisting of Disertation upon the true Original
       of the French by a Parallel of their Manners with those of the Ger-
       mans; Salique Laws; On the Sainte Ampoulle; Antient Form of
       Oaths, . . . Done from the French by John Henley.   8vo.   London.

1723-26   BREVAL, JOHN DURANT.   Remarks on several Parts of Europe:
       relating chiefly to the History, Antiquities, and Geography of France,
       the Low Countries, Lorrain, Germany, Savoy, Tyrol, Switzerland,
       Italy, and Spain.   2 vols.   4to.   London.

> Vol. I appeared in 1723, and vol. II in 1726. Reprinted in 2 vols., fol. Lon-
> don, 1738.
> Breval was a hackwriter for the "unspeakable Curll." For some ridicule which
> he cast on Pope the latter put him in the *Dunciad*.

1725   MACKY, JOHN.   A Journey through the Austrian Netherlands, Contain-
       ing the Modern History and Description of all the Provinces, Towns,
       Castles, Palaces, . . . of that Fruitful, Populous Country, so long the
       Scene of Wars and dreadful Ravages, till it was by the Treaty of
       Utrecht yielded to the Emperor of Germany. With an Account of all
       the Remarkable Battels and Sieges; taken from the most authentick
       Narratives. To which is prefixed, An Introduction, containing the
       Ancient History of the whole Seventeen Provinces.   London.

> 2nd edit., 8vo. London, 1732.

Travels through Flanders, Holland, Germany, Sweden, and Denmark; containing an Account of what is most remarkable in those Countries, particularly a Description of those fortified Towns in Flanders and Holland, with exact Draughts of Dunkirk, Maestricht, Charleroi, Gent, and Ath, together with necessary Instructions for Travellers. 5th edit. much enlarged. Written by an English Gentleman, who resided many years in Holland in a publick Capacity.

This may be the same work as that listed under 1691 above: *An Accurate Description of the United Netherlands.*

1726 BROCKWELL, C. Natural and Political History of Portugal, . . . To which is added, The History of Brazil, and all other Dominions subject to the Crown of Portugal in Asia, Africa, and America. Maps of Portugal and Brazil and 1 plate. London.

Letters describing the Character and Customs of the English and French Nations, with a curious Essay on Travelling; and a Criticism on Boileau's Description of Paris. Translated from the French. 8vo. London.

Versailles Illustrated. Plates. London.

1728 BURRISH, ONSLOW. Batavia Hemstuata, or, A View of the Policy and Commerce of the United Provinces, Particularly of Holland, with an Enquiry into the Alliances of the States general with the Emperor, France, Spain and Great Britain. 8vo. London.

Reprinted, London, 1731, with title, *Batavia Illustrata.*
Part I describes the country and its government; part II the fisheries, manufactures and commerce, including the East and West India Companies; part III the alliances with foreign states.

1730 BEHRENS, GEORGE HENNING. The Natural History of Hartz Forest, in Germany, translated by John Andres. 8vo. London.

WRIGHT, EDWARD. Some Observations Made in Travelling through France, Italy, . . . in 1720-22. 42 folding plates by Van der Gucht. 2 vols. 4to. London.

2nd edit., 4to, London, 1764 (without the plates).

1731 Some Short Reflections on the Situation of Gibraltar, and its Importance to the Trade and maritime Force of this Kingdom, with a Proposal for rendering the late Works of the Spaniards near that Fortress, ineffectual. (16 pp.) 4to. London.

1732 BOLLAND, RICHARD (Captain). A Draught of the Streights of Gibraltar, with some Observations upon the Currents thereunto belonging. In Churchill IV, 782-784.

> This "draught" was made in July, 1675.

CARERI, JOHN FRANCIS GEMELLI (Dr.). Travels through Europe in several Letters to the Counsellor Amate Danio. In Churchill VI, 41-142.

> 1st letter dated Venice, Jan. 25, 1686. It covers parts of Italy, Savoy, Paris, England, the Low Countries, and Germany, and is concerned with matters of historical interest and general information. The last letter is dated Vienna, July 14. 1686. See also Careri under 1732, FAR EAST.

MERIN, JOHN BAPTIST (M.D.). A Journey of John Baptist Merin to the Mines of Hungary: with an Account of his Observations made there, in relation to them, and subterraneous Passages in general. In Churchill IV, 762-767.

> This journey was made in 1615.

SKIPPON, PHILIP. An Account of a Journey made Thro' a Part of the Low Countries, Germany, Italy, and France. In Churchill VI, 359-736.

> Abstract in Harris II, 715-727. See below.
> The author travelled in company with Ray, Willoughby, and Bacon. They set out from London, April 17, 1663. He was Ray's companion from the time he left England until he separated from the latter at Paris to return to England. Being an inquisitive traveller, he kept an exact account of everything he saw, and what he missed was not likely to be observed by other travellers. But he gave little or no personal narrative.

> 1744-48 SKIPPON, SIR PHILIP. The Travels of Sir Philip Skippon and the Reverend John Ray through the best Part of the Kingdom of France; interspersed with a great Variety of historical and political, philosophical and mechanical Remarks and Observations. Collected from the Journals of those ingenious Persons. In Harris II, 715-727.

1735 FRANK, THOMAS. Tour through France, Flanders, and Germany. London.

1737 DE VEIL, HANS. Les Amusemens de Spa, or the Gallantries of the Spaw in Germany, containing the Virtues of every Spring, Nature and Uses, the Reasons why frequented by Persons of the first Distinction, the various Diversions and Amusements, many entertaining Histories of Persons resorting to Spaw, intermix'd with several others of Wit, Humor, Gaiety, . . . 2 vols. 8vo. London.

1738 LEDIARD, THOMAS. The German Spy. In Familiar Letters from Munster, Paderborn, Osnabrug, Minden, Bremen, Hamburg, Gluckstadt, Helgoland, Stade, Lubeck, and Rosrock. Written by a Gentleman on his Travels, to his Friend in England. With a Prefatory Account of these Letters, and Explanatory Notes, by Thomas Lediard. London.

> An edition in 1740 cited by Pinkerton XVII.
> Lediard was a miscellaneous writer of historical and biographical works. He was attached to the staff of the Duke of Marlborough and accompanied him on his visit to Charles XII of Sweden. He also wrote an English opera, "Britannia."—D.N.B.

1739 CAMPBELL, JOHN. For his travels in France, Italy, Malta, see his *The Travels and Adventures of Edward Brown*, under GENERAL TRAVELS AND DESCRIPTIONS.

DE TOT, C. DE FERRARE. Political Reflections upon the Finances and Commerce of France, shewing the Causes which formerly obstructed the Advancement of her Trade, . . . Translated from the French. 8vo. London.

WHATLEY, ROBERT (Rev.). Three Letters giving an Account of his Travels into Germany, . . . in 1721-22.

> The author was a prebendary of York.

1740 RIPPERDA, DUKE DE. Memoirs of the Duke de Ripperda: first Embassador from the States-General to his Most Catholick Majesty, then Duke and Grandee of Spain; afterwards Bashan and Prime Minister to Muly Abdulla, Emperor of Fez and Morocco. Containing a succinct Account of the most Remarkable Events which happen'd between 1715 and 1736. Interspers'd throughout with several Curious Particulars relating to the Cardinals Del Guidice and Alberoni, the Princess of Ursino, Prince Cellamere, the Marquis Beretti Landi, M. De Santa Cruz, . . . As also a Distinct and Impartial Detail of the Differences between the Courts of London and Madrid. To which is annexed an Appendix, containing some Papers on the Balance of Europe, the Present State of Spain, and the Consequences of a War in the West Indies. 8vo. London.

1741 A Short Account of a late Journey to Tuscany, Rome, and other Parts of Italy. London.

1742 An Inquiry into the Revenue, Credit and Commerce of France. 8vo. London.

POOLE, ROBERT (M.D.). A Journey from London, to France and Holland; or, The Traveller's Useful Vade Mecum. 2 vols. 8vo. London.

> Reprinted, London, 1746, the second volume of which appeared in 1750.
> In 1741 Poole set out for France to get a degree in medicine from the University of Rheims, but he returned in three months. The above account contains a minute journal of his travels with interesting remarks on Paris hospitals. The bulk of the book is taken up with a French grammar, a sort of gazetteer of Europe, and other information for travellers. See his *Beneficent Bee* under 1753, WEST INDIES.

1743 A Description of Holland and the United Provinces. London.

1743-45 BLAINVILLE, M. DE. Travels through Holland, Germany, Switzerland and other Parts of Europe, but especially Italy. Translated from the French by Turnbull and Guthrie. Maps. 3 vols. 4to. London.

> Reprinted, 3 vols., 4to, London, 1749.
> These travels, though praised by Dr. Johnson, are now held in little esteem. —Lowndes.

1744 MARTEL, PETER. An Account of the Glaciers, or Ice Alps in Savoy. In Two Letters, One from an English Gentleman to his Friend at Geneva; the other from Peter Martel, Engineer, to the said English Gentleman. 2 folding plates. 4to. London.

> The English Gentleman was W. Windham and the Friend at Geneva was the miniature painter, M. Arlaud, a friend of Sir Isaac Newton. This account of Windham's is reproduced in de Beer's *Early Travellers in the Alps*. De Beer points out that the honor of discovering Chamonix as the goal for tourists belongs to a group of Englishmen who were staying at Geneva in 1741. This letter produced results at once. The first to be lured thither was Peter Martel who describes his journey in the letter to Windham cited above. His account is of interest in that it makes the first known mention of Mont Blanc. The Alps, especially in the region of Mont Blanc, were now to become a really fashionable resort. De Beer states that in the eighteenth century more than a hundred accounts of journeys through the Alps appeared.

THOMPSON, CHARLES. The Travels of the late Charles Thompson, containing his Observations on France, Italy, . . . 3 vols. Reading.

> Another edition, London, 1748.

1744-48 Travels through Hungary into Thessaly; a Description of the City of Larissa, and of the Grand Seignor's Court there, with other curious Particulars; together with a Description of other Parts of Hungary, more especially of the Gold Mines, and some Remarks upon the adjacent Countries, then and now making Part of the Hereditary Dominions of the House of Austria. In Harris II, 765-789.

> The writer was a student of physics, botany, anatomy, natural history, and "chymistry." He travelled for the sake of extending his knowledge of things—so he tells us.

Travels through Portugal and Spain, with a distinct Description of the principal Cities in both Kingdoms; particularly Lisbon, Coimbra, Porto, and Braga, in the former; Madrid, Valubra, Alicant, . . . in the latter; with a curious and correct Detail of the Curiosities in the Escuriel, and a Succinct Description of the Royal Palaces of their Catholick Majesties. By an English Gentleman. In Harris II, 705-714.

> The author embarked for Portugal in 1693. He comments on the large spectacles fastened to the ears of many young and old people of Portugal.

1745 DAVIS, WILLIAM. A True Relation of the Travels and most miserable Captivity of William Davis, Barber-Surgeon of London, under the Duke of Florence. Wherein is truly set down the Manner of his Taking, the long Time of his Slavery, and Means of his Delivery, after Eight Years and Ten Months Captivity in the Gallies. Discovering many Main Lands, Islands, Rivers, Cities and Towns, the Condition of the People of the Christians and Infidels, . . . In Osborne I, 476-488.

> The victim of these hardships set out from England, January 28, 1597. Taken prisoner by one of the Duke of Florence's gallies, he was made to toil several years at the oars. His description of the Italian character and his animus against papists both English and Italian are justifiably bitter.

Flanders Delineated: or, A View of the Austrian and French Netherlands, . . . By an Officer of the Allied Army now in Flanders. To which is prefix'd a Summary of the History of the Low Countries in general. Maps and a folding plate. 8vo. Reading.

The Theatre of the Present War in the Netherlands and upon the Rhine, containing a Description of all the Divisions, Fortified and other Towns in the Provinces, South-West Germany, Frontiers of France and Lorrain. Also Introduction to the Art of Fortification and Military Dictionary. Map and plates. 8vo. London.

1749 CAREW, GEORGE. A Relation of the State of France with the Character of Henry IV, and the Principal Persons of that Court. London.

> This is probably Sir George Carew (d. 1612) who was an envoy to France in 1605-09.

Letters on the French Nation, by a Sicilian Gentleman, translated from the French. 8vo. London.

NUGENT, THOMAS. The Grand Tour; Or, a Journey through the Netherlands, Germany, Italy and France. Containing: I. A Description of the principal Cities and Towns, their Situation, Origin, and Ancient Monuments. II. The public Edifices, the Seats and Palaces of the Princes of the Nobility, their Libraries, Cabinets, Paintings, and Statues. III. The Produce of the Countries, the Customs and Manners of the People, the different Coins, their Commerce, Manufactures, Learning, and present Government. IV. An exact List of the Post-Routes, and of the different Carriages by Water and Land, with their settled Prices. 12mo. London.

> 2nd edit., corrected and considerably improved: To which is added, The European Itinerary, 4 vols., London, 1756; a later edition, 4 vols., London, 1778.
> Nugent was a voluminous translator of French works. His *Grand Tour* has become a source book for all studies in this field. It is one of the chief witnesses to the seriousness with which the young English gentleman was supposed to regard his travels abroad.

The Present State of Holland, or a Description of the United Provinces; wherein is contained a Particular Account of the Hague, and the Principal Cities and Towns of the Republick. 12mo. The Hague.

RHYS, UDALL (Price). An Account of the most Remarkable Places and Curiosities in Spain and Portugal. 8vo. London.

1750 CLANCY, Michael (M.D.). Memoirs, containing his Observations on many Countries in Europe. 2 vols. Dublin.

RUSSELL, JONATHAN. Letters from a Young Painter Abroad to his Friends in England. Folding copperplate engravings. 2 vols. 8vo. London.

> A scarce and valuable art book, by some ascribed to Sir Joshua Reynolds.— Bookseller's Note.

A Trip to the Jubilee, by a Gentleman that was at the late Grand one at Rome. Containing a Diverting Account of his most remarkable Travels through France, Milan, . . . 8vo. London.

Voyage en Hollande et sur les frontières occidentales de l'Allemagne, traduit l'anglais par Cantwel. (Place and date?).

> What is the English original? D.N.B. cites an Andrew Cantwell, an Irishman, who studied medicine on the Continent and practiced surgery at Paris from 1742 on.

1751 CLEGHORN, GEORGE. Observations on the epidemical Diseases in Minorca, in the years 1744 and 1749; to which is prefixed a short Account of the Climate, Productions, Inhabitants, and endemical Distempers of the Islands. London.

A Description of the City House of Amsterdam. Amsterdam.

1752 ARMSTRONG, JOHN. The History of the Island of Minorca, Trade, Customs, Antiquities, . . . Map and plates. 8vo. London.

> 2nd edit., with large additions, 8vo, London, 1756. Translated into French, Amsterdam and Paris, 1769. See below.

> 1769 (In French.) Histoire naturelle et civile de l'Isle de Minorque. Traduit sur la 2e édit. angloise. 12mo. Amsterdam and Paris.

1753 BELLICARD, ——. Observations upon the Antiquities of Herculaneum. 42 plates. 8vo. London.

> An ingenious work, containing some particulars which escaped the observations of former writers.—Lowndes. Herculaneum and Pompeii came to the notice of the curious in 1738 and 1748 respectively, though it was not until 1763 that excavations were begun at the latter place.

A Brief Account of the Vaudois, His Sardinian Majesty's Protestant subjects in the Valleys of Piedmont, in a letter from a Gentleman on his Travels in Italy. London.

HANWAY, JONAS. For an account of his travels in Germany and Holland see his *An Historical Account of the British Trade over the Caspian Sea*, under CENTRAL ASIA.

The Traveller's Companion and Guide through France, Flanders, Brabant and Holland. London.

1754 DRUMMOND, ALEXANDER. For accounts of the cities of Germany and Italy see his *Travels through different Cities of Germany, Italy, Greece*, under NEAR EAST.

DUCAREL, ANDREW COLTEE. A Tour through Normandy, described in a Letter to a Friend. 4to. London.

> Another edition, considerably enlarged, fol., London, 1767. See below.
> Though born in Normandy, the author was educated in England and became an enthusiastic student of antiquities. George North, an antiquarian, to whom Ducarel submitted his Account of his tour, criticises it for having "too many repetitions appear in it, especially of the words, *there are,* which render the narrative flat and unenlivening, and make too many breaks in it. With these expunged, and the sentences made to run off a little more roundly in a more

continued flow, the pleasure would be greatly heightened to the reader, etc."—
From Nichols, *Literary Anecdotes*. Ducarel made this tour into Normandy to in-
spect its antiquities. Lowndes characterises it as a meagre composition, with
wretched plates.

1767 DUCAREL, ANDREW COLTEE. Anglo-Norman Antiquities consid-
      ered in a Tour through Part of Normandy. 27 copperplates. Fol.
      London.

MAJOR, THOMAS. The Ruins of Paestum, otherwise Posidonia in
Magna Graecia. 25 copperplates. Fol. London.

    2nd edit., fol., London, 1768. Translated into French, with additions (by
Thomas Major), London, 1768; again by Dumont, with his additions, and other
plates of Herculaneum and antiquities of Naples, in all 18 plates, Paris, 1769.
    Major was an engraver who lived and worked for some time in Paris. He
was the first engraver to be elected R.A.—D.N.B.

1755 FIELDING, HENRY. Journal of a Voyage to Lisbon. 12mo. London.

    Other editions: 12mo, Dublin, 1756; London, 1785; a modern reprint, Lon-
don, 1892; edited for the Oxford Classics by Austin Dobson, Oxford, 1907.
Translated into German, Altona, 1764. See below.
    This work as originally printed contained some libelous matter relating to
the conduct of the captain of the ship. The whole edition was withheld and a
revised one printed. The book is a most readable account of a voyage by sea in
the days when ships had to wait for "fair winds" before they could leave port.
Fielding was suffering from dropsy and made this voyage in the hope of regaining
his health. Both hopes and remedy, however, proved vain, for, as is well known,
Fielding died shortly after reaching Lisbon and was buried there.

1756 FIELDING, HENRY. Journal of a Voyage to Lisbon. With a Frag-
      ment of a Comment on Lord Bolingbroke's Essays. 12mo. Dublin.

1764 (In German.) Herrn Heinrich Fieldings, Esq. Reise nach Lisbon. Von
      ihm selbst beschrieben. Aus dem Englischen übersetzt. Nebst einer
      Nachricht von dem Lebensumstanden dieses berühmten Schriftstellers.
      Altona.

1917 DICKSON, F. S. The Early Editions of Fielding's Voyage to Lisbon;
      The Chronology of Tom Jones; 2 items. 8vo. Reprinted from the
      Library, January and July, 1917. London.

1756 The Importance of the Island of Minorca and Harbour of Port Mahon,
    with a History and Description of both. In a Letter from a Merchant
    to a Noble Lord. 8vo. London.

KEYSLER, JOHANN GEORG. Travels through Germany, Bohemia,
Hungary, Switzerland, Italy, and Lorraine, giving a True Description
of their Present State. (Translated from the German.) 7 engraved
plates. 4 vols. 4to. London.

    3rd edit., London, 1760. German original, Hanover, 1740. See below.
    This work, though heavy, is interesting from the picture it exhibits of Ger-
many, etc., in the middle of the 18th century. The author's judgments on antiquities

have been questioned.—Lowndes. The volumes deal with the natural history, manners, commerce, manufactures, laws, antiquities, etc., and close with an appendix of roads, post stages, etc.

1740 KEYSLER, JOHANN GEORG. Neueste Reise durch Teutschland, Böhmen, Ungarn, die Schweitz, Italien und Lothringen. 3 copperplates and a map of central Europe. 4to. Hannover.

STEVENS, SACHEVERELL. Miscellaneous Remarks made on the Spot, in a late Seven Years' Tour through France, Germany and Holland. London.

> Reprinted in the *World Displayed*, XIX, London, 1761.
> The author was in Paris in 1738 and 1739. He had many complaints to make of the exorbitant prices of inns, the rapacity of the sailors, the bad faith of French valets, the insolence of beggars in Paris, and such like. The English traveller, like the modern American, was always supposed to be rich and hence was much imposed upon. Stevens was full of prejudices but was often an original observer. The people of France he found combined the utmost gaiety with the greatest poverty.

1757 CAMPBELL, JOHN. The Present State of Europe; Interests, Political and Commercial Views, Constitutions, . . . 8vo. London.

CARLETON, SIR DUDLEY. Letters from and to Sir Dudley Carleton, Knt., during his Embassy in Holland, from January, 1615-16, to December, 1620. 4to. London.

1761 JEFFERYS, THOMAS. A Description of the Maritime Parts of France, containing a particular Account of all the Fortified Towns, Forts, Harbours, Bays and Rivers, with their Tides, Currents, Soundings, Shoals, . . . 88 maps and plans. 2 vols. 4to. London.

> Another edition, 2 vols., London, 1774.

KEATE, GEORGE. A Short Account of the ancient History, present Government, and Laws of the Republic of Geneva. Map. 8vo. London.

> Keate is better known through his *Account of the Pelew Islands*. See under 1788, SOUTH SEAS. He also wrote poems on the Alps and on Italy.

TAYLOR, JOHN (Chevalier). The History of the Travels and Adventures of the Chevalier John Taylor, Ophthalmiater Pontifical—Imperial and Royal, to the Kings of Poland, Denmark, Sweden, The Electors of the Holy Empire, . . . Author of 45 Works in different languages; the Produce for upwards of thirty Years, of the greatest practice in the Cure of distempered Eyes, of any in the Age we live—Who has been in every Court, Kingdom, Province, State, City, and Town of the least

Consideration in all Europe, without Exception. Written by Himself. This Work contains all the most worthy the Attention of a Traveller. . . . 3 vols. 8vo. London.

> The full title of this curious work is set forth in Nichols, *Literary Anecdotes* VIII, 410. Taylor was a quack oculist, of much notoriety in his day. Though he is allowed by Dr. King, in his *Political and Literary Anecdotes,* to have possessed professional talents, yet his strange farrago, which he calls the History of his Travels, shows him as a charlatan and coxscomb. The work is now very scarce, being bought up by some descendant or connexion of the family.—Lowndes. He was the subject of many satires and the author of treatises on the eye and a bombastic autobiography.—D.N.B.

1762 GOLDSMITH, OLIVER. See the *Bee* No. 2, in which he traces the character and the manners of Frenchmen in several satirical sketches. See also the *Citizen of the World,* ch. lxxviii, and the *Traveller.* For the most part Goldsmith had a keen appreciation and sympathy for France, its life and taste.

VENUTI, R. Collection of some of the Finest Prospects in Italy, with Short Remarks on them, engraved by various celebrated Engravers at Rome. 2 (?) vols. 8vo. London.

> Letterpress descriptions are given in English, Italian, and French.

1763 ANTONINI, —— (Abbé). A View of Paris, describing all the Churches, Palaces, Public Buildings, and fine Paintings, by the Abbé Antonini, in French and English. 2 vols. 12mo. London.

CLARKE, EDWARD (Rev.). Letters concerning the Spanish Nation, written at Madrid during the Years 1760 and 1761. 4to. London.

> An abridged version in Knox V, 389-433, 1767. Translated into German, Lemgo, 1765; into French, Paris, 1770. See below.
> The author was chaplain to George William, Earl of Bristol, Ambassador Extraordinary to Spain. During his two years' residence there he collected much information, hints, and materials relative to the existing state of Spain, as might "either gratify the curiosity of his friends, or prove of some utility to the publick in general."—Nichols, *Literary Anecdotes.* Several letters describe celebrated libraries, but mostly they have to do with various aspects of local life of the time in Spain.

> 1765 (In German.) Briefe von dem gegenwärtigen Zustande des Königreichs Spanien geschrieben zu Madrid in den Jahren 1760 und 1761 von Edward Clarke, Magister der Weltweisheit, Mitglied des St. Johann Collegii zu Cambridge und Rektors zu Pepperharrow in der Grafschaft Surry damaligen Gesandtschaftsprediger bey dem Grossbritannischen Gesandten dem Grafen von Bristol. In das Deutsche übersetzt und hin und wieder erläutert von Johann Tobias Köhler, Professor zu Göttingen und Mitglied der Churmannzischen Gesellschaft der Wissenschaften zu Erfurth. 8vo. Lemgo.

1770 (In French.) Etat présent de l'Espagne et de la nation espagnole, ou Lettres écrites à Madrid pendant les années 1760 et 1761 par le Rev. Edouard Clarke. Traduit de l'anglois. 2 vols. Paris.

> The translator is said to be Guillaume Imbert. The French version was prohibited in France, because possibly the criticism of Charles III could appear to be addressed to Louis XIV.—From Foulché-Delbosc.

CONDAMINE, M. DE LA. Journal of a Tour to Italy. 8vo. London.

> This work contains, among many other interesting and curious particulars, accounts of the Leaning Towers of Pisa and Bologna, Eruptions of Mount Vesuvius, Detection of the Impositions used in the pretended liquefying of the Blood of St. Januarius, Parallel between the Horse-Races at Rome and Newmarket, etc.—Bookseller's Note.

MAIHOWS, —— (Dr.). Travels in France, Italy and the Archipelagus, or Letters written from several Parts of Europe in 1750. 4 vols. London.

> Translated into French, 4 vols., Paris, 1763; and again in 1767. See below. Pinkerton XVII gives the name of the writer as Matthews.
>
> The first volume is given up entirely to a description of France. The author crossed France in 1750 on his way to the Near East. He describes conscientiously but without originality the principal monuments of a city.

1767 (In French.) Voyage en France, en Italie et aux îles de l'archipel. Traduit de P. F. de Puisieux. 4 vols. 12mo. Paris.

MONTAGUE, LADY MARY WORTLEY. For her letters from various parts of Europe see her *Letters written during her Travels in Europe, Asia, and Africa,* under NEAR EAST.

1764 An Account of the Southern Maritime Provinces of France, representing the Distress to which they are reduced at the Conclusion of the War in 1748, with Supplement, and Remarks on the Marine of France. 2 folding plans of Toulon. 4to. London.

ADAM, ROBERT. A Picturesque Journey in Istria and Dalmatia. London.

> Adam was the famous architect, one of four brothers in the same profession, whose best known work was the Adelphi Terrace in London. This trip to Dalmatia led to a study of the palace of Diocletian, which resulted in a finer use of Greek architectural style for domestic purposes in England.

1766 NORTHALL, JOHN (Captain). Travels through Italy. Containing New and Curious Observations on that Country. London.

> These travels took place in 1752. The author was a captain in the army service

SHARP, SAMUEL (M.D.). Letters from Italy, describing the Customs and Manners of that Country, in the Years 1765 and 1766; to which is annexed, an Admonition to Gentlemen who pass the Alps, in their Tour through Italy. 8vo. London.

> 2nd edit., London, 1767.
> Sharp was surgeon to Guy's Hospital and an eminent writer on surgery. These Letters are the outcome of a journey to Italy for his health. They were attacked by Baretti, between whom and Sharp, arose a great "book fight," as Fanny Burney called it, over some opinions expressed. Baretti followed his first attack in his *Frustra Letteraria* with his *Account of the Manners and Customs in Italy* (1768). Sharp replied in the same year with his *Views of the Customs, Manners, Drama, . . . of Italy*. See 1768 below. Dr. Johnson remarked of these Letters (1776), "I read Sharp's Letters from Italy over again when I was at Bath. There is a great deal of matter in them." Modern opinion regards them as rather superficial.

SMOLLETT, TOBIAS (Dr.). Travels through France and Italy, containing Observations on Character, Customs, Religion, Government, Police, Commerce, Arts and Antiquities. With a particular Description of Nice. 2 vols. 8vo. London.

> An edition, 2 vols., Dublin, 8vo, 1766; another, London, 1778; edited for the World's Classics by Thomas Seccombe, Oxford, 1907, 1919. Reprinted in various collected editions of his works.
> Smollett was probably the most embittered and cantankerous Englishman that ever travelled abroad. Everything and everybody conspired to excite his irascibility. The food and the inns were bad, the accommodations were damp, dirty, and dark; the postillions, innkeepers, and the whole crew of caterers to travellers combined to irritate him with their sharp practices and outrageous extortions. Sterne met him at Turin and has left this memorable account of him: "The learned Smelfungus travelled from Boulogne to Paris, from Paris to Rome, and so on, but he set out with the spleen and jaundice, and every object he passed by was discolored or distorted. He wrote an account of them, but 'twas nothing but the account of his miserable feelings." But Smollett was sick when he left England and still sick when he returned home. He realized himself that the cause of his discomforts lay largely in his poor health as well as in his inability to adapt himself to foreign ways. Nevertheless, being an acute observer, he saw much more than he was given credit for.

THICKNESSE, PHILIP. Observations on the Customs and Manners of the French Nation; in a Series of Letters in which that Nation is vindicated from the Misrepresentations of some late Writers. London.

> 2nd edit., London, 1779; 3rd, London, 1789, with considerable additions, together with the routes through Germany, Holland, Switzerland, differences of money, etc.
> Thicknesse travelled widely and encountered a variety of experience. He went out with Oglethorpe to Georgia in 1735, became Lieut.-Governor of Landguard Fort in 1766, was a patron of Gainsborough, and thought he had discovered the author of the *Letters of Junius* in the person of Horne Tooke. See also under 1769, 1777, and 1788 below.

1766-1773 NUGENT, THOMAS. The History of Vandalia, containing the Ancient and Present State of the County of Mecklenburg; its Revolutions under the Vandals, the Venedi, and the Saxons; with the Succession and memorable Actions of its Sovereigns. 3 vols. 4to. London. (See under 1768 below.)

1767 CORIAT, JUNIOR. Another Traveller; or, Cursory Remarks and Tritical Observations made upon a Journey through Part of the Netherlands in 1766 by Coriat Junior. 2 vols. 12mo. London.

> The author was Samuel Paterson, the celebrated auctioneer and bookseller. His talent for cataloguing was unrivalled. . . . Few men of this country had so much bibliographical knowledge; and perhaps we never had a Bookseller who knew so much of the contents of books generally; and he was particularly well acquainted with our English Poets.—From Nichols, *Literary Anecdotes.* Of this work Dr. Johnson said, "This book was in imitation of Sterne and not of Coriat, whose name Paterson had chosen as a whimsical one." Paterson, in a pamphlet entitled "An Appeal," etc., by Coriat Junior, 12mo, produced some evidence to show that his work was written before Sterne's *Sentimental Journey* appeared.— Bookseller's Note.

STEPHENS, P. 150 Views in Italy, etched by various Artists and Amateurs on the Spot. 4to. London.

1768 BARETTI, JOSEPH. An Account of the Manners and Customs of Italy, with Observations on the Mistakes of some Travellers with Regard to that Country. 2 vols. in 1. 8vo. London.

> 2nd edit., corrected, with notes and appendix, 2 vols., 8vo, London, 1769.
> For his controversy with Samuel Sharp, see the latter under 1766 and 1768. Baretti was one of the best known Italian literati of his day. He resided a long time in London, where he became quite intimate with the Johnson circle. He made a name for himself in England with his Italian Dictionary. For his *Travels in Spain and Portugal* see under 1770 below.

BOSWELL, JAMES. An Account of Corsica: the Journal of a Tour to that Island, and Memoirs of Pascal Paoli. Folding map. 8vo. London.

> 2nd edit., 8vo, London and Glasgow, 1768; 4th Irish edit., 8vo, Dublin, 1768. Translated into French, German, Dutch, and Italian. See also *Gentlemen's Magazine,* June, 1795. For the Italian and French versions see below. A modern reprint, edited by S. C. Roberts, Cambridge, 1923.
> This work made Boswell famous. It is a lively account of his Quixotic adventures in Corsica and his associations with General Paoli, whom he later exhibited in London, and for whom he endeavored to get official British assistance. His childish pleasure in being the chief sponsor of this wild island struggling to become a nation led him to wear a Corsican costume at Garrick's anniversary celebration in honor of Shakespeare held in 1769 at Stratford-on-Avon. Dr. Johnson praised his Tour in these words: "Your History is like other histories, but your Journal is in a very high degree curious and delightful . . . Your History was copied from books; your Journal rose out of your own experience and observation."

1768 (In Italian.) Osservationi di un Viaggiatore Inglese sopra l'Isola de Corsica, scritte in Inglese sul luogo, e tradotte in Italiano. London.

1769 (In French.) Relation de l'Isle de Corse, Journal d'un Voyage dans cette Isle, et Mémoires de Pascal Paoli. Par Jacques Boswell, Ecuyer. Enrichie d'une nouvelle et très exacte Carte de la Corse. . . . Traduit de l'Anglois. Sur la seconde Edition.. Par J. P. I. Du Bois. Folding map. 8vo. The Hague.
This is the first edition of the second French translation.

NUGENT, THOMAS. Travels through Germany; with a particular Account of the Court of Mecklenburgh. 2 vols. London.

See Nugent under 1766-1773 above.

SHARP, SAMUEL. A View of the Customs, Manners, Drama, . . . of Italy, as they are described in the Frustra Litteraria and in the Account of Italy in English, written by Mr. Baretti; compared with the Letters from Italy, written by Mr. Sharp. 8vo. London.

Baretti's *Frustra Litteraria* were written at Venice in 1763-1765, while he was carrying on a paper there. See Baretti under 1768 and Sharp under 1766 above.

STERNE, LAURENCE. A Sentimental Journey through France and Italy. By Mr. Yorick. 2 vols. in 1. 12mo. London.

This work is too well known to need description. Sterne, unlike Smollett, found amiability, courtesy, urbanity, dignity, cordiality, and sentiment everywhere and among all classes of Frenchmen. At the same time he was not blind to their defects, such as the abuses of power, for the Bastile was too obvious a fact to be ignored. This work was very popular in France. For a "Continuation" of the book see Stevenson under 1769 below.

TALBOT, SIR R. (?). Journey through France. Amsterdam.

So cited by Pinkerton XVII.

WOLF, JOHN. Sketches and Observations taken in a Tour through a Part of the South of Europe in 1757. London.

1769 GROSLEY, PIERRE JEAN. New Observations on Italy. Translated by Thomas Nugent. 2 vols. London.

French original, London and Paris, 1764. See below.
Since the publication of Misson, this work met with great success, till it was superseded by those of Lalande and Richard.—Pinkerton XVII. This work is chiefly political and anecdotal; and in some parts of doubtful authority.—Lowndes.

1764 GROSLEY, PIERRE JEAN. Nouveaux Mémoires sur l'Italie et les Italiens, par deux Gentilhommes Suédois: traduit du Suédois. 3 vols. London and Paris.

Letters concerning the present State of the French Nation . . . With a compleat Comparison between France and Great Britain. London.

STEVENSON, JOHN HALL. Yorick's Sentimental Journey, continued. To which is prefixed some Account of the Life and Writings of Mr. Sterne. 2 vols. in 1. London.

> Stevenson was a friend of Sterne and the "Eugenius" of the *Sentimental Journey*.—Quaritch.

THICKNESSE, PHILIP. Remarks on the Character and Manners of the French, in a Series of Letters written during a Residence of twelve Months in Paris and its Environs. London.

> Reprinted, 2 vols., London, 1770.

1770 An Account of the Character and Manners of the French, with Occasional Observations on the English. 2 vols. 8vo. London.

BARETTI, JOSEPH. A Journey from London to Genoa through England, Portugal, Spain and France. 4 vols. 8vo. *London.

> Two other editions appeared the same year. Italian original, Milan, 1761. See below.
> This work was suggested to Baretti by Dr. Johnson, who advised him on the method he should adopt. "It was he," says Baretti in his preface, "that exhorted me to write daily, and with all possible minuteness: it was he that pointed out the topics which would most interest and most delight."—Bookseller's Note. The greater part of these travels have to do with Portugal and Spain. The personal adventures and observations of people and incidents are delightful reading. According to some critics the original Italian version has a freshness and vividness that is not quite reproduced in the English. In his Memoirs Baretti says that the English version is not merely a simple translation of the Italian, but is almost a new work. It contains an appendix which lists several itineraries in the interior of Spain and gives a brief recital of what he had observed during a new voyage he had made in December, 1768, to February, 1769. According to Foulché-Delbosc, the Italian edition contained only 47 letters, whereas the English had 89.

> 1761 BARETTI, JOSEPH. Lettere familiari di Giuseppe Baretti ai suoi tre fratelli Filippo, Giovanni e Amadeo. 2 vols. Milan.
>
> Many later editions of this work were published.

BOCAGE, MADAME DU. Letters concerning England, Holland, and Italy. 2 vols. 12mo. London.

> An entertaining work.—Lowndes.

MILLARD, JOHN. The Gentleman's Guide in his Tour through France, wrote by an Officer in the Royal Navy, with a correct Map of all the Post-Roads. Distances of Towns, Expence of Travelling, . . . 8vo. London.

> The 9th edit., with additions by T. Martyn, London, 1787.

WILKINSON, J. L. Excursions in France. London.

Reprinted, 2 vols., London, 1775.

1771 ARMSTRONG, JOHN (Dr.) A Short Ramble through France and Some Parts of Italy. London.

For an account of his personality, see Fanny Burney's *Diary* under date of Sept. 15, 1771. She reports him as being past the age of enjoying foreign countries and foreign manners. He travelled with the painter Fuseli. As is usual with travellers in pairs, they quarreled and parted at Genoa. He used the pseudonym "Lancelot Temple." To students of eighteenth century literature Armstrong is known for his didactic poem, "The Art of Preserving Health."

BURNEY, CHARLES (Dr.). The Present State of Music in France and Italy: or, The Journal of a Tour Through Those Countries, Undertaken to Collect Materials for a General History of Music. London.

2nd edit., London, 1773. Translated into German by Ebeling, Hamburg, 1772. For further details see his Tour under date of 1773 below.

JAMES, THOMAS (Lieut.-Colonel). The History of the Herculean Straits, now called the Straits of Gibraltar; including those Parts of Spain and Barbary that lie contiguous thereto. 2 vols. 4to. London.

TALBOT, SIR R. Letters on the French Nation. 2 vols. London.

See Talbot under 1768 above. The two items may be the same.

WINCKELMAN, JOHN (Abbé). A Critical Account of the Situation and Destruction by the First Eruption of Mount Vesuvius, of Herculaneum, Pompeii and Stabia . . . in a Letter to Count Bruhl. (Translated with notes from the German.) London.

1772 HAMILTON, SIR WILLIAM. Observations on Mount Vesuvius, Mount Etna, and other Volcanos, with explanatory Notes by the Author, hitherto unpublished. 5 copperplates of volcanoes and folding map. 8vo. London.

2nd edit., 8vo, London, 1773; 3rd and last, 8vo, London, 1774. Translated into German, Berlin, 1773. See below. For another account of volcanoes see under 1776-79 below.

The author was the well known British envoy at the Court of Naples, art enthusiast and collector. "Two points in his description are of especial interest, one referring to the changes which occurred in the central cone, the other to the actual outbreak of the great lava-flood to which he was a witness."—Prof. Bonney, quoted by Sotheran. His works are in high and merited repute among the learned; as were for many years the hospitalities of himself and Lady Hamilton to every British Traveller of Distinction. Their services to the publick in assisting the immortal Nelson will never be forgotten.—From Nichols, *Literary Anecdotes*.

1773 HAMILTON, SIR WILLIAM. Observations on Mount Vesuvius, Mount Etna, and other Volcanoes; in a Series of Letters, addressed to the Royal Society, from the Hon. Sir W. Hamilton, to which are added Explanatory Notes by the Author. Plates. 8vo. London.

1773 (In German.) Beobachtungen über den Vesuv, den Aetna und andere Vulkane, nebst neuen erläuternden Anmerkungen des Herrn Verfassers. 5 copperplates and folding map. 12mo. Berlin.

A Tour of Holland, Dutch Brabant, the Austrian Netherlands and Part of France; in which is concluded a Description of Paris and its Environs. Folding map. 8vo. London.

Another edition, London, 1788.

WRAXALL, NATHANIEL WILLIAM. A Tour through the Western, Southern, and Interior Provinces of France. London.

Another edition, with added matter, 2 vols., 8vo, London, 1777; again in 1785. Translated into French, Paris, 1777. See below.
Wraxall is almost the only modern traveller who has visited any large portion of France, except Young; but his observations are generally too much confined to the history of the parts he visited.—Pinkerton XVII. He followed routes usually neglected by his compatriots. He admired the country more than the cities, which he generally found poorly built. He noticed the poverty and the oppression of the inhabitants, which seem to consort ill with the appearance of happiness he observed prevalent among the peasants.

1777 WRAXALL, NATHANIEL WILLIAM. Memoirs of the Kings of France of the Race of Valois, with a Tour through the Western, Southern and Interior Provinces of France. 2 vols. 8vo. London.

This work was reissued in 1785 as *The History of France . . . from the Accession of Charles V*, etc.

1777 (In French.) Tournée dans les provinces occidentales, méridionales et intérieures de la France, faite par M. N. Wraxall, junior. Traduite de l'anglais. 12mo. Paris.

1773 Antiquities of Herculaneum; translated from the Italian by Thomas Martyn and John Lettice. 4to. London.

Only this volume, containing the pictures, was published.—Lowndes.

BRYDONE, PATRICK. A Tour through Sicily and Malta, in a Series of Letters to William Beckford. Folding map. 2 vols. 8vo. London.

2nd edit., corrected, 2 vols., 8vo, London, 1774; another edition, London, 1790. Translated into French, Amsterdam, 1775; London and Paris, 1776. A Supplement in French by Comte de Bolch, Turin, 1782. See below. Noticed in the *Journal des Scavans*, 1776, II, 7.
Liveliness of description of manners and scenery, couched in an easy and elegant style, has rendered these volumes extremely popular, notwithstanding they do not display much learning or knowledge and are even sometimes superficial and inaccurate.—Lowndes. Fanny Burney, in her *Diary,* under date of March 3, 1773, speaks highly of this work: "I have received very great pleasure from this

book. . . . It discovers throughout a liveliness of imagination, and insatiate curiosity after knowledge and the most vehement desire of instruction." This last quality may have been its chief merit in her eyes. Boswell criticises it because, though entertaining, it introduces an "anti-mosaical remark," having to do with the age of the earth as calculated from evidences of volcanoes. Dr. Johnson thought Brydone would have been a great traveller, if he had been more attentive to the Bible. These travels were made in 1765-1771.

1776 (In French.) Voyage en Sicile et à Malthe, traduit de l'anglais par Demeunier. 8vo. London.

1782 BORCH, COMTE DE. Lettres sur la Sicile et l'Isle de Malte, pour servir de Supplement au Voyage de Brydone. 2 vols. 8vo. Turin.

BURNEY, CHARLES (Dr.). Travels through the Low-Countries, Holland and Germany. London.

    Those portions of his journals concerned with his musical experiences have been selected and edited by C. H. Glover, London, 1927. This 2nd tour translated into German by Bode, Hamburg, 1773; into Dutch, with notes, by J. W. Lustig, Groningen (?), 1786.
    Burney states that his object in travelling was to get what information he could relative to the music of the ancients; "and to judge with my own eyes the *present* state of modern music in the places through which I should pass, from the performance and conversation of the first musicians in Italy." His journals of his first tour to France and Italy (see under 1771 above) and the present one here cited contain interesting records of meetings with noted men of his day, and of his adventures on his travels, of the discomforts he endured on the road, and of the devastations wrought by the Seven Years' War. Among the famous musicians finding mention in his books are Bach, Handel, Tartini, Boccherini, Galuppi, Scarlatti, and the boy prodigy Mozart whom he had heard play in London. His descriptions of the various orchestras attached to the petty courts of Germany and of the unsatisfactory performance of the woodwind instruments have some bearing on the practice of modern conductors in enlarging the orchestration of eighteenth century compositions.

1927 BURNEY, CHARLES, (Mus. D.). Continental Travels, 1770-72; compiled from his Journals, . . . Edited by C. H. Glover. 8vo. London.

CORKE AND ORRERY, JOHN, EARL OF. Letters from Italy in the Years 1754-55, published from the Originals, with explanatory Notes by Rev. John Dunscombe. 8vo. London.

    2nd edit., 8vo, London, 1774.

RIEDELSEL, JOHANN HERMANN, BARON VON. Travels through Sicily and that part of Italy called Magna Graecia; and a Tour through Egypt. Translated from the German by J. R. Forster. 8vo. London.

    German original, Zurich, 1771. See below.

1771 RIEDELSEL, JOHANN HERMANN, BARON VON. Reise durch Sicilien und Grossgriechenland. 8vo. Zurich.

1774 The Roads of Italy, engraved on 26 copper-plates from the MS. Drawings of a Nobleman of Distinction, wherein are found all the Cities, Towns, Villages, Rivers, . . . Map and plates. 8vo. London.

1775 BOURRIT, MARC THEODORE. Relation of a Journey to the Glaciers in the Duchy of Savoy, translated (from the French) by C. and F. Davy. 8vo. London.

> 2nd edit., 12mo, London, 1776. A French edition, embodying later journies, Geneva, 1785. See below.
> The author, who was precentor of the Cathedral of Geneva, made innumerable trips in this region of the Alps, attempting on several of them to achieve the ascent of Mont Blanc. In 1787 he all but accomplished his ambition. There is a good account of his efforts and explorations in de Beer's *Early Travellers in the Alps.*

> 1785 BOURRIT, MARC THEODORE. Nouvelle Description des Glacières de Savoye, particulièrement de la vallée de Chamount et du Mont-Blanc. Map and 4 plates. 8vo. Geneva.

A Brief Account of the Roads of Italy for the Use of Gentlemen who travel with the Post, with a full Description of the Cities, Towns, Villages and Rivers, . . . London.

> See *The Roads of Italy* under 1774 above.

E., W. B. A Letter to the late Lord Lyttleton, containing a Description of the Last Great Eruption, . . . of Mount Aetna, A. D., 1766. (With an etched plate of a new view of the Simplon by J. T., 1775.) London.

TIMBERTOE, TIMOTHY. A Trip to Calais. London.

> Cited in Ponton's Catalogue.

TWISS, RICHARD. Travels through Portugal and Spain, in 1772 and 1773. With . . . an Appendix. Map and plates. 4to. London.

> Issued also in 2 vols., 12mo, Dublin, 1775. Translated into French, Berne, 1776; into German, Leipzig, 1776. See below.
> Fanny Burney records meeting Twiss at the Burney house under date of March 17, 1774. In 1776, Twiss wrote, "I have now visited the greatest part of England, Scotland, Ireland, Germany, Bohemia, Italy, Portugal and Spain, and including sea voyages, have journeyed about 27,000 miles, which is 2000 more than the circumference of the earth." He gives very fair reasons against travelling with companions, or tutors, and seems to have been by no means extravagant in his expenses.—Note by the editor of the Burney *Diary.* Of these Travels Dr. Johnson remarked, "They are as good as the first book of travels that you will take up. They are as good as those of Keysler or Blainville: nay, as Addison's, if you except the learning. They are not as good as Brydone's, but they are better than Pococke's."

> 1776 (In French.) Voyage en Portugal et en Espagne fait en 1772 et 1773, par Richard Twiss, gentilhomme anglois, Membre de la Société Royale. Traduit de l'anglois et orné d'une carte des 2 royaumes. 8vo. Berne.

> 1776 (In German.) Reisen durch Portugal und Spanien in den Jahren 1772 und 1773. Aus dem Englischen von Christoph Daniel Ebeling. 8vo. Leipzig.

1776 FERBER, J. J. Travels through Italy in the years 1771 and 1772, Described in a Series of Letters to Baron Bern on the Natural History,
particularly the Mountains and Volcanoes of that Country. Translated
by R. E. Raspe. 8vo. London.

> German original, Prague, 1773.
> For Raspe on volcanoes see this date below. See also under Born, 1777, below.

MARSHALL, JOSEPH. Travels through France and Spain, in the
years 1770 and 1771. In which is particularly minuted the present
State of those Countries, respecting their Agriculture, Population,
Manufactures, Commerce, the Arts and Useful Undertakings. 8vo.
London.

> This is vol. IV of *Travels through Holland, Flanders,* etc., published in 1772.
> See Marshall under 1772, CONTINENTAL EUROPE. Translated into German,
> Danzig, 1778. See below.

> 1778 (In German.) Reisen durch Frankreich und Spanien . . . 8vo. Danzig.

PALMER, JOSEPH. Four Months' Tour through France. London.

> The author was Dean of Cashel, Ireland.

RASPE, RUDOLPH ERICH. An Account of some German Volcanoes,
and their Productions, with a new Hypothesis of the Prismatical Basaltes; established upon Facts: being an Essay of Physical Geography.
. . . Folding plates. 8vo. London.

> Raspe was one of the first geologists to adopt the view that basalt was of
> volcanic origin. This work, unknown to Poggendorff, is also of interest for the
> personality of the author, a German Professor at Cassel, who fled to England in
> 1775 to avoid punishment for theft. He was elected Fellow of the Royal Society,
> but was expelled when his antecedents became known. He was the author of the
> original "Baron Munchausen," and a swindler of a most interesting type, on whom
> the character of "Dousterswivel" and the incidents connected with him, are based
> in Scott's *Antiquary.*—Sotheran.

RIGGS, ANNA (Lady Anne Millar). Letters from Italy, Describing the
Manners, Customs, Antiquities, Paintings, . . . of that Country, in the
Years 1770 and 1771. London (?) or Bath (?).

> This, the first edition, was published anonymously. 2nd edit., revised and cor-
> rected, 2 vols., 8vo, London.
> The author is the Lady Anne Millar who instituted the literary salon at her
> place in Batheaston, where each guest was invited to contribute an original poem,
> the winner being appropriately crowned. An amusing account of one of her as-
> semblies is to be found in Madame D'Arblay's *Diary.* She was also the butt of
> Horace Walpole's wit.

1776-1779 HAMILTON, SIR WILLIAM. Campi Phlegraei: Observations on the Volcanoes of the Two Sicilies (with Supplement to the Campi Phlegraei). 59 plates, colored like drawings, of ships, volcanoes, views, geological specimens, etc., and one double page colored map of the Bay of Naples. 3 vols. in 1. Fol. London.

> The supplementary volume was added in 1779. The text is in French and English.
> For his observations on Mount Vesuvius, etc., see under 1772 above. His leisure was chiefly occupied in the study of volcanic phenomena, and in the formation of his remarkable collection of antiquities. Within four years he had ascended Vesuvius twenty-two times, more than once at great risks, making himself or causing Fabris, an artist trained in the work by him, to do numberless sketches at all stages of the eruptions. He witnessed and described the eruptions of 1776 and 1777.—D.N.B.

1777 BLANKETT, JOHN. Letters from Portugal, on the late and present State of that Kingdom. London.

> Translated into French, London and Paris, 1780; into German, from the French edition, Leipzig, 1782. See below. The date of the original English edition is in doubt.
> According to Barbier, the author of these Letters was a Miss Philadelphia Stevens (or Stephens), of whom one finds no mention in English bibliographies. Halkett and Laing attribute them to Lieutenant (later Admiral) Blankett, as seems more likely.—Foulché-Delbosc.

> 1780 (In French.) Lettres écrites de Portugal, Sur l'état ancien et actuel de ce Royaume Traduites de l'anglois. Suivies du portrait historique de M. le Marquis de Pombal. 8vo. London and Paris.
>
> > The translator is H.-J. Jansen, to whom has been attributed the "Portrait."—Foulché-Delbosc.

> 1782 (In German.) Briefe über Portugal nebst einem Anhang über Brasilien. Aus dem Französischen. Mit Anmerkungen herausgegeben von Matthias Christ. Sprengel, Professor der Geschichte in Halle. 8vo. Leipzig.

BORN, BARON INIGO. Travels through the Bannat of Temeswar, Transylvania and Hungary, in 1770. To which is added, J. J. Ferber's Mineralogical History of Bohemia. Translated from the German, with some explanatory Notes, and a Preface on the Mechanical Arts, the Art of Mining and its present State and future Improvement, by R. E. Raspe. 8vo. London.

> A very valuable mineralogical tour, likewise containing some curious notices respecting the tribes inhabiting Transylvania and the adjacent districts.—Lowndes.

CARTER, FRANCIS. A Journey from Gibraltar to Malaga; with a View of that Garrison and its Environs; a Particular Account of the Towns in the Hoya of Malaga; the Ancient and Natural History of those Cities, of the Coast between them, and the Mountains of Ronda.

Illustrated with medals of each municipal town; and a chart, perspective and drawings, taken in the year 1772. 3 vols. 8vo. London.

A volume of plates was sold separately. Reprinted in 1778 with the plates inserted.—Nichols, *Literary Anecdotes.* 2nd edit., 2 vols., 8vo, London, 1780. Translated into German, Leipzig, 1779. See below.

"A very curious Journey from Malaga to Gibraltar, through the Moorish part of Spain, by a Mr. Carter, is printing with all speed, and correcting by Arabic Jones (doubtless Sir William Jones). Much is expected of it."—From Richard Gough to Rev. Michael Tyson, Mar. 6, 1776, quoted by Nichols, *Literary Anecdotes.* The many coins engraved in this work were from the Collection of the celebrated Spanish medallist Flores, whose cabinet Mr. Carter purchased on his death, and disposed of the duplicates to Dr. Hunter.—Nichols.

1779 (In German.) Reise von Gibraltar nach Malaga im Jahr 1772. Aus dem Englischen. 2 vols. 8vo. Leipzig.

CAYLEY, CORNELIUS. A Tour through Holland, Flanders and Part of France (in 1772). Leeds.

DALRYMPLE, WILLIAM (Major). Travels through Spain and Portugal, in 1774; with a Short Account of the Spanish Expedition against Algiers in 1775. Map and frontispiece. 12mo. Dublin.

Printed in London the same year. Translated into German, Leipzig, 1778; Berlin, 1784; into French, Paris, 1783; Paris and Brussels, 1787. See below.

1778 (In German.) Reisen durch Spanien und Portugal im Jahr 1774; nebst einer Kurzen Nachricht von der spanischen Unternehmung auf Algier im Jahr 1775. Aus dem Englischen übersetzt mit einiger Anmerkungen und Zusätzen. 8vo. Leipzig.

1783 (In French.) Voyage en Espagne et en Portugal dans l'année 1774. Avec une Relation de l'Expédition des Espagnols contre les Algeriens en 1775. Par le Major W. Dalrymple. Traduit de l'Anglois par un Officier Francois. 8vo. Paris.

The French translator was the Marquis Germain Hyacinthe de Romance de Mesmon.

The Englishman's Fortnight in Paris, or the Art of Ruining Himself there in a few Days. By an Observer. Translated from the French. 8vo. London.

The French original seems to have been attributed to Sterne. See below.
"This work may be had of the booksellers in French printed from the Paris edition, which was suppressed in that country."—Quoted by Bookseller.

1776 STEARNE, DOCTEUR. La Quinzaine Angloise à Paris ou L'Art de S'y Ruiner en Peu de Tems. Ouvrage posthume du Docteur Stearne, traduit de l'Anglois par un Observateur. 8vo. Londres.

Is this another hoax of this century of hoaxes?

FERBER, JOHN JAMES. Mineralogical History of Bohemia. See Born, *Travels through the Bannat of Temeswar,* under this date above.

FOURMONT, ——.   Travels in France.   London.

So cited by Pinkerton XVII.

HOWARD, JOHN.   The State of the Prisons in England, Wales . . . and an Account of some foreign Prisons and Hospitals.   Plates.   Warrington.

> 2nd and 3rd editions, with additions, 4to, Warrington, 1780 and 1784. Subsequent observations were embodied in a volume called *An Account of the Principal Lazarettos in Europe,* Warrington, 1789. A second volume of this was published in 1791, and a 4th edit. of the *State of the Prisons,* a reprint of the 3rd, in 1792. Modern edition in Everyman's Library, somewhat abridged, London, 1929.
> The author is the well known prison reformer and philanthropist, whose wealth and position as Sheriff of Bedfordshire enabled him to effect considerable improvement even during his own lifetime in the management, sanitation, and treatment of prisoners. Before he put his investigations into print he visited every English prison two or three times, and then toured Europe twice, "conjecturing that something useful to my purpose might be collected abroad." In all he made five journies abroad. He died in far off Crimea on an errand of mercy and was buried at Cherson, fifteen hundred miles away from his home in Bedfordshire. Compassion like his for the miserable and the outcast was seldom met with in his century. In 1780, while he was yet alive, Burke described his mission in these words: "To dive into the depths of dungeons and plunge into the infection of hospitals; to survey the mansions of sorrow and pain; to take the gauge and measure of misery, depression, and contempt; to remember the forgotten, to attend to the neglected, to visit the forsaken, and compare and collate the miseries of all men in all countries." See the Introduction to the edition in Everyman's Library.

JONES, WILLIAM (Rev.).   Observations in a Journey to Paris, by Way of Flanders, in the month of August, 1776.   2 vols.   12mo.   London.

MELMOTH, COURTNEY.   Travels for the Heart, written in France.   2 vols.   London.

> Author's real name was Samuel Pratt; he will be remembered as being the object of Dr. Johnson's derision. He was an acquaintance of Mrs. Thrale's at Bath. He also translated some Pliny and Cicero.

SANDBY, PAUL.   Sixteen Views in Naples and other Parts of Italy.   Fol.   London.

> Sandby was a well known water color painter and engraver. He introduced the aquatint process of engraving into England, which was so largely used in illustrated books of scenery at the time.

THICKNESSE, PHILIP.   A Year's Journey through France and Part of Spain.   Engravings.   2 vols.   8vo.   London and Bath.

> 2nd edit., with additions, 2 vols., London, 1778; 3rd edit., with plates and music, 2 vols., London, 1789. Translated into German, Leipzig, 1778. See below and also under 1766 above.
> Disappointed in the expectation of falling heir to some property, in 1775, "driven out of his own country with eight children in his train," he removed himself to Spain, where he thought he could live more cheaply than in England.

This trip employed him until November, 1776, and produced the above book. Boswell records under April 3, 1778: "Johnson.—I have been reading Thicknesse's Travels, which I think are entertaining. Boswell.—What, Sir, a good book? Johnson.—Yes, Sir, to read once; I do not say that you are to make a study of it, and digest it." Fanny Burney notes some unfavorable comments by Johnson on Thicknesse.

1778 (In German.) Reisen durch Frankreich und einen Theil von Katalonien. Aus dem Englischen. 8vo. Leipzig.

1778 AYSCOUGH, GEORGE. EDWARD. Letters from an Officer in the Guards to his Friend in England, containing some Accounts of France and Italy. 8vo. London.

The author was a dramatist who produced a version of Voltaire's "Semiramis" at Drury Lane, in 1776.

FORTIS, ALBERTO (Abbé). Travels into Dalmatia: containing General Observations on the Natural History of that Country and the Neighboring Islands: The Natural Productions, Arts, Manners and Customs of the Inhabitants; in a Series of Letters to the Earl of Bute, the Bishop of Londonderry, John Strange, . . . to which are added by the same Author, Observations on the Islands of Cherso and Osero, translated from the Italian, with an Appendix and Other Additions. 20 copperplates. 4to. London.

This work treats principally of the geology, natural history and antiquities of the country with notices of the singular races which inhabit it . . . His work is very erroneous.—Lowndes.

The Grand Tour, or a Journey through the Netherlands, Germany, Italy, and France. 4 vols. 8vo. London.

HULL, THOMAS. Select Letters between the late Duchess of Somerset, Lady Luxborough, Miss Dolman, Mr. Whistler, Mr. R. D. Dodsley, Wm. Shenstone, Esq., and others. 2 vols. 8vo. London.

In these volumes will be found a sketch of the manners, laws, etc., of the republic of Venice.—Lowndes.

1779 BOURGET, JOHN (Dom.). History of the Royal Abbey of Bec, near Rouen in Normandy. Translated from the French (by Dr. Ducarel). Plates. 8vo. London.

This work is usually appended to Gough's *Alien Priories.*—Lowndes.

COXE, WILLIAM. Sketches of the Natural, Civil and Political State of Swisserland; in a Series of Letters to William Melmoth. 8vo. London.

Translated into French, Paris, 1781, and 1787, with additions by the translator (Ramond de Carbonnières). See below. For his later account of Switzerland see under 1791 below, and for general travels over other parts of Europe under 1784, NORTH EUROPE.

Archdeacon Coxe made four trips to Switzerland—in 1776, 1779, 1785, and 1786, which are all combined as one account in the second and succeeding editions of this book. While his chief interest was in the political constitutions of the Swiss cantons, he did a great deal of sight-seeing, visited many shrines, and observed acutely the disposition of the inhabitants. At Zug his curiosity was much piqued by discovering that the patron saint of the church was the old Northumbrian king, Oswald. One concludes from a reading of this tireless traveller that Switzerland must have been a most baffling complexity of boundaries, languages, faiths, and localisms.

1781   (In French.) Lettres de M. W. Coxe à M. W. Melmoth sur l'état politique, civil et naturel de la Suisse. Traduit de l'anglois augmentée des observations faites dans le même pays, par le traducteur (Ramond de Carbonnières). 12mo. Paris.

Ramond made a visit to Switzerland in 1777. This remarkable man, one of the founders of French geology, was Counsellor to the Cardinal de Rohan and was employed by him in his relations with the extraordinary charlatan, Balsamo or Cagliostro, and was sent on a mission to England to trace the Queen's necklace, immortalised by Alexander Dumas. . . . His translation of Coxe was utilised by Wordsworth in his *Descriptive Sketches.*—From de Beer, *Early Travellers in the Alps.*

MOORE, JOHN (Dr.). A View of Society and Manners in France, Switzerland and Germany: with Anecdotes relating to some Eminent Characters. By a Gentleman who resided several years in those Countries. 2 vols. 8vo. London.

Several editions followed, the 4th being in 3 vols., Dublin, 1792; 9th edit., 2 vols., London, 1800. Translated into French, Geneva, 1781. See below. For his *View of Italy* see under 1781 below. Noticed in the *Journal des Scavans,* 1779, VI, 517.

The author was a surgeon and a man of letters. He served as surgeon's mate in the Duke of Argyll's regiment in Holland in 1747; took his medical degree at Glasgow in 1770; travelled with Douglas, 8th Duke of Hamilton, in 1772-78; and was the friend, physician, and editor of Smollett.—D.N.B. He carried with him many preconceptions, such as the belief that the lower classes of France lived in a state of oppression. But he was forced to admit that the condition of the people, especially in Paris, was superior to what he found in several other countries of Europe. He pays tribute to the universal politeness of the French and to their gaiety. Of the cities he saw only Paris, Lyons, and Strassburg.

1781   (In French.) Lettres d'un voyageur sur la France, la Suisse et l'Allemagne. Traduites de l'anglais. 2 vols. 8vo. Geneva.

SHERLOCK, MARTIN (Rev.). Letters from an English Traveller, written from Berlin, Dresden, Vienna, Rome, Naples, and France, in 1776, 1777, and 1778. Translated from the French by the Rev. John Dunscombe. London.

Revised by the author, London, 1780. Reissued, with New Letters, London, 1780; these republished, London, 1781. French original, Geneva, 1779; another French version, London and Paris, 1780. See below.

The first English edition contained 27 letters, "the quintessence of 200 which this lively Traveller had written; originally published in French, that the connoisseurs on the Continent might not be deprived of the pleasure of perusing them. They are dated in the years 1776, 1777, and 1778, from Berlin, Dresden, etc. . . .

He describes every object in a striking point of view, which gives an air of novelty to observations that would otherwise be familiar to many readers." He was an eccentric and original writer, very solicitous of fame and report about himself.—From Nichols, *Literary Anecdotes*. He enjoyed the theaters and the society of French men of letters, and was much struck with the amiability of the French people.

1780 SHERLOCK, MARTIN (Rev.). Letters (with New Letters) from an English Traveller. Translated from the French Original, . . . with Notes. New Edition, revised and corrected. 8vo. London.

1781 SHERLOCK, MARTIN (Rev.). New Letters from an English Traveller, written originally in French, and now translated into English by the Author. 8vo. London.

> This collection contains 44 letters, which were as well received in all the foreign journals as the author seems to have been in foreign courts.—From Nichols, *Literary Anecdotes*.

1779 SHERLOCK, MARTIN. Lettres d'un voyageur anglais. 12mo. Geneva.

> A French version, London, 1780. What is called a 2nd edit., 8vo, Paris, 1780.

SWINBURNE, HENRY.   Travels through Spain, in the Years 1775 and 1776.   In which several Monuments of Roman and Moorish Architecture are illustrated by accurate Drawings taken on the Spot.   4to. London.

> 2nd edit., with additions, 2 vols., London, 1787; an edition 2 vols., 8vo, Dublin, 1783-86. Translated into French, Paris, 1787. See below. Noticed in the *Journal des Scavans*, 1780, II, 219.
> The plates are of great excellence. His drawings were faithful to fact and elegant in design.—D.N.B. "Henley has announced to me Swinburne's Travels, to which he performed the part of midwife. This circumstance, together with my fondness for the principal subject of the Travels (the Architecture), has made me purchase the book. . . . I am much pleased with his plates of that wonderful building, the Alhambra; but I draw a different conclusion from them. Swinburne thinks our Goths borrowed nothing from them; I think even the leading feature, the Pointed Arch, was taken from the Saracen."—Rev. M. Tyson to R. Gough, dated March 29, 1779; quoted by Nichols, *Literary Anecdotes*. For the author's travels in the Sicilies see under 1783-85 below. Swinburne also made several trips to France from 1771 to 1791. Being a Catholic he was educated in France. These trips were preserved in letters and published in London, 1841, under the title, *The Courts of Europe at the Close of the last Century*. He was a somewhat superficial man of the world, but he observed a great variety of things and for this is interesting. He cared little for the countryside or for French peasant life. He is best in describing cities and society.

1787 SWINBURNE, HENRY. Travels through Spain, in the Years 1775 and 1776. In which several Monuments, . . . To which is added, A Journey from Bayonne to Marseilles. 2 vols. London.

1787 (In French.) Voyage de Henri Swinburne en Espagne en 1775 et 1776, traduit de l'anglais. 8vo. Paris.

> The French translator was Jean-Benjamin de la Borde.

1780 A Collection of the most remarkable Ruins of Lisbon, as they appeared immediately after the Great Earthquake and Fire which destroyed that City November 1, 1755, by Messieurs Paris and Pedagache. Colored and plain plates. Fol. London.

DILLON, JOHN TALBOT. Travels through Spain, with a View to illustrate the Natural History and Physical Geography of that Kingdom, in a Series of Letters. Including the most interesting Subjects contained in the Memoirs of Don Guillermo Bowles, and other Spanish Writers. Interspersed with historical Anecdotes. Adorned with Copperplates and a new Map of Spain. With Notes and Observations relative to the Arts, and descriptive of modern Improvements. Written in the Course of a late Tour through that Kingdom by John Talbot Dillon, Knight and Baron of the Sacred Roman Empire. Map of the Peninsula. Plates. 4to. London.

> Later editions: 8vo, Dublin, 1781 and 1782; 4to, London, 1783. Translated into German, Leipzig, 1782. See below.
> For his volume dealing with Spanish poetry see under 1781 below.

> 1782 (In German.) Dillon's Reise durch Spanien welche wichtige Beobachtung auf der Naturgeschichte, über den Handel, die Fabriken, den Ackerbau, nebst einem Auszug der merkwürdigen Sachen aus Don Guillermo Bowles Einleitung in die Naturgeschichte und physikalische Erdbeschreibung von Spanien enthält. Aus dem Englishchen übersetzt und mit übrigen Nachrichten des Herrn Bowles vermehrt. 2 vols. 8vo. Leipzig.
>
> > The translator's preface is signed J. A. Engelbrecht.—Foulché-Delbosc. The original was noticed in the *Journal des Scavans*, 1780, VII, 215; 449.

1781 DILLON, JOHN TALBOT. Letters from English Traveller in Spain, in 1778, on the Origin and Progress of Poetry in that Kingdom; with occasional Reflections on Manners and Customs; and illustrations of the Romance of Don Quixote. Adorned with Portraits of the most Eminent Poets. 8vo. London.

> The greater part of this work is borrowed from *Origines de la Poesia castellana* of Velasquez and from Sarmiento and Sedano.—Foulché-Delbosc.

PARKER, GEORGE. A View of Society and Manners in High and Low Life: being the Adventures in England, Ireland, Scotland, Wales, France, . . . of Mr. G. Parker: in which is comprised a History of the Stage Itinerant. 2 vols. 12mo. London.

> Republished under the following title: Life's Painter of variegated Colours in public and private Life, to which is added, A Dictionary of Modern Flash or Cant Language. London, n.d. Another edition, 18mo, London, 1789.—Lowndes.
> Parker was a soldier, actor, lecturer, and sergeant in the Seven Years' War. As an actor and lecturer he was not a success. Though patronized by Goldsmith, Johnson, and Reynolds, he sank into poverty. His autobiography is not regarded as trustworthy.—D.N.B.

RICHARD, —— (Abbé). For his account of Italy see below under the French title.

> This work was published in English, London, 1781, according to Pinkerton XVII. But this is the only mention of the work that has come to the notice of the editor.

> 1768 RICHARD, M. L'ABBE. Description historique et critique de l'Italie, ou nouveaux mémoires sur l'état actuel de son gouvernement, des sciences, des arts, du commerce, de la population, et de l'histoire naturelle. 6 vols. Paris.
>
> > This is the 2nd edition. These travels were performed about the year 1764 and the first edition appeared in 1766, but it was much enlarged in that of 1768. Notwithstanding several omissions and some ill-judged descriptions of works of art, the work met with great success.—Pinkerton XVII.

1782 CHARINGTON, LORD. Memoirs of the late Right Honourable Lord Charington; containing a genuine Description of the Government and Manners of the present Portuguese. London.

Danverian History of the Affairs of Europe for 1731. With the Present State of Gibraltar and an Exact Description of it, and of the Spanish Works before it; Also of Dunkirk, and the Late Transactions there. Folding plates of both these places. 8vo. London.

——, J. Travelling Anecdotes through Various Parts of Europe, Vol. I (all published). 6 plates, one folding. 8vo. Rochester.

> See Douglas under 1785 below.—Written much in the manner of Sterne; the humorous plates are drawn by the author.—Bookseller's Note.

Letters from Minorca; describing the Constitution, Government, Produce, Antiquities and Natural History, of that Island; with an accurate Description of the Town, Harbour, and Fortifications of Mahon; and the Trade, Customs, and Manners, of the Minorquins. Map. Dublin.

PEYRON, JEAN-FRANCOIS. Nouveau voyage en Espagne fait en 1777 et 1778; dans lequel on traite des Moeurs, du Caractère, des Monuments anciens et modernes, du Commerce, du Théatre, de la Législation des Tribunaux particuliers à ce Royaume, et de l'Inquisition; avec de nouveaux détails sur son état, et sur une Procédure récent et fameuse. 2 vols. 8vo. London and Paris.

> Another edition, 2 vols., 8vo, London and Liege, 1783. This work appeared first under a slightly different title at Geneva, 1780. For an English rendering of portions of this work, see Bourgoing under 1789 below.
> Bourgoing states that the description of the kingdom of Granada is the most interesting part.—Foulché-Delbosc.

RIVERS, LORD.   Briefe von und an denselben während seines zweiten Aufenthalts in Deutschland, . . . Translated from his original Papers. Leipzig.

> So cited by Pinkerton XVII.

The Traveller's Vade Mecum through the Netherlands, and Parts of France and Germany, Designed principally for those who visit the Continent by way of Margate and Ostend.   Canterbury.

1783   BARRAL, ——.   Mémoire sur l'histoire naturelle des Corses.   London (Paris).

> So cited by Pinkerton XVII.

The Female Spy, Or Mrs. Tonkins' Journey through France in the late War, undertaken by the express Order of Rt. Hon. Chas. Jas. Fox. London.

1783-85   SWINBURNE, HENRY.   Travels in the Two Sicilies, in the Years 1777, 1778, 1779, and 1780.   4 vols.   8vo.   London.

> 2nd edit., 4 vols., 8vo, London, 1790; a new edition, London 1795. Translated into French, Paris, 1785. See below.
> "The warmth and animation of his descriptions discover an imagination highly susceptible of every bounty of Nature or Art; and, if he had a fault, it was the being too apt to relinquish simplicity for profusion of ornament, but, from this fault what Traveller is free?"—Nichols, *Literary Anecdotes*.
>
> 1785   (In French.) Voyages dans les deux Siciles de M. Henri Swinburne, dans les années 1777, 1778, 1779, & 1780, traduits de l'Anglois par Mlle. de Keralio.   8vo.   Paris.
> Noticed in the *Journal des Scavans*, 1786, I, 285.

1784   An Accurate Description of the Island and Kingdom of Sicily.   8vo.   Falkirk.

> Another edition, with slightly enlarged title, appearing as a translation, London, 1786. See below.
>
> 1786   An Accurate Description of Sicily: Provinces, Towns, Public Roads, . . . with a Narrative of Sardinia. Translated by D. Macnab.   8vo.   London.

THICKNESSE, PHILIP.   A Year's Journey through the Pais Bas and Austrian Netherlands.   Vol. I (all published).   London.

> 2nd edit., London, 1786, with considerable additions, such as the routes through Germany, Holland and Switzerland, differences of money, etc.

1785 ANDREWS, JOHN (LL.D.). A Comparative View of the French and English Nations in their Manners, Politics and Literature. London.

> Andrews also wrote a work called *Remarks on French and English Ladies.* London, 1783.

DOUGLAS, JAMES. Travelling Anecdotes through several Parts of Europe. Frontispiece. 8vo. London.

> This may be the 2nd edition of the work listed as *Travelling Anecdotes* under 1782 above. 3rd edit., 8vo, London, 1786.

HERVEY, CHRISTOPHER. Letters from Portugal, Spain, Italy and Germany, in the Years 1759 to 1761. 3 vols. 8vo. London.

1786 FLEURIOT, JEAN-MARIE-JEROME. (dit Marquis de Langle). A Sentimental Journey through Spain; written in French, by the Marquis de Langle, and translated from the Paris Edition, That was burnt by the common Hangman. 2 vols. 8vo. London.

> 1st French edit., 12mo, Saint-Malo, with the title, *The Voyage de Figaro, en Espagne,* 1784. The edition which first bears the imprint of Paris was that of 1796. Probably the one referred to in the English version was the 3rd, of 1785 which has no place of publication designated. For the numerous French editions of this work and its history, see Foulché-Delbosc, under No. 188. French original, 1785. See below.
> Concerning the burning of his book, the author observes, "The reader loves a burned book; so does the bookseller, and so does the author." The work was very sarcastic in its criticisms of the manners and customs of the Spanish nation, and aroused the repercussion noted. Ticknor says of it, "A poor imitation of Sterne's Sentimental Journey, and as immoral and irreligious as its date may seem to imply." For Fleuriot's description of Switzerland see under 1791 below.

> 1785 FLEURIOT, JEAN-MARIE-JEROME. Voyage en Espagne, par M. le Marquis de Langle. 2 vols. 8vo. (No place.)

RUSSELL, FRANCIS (5th Duke of Bedford). A Descriptive Journey through the interior Parts of Germany and France, including Paris, by a young English Peer of the highest Rank. 12mo. London.

SHAW, J. Sketches of the History of the Austrian Netherlands, with Remarks on the Constitution, Commerce, Arts, and General State of the Provinces. 8vo. London.

A Trip to Holland; containing a Sketch of the Character of the People. 2 vols. London.

1787 COSTIGAN, ARTHUR WILLIAM. Sketches of Society and Manners in Portugal. In a Series of Letters from Arthur William Costigan, Esq., late a Captain of the Irish Brigade in the Service of Spain, to his Brother in London. 2 vols. 8vo. London.

> The work bears no date on the title page, but the preface, written by the author's brother, Charles Costigan, gives 1787. Another edition, 2 vols., 8vo, London, 1788. Translated into German, Leipzig, 1788-89; into French, with additions from other writers, Paris, 1804. See below.
> According to Francisque Michel, this work was composed by the brigadier Ferriere.—Foulché-Delbosc.

> 1788-89 (In German.) Captain Costigan. Skizzen der Sitten und des gesellschaftlichen Lebens in Portugal. Aus dem Englischen. 2 vols. 8vo. Leipzig.

MARTYN, THOMAS. The Gentleman's Guide in his Tour through Italy. 8vo. London.

> Reprinted, with a different title, London, 1791. Translated into French, (place ?), 1791. See below.
> In 1778, Martyn, who was the son of the professor of botany at Cambridge and himself somewhat proficient in that science, started on a tour of the Continent. He visited Germany, Flanders, and Holland, but spent most of his time in Italy. He kept a journal of his travels, part of which he published anonymously under the above title. His name appears on the title-page of the 1791 edition.

> 1791 MARTYN, THOMAS. A Tour through Italy; containing full Directions for travelling in that interesting Country; with ample Catalogues of every Thing that is curious in Architecture, Painting, Sculpture, . . . Some Observations on the Natural History, and very particular Descriptions of the four principal Cities, Rome, Florence, Naples, and Venice, with their Environments. Colored chart. 8vo. London.

> 1791 (In French.) Guide du Voyageur en Italie. Traduit de l'anglais de M. Thomas Martyn. 2 parts in 1. (Place ?.)

MARTYN, THOMAS. Sketch of a Tour through Switzerland, with an accurate map. London.

POWNALL, THOMAS. Notices and Descriptions of Antiquities of the Provincia Romana of Gaul, now Provence, Languedoc and Dauphine: With Dissertations on the Subjects of which those are Exemplars. And an Appendix, describing the Roman Baths and Thermae discovered in 1784, at Badenweiler. 7 engraved plates. 4to. London.

> This work professes to give a particular account of such monuments of Roman Antiquity as are yet remaining in so fine a part of the Roman Empire, so cultivated and improved, but which have remained nondescript, or imperfectly and wrongly described till now, at length, a spirit of literary curiosity has arisen in the country itself.—From *Gent. Mag.* LVII, 990, quoted by Nichols, *Literary Anecdotes.* Pownall was Governor of Massachusetts in 1757.

RIESBECK, BARON. Travels through Germany, in a Series of Letters, translated by Paul Henry Maty, Assistant Librarian, British Museum. 3 vols. 8vo. London.

> Reprinted in Pinkerton VI, 1-292.
> In the German original the author assumed the character of a French traveller to secure himself from the probable effects of his severe remarks on the government, manners and customs of Germany.—Lowndes. The date of the first letter is April 3, 1770.

A Tour through Part of the Austrian Netherlands, and great Part of Holland, . . . in 1785. By an English Gentleman. London.

WALKER, ADAM. A Hasty Sketch of a Tour through Part of the Austrian Netherlands, . . . London.

> This may be identical with the item just preceding. It was issued anonymously.

1788 BOWDLER, THOMAS (F.R.S.). Letters written in Holland, in September and October, 1787; with other Papers relating to the Journey of the Princess of Orange, on the 28th June, 1787. Maps. 8vo. Bath.

> The author is the famous "Bowdleriser" of Shakespeare.

JARDINE, ALEXANDER (Lieut.-Colonel). Letters from Barbary, France, Spain and Portugal, . . . by an English Officer. 2 vols. 8vo. London.

> An edition, 2 vols., 8vo, Dublin, 1789 (probably pirated) ; 2nd edit., corrected, 2 vols., 8vo, London, 1790; again in 1793 and 1794. Translated into German, Leipzig, 1790. See below.
> The author had been sent on a mission to Morocco.

> 1790 (In German.) Bemerkungen über Maroko, desgleichen über Frankreich, Spanien und Portugall. Von einem englischen Offizier während seinen Reisen durch diese Länder. Ein gedrängter Auszug aus dem Englischen. Leipzig.

PECKAM, ——. Travels through Holland and Brabant. London.

ST. JOHN, JAMES. Letters from France to a Gentleman in the South of Ireland written in 1787. 2 vols. Dublin.

THICKNESSE, PHILIP. Memoirs and Anecdotes of Philip Thicknesse, late Lieutenant-Governor of Land Guard Fort, and unfortunately father to George Touchet, Baron Audley. 8vo. London.

> See under 1766 and 1777 above.

1788-1791 GARDNOR, JOHN (Rev.). Views taken on and near, the River
Rhine, at Aix-la-Chapelle, and on the River Maese, by the Rev. J.
Gardnor. Engraved in Aqua Tints by William and Elizabeth Ellis.
32 large plates. Fol. London.

> Another edition, 4to, London, 1792.
> An elegant work, . . . There are proofs before the letters. Some copies are
> colored.—Lowndes.

1789 BOURGOING, JEAN-FRANCOIS DE. Travels in Spain: containing
a new, accurate and comprehensive View of the Present State of that
Country. By the Chevalier de Bourgoanne. To which are added, Copious Extracts from the Essays on Spain of M. Peyron. 12 copperplates. Translated from the French. 3 vols. 8vo. London.

> Several reprints appeared in various collections after 1800, one of which is
> in Pinkerton V, 298-639, taken from the French of the 3rd edition of 1803. The
> French original, Paris, 1788. See below. For full details of various editions and
> an analysis of the nature of the work, see Foulché-Delbosc, item No. 189.
> Bourgoing was twice in Spain, from 1777 to 1785, and from 1792 to 1793.

> 1788 BOURGOING, JEAN-FRANCOIS DE. Nouveau Voyage en Espagne,
> ou Tableau de l'état actuel de cette monarchie; Contenant les détails
> les plus récens sur la Constitution, Politique, les Tribunaux, l'Inquisi-
> tions, les Forces des terres et de mer, le Commerce et les Manufactures,
> . . . enfin, sur les Moeurs, la Littérature, les Spectacles, sur le dernier
> siége de Gibraltar et le voyage de Monseigneur Comte d'Artois; Ouv-
> rage dans lequel on a présenté avec impartialité tout ce qu'on peut
> dire de plus neuf, de plus averé et de plus intéressant, sur l'Espagne,
> depuis 1782 jusqu'à présent; Avec une carte enluminée, des Plans et des
> Figures en taille-douce. 3 vols. 8vo. Paris.

> > According to Foulché-Delbosc, it was not in 1782 but in 1777 that
> > Bourgoing made his visit to Spain. The later date was given to con-
> > ceal the authorship.

COXE, WILLIAM. Travels in Switzerland and in the Country of the
Grisons, in a Series of Letters to W. Melmoth. Plates, some folding.
3 vols. 8vo. London.

> Another edition, London, 1791. In Pinkerton V, 640-992. See also under
> 1779 above.

DU PATY, J. B. MERCIER (President). Travels through Italy, in a
Series of Letters written in 1785, translated by an English Gentleman
from the French. 8vo. Dublin.

> Another translation, by J. Povoleri, entitled *Sentimental Letters on Italy*,
> appeared in 2 vols., 12mo, London, 1789. French original, Rome and Paris, 1788.
> See below.

> 1788 DU PATY, J. B. MERCIER (President). Lettres sur l'Italie en 1785.
> 2 vols. 8vo. Rome and Paris.

PIOZZI, HESTER LYNCH. Observations and Reflections made in the Course of a Journey through France, Italy, and Germany. 2 vols. 8vo. London.

> Another edition, 8vo, Dublin, 1789.
> An agreeable and amusing tour.—Lowndes. Mrs. Piozzi wrote wittily, describing scenes vividly, relating anecdotes with humour and point, never allowing her English prejudices to interfere with her judgment or spoil her enjoyment of the scenes so new to her. Her book remains a most valuable record of Italian society in the 18th century.—M. S. Stillman, quoted in Bookseller's Note. She will be remembered as the former Mrs. Thrale, whose marriage to the Italian musician Piozzi so highly scandalised the Johnson circle.

SAINT-NON, RICHARD DE. According to Pinkerton XVII an English version of the following French item was printed at London in 1789. See below.

> 1781 SAINT-NON, RICHARD DE. Voyage pittoresque, ou Description des Royaumes de Naples et de Sicile; ornées de cartes, plans, vues, figures, vignettes, et cul-de-lampes. 5 vols. Fol. Paris.
>
> > The French edition of this work, when compleat and containing the 14 plates of medals of the ancient Sicilian cities, is worth 600 francs and upwards. A copy of great magnificence was even sold for 1650 francs. The traveller visited these kingdoms in 1777, accompanied by several artists, and engaged others resident in them.—Quoted by Pinkerton XVII.

A Tour to Ermonville; containing besides, an Account of the Palace, Gardens, and Curiosities of Chantilly; a particular Description of the Tomb of Rousseau. London.

> The magnificent gardens at Chantilly were soon to suffer utter destruction during the French Revolution.

VILLIERS, JOHN CHARLES (3rd Earl of Clarendon). A Tour through Part of France, Containing a Description of Paris, Cherbourg, and Ermonville. London.

1790 GARDNOR, JOHN (Rev.). A Picturesque Tour by Manheim, Mentz, Aix-la-Chapelle, Brussels, . . . Plates. London.

> Probably issued in 1790.

IRELAND, SAMUEL. A Picturesque Tour through Holland, Brabant, and Part of France made in the Autumn of 1789. Aquatint plates. 2 vols. 8vo. London.

> 2nd edit., with additions, 2 vols. in 1, 8vo, London, 1796.
> A series of these picturesque tours were published in detached volumes, and were formerly in great request. This Ireland was the father of the forger of Shakespearian texts. He was an engraver and issued views of his tours etched from his own works.

MACDONALD, JOHN. For his account of Spain see his *Travels in various Parts of Europe, Asia, and Africa,* under GENERAL TRAVELS AND DESCRIPTIONS.

PUTTER, JOHN STEPHEN. An Historical Development of the present political Constitution of the Germanic Empire, translated from the German, with Notes, . . . by Josiah Dornford. 3 vols. 8vo. London.

A valuable work.—Lowndes.

WALKER, ADAM. Ideas suggested in an Excursion through Flanders, Germany, Italy and France. 8vo. London.

The author, a self-taught man, was for a while a mathematical tutor in the North of England, and later became a travelling lecturer on physics.—D.N.B.

1791 FLEURIOT, JEAN-MARIE-JEROME (Marquis de Langle). A Picturesque Description of Switzerland, translated from the French. Engraved view. 12mo. London.

There is some question of the exact date of publication of this work. Marquis de Langle is a pseudonym. See also Fleuriot under 1786 above.

JENNER, MATTHEW. For his route through France, Germany, Hungary, etc., to India, see his *Route to India,* under NEAR EAST.

TOWNSEND, JOSEPH (Rev.). A Journey through Spain in the years 1786 and 1787; with particular Attention to the Agriculture, Manufactures, Commerce, Population, Taxes, and Revenue of that Country; and Remarks in passing through a Part of France. 3 vols. 8vo. London.

2nd edit., London, 1792. Translated into German, Leipzig, 1791. See below. This work has been highly commended.

1791 (In German.) Jos. Townsend's Reise durch Spanien und einen Theil von Frankreich in den Jahren 1786 und 1787. Aus dem Englischen übersetzt. 3 vols. Leipzig.

1791-92 GARDENSTONE, LORD. Travelling Memorandums, made in a Tour upon the Continent of Europe, 1786-88. 2 vols. 8vo. Edinburgh.

2nd edit. of vol. I, Edinburgh, 1792; after the author's death in 1793, a 3rd vol. was printed, containing his life.—Lowndes.
The author was Francis Garden, a Scottish judge. Among the well known men he met whose acquaintance he enjoyed was the Abbé Raynal. See Raynal under 1776, WEST INDIES.

1792 BEAUMONT, SIR ALBANIS. An Historical and Picturesque Description of the Country of Nice. 12 etchings finished in water colors. Fol. London.

> A French version, probably the original, Geneva, 1787. See below.
> The author was an engraver and landscape painter, born in Piedmont. For later publications of travels and views see 1794-95 and 1800 below.

> 1787 BEAUMONT, SIR ALBANIS. Voyage Historique et Pittoresque du Comte de Nice. Map and 12 colored engravings. Fol. Geneva.

BEAUMONT, SIR ALBANIS. Travels through the Rhetian Alps in 1786, from Italy to Germany, through Tyrol. Map and 10 large aquatint views by C. Apostool, printed in sepia, after drawings by the author. Fol. London.

HILL, BRIAN (Rev.). Observations and Remarks in a Journey through Sicily and Calabria in the year 1791. 8vo. London.

> With a postscript containing some account of the ceremonies of the last holy week at Rome and of a short excursion to Tivoli.—Lowndes.

WALKER, ADAM. An Excursion to Paris in 1785. (In *A Tour from London to the Lakes of Westmoreland and Cumberland*, 1791.)

> See Walker under 1790 above.

WESTON, STEPHEN. Letters from Paris during the Summer of 1791. London.

> The author was an antiquarian and man of letters. He published notes of travel, classical texts and annotations, notes on Shakespeare, scriptural annotations, and translations from the Arabic, Chinese, and Persian.—D.N.B.

YOUNG, ARTHUR. Travels during the years 1787, 1788 and 1789, undertaken more particularly with a View of ascertaining the Cultivation, Wealth, Resources, and National Prosperity, of the Kingdom of France. To which is added, the Register of a Tour into Spain. 2 vols. 4to. Bury St. Edmunds.

> 2nd edit., 2 vols., with maps, 4to, Bury St. Edmunds, 1794; 3rd edit., edited by Matilda Betham Edwards, London, 1890, with several editions since, among them one in Everyman's Library. An edition, probably pirated, Dublin, 1793. Translated into French, 6 vols., Paris, 1793. See below. The Voyage to Italy published separately in French, Paris, 1796. Reprinted in Pinkerton IV, 77-676.
> Young's accounts of his travels are deservedly among the most famous that the century produced. He made three trips to the Continent, the first to the Pyrenees in 1787, the second to France in 1788, and the third, which included Italy, in 1789. He is unexcelled in relating personal adventures, in observations of the agricultural situation, and in descriptions of the many friends he met. He was near enough to the outbreak of the French Revolution to perceive that something unusual was astir, and even experienced some personal contacts with the

disordered state of affairs. He was known in England and France as the chief authority on agriculture, yet, as has often been pointed out, his own farming was a failure. He was often consulted by "Farmer George" (George III). In 1793 he was made Secretary to the Board of Agriculture, and worked tirelessly publishing articles on the subject. He also wrote accounts of his tours in England and Ireland in the interest of agriculture. His Autobiography, edited by Matilda Betham Edwards (London, 1898), is an absorbing account of his life and of the century in which he lived. Especially pathetic is the story of the distressful mental aberration which darkened the close of his days.

1793 (In French.) Voyage en France pendant les années 1787-1790 entrepris plus particulièrement pour s'assurer de l'état de l'agriculture, des richesses, des resources et de la prosperité de cette nation. Traduit de l'anglais par F.-S. Francois Soulés. 6 vols. 8vo. Paris.

> Vols. I-III contain the journey in France, with notes by M. de Casaux; vol. IV the voyage to Italy; vols. V-VI the voyage to Ireland.

1796 (In French.) Voyage en Italie pendant l'année 1789, traduit par Francois Soulés. 8vo. Paris.

1792-96 SMITH, JOHN. Select Views in Italy. 72 engraved plates by Landseer and others after John Smith. Topographical and Historical Descriptions in English and French. (Also 6 uncolored aquatint views of South Wales by Smith.) 2 vols. in 1. Fol. London.

1793 BEAWES, W. A Civil, Commercial, Political and Literary History of Spain and Portugal. 2 vols. in 1. Fol. London.

> Includes chapters on the military orders, governors, etc., in Europe and America, on Spaniard's dress, customs, diversions, etc., also on the Atlantic Islands belonging to Portugal.—Bookseller's Note.

BISANI, ALEXANDER. A Picturesque Tour through Part of Europe, . . . London.

DRINKWATER, JOHN. A History of the late Siege of Gibraltar; with a Description and Account of that Garrison, from the Earliest Periods, and a copious Table of Contents. Frontispiece and folding plate. 8vo. Dublin.

Letters from Paris, during the Summers of 1791 and 1792, with Reflections. 2 vols. 8vo. London.

MOORE, EDWARD (M.D.). The Journal of a Residence in France, from the Beginning of August to the Middle of December, 1792. 2 vols. London.

> This very interesting production has been translated into French, German, Dutch, and other Languages.—Pinkerton XVII.

A Ramble through Holland, France, and Italy, 1793. 2 vols. London.

SMITH, SIR JAMES (M.D.). A Sketch of a Tour on the Continent in the Years 1786 and 1787. 3 vols. 8vo. London.

A Tour through Germany, containing full Directions for travelling in that interesting Country, . . . Chart. London.

A Tour through the Theatre of War (i. e., France) in the Months of November and December, 1792, January, 1793, with Curious Military Anecdotes; also Accounts of the Death of Louis XVI. 8vo. London.

TWISS, RICHARD. A Trip to Paris in 1792. London.

> See Twiss under 1775 above.

WESTON, STEPHEN. Letters from Paris during the Summer of 1792. London.

> See Weston under 1792 above.

WORDSWORTH, WILLIAM. Descriptive Sketches in verse taken during a Pedestrian Tour in the Italian, Grison, Swiss, and Savoyard Alps by W. Wordsworth, B.A., of St. John's, Cambridge. London.

> A poetical record of a pedestrian tour with Robert Jones in France and Switzerland during the summer of 1790. Their way of touring was rather unprecedented in that each had only twenty pounds in his pocket and his baggage tied up in a pocket handkerchief. This tour is in part described in Book VI of the *Prelude* and more fully in a letter to his sister Dorothy. See Harper's *Wordsworth*, I, 93-94.

1793-96 WILLIAMS, HELEN MARIA. Letters written in France in 1790, 1793, and 1794, to a Friend in England, containing Anecdotes relative to the French Revolution; concerning important Events, particularly relating to the Campaign of 1792; A Sketch of the Politics of France during 1793-4, and Scenes in the Prisons of Paris. 7 vols. in 3. 12mo. London.

> See under 1796 below.

1794 ASTLEY, PHILIP. A Description and Historical Account of the Places now the Theatre of War in the Low Countries. Frontispiece and plans of the principal fortified places. 8vo. Dublin.

BEAUMONT, SIR ALBANIS. A Picturesque Tour from Geneva to the Pennine Alps. Translated from the French. 12 plates. Fol. London.

> French original, Geneva, 1787. See below.
> This is a companion volume to the *Description of the Country of Nice*. See under 1792 above.

1787 BEAUMONT, SIR ALBANIS. Voyage Pittoresque aux Alpes Pennines, précédé de quelques observations sur les hauteurs de montagnes, glaciers, & des différens villages, qui se trouvent sur cette route. . . . Geneva.

COGAN, THOMAS. The Rhine; or, a Journey from Utrecht to Frankfort, 1791-92. Map and views. 2 vols. 8vo. London.

> The style of the work is lively and interesting; the pictures of manners and scenery good; and it contains a learned dissertation on the origin of printing.— Lowndes.

ESTE, C. A Journey in the year 1793 through Flanders, Brabant, and Germany to Switzerland. London.

> Reprinted, London, 1795 and 1800.
> Este states that half of the inhabitants of the Palatinate had emigrated to Pennsylvania to escape the excessive taxes and other unbearable conditions of life.

GRAY, ROBERT. Letters during a Journey through Germany, Switzerland, and Italy, in the years MDCCXCI, and MDCCXCII. 8vo. London.

MAJOR, J. H. Two Letters on Norman Tiles, stained with Armorial Bearings. 8vo. London.

> The work contains engravings of 16 painted tiles from the pavement of the palace of the Dukes of Normandy at Caen.

A Peep into Paris: amusing and incidental French Anecdotes, with a Description of the Parisian Theatres, and a comparative View of the French and English Actors, by the Author of TANCRED. London.

1794-95 BEAUMONT, SIR ALBANIS. Travels (in 1794) through the Maritime Alps from Italy to Lyons across the Col de Tende, by Way of Nice, Provence, and Languedoc, with topographical and historical Descriptions. 19 plates, all but one being aquatint in brown. Select Views of the Antiquities and Harbours in the South of France. 15 plates, of which 13 are in aquatint. 2 vols. in 1. Fol. London.

1795 FREDERICK, (Colonel of the late Theodore, King of Corsica). Description of Corsica; with an Account of its Union to the Crown of Great Britain, including the Life of General Paoli, and the Memorial presented to the National Assembly of France, upon the Forests, . . . London.

A History and Description of the Royal Abbaye of Saint Denis, with an Account of the Tombs of the Kings and Queens of France, . . . 8vo. London.

MURPHY, JAMES. Travels in Portugal; through the Provinces of Entre Douro e Minno, Beira, . . . in the Years 1789 and 1790. Consisting of Observations on the Manners, Customs, Trade, Public Buildings, Arts, Antiquities, . . . of that Kingdom. Illustrated with 24 plates of views, characters, antiquities, etc., by James Murphy, Architect. 4to. London.

> Translated into French, Paris, 1797. See below.
> Murphy was an architect who studied Moorish architecture at Cadiz. He also wrote on Arabian antiquities.—D.N.B. For another work on Portugal see under 1798 below.

> 1797 (In French.) Voyage en Portugal à travers les provinces d'entre Douro et Minno, de Beira, d'Estramadure et d'Alenteju, dans les années 1789 et 1790. Contenant des observations sur les moeurs, le commerce, les edifices, les antiquités, . . . Traduit de l'anglais. 23 engraved copperplates. 2 vols. 8vo. Paris.

> The French translator was Lallemant.

PRATT, SAMUEL JACKSON. Gleanings through Wales, Holland and Westphalia. 3 vols. London.

RADCLIFFE, ANN. A Journey made in the Summer of 1794 through Holland and the Western Frontier of Germany, with a Return down the Rhine, with Observations during a Tour to the Lakes of Lancashire, Westmoreland, and Cumberland. 4to. London.

> This is by the author of the *Mysteries of Udolpho*. Her travels were undertaken after she had written the novels whose romantic settings in forests and mountains of Italy so delighted her readers. Though she had not visited Italy, yet she, like her audience, was sufficiently familiar with the paintings of the "savage Rosa" and the "gentle Claude" and with the general requirements of the picturesque as to know what was called for in recreating visions of foreign lands. Concerning her account of her travels Dr. Garnett says, "(It) is rich in pictorial description, and also in political and economic observations, probably contributed by her husband."—Quoted by Sotheran.

SPALLANZANI, LAZZARO (Abbé). Tour to Vesuvius, Oetna, . . .
8vo. London. Bound up with the 1795 edition of Este's *Journey in
1793 through Flanders,* etc. See Este under 1794 above and Spallanzani under 1798 below.

WILKINSON, JOSHUA LUSCOCK. The Wanderer: or, a Collection
of Anecdotes and Incidents, with Reflections, political and religious,
during two Excursions, in 1791 and 1793, in France, Germany, and
Italy. 2 vols. 12mo. London.

> Reprinted, 2 vols., London, 1798.

1796 GIBBON, EDWARD. Autobiography. Edited in *Miscellaneous Works,*
by Lord Sheffield. London.

> Gibbon's *Memoirs* were edited by G. Birkbeck Hill, London, 1900. The Auto-
> biography is reprinted in the Oxford Classics, Oxford, 1923.
> This work contains interesting descriptions of the region around Lausanne,
> where Gibbon lived while writing his *Decline and Fall.*

Journal du voyageur neutre, depuis son depart de Londres pour Paris, le
18 Nov., 1795, jusqu'à son retour à Londres, le 6 Févr., 1796. London.

MERIGOT, J. Views and Ruins in Rome and its Vicinity, recently ex-
ecuted from drawings made upon the Spot in 1791. Description in
English and French. 62 aquatint plates of architecture and scenery.
Fol. London.

> Another edition, London, 1797-99.

OWEN, JOHN (Rev.). Travels into different Parts of Europe in the
years 1791-92, with Familiar Remarks on Places, Men, and Manners.
2 vols. 8vo. London.

Select Views in Italy, with Topographical and Historical Descriptions in
English and French. With india proof engravings drawn by J. Smith.
8vo. London.

TENCH, WATKIN. Letters written in France to a Friend in London,
1794-95. London.

> For his *Narrative of the Expedition to Botany Bay* see under 1789, AUS-
> TRALIA. Tench was made a prisoner twice, once by the Americans in 1778,
> during the American Revolution, and again by the French in 1794.

WILLIAMS, HELEN MARIA. New Travels in Switzerland, containing a Picture of the Country, the Manners and the actual Government. 2 vols. London.

> Another edition, London, 1798. See below.
> Miss Williams was the poetess to whom Wordsworth addressed some of his early poems. After 1788 she lived largely in France, where she took up the cause of the Girondists and narrowly escaped execution at the hands of Robispierre. See also under 1793-96 above.

> 1798 WILLIAMS, HELEN MARIA. A Tour in Switzerland; Or, a View of the Present State of the Governments and Manners of those Cantons; with Comparative Sketches of the present State of Paris. 2 vols. 8vo. London.

1796-97 STOLBERG, FREDERICK LEOPOLD, GRAF VON. Travels through Germany, Switzerland, Italy, and Sicily, translated by Thomas Holcroft. Folding map and 18 plates of views. 2 vols. 4to. London.

> German original, Königsberg, 1794. See below.
> The translator was Holcroft the dramatist and novelist. He performed the remarkable feat of memorising the *Marriage of Figaro,* after having seen it a few times in Paris, and so bringing it home to London audiences.

> 1794 STOLBERG, FREDERICK LEOPOLD, GRAF VON. Reisen des Grafen von Stolberg im Deutschland, Italien, und Sicilien. 4 vols. Königsberg.

1797 GIFFORD, JOHN. A Residence in France, during the Years 1792-95. Described in a Series of Letters from an English Lady. With general and incidental Remarks on the French Character and Manners. 2 vols. 8vo. London.

> The real name of the author was John Richard Green, who assumed the pseudonym of Gifford to deceive his creditors. Notwithstanding, he became a London police magistrate. He also edited the *Anti-Jacobin Review* in imitation of Wm. Gifford's *Anti-Jacobin.*

LUMISDEN, ANDREW. Remarks on the Antiquities of Rome and its Environs; being a classical and topographical Survey of the Ruins. Numerous plans, engravings, and views, some in aquatint. 4to. London.

> Sometimes this work is illustrated with Merigot's Views in Rome, consisting of 60 plates in aquatint.—Lowndes. Lumisden was a Jacobite who became private secretary to Prince Charles Edward. He was at the battle of Culloden but escaped to France. In 1773 he was allowed to return to England.

REYNOLDS, SIR JOSHUA. Works . . . containing his Discourses, Idlers, A Journey to Flanders and Holland (now first published), and his Commentary on Du Fresnoy's Art of Painting: printed from his Revised Copies (with his corrections and additions) . . . To which is

Prefixed an Account of the Life and Writings of the Author, by Edmund Malone, Esq. (First collected edition.) Portrait, 2 vols. 4to. London.

> Reprinted in Bohn's edition of Reynolds' works, London, 1852.
> This journey, which took place in 1781 and lasted not quite two months, was made largely for the purpose of inspecting the paintings of these countries.

Sketches and Observations made on a Tour through various Parts of Europe, in the years 1792-94. London.

SOUTHEY, ROBERT. Letters written during a Short Residence in Spain and Portugal, with some Account of Spanish and Portuguese Poetry. 8vo. Bristol.

> 2nd edit., Bristol and London, 1798.

TOWNSON, ROBERT. Travels in Hungary, with a Short Account of Vienna in the year 1793. 16 copperplates and map. 4to. London.

> This is the best English work respecting Hungary. It has been translated into both French and German.—Pinkerton XVII. A work valuable to the natural historian, particularly the mineralogist; it also contains a very particular account of the Tokay wines.—Lowndes. Townson was the author of a work called the *Philosophy of Mineralogy* (1798).

1798 CLUBBE, WILLIAM. The Omnium; containing the Journal of a late three Days' Tour into France; curious and extraordinary Anecdotes, Critical Remarks and other Miscellaneous Pieces in Prose and Verse. 8vo. Ipswich.

> The author was vicar of Brandeston in Suffolk, and a writer of minor verse.

MURPHY, JAMES. A General View of the State of Portugal; containing a Topographical Description thereof. In which are included, an Account of the Physical and Moral State of the Kingdom; together with Observations on the Animal, Vegetable, and Mineral Productions of its Colonies. The Whole compiled from the best Portuguese Writers, and from Notices obtained in the Country by James Murphy. 16 plates. 4to. London.

> See also Murphy under 1795 above.

A Sketch of Modern France in a Series of Letters to a Lady of Fashion, written in the Years 1796 and 1797, during a Tour through France by a Lady. London.

> It is stated that these Letters were edited by C. L. Moody.

SPALLANZANI, LAZZARO (Abbé). Travels in the Two Sicilies, and some Parts of the Appennines, translated from the original Italian. 11 plates. 4 vols. 8vo. London.

> A translation from the original Italian version of 1788 is printed, with some omissions, in Pinkerton V, 1-272. An Italian version, Pavia, 1792-97. See below.
> The author was a scientist of note, greatly interested in volcanoes and their geology. He was also known for his experiments in spontaneous generation. He did considerable travelling for the purpose of collecting material for the Public Imperial Museums of Natural History in the University of Pavia. See also under 1795 above.

> 1792-97 SPALLANZANI, LAZZARO (Abbé). Viagge alle due Sicilie ed in alcune parte degli Apennini. Pavia.

1799 CROKER, RICHARD. Travels through several Provinces of Spain and Portugal. 8vo. London.

MATTHISON, FREDERICK. Letters written from various Parts of the Continent (Germany, Switzerland, the South of France, etc). Translated by A. Plumptree, from the German. 8vo. London.

> In the Appendix are included three letters of the poet Gray never before published in this country.—Lowndes.

1800 An Account of the Republic of Geneva. London.

> So cited by Pinkerton XVII.

BEAUMONT, SIR ALBANIS. Travels from France to Italy through the Lepontine Alps: or, an Itinerary of the Road from Lyons to Turin by way of the Pays de-Vaud, the Vallais, and the Monts Great St. Bernard, Simplon, and St. Gothard, with topographical and historical Descriptions, the Natural History, and Remarks on the Course of the Rhone. 27 aquatint views, printed in brown, after the author. Fol. London.

HAGER, —— (Dr.). Pictures of Palermo: Translated by Mrs. Robinson. London.

> German original, Berlin, 1799. See below.

> 1799 HAGER, —— (Dr.). Gemälde von Palermo. Berlin.

MERCIER, ——. New Pictures of Paris, translated from the French. 2 vols. 8vo. London.

MOORE, JOHN (Mordaunt). Sketches of Life, Characters and Manners in various Countries, including the Memoirs of a French Lady of Quality, by the Author of Zeluco and Edward. 3 vols. 8vo. London.

Apparently the name Mordaunt was used to indicate the authorship of this work.

RENDER, ——. Tour through Germany. 3 vols. London.

So cited by Pinkerton XVII. Possibly the author is William Render, a German who came to London in 1790. He was a grammarian and a translator of Goethe and Kotzebue.

SALMON, J. An Historical Description of ancient and modern Rome; also of the works of Art, particularly in Architecture, Sculpture, and Painting; to which is added, a Tour through the Cities and Towns in the Environs of that Metropolis, and an Account of the Antiquities found at Gabia. 2 vols. 8vo. London.

STARKE, MARIANA. Letters from Italy between the Years 1792 and 1798. 2 vols. London.

STARKE, MARIANA. Travels on the Continent for the Use and Particular Information of Travellers. London.

STOCKDALE, JOHN. A Geographical, Historical, and Political Description of the Empire of Germany, Holland, the Netherlands, Switzerland, Prussia, Italy, Sicily, Corsica, and Sardinia, with a Gazetteer of Reference to the principal Places in those Countries; to which are added, Statistical Tables of all the States of Europe. Folding maps. 4to. London.

WALSH, EDWARD. Narrative of the Expedition to Holland in the Autumn of 1799. Map and 7 views by Heath, after the author. 4to. London.

WRAXALL, NATHANIEL WILLIAM. Memoirs of the Courts of Berlin, Dresden, Warsaw, and Vienna, 1777-79. 2 vols. 8vo. London.

See also Wraxall under 1815 below.

ADDENDA

BROOKE, ——. A Journey from Naples into Tuscany before the French Invasion of Italy. London.

Cited by Pinkerton XVII without date.

1803 MUIRHEAD, LOCKHART. Journals of Travels in Parts of the late Austrian Low Countries, France, . . . in 1787 and 1789. London.

1805 BECKFORD, PETER. Familiar Letters from Italy in 1787. 2 vols. 8vo. London.

The author published several works on hunting and fox hounds.

1808-1814 DE SAUSSURE, HORACE BENEDICT. An Account of the Attempts that have been made to attain the Summit of Mont Blanc. Written in the Years 1786, 1787. Translated from his *Voyages dans les Alps,* II, 556 ff. In Pinkerton IV, 677-709.

French original, Neuchâtel and Geneva, 1779-1796. See below.

De Saussure has been called the greatest of all Alpine tourists. Of the numerous journies he made in the Alpine regions, seven are narrated in his book. He was interested in everything he saw: the rocks of the earth's crust, the nature of electricity and heat, why the tops of mountains and the bottoms of lakes are cold, why the inhabitants of some valleys suffer from goitre, etc. On the summit of Mont Blanc, which he reached on his fourth trip in 1787, he made all sorts of experiments: the readings of the barometer, thermometers, hygrometers, and electrometers, the temperature at which water boiled, the variation of the magnetic needle, the beat of the pulse, etc. On other trips he measured the heights of various mountains, investigated the various dialects of different valleys, and proposed explanations of glacial phenomena. The modesty of the scientist is fitly expressed in his own words: "Placed on this planet since yesterday, and only for one day, we can but desire knowledge to which, seemingly, we shall never attain." —Taken from De Beer, *Early Travellers in the Alps.*

1779-1796 DE SAUSSURE, HORACE BENEDICT. Voyages dans les Alps. Neuchâtel and Geneva.

DOLOMEN, DEODATUS DE. A Dissertation on the Earthquake in Calabria Ultra, which happened in the Year 1783. Translated from the Italian of 1784. In Pinkerton V, 273-297.

1809 COLERIDGE, SAMUEL TAYLOR. Satyranes Letters. London.

A selection from the letters he wrote home from Germany (1798-99), which he thought likely to be most interesting and at the same time most pertinent to the title of his *Biographia Literaria,* in which he included them. They were first published in the *Friend,* Nov.-Dec., 1809.

PENNINGTON, THOMAS (Rev.). Continental Excursions, or Tours into France, Switzerland and Germany in 1782, 1787 and 1789. 2 vols. London.

1813 RERESBY, SIR JOHN. Travels and Memoirs, the former exhibiting a View of the Government and Society in the principal States and Courts of Europe, during the Time of Cromwell's Usurpation; the latter containing Anecdotes, and Secret History of the Courts of Charles II and James II. 40 portraits and plates, some in colors. 8vo. London.

> A modern reprint, London, 1904. See below.
> Reresby travelled on the Continent at the time of the Commonwealth, and in 1675 he entered Parliament. His Memoirs appeared in 1734 and together with his Travels in 1813.

> 1904 RERESBY, SIR JOHN. The Memoirs and Travels of Sir John Reresby, Bart., edited by Albert Ivatt, M.A. In Dryden House Memoirs Series. Reprint of the 1813 issue. London.

1815 WRAXALL, SIR NATHANIEL WILLIAM. Historical Memoirs of My Own Time, from 1772 to 1784. 2 vols. 8vo. London.

> 2nd edit., London, 1815. A modern reprint, in the Dryden House Memoirs Series, edited by Richard Askhan, London, 1904.
> This work was severely criticised in the *Edinburgh Review*, vol. 25, the *Quarterly*, vol. 13, and other reviews, and the author was prosecuted and imprisoned for a libel on Prince Gortschakeff. Wraxall published two answers to the attacks made on him. The first edition contained passages that were afterwards suppressed.—Lowndes. This work gives the reader a good introduction to the most important personages of the period.

1820 DOUGLAS, JOHN (Bishop of Carlisle and later of Salisbury). Journal of a Tour through Germany, Holland and France, July 5, 1748 to October, 1749. Printed in *Select Works*. Edited by Ed. W. Macdonald. Salisbury.

1834 BECKFORD, WILLIAM. Italy; with Sketches of Spain and Portugal By the Author of *Vathek*. 2 vols. London.

> A modern reprint, 2 vols., edited by Guy Chapman, London, 1928.
> Beckford made three visits to the Spanish Penninsula: the first in 1787-88; the second in 1791-96; and the third in 1798-99. The volumes listed above do not contain the details of his last visit, during which time he resided in Portugal entirely.—Foulché-Delbosc.

1835 BECKFORD, WILLIAM. Recollections of an Excursion to the Monasteries of Alcobaca and Batalha. By the Author of *Vathek*. London (?).

1836 BROWNE, EDWARD. Journal and Letters of Edward Browne in Sir Thomas Browne's *Works,* vol. I. Edited by Simon Wilkin. London.

> See also Browne under 1673, CONTINENTAL EUROPE.

1844 BRERETON, SIR WILLIAM. Travels in Holland, United Provinces, England, Scotland, and Ireland, 1634-35. Edited by S. Hawkins, Chetham Society, vol. I. Manchester.

1857 BUSINO, HORATIO. Journey from Venice to London, 1617. Record Office, Venetian Transcripts, vol. CXLII, 1-46.

> The translation was made by Rawdon Brown. See *Quart. Rev.,* Oct., 1875, and Lett's abstract in *Notes and Queries,* 2nd ser., I, 61 ff.

1867 The Stacions of Rome (in verse from the Vernon MS., c. 1370, and in prose from the Porkington MS., c. 1460-1470), and the Pilgrims Sea-Voyage and Sea-Sickness (from the Trinity College Library MS. R, about the time of Henry VI). Edited for the Early English Text Society by F. J. Furnivall, original series, no. 25. London.

1880 RIGBY, EDWARD (Dr.). Letters from France, . . . in 1789. Edited by his daughter, Lady Eastlake. London.

> Rigby was the exact opposite of Smollett in temperament, being an optimist, but at the same time an intelligent and sincere witness of things and events. His book makes a good supplementary volume to the travels of Arthur Young (see under 1792 above).

1884 CALDERWOOD, MRS. (of Polton). Letters and Journals from England, Holland, and the Low Countries in 1756. Edited by Alex. Ferguson. 5 illus. 8vo. London.

> Vigorous in speech and pawky in her observations, she writes a very entertaining account of her experiences in Catholic lands. Her language preserves many Scottish idioms of her day.

1885 TEMPLE, HENRY (2nd Viscount Palmerston). Diary in France during July and August, 1791. Printed as an Appendix to the Dispatches of Earl Gower, English Ambassador at Paris, 1790-92. Edited by O. Browning. Cambridge.

1888 ESSEX, JAMES. Journal of a Tour through Part of Flanders and France in August, 1773. Edited by W. M. Fawcett, Cambridge Antiquarian Society, No. XXIV, pp. 12 ff. Cambridge.

1889 FRASER, (Major). Fraser's Manuscript: his Adventures in Scotland and England; his Mission to, and Travels in, France in Search of his Chief; his Services with Simon Fraser, Lord Lovat, 1697-1737; edited by A. Fergusson. 2 vols. 8vo. Edinburgh.

1894 FERRIER, RICHARD, F. E., and JOHN H. H. The Journal of Major Ferrier, M. P., while travelling in France in the year 1687. With a brief Memoir of his Life. Camden Society, vol. IX. London.

1900-1912 GRAY, THOMAS. Letters of Thomas Gray. Edited by D. C. Tovey. 3 vols. London.

> The poet travelled on the Continent with Horace Walpole in 1739-1740, but the two parted company because of incompatibility. As a letter writer Gray ranks high, and his descriptions of wild mountain scenery with its sounds of falling waters marks the turning point in the romantic appreciation of mountains. After returning from his visit to Scotland, he said that one ought to visit the Highlands once a year.

1902 PARMINTER, JANE. Extracts from a Devonshire Lady's Notes of Travel in France in 1784. Edited by Rev. O. Reichel for the Devonshire Association for the Advancement of Science, Literature, and Art, XXXIV. Plymouth.

1903 MONTAIGNE, MICHEL EYQUEM, SEIGNEUR DE. Journal of Montaigne's Travels in 1580 and 1581. Translated and edited with an Introduction and Notes by W. G. Waters. Illus. 3 vols. 8vo. London.

1905 KNIGHT, LADY PHILIPPINA. Letters from France and Italy, 1776-1795. Edited by Lady Eliott-Drake. 8vo. London.

1908 WALPOLE, HORACE. Letters on France, 1774-1796. London.

> See also his *Letters*, edited by Peter Cunningham, 9 vols., London, 1891.
> Walpole made several visits to France. Being free from the prejudices of Smollett and Moore, perfectly at home among people of taste, and a thorough adept in the social graces, he opens to us the doors of the salons and lets us see for ourselves what it was that made Paris the capital of Society.

1909 CUST, MRS. HENRY. Gentlemen Errant, being the Journeys and Adventures of Four Noblemen in Europe during the Fifteenth and Sixteenth Centuries. Illus. 8vo. London.

1923 BROWNE, EDWARD. Journal of a Visit to Paris, 1664. Edited by Geoffrey Keynes in St. Bartholomew's *Hospital Reports,* vol. LVI. Reprinted separately. London.

1925 BOWREY, THOMAS. The Papers of Thomas Bowrey, 1669-1713. Part I, Diary of a Six Weeks Tour in 1698 in Holland and Flanders; Part II, the Story of the *Mary Galley,* 1704-1710. Edited by Lieut.-Col. Sir Richard C. Temple, Bart., C.B., C.I.E., F.B.A., F.S.A. 5 maps and 9 plates. Hak. Soc., ser. II, vol. 58. London.

> The Diary is of especial interest for its accounts of Amsterdam and other cities of the Low Countries at the end of the seventeenth century, and of the monetary system of the time.—Quoted from Notice of the volume.

BUTLER, ALBAN (Rev.). Travels through France and Italy, and part of the Austrian, French, and Dutch Netherlands, during the year 1745-46, by the late Rev. Alban Butler, Author of the Lives of the Saints. (Place and date ?.)

> The notes of these tours left by the author were collected and published by a nephew, Charles Butler, probably before 1800. The existence of this work is mentioned by Robert Bracey, together with an account of Alban Butler, in his *Eighteenth Century Studies,* Oxford, 1925. Butler was guide and tutor to the Earl of Shrewsbury's sons, and professor of philosophy and divinity at Douay.

MORTOFT, FRANCIS. Francis Mortoft: His Book. Being his Travels through France and Italy in 1658-59, from a manuscript at the British Museum. Edited by Malcom Letts, F.R. Hist. S. 2 maps and 1 plate. Hak. Soc., ser. II, vol. 57. London.

> A lively journal by a typical tourist of the period containing, among other items of interest, a detailed description of Rome in the seventeenth century.—Quoted from Notice of the volume.

1928 GARRICK, DAVID. The Diary of David Garrick: being a Record of his memorable Trip to Paris in 1751. Edited by R. C. Alexander. 8vo. London.

> This visit was one of the triumphs of Garrick's career. It made French actors sadly realise the difference of social status obtaining among the acting profession in England as compared with that of France. The Diary had been lost for a long time.

1931 BLAIKIE, THOMAS. The Diary of a Scotch Gardener, 1775-1792. Edited, with an Introduction, by Francis Birrell. 8vo. London.

> His experiences in France, where he was professionally employed, and his couthy observations on French gardens and gardening ways make this volume of great interest.

COLE, WILLIAM (Rev.). A Journal of my Journey to Paris in the
Year 1765. Edited from the original MS. in the British Museum by
Francis Griffin Stokes, with an Introduction by Helen Waddell. 8vo.
London.

> Cole was rector of Bletchley, and a friend of Horace Walpole. His Diary
> makes a good guide to the older Paris of the eighteenth century.

VI.

North Europe

1561 NORTH, GEORGE. The Description of Swedland, Gotland, and Finland, the auncient estate of theyr Kynges, the moste horrible and incredible tiranny of the second Christiern, kyng of Denmarke, agaynst the Swecians, the poleticke attaynyng to the Crowne of Gostane, wyth hys prudent prouidyng for the same. Collected and gathered out of sundry laten Aucthors, but chieflye out of Sebastian Mounster. By George North. Set forth accordyng to the order in the Quenes Maiesties Iniunction. 4to. London.

> For Sebastian Munster see under 1572, GEOGRAPHY.—Apparently this is the only edition and is extremely rare.—Quaritch. It is mainly historical in content.—Parks.

1658 MAGNUS, OLAUS (Archbishop). A Compendious History of the Goths, Swedes, and Vandals, and other Northern Nations, written by Olaus Magnus, Archbishop of Upsall and Metropolitan of Sweden. Fol. London.

> Latin original, Rome, 1555. See below.
> This work long remained for the rest of Europe the chief authority on Swedish matters, and is still a valuable repository of much curious information in regard to Scandinavian customs and folk-lore.—Quoted by Maggs, No. 442. It was a favorite work of Sir Walter Scott, who described in his *Pirate* the Udaller inspecting this curious volume. It is the most remarkable work published on Scandinavia, full of curious matter, embracing manners, customs, occupations, weapons, legends, myths and superstitions; a detailed description of the birds, animals and fish, and interspersed with historical anecdotes and some quaint stories; together with "horrid apparitions of divels, the antick prestigation of conjurors and Magical Inchantments."—Bookseller's Note. Olaus Magnus was at the Council of Trent, and distinguished himself by opposing the Reformation in Sweden.— Maggs, No. 505. The translator was J. Streater.

> 1555 MAGNO, OLAO. Historia de Gentibvs Septentrionalibvs, earvmque diversis statubvs, conditionibvs, moribvs, ritibvs, svperstitionibus disciplinis exercitiis regimine victu, bellis, structuris, instrumentiis, ac mineris metallicis, & rebus mirabilibus, necnon vniuersis pene animalibus in Septentrione de gentibus eorumque natura. Opus ut varivm plvrimarvmqve rervm cognitione refertvm atqve cvm exemplis externis tum expressis rerum internarum picturis illustratum, cum indice. Many woodcuts and initial letters. Fol. Rome.

1674 MARTINIERE, PIERRE MARTIN DE LA. Travels into the Northern Countries; being a Description of the Manners, Customs, Superstitions, Buildings, and Habits of the Norwegians, Laponians, Kilops, Borandians, Siberians, Samoiedes, Zemblans and Icelanders; with Reflections upon an Error in our Geographers, about the Situation and Extent of Greenland and Nova-Zembla. 12mo. London.

> Later edition, with additions, 8vo, London, 1706. French original, Paris, 1671. See below.

1706 MARTINIERE, PIERRE MARTIN DE LA. A New Voyage to the North, containing a full Account of Norway, the Laplands, . . . of Borandia, Siberia, Samojedia, Zembla, and Iseland, with the Description of the Religion and Customs of these several Nations; to which is added, a Particular Relation of the Court of the Czar, of the Religion and Customs of the Muscovites, and a short History of Muscovy, now done into English. Folding frontispiece containing 20 figures. 8vo. London.

1671 MARTINIERE, PIERRE MARTIN DE LA. Voyage des Pays septentrionaux dans lequel se voit les moeurs, manière de vivre et superstitions des Norvéguiens, Lappons, Kiloppes, Borandiens, Sybériens, Samoyèdes, Zembliens et Islandois. 11 copperplates. 12mo. Paris.
La Martinière est, selon toutes les apparences, né à Rouen. C'est le premier Francais qui ait publié un voyage maritime le long des côtes boréales de l'Europe.—Bookseller's Note.

SCHEFFER, JOHN.   The History of Lapland; wherein are shewed the Original Manners, Habits, Marriages, Conjurations, Employments, . . . of that People. Map and a large number of woodcuts. Fol. Oxford.

Another edition, with additions, London, 1703; again, London, 1751. Latin original, Upsala, 1670. See below.
Portions of this work are translated into verse. The author, a German by birth, wandered to Sweden in 1648, where he was hospitably received by Queen Christina, who was already acquainted with his works, and loaded with honors. This history long remained the main source of information on Lapland.

1703 SCHEFFER, JOHN. The History of Lapland; containing a Geographical Description, and a Natural History, of that Country; with an Account of the Inhabitants, their Original, Religion, Customs, Habits, Marriages, Conjurations, Employments, . . . Written by John Scheffer, Professor at Upsalla in Sweden, Translated from the last Edition in Latin: and illustrated with 28 Copper Cuts. To which is added, The Travels of the King of Sweden's Mathematicians into Lapland. The History of Livonia, and the Wars there. Also a Journey into Lapland and Finland, . . . Written by Dr. Olof Rudbeck, in the Year 1701. 8vo. London.

1751 SCHEFFER, JOHN. The History of Lapland, shewing the original Manners, Habits, Religion, and Trade of that People, with a particular Account of their Gods and Sacrifices, Marriage Ceremonies, diabolical Rites, . . . 8vo. London.

1670 SCHEFFER, JOHN. Lapponia id est, regionis Lapponum et gentis nova et verissima descriptio. In qua multa de origine, superstitione, sacris magis, victu, cultu, negotiis Lapponum, item animalium, metallorumque indole, in terris eorum proveniunt, hactenus incognita produntur, et eiconibus adjectis cum cura illustrantur. Upsala.

1676 DEBES, LUCAS JACOBSON. Faeroae et Faeroa reserata: that is, a Description of the Islands and Inhabitants of Foeroe, being seventeen Islands subject to the King of Denmark, lying under 62 degrees 10 min. of North Latitude. Wherein several Secrets of Nature are brought to Light, and some Antiquities hitherto kept in Darkness, discovered. Englished by J(ohn) S(terpin). 12mo. London.

1675 is the date given in the *Term Catalogues*. Danish original, Copenhagen, 1673. See below.

1673 DEBES, LUCAS JACOBSON. Faeroae et Faeroa reserata. Det er: Faeroernes oc Faeroeske Indbyggeres Beskrifvelse, udi hvilken foris til Liuset adskillige Naturens Hemeligheder, oc nogle Antiqviteter, som her til Dags udi Morcket hafve vaeret indelugte, oc nu her opladis, Alle curieuse til Velbehagelighed. 8vo. Copenhagen.

1683 MIEGE, GUY. The Present State of Denmark. 12mo. London.

> French original, Rouen, 1670.
> The author was a native of Lausanne, who settled in England and became a member of the household of Charles Howard, Earl of Carlisle, and Ambassador Extraordinary to Russia, Sweden, and Denmark.

PIERREVILLE, G. The present State of Denmark; and Reflections upon the ancient State thereof. Together with a particular Account of the Birth, Education, and Martial Atchievements of his Royal Highness Prince George, only Brother to his present Majesty of Denmark. 8vo. London.

> The author was secretary to the King's Minister to Denmark.

1691 For travels to Sweden and Denmark see *An Accurate Description of the United Netherlands,* under WEST EUROPE.

1694 KING, WILLIAM. Animadversions on a Pretended Account of Danmark. 8vo. London.

> This probably refers to Molesworth's account. See following item, which provoked a number of replies.

MOLESWORTH, ROBERT (First Viscount). An Account of Denmark, as it was in the year 1692; more particularly of the Form of Government, how it became hereditary and absolute; the Conditions, Customs, and Temper of the People; of the Revenue, Army, Fleet, Fortresses, Court; Disposition and Inclination of the King of Denmark towards his Neighbors; the manner of disposing and restoring the Duke of Holstein Gottorp; the Interest of Denmark with other States; of the Clergy, Laws, Learning, . . . 8vo. London.

> Another edition, London, 1697; 4th edit., with added matter, London, 1738; abbreviated reprint in Harris II, 501-507. See below.
> This book so much exasperated the Danish sovereign that he demanded the punishment of the author, who had been ambassador at his court. On being told that English laws did not permit reprisals of this kind, he said, as we are informed by Count Suhm, that if such a work had been published in his dominions against England, the author should have been executed for it.—Quoted. Molesworth resided in Denmark during the reign of William III. He explains how the great revolution took place by which the Danish kings, hitherto elected and limited, became hereditary and absolute monarchs. The observation is made that this is the only legal absolute monarchy in the world, the King having been declared such by the States of that Kingdom, which had such power under the Constitution. Hence the Danish Government is represented as being arbitrary and tyrannous,

and is held up as an object lesson to men of enlightenment. Being anti-clerical in tone, the book at once obtained popularity and distinction. It was highly approved by Shaftsbury and Locke. See Maggs, No. 594.

> 1738 MOLESWORTH, ROBERT (First Viscount). An Account of Denmark as it was in the year 1692. An Account of Sweden as it was in 1688. A Short Narrative of the Life and Death of John Rhinbald, Count Pathul. . . . 8vo. London.
>
> Said by Lowndes to be the best edition of this work.

Denmark Vindicated; being an Answer to a late Treatise, called An Account of Denmark as it was in the year 1692. Sent from a Gentleman in the Country to his Friend at London. (By Jodocus Crull.) 8vo. London.

> This is a criticism of Molesworth's book above.

ROBINSON, JOHN (Bishop of London). An Account of Sueden, with an Extract of the History of that Kingdom. 8vo. London.

> The author spent more than 25 years at the Swedish court as chaplain to the English embassy. This little work is stored with useful information set forth in a style not unlike that of a modern consular report, and its value was recognized in diplomatic circles both in England and abroad. Marlborough wrote of Robinson's excellent influence at the Swedish court in 1704, and in 1707 thought of employing him to appease the Swedish King, who cherished grievances against the Allies.—D.N.B., quoted by Sotheran.

1695   CARR, WILLIAM. For western and northern Europe see his *Travellour's Guide,* under GENERAL TRAVELS AND DESCRIPTIONS.

1697   Travels through Denmark and some Parts of Germany: translated from a Manuscript in French. London.

1698   BILBERG, JOHN. A Voyage of the late King of Sweden, and another of Mathematicians sent by him; in which are discovered the refraction of the Sun, which sets not in the northern Parts at the Time of the Summer Solstice, Variation of the Needle, Latitude of Places, Season, . . . of those Countries. By the Command of the most serene Charles XI, King of Sweden, . . . Faithfully Englished. 8vo. London.

1699   ALLISON, THOMAS. For his voyage from Archangel to the North Cape see under EAST EUROPE.

1702   BROMLEY, WILLIAM. For an account of travel in Denmark and Sweden see his *Several Years' Travels through Portugal,* under WEST EUROPE.

1703 RUDBECK, OLOF. For a journey into Lapland and Finland see under Scheffer, 1674 above.

> Swedish original, Upsala, 1701.

1707 Travels through Denmark and some Parts of Germany. By way of a Journal in the Retinue of the English Envoy in 1702. With Extracts of several Laws, relating to the absolute Power of the King. Religion and Civil Government of the Country. Including the Military and Maritime State thereof: the whole illustrated with divers curious Remarks. 8vo. London.

1714 WHITELOCK, BULSTRODE. Account of his Embassy to Sweden, deliver'd to the Parliament in the year 1654: together with the Defensive Alliance concluded between Great Britain and Sweden in the year 1700, under the reign of the late King William. 8vo. London.

> This is a short pamphlet of 24 pp., and is probably not by Whitelocke. For his own journal see under 1772 below.

1720 LEOPOLD, J. F. Relatio epistolica de Itinere suo Suedico 1707 facto, ad J. Woodward. London.

1725 For an account of Sweden and Denmark see *Travels through Flanders, Holland, Germany,* etc., under WEST EUROPE.

1732 (?) A Description of the Islands and Inhabitants of Faeroe. Written in Danish and translated into English. 12mo. London (?).

> Cited in Churchill's Introduction, which goes on to say: The description is very particular and curious and indeed more than could be expected of those miserable northern islands; but the author was provost of the churches there, and had time to gather such an account, . . . His character of the people is very favorable and savours more of affection than sincerity; but the worst part of this small book, is first a collection of some romantick stories of the ancient inhabitants of Faero; and in the next place, what is yet worse, a parcel of insignificant tales of spectres and illusions of Satan, as the author calls them.—It is apparent that the editor of Churchill was no folk lorist. No date is assigned to this work. Perhaps it is Debes's. See 1676 above.

PEYRERE, ISAAC DE LA. An Account of Iseland sent to Monsieur de la Mothe de Vayer. In Churchill II, 383-395.

> This account is dated Dec. 8, 1644, Copenhagen. It may have been abstracted by the editors of Churchill from Peyrère's *Relation du Groenland,* which was published at Paris, 1647. See the Hakluyt Society volume under 1850, ARCTIC REGIONS.

1738   An Account of Sweden as it was in the year 1688. See under Molesworth, 1694 above.

1744-48   A Succinct Account of the Kingdom of Sweden, with respect to its Climate, Soil and Produce; as also of the Temper, Genius, Customs, Policy, Form of Government, Force, and Trade of its Inhabitants. Collected from the Writings of an English Minister residing there. In Harris II, 493-501.

>   This is a generalised account. The minister was one sent by William III to Charles XI of Sweden.

A Voyage to the North, containing an Account of the Sea Coasts, Mines of Norway, the Danish, Swedish, and Muscovite Laplands; Borandia, Siberia, Samojedia, Zemilla and Iceland; with some very curious Remarks on the Norwegians, Laplanders, Russians, Poles, Circassians, Cossacks, and other Nations. Extracted from the Journal of a Gentleman, employed by the North Sea Company, at Copenhagen; and from the Memoirs, of a French Gentleman, who, after serving many years in the Armies of Russia, was at last banished into Siberia. In Harris II, 457-492.

>   The occasion of this voyage was the desire of the North Sea Trading Company to extend its commerce by voyages of discovery. For this purpose a petition was presented to Frederick III, King of Denmark, Feb., 1653. Permit was secured and several ships were fitted out. The author, being of a curious mind and residing at Copenhagen at the time, took a fancy to the voyage and went as surgeon to the ships. It is an interesting narrative given generally in the first person.

1745   STORY, JOHN. Travels through Sweden: Containing a short Survey of that Kingdom; and a Brief Description of all its Provinces: as also Their Riches, Antiquity, Nature, and Manners; together with the Government of this Realm, Might and Power of this great King, as well by Sea as Land, his great Officers, Customs, and Revenues of the Crown: Likewise a Catalogue of many of the Kings of Sweden . . . In Osborne I, 209-237.

>   This account comes down "to the present year 1632." There is no narrative; the contents could have been compiled from books. The author was obliged to travel "to avoid the persecutions of the iniquitous court of Star-Chamber."—Quoted from Osborne.

1748   An Historical Abridgement of the Present State of Sweden. 2 vols. 12mo. London.

>   This treats of the interval between 1680 and 1743. Very concise, but not always correct, and of small esteem.—Pinkerton VI.

1755 PONTOPPIDAN, ERIC (Bishop of Bergen). The Natural History of Norway. Folding map and 28 plates. 2 vols. Fol. London.

> Danish original, Copenhagen, 1752-54. See below.
> Notwithstanding Pontoppidan is occasionally betrayed into error by his credulity, his account of the country and its natural history is very valuable, and in general correct.—Pinkerton XVII.

> 1752-54 PONTOPPIDAN, ERIC. Forsög til Norges naturlige Historie. 2 vols. 30 plates. Copenhagen.

1758 HORREBOW, NIELS. The Natural History of Iceland; containing a Particular Account of the different Soils, Burning Mountains, Minerals, Vegetables, Metals, Beasts, Birds and Fishes, with the Disposition, Customs, and Manner of Living of the Inhabitants. Interspersed with an Account of the Island by Mr. Anderson . . . Translated from the Danish Original (by Mr. Anderson). Large folding map. Fol. London.

> Danish original, Copenhagen, 1750. See below.
> Boswell reports that Bennet Langton had said to him that Johnson could repeat a complete chapter from this work, "the whole of which was exactly this: Chap. LXXII. Concerning Snakes. 'There are no snakes to be met with throughout the whole Island.'"

> 1750 HORREBOW, NIELS. Tilforladelige efterretninger om Island. 8vo. Copenhagen.

1770 MALLET, PAUL HENRY. A Description of the Manners, Customs, Religion, and Laws of the Ancient Danes, and other Northern Nations, including those of our own Saxon Ancestors; with a Translation of the Edda, or System of Runic Mythology, and other Pieces from the Ancient Islandic, with Additional Notes and Goranson's Latin Version of the Edda. 2 vols. 8vo. London.

> An edition in Bohn's Library, 2 vols., London, 1847. See below. French original, Copenhagen, 1755-56. See below.
> This work is a translation from the French by Bishop Percy, editor of *Reliques of Ancient English Poetry*. It contributed to the nourishment of romantic longings for the distant in time and place, and continued the interest in Norse mythology and literature of which Gray's "Runic Poems" are the finest expression in the literature of the day. Mallet was tutor to Christian VII of Denmark. During his residence in that country he was engaged by Frederick II to write a history of Denmark in French. The above work was intended as a prefatory volume to the History, but it has merit as an independent work.

> 1847 MALLET, PAUL HENRY. Mallet's Northern Antiquities; or, an Historical Account of the Manners, Customs, Religions and Laws, Maritime Expeditions and Discoveries, Language and Literature of the Ancient Scandinavians. Translated by Bishop Percy. New edition, revised by I. A. Blackwell. 8vo. Bohn's Library. London.
>
> > This work is considerably enlarged with a translation of the Prose Edda from the original old Norse text, with notes. To this is added an abstract of the Eyrbyggja Saga, by Sir Walter Scott.

1755-56 MALLET, PAUL HENRI. Introduction à l'histoire du Danemarck où l'on traite de la religion, des moeurs, des lois, et des usages des anciens Danois. (Part II.) Monuments de la mythologie et de la poesie de Celtes, et particulièrement des anciens Scandinaves. 2 parts. Copenhagen.

1772   MARSHALL, JOSEPH. For travels in Denmark and Sweden in 1768, see under CONTINENTAL EUROPE.

WHITELOCK, BULSTRODE. A Journal of the Swedish Embassy in 1653 and 1654 from the Commonwealth of England, Scotland, and Ireland, with Appendix of Original Papers. 2 vols. 4to. London.

> This was published by Charles Morton from the original manuscript. It was revised and reprinted by Henry Reeves, 2 vols., 8vo, London, 1855. See also *Memoirs, Biographical and Historical*, by R. H. Whitelock, London, 1860.
> Whitelock, the English Ambassador to Sweden, 1653-54, was appointed to many commissions during the Protectorate and served on all kinds of committees. Sweden was then at the height of its power. The pictures he gives us of its great personalities—Christina, Oxenstierna, and others, his conversations with Cromwell, are all highly interesting and of permanent value. The book has also been translated into Swedish.—From D.N.B. By modernising the spelling in his edition of 1855, Henry Reeves destroyed the original flavor of the work.—Sotheran.

1773   Letters from an English Gentleman during his Travels through Denmark. London.

OROSIUS. The Anglo-Saxon Version from the Historian Orosius by Alfred the Great. This together with an English Translation from the Old English by Daines Barrington. 8vo. London.

> Also in Hakluyt's *Principal Voyages,* said to be by Dr. Caius. Not regarded as accurate and considered to be of little value.—Pinkerton XVII.
> Among the men whom King Alfred gathered around him in the cause of learning were the Norseman Ohthere and the Dane Wulfstan, whose voyages to the White Sea and the region of Archangel and to the eastern part of the Baltic respectively were used by the great king in his translation of Orosius' *General History*. The discoveries of these men enabled him to rectify the geography of the Germanic, Baltic, and Northern regions. The title of Orosius' work was *Historiae adversum Paganos.* It was suggested to him by St. Augustine, and was the first attempt to write the history of the world as a history of God guiding humanity. Nearly 200 MSS. are extant. Alfred's version is a free, abridged translation. The Old English text with the Latin original was edited by Henry Sweet in 1883. Daines Barrington's eighteenth century version is evidence of the growing interest the age was manifesting in Old English language and literature.

1775   WRAXALL, NATHANIEL. A Tour through some of the Northern Parts of Europe, particularly Copenhagen, Stockholm, and Petersburgh, in a Series of Letters. Map. 8vo. London.

> 3rd edit., corrected, London, 1776.
> Wraxall covered a distance of 2000 miles around the Baltic Sea in five months' time. He was a tireless traveller. See under date 1800, WEST EUROPE.

1777 WILLIAMS, JOHN. For a generalized description of Denmark and Sweden, see under CONTINENTAL EUROPE.

1780 BANKS, JOSEPH (and Others). Letters on Iceland. See under Uno von Troil this date below.

COXE, WILLIAM. An Account of the Prisons and Hospitals in Russia, Sweden, and Denmark. With occasional Remarks on the different Modes of Punishments in those Countries. 8vo. London.

TROIL, UNO VON. Letters on Iceland: containing Observations on the Civil, Literary, Ecclesiastical, and Natural History; Antiquities, Volcanoes, Basaltes, Hot Springs; Customs, Dress, Manners of the Inhabitants, . . . Made during a Voyage undertaken in the Year 1772, by Joseph Banks, Esq., P.R.S., assisted by Dr. Solander, F.R.S., Dr. J. Lind, F.R.S., Dr. Uno von Troil, and several other Literary and Ingenious Gentlemen. . . . Map and 1 plate. 8vo. London.

> 2nd edit., London, 1780; the whole revised and corrected by E. Mendes da Costa, with map, Dublin, 1780; this again, London, 1783. In Pinkerton I, 621-734, with additions. Swedish original, Upsala, 1777. See below.
> According to Pinkerton, the most valuable version of these letters is the French translation by Lindholm, Paris, 1781, for which the Swedish original was revised by von Troil, and to which he added notes from the English and German editions. Banks and Solander will be remembered as members of Cook's first expedition to the South Seas.

> 1808-1814 TROIL, UNO VON. Letters on Iceland, . . . to which are added, the Letters of Dr. Ihre and Dr. Bad to the Author, concerning the Edda, and the Elephantiasis of Iceland; also Prof. Borgman's curious Observations and Chemical Examination of the Lava and other Substances produced on the Island. In Pinkerton I, 621-734

> 1777 TROIL, UNO VON. Bref rörende en Resa til Island in aaren 1772. Upsala.

1782 SHERIDAN, T. R. A Full and Genuine Account of the Revolution in the Kingdom of Sweden . . . to which is added Facts concerning the Extent, Power, Government, Religion, Literature, and Manners of the Swedish Nation. Folding maps and plate (view of Stockholm). 8vo. London.

1784 COXE ,WILLIAM. Travels into Poland, Russia, Sweden, and Denmark, with Historical Relations. Maps, plans, portraits, and other engravings. 2 vols. 4to. London.

> Reprinted in 5 vols., London, 1787-1791; again, London, 1792. Sections on Sweden and Denmark reprinted in Pinkerton VI, 293-372. Translated into French, Geneva, 1786. See below and also this date under EAST EUROPE.

1786   (In French.)   Voyage en Pologne, Russie, Suède, Dannemarc, . . . Traduit de l'anglais par P. H. Mallet. Map, plans, and portraits. 2 vols. 4to. Geneva.

1789   CONSETT, MATTHEW. A Tour through Sweden, Swedish Lapland, Finland, and Denmark; in a Series of Letters. Engravings. 4to. London.

> Translated into German, Nürnberg, 1790.
> Consett accompanied Sir H. G. Liddell, Bart., and Mr. Bowes on this trip. Lowndes considers it to be a hasty tour containing, however, many amusing observations, anecdotes, and little descriptive sketches.

1790   A Voyage in Sweden, containing the State of its Population, Commerce, Finances, with several particulars concerning the History of Denmark, by a Dutch Officer. Translated into English by W. Radcliffe (with additions of particulars concerning the life of Count Struensee). London.

> French original, the Hague, 1789. See below.
> These travels contain an accurate and interesting account of Sweden.—Pinkerton XVII.

> 1789 Voyage en Suède; contenant un état de sa population, de son commerce, des ces finances, avec quelques particularités concernant l'histoire du Dannemarck, par un Officier Hollandais. The Hague.

1792   SWINTON, ANDREW. Travels into Norway, Denmark, and Russia, 1788-1791, with Vocabulary. Dublin.

> Translated into French, Paris, 1798. See below.
> This work contains a variety of amusing information, written in rather a flippant style. There is an Appendix of words common to the Scotch, Icelanders, and Danes.—Lowndes.

> 1798 (In French.) Voyage en Norvège, en Dannemarck et en Russie. Traduit par P. F. Henry. 2 vols. Paris.

1796   Letters from Scandinavia, on the Past and Present State of the Northern Nations of Europe. 2 vols. 8vo. London.

> A valuable and authentic work.—Lowndes.

WOLLSTONECRAFT, MARY. Letters written during a short Residence in Sweden, Norway and Denmark. 8vo. London.

> This is by the famous author of the *Vindication of the Rights of Women,* later to become the wife of William Godwin. "She appears to have been grossly irreligious, indelicate and dissolute."—London Gentleman's Magazine, June, 1836. Quoted by Bookseller.

1800   A Journey through Sweden. London.

> So cited by Pinkerton XVII.

·ADDENDA

1802 ACERBI, JOSEPH. Travels through Sweden, Finland and Lapland, to the North Cape, in the years 1798 and 1799. Folding map and engraved plates (natural history plates in color). 2 vols. 4to. London.

> Translated into German, Berlin, 1803; into French, 3 vols., Paris, 1804; into Dutch, 4 vols., Haarlem, 1804-06.
> The accounts of Finland, which has been little visited by travellers, and the additional information respecting Lapland contained in this work, bestow a great value on it.—Pinkerton XVII.

1805 OLAFSEN and POVELSEN. Travels in Iceland 1800-01. Voyages and Travels. A Collection II.

> So cited in Chavanne.

1808-1814 EHRENMALM, ARWID. The Travels of Arwid Ehrenmalm into the Western Nordland and the Lapland Province of Asehle, or Aughermanland, in the Month of June, 1741. Translated from the *Histoire Générale des Voyages,* XXV, 464 ff. In Pinkerton I, 337-375.

FORTIA, M. Travels in Sweden. Translated from the French *Voyage de deux Francais en Allemagne, Danemarck, Suède, Russie, et Pologne fait en 1790-92* (Paris, 1796). In Pinkerton VI, 373-569.

KERGUELEN-TREMAREC, IVES JOSEPH DE. For his voyage along the coasts of Norway see his *Relation of a Voyage in the North Sea, under* ARCTIC REGIONS.

LEEMS, KNUD. An Account of the Laplanders of Finmark, their Language, Manners and Religion. By Knud Leems, Professor of the Laplandic, with the Notes of Gunner, Bishop of Drontheim, and a Treatise by Jessen, on the Pagan Religion of the Finns and Laplanders. Originally in Danish and Latin, Copenhagen, 1767. New translated into English. In Pinkerton I, 376-490.

> Danish original, Copenhagen, 1767. See below.

> 1767 LEEMS, KNUD. Beskrivelse oefwer Finmarkens Lapper. 4to. Copenhagen.

MAUPERTUIS, PIERRE-LOUIS MOREAU DE. Memoir read before the Royal Academy of Sciences, Nov. 13, 1737, on the Measure of a Degree of the Meridian at the Polar Circle. With his Journey to the Polar Circle and his Journey to the Extremity of Lapland for the purpose of finding an ancient Monument. Newly translated. In Pinkerton I, 251-258.

> French original, Paris, 1738. See below.
> The other half of this project was the measurement of a degree of the meridian in the equatorial region, which was carried out in La Condamine's Voyage (see under 1747, SOUTH AMERICA). In company with Maupertuis were Outhier (see below), Clairault, Camus, and Monnier, assisted by the Swedish astronomer Celsius.

1738 MAUPERTUIS, PIERRE-LOUIS MOREAU DE. Sur la figure de la Terre. 12mo. Paris.

OUTHIER, REGNAULD (Abbé). Journal of a Voyage to the North in the Years 1736 and 1737. Newly translated from the original. In Pinkerton I, 259-321.

> French original, Paris, 1744. See below.
> This is the same voyage as that reported on by Maupertuis.

1744 OUTHIER, REGNAULD (Abbé). Journal d'un voyage au Nord en 1736-37, par M. Outhier, prêtre du diocèse de Besancon. Illus. 4to. Paris.

1811 LINNAEUS, CARL. Lachesis Lapponica; or A Tour in Lapland, now first published from the original Manuscript Journal of the celebrated Linnaeus; by James Edward Smith. Proof portrait of Linnaeus and various cuts in the text. 2 vols. in 1. 8vo. London.

> An important and interesting work on Lapland and parts of Norway and Sweden.—Maggs, No. 499. This famous botanist was himself the instigator of a large number of scientific voyages.

VII

East Europe

1568-69 TURBERVILLE, GEORGE. Certaine Letters in Verse. Written by Master George Turberuile, out of Moscouia, which went as Secretare thither with Master Tho. Randolph, her Maisties Embassadour to the Emperor, 1568, to certain friends of his in London, describing the manners of the Country and People. London.

> Referred to in vol. 10, Hakluyt Society, 1851. See under this date, ADDENDA.

1591 FLETCHER, GILES. Of the Russe Common Wealth. Or Maner of Gouernement by the Russe Emperour . . . with the manners, and fashions of the people of that Countrey, . . . 8vo. London.

> Reprinted in Hakluyt, 1599; in Purchas, 1625; 18mo, London, 1643. Edited for the Hakluyt Society, London, 1857. See below.
> This, the first edition, is very rare. The dedication to the Queen is omitted in subsequent reprints. From it we learn that Fletcher, who had been sent on a special embassy to Russia in 1588, prepared his notes during his sojourn in that country, and whiled away the time on the return journey by putting them into the above shape. He had to endure many indignities from the Russian authorities and, although he obtained several concessions for English merchants, he expressed his bad opinion of Russia so strongly that the Eastland merchants were alarmed. They accordingly petitioned Lord Burghley, and the book was suppressed. It was so much esteemed, however, that with the omission of several passages it was reprinted in Hakluyt and Purchas.—From Quaritch.

> 1857 Russia at the Close of the Sixteenth Century, Comprising the Treatise, "The Russe Commonwealth" by Dr. Giles Fletcher, and the Travels of Sir Jerome Horsey, Knt., now for the first time printed entire from his own MS. Edited by Sir Edward Augustus Bond, K.C.B., Principal Librarian of the Brit. Mus. Hak. Soc., ser. I, vol. 20. London.

1602 A Lamentable report of the miserable State of Liuonia or Lyffeland concerninge great Dearth and famine by reason of the Warres there. With newes of the Ouerthrowe of the Turkes by the Persians this yere 1602. London.

> So entered in the *Stationers' Register.*

1605 SMITH, SIR THOMAS. Sir Thomas Smithes Voiage and Entertainment in Russia. With the tragicall ends of two Emperors and one Empresse . . . And the miraculous preseruation of the now raigning Emperor, esteemed dead for 18. yeares . . . 4to. London.

> Very rare. The author is unknown. From reading it one would suppose that he was one of Sir Thomas Smith's suite, but in the address to the reader he says: "But I taking the truth from the mouths of diuers gentlemen that went in the Iourney, and having som good notes bestowed upon me in writing, wrought them into this body, because neither thou shouldst be abused with false reports, nor the Voyage receiue slaunder." He was evidently a man well acquainted with

the literary London of his time, for he mentions Sir Philip Sidney, Fulke Greville, and Ben Jonson ("our Lawreat worthy Beniamen") by name; and there is an allusion to the play of *Hamlet,* suggested by the supposed sudden poisoning of the Czar Ivan.—Quaritch. Smith was apparently much interested in trade and discovery.

1662 OLEARIUS, ADAM. For his travels in Russia see his *Voyages and Travels of the Ambassadors,* under CENTRAL ASIA.

1669 HOWARD, CHARLES (First Earl of Carlisle). The Earl of Carlisle's Relation of three Embassies from his Majesty Charles II to the Duke of Muscovy, the King of Sweden, and the King of Denmark, in 1663 and 1664. 8vo. London.

> Translated into French, Rouen and Amsterdam, 1669-1670. See below.
> This was written by an attendant on the Embassies; and published with his Lordship's approbation.—Pinkerton XVII.

> 1669-1670 (In French.) Relation des trois ambassades de M. le comte (Ch. Howard) de Carlisle de la part de Charles II, roy de la Grande-Bretagne, vers le grand duc de Moscovie, le roy de Suède et le roy de Danemark, de 1663-65, avec une description de la Moscovie. Traduit par Guy Miège. 2nd edition (made on that of Rouen). 12mo. Amsterdam.

1671 COLLINS, SAMUEL. The Present State of Russia, in a Letter to a Friend at London; written by an Eminent Person residing at the Great Tzars Court at Mosco for the space of nine years. Copperplates, including a portrait of Czar Alexei Michailovitch. 12mo. London.

> Translated into French, Paris, 1679. See below.
> This is a very entertaining account of life in the Russian court, . . . Dorman Newman, the original publisher, according to his own statement, received the manuscript from "a gentleman that attended upon the learned Dr. Collins all the time of his being with the emperor of Russia."—D.N.B., quoted by Sotheran. Collins was physician to the Czar of Russia.

> 1679 (In French.) Relation de la Russie, par un Anglais qui a été neuf ans à la cour du grand Czar. Avec figures. Paris.

>> The name of the author of this work is catalogued as Antoine Desbarres. But the wording of the title suggests that it is evidently a translation of Collins' work.

1672 CHEVALIER, PIERRE. A Discourse of the Original, Countrey, Manners, Government and Religion of the Cossacks, with another of the Procopian Tartars. And the History of the Wars of the Cossacks against Poland. (Translated from the French by Edward Browne.) 8vo. London.

> The translator was a son of Sir Thomas Browne and a traveller himself. See Browne under 1673, CONTINENTAL EUROPE.

1682 MILTON, JOHN. A Brief History of Muscovia; and of other less known Countries lying Eastward of Russia, as far as Cathay. Gathered from the Writings of several Eye Witnesses. By John Milton, before he lost his Sight. London.

1689 BOUVET, J. (Father). The Present Condition of the Muscovite Empire till the Year 1689. 8vo. London.

1697 The Ancient and Present State of Poland drawn out of their best Historians. London.

1698 CONNOR, BERNARD. The History of Poland, in several Letters to Persons of Quality; giving an Account of the ancient, and present, State of that Kingdom, Historical, Geographical, Physical, Political, and Ecclesiastical, viz., Its Origin and Extent, with a Description of its Towns and Provinces; the Succession and remarkable Actions of all its Kings, . . . the Election, Power, and Coronation of the King; the Diet and Form of Government. The Privileges of the Gentry; their Religion, Learning, Language, Customs, Habit, Manners, Riches, Trade, and military Affairs; together with the state of Physick and natural Knowledge: . . . With sculptures, and a new Map after the best Geographers; with several Letters relating to Physick . . . 2 vols. 8vo. London.

> Reprinted in part in Harris II, 508-515.
> Connor lived for some time in Poland as physician to King John Sobieski.

CRULL, JODOCUS. The Antient and Present State of Muscovy. 8vo. London.

DE HAUTEVILLE, ——. An Account of Poland; containing a Geographical Description of the Country; the Manners of the Inhabitants, and the Wars they have been engaged in; the Constitution of that Government, . . . with a brief History of the Tartars. . . . To which is added, A Chronology of the Polish Kings. . . . The whole comprehending whatsoever is curious and worthy of remark in the former and present State of Poland. London.

> De Hauteville is a pseudonym for Gaspars de Tende, "who resided about 25 Years in that Kingdom."

An Historical Account of Russia; containing the Customs and Manners of the People, and a Description of the vast Dominions subject to His Imperial Majesty the Czar of Muscovia. 8vo. London.

LUDOLF, H. W.   Curious Observations concerning the Products of Russia. 12mo. London.

> This account is found added to Adam Brand's *Journal of the Embassy from their Majesties John and Peter Alexievitz, Emperors of Muscovy.* See Brand this date under FAR EAST.

1699   ALLISON, THOMAS.   An Account of a Voyage from Archangel in 1697; also, Remarkable Observations of the Climate, Country and Inhabitants. 2 charts. 8vo. London.

> Reprinted in Pinkerton I, 491-521.
> This voyage extended from Archangel to the neighborhood of the North Cape.

NEUVILLE, FOY DE LA.   An Account of Muscovey, as it was in the Year 1689, in which the Troubles that Hapned in that Empire, from the present Czar Peter's Election to the Throne to his being firmly settled in it, are particularly related. With a Character of Him and his People. 8vo. London.

> This is an interesting personal account of the primitive conditions then prevailing in Russia, and of the early years of the Czar Peter the Great before he left on his European tour and introduced reforms into Russia.—Sotheran. The author lived at Moscow at the time of his writing his report.

1701   BLOMBERG, —— DE.   An Account of Livonia, with a Relation of the Rise, Progress, and Decay of the Marian Teutonick Order, the Revolutions that have happen'd there, Account of the Dukedoms of Courland, Semigallia, and Provinces of Pilten; to which is added the Author's Journey from Livonia to Holland in 1698, sent in Letters to his Friend in London. Frontispiece. 8vo. London.

1703   RUDBECK, OLOF.   For Livonia and its Wars see under NORTH EUROPE.

1706   MARTINIERE, PIERRE MARTIN DE LA.   For an account of the Czar of Russia and his court see his *Travels into the Northern Countries,* under 1674 (the 1706 edition), NORTH EUROPE.

1716   PERRY, JOHN (Captain).   The State of Russia, under the present Czar. In Relation to the several great and remarkable Things he has done . . . particularly those Works on which the Author was employ'd with the Reasons of his quitting the Czar's Service after having been Fourteen Years in that Countrey. . . . Also an Account of those Tartars, and other People who border on the Eastern and extreme Northern Parts of the Czar's Dominions, their Religion and Manner of Life: to which is annexed, a more accurate Map of the Czar's Dominion than has hitherto been extant. Folding map by Moll. 8vo. London.

"This ingenious officer and mechanic" was engaged by the Russian Ambassador, at a salary of 300 pounds a year, to superintend in particular a communication then making between the Volga and the Don. In an introduction to this work Perry gives an account of the many disappointments he experienced during fourteen years of residence in Russia, which he was finally forced to quit without receiving his expected remuneration. Of the country itself, and of the various plans of the Czar for its improvement, a pleasing account is given.—From Nichols, *Literary Anecdotes.*

1717 SOUTH, —— (Dr.). Travels into Poland with the Earl of Rochester, in the year 1674. London.

This work is referred to in Hearne's *Remains.*

1720 LE BRUN, CORNELIUS. For his travels in Russia see his *Voyage to the Levant,* under CENTRAL ASIA.

1722-23 WEBER, F. C. The Present State of Russia, being an Account of the Government of that Country, Civil and Ecclesiastical, . . . being the Journal of a Foreign Minister who resided in Russia at that Time, with a Description of Petersburg and Cronstot, and other Pieces relating to the Affairs of Russia, translated from the High Dutch. Maps. 2 vols. 8vo. London.

This work contains also Lange and Le Brun, *Travels through Russia to China and Siberia.* See Lange this date under FAR EAST.

1729 CONSETT, T. The Present State and Regulations of the Church of Russia, established by the late Tsar's Royal Edict; also a Collection of several Tracts relating to Fleets, Expeditions to Derbent, . . . translated from the Originals in the Slavonian and Russian Languages, with an accurate map of the Caspian Sea. 2 vols. in 1. 8vo. London.

1732 BEAUPLAN, GUILLAUME LEVASSEUR, SIEUR DE. A Description of Ukraine, Containing several Provinces of the Kingdom of Poland, Lying between the Confines of Muscovy, and the Borders of Transylvania. Together with their Customs, Manner of Life, and how they manage their Wars. (Translated from the French.) In Churchill I, 515-551.

Abstract in Harris II, 516-520. French original, Paris, 1660. See below.
The author served 17 years in the Ukraine as engineer to the King of Poland. He gives interesting pictures of the ways of life among the Cossacks and Tartars. He states that the Crimean Tartars do not open their eyes for several days after they are born. The period of his stay in the country was in the middle of the 17th century.

1660 BEAUPLAN, GUILLAUME LEVASSEUR DE. Description de l'Ukraine, qui sont plusieurs provinces du royaume de Pologne contenuas depuis les confins de la Moscovie jusques aux limites de la Transylvanie, ensemble les moeurs, facon de vivre et de la faire le guerre. 4to. Paris.

MOTRAYE, AUBRY DE LA. Travels in several Provinces of ducal and royal Prussia, Russia, and Poland. The Hague, London, and Dublin.

So cited in Pinkerton XVII. For Motraye's general travels through Europe, Asia, and Africa see under 1723, GENERAL TRAVELS AND DESCRIPTIONS.

1734 A Particular Description of the City of Dantzick, its Fortifications, Extent, Trade, Government, Religion, . . . with many other remarkable Curiosities. By an English Merchant, lately resident there. 8vo. London.

1736-38 STRAHLENBURG, PHILIP JOHANN VON. Historico-Geographical Description of the North and Eastern Parts of Europe and Asia, but more particularly of Russia, Siberia and great Tartary, translated from the original German into English. Maps and plates. 2 vols. 4to. London.

An edition in 1 vol. is listed under 1738. German original, Stockholm and Leipzig, 1730. See below.
The author was a Swede who had fallen prisoner to the Russians after the defeat of Charles XII. The name he bore first was Philipp Johann Tabbert; he later adopted the name listed above after he had been ennobled upon his return to Sweden. Together with the Prussian naturalist Messerschmidt, he explored the lower basins of the Obi and Yenesei river systems. His map of Northern Asia for a long time served as the chief guide to this region.

1730 STRAHLENBURG, PHILIP JOHANN VON. Das Nord- und Oestliche Theil von Europa und Asia, insoweit solches das ganze Russische Reich mit Siberien und der grossen Tartarey in sich begreiffet. Copperplates. 2 vols. Stockholm.

1739 JUSTICE, ELIZABETH. A Voyage to Russia: Describing the Laws, Manners and Customs, of that Great Empire, as govern'd, at this present, by the Excellent Princess, the Czarina. Shewing The Beauty of Her Palace, the Grandeur of Her Courtiers, the Forms of Building at *Petersburgh,* and other Places: With several Entertaining Adventures, that happened in the Passage by Sea, and Land. . . . To which is added, Translated from the Spanish, A Curious Account of the Relicks, which are exhibited in the Cathedral of Oviedo, A City of Spain. Numerous woodcuts. 8vo. London.

Another edition, London, 1746.

1742 SPILMAN, JAMES. For his travels in Russia see his *Journey through Russia into Persia,* under CENTRAL ASIA.

1744-48 For an account of the Russians, Poles, Circassians, and Cossacks see *A Voyage to the North* this date under NORTH EUROPE.

1745 A Description of Moscovy: Containing I, Its ancient and modern State, Situation, Extent, Latitude, Division into Provinces, . . . II. Its Cities and Towns, Fortification, and Manner of Building; the first Discovery made by the English, . . . III. Their Religion, Marriages, Obedience of the Women to their Husbands, their Diet, . . . IV. The Government of the Provinces, . . . V. Their Military Affairs, . . . VI. Strange Fish, Beasts, Fowl, and other Rarities of Moscovy. VII. The Succession of the Royal House of Moscovy, . . . In Osborne I, 239-250.

1745-47 JENKINSON, ANTHONY. For his travels in Russia see *The Voyages and Travels of Anthony Jenkinson from Russia to Boghar,* under CENTRAL ASIA.

1753 HANWAY, JONAS. For his voyage down the Volga see his *An Historical Account of the British Trade over the Caspian Sea,* under CENTRAL ASIA.

1758 WHITWORTH, LORD CHARLES. An Account of Russia as it was in the Year 1710. 8vo. London.

> The introduction was written by Horace Walpole and the work printed at the Strawberry Hill Press. The author served as Minister at the courts of Poland and St. Petersburg.

1763 BELL, JOHN (of Auchtermony). For his travels in Russia see his *Travels from St. Petersburgh in Russia to several Parts of Asia,* under CENTRAL ASIA.

1764 Anecdotes russes ou Lettres d'un officer Allemand à un gentilhomme Livonien, écrites de Petersbourg en 1762, tems du regne et du detronement de Pierre III, . . . et publiés par C.F.S. de la Marche. 8vo. Londres.

1770 CHAPPE D'AUTEROCHE, JEAN (Abbé). For an account of the manners and customs of the Russians see his *Journey into Siberia,* under SIBERIA.

COOK, JOHN (M. D.). Voyages and Travels through the Russian Empire, Tartary, and part of Persia (made in 1739 and 1750). 2 vols. 8vo. Edinburgh.

MANSTEIN, CHRISTOPH HERMANN VON (General). Memoirs of Russia, Historical, Political, and Military, 1727-1744, a period Comprehending many Remarkable Events, in particular the Wars of Russia with Turkey and Sweden, . . . the State of the Military, Marine, Commerce, . . . Translated from the original Manuscript. Maps and plans. 4to. London.

> 2nd edit., corrected and improved, London, 1773.
> A work of authority. The recommendatory advertisement was written by David Hume.—Lowndes. C'est un morceau d'histoire aussi précieux par la sincérité de l'écrivain, temoin des faits qu'il raconte, qu'intéressant par rapport aux faits eux-mêmes.—*Biog, Gén.,* quoted by Sotheran.

1772 BRUCE, PETER HENRY. For an account of his travels in Russia see his *Memoirs of Peter Henry Bruce,* under GENERAL TRAVELS AND DESCRIPTIONS.

1773 LIND, JOHN. Letters concerning the Present State of Poland. 8vo. London.

> The author was tutor to Prince Stanislaus Poniatowski, and was appointed governor of an institution for the education of four hundred cadets. He returned to England in 1773.—D.N.B.

MARSHALL, JOHN. For his travels through Russia and Poland see his *Travels through Holland, Germany, Russia, Sweden, Poland,* under CONTINENTAL EUROPE.

1775 VIGOR, (Mrs.) WILLIAM. Letters from a Lady who resided many years in Russia, to her Friend in England; with Historical Notes. 8vo. London.

> The writer, whose third husband was William Vigor, was first married to Thomas Ward, Esq., consul-general of Russia in 1731. Her second husband was Claudius Rondeau, Esq., resident of that court. There she wrote these highly interesting and entertaining letters, which were published by Dodsley. Her account of the court of Russia is extremely curious, and the secret history of it quite new; and nowhere else, perhaps, so exactly pictured.—From Nichols, *Literary Anecdotes.*

WRAXALL, NATHANIEL. For an account of St. Petersburg see his *Tour through some of the Northern Parts of Europe,* under NORTH EUROPE.

1778 KING, JOHN GLEN. A Letter to the Right Rev. the Lord Bishop of Durham; containing some Observations on the Climate of Russia and the Northern Countries. London.

> The author was chaplain to the English Factory at St. Petersburg.

1780 COXE, WILLIAM. See his *Account of the Prisons and Hospitals in Russia, Sweden, and Denmark,* under NORTH EUROPE.

RICHARD, JOHN. A Tour from London to Petersburg and Moscow, and Return to London by the way of Curland, Poland, Germany, and Holland. London.

> Another edition, 12mo, Dublin, 1781.

1780-83 GEORGI, ——. Russia: or, A Complete Historical Account of all the Nations, which compose that extensive Nation. (Translated from the German.) 4 vols. 8vo. London.

> Vols. 1-3 appeared in 1780; vol. 4 in 1783. German original, Frankfurt, 1777. See below. See also Tooke under 1799 below.
> The translator, Rev. William Tooke, was for many years chaplain to the English Factory in Russia.

> 1777 GEORGI, ——. Merkwürdigkeiten verschiedener unbekannter Völker des russischen Reiches. Ein Auszug auf den Bemerkungen desselben. Frankfurt.

1784 COXE, WILLIAM. For his travels in Poland and Russia see his *Travels into Poland, Russia, Sweden, and Denmark,* under NORTH EUROPE. The sections dealing with Russia are reprinted from the 1802 edition in Pinkerton VI, 570-913.

RANDOLPH, ——. For Russia see his *Observations on the Present State of Denmark, Russia, and Switzerland,* under CONTINENTAL EUROPE..

RICHARDSON, WILLIAM. Anecdotes of the Russian Empire in a Series of Letters written from St. Petersburgh. 8vo. London.

1789 CRAVEN, LADY ELIZABETH (Margravine Anspach). A Journey through the Crimea to Constantinople in a Series of Letters written in the Year 1786. Map and plates. 4to. London.

> Reprinted, Dublin, 1789. A modern edition, London, 1914. Translated into French, London and Paris, 1789. See below.
> Lady Craven is said to have been the first woman that descended into the

grotto of Antiparos. "She has, I fear, been *infinitamente* indiscreet, but what is that to you or me?"—Horace Walpole, quoted. She was the author as well of several dramas which were produced at Drury Lane and Covent Garden theaters.

1914   CRAVEN, LADY ELIZABETH. The Beautiful Lady Craven, the Original Memoirs of Elizabeth Baroness Craven, afterwards Margravine of Anspach and Bayreuth and Princess Berkeley of the Holy Roman Empire (1750-1828), edited with notes and biographical and historical introduction, containing much unpublished matter, by A. M. Broadley and Lewis Melville. Portraits. 2 vols. 8vo. London.

    1789   (In French.) Voyage en Crimée et à Constantinople, en 1786. Traduit de l'anglois par Guedon de Berchère. Map and 6 plates. 8vo. London and Paris.

1792   PLESCHEEF, F.   A Survey of the Russian Empire, translated, with Additions, by James Smirnove. Folding map and large colored plates. 8vo. London.

SWINTON, ANDREW. For his travels in Russia see his *Travels in Norway, Denmark, and Russia,* under NORTH EUROPE.

1794   CHANTREAU, P. N.   Philosophical, political and literary Travels in Russia, 1788. Translated from the French. 2 vols. 8vo. Perth.

    Another edition, London, 1794. French original, Paris, 1794. See below. Replete with curious and original information.—Lowndes.

    1794   CHANTREAU, P. N. Voyage philosophique, politique, et literaire fait en Russie dans les années 1788 et 1789: ouvrage dans le lequel on trouve avec beaucoup d'anecdotes, tout ce qu'il y a de plus intéressant, et de vrai sur les moeurs des Russes, leur population, leurs opinions, religieuses, leurs prejugés, leurs usages, leurs institutions politiques, leurs forces de terre et de mer, et le progres qu'ils ont faits dans les sciences: traduit du Hollandais, avec des augmentations considérables. 2 vols. 8vo. London.

        A great part of this pretended translation from the Dutch is merely copied from Coxe.—Pinkerton XVII.

1795   JONES, STEPHEN.   The History of Poland, from its Origin as a Nation to 1795, with its Geography and Government, and Customs of its Inhabitants. Map. 8vo. London.

1799   TOOKE, WILLIAM (Rev.).   A View of the Russian Empire during the Reign of Catherine II, and to 1798: Manufactures, Commerce, . . . Map. 3 vols. 8vo. London.

    2nd edit., 3 vols., 8vo, London, 1800. This last edition translated into French. Paris, 1801.

1800 GUTHRIE, MARY. A Tour performed in the years 1795 and 1796, through Tauridia or Crimea, and all the other Countries on the North Shore of the Euxine, ceded to Russia by the Peace of Kaidnarga and Jaffy. Map and engravings. 2 vols. London.

MASSON, CHARLES F. P. Secret Memoirs of the Court of Petersburg, particularly towards the End of the Reign of Catherine II, and the Commencement of that of Paul I. 2 vols. 8vo. London.

ADDENDA

1802-03 PALLAS, PETER SIMON. Travels through the Southern Provinces of the Russian Empire, in the years 1793 and 1794. Translated from the German of P. S. Pallas. 25 full paged colored plates, 14 colored vignettes, and 3 maps. 2 vols. 4to. London.

> German original, Leipzig, 1799-1801. See below.
> These travels of Professor Pallas into the Crimea and to the Caucasus are less confined to scientific objects and therefore are more generally interesting than his former work.—Pinkerton XVII. Pallas was one of the savants chosen by the St. Petersburg Academy to carry on the work of examining the resources of the far distant parts of the Russian Empire. He left St. Petersburg in 1768 and spent full six years investigating various districts of Siberia—the Urals, the Caspian, Tobolsk, Lake Baikal, the Lower Volga, etc. His reports on the geology, fauna and flora are of great scientific value.

> 1799-1801 PALLAS, PETER SIMON. Bemerkungen auf einer Reise in der südlichen Statthalterschaften der Russischen Reiche, 1793-94. Plates and maps. 2 vols. 4to. Leipzig.

1851-52 HERBERSTEIN, BARON SIGISMUND VON. Notes upon Russia, being a Translation from the earliest Account of that Country, entitled Rerum Muscoviticarum Commentarii, by the Baron Sigismund von Herberstein, Ambassador from the Court of Germany to the Grand Prince Vasiley Ivanovich, in the years 1517 and 1526. Translated, with Notes and Introduction, by Richard Henry Major, F.S.A., Keeper of Maps, Brit. Mus., Sec. R.G.S. 2 illus. 2 vols. Hak. Soc., ser. I, vols. 10 and 12. London.

1854 HAMEL, JOHN (Dr.). England and Russia compared: comprising the Voyages of John Tradescant the Elder, Sir Hugh Willoughby, Richard Chancellor, Nelson, and others to the White Sea. Translated by J. S. Leigh. Portrait and plates. 8vo. London.

1857 HORSEY, SIR JEROME. Travels of Sir Jerome Horsey, Knt. See Hakluyt Society edition this date, under Fletcher, 1591, above.

1886 CHANCELLOR, RICHARD. Chancellor's Voyage to Muscovy; being
Clement Adam's Anglorum Navigatio ad Muscovitas taken from Res-
publica Muscoviae (1630). To which is added a very rare tract De
Moneta Russica, Elzevir, 1630, with English Translation by J. M'Crin-
dle. 8vo. London.

> Chancellor was "pilot-major" of an expedition of three ships, which was sent
> out, under the instigation of Sebastian Cabot, to make discoveries and trade con-
> nections with the East by way of the Northeast Passage. The preparations were
> most elaborate; the ships sailed in May, 1553, amid salutes, salvoes and prayers.
> But the attempt turned out most disastrously, for two ships were lost in the ice
> and the crews starved to death. Among those who never returned was Sir Hugh
> Willoughby. Chancellor's ship managed to make the mouth of the River Dvina.
> He and his men finally reached Moscow and became the instruments for the de-
> velopment of trade between England and Russia. Chancellor was drowned on a
> later voyage. His account is the earliest first-hand report of Russia to English-
> men. The story is well told in Hakluyt.

1919 BADDELEY, JOHN F. See his *Russia, Mongolia, and China,* under
FAR EAST.

VIII

Near East

1511 GUYLFORDE, SIR RICHARD. This is the begynnynge of the Pyl-
grymage of Sir R. Guylforde Knyght. 4to. London.

> Printed by Pynson. A modern reprint issued by the Camden Society, London,
> 1851. See below.
> This was a pilgrimage made to Palestine in 1506 at a time when such expedi-
> tions were generally in decline. The latest journey of this kind is believed to be
> Sir Richard Torkington's to Jerusalem in 1517. See below under 1883. The author
> of the above work, whose name is unknown, was chaplain to Sir Richard. The
> latter died in Palestine and was buried on Mount Sion.

> 1851 GUYLFORDE, SIR RICHARD. The Pylgrymage of Sir Richard Guly-
> ford (sic) to the Holy Land A.D. 1506, from a copy believed to be
> unique from the press of Richard Pynson. Edited by Sir Henry Ellis.
> 4to. Camden Society, vol. 51. London.

1529 HAYTON (HATTO, HAITON, HAYCON, AITHON), NIC. Here
begynneth a lytell cronycle translated and imprinted at the cost and
charge of Richard Pynson, by the commandement of the right high
and mighty Prince Edward duke of Buckingham, yerle of Gloucestre,
Staffarde and of Northampton. Fol. London.

> It is stated in the colophon that this chronicle was translated out of French.
> According to Ibrahim-Hilmy the English version was made in 1520 by Alexander
> Barclay, the translator of Brant's *Narrenschiff*. The date of the supposed French
> original is given as 1300 and that of the first Latin translation as 1307. The preface
> to the Latin edition of 1529 says that this work was composed by Haytho, adding,
> "Which I, Nicholas Salconi, by command of Pope Clement V, first wrote in the
> French language . . . as the said Friar Haytho dictated it to me, without note
> or copy, and from the French I have translated it into Latin in the year 1307."
> Various editions in French and Latin followed, of which that in French of 1529
> is cited below. Hayton, whose name is variously spelled, was king of Little
> Armenia or Cilicia from 1224 to 1269. He became a monk and abdicated, lived
> on good terms with the Mongol Princes Batu, Kuyuk, Hulugu, and Mangu, and
> travelled extensively in central and western Asia. He finally came to Poictiers in
> France, where at the request of Pope Clement V, he dictated in French the his-
> tory of the East from the time of the appearance of the Mongols down to his
> day. Part VI tells of Syria and the towns on the sea coast, Egypt, the desert
> of Mt. Sinai, Arabia, and the Holy Land. See Hak. Soc. ser. I, vol. 7, and the
> *Encyclopedia Britannica*, 14th edit.

> 1529 HAYTON, NICHOLAS. L'Hystoire merveilleuse, plaisante et recreative
> du grand empereur de Tartarie, seigneur des Tartares, nommé le grand
> Can. Pour Jehan S. Denys (à la fin) ; Cy finist l'histoire merveilleuse
> . . . Fol. Paris.

> > Ce livre est une traduction du Latin, fait en 1351, par Jehan de
> > Longdit, né à Ypres, moine de l'abbaye de Saint-Bertin, à Saint-Omer,
> > de l'ordre de S. Benoit.—Bookseller's Note.

1542 The Order of the Greate Turckes Courte, of the Menne of Warre, and
of all hys Conquestes, with the Summe of Mahumetes Doctrine. Translated out of Frenche (by Richard Grafton). 16mo. London.

> Grafton was the King's Printer. Together with Edward Whitchurch he
> issued in 1539 the "Great Bible," which was suppressed in Paris but ordered to
> be purchased by every parish in England. He also put out the Prayer Book of 1549.

1577 NEWTON, THOMAS (the Elder). A Notable Historie of the Saracens. Briefly and faithfully descrybing the originall beginning, Continuance and Successe as well of the Saracens, as also of Turkes, Souldans, Mamalukes, Assassines, Tartarians and Sophians. With a Discourse of their Affaires and Actes from the Byrthe of Mahomet their first pee-uish Prophet and Founder for 700 yeeres space. Whereunto is an-nexed a Compendious Chronycle . . . from . . . Mahomets time tyll . . . 1575. Drawn out of Augustine Curio and sundry other Authours by Thomas Newton. 4to. London.

> Apparently this is the only edition of this rare book. It is dedicated to Charles Howard, Baron Howard of Effingham, in an address which plainly shows that Newton had no love for "Saracens, Turks, and other Reprobates of the same stamp and Lyuery."—Quaritch.

VARTHEMA, LUDOVICO DI. For his travels in Arabia, Syria, and other parts of the Near East, see under EAST INDIES.

> In this part of his travels he visited Alexandria and Cairo, Damascus, Me-dina, Mecca, Yemen, and Aden. He was the first European to visit Mecca with a caravan and write an account of the journey.—Bookseller's Note.

1584 SAUNDERS, THOMAS. A most lamentable Voyage made into Tur-kye. Compiled by Thomas Saunders, Captyve. London.

> Cited in the *Stationers' Register*.

1585 NICHOLAY, NICHOLAS DE, SIEUR D'ARFEVILLE. The Naviga-tions, Peregrinations and Voyages, made into Turkie by Nicholas Nich-olay, . . . conteining sundry singularities which the Author hath there seene and observed; Deuided into foure Bookes, With threescore figures, naturally set forth as well of men as women . . . with divers faire and memorable Histories, happened in our Time. Translated out of French by T. Washington, the younger. 60 woodcut figures. 4to. London.

> 2nd edit. of the French original, Anvers, 1576. See below. Reprinted in Os-borne I, 553-708 (pp. 631-698 not in this volume, but their lack may be due to an error in pagination).
> The occasion of this voyage was an embassy from the French king to the Sultan at Constantinople. Part I relates the adventures on the voyage thither, in which occurs the usual set-to with the Barbary corsairs; the other books de-scribe the cities, countries, states, natives, dress, etc., of the inhabitants of the Turk-ish empire. The woodcuts, which have been attributed to Titian, are said to give a graphic idea of the inhabitants of the East.

> 1576 NICOLAY, NICOLAS DE. Les Navigations, Périgrinations et voyages, faicts en la Turquie, par Nicholas de Nicolay, Daulphinoys seigneur d'Arfeuille, valet de chambre et géographe ordinaire du roy, . . . 4to. Anvers.

1587   The Policy of the Turkish Empire.   4to.   London.

Pollard cites this as of the date 1590.

1590   WEBBE, EDWARD.   The rare and most vvonderful thinges which Edward Webbe an Englishman borne, hath seene and passed in his trouble-
some trauailes, in the Citties of Ierusalem, Dammasko, Bethelem and
Galely; and in the Landes of Iewrie, Egipt, Grecia, Russia, and in the
Landes of Prester Iohn. Wherein is set foorth his extreame slauerie
sustained many yeres togither, in the Gallies and wars of the great
Turk against the Landes of Persia, Tartaria, Spaine and Portugall,
with the manner of his releasement, and comming into Englande in
May last.   4to.   London.

Reprinted, London, 1590; 2nd edit., enlarged and corrected by the author,
London, 1590. Another edition, London, 1600. Reprinted in Arber *Reprints,* London, 1895.
One closes Webbe's account doubting whether to wonder more at the brutal-
ities of man or at the indomitableness of his spirit.

1594   GLEMHAM, EDWARD.   Newes from the Levant Seas. Discribing the
. . . voyage of E. Glemham, Esquire, made . . . 1593 into the Levant
Seas. By H. R.   4to.   London.

The name is spelled Glenham by Parks. The author afterwards made a
second voyage. His adventures are described in black letter pamphlets, which
were reprinted in 1829 and 1866.—D.N.B.

1595   ADRICHOMIUS, CHRISTIANUS.   A Brief Description of Hierusalem
and of the Suburbs thereof, as it florished in the time of Christ, with
a Short Commentarie, translated out of Latin, by T. Tymme.   Map.
4to.   London.

The Estate of the Christians living under the Subjection of the Turke;
also the Warres between the Christians and the Turke, 1592-93.   4to.
London.

MINADOI, GIOVANNI TOMMASO.   The History of the Warres betweene Turkes and the Persians. Translated by A. Hartwell.   4to.
London. See under EAST INDIES.

1598   BUNTYNGE, HENRY.   Itinerarium Sacrae Scripturae that is a Voyage of the whole Travelles of the Holy Scriptures devided into twoo
Bookes. In the ffirst is conteyned all the Travelles of the Patryarches,
Judges, Kinges, Prophets, prynces, . . . collected into Dutche myles
together with the Landes, Townes, Waters, Hilles, and Vallies that

are mencioned and sett downe with the Scriptures, with the Hebrewe and Greeke Names translated into Inglishe, with diverse brief Allegories and Spirituall. The seconde concerneth the newe Testament wherein is Declared howe the Virgin Marye, Joseph, The Three Wise Men, that came out of the East, our Saviour Jhesus Christ and all the Apostles have travailed, collected out of the most credible and worthiest wryters, calculated in a geometricall proporcion. . . .

> So cited in the *Stationers' Register.* Another edition, 4to, London, 1619; still later, 8vo, London, 1636. German original, Magdeburg, 1585. See below.

1619   BÜNTING, HEINRICH. Itinerarium totius Sacrae Scripturae; or the Travels of the Holy Patriarchs, Prophets, Judges, Kings, our Saviour Christ, and his Apostles, as they are related in the Old and New Testaments. With Descriptions of the Towns and Places to which they travelled. . . . Also a short Treatise of the Weights, Monies and Measures mentioned in the Scriptures. . . . Collected out of the works of H. Bünting, and done into English (with a preface) by R. B. 4to. London.

1585   BÜNTING, HEINRICH. Itinerarium Sacrae Scripturae: das ist, Ein Reisebuch über die gänzte heilige Schrifft, in zwey Bücher getheilet . . . Auffs new widerumb übersehen und vermehret, Sampt angehengten Büchlin, De Monetis et mensuris . . . Mit einer Vorrede . . . M. Chemnitii. 3 Parts. Fol. Magdeburg.

1600   The Mahumetane or Turkish Historie containing three bookes; translated from the French by R. Carr. 4to. London.

1603   KNOLLES, RICHARD.   The Generall Historie of the Turkes, from the first beginning of that Nation to the rising of the Ottoman Familie, with all the notable Expeditions of the Christian Princes against them together with the Lives and Conquests of the Ottoman Kings and Emperours; faithfullie collected out of the best Histories, both auntient and moderne, and digested into one continual Historie until this present yeare 1603. Fol. London.

> Successive editions as follows: 1610, 1621, 1631, 1638, 1687, and 1700, all folios, London, some with continuations. See below, and also Rycaut, under 1666 below.
> This book long continued to hold high repute, by reason of the fact that it was written in excellent prose and opened a new field to the English student.— Cam. Hist. IV, v. It was lavishly praised by Dr. Johnson in his *Rambler* No. 122. Byron said it was an early favorite of his and that it influenced him greatly in his desire to visit the Levant. He admitted that it "gave perhaps the oriental colouring which is observed in my poetry."

1631   KNOLLES, RICHARD. The Generall Historie of the Turkes, . . . With a new Continuation, from ye yeare of our Lord 1621, vnto the yeare 1629, faithfully collected. Numerous portraits. Fol. London.

1638   KNOLLES, RICHARD. The Generall Historie . . . With a new Continuation, from the yeare of our Lord 1629 unto the yeare 1638. . . . Fol. London.

1687-1700 KNOLLES, RICHARD, and RYCAUT, SIR PAUL. The Turkish History, from the Original of that Nation to the growth of the Otto-man Empire, with the Lives and Conquests of their Princes and Emper-ors, by R. Knolles. With a Continuation to 1687, whereunto is added the Present State of the Ottoman Empire by Sir P. Rycaut. 2 vols. 1687. Together with the third volume: The History of the Turks, be-ginning with the Last Troubles in Hungary, with the sieges of Vienna, and Buda, and all the Battles both by Sea and Land, between the Christians and the Turks, until the Peace, 1700. 3 vols. Fol. London.

1603 TIMBERLAKE, HENRY. A Trve and straunge Discourse of the Tra-uailes of two English Pilgrimes: what Admirable Accidents befell them in their Iourney towards Jerusalem, Gaza, Grand Cairo, Alexan-dria, and other Places. 4to. London.

> By 1629 this work had run through six editions. Further issues followed in 1631, 1683, 1692, 1744 (*Harl Misc.*), and 1759. This item, together with *The Trav-els of Fourteen Englishmen* (1672), and other matter, printed in one volume, 1683. See this date below.
> The two pilgrims were Timberlake himself and John Burrell.

1608 MUNDAY, ANTHONY. The admirable Deliverance of 266 Christians by J. Reynard (*i. e.,* J. Fox), Englishman, from the Turkes. 4to. London.

> Pollard cites Munday as the author of this anonymous work.

1609 BIDDULPH, WILLIAM. The Travels of certaine Englishmen into Africa, Asia, Troy, Bythinia, Thracia, and the Blacke Sea, and into Syria, Cilicia, Pisidia, Mesopotamia, Damascus, Canaan, Galile, Sam-aria, Judea, Palestina . . . to the Red Sea, and to sundry other places. Begunne in 1600 and by some of them finished this yeere 1608. Edited by Theoph. Lavender, B.L. 4to. London.

> Another edition, 4to, London, 1612, with the change "and by some of them finished in the yeere 1611, and others not yet returned." Reprinted in Osborne I, 761-830, with the statement, "Begun in the Year of Jubilee, 1600, and by some of them finished in the Year 1611. Very profitable for the help of Travellers." Here the opening sentence runs, "The Travels of Four Englishmen and a Preach-er." This is likewise the opening phrase of the title of the 1612 edition.
> These five travellers were Wm. Biddulph, preacher to the company of Eng-lish merchants at Aleppo, Jeffery Kirbie, merchant, John Elkin, gentleman, Ed-rrond Abbot, merchant, Jasper Tyon, jeweler, all men of learning, "sound judg-ment and veracity." The book consists of four letters, two from Constantinople, one from Aleppo, and one from Jerusalem. The subject matter is the history, antiquities, buildings, voyages, country-side, manners, customs, government, etc., of the places visited.

1611 CARTWRIGHT, JOHN. The Preachers Travels. Wherein is set downe a true Iournall to the Confines of the East Indies, through the great Countreyes of Syria, Mesopotamia, Armenia, Media, Hircania, and Parthia. With the Authors returne by the way of Persia . . . and Arabia . . . also a true Relation of Sir Anthony Sherley's Entertainment in the Court of the King of Persia. Description of the Port in the Persian Gulf commodious for the East-India Merchants of England. Rehearsal of some gross absurdities in the Turkish Alcoran. Penned by I. C. sometime student in Madgalen Colledge in Oxford. 4to. London.

> Reprinted in Osborne I, 709-752.
> This is one of the most interesting and valuable accounts of old English travels in the East that we possess. The occasional Christian comments on Mohammedan darkness are not accompanied by any prejudices in the narrative, which is especially circumstantial concerning the Persian Empire, then very powerful. It is not clear why the title runs, "The Preachers Travels," as Cartwright, who went to Ispahan, and his companion John Mildenab, who travelled on to Lahore, seem to have been merchants. See Collier, *Rarest Books in the English Language,* vol. I.—Robinson, No. 19.

1615 SANDYS, GEORGE. A Relation of a Journey begun An. Dom. 1610. Foure Bookes. Containing a Description of the Turkish Empire, of Egypt, of the Holy Land, of the Remote Parts of Italy and Ilands adioyning. Plates. Fol. London.

> 2nd edit., fol., London, 1621; other editions 1627, 1632, 1652, 1658, 1670, 1672, some with slightly different titles; see below. Translated into Dutch, Amsterdam, 1653; into German, Frankfurt, 1669; into Latin, London, 1645. See below.
> Sandys was equally well known for his translation of Ovid's *Metamorphoses,* 1621-26. He also travelled to Virginia and became treasurer to the Virginia Company.

> 1670 SANDYS, GEORGE. Travels: containing an History of the Original of the Turkish Empire; their Laws, Government, Policy, Military Force, Courts of Justice and Commerce, the Mahometan Religion, and Ceremonies; a Description of Constantinople; the Grand Seignor's Seraglio, and his manner of living; also of Greece, with the Religion and Customs of the Grecians of Egypt; the Antiquity, Hieroglyphicks, Rites, Customs, Discipline, and Religion of the Egyptians; a Voyage to the River Nilus, of Armenia, Grand Cairo, Rhodes, the Pyramides, Colossus; the former flourishing and present State of Alexandria; a Description of the Holy Land, . . . Italy described, and the Islands adjoining, as Cyprus, Crete, Malta, the Aeolian Islands, of Rome, Venice, Naples, . . . and other Places of Note. 50 engraved maps and plates. London.

> 1653 (In Dutch.) Voyagien behelsende een Historie van de oorspronkelycke . . . Standt de Tirksen Rijks . . . als mede van Aegypten; d'Antiquiteyt . . . Costuymen . . . Religie der Aegyptenaren, enz. (Translated from the English by J. Glazemaker.) 4to. Amsterdam.

> 1669 (In German.) Reisen, inhaltende: die Historie von dem Stand des Türkischen Reiches, die Beschreibung von Constantinopel. Zugleich einer Reisebeschreibung des gelobten Landes. . . . Endlich eine Beschreibung Italiens. Copperplates. 12mo. Frankfurt.

1618 HAGA, CORNELIUS. A true Declaration of the Arrival of Cornelius Haga, Ambassador for the General States of the United Netherlands at Constantinople. . . . Translated from the Dutch. 4to. London.

> Reprinted in *Harl. Misc.,* London, 1744.

1628 ROBSON, CHARLES. Newes from Aleppo. A Letter . . . Containing many remarkable Occurences observed by him in his Journey hither. 4to. London.

1633 MARSH, HENRY. A New Survey of the Turkish Empire and Government . . . with their Laws, Religion and Customs. . . . London.

> Another edition, 12mo, London. 1663; followed by a 2nd part, 12mo, London, 1664. See below.

> 1663 MARSH, HENRY. A New Survey of the Turkish Empire and Government, in a brief History deduced to the present Time, with their Laws, Religion and Customs, also an Account of the Siege of Neuhausel. Portrait of Mahomet IV, and plate of slaves ploughing. 12mo. London.

> 1664 MARSH, HENRY. The Second Part of the New Survey of the Turkish Empire, History and Government compleated. Being an Exact and absolute Discovery of what is worthy of Knowledge, or any way satisfactory to Curiosity· in that mighty Nation. With several Brass Pieces lively expressing the most eminent Personages concerned in this subject. 2 engraved portraits and 2 other plates. 12mo. London.

> > The Epistle to the Reader is signed H. M. (Henry Marsh), for whom the work was printed. This does not mean, however, that Marsh was not the author of the volume.

1635 BAUDIER, MICHEL. The History of the Imperiall Estate of the Grand Seigneurs: Their Habitations, Lives, Titles, Qualities, Exercises, Workes, Revenues, Habits, Discent, Ceremonies, Magnificence, Judgements, Officers, Favourites, Religion, Power, Government and Tyranny. Translated out of French by E(dward) G(rimstone), S(ergeant at) A(rms). 4to. London.

> Bound up with this work is, The History of the Court of the King of China. Written in French by the Seigneur Michael Baudier of Languedoc. Translated by E. G. French original, Paris, 1626. See below.

> 1626 BAUDIER, MICHEL. Histoire générale du sérail et de la cour de l'empereur des Turcs. Paris.

1636 BLOUNT, HENRY. A Voyage in the Levant, being a brief Relation of a Journey from England to Great Cairo, through Venice, Dalmatia, Croatia, Slavonia, Bosnia, Hungary, Macedonia, Thessaly, Thrace, the Isle of Rhodes, and Egypt; with Observations on the Present State of the Turks, and other Subjects of that Empire. 4to. London.

> There were eight editions of this work between 1636 and 1671; reprinted in Osborne I, 511-552, and in Pinkerton X, 222-271. Translated into German, Helmstadt, 1687; into Dutch, Leyden, 1707. See below.
> The worth of this work is variously estimated. Of little value or authority. —Lowndes. The whole is very concise, and without any curious observations, or any notable description; . . . the language mean, and not all of it to be relied upon. —Churchill, *Introduction*. The voyage at once established Blount's fame as an author and traveller. Altogether it occupied over eleven months, he having journied

above 6000 miles.—Maggs, No. 519. Blount sailed from Venice for the Levant, May 7, 1634. The power of the Turkish empire at that period excited tremendous interest in the lands and peoples subject to the Sultan. The author was held in high esteem by his countrymen for his native talents and good judgment.

1687   (In German.)   Morgenländische Reise durch Dalmatien, Sklavonien, Thrazien und Aegypten . . . in welcher die Grundfeste des Türkischen Staates genausichtig untersuchet wird, erstlich von ihm in Englisch verzeichnet, nun aber in die Reine hochteutsche Sprache übersetzt von G.C.S.A.T. Nebst einem Bedenken über diese Betrachtungen, worinnen zugleich die Ursachen des jetztigen Unfals dieses mächtigen Reiche gesucht werden. 4to. Helmstadt.

1707   (In Dutch.)   A Dutch version of this work is included in Pieter van der Aa's *Naaheurige Versameling der Zee en Land-Reysen zedert het jaar 1616 tot 1634.* Leyden.

1648   BENDISH, SIR THOMAS.   Newes from Turkie, or, A True Relation of the Passages of the Right honourable Sir Tho. Bendish, Baronet, Lord Ambassadour with the Grand Signeur at Constantinople, his Entertainment and Reception there. Also a true Discourse of the unjust Proceedings of Sir Sackville Crow, former Ambassador, and Sir Sackvilles Imprisonment, and in his Returne, his wretched betraying the Captain of the Ship, and some English Merchants, at Alicant in Spain, to the Inquisition; Lastly his Comitment to the Tower of London, where he now is. 4to. London.

   The tract throws some interesting sidelights on the state of English trade in the Near East at that period.—Robinson, No. 48.

1650   FULLER, THOMAS.   A Pisgah-Sight of Palestine and the Confines thereof, with the History of the Old and New Testament acted thereon. Folding maps and plates. Fol. London.

      Another edition, London, 1662.
      A curious book, containing many things relating to Jewish antiquities, and to the manners and customs of the People.—Bookseller's Note.

      GREAVES, JOHN.   Descriptio Chorasmiae et Mawarolnohrae (i. e., regionum extra Oxum), Arabici cum versione J. Gravii. 4to. London.

         Reprinted in *Geographiae veteris Scriptores Graeci Minores,* 1698-1712, Oxford. See Hudson under 1698 below.
         Greaves was a mathematician, oriental traveller, and collector of gems, coins, oriental manuscripts, and the author of various scientific works.

      LEO MODENA.   The History of the Rites, Customes, and Manner of Life, of the Present Jews throughout the World. Written in Italian, by Leo Modena, a Rabbine of Venice. Translated into English by Edmund Chilmead. 12mo. London.

WITHERS, ROBERT. A Description of the Grand Signor's Seraglio, or Turkish Emperour's Court. 12mo. London.

> The title of this work is almost an exact translation of a French work attributed to Michel Baudier. See Baudier under 1635 above.
> Withers lived for some years in Turkey, and through the favor of the English Ambassador he was able to procure admission to the Seraglio.—Maggs, No. 519.

1651 GREGORII ABUL-PHARAGII. Specimen Historiae Arabum, seu de origine et Moribus Narratio; Arab. et. Lat. in Linguam Latinam conversa, et notis illustrata, opere Edward Pococke. Oxford.

> So cited by Pinkerton XVII.

1656 MACHIAVEZ, NICOLAS. Political Reflections upon the Government of the Turks. The King of Sweden's Descent into Germany . . . 12mo. London.

1661 ABU-ISMAEL. Carmen Tograi, una cum versione Latina et Notis, Opera Edv. Pocockii. Accessit Tractatus de Prosodia Arabica. 12mo. Oxford.

> Translated into English, Cambridge, 1758. See below.

> 1758 ABU-ISMAEL. The Traveller; an Arabic Poem, intitled Tograi, written by Abu-Ismael; translated into Latin and published with Notes in 1661, by Edward Pocock, D.D. Now rendered into English in the same Iambic Measure as the Original; with some additional Notes to illustrate the Poem, by Leonard Chappelow, B.D. 4to. Cambridge.
>
> > Pococke was an oriental scholar of European fame. He collected many eastern manuscripts and edited numerous Hebrew and Arabic texts.

FINCH, HENEAGE (2nd Earl of Winchelsea). A Narrative of the Successe of his Embassy to Turkey. 4to London.

> Finch was Ambassador to Turkey from 1661 to 1669.

1665 VALLE, PIETRO DELLA. For an account of Arabia Deserta see his *Travels of Signor Pietro della Valle, noble Roman, into East India,* under EAST INDIA.

1666 PALMER, ROGER (Earl of Castlemaine). An Account of the Present War between the Venetians and Turks; with the State of Candia (in a Letter to the King, from Venice). Portrait, map and plans. 8vo. London.

> The Earl of Castlemaine was a linguist, mathematician and political pamphleteer, who was mixed up in a number of intrigues under Charles II, at Rome, and under William III, at home. He was indicted for treason in 1695, but was released without trial on condition of going overseas.—D.N.B.

RYCAUT, SIR PAUL. The History of the Present State of the Ottoman Empire, containing the Maxims of the Turkish Politie, the most
material Points of the Mahometan Religion, their Sects and Heresies,
their Convents and Religious Votaries, their Military Discipline, with
an exact Computation of their Forces by Land and Sea. Fol. London.

> Subsequent editions in 1668, 1670, 1675, 1680, 1682, 1686, and 1700, all London
> imprints. The last one listed is combined with Knolles, *The Turkish History;*
> see under Knolles, 1603, above. Translated into French, Rouen, 1677. See below.
> Rycaut, from his long residence and connexion with the Embassy, was well
> qualified to delineate Levantine customs. It is faithful but dull.—Dalrymple. This
> work is regarded as one of the best of its kind with respect to the religious and
> military state of Turkey. According to the D.N.B., it long proved a useful com-
> panion to Richard Knolles' *History,* while the writer's impartiality renders it of
> interest to the modern reader. It was quoted by Gibbon in his account of the rise
> of the Ottomans. The author was secretary to Heneage Finch, Earl of Winchelsea,
> during his embassy at Constantinople, and consul of the Levant Company at Smyr-
> na in 1668.

> 1687-1700 RYCAUT, SIR PAUL, and KNOLLES, RICHARD. The Turkish
> History, from the Original of that Nation, to the Growth of the Ot-
> toman Empire: with the Lives and Conquests of their Princes and
> Emperors, with a Continuation to 1687, and an Account of the Present
> State of the Ottoman Empire, 6th edit., 2 vols.; also The History of
> the Turks beginning with the year 1679, being a full relation of the Last
> Troubles in Hungary, the Sieges of Vienna and Buda, . . . until the End
> of the years 1698 and 1699, by Sir P. Rycaut; together 3 vols. Fol.
> London.

1670   A Description of Candia, in its Ancient and Modern State: with an Account of the Siege thereof, begun by the Ottoman Emperour, in the
Year 1666, continued in 1667 and 1668, and surrendered the latter end
of 1669. The most Part collected from private Letters, during the
Siege, sent by one in the Services of the Republique (of Venice). . . .
12mo. London.

A Relation of the Siege of Candia, etc. See under MILITARY EXPE-
DITIONS.

1671   BURBURY, JOHN. Relation of a Journey of the Right Honourable
My Lord Henry Howard, from London to Vienna, and thence to Con-
stantinople; in the Company of his Excellency Count Lesley . . . Coun-
cellour of State to his Imperial Majesty,'. . . and to the Grand Signior,
Sultan Mahomet Hau the Fourth. Written by John Burbury. 12mo.
London.

1672   A Journey to Jerusalem, or, A Relation of the Travels of Fourteen Englishmen, in the year 1669, from Scanderoon to Tripoly, Joppa, Ramab,
Jerusalem, Bethle(he)m, Jeric(h)o, the Dead Sea; and back again to

Aleppo. With an exact Account of all the remarkable Places and Things in their Journey. London.

> This work contains remarks on the antiquities, monuments, and memorable places mentioned in the Scriptures; on the Jewish nation, the Holy Land, the captivities of the Jews, the fate of the Ten Tribes, etc.

1673 BROWNE, EDWARD. For an account of his travels in northern Greece see his *Brief Account of Some Travels,* under CONTINENTAL EUROPE.

1674 SMITHII, THOMAE. Epistolae de Moribus et Institutis Turcarum; accessit brevis Constantinopoleos Notitia. Oxford.

> So cited by Pinkerton XVII. See Smith under 1678 below.

1675 ADDISON, LANCELOT. The Present State of the Jews; wherein is contained an Exact Account of their Customs, Secular and Religious . . . London.

> 3rd edition, 12mo, London, 1682. Relates particularly to those of Barbary.

1676 GUILLATIERE, M. DE LA. An Account of a late Voyage to Athens; containing the Estate, both Ancient and Modern, of that famous City, and of the present Empire of the Turks. The Life of the now Sultan Mahomet IV; with the Ministry of the Grand Vizier. Also the most remarkable Passages in the Turkish Camp at the Siege of Candia. . . . By Monsieur de la Guillatière. Now Englished. 12mo. London.

> This work is dated 1677 by Lowndes. French original, Paris, 1675.
> The aim of the author was to present the popular life of Greece as it was lived from day to day, intermixed with numerous anecdotes about the Turks.—Iorga, *Les Voyageurs Francais.*

1677 The History of the Grand Viziers, Mahomet and Achmet Coprogli, of the three last Grand Signors, their Sultans' chief Favourites; with the most sacred Intrigues of the Seraglio. Besides several other particulars of the Wars of Dalmatia, Transylvania, Hungary, Candia, and Poland. Englished by John Evelyn, Junior. 8vo. London.

1678 GEORGIRENES (Archbishop of Samos). Description of the State of Samos, Nicaria, Pathmos, and Mount Athos by . . . now living in London; translated from the vulgar Greek (by Henry Denton). 12mo. London.

> This prelate long resided as Archbishop at Samos and saw Nicaria as a dependance of his diocese, but being weary of that function, he retired to Patmos, where he remained for some time. Later he visited Mt. Athos. So that all he delivers of these places is as an eye-witness, and indeed the most particular account of them we have . . . The Preface to the Reader, it must be observed, is the translator's.—Churchill, *Introduction.*

SMITH, THOMAS. Remarks upon the Manners, Religion, and Government of the Turks; together with a Survey of the Seven Churches of Asia as they now lye in their Ruines, and Brief Description of Constantinople. 12mo. London.

> This may be a translation or English version of the Latin item cited under Smithii, 1674, above.

WHELER, GEORGE, and SPON, JACOB. A Journey into Greece by George Wheler, Esq., in company of Dr. Spon, of Lyons. In Six Books. Containing: I. A Voyage from Venice to Constantinople; II. An Account of Constantinople and the Adjacent Places; III. A Voyage through Lesser Asia; IV. A Voyage from Zant through several Parts of Greece to Athens; V. An Account of Athens; VI. Several Journies from Athens into Attica, Corinth, Boeotia, . . . Numerous maps and engravings. Fol. London.

> Subsequent editions: London, 1688; in Ray's Collection, 1693. Spon's account was published in French, Lyons, 1678. Wheler's work was translated into French, Amsterdam, 1689. See below.
> This was the first antiquarian expedition into those parts of which careful record has been kept. After the two parted company, Wheler continued his travels, directing his attention to other matters besides antiquarian, which had been the chief pursuit of Spon.

1689   (In French.) Voyage de Dalmatie, Grèce et du Levant, avec la description des coûtumes, des villes, rivières, ports de mer, et de ce que s'y trouve de plus remarquable. Traduit de l'anglois (de 1682). 2 vols. 12mo. Amsterdam.

1678   SPON, JACOB. Voyage de Dalmatie, du Grèce, et du Levant, fait aux années 1675 et 1676, par Jacob Spon et George Wheler; avec le portrait de l'Auteur, et plusieurs plans, gravures et médailles. 2 vols. Lyons.

1683   CAOURSIN, GULIELMUS, and AFENDY, RHODIGA. The History of the Turkish War with the Rhodians, Venetians, Egyptians, Persians, and other Nations. . . . Written by W. C. . . . and Rhodiga (Khodiga) Afendy. 8vo. London.

GRELOT, WILLIAM JOSEPH. A Late Voyage to Constantinople containing an exact Description of the Propontis and Hellespont, with the Dardanels, and what else is remarkable in those Seas; as also of the City of Constantinople, wherein is particularly described the Grand Seraglio and Chief Mosquees. Likewise an Account of the Ancient and Present State of the Greek Church with the Religion and Manner of Worship of the Turks, . . . Illustrated with maps and curious and exact Draughts of the Hellespont, Propontis, Seraglio and other chief Mosquees, . . . with the Several Postures of the Turks in Prayer Time in fourteen copperplates. The Like never done before. Published by

Command of the French King by Monsieur William Joseph Grelot. Made English by J. Philips. Engraved frontispiece of Mahomet IVth. 8vo. London.

> French original, Paris, 1680. See below.
> Grelot disguised himself as a Turk and thus attired travelled over the greater part of the Turkish Empire. He even pretended that he had been in Paris in the suite of Mustapha-Aga. Knowing the language of the Turks he was enabled to wander about the city of Constantinople as he pleased, to mingle with the inhabitants, and to make sketches of interesting objects. He did not gain admission to the Seraglio, for he affirmed that it would cost more than "the Empire of the Grand Signior." Anyway it cannot compare with the Tuilleries or Versailles or Fontainebleau. By judicious bribing he gained entrance to St. Sophia, of which he made sketches. The work has been reckoned to be one of the best books of travel.—From Iorga, *Les Voyageurs Francais.*

1680 GRELOT, WILLIAM JOSEPH. Relation nouvelle d'un voyage à Constantinople, enrichie de plans levéz par l'auteur sur les lieux, et des figures de tout ce qu'il a de plus remarquable dans cette ville. 12 plates. 4to. Paris.

> The original edition was much sought after on account of the accurate views made on the spot.

Historical and Political Observations upon the Present State of Turkey; describing the Policy, Religion, Manners, Military Discipline of the Turks; with an Account of the Battels, Sieges, and other remarkable Transactions which have hapned from the beginning of the Ottoman Empire to this present Grand Seignior. To which is added, His Life, and the material Occurences of his Reign; with the present State of Hungary, and the History of these Wars there. 12mo. London.

> This may be an edition of Rycaut. See under 1666 above.

The History of the Turks from the first Founders to the Year 1683. Portrait of the Sultan. 8vo. London.

> This may likewise be an edition of Rycaut.

The Present State of the German and Turkish Empires, with Reflections thereupon; as also some Reflections on the Interest of the Christian Princes; with Memoirs of the Siege of Vienna, by an eminent Officer in that City. With a true Account of the great Success of the Christian Forces in taking Barkan, Gran, . . . Also an historical preface of the Rise and Growth of the Turkish Empire. London.

Two Journies to Jerusalem: containing, I. A Strange Account of the Travels of two English Pilgrims, and what Accidents befel them in their Journey to Jerusalem, Grand Cairo, Alexandria, . . . With the Wonderful Manner of hatching thousands of Chickens at once in Ovens. II. The Travels of fourteen Englishmen in 1669, from Scanderoon to

Tripoly, Joppa, Ramah, Jerusalem, Bethlehem, Jericho, the River Jordan, the Lake of Sodom and Gommorrah; and back again to Aleppo. . . . To which is added, A Relation of the great Council of the Jews assembled in the plains of Ajayday in Hungary, 1650. By S(amuel) B(rett), an Englishman there present. . . . Beautified with Pictures. 8vo. London.

> Other editions, London, 1684 and 1692, with the addition: The Delusion of the Jews concerning a Messiah in 1668, . . . Collected by R. B. Thomas Hearne cites the title, *Two Journies to Jerusalem,* in a list of "Cheap Books," with the dates, 1683, 1685, 1692, 1730, 1738, 1759. See *Remains of Thomas Hearne,* vol. III, app. viii, 234-5.
> The first part of this work is by Timberlake. See under 1603 above. The second part is cited under 1672 above; the "Council of the Jews" by Samuel Brett; and the "Delusion" by Richard Burton.

1686 RANDOLPH, BERNARD. The Present State of the Morea, called anciently Peloponnesus: which hath been near Two Hundred Years under the Dominion of the Turks; and is now very much Depopulated. Together with a Description of the City of Athens, Islands of Zant, Strafades, and Serigo. 4to. London.

> 3rd edit., London, 1689.
> The work by Randolph cited under 1687 below, though printed a year later, is a companion volume to the above, thus making two volumes.—These two volumes contain an admirable account of the state of the country about the Aegean Sea, and are valuable for the light they throw on the Ottoman Empire in the early stages of its decadence.—D.N.B., quoted by Sotheran.

1687 CORONELLI, P. M. An Historical and Geographical Account of the Morea, Negropont, and the Maritime Places, as far as Thessalonica. . . . Written in Italian by P. M. Coronelli. . . . Englished by R. W., Gent. 42 maps and plates. 12mo. London.

RANDOLPH, BERNARD. The Present State of the Islands in the Archipelago (or Arches), Sea of Constantinople, and Gulph of Smyrna, with the Islands of Candia and Rhodes, with Index of the Longitude and Latitude of the Places in the New Map of Greece. Map and plates. 4to. London.

THEVENOT, JEAN. The Travels of Monsieur de Thevenot into the Levant. In Three Parts. Viz. into I. Turkey. II. Persia. III. The East Indies. Newly done out of French. . . . 3 vols. in I. Portrait and plates. Fol. London.

> The Near East portion of these travels are to be found in Harris II, 790-841. See below. French original, Paris, 1674.
> The author was of the same family as Melchizidec Thevenot, who published a large collection of Travels, Paris, 1663. The elder Thevenot travelled extensively in Europe but printed nothing about his journies. The younger Thevenot was

equally curious about seeing the sights and travelled much farther afield. He became particularly fascinated by the Orient through his acquaintance with the famous orientalist Herbelot whom he met in Rome. He left this city for the East May 1, 1655. As a traveller he was quite free from the prejudices of the day, and has left very interesting observations on the mentality of the Turks. He is said to have introduced coffee into France. See also under CENTRAL ASIA and 'EAST INDIES.

1744-48 THEVENOT, JEAN. The Voyages and Travels of the celebrated Mr. John Thevenot, from Italy to Constantinople, including very curious and extraordinary Descriptions of the several Places he touched at in his Passage; a most exact View of Constantinople, at the Time he visited it. Interspersed with a great variety of Historical and political Remarks, equally instructive and entertaining. Extracted from the last Edition of the Author's Travels, printed at Amsterdam, 1727. In Harris II, 790-822.

1744-48 THEVENOT, JEAN. An Account of several of the most remarkable Cities of Asia, of various Islands in the Archipelago, and of Things most observable in them, both with respect to their ancient and present Condition; with Remarks Historical, Physical and Geographical. Intermixed Accounts from Wheler and Lebrun. In Harris II, 822-841.

1688 DU VIGNAU, ——. A New Account of the Present Condition of the Turkish Affairs, with the Causes of the Decay of the Ottoman Power. Portrait of Soliman III. 12mo. London.

1689 HELIOGENES DEL EPY. For an account of part of Greece and Turkey see his *A Voyage into Tartary*, under CENTRAL ASIA.

OSBORNE, FRANCIS. Reflections on the Government of the Turks, ... In *Works*. 8vo. London.

1693 ALPINUS. Travels in Greece, Asia Minor, ... In Ray's Collection. London.

BELON, PIERRE. Travels in Greece, Asia Minor, ... In Ray's Collection. London.

French original, Paris, 1550. See below.
Belon was a French physician and an industrious herbalist who travelled extensively in the Near East. He was an accurate observer, and reported faithfully on the manners, the government, and particularly the natural history of the countries he visited. His remarks have generally been found reliable by subsequent travellers.

1550 BELON, PIERRE DU MANS. Les observations de plusieurs singularitéz et choses memorables, trouvées en Grèce, Asie, Judée, Egypte, Arabie, e. a. pays étranges, redigées, en trois livres. 8vo. Paris.

The edition published in 4to in 1558 is considered more desirable for its two large maps of Lemnos and Mount Sinai.

1693   RAUWOLF, LEONHART (Dr.).   Itinerary into the Eastern Countries, as Syria, Palestine, Armenia, Mesopotamia, . . . translated by Nicholas Staphorst.   In Ray's Collection II.

> German original, Augsburgh, 1581. See below.
> This account makes up vol. II of John Ray; *Travels through the Low Countries, Germany, Italy,* 1738 edition. See Ray under 1673, WEST EUROPE.

> 1581   RAUWOLF, LEONHARD.   Aigentliche Beschreibung der Reise, so er vor dieser Zeit gegen Aufgang in die Morgenländer, fürnemlich Syriam, Judaeam, Arabiam, Mesopotamiam, Babyloniam, Assyriam vollbracht.   4to.   Augsburgh.

VENNER, ——.   Travels in Greece, Asia Minor, . . . In Ray's Collection. London.

1694   BUSBECQ, OGIER GHISELIN DE.   Travels into Turkey: Containing the most accurate Account of the Turks and neighboring Nations, Their Manners, Customs, Religion, Superstition, Policy, Riches, Coin, . . . Translated from the Latin.   London.

> 2nd edit., London, 1744; 3rd edit., (translated from the original Latin), Glasgow, 1761. Modern editions: 2 vols., London, 1881; Oxford, 1927. See below. Latin original, 1633. The Latin edition contains the Baron's account of his embassy to France as well as to Turkey. Earlier editions, Antwerp (the first Letter), 1581; Paris, 1589 (complete four Letters).

> 1881   BUSBECQ, OGIER GHISELIN DE.   The Life and Letters of Ogier Ghiselin de Busbecq, Seigneur of Bousbecque, Knight, Imperial Ambassador, by C. T. Forster and F. H. Blackburne Daniell.   2 vols.   8vo. London.
>
> > This contains a bibliography of the various editions and translations.

> 1927   BUSBECQ, OGIER GHISELIN DE.   The Turkish Letters of Ogier Ghiselin de Busbecq, Imperial Ambassador at Constantinople 1554-1562. Newly translated from the Latin of the Elzevir Edition of 1633, by Edward Seymour Forster.   Illus. and maps.   8vo.   Oxford.

1695-97   HALIFAX, WILLIAM (Rev.).   A Relation of a Voyage from Aleppo to Palmyra in Syria; sent by the Rev. Wm. Halifax to Dr. Edw. Bernard (late) and by him communicated to Dr. Thomas Smith.   In *Philos. Trans. of the Royal Society,* XIX, 83-110; 129-160.   Edinburgh.

> Reprinted separately, London, 1705; and in *Misc. Curiosa,* London, 1708. See below.

> 1705   HALIFAX, WILLIAM.   Travels to Tadmor (Palmyra).   London.

> 1708   HALIFAX, WILLIAM (Rev.).   A Relation of a Voyage from Aleppo to Palmyra in Syria. . . . Also an Extract of the Journals of two several voyages of the English Merchants of the Factory of Aleppo to Tadmor, anciently call'd Palmyra.   In *Misc. Curiosa,* vol. III, 84-110, 129-160. London.

1696 DU MONT, SIEUR JEAN. A New Voyage to the Levant; containing an Account of the most Remarkable Curiosities in Germany, France, Malta and Turkey; with Historical Observations relating to the Present and Ancient State of those Countries. Done into English, and adorn'd with Figures. London.

> Another edition, London, 1702; 4th edit., London, 1705. French original, the Hague, 1699. See below.
> Du Mont was present at the reception of the new French Ambassador Chateauneuf, and witnessed the formal entrance of the Sultan. His account is richer in historical details of the day than in the relics of antiquity.—Iorga, *Les Voyageurs Français.*

1699 DU MONT, SIEUR JEAN. Voyage de M. Du Mont en France, en Italie, en Allemagne, à Malthe et en Turquie, contenant les recherches et observations curieuses qu'il a faites en tous ces païs, tant sur les moeurs, les coûtumes des peuples, leur différens gouvernements et leurs religions, que sur l'histoire ancienne et moderne, la philosophie ancienne et moderne, la philosophie et les monuments antiques. 4 vols. 12mo. The Hague.

SELLER, ABRAHAM. The Antiquities of Palmyra; containing the History of the City and its Emperors, from its Foundation to the present Time; with an Appendix, of critical Observations on the Manners, Religion, and Government of the Country, and a Commentary on the Inscriptions lately found there. 8vo. London.

> 2nd edit., 8vo, London, 1706.
> Far outdoing this work in thoroughness and importance is that of Robert Wood. See his *Ruins of Palmyra* under 1753 below.

1697 POTTER, JOHN. Archaeologiae Graecae, or the Antiquities of Greece. Plates. 8vo. London.

> A 2nd vol. appeared, London, 1698. Another edition, 2 vols., London, 1764.
> The work deals with the invention and different sorts of ships, marriage ceremonies, etc. The author became Archbishop of Canterbury in 1737; he was the editor of several Greek texts.

1698 DANDINI, GIROLAMO. A Voyage to Mount Libanus; wherein is an Account of the Customs, Manners, . . . of the Turks. Also a Description of Candia, Nicosia, Tripoly, Alexandretta, . . . with curious Remarks upon several Passages relating to the Turks and Maronites. Written originally in Italian. 8vo. London.

> Reprinted in Osborne I, 831-873; in Pinkerton X, 272-304. Italian original, Cesana, 1656. See below.
> The author was teaching philosophy at Perugia when he received word that he had been appointed (1586) papal nuncio by Clement VIII to the sect of Maronites living in the Mount Lebanon region of Syria. He was to investigate the charges of errors in belief and dogma attributed to them and to determine who should be sent to the college at Rome and what employment could be found for these on their return. Pinkerton regards the account of the Maronites to be the only valuable portion of the book.

1656 DANDINI, GIROLAMO. Missione apostolica al Patriarca a Maroniti del Monte Libano. Cesana.

1698 HUDSON, JOHN. Descriptio Peninsulae Arabiae. Printed with Descriptio Chorasmiae, in vol. III. of *Geographiae veteris Scriptores Graeci Minores.* 8vo. Oxford.

> Hudson was a classical scholar and editor of several Greek texts. He became Bodleian librarian in 1701. The editing of the *Geographiae* took him until 1712 to complete. See the same under GEOGRAPHY. See also Greaves, under 1650 above.

1699 ROBERTS, ——. Adventures among the Corsairs of the Levant; his Account of their Way of Living; Description of the Archipelago Islands, Taking of Scio, . . . Maps and draughts. In Hacke's Collection.

1701 SAVAGE, JOHN. The Turkish History, abridged from Knolles and Rycault. 2 vols. 8vo. London.

> See Rycaut unnder 1666 above.

VERYARD, ELLIS (M.D.). An Account of divers Choice Remarks, as well Geographical as Historical, Political, Mathematical, Physical and Moral; Taken in a Journey through the Low-Countries, France, Italy, and Part of Spain; with the Isles of Sicily and Malta. As also, A Voyage to the Levant: A Description of Candia, Egypt, the Red-Sea, the Deserts of Arabia, Mount-Horeb, and Mount-Sinai; the Coasts of Palestine, Syria, and Asia-Minor; the Hellespont, Propontis, and Constantinople; the Isles of the Carpathian, Egean, and Ionian Seas. Wherein, Their present State, Interest, Customs, Manners, and Religion; their Learning and Learned Men; with the most celebrated Pieces of Sculpture, Painting, . . . are more accurately set forth, than hath hitherto been done. With an Account of divers Sorts of Shell-like Bodies found at great Distances from the Seas; with Remarks thereon, in a Way to discover their Original. And what else occurr'd Remarkable in Thirteen Years Travels. Illustrated with divers figures. Fol. London.

1702 LE BRUN, CORNEILLE. A Voyage to the Levant, translated out of French into English by W. J. Map and plates. Fol. London.

> Later editions: 3 vols., London, 1720, where it is combined with his travels in Moscovy, Persia, and the East Indies; 2 vols., fol., London, 1737. French original, Delft, 1700. See below.
> The name of the author is also spelled Le Bruyn and Lebrun. His book is said to be one of the best illustrated works on the Levant; although Dalrymple, a traveller to the East in the late eighteenth century, denies that the views are accurate representations. The illustrators were two painters, one a Fleming, the other an Italian. These travels were begun in 1674.

> 1720 LE BRUYN, CORNEILLE. Voyage to the Levant and Travels into Moscovy, Persia, and the East Indies. Numerous plates. 3 vols. London.

700 LE BRUN, CORNEILLE. Voyage au Levant, c'est à dire dans les
principaux endroits de l'Asie mineure, dans les Isles de Chio, de
Rhodes, de Chypre, . . . de même que dans les plus considérables villes
d'Egypte, de Syrie et de la Terre Sainte. Numerous plates. Fol.
Delft.

> This French version is a translation from the Dutch. It bears the
> name of Lebrun.

1703 MAUNDRELL, HENRY. A Journey from Aleppo to Jerusalem, at
Easter, 1697, with Appendix. Plates. 8vo. Oxford.

> 3rd edit., with additions, 8vo, Oxford, 1714; again in 1721, 1732, 1740, 1749,
> Oxford; in Harris II, 841-861, and in Pinkerton X, 305-385. Translated into
> French, Utrecht, 1705, and into German and Dutch. See below. It was noticed
> in the *Journal des Scavans*, 1706, I, 306.
> Bishop Newton observes of the work and its author, "whom it is a pleasure
> to quote as well as to read, and whose Journal from Aleppo to Jerusalem, though
> a little book, is yet worth a folio, and is so accurately and ingeniously written, that
> it might serve as a model for all writers of travels."—Quoted by Maggs, No. 505.
> The antiquarian Hearne (*Remains* II, 59) refers to it as "a very good book,
> written in a good plain style, which shews the author to have been a clear-headed,
> rational man, and a very good scholar." Maundrell was so eager to travel that
> he seized the opportunity to become chaplain to the English Factory at Aleppo.
> He set out from that city with fourteen other English gentlemen, Feb. 26, 1697,
> to visit the Holy Land at the coming Easter, the ceremonies of which greatly
> interested him.

> 1714 MAUNDRELL, HENRY. A Journey from Aleppo to Jerusalem, at
> Easter, 1697. Third edition, with an Account of the Author's Journey
> to the Banks of the Euphrates at Beer, and to the Country of Mesopo-
> tamia. Folding plates and other illustrations. 8vo. London.

> 1744-48 MAUNDRELL, HENRY. A Journey from Aleppo to Jerusalem,
> containing a curious and accurate Description of the Holy Land and
> City, interspersed throughout with a Great Variety as well of Phil-
> ology, Physics, and Philosophy; as Historical and Critical Remarks. In
> Harris II, 841-861.

> 1705 (In French.) Voyage d'Alep à Jérusalem (1697) par Henry Maundrell,
> Membre du College d'Exeter et Chapelin de la Facture Anglois à
> Alep. Traduit de l'Anglois. 12mo. Utrecht.

1704 PITTS, JOSEPH. For a description of Mecca, Medina and Mahomet's
Tomb, see his *A Faithful Account of the Religion and Manners of the
Mahometans,* under AFRICA.

1707 DANIEL, SAMUEL. A Voyage to the Levant, giving an Account of
each Place, their Inhabitants, Language, Coins, Weights and Measures;
their Provisions and Prices, . . . In the *Monthly Misc.,* or *Memoirs for
the Curious,* May, 1707, London.

1708-1718 OCKLEY, SIMON. The Conquest of Syria, Persia, and Egypt, by the Saracens. 2 vols. London.

> 3rd edit., Cambridge, 1757. Translated into French, Paris, 1748. See below.
> The author was an orientalist and professor of Arabic at Cambridge. This history was the main source of the general notions of Mohammedan activities for generations.—D. N. B.

> 1757 OCKLEY, SIMON. The Conquest of Syria, Persia, and Egypt by the Saracens. To which is prefixed, An Account of the Arabians or Saracens, of the Life of Mahomet and the Mahometan Religion, by Dr. Long; with a plan of the Ca'aba or Temple of Mecca, from a MS. in the Bodleian Library. 2 vols. 8vo. Cambridge.

> 1748 (In French.) Histoire des Sarrazins et de leurs Conquêtes sous les onze premiers Califs, par Fr. Jault. 2 vols. 12mo. Paris.

1709 HILL, AARON. A Full and Just Account of the Present State of the Ottoman Empire in all its Branches of the Government, Policy, Religion, Customs and Way of Living of the Turks in General; faithfully related from serious Observations taken in many years' Travels through those Countries. Portrait and plates. Fol. London.

> Another edition, London, 1733. Noticed in the *Journal des Scavans,* 1710, I, 548.
> This poet and dramatist was also a traveller. He is better known for Pope's attacks on him and his counter-attacks, and the rather unusual amicable relationship existing between them later.

1714 RELAND, HADRIAN. Palaestina ex monumentis veteribus illustrata. Maps and plates. 2 vols. 8vo. London (?).

> The same work is also cited as having been printed at Utrecht, 1714.

1718 D'ARVIEUX LAURENT (Chevalier). Travels in Arabia the Desart; written by Himself, and Publish'd by Mr. De la Roque: Giving a very accurate and entertaining Account of the Religion, Rights, Customs, Diversions, . . . of the Bedouins, or Arabian Scenites. Undertaken by Order of the late French King. To which is added, A General Description of Arabia, by Sultan Ishmael Abulfeda, translated from the best MSS.; with Notes. Done into English by an Eminent Hand. 12mo. London.

> 2nd edit., London, 1723; again, 12mo, London, 1732. French original, Paris, 1717. See below.
> At the commencement of these travels in 1653, the author was not more than eighteen years old. He was subsequently charged with missions to the Porte and appointed consul to Aleppo, Tripoli, and other places in the Orient. According to Iorga, he gives a good description of Adrianople and Constantinople, of the Turkish army when engaged in warfare against Poland, and of the Sultan Mohammed, then thirty-three years old, towering high amid his jannisaries and spahis, with "his dark, very large eyes almost darting from his head." His residence in Barbary and among the Bedouin Arabs enabled him to give a reliable account of those regions and peoples. Dalrymple, however, with his usual depreciation, characterises his work as "multifarious and amusing but not infallible."

1718 D'ARVIEUX, LAURENT (Chevalier). Voyage fait par ordre du roy Louis XIV. dans la Palestine, vers le grand émir, chef des princes Arabes du Désert. . . . Avec la description générale de l'Arabie, faite par le Sultan Ismael Abulfeda, traduite en Francois avec des notes. Par Monsieur D. L. R. (De la Roque). 12mo. Paris.

TOURNEFORT, JOSEPH PITTON DE. A Voyage into the Levant: the State of the Islands, Constantinople, Armenia, Georgia, the Frontiers of Persia, . . . Numerous maps and engravings of views, costumes, plants, etc. With Life by Lauthier. 2 vols. 4to. London.

> Another edition in 3 vols., 8vo, London, 1741. French original, Paris, 1717. See below.
> Dalrymple discounts the praise given to this work with the remark, "His botanical discoveries and researches are justly commended, but the other descriptions are a mere collection from his predecessors." Tournefort's objectives are set forth in his opening sentence: "The Count de Pontchartrain, Secretary of State, to whose care the Academies are committed, and who is ever intent upon promoting the Sciences, moved his Majesty, towards the end of the year 1699, to send abroad into foreign Countries some Persons that were capable of making pertinent Observations, not only upon the Natural History, old and new Geography, of those parts, but likewise in relation to the Commerce, Religion, Manners of the different people inhabiting those." He took with him a physician and a painter, Aubriet, to enrich the collections of the king and those of the Academy. His rigid determination to stick closely to his scientific aims prevented him from noting many things that a more naive traveller would have described.

1717 TOURNEFORT, JOSEPH PITTON DE. Relation d'un voyage du Levant fait par ordre du Roy: contenant l'histoire ancienne et moderne de plusieurs Isles de l'Archipel, de Constantinople, des Côtes de la Mer Noire, de l'Arménie, de la Georgia, des Frontières de Perse et de l'Arménie, de la l'Asie Mineure, avec les Moeurs, le Commerce et la Religion des différens Peuples. Numerous illustrations, views, costumes, characters, and natural history, plans, etc. 2 vols. 4to. Paris.

1719 The History of the Turks. Maps and portraits. 4 vols. 8vo. London.

1721-25 MONTFAUCON, BERNARD DE. Antiquity explained, and represented in Sculptures. Translated into English by D. Humphreys. 5 vols. Supplement, 5 vols. 4to. London.

> French original, Paris, 1719-1724. See below.

1719-1724 MONTFAUCON, BERNARD DE. L'Antiquité expliquée et représentée en Figures. Plates. 15 vols. Fol. Paris.

1725 MOTRAYE, AUBRY DE LA. For an account of Turkey, Greece Crimea, Noghai Tartary, Circassia, see his *Travels through Europe, Asia, and into Part of Africa,* under GENERAL TRAVELS AND DESCRIPTIONS.

> Motraye's close association with the unfortunate Charles XII of Sweden, whom he met in 1714 at Bender, makes him an authority of the first rank on the Scandinavian king's sojourn in Turkey. The life of the miserable king of Hungary, Tokoly, whom Motraye sought out in Nicomedia, could be rewritten with the aid of this tireless reciter's account. Besides he was a good witness of all that went on in Turkish society at Constantinople and elsewhere.—From Iorga, *Les Voyageurs Français.*

SAINT-MAURE, C. DE. A New Journey through Greece, Egypt, Palestine, Italy, 1721-23, . . . by a French Officer. Translated from the French. 8vo. London.

1726 LA ROQUE, JEAN DE. A Voyage to Arabia the Happy, by the Eastern Ocean and the Streights of the Red Sea, perform'd by the French for the first Time, 1708-1710, with a Journey from Moka to the King of Yemen, 1711-13; also an Account of the Coffee-Tree, with an Historical Treatise of Coffee. Map and 3 folding copperplates of the coffee-plant. 12mo. London.

> Other editions: 8vo, London, 1732; 8vo, London, 1742, with added matter. French original, Paris, 1715. See below.
> The travels are particularly full respecting the history of coffee in Asia and Europe.—Lowndes.

> 1742 LA ROQUE, JEAN DE. A Voyage to Arabia Felix. . . . To which is added, An Account of the Captivity of Sir Henry Middleton at Mokha by the Turks, in 1612. 8vo. London.

> 1715 LA ROQUE, JEAN DE. Voyage de l'Arabe heureuse par l'Océan Oriental, et le Détroit de la Mer Rouge, 1708-1710. Avec la relation d'un voyage fait du Port de Moka à la cour de roy d'Yémen 1711-13. Un Mémoire concernant l'arbre et le fruit du Café. 3 plates and 1 map. Paris.

> Quaritch gives the date as 1716. There was another French edition printed at Amsterdam in 1716.

1729 GYLLIUS, PETRUS. The Antiquities of Constantinople. With a Description of its Situation, the Conveniences of its Port, its Public Buildings, the Statuary, Sculpture, Architecture, and other Curiosities of that City. With Cuts explaining the chief of them. In Four Books. Written originally in Latin by Petrus Gyllius, a Byzantine Historian. Now translated into English, and enlarged with an antient Description of the Wards of that City, as they stood in the Reigns of Arcadius and Honorius. With Pancirolus's Notes thereupon. To which is added, A Very curious Passage of Nicelas Choniat, relating to the Statues of that City, which were demolished by the Latins, when they took Constantinople, taken out of a MS. in the Bodleian Library; and an explanatory Index. 8vo. London.

> Latin original, Lyons, 1561. See below.
> The translator was John Ball, formerly of Christ Church College, Oxford. Gyllius was a French physician said to have been commissioned by Francis I to collect manuscripts at Constantinople early in the sixteenth century. He compiled during his residence there two treatises on antiquities, *Topographia Constantinopoleos* and *De Phosophora*, chiefly collected from a poem by Dionysius of Byzantium.—Dalrymple. "This book is beautifully adorned with cuts of the Buildings, the Statuary, and Sculpture of that City. The whole impression being near disposed of, the remainder may be had, . . . at the Oxford Arms in Warwick Lane."—Evening Post, Aug. 16, 1729. Quoted by Nichols, *Literary Anecdotes.* Gyllius may well be counted among the representative spirits of the Renaissance at

that epoch. He has given us the first circumstantial account of the antiquities of Constantinople and may be considered the founder of Byzantine archaeology.—From Iorga, *Les Voyageurs Français.*

1561 GYLLIUS, PETRUS. De topographia Constantinopoleos et de illius antiquitatibus. Lyons.

1732 BAUMGARTEN, MARTIN. The Travels of Martin Baumgarten, a Nobleman of Germany, Through Egypt, Arabia, Palestine, and Syria. In 3 Books. Giving an Account of the Situation, Nature, Monuments and Ruins of those Countries; and of the Islands, Cities and Temples therein; of their Manners and Customs; of the Rise, Increase, and Actions of some foreign Princes; And of the Properties of several Animals, with other added things. In Churchill I, 382-452.

> Reprinted in Moore II. A Latin version, Nuremberg, 1594. See below.
> The knight died in 1532, aged 62 years. The account of his travels was compiled from his diary and that of his servant.

1594 BAUMGARTEN, MARTIN. Peregrinatio in Aegyptum, Arabiam, Palaestinam et Syriam, . . . Nuremberg.

ROLAMB, NICHOLAS. A Relation of a Journey to Constantinople; giving an Account of divers Occurrences; . . . being a Report made to the most Potent Prince Charles Gustavus, King of the Swedes, Goths, and Vandals, by . . . Nicholas Rolamb, formerly Envoy Extraordinary to the Ottoman Porte. Translated from a Copy printed in Swedish at Stockholm. In Churchill V, 669-716.

> The author, a Swedish nobleman, was sent to Constantinople to remove the fears of the Porte over the Swedish successes in Poland.

1734 CANTEMIR, D. The History of the Growth and Decay of the Othman Empire. Portraits. Fol. London.

> This was a translation into English by N. Tindal.—Bookseller's Note.

1736. GREEN, J. A Journey from Aleppo to Damascus in 1725; with a Description of those two Capital Cities, and the neighboring Parts of Syria. Engraved map. 8vo. London.

> Pinkerton XVII lists an anonymous work of the same date and title with the addition: To which is added, An Account of the Maronites inhabiting Mount-Lebanon.

1738 SHAW, THOMAS. For his travels in the Levant see his *Travels, or Observations relating to several Parts of Barbary,* under AFRICA.

1739 CAMPBELL, JOHN. For travels in the Orient see his *The Travels and Adventures of Edward Brown,* under GENERAL TRAVELS AND DESCRIPTIONS.

1740 ROE, SIR THOMAS. The Negotiations of Sir Thomas Roe, in his Embassy to the Ottoman Porte, from the years 1621 to 1628 inclusive; Containing a great Variety of curious and important matters relating not only to the Affairs of the Turkish Empire, but also to those of the other States of Europe, in that Period. Portrait. Fol. London.

> This was printed by Samuel Richardson, the novelist, with a special dedicatory epistle by him to the King.—Maggs, No. 521. See also Rice, *English Travelers in Greece,* for an account of the Arundel Marbles.

1743 PERRY, CHARLES (M. D.). A View of the Levant: particularly of Constantinople, Syria, Egypt and Greece, in which their Antiquities, Government, Politics, Maxims, Manners and Customs (with many other Circumstances and Contingencies), are attempted to be described and treated on. Numerous plates and map. Fol. London.

> Another edition, 3 vols., London, 1773.
> This work, which has been twice translated into German, is much less known than it deserves to be.—Lowndes. It is curious that no French translation was ever made.

1743-45 POCOCKE, RICHARD. Description of the East, and some other Countries: Egypt, Palestine, Mesopotamia, Cyprus, Candia, Greece, Asia Minor, . . . 178 large plates of views, plans, details, plants, etc. 2 vols. Fol. London.

> 2nd edit., London, 1771; reprinted entire in Pinkerton X, 406-770, and XV, 163-402. Translated into German, Erlangen, 1754-55; into French, Paris, 1772-73; into Dutch, Utrecht, 1776-1786. See below.
> Pococke was a great traveller and visited many other places besides the East. He toured the British Isles as well, but his account of these journies was not published until 1888-1891. He visited Egypt in 1737-38, ascending the Nile as far as Philae, and then passed into Palestine and the other places mentioned above, in 1738-1740. The work attained great celebrity. Hallam regarded Pococke as the equal of any oriental scholar. Gibbon (*Decline and Fall* LI, note 60) described his book as of "superior learning and dignity," though he objected to the confusion between what the author saw and what he heard. He became bishop of Ossory in 1765.

> 1754-55 (In German.) Beschreibung des Morgenlandes und einiger andern Länder, übersetzt von (Christ. Ernst von) Windheim. Plates. 3 vols. 4to. Erlangen.

> 1772-73 (In French.) Voyages dans l'Egypte, l'Arabie, la Palestine, la Syrie, la Grèce, la Thrace, . . . contenant une description exacte de l'Orient et de plusieurs autres contrées: comme la France, l'Italie, l'Allemagne, la Pologne, la Hongrie, . . . et des observations intéressantes sur les moeurs, la religion, les lois, le gouvernement, les arts, les sciences, le commerce, la géographie et l'histoire naturelle et civile de chaque pays,

et généralement sur toutes les curiosités de la nature et de l'art qui s'y trouvent; traduits de l'Anglais sur seconde édition, par une société de gens de lettres (redigés par De la Flotte, ou Ant. Eidous). 7 vols. 12mo. Paris.

1776-1786 (In Dutch.) Beschryving van het Oosten, en van eenige andere Landen. 3 deelen in 6 stukken. Uit het Engelsch overgezet en met aantekingen voorzien door E. W. Cramer. Maps and plates. 4to. Utrecht.

1744 THOMPSON, CHARLES. For his observations on the Near East see his *Travels, containing his Observations on France, Italy, Turkey, etc.,* under GENERAL TRAVELS AND DESCRIPTIONS.

1745 A General Account of the Turkish Empire. In Osborne I, 502-510.

This is probably by the editor of this collection. It is used as an introduction to the voyages to the Near East which follow in this volume.

USHER, JAMES (Archbishop of Armagh and Primate of Ireland). A Geographical and Historical Disquisition touching the Asia properly so called, the Lydian Asia (which is the Asia so often mentioned in the New Testament), the Proconsular Asia, and the Asian Diocese. In Osborne I, 490-500.

This deals largely with Roman Asia, with a few remarks on the modern state of this part of the continent.

1745-47 ABU 'LFEDA. A Description of the Sea of Kolzum commonly called the Arabic Gulf, or Red Sea: from Abu 'lfeda's Geography. In Astley I, 130-132.

Abu wrote this geography in 1321. It consists of Tables of the Longitude and Latitude of places (in imitation of Ptolemy), with their descriptions under the title of Takwim al Boldan. Part of the Tables were published in Thevenot's Collection; part with Latin translation by Dr. Greaves in 1650 (see this date above); and more in Hudson's *Lesser Geographers* in 1612 (see under GEOGRAPHY).

1747 CHISHULL, EDMUND. Travels in Turkey and Return back to England. Fol. London.

The author, who had antiquarian interests, was chaplain to the Factory of the Worshipful Turkey Company at Smyrna, 1698-1702. During his residence at Smyrna he made various expeditions in Asia Minor and Turkey, which make up the matter of the above volume. His account is said to have been of value to later explorers in those regions.

1750 VENUTI, DON MARCELLO DI. A Description of the first Discoveries of the ancient City of Heraclea, translated from the Italian by Wickes Skurray. 8vo. London.

1751 DALTON, RICHARD. Antiquities and Views in Greece and Egypt, with the Manners and Customs of the Inhabitants, from Drawings made on the Spot, A.D., 1749. 52 plates. Fol. London.

> This is a series of engravings representing views of places, buildings, antiquities, etc., in Sicily, Greece, Asia Minor, and Egypt. Dalton was a draughtsman, engraver and librarian, and keeper of pictures and antiquities to George III. He accompanied Lord Charlemont to Greece in 1749, where he made several drawings of Athenian antiquities. They are said to possess little value, however, either for art or archeology. See also Dalton under dates 1781 and 1790, AFRICA.

1751-58 CLAYTON, ROBERT (Bishop of Clogher). Journal of a Voyage from Grand Cairo to Mount Sinai and Back: translated from a Manuscript written by the Prefetto of Egypt with Remarks on the Origin of Hieroglyphics. 2 plates. 8vo. London.

> 2nd edit. corrected, 4to, London, 1753. Reprinted in Pinkerton X, 386-405. Translated into German, Hanover, 1754; into French, Amsterdam, 1759. See below.
> To the Society of Antiquaries, to whom this work was inscribed, Bishop Clayton observes, "that as the Journal particularly describes many places in the Wilderness, where great numbers of antient characters are hewn in the rocks; if a person was sent to live some time among the Arabs, he might get copies of the characters, and some help, by which the antient Hebrew characters, now lost, may be recovered." These characters, which were cut in the solid rock twelve and fourteen feet high, were examined by Wortley Montagu in 1765, and appeared to be nothing more than the work of Christian converts, pilgrims to Mount Sinai. Niebuhr declared them to be only the names of persons that had passed that way. —From Nichols II, *Literary Anecdotes*.

> 1808-1814 CLAYTON, ROBERT (Bishop of Clogher). A Journal from the Grand Cairo to Mt. Sinai and back again in Company with some Missionaries de propoganda fide at Grand Cairo. Translated from a MS. by the Prefetto of Egypt by Right Rev. Robert Clayton, Bishop of Clogher. (The MS. was mentioned by Richard Pococke in his *Travels through the East;* see 1743-45 above.) In Pinkerton X, 386-405.

> The Prefetto set out from Cairo Sept. 1, 1722.

> 1754 (In German.) Tage-Reisen von Gross-Kairo nach dem Berge Sinai und wieder zurück. Aus einer Handschrift des Präfektus der Franciskaner in Egipten. Mit Anmerkungen über den Ursprung der Hieroglifen und Mythologie der alten Heiden, ... von ... R. C. 8vo. Hanover.

> 1759 (In French.) Journal d'un voyage du Grand Cairo au mont Sinaï, et retour, en 1722, par un envoyé du préfet d'Egypte: copie d'un MS. contenant en outre des remarques sur l'origine des Hiéroglyphes et des notions fabuleuses des anciens peuples, traduit de l'Anglais de (Robert) Clayton, par J. J. Dusterhopp, en Hollandais. 8vo. Amsterdam.

1753 FALCONER, DAVID. A Journey from Joppa to Jerusalem in May, 1751. 4to. London.

> An amusing narrative.—Lowndes.

Letters from Several Parts of Europe and the East, written in the years 1750, ... on the Productions of Nature, the Monuments of Art, and the manners of the Inhabitants. 2 vols. 8vo. London.

WOOD, ROBERT. The Ruins of Palmyra, otherwise Tadmor, in the Desert. 57 large engraved plates of architecture and inner decorations, and large panoramic view, by P. Fourdrinier and T. M. Müller, after G. B. Borra. Fol. London.

> No new edition of this work was published until 1827. There was a French translation printed in 1753.
> "The beautiful editions of Baalbec and Palmyra, illustrated by the classic pen of Robert Wood, supply a nobler and more lasting monument, and will survive those august remains." Horace Walpole's inscription on Wood's monument, quoted by Sotheran. Wood was a member of the Society of Dilettanti, which took a great interest in the progress of the work and its publication. He and Dawkins set out on their journey of exploration through the western portion of Asia Minor in 1750. His exact measurements of the ruined columns, arcades, architraves, and other details of classic architecture at Palmyra provided his countrymen at home with examples of a purer Hellenic style than they had hitherto obtained through Roman copies.

1754 DRUMMOND, ALEXANDER. Travels through different Cities of Germany, Italy, Greece, and several parts of Asia as far as the Banks of the Euphrates. 34 maps and curious copperplates. Fol. London.

> The illustrations include three large folding maps of Cyprus, part of Syria and Aleppo to the Euphrates, and a large folding view of the city and Castle of Aleppo. The author was consul at Aleppo, 1754-56.

1756 RUSSELL, ALEXANDER (F.R.S.). The Natural History of Aleppo, and Parts adjacent, with the Climate, Inhabitants, and Diseases, particularly the Plague, with Methods used by Europeans for their Preservation. Folding and other copperplates of Eastern customs, natural history, etc. 4to. London.

> 2nd edit. (considered the best), London, 1794. See below.
> Russell was physician to the English Factory at Aleppo, and afterwards physician to St. Thomas's Hospital. This work, which has been described as "one of the most complete pictures of Eastern manners extant," was reviewed by Dr. Johnson in the *Literary Magazine*, and was translated into German by Gronovius.—D. N. B. Speaking of the *Arabian Nights*, the author says, "It is a scarce book at Aleppo, I found only two volumes, containing two hundred and eighty nights, and with difficulty obtained liberty to have a copy taken."—Quoted by Sotheran. For a description of Russell, see Fanny Burney, *Early Diary*, for April 3, 1775.

> 1794 RUSSELL, ALEXANDER. The Natural History of Aleppo, . . . by Patrick Russell, the Author's half-brother, with the same illustrations, also a folding plate of Aleppo and two other plates. 4to. 2 vols. London.

1757 ELIOT, —— (Captain). Directions for passing over the Little Desart, from Busserah, by way of Bagdad, Orsa and Aleppo. 12mo. London.

> This is appended to Plaisted's work listed just below. Probably it should read the Great Desart instead of the Little Desart.

PLAISTED, BARTHOLOMEW. Journal from Calcutta, by Sea, to Busserah, from thence Across the Great Desart to England in 1750. Map of Bengal. 12mo. London.

See the same under EAST INDIES, for further details and editions.

WOOD, ROBERT. The Ruins of Balbec, otherwise Heliopolis in Coelo-Syria; taken from Botra, Bouverie, and Dawkins. 46 plates. Fol. London.

See Wood under 1753 above.

1758 MARIGNY, —— DE (Abbé). The History of the Arabians under the Government of the Caliphs, from Mahomet, their Founder, to the Death of Mostazem, the Fifty-sixth and last Abassian Caliph, translated from the French, with Additional Notes by Nugent. 4 vols. 8vo. London.

French original, Paris (?), 1750. See below.

1750 MARIGNY, —— DE (Abbé). Histoire des Arabes sous le Gouvernement des Califes, . . . 4 vols. 8vo. Paris (?).

1758 Travels in Egypt, Turkey, Syria, and the Holy-Land by an English Merchant; with Notes by a Gentleman of Oxford. 8vo. London.

1759 EGMONT, J. AEGIDIUS VAN, and HEYMANN, JOHN. Travels through Part of Europe, Asia Minor, the Islands of the Archipelago; Syria, Palestine, Egypt, Mount Sinai, . . . Giving a particular Account of the Most remarkable Places, Structures, Ruins, Inscriptions, . . . in these Countries. Together with the Customs, Manners, Religion, Trade, Commerce, Tempers, and Manners of Living of the Inhabitants. By the Honourable J. Aegidius van Egmont, Envoy Extraordinary from the United Provinces to the Court of Naples; and John Heymann, Professor of the Oriental Languages in the University of Leyden. Translated from the Low Dutch. Plates. 2 vols. 8vo. London.

Another edition, London, 1772. Dutch original, Leyden, 1757-58. See below.

1757-58 EGMONT VAN DER NYENBERG, J. AEGIDIUS VAN, and HEY-MANN, JAN. Reyzen door een gedeelte van Europa, Klein Asia, verscheyde Eylanden van t'Archipal, Syrien, Palaestina in het H. Land, Egyptian, den Berg Sinai, nyt beider nagelaaten Schriften (from the years 1700 to 1709 and 1720) samen gestelt door Jon. Wilh. Heymann. 11 Deele. 4to. Leyden.

LE ROY, ——. The Ruins of Athens, with Remains and other valuable Antiquities in Greece. (Translated into English by Robert Sayer.) Plates. Fol. London.

Le Roy had been led to undertake an expedition to Athens in the interest of France in rivalry with that of Wood's and Dawkins's. Le Roy left Rome for Athens in 1753. Sayer's translation was also intended to anticipate the projected work of Stuart and Revett. See below.

1762-1794 STUART, JAMES, and REVETT, NICHOLAS. The Antiquities of Athens, measured and delineated by James Stuart, F.R.S., and Nicholas Revett. Over 200 large folding and full page engravings of views, architecture, sculpture, antiquities, etc., and numerous head and tail pieces, all by the best artists of the time, letter press historical and descriptive. 3 vols. Fol. London.

An additional volume was published in 1814, edited by Jos. Wood, containing biographies of Stuart and Revett, and numerous extracts from their notes and journals; and a fifth volume appeared in 1830.

In preparation for this work the authors spent six or seven years at Rome in the study of painting. Their labors were much indebted to the Society of Dilettanti, who both financed the expedition and went to the expense of engraving a great number of plates from original drawings in their possession. Several of the members of the Society interested themselves individually in promoting the publication of the volumes. For the story of this fascinating expedition one should consult *The History of the Society of Dilettanti* compiled by Lionel Cust and edited by Sir Sidney Colvin (London, 1914). After his return from Greece, Stuart became generally known as "Athenian Stuart." As a result of the publication of his work London saw an increase in the number of houses built in the Greek style.

1763 BELL, JOHN. For his journey from St. Petersburg to Constantinople (in 1737-38) see his *Travels from St. Petersburg in Russia, to Diverse Parts of Asia,* under CENTRAL ASIA.

MONTAGUE, LADY MARY WORTLEY. Letters written during her Travels in Europe, Asia and Africa. 8vo. London.

Later editions: London, 1767; London, 1769; London, 1789. Translated into most of the European languages: German, Leipzig, 1764; French, Amsterdam, 1763, Paris, 1764. See below.

Lady Mary accompanied her husband, Edward Montague, on his diplomatic mission to Constantinople, making the journey overland. When she left Vienna she received as many admonitions as though she were journeying to the ends of the earth. The letters she wrote back home are justly ranked among the most celebrated of their kind in a century richly endowed with excellent letterwriters. It has been hinted that she expected at the time of writing to see them in print later. But in this respect she was not an exception in the eighteenth century. Her part in introducing the practice of inoculating against small-pox is well known.

1769 MONTAGUE, LADY MARY WORTLEY. Letters . . . containing among other curious Relations Accounts of the Policy and Manners of the Turks. 3 vols. in 1. 8vo. London.

1789 MONTAGUE, LADY MARY WORTLEY. Letters written . . . to Persons of Distinction, . . . A New Edition with Poems by the same Author. Portrait. 12mo. London.

1763   (In French.)   Lettres écrites pendant ses voyages en Europe, en Asie et en Afrique, . . . traduites de l'anglais sur la seconde édition.   12mo.   Amsterdam.

It is stated that there were five translations of these letters into French. The one above was made by Father Jean Brunet, a Dominican Friar.

1764   (In French.)   Lettres de milady Worthley Montague, écrites en diverses parties du monde, traduites de l'anglois, troisième partie pour servir de supplément aux deux prémières. On y a joint une reponse à la critique que le Journal encyclopédique a fait des deux prémières, par P. J. Brunet. 2 vols. 12mo. Paris.

1764   (In German.)   Briefe während ihrer Reise durch Europa, Asien, und Afrika. Aus dem Englischen übersetzt. 8vo. Leipzig.

1765 LYTTLETON, CHARLES. An Account of the Plague at Aleppo. London.

Noticed in the *Journal des Scavans,* 1765, III, 257.

1766 CARMICHAEL, JOHN. A Journey from Aleppo over the Desert to Basserah, Oct. 21, 1751.

This is printed as an Appendix to John Henry Grose's *Voyage to the East Indies,* 2nd edit. See the latter under 1757, EAST INDIES. An abridged version of Carmichael appeared in the *Philos. Trans. Roy. Soc.,* LVII, 38 ff., 1791-96.

HASSELQUIST, FREDERICK (M.D.). Voyages and Travels in the Levant, 1749-1752: Natural History, Physick, Agriculture, . . . Map. 8vo. London.

Original Swedish, Stockholm, 1757. See below.
The author was one of that zealous band of students who, fired by the genius of Linnaeus, scattered over different parts of the world in pursuit of natural history. Like many others, Hasselquist died while on the quest. His own profession was medicine. The first part of this work is a journal of travel and correspondence, the second observations on mineralogy, botany, zoology, diseases, commerce, etc. He visited Smyrna, Magnesia, Alexandria (remaining a year in Egypt), the Holy Land, Cyprus, but omitted Constantinople on account of the plague raging there. He died in 1752 at Smyrna. His work is uncommonly interesting and valuable to the natural historian.

1757 HASSELQUIST, FREDERICK. Iter Paloestinense, . . . forroetad ifran 1749 til 1752. 8vo. Stockholm.

1767 BRYANT, JACOB. Observations and Inquiries relating to various parts of Ancient History, containing Dissertations on the Wind Euroclydon and on the Island Melite, . . . Folding maps. 4to. Cambridge.

Bryant comes in for a scathing remark in Byron's *Don Juan.*

CALVERT, FREDERICK (Sixth Baron Baltimore). A Tour in the East in years 1763 and 1764, with Remarks on the City of Constantinople and the Turks, by the Lord Baltimore. Plates and a colored folding plan of Constantinople. 8vo. London.

Another edition, Dublin, 1768.

1768 PORTER, SIR JAMES. Observations on the Religion, Laws, Government and Manners of the Turks. 2 vols. 8vo. London.

2nd (and best) edit., London, 1771. Translated into French, London, 1768. See below.
The author was ambassador at Constantinople, 1746-1762.

1771 PORTER, SIR JAMES. Observations on the Religion, Laws, Government and Manners of the Turks, to which is added, the State of the Turkey Trade from its Origin. 8vo. London.

1768 (In French.) Observations sur la Religion, les Loix, le Gouvernement, les Moeurs des Turcs. Traduit de l'Anglois. 2 vols. 12mo. London.

Noticed in the *Journal des Scavans,* 1770, IV, 291.

1769 CHANDLER, RICHARD. Ionian Antiquities: published by order of the Society of Dilettanti.

A second volume was published as a continuation, London, 1797.
This work, together with *Inscriptiones Antiquae* (1774), were the published results of Chandler's archaeological expedition to Greece and the adjacent regions made under the auspices of the Society of Dilettanti. For an account of his travels see under 1775.

1772 BOS, LAMBERT. Antiquities of Greece, with the Notes of Frederick Leisner, translated by Percival Stockdale. 8vo. London.

This is a work intended principally for the use of schools.—Lowndes.

GUYS, PIERRE-AUGUSTIN. A Sentimental Journey through Greece, in a Series of Letters . . . to M. Bourlaι de Montredon, translated from the French. 3 vols. 12mo. London.

The author was a physician of Lyons who with his family made a long stay in the Orient. His aim was to show that in order to know the life of the ancient Greeks it was necessary to attire oneself in the costume of the modern Greek. Probably this was the first and also the last time that such an idea was bruited in the eighteenth century. He possessed an admirable knowledge of Greek antiquity as well as a familiarity with the modern Greek and Turkish languages. In his book he included specimens of songs from both those peoples. He may be said to have been the first folklorist who directed his attention towards the Orient. His work is written in such an agreeable style, his observations so delicate and his comparisons so subtle that it makes excellent reading even today. From Iorga, *Les Voyageurs Français.*

1775 CHANDLER, RICHARD. Travels in Asia Minor, or an Account of a Tour made at the expense of the Society of Dilettanti. Map. 4to. Oxford.

> The 2nd part of his Travels came out, Oxford, 1776. Reprinted, Dublin, 1775 and 1776. No French translation appeared until 1806. The work was noticed in the *Journal des Scavans*, 1776, I, 542.
> Chandler, who was a good Greek archaeologist, was sent to Greece in 1764 by the Society of Dilettanti to copy inscriptions and to finish the task left uncompleted by Stuart. He returned to England in 1774. He was a neighbor and correspondent of Gilbert White, author of the *History and Antiquities of Selbourne*.

1777 RICHARDSON, JOHN. Dissertations on the Languages, Literature, and Manners of Eastern Nations. 8vo. Oxford.

1780 IRWIN, EYLES. A Series of adventures in the Course of a Voyage up the Red Sea, on the Coasts of Arabia, and of a Route through the Desarts of Thebais, hitherto unknown to the European Traveler, in the year 1777, in Letters to a Lady. Maps and plates. 4to. London.

> Later editions: London, 1781, with additions; 2 vols., 8vo, London, 1784; 2 vols., 8vo, London, 1787. Translated into German, Leipzig, 1781; into French, Paris, 1792. See below.
> This work is chiefly valuable for the information which his personal adventures necessarily give of the manners, etc., of the Arabians.—Lowndes. The author was superintendent of Madras, 1771; dismissed for protest against the deportation of Lord Pigot, he was returned to India, 1780, on being reinstated, and filled other positions afterwards.—D. N. B.

> 1781 IRWIN, EYLES. A Series of Adventures in the course of a Voyage up the Red Sea, . . . with a Supplement of a Voyage from Venice to Latichea, and of a Route through the Desarts of Arabia, by Aleppo, Bagdad, and the Tygris, to Busrah, in the years 1780 and 1781, in Letters to a Lady. Plates. 4to. London.

> 1781 (In German.) Begebenheiten einer Reise auf dem Rothen Meere, und auf der Arabischen und Aegyptischen Küste, ingleichen durch die Thebaische Wüste. Aus dem Englischen von J. A. Engelbrecht. Map and plates. 8vo. Leipzig.

> 1792 (In French.) Voyage à la Mer Rouge, sur les côtes de l'Arabie, en Egypte et dans les Déserts de la Thebaide suivi d'un Voyage à Bassorah, . . . en 1780 et 1781. Traduit de l'anglais, sur le 3me édition, par J. P. Parraud. 2 vols. Maps. 8vo. Paris.

WALKIN, ——. Travels to Constantinople and in the Crimea. 2 vols. London.

> So cited by Pinkerton XVII. Both the name and the date are in doubt.

1782 BRUCE, PETER. For his travels in Turkey see his *Memoirs of Military Service in Prussia, Russia*, etc., under GENERAL TRAVELS AND DESCRIPTIONS.

1783 CAPPER, JAMES. Observations on the Passage to India (in the year 1779) through Egypt; also by Vienna through Constantinople to Aleppo, and from thence by Bagdad, and directly across the Grand Desert to Bassora. Maps. 4to. London.

> Another edition enlarged, 4to, London, 1784. Translated into French, London and Paris, 1786. See below.
> Capper was also the author of several works on meteorology.

> 1786 (In French.)· Voyages du Colonel Capper dans les Indies, au travers de l'Egypte et du grand désert, par Suez, en 1779. Traduits de l'Anglois, et accompagnés de notes sur l'original et des cartes géographiques. 2 vols. 8vo. Londres et Paris.
>
>> This translation appeared in the same volume with the French version of James Mackintosh's *Travels in Europe, Asia, and Africa*. For the latter see under 1782, GENERAL TRAVELS AND DESCRIPTIONS.

LUSIGNAN, S. For a description of Palestine and Syria, and the Journal of a Gentleman who travelled from Aleppo to Bassora, see his *History of the Revolt of Ali Bey*, under AFRICA.

ROOKE, HENRY. Travels to the Coast of Arabia Felix, and from thence, by the Red Sea and Egypt, to Europe, containing a short Account of an Expedition undertaken against the Cape of Good Hope; in a series of Letters. 8vo. London.

> 2nd edit., with additions, 8vo, London, 1784. Translated into German, Leipzig, 1787; into French, Paris, 1788. See below.

> 1787 (In German.) Reisen nach den Küsten des glücklichen Arabiens und von da über das Rothe Meer und Aegypten nach Europa zurück; worin ein kurzer Bericht von einem gegen das Vorgebirge der guten Hoffnung unternommen Seezüge geliefert wird. In einer Reihe von Briefen. Nach der 2 verm. Eng. Ausgabe übersetzt. 8vo. Leipzig.

> 1788 (In French.) Voyage sur les Côtes de l'Arabie Heureuse, sur la Mer Rouge et en Egypte, . . . ; avec une Notice sur l'Expédition de M. Suffrein au Cap de Bonne-Espérance. Traduit de l'Anglois (par M. L. M. Langlès). 8vo. Paris.

1784 EVERS, SAMUEL (Lieut.). A Journal kept on a Journey from Bassora to Bagdad, through the Little-Desert, to Aleppo, Cyprus, Rhodes, Zante, Corfu, and Otrante, in the year 1779 by a Gentleman. Horsham.

HABESCI, ELIAS. The Present State of the Ottoman Empire . . . including a particular Description of the Court and Seraglio of the Grand Signor. Translated from the French Manuscript of Elias Habesci. 8vo. London.

> Habesci was for many years resident at Constantinople, in the service of the Grand Signor.—Lowndes. The real name of the author, who assumed the title of Count, was, according to Major Taylor, Gica.—Pinkerton XVII.

1785 TOTT, FRANCIS, BARON DE. Memoirs of Baron de Tott, containing the State of the Turkish Empire and the Crimea during the late War with Russia, with numerous Anecdotes, Facts and Observations on the Manners and Customs of the Turks and Tartars. Translated from the French by an English Gentleman at Paris, under the immediate Inspection of the Baron. 2 vols. 8vo. London.

> 2nd edit., with Strictures subjoined by M. Peyssonnel, London, 1786. French original, Amsterdam, 1784. See below.
> Eton asserts Baron Tott's Account of Turkey, and of its inhabitants, to be the best and most exact. There are, however, several exaggerations and inaccuracies in the work, as may be easily conceived from the character of the author. The description of the Crimea, and its inhabitants, is, perhaps, the most interesting. —Pinkerton XVII. The account is marked by sprightly egotism, an apparent disregard for truth and a love of exciting surprise. This depreciates in the public eye the value of that singular nation with which he was so intimately conversant. —Dalrymple. This odd traveller was the son of an Hungarian refugé in the suite of the pretender Rakoczy, but owing to a sprightliness of disposition and a French education, he became essentially French in spirit. He passed some time among the Tartars and in the Crimea, traversed Moldavia and Wallachia, and finally reached Constantinople, where he undertook a very peculiar mission. At that time Selim III was desirous of introducing the European dress, hoping by a reform, especially in the army, to win out in the struggle with Russia. Despite bickerings with the Turks, De Tott managed to impart something of western military technique. His book went through three editions.—From Iorga, *Les Voyageurs Français*.

1784 TOTT, FRANCIS, BARON DE. Mémoires sur les Turcs et les Tartares. 3 parts in 2 vols. 8vo. Amsterdam.

> Dans cet ouvrage, Tott précéda Anquetil-Duperron, Savary et Volney. Il est le premier qui ait debrouillé avec exactitude et impartialité le chaos de notions fausse sous lequel restait voile pour l'Europe cette partie du monde.—Gamber.

1785 PEYSSONNEL, CHARLES DE. Lettres de M. Peyssonnel à le Marquis . . . contenant quelque observations relatives aux Mémoires qui ont paru sous le nom de M. le Baron de Tott. Paris.

> Peyssonnel resided some time at Constantinople from 1735 on and there carried on the practice of law. His archaeological and commercial studies of the Tartars, of the Isle of Crete, the Black Sea, Smyrna, and Candia are of great value for the period.—From Iorga, *Les Voyageurs Français*.

1786 A Description of the Holy Places of Jerusalem and the Objects visited by Pilgrims in Judea and Galilee, by the Reverend Fathers of the Latin Convent at Jerusalem. Translated from the Latin by W. Witman. London.

> The date given is a guess based on Pinkerton, who, however, is often unreliable. Wittman travelled in Turkey, Syria, and adjacent places during the years 1799, 1880, and 1801, in company with the Turkish army and the British military mission. It is probable that this translation is the result of contacts made during those years and hence would be of a much later date. See Wittman under 1803 below.

1787 VOLNEY, CONSTANTINE FRANCOIS CHASSEBOEUF, COMTE DE. Travels through Syria and Egypt 1783-85, containing Observations on their Commerce, Arts, Politics, . . . Maps and plates. 2 vols. 8vo. London.

> Another edition, 2 vols., 8vo, Dublin, 1788. French original, Paris, 1787. Two volumes were made up in the French edition by the addition of matter concerning the war between the Russians and the Turks. This appeared at Paris, 1788. See below.
>
> One of the most exact and valuable works of the kind ever published, all personal details being eliminated "to economise the time of readers."—Chambers, quoted by Sotheran. Volney was a member of the States General and later of the Constituent Assembly. He had a varied career during the Revolution, once narrowly escaping the guillotine. He won the favor of Napoleon, who made him a count and put him in the Senate. His chief work was *Les Ruines, ou meditations sur les révolutions des empires,* known in English as *The Ruins of Empires,* which appeared first in Paris, 1791. He tried to put his political philosophy into practice on an estate which he bought in Corsica. He died in 1820.

> 1787 VOLNEY, CONSTANTIN FRANCOIS CHASSEBOEUF, COMTE DE. Voyage en Syrie et en Egypte, pendant les années 1783, 1784, et 1785. 2 vols. 8vo. Paris.

1788 ELLIS, GEORGE. Memoir of a Map of the Countries comprehended between the Black Sea and the Caspian; with an Account of the Caucasian Nations, and Vocabularies of their Languages. 4to. London.

HOWEL, THOMAS (M. D.). Journal of a Passage from India by a Route partly unfrequented through Armenia and Natolia or Asia Minor. Map. 8vo. London.

> Another edition, 8vo, London, 1790. Translated into French (with Capper's Voyage), Paris, 1797. See below.
> For this overland journey from India the author recommends a very miscellaneous equipment, including "a small tin tea pot" and "a Broad Sword."—Sotheran.

> 1790 HOWEL, THOMAS. Journal of a Passage from India, by a Route partly unfrequented, through Armenia and Natolia, or Asia Minor, with Instructions for those who intend to travel, either to or from India, by that Route. Large folding map. 8vo. London.

> 1797 (In French.) Voyage en retour de l'Inde par une route en partie inconnue jusqu'ici, suivi d'observations sur le passage dans l'Inde par l'Egypte et le grand désert, par James Capper. Traduit de l'anglois, par Th. Mandar. Impr. de la Republique an V. Plates. 4to. Paris.

> > Les pp. 328-385 sont occupées par l'itinéraire de l'Arabie déserte, ou lettres sur en voyage de Bassora à Alep par le Grand et le Petit Désert, publié en 1750 par MM. Plaisted et Eliot.—Bookseller's Note.

LUSIGNAN, S. Letters addressed to Sir William Fordyce, F.R.S., containing a Voyage from England to Smyrna; from thence to Constantinople, and from that Place over Land to England; likewise an Account of the Cities, Towns, and Villages, through which the Author passed, . . . With a short Answer to Volney's Contradictions on Ali Bey's History and Revolt, and Appendix on the Holy Land. 2 vols. 8vo. London.

For Lusignan's account of Ali Bey see under 1783, AFRICA.

SAVARY, CLAUDIO ESTEBAN. Letters on Greece, translated from the French. 8vo. London.

French original, Paris, 1788. See below.
This French orientalist left for Egypt in 1776 and spent three years there studying costumes and monuments. For his Letters on Egypt see under 1786, AFRICA.

1788 SAVARY, CLAUDIO ESTEBAN. Lettres sur la Grèce. Paris.

1789 CRAVEN, LADY ELIZABETH (Margravine Anspach). For her journey from the Crimea to Constantinople, see under EAST EUROPE.

1790 SUTHERLAND, DAVID (Captain). A Tour up the Straits, from Gibraltar to Constantinople, with the leading Events in the present War between the Austrians, Russians, and the Turks, to the Commencement of the Year 1789. 4to. London.

1791 ANACHARSIS THE YOUNGER. Maps, Plans, Views, and Coins illustrative of the Travels of Anacharsis the Younger in Greece, during the middle of the Fourth Century before the Christian Era. 4to. London.

See Barthélemy under 1793-94 below.

DALRYMPLE, RICHARD. Antiquities and Views in Greece and Egypt, with the Manners and Customs of the Inhabitants, from Drawings made on the Spot. Fol. London.

Held in little esteem.—Lowndes. A similar judgment was passed by Dalrymple himself on most of his predecessors in the same field.

JENNER, MATTHEW. The Route to India through France, Germany, Hungary, Turkey, Natolia, Syria, and the Desert of Arabia. London.

LE CHEVALIER, (Citizen). Description of the Plain of Troy, by Citizen Le Chevalier, translated from the French. Maps. 4to. London.

2nd edit. of French original, Paris, 1799. See below.
The author was secretary to the prince of Moldavia; he disappeared during the war between Russia and Turkey, begun in 1788. The above work is a laborious effort to identify ancient localities in the Troad. He also describes the Turk-

ish monuments in Constantinople, the manners and customs of the inhabitants, the defenses of the city, the Greek churches, etc.—From Iorga, *Les Voyageurs Français.* The date given above is taken from Pinkerton and is open to suspicion.

1799 LE CHEVALIER, (Citizen). Voyage dans le Troad, ou Tableau de la Plaine de Troie dans son Etat actuel. 2nd edit. Map and plates. Paris, An VII.

MARITI, GIOVANNI (Abbé). Travels through Cyprus, Syria, and Palestine, with a general History of the Levant (translated from the French). 3 vols. London.

> This is a literal translation of the French translation (Paris, 1791), which is anything but literal. Another version asserted to be a translation from the Italian original (vol. I only), Dublin, 1792. A modern edition made from the Italian original, Cambridge, 1895; 2nd edition of the same, Cambridge, 1901. Italian original, Lucca, 1769. See below.
> The Ottoman conquest of Cyprus in 1571 found a goodly number of chroniclers, some of them eye-witnesses. In Cobham's volume are included two of them. Mariti, who was an official of the Imperial and Tuscan consulates, gives an excellent account of the condition of Cyprus during the third quarter of the eighteenth century, which is based mainly on his own observations. See the preface to Cobham's edition.

1909 COBHAM, C. B. (C. M. G.). Travels in the Island of Cyprus, 1760-67, translated from the Italian of Giovanni Mariti, with contemporary Accounts of the Sieges of Nicosia and Famagusta by Conterini and Martinengo, with prefatory Notes and Index. 2nd edit., enlarged. 8vo. Cambridge.

1769 MARITI, GIOVANNI (Abbé). Viaggi per l'isola di Cipro, . . . Lucca.

1791 MARITI, GIOVANNI (Abbé). Voyage dans l'isle de Chypre, la Syrie et la Palestine, avec l'histoire générale du Levant. Tome 1-2 (tout ce qu'il a paru). Paris.

1792 EMIN, JOSEPH. Life and Adventures, 1726-1809. 8vo. London.

> The author, an American, was a great friend of Lady Mary Montague. He spent some time in Armenia.

NIEBUHR, CARSTEN. Travels through Arabia and other Countries in the East: Hedjas, Yemen, Oman, . . . Translated by Robert Heron, with Notes and illustrated with engravings and maps. 2 vols. 8vo. Edinburgh.

> Another edition, 2 vols., London, 1799. Abridged in Pinkerton, X, 1-221. German original, Copenhagen, 1772, and 2nd Part, Copenhagen, 1774-78. See below.
> This is a justly famous and popular work. Niebuhr, though German born, took part as astronomer and naturalist in the Royal Danish expedition to Arabia, 1763-67. His accounts are probably the best and most authentic of their day. Though Arabia was his chief concern, his travels extended into Egypt, Persia, and Hindustan. His translator, Robert Heron, was one of the early biographers of Burns.

1772 NIEBUHR, CARSTEN. Beschreibung von Arabien, aus eigenen Beobachtungen und im Lande selbst gesammelten Nachrichten. Copenhagen.

1774-78 NIEBUHR, CARSTEN. Reisebeschreibung nach Arabien, und andern umliegenden Ländern. Copenhagen.

1792 WATKINS, THOMAS. For his travels to Constantinople and the Grecian Isles, see his *Travels in* 1787-89, under CONTINENTAL EUROPE.

1792-96 Dissertations and miscellaneous Pieces relating to the History and Antiquities, . . . of Asia. 3 vols. 8vo. London.

> This is a selection of essays from the *Asiatic Researches.*—Lowndes.

1793-94 BARTHELEMY, JEAN JACQUES (Abbé). Travels of Anacharsis the Younger in Greece during the Middle of the Fourth Century before the Christian Aera, translated (by William Beaumont). 2nd edit., enlarged. 7 vols. Atlas, containing numerous plates of views and coins, plans and maps. 4to. Together 8 vols. London.

> Date of 1st edit. may be 1791; see Anacharsis under 1791 above. Another edition, 5 vols., 8vo, Dublin, 1795; abridged to 1 vol., 8vo, London, 1797; 3rd edit., abridged, 8vo, London, 1800. French original, Paris, 1784. Another edition in French, London, 1796. See below.
>
> Anacharsis the Younger was the name assumed by the author. This very popular work describes Greece as seen by a barbarian Scythian, who commits the anachronism of visiting Athens a few years before the birth of Alexander the Great and of conversing with Phocion, Epaminondas, Xenophon, Plato, Aristotle, and Demosthenes. In his travels through the provinces he makes note of the manners, morals, and customs of the inhabitants and takes part in their festivals. The work furthered contemporary knowledge of ancient Greece and gave rise to many imitations. The *Monthly Review* insinuated that the author borrowed largely from the *Athenian Letters* (Cambridge, 1741), but Barthélemy denied knowledge of that work.

> 1784 BARTHELEMY, JEAN JACQUES (Abbé). Voyage du jeune Anacharsis en Grèce, dans le millieu du quatrième siècle avant l'ère vulgaire. Plates. 4 vols. 8vo. London.

1794 PAUSANIUS. The Description of Greece by Pausanius; translated from the Greek, with Notes, by Thomas Taylor. Maps and views. 3 vols. 8vo. London.

> Taylor was a well known Platonist and translator of many Greek works. He is also remembered for some interesting associations with Wordsworth.

1796 CAMPBELL, DONALD. For his journey to India by way of Aleppo, Mosul, Bagdad see his *Journey overland to India,* under EAST INDIES.

1797 DALLAWAY, JAMES. Constantinople, ancient and modern, with Excursions to the Shores and Islands of the Archipelago and to the Troad. 10 colored aquatint views. 4to. London.

> Translated into French, Paris, 1799. See below.
> This very excellent and circumstantial account of Constantinople has been reproached with a want of arrangement approaching confusion. A great share of the work refers to Asiatic Turkey.—Pinkerton XVII.

> 1799 (In French.) Constantinople ancienne et moderne, et description des côtes et isles de l'Archipel et de la Troade; traduit de l'anglais par André Morellet. An VII. 2 vols. 8vo. Paris.

1798 ETON, WILLIAM. A Survey of the Turkish Empire; its Government, the State of the Provinces, the Causes of the Decline of Turkey, the British Commerce with Turkey. 8vo. London.

> 2nd edit., 8vo, London, 1799. See below.
> A work remarkable for nothing but the enthusiasm with which the author maintains the necessity of bringing about the restoration of the Greeks.—Lowndes.

1799 BROWNE, WILLIAM G. For his travels in Syria see his *Travels in Africa, Egypt, and Syria,* under AFRICA.

JACKSON, JOHN. A Journey from India to England in the year 1797, by a Route commonly called Overland, through Countries not much frequented and many of them hitherto unknown to Europeans, particularly those between the Euphrates and the Tigris, Curdistan, Diarbekir, Armenia, and Anatolia in Asia; and Romelia, Bulgaria, and Transylvania in Europe. London.

LANTIER, E. F. The Travels of Antenor. Translated from the French of E. F. Lantier. With additional Notes by the English translator. 3 vols. 8vo. London.

> 6th edit. of French original, Paris, 1802. See below.

> 1802 LANTIER, E.F. Les Voyages d'Antenor en Grèce et en Asie, avec des notions sur l'Egypte; manuscript Grec trouvé à Herculanum, traduit (or rather written) par E. F. Lantier. 6th edit. 5 vols. 16mo. Paris.

1800 FRANCKLIN, WILLIAM (Captain). Remarks and Observations on the Plain of Troy, made during an Excursion in June, 1799. 4to. London.

ADDENDA

1803 WITTMAN, WILLIAM (M. D.). Travels in Turkey, Asia-Minor, Syria, and across the Desert into Egypt, during the years 1799, 1800, and 1801, in company with the Turkish Army and the British Military Mission; to which are annexed Observations on the Plague, and on the Diseases prevalent in Turkey, and a meteorological Journal, by William Wittman, M. D. Many colored plates of Turkish and Egyptian costumes. 4to. London.

1804 CALDWELL, ANDREW. An Account of the extraordinary Escape of James Stuart, Esq. ("Athenian Stuart"), from being put to Death by some Turks, in whose Company he happened to be travelling. Fol. London.

> Privately printed.—Lowndes.

1805 ARRIAN. Voyage round the Euxine Sea translated; and Accompanied with a Geographical Dissertation, to which are added three Discourses: I. On the Trade to the East Indies by means of the Euxine Sea; II. On the Distance which Ships of Antiquity usually sailed in 24 Hours; III. On the Measure of the Olympic Stadium. Maps. 4to. London.

1807 BROQUIERE, BERTRANDON DE LA. Travels to Palestine, and Return from Jerusalem overland to France, during the years 1432 and 1433, translated by Thomas Johnes, from a MS. in the National Library at Paris. Map of Tartary. 8vo. Hafod Press.

> Reprinted in Wright's *Early Travels in Palestine,* London, 1848.

1829-1836 MACARIUS. The Travels of Macarius, Patriarch of Antioch, written by his attendant Archdeacon Paul of Aleppo, in Arabic. Translated by F. C. Belfour. 9 parts in 7 vols. 4to. London.

> Published by the Oriental Translation Fund.

1843-49 FABRI, FELIX. Fratris Felicis Fabri Evagatorium in Terrae Sanctae, Arabiae et Egypti Peregrinationem. Edidit C. D. Hassler. 3 vols. 8vo. London.

> A modern edition in English, London, 1892-93. A German version (place?), 1556. See below.

> 1892-93 FABRI, FELIX. Book of the Wanderings of Brother Felix Fabri (to the Holy Land, . . . circa 1480-83). Translated by A. Stewart. 4 vols. 8vo. London.

> 1556 FABRI, FELIX. Eigentliche Beschreibung der Hin und Wiederfahrten zu dem Heilige-Lande und Jerusalem. 4to. (Place?)

1848 WRIGHT, THOMAS. Early Travels in Palestine. Comprising the Travels of Bishop Arculf, in the Holy Land, towards A. D. 700; The Travels of Willibald, 721-727; The Voyage of Bernard the Wise, 867; The Travels of Saewulf, 1102 and 1103; The Saga of Sigurd the Crusader, 1107-1111; The Travels of Rabbi Benjamin, Tudela, 1160-1173; The Book of Sir John Maundeville, 1322-1356; The Travels of Bertrandon de la Broquiere, 1432 and 1433; The Journey of Henry Maundrell, from Aleppo to Jerusalem, 1697. 8vo. Bohn's Library. London.

> Although this work is a collection of travels, it is put here because its contents have all been selected for their bearing on the Near East. In his Introduction Wright accounts for the sources of his texts.

1857 WEY, WILLIAM. The Itineraries of William Wey. Edited for the Roxburghe Club. London.

> This pilgrim to Palestine left a pretty full account of the routes he followed on his way to the Holy Land in 1458 and 1462. He advises others how to travel and describes various places he passes by, but he has no interest in relics of classical antiquity. Among his aids to travellers is a vocabulary of useful phrases in the Greek of the day. —From Rice, *English Travellers in Greece.*

1862 WRATISLAW, BARON WENCELAS (of Mitrowitz). Adventures of Baron Wencelas Wratislaw: What he saw in the Turkish Metropolis, Constantinople, Experiences in his Captivity, and after his happy Return to his Country, committed to Writing in 1599. Literally translated from the original Bohemian by A. H. Wratislaw. London.

1870 BORDE, ANDREW. Fyrst Boke of the Introduction of Knowledge, made by Andrew Borde, a Physycke Doctor. Edited by F. J. Furnivall. Early English Text Society. New Ser., vol. 10. London.

> Reprinted by the same, London, 1893. Original printing, London, 1547.
> Furnivall, in his Introduction, discusses at some length the probable date of printing, and concludes that the dedication to Princess (later Queen) Mary was written in 1542, but that the book was not published until 1547. Like Wey's *Itineraries* cited above, it is more of an aid to travellers than a description of a journey.

1883 TORKINGTON, SIR RICHARD. Ye Oldest Diarie of Englysshe Travell: being the hitherto unpublished Narrative of the Pilgrimage of Sir Richard Torkington to Jerusalem in 1517. Edited by W. J. Loftie. 12mo. London.

> This purports to be an account of a journey made to Jerusalem in 1517; but its author has copied the largest portion of his "diary" verbatim from Guylforde's Pylgrymage, . . .—Rice, *English Travellers in Greece.*

1890 LE STRANGE, GUY. Palestine under the Moslems. A Description of Syria and the Holy Land from A. D. 650 to 1500, translated from the works of the medieval Arab Geographers. Maps and illus. 8vo. London.

> The object of the author was to translate, systematise, and bring into comparison and chronological order, all the various accounts given by Arab geographers, of the cities, Holy Places, and districts of Palestine and Syria.—Bookseller's Note.

1890-97 Palestine Pilgrims' Text Society Publications. 14 vols. Numerous maps and illus. 8vo. London.

> This valuable and unique collection of early descriptions of the Holy Places and of the topography of Palestine from the earliest times to the period of the Crusades consists of about thirty-four accounts of pilgrimage, translated from the Greek, Latin, Arabic, Old-French, and Old-German originals.—Heffer. For partial contents see below.

> 1897 The Churches of Constantin at Jerusalem. The Bordeaux Pilgrim. The Pilgrimage of S. Silvia to the Holy Places. The Letter of Paula and Eustochium to Marcella. The Pilgrimage of Holy Paula, by S. Jerome. Vol. I. 1897.

> 1897 The Epitome of S. Eucherius. The Breviary or Short Description of Jerusalem. Theodosius on the Topography of the Holy Land. The Buildings of Justinian by Procopius. The Holy Places visited by Antoninus Martyr. Vol. II.

> 1897 The Pilgrimage of Arculfus. The Hodieporicon of S. Willibald. Description of Syria and Palestine by Mukkadasi. The Itinerary of Bernard the Wise. Vol. III.

> 1897 Journey through Syria and Palestine by Nasir-i-Khusrau. The Pilgrimage of Saewulf to Jerusalem. The Pilgrimage of the Russian Abbot Daniel. Vol. IV.

1892 Early Voyages and Travels in the Levant. I. The Diary of Master Thomas Dallam, 1599-1600. II. Extracts from the Diaries of Dr. John Covel, 1670-1679. With some Account of the Levant Company of Turkey Merchants. Edited by James Theodore Bent, F.S.A., F.R.G.S. Illus. Hak. Soc. ser. I, vol. 87. London.

1893 Information for Pilgrims into the Holy Land, edited by E. Gordon Duff. 4to. London.

> A facsimile reproduction of the unique copy of 1498.
> This book was first printed in 1498. As its title implies, it was intended to serve as an aid to travellers to the Holy Land. To this end it includes useful directions and a set of phrases needed by travellers.—See Rice, *English Travellers in Greece.*

1897 COSMAS INDICOPLEUSTES. The Topographia Christiana of Cosmas Indicopleustes. Translated from the Greek and edited by John Watson McCrindle, M.A. 4 illus. Hak. Soc., ser. I, vol. 98. London.

> An edition under a different editor, London, 1909. See below.
> This work was written about the year 547. It was termed by Professor Beazley "systematic nonsense," a label it seems to deserve, for it is a curious mixture of theological argument for a flat earth with Jerusalem at its center and Cosmas' own knowledge of geography. It had little bearing on the progress of geography of the time. See Baker, *Geographical Discovery.*
>
> 1909 COSMAS INDICOPLEUSTES. The Christian Topography of Cosmas Indicopleustes, edited with geographical notes by E. O. Winstedt. 8vo. London.

1900 LE STRANGE, GUY. Baghdad during the Abbasid Caliphate from contemporary Arabic and Persian Sources. 8 plans. 8vo. London.

1901 TEIXEIRA, PEDRO. The Journey from India to Italy by Land, 1604-05; With his Chronicle of the Kings of Ormus. Translated and Edited by William Frederick Sinclair, late Bombay C.S., with additional Notes, etc., by Donald William Ferguson. Hak. Soc., ser. II, vol. 9. London.

1902 BODENHAM, ROGER, (Captain). Voyage to Scio, 1551. In Beazley, *Voyages and Travels,* vol. I (from Hakluyt, 1599-1600). London.

CAMPION, JASPER. The English Trade to Scio in 1539-1570. In Beazley I (from Hakluyt, 1599-1600). London.

1907 CASOLA, PIETRO (Canon). Pilgrimage to Jerusalem in the year 1494. Translated, with Introduction, by M. M. Newett. 8vo. London.

> A later edition, London, 1929. See below.
>
> 1929 The Casale Pilgrim, a Sixteenth-Century Illustrated Guide to the Holy Places, reproduced in facsimile, with introduction, translation and notes, by Cecil Roth. Illus. in color. 4to. London.

IBN JUBAYR. Travels. Edited from a MS. in the University of Leyden by W. Wright. 2nd edit., revised by M. J. De Goeje. 8vo. London.

> This is the best edition of the Arabic text of this famous Moslem traveller of the 12th century.—Bookseller's Note.

1911   BREYDENBACH, BERNHARD VON. Bernhard von Breydenbach
       and his Journey to the Holy Land, 1483-84. A Bibliography. Com-
       piled by Hugh W. Davies. 60 pp. of reproductions. 4to. London.

> Latin original, Mainz, 1486. See below.
> This book, one of the earliest accounts of travel that have come down to us,
> gives the salient facts and fancies of a voyage undertaken by Bernhardus de Brey-
> denbach, an official of the Archbishop of Mainz, with two other knights to the
> Holy Land. Reuwich went with them as artist to the expedition and designed the
> drawings of the places they visited, besides smaller ones of costumes, etc. On ac-
> count of the length of some of the cuts—the Venetian panorama measuring over
> five feet, and one of the Palestine over four—copies of this book with the cuts
> quite complete are of the greatest rarity. The illustrations mark a new era in the
> history of wood-engraving and book illustration, and their designer, Erhard Reu-
> wich of Utrecht, ranks with the first of his time. The engraver, whose name is
> unfortunately unknown, is entitled to equal credit. They are the best illustrations
> in any medieval book, being among the first woodcuts in which shading is used in
> masses and not merely to help the outlines, . . . being the first definite attempt to
> represent places and persons in a life-like way, and drawn from the life.—From
> Bookseller's Notes. The book was frequently translated.

> 1486—BREYDENBACH, BERNHARDUS DE. Sanctarum Peregrinatium in
>   Montem Sinai ad venerandum Christi Sepulcrum atque in Montem Sinai
>   ad divam Virginem et Martyrem Catharinam: opusculum Bernh. de
>   Breydenbach. Mentz.

1920   ABBOTT, G. F. Under the Turk in Constantinople, a Record of Sir
       John Finch's Embassy, 1674-1681. Illus. 8vo. London.

1926   TAFUR, PERO. Travels and Adventures, 1435-1439. Translated from
       the Spanish, with Introduction by M. Letts. 3 plates. Broadway
       Travellers. 8vo. London.

> Spanish original, Madrid, 1874. See below.
> Tafur was a Spanish knight who travelled as far east as Constantinople and also
> visited the great trading centers of medieval Europe, such as Antwerp, Ghent, etc.,
> when these towns were at the height of their commercial supremacy. He greatly
> admired the Venetians and the Flemings. At the time of his visit Constantinople
> was very much in decay.

> 1874 TAFUR, PERO. Andanças e viajes de Pero Tafur por diversas partes
>   del mundo avidos. Madrid.

>> No complete translation had hitherto appeared, though portions had
>> been translated into German earlier. Only one manuscript is known to
>> be extant, and that one is some centuries later than the time of the
>> travels themselves.

1928   The Desert Route to India, being the Journals of four Travellers by the
       great Desert Caravan Route between Aleppo and Basra, 1745-1751.
       Edited by Douglas Carruthers. Map and plates. Hak. Soc. ser. II,
       vol. 63. London.

1931 MAKHAIRAS, LEONITOS. Recital concerning the Sweet Land of Cyprus entitled "Chronicle," edited with a translation by R. M. Dawkins. Map. 2 vols. 8vo. London.

> The Chronicle of Leonitos Makhairas deals with the history of Cyprus to the year 1458 and principally with the hundred years immediately preceding that date. It was last edited, with a French translation, in 1881; the present edition offers a text based upon a fresh collation of the two existing manuscripts, and provides it for the first time with an English translation and notes. The first volume contains text and translation, the second, the Introduction, Commentary, Glossary and Indexes.—Bookseller's Note.

SANDERSON, JOHN. Selections from the Papers of John Sanderson, Levant Merchant, 1560-1627, including his Travels in Palestine, etc. Edited by Sir William Foster, C.I.E. Hak. Soc., ser. II, vol. 68. London.

IX

Central Asia

1577 VARTHEMA, LUDOVICO DI. For his account of Persia see his *Navigation and Vyages of Lewes Vertomannus,* under EAST INDIES.

1580 FRAMPTON, JOHN. A Discourse of Tartaria, Scithia, . . . 12mo. London.

The Region of Tartaria and of the Lawes and Power of the Tartares, of the Cuntrey of Scithia and the Manner of the Scithians, of the Cuntrey called the other side of Gange, of Cataia and the Region of Sina, a cuntrey of the Great Cham and of the mervulous wonders that haue ben seene in those Cuntreyes. London.

> Taken from the *Stationers' Register.* This work may be that listed under Frampton above.

1590 BEROALDUS, MATTHAEUS. A Short View of the Persian Monarchie and of Daniels Weekes. Translated by H. Broughton. 4to. London.

1595 MINADOI, GIOVANNI THOMASCO. The History of the Warres between the Turks and the Persians. Containing the Description of all such Matters, as pertaine to the Religion, to the Forces, to the Government, and to the Countries of the Kingdome of the Persians. . . . And last of all, a Letter of the Authors, wherein is discoursed, what Cittie it was in the old time, which is now called Tauris. Translated into English by Abraham Hartwell. Folding map of Persia. 4to. London.

> Italian original, Venice, 1594. See below.
> Minadoi was an Italian doctor of medicine attached to the Venetian Consulate in Constantinople and Syria. He was able to gain much valuable information on the war between Turkey and Persia during the years 1576-1588.—Maggs, No. 519.

> 1594 MINADOI, GIOVANNI THOMASCO. Historia della Guerra fra Turchi et Persiani, divisa in libri none. Folding map of Persia and Turkey. 4to. Venice.

1601 SHERLEY, SIR ANTHONY. A New and large Discourse of the Travels of Sir Anthony Sherley, Knight, by Sea, and over Land, to the Persian Empire. Wherein are related many Straunge and wonderfull accidents; and also, the Description and Condition of those Countries and

People he passed by; with his returne into Christendome. Written by William Parry, Gentleman, who accompanied Sir Anthony in his Travels. 4to. London.

Sir Anthony published his own Relation in 1613. Parry's account reappears in Anthony Nixon's *The Three English Brothers*, London, 1607. Reprinted in Collier's Reprints, Red Series. The Travailes of the three English Brothers dramatised by John Day, 1607. Translated into Dutch, Leyden, 1706. See below.

Parry's account is an exceedingly scarce work, being much rarer than Sherley's. It is a most interesting and well-written little volume. Among one of the wonders that Sherley hardly expects people to believe is that Turkish merchants make use of a pigeon post from Mecca to Aleppo and train their pigeons to carry letters concerning the state of the markets from places three months' camel journey away. He gives a curious description of the manners and customs of the Persians. Among the interesting items is his relation concerning petroleum found at Baku. The Shah took a great liking to him and sent him as ambassador to Moscow, where, however, he was given a bad reception by the Russians.—Maggs, No. 519. His career was one of travels, adventures, dangers and varying fortunes. He ended his days in poverty at Madrid.

1607 NIXON, ANTHONY. The Three English Brothers. Sir Thomas Sherley his Travels, with his three Yeares Imprisonment in Turkie. Sir Anthony Sherley his Embassage. Master Robert Sherley, his Wars against the Turkes, and Marriage to the Emperor of Persia's Niece. 4to. London.

1607 DAY, JOHN. The Travailes of the three English Brothers, Sir Thomas, Sir Anthony, and Mr. Robert Shirley. As it is now play'd by her Maiesties Seruantes. 4to. London.

> This play is dedicated "To honours fauorites, and the intire friends of the familie of the Sherley's," by John Day, William Rowley and George Wilkins.—Lowndes.

1706 (In Dutch.) Opmerkelyke Reystogten van den heer Anthony Sherley, gedaan in den Jare 1599, na Persien. Map and plates. 12mo. Leyden.

1611 CARTWRIGHT, JOHN. For an account of Sir Anthony Sherley's Entertainment at the Court of Persia, see *The Preachers' Travels,* under NEAR EAST.

1613 SHERLEY, SIR ANTHONY. Relation of his Travels into Persia, the Dangers and Distresses which befell him in his Passage . . . his Magnificent Entertainment in Persia . . . 2 portraits. 4to. London.

> Reviewed by Collier in his *Rarest Books in the English Language*. Modern edition, London, 1933.

> 1933 Sir Anthony Sherley and his Persian Adventure. Including some Contemporary Narratives relating thereto. Edited by Sir E. Denison Ross. 8 plates and 2 maps. London.

1625 ROE, SIR THOMAS. For an account of Persia see his *The Embassy of Sir Thomas Roe to the Court of the Great Mogul,* under EAST INDIES.

1634 HERBERT, SIR THOMAS. A Description of the Persian Monarchy
Now beinge: The Orientall Indyes, Iles, & other part's of the Greater
Asia, and Africk'. (Second title.) A Relations of some Yeares Travaile, begynne Anno 1626. Into Afrique and the greater Asia, especially
the Territories of the Persian Monarchie: and some parts of the Orientall Indies, and Iles adiacent. . . . Fol. London.

> Four English editions appeared during the author's lifetime: the 2nd in fol.,
> London, 1638, revised and enlarged by the author; the 3rd, London, 1665; the 4th,
> London, 1677, further amplified, with a chapter on the discovery of America by
> the Welsh Prince Madoc in the twelfth century. This last edition, much pared
> down, was published in the Broadway Travellers' Series, edited by Sir William
> Foster, London, 1928. Translated into Dutch, Dordrecht, 1658; into French,
> Paris, 1663. See below.
> Herbert's narrative "is of considerable importance from an historical point of
> view, as giving us the only detailed account available of the first English Em-
> bassy to Persia, to say nothing of the information afforded concerning the re-
> doubtable Shah Abbas and his chief servants."—From Sir William Foster's Intro-
> duction. He commenced his travels in 1626/7 and returned to England in Decem-
> ber, 1629. He went out to Persia in the train of Sir Dodmore Cotton, ac-
> credited as Ambassador to the Shah of Persia. He also visited the Cape of Good
> Hope, Madagascar, and Surat, and coasted the eastern shores of North America
> on his return to England. His account of these travels is written in a lively and
> agreeable style. To prove that the Welshman Madoc ap Owen discovered Amer-
> ica, he quotes the Welsh bards in evidence. It is amusing that he points to the
> name of Cape Breton as a proof that his countrymen were there in the ninth
> century.—From Robinson, No. 20.

1638 HERBERT, SIR THOMAS. Some Yeares Travels into Divers Parts of
Asia and Afrique. Describing especially the two famous Empires, the
Persian, and the great Mogull . . . As also, many rich and spatious
Kingdomes in the Orientall India, and other parts of Asia; Together
with the adjacent Isles. . . . With a revivall of the first Discoverer of
America. Revised and Enlarged by the Author. Fol. London.

1658 (In Dutch.) Zee-en Lant-Reyse Na verscheyde Deelen van Asia en Africa
Beschryvende Voornamelijck de twee bevremde Rijcken van den Per-
siaen, en den Grooten Mogul . . . Beneffens een Verhael van den
eersten Vinder van America. Uyt het Engels in de Nede landtsche
Tale vvergeset door L(ambert) van den Bosch. 4to. Dordrecht.

1663 (In French.) Relation du Voyage de Perse et des Indes-Orientales: traduit de l'anglais de Thomas Herbert (par Wiquefort); avec le Révolutions arrivées au Royaume de Siam l'an 1647; traduites du Flammand
de Jeremie van Vliet (par le même). 4to. Paris.

1662 MANDELSLO, JOHANN ALBRECHT VON. For his travels in Persia see his *The Voyages and Travels of,* under EAST INDIES, and
also Olearius below.

OLEARIUS, ADAM. Voyages and Travels of the Ambassadors to the
Great Duke of Muscovy and the King of Persia, rendered into English by J. Davies. Portraits and maps. Fol. London.

> 2nd edit., fol., London, 1669. German original, Sleswick, 1647. See below.
> The occasion of this journey was an embassy sent by the Duke of Holstein
> to the Duke of Moscovy and the King of Persia in the years 1633-1639. Olearius
> was its secretary. For further detail see under the edition of 1669 below. Moscow
> was reached in the first expedition, 1633-35; and Persia in the second, 1635-39.

1669 OLEARIUS, ADAM. The Voyage and Travells of the Ambassadors sent by Frederick, Duke of Holstein, to the Great Duke of Muscovy and the King of Persia, containing a compleat history of Muscovy, Tartary, Persia and other adjacent Countries; whereunto are added the Travels of John Albert de Mandelslo from Persia into the East Indies, containing a particular description of Indosthan, the Mogul's Empire, the Oriental Islands, Japan, China, . . . Portraits and folding maps. 2nd edition, corrected. Fol. London.

> The work is of importance cartographically (especially for its map of the river Volga), and contains moreover many valuable magnetic and orographical observations. The Portion dealing with Mandelslo has a separate title and pagination.—Bookseller's Note. Goethe described the work as "höchst erfreulich und belehrend." Olearius and Mandelslo parted at Ispahan, the latter proceeding on to India.

1647 OLEARIUS, ADAM. Muskowitische oft begehrte Beschreibung der neuen orientalischen Reise an den König von Persien: item, ein Schreiben des J. A. Mandelslo, worinn eine Ostindianische Reise über Oceanum enthalten. Fol. Sleswick.

1665 VALLE, PIETRO DELLA. For a description of Persia see his *The Travels of*, under EAST INDIA.

1673 OGILBY, JOHN. Asia, the first part, being an Accurate Description of Persia, the Vast Empire of the Great Mogul, and other Parts of India. . . . London. (See under EAST INDIES.)

1678 TAVERNIER, JEAN BAPTISTE. The Six Voyages of Jean Baptiste Tavernier, Baron of Aubonne, through Turkey into Persia and the East Indies, for the space of forty years; giving an Account of the Present State of those Countries, viz., of the Religion, Government, Customs, and Commerce, of every Country; and the Figures, Weights, and Value of the Money current all over Asia. To which is added, A New Description of the Seraglio; made English by J(ohn) P(hillips). With a Description of the Kingdoms which encompass the Euxin and Caspian Seas, . . . by an English Traveller: never before printed. Fol. London.

> For further detail see under EAST INDIES. A modern French edition of the portion relating to Persia, published by Pascal Pia, 4to, Paris, 1931.

1684 STRUYS, JEAN. For his travels through Tartary see his *Voyages and Travels through Muscovia, etc.,* under GENERAL TRAVELS AND DESCRIPTIONS

1686 CHARDIN, SIR JOHN. Travels into Persia and the East-Indies, the first volume containing the Author's Voyage from Paris to Ispahan: to which is added, the Coronation of this Present King of Persia, Solyman the Third. Portrait, map, and numerous plates. Fol. London.

Later English editions: 2 vols., 4to, London, 1711; London, 1724; the portion on Persia in Harris II, 862-876; reprinted in abstract in Pinkerton VIII, 138-167; Argonaut Press, London, 1925. In French, 2 vols., London, 1686; 2 vols., Amsterdam and Lyons, 1686; these editions contain only the journey from Paris to Ispahan. Other parts of his travels were published entire in the edition of Amsterdam, 10 vols., 1711; 10 vols., Paris, 1723. An enlarged edition, 4 vols., Amsterdam, 1735. For some of these see below.

Chardin was a Huguenot who was forced to emigrate to England. He was knighted by Charles II and on his death was buried in Westminster Abbey. His first visit to the East was made in 1665, at the age of twenty-two, when he both gratified a love of travelling and carried on his trade as a dealer in jewels. His more important voyage was made in 1671. His route differed from that usually taken by travellers to the East Indies in that he proceeded by way of the Black Sea and the countries bordering thereon. His account of the Persian court and of his business transactions with the Shah are of great interest. Sir William Jones regarded his narrative as the best yet published on the Mohammedan nations.

1744-48   CHARDIN, SIR JOHN.   The Travels of Sir John Chardin, by the Way of the Black Sea, through the Countries of Circassia, Mingrelia, the Country of the Abcas, Georgia, Armenia, and Media, into Persia Proper; with a very curious and accurate Account not only of the Countries through which he travelled but of the Manners and Customs, Religion and Government, Commerce and Inclinations of the several Nations that inhabit them; Relations so much the more curious, as these Countries, and the People, dwelling in them, had not been tolerably described before by any Author. In Harris II, 862-876.

1686   (In French.)   Journal du Chevalier Chardin en Perse, et aux Indes-Orientales, par la Mer-Noire. Londres.

1723   (In French.)   Voyages en Perse et autres lieux de l'Orient. 77 plates and 1 map. 10 vols. Paris.

1687   THEVENOT, JEAN.   For his travels in Persia see his *Travels into the Levant,* Part II, under NEAR EAST.

1689   HELIOGENES DEL EPY.   A Voyage into Tartary; containing a curious Description of that Country, with part of Greece and Turkey; the Manners, Opinions, and Religion, of the Inhabitants therein; with some other Incidents.   London, 1689.

The date 1688 is also given for this work.

1695   SANSON, ——.   The Present State of Persia; with a faithful Account of the Manners, Religion, and Government of that People.   Illus. Done into English by John Savage.   12mo.   London.

French original, Paris, 1695. See below.
In his preface the author says: "I was sent to Persia in 1683 to work in the Missions. . . . I had access to the Palace such as was not accorded to the great Lords of Persia; I assisted at all the audiences that the king gave, and I had my place at the festivals."—Quoted.

1695   SANSON, ——.   Voyage ou Relation de l'Etat Présent du Royaume de Perse. Avec une dissertation curieuse sur les Moeurs, Religion et Gouvernement de cet Etat. 6 copperplates of views and costumes. 12mo. Paris.

1698 FRYER, JOHN. For his travels into Persia see his *New Account of East-India and Persia,* under EAST INDIES.

1715 STEVENS, JOHN (Captain). The History of Persia, containing a curious Account of India, China, Tartary, Kermon, Arabia, . . . and the Manners and Customs of those People, Persian Worshippers of Fire. . . . To which is added, An Abridgement of the Lives of the Kings of Harmuz, or Ormuz. The Persian History written in Arabick, by Mirkond, . . . that of Ormuz, by Torunxe, . . . both of them translated into Spanish, by Antony Teixeira, . . . and now render'd into English by Captain John Stevens. Frontispiece, 8vo. London.

> For Teixeira see also under 1901, NEAR EAST, and Stevens, 1708-1710, EAST INDIES.

1720 LE BRUN, CORNELIUS. Voyage to the Levant and Travels into Moscovey, Persia and the East-Indies. Numerous cuts. 3 vols. London.

> The edition of Le Brun of 1702 contained his travels into the Levant. See under NEAR EAST, this date. An edition limited to his travels in Persia and the East Indies in 2 vols., London, 1737; another edition, fol., translated by M. Powis, London, 1759. The French original of these travels, Amsterdam, 1718. See below.

> 1737 LE BRUN, CORNELIUS. Travels into Muscovy, Persia, and part of the East-Indies. Containing an accurate Description of whatever is most remarkable in those Countries. To which is added, An Account of the Journey of Mr. Isbrants, Ambassador from Moscovy, through Russia and Tartary to China; together with Remarks on the Travels of Sir John Chardin and Mr. Kaempfer, and a Letter written to the Author on that Subject. Translated from the original French. Portrait, 3 maps, 131 plates, and numerous engravings in the text. 2 vols. Fol. London.

> 1759 LE BRUN, CORNELIUS. A new and more correct Translation than has been hitherto published of Mr. Cornelius Le Brun's Travels into Muscovey, Persia and divers parts of the East-Indies. Portrait and 47 illus. Fol. London.

> > This translation is by M. Powis.

> 1718 LE BRUN, CORNEILLE. Voyage de Corneille Le Brun par la Moscovie, en Perse, et aux Indes Orientales. 2 vols. Fol. Amsterdam.

> > This edition also contains Isbrant's route as well as the remarks on Chardin and Kaempfer.

1722-23 LANGE, LAURENCE. For an account of Tartary see his *Travels through Russia to China and Siberia,* under FAR EAST.

1723 CHEREFEDDIN ALI. The History of Timur-Bec, known by the Name of Tamerlain the Great, Emperor of the Moguls and Tartars: being an historical Journal of his Conquests in Asia and Europe. Written in

Persian by Cherefeddin Ali, his Contemporary. Translated into French by Petis de la Croix, now rendered into English. Maps. 2 vols. 8vo. London.

1727   An Historical Account of the Revolutions in Persia in the Years 1722-25. . . . Together with a Relation of the Miseries occasion'd by the Siege of Ispahan. . . . Written by a French Missionary . . . , To which is prefix'd a Genealogical Account of the Royal Family of Persia by the Translator. 8vo. London.

1729-1730   General History of the Turks, Moguls and Tatars, vulgarly called Tartars; together with a Description of the Countries they Inhabit. 2 vols. 8vo. London.

1730   ABU'L GHAZI. The Genealogical History of the Tatars. Translated from the Tatar manuscript written in the Mogul Language by Abu'l Ghazi Bahader, Khan of Khowarazm, containing the Antiquities of the Moguls and Tatars from Adam. A curious description of all the Tribes into which the Turkish Nation is divided, the Life of Zinghiz Khan the Great and his successors. With a complete History of the Uzbek Khans, the Khans of Great Bukharia from the first Conquest of those countries to the Death of Abu'l Ghazi in 1663. The whole made English. Map. 2 vols. 8vo. London.

>   The author dying in 1663, his son and successor, Anusha Mahomet, supplied what was left to be done in 1665. This history, he tells us, was extracted from books on the subject and partly from particular Memoirs of divers Mogul tribes.

1736   KAEMPFER, ENGELBERT. Travels in Persia, and other Countries of the East. 2 vols. London.

>   Cited by Pinkerton XVII, who adds, "these are both works of great merit and scarcity."

1736-38   STRAHLENBURG, PHILIP JOHANN VON. For his account of Great Tartary see his *Historico-Geographical Description of the North and Eastern Parts of Europe*, under EAST EUROPE.

1739   Persepolis Illustrata; or, Account of the Ancient and Royal Palace of Persepolis in Persia, destroyed by Alexander the Great; with particular Remarks concerning that palace, and an Account of the ancient authors; illustrated and described in 21 copper-plates. Fol. London.

1742 FRASER, JAMES. The History of Nadir Shah, formerly called Thamas Kuli Khan, the present Emperor of Persia; to which is prefix'd a short History of the Moghol Emperors. Map. 8vo. London.

SPILMAN, JAMES. A Journey through Russia into Persia; by Two English Gentlemen, who went in the Year 1739, from Petersburgh in order to make a Discovery how the Trade from Great Britain might be carried on from Astracan over the Caspian. To which is annexed, A Summary Account of the Rise of the famous Kouli Kan (i. e., Nadir Shah), and his Successes, till he seated himself on the Persian Throne. 8vo. London.

A Copious and circumstantial Description of the Great Empire of Persia, its Situation, Extent, Distribution of its Provinces, Climate, Rivers, Seas, Soil, Produce, and the chief Cities throughout the Country, so as to afford a perfect Idea of its Condition, in past and present Times. Collected from the Writings of the most famous Travellers, particularly from those of Herbert, Chardin, Tavernier, Thevenot, Le Brun, and others, their several Remarks and Observations being all digested into a regular and easy Method. In Harris II, 876-891.

1744-48 Of the Disposition and Temper of the Persians, their Persons, Habits, Manner of Living, their Artifices and Mechanicks, the Respect paid to Merchants, the Methods in which their Inland Trade is carried on, the past and present State of the English Commerce, and other Particulars, together with some curious Observations on the Nature of the silk Trade, and a Computation of the annual Balance in Favour of Persia. Collected as well from private Memoirs, as from Accounts that have been published. In Harris II, 891-897.

Containing an Account of the Government and Constitutions of Persia, the Nature of the Shah's Power, the Distribution of Civil, Ecclesiastical and Military Offices, the interior Policy of the Empire, the regular Forces kept there, both Horse and Foot, and the Nature and Amount of the publick Revenues. The Whole digested into Order from the Best Authorities. In Harris II, 897-906.

A succinct View of the Persian History from the earliest Accounts down to the present Time; in which is contained a concise Representation of the several remarkable Revolutions in that Empire, ancient and modern, the Conquests thereof by several Nations, and the Succession of their respective Monarchs, so as is necessary to illustrate what has been delivered in the foregoing sections. Collected as well from the Oriental Writers, as from the Greek and Latin Historians. In Harris II, 907-917.

1745-47   Accounts of Independent Tartary. Abstract in Astley IV, 476-514.

> Reprinted in Pinkerton VIII, 310-385.

ASCELIN, Friar. The Travels of Friar Ascelin and his Companions, towards the Tartars in 1247. Generalized account in Astley IV, 550-552.

> This relation is taken from the Memoirs of Friar Simon de St. Quintin, inserted in the 32nd Book of *Speculum Historiale* of Vincent of Beauvais. Purchas has also made an abstract of it. These friars were sent on an embassy from the Pope to solicit more mercy from the Tartars towards the Christians. But their embassy was fruitless; even they themselves were subjected to maltreatment.

A General Description of Tartary, subject to China. Taken from various sources. In Astley IV, 348-362.

A General Description of Western Tartary. Taken from various sources, some of them freely translated from the French. In Astley IV, 367-449.

A General Description of Turkestan, taken from various sources. In Astley IV, 536-541.

A generalized Description of Great Bukharia from various sources. In Astley IV, 514-525. Followed by a brief description of Little Bukharia, or the Kingdom of Kashgar. In Astley IV, 526-536.

A generalized Description of the Kingdom of Karazm from various sources. In Astley IV, 476-514; 552-580.

JENKINSON, ANTHONY. The Voyages and Travels of Anthony Jenkinson from Russia to Boghar, or Bokhara in 1577. Abstract in Astley IV, 632-642.

> Reprinted in Pinkerton VIII, 386-394. Published by the Hakluyt Society for 1885. Translated into French in Thevenot's Collection, Part I. See below. Also found in Hakluyt and Purchas.
> Jenkinson, an intelligent merchant, was sent by the Muscovy Company, by way of Russia, to discover the road to Bokhara and to settle a trade, if convenient and advantageous, in that country. He left Gravesend in 1557. Sailing around Norway he arrived at St. Nicholas in Russia and proceeded thence to Moscow. Having obtained letters from the Czar to several princes, he travelled on with

three servants to Bokhara. He afterwards made three voyages to Russia, on one of them as Ambassador from Queen Elizabeth to the Russian Court.

1885 JENKINSON, ANTHONY. Early Voyages and Travels to Russia and Persia. By Anthony Jenkinson and other Englishmen, with some account of the first Intercourse of the English with Russia and Central Asia by way of the Caspian Sea. Edited by Edward Delmar Morgan and Charles Henry Coote. 2 maps and 2 illus. 2 vols. Hak. Soc., ser. I, vols. 72-73. London.

1666 (In French.) Voyage d'Antoine Jenkinson, pour découvrir le Chemin de Catay par la Tartarie, écrit par lui-même aux Marchands Anglais de la Compagnie de Moscou, qui l'aboient de faire ce voyage (en 1558). In Thevenot. Paris.

RUBRUQUIS, WILLIAM DE. For the Travels of William de Rubruquis to Tartary and to China see under FAR EAST. For those of Carpini see likewise this date under FAR EAST.

1746 CEREAU, J. K. DU. Nadir-Shah (Vely Neamen: formerly called Thamus Kuli Khan: usurper of Persia). The Compleat History of, I. Containing a Description of the Persian Empire, the Lives of Cyrus and his Descendents (*sic*); II. Containing a Description of the Empire of Indostan, some Account of all the Great Moguls from Tamerlane, ... written in French (by J. K. du Cereau), and rendered into English. 2nd edit., with Appendix. Portrait of Nadir-Shah by Boitard and map. 12mo. London.

Published in the year preceding the death of this terrible murderer, blinder of his own son, and massacrer of the people of Delhi, where he captured booty amounting to £20,000,000, and including the Koh-i-nur diamond.—Sotheran.

1753 HANWAY, JONAS. An Historical Account of the British Trade over the Caspian Sea, with the Author's Journals of Travels through Russia into Persia, and back through Russia, Germany and Holland, to which are added, the Revolutions of Persia during the Present Century, with the History of Nadir Kouli. Numerous plates of views, portraits, and maps. 4 vols. in 3. 4to. London.

2nd edit., revised, 2 vols., 4to, London, 1754; also in Dublin, 1754; 3rd edit., revised and corrected, 2 vols., 4to, London, 1762. A Life by John Pugh, London, 1787. Translated into German, Hamburg, 1754. See below.
Hanway was a well known traveller and philanthropist, popularly remembered as the pioneer user of the umbrella. Readers of Boswell will recall Johnson's severe criticism of his essay attacking tea-drinking. As a partner of a St. Petersburg merchant, he made a journey in 1743 down the Volga and by the Caspian Sea to Persia with a caravan of woolen goods, and returned in 1745 by the same route after many perilous adventures. He reached London in 1750. He later filled several public positions, and had a street named after him in London and a monument erected to him in Westminster Abbey. Dr. Johnson said of him, "that he acquired a reputation travelling abroad, but lost it all by travelling at home." This was in reference to his "Eight Days'" trip in England. There is a pleasant essay on him by Austin Dobson in *Eighteenth Century Vignettes*.

1754 HANWAY, JONAS. An Historical Account of the British Trade over the Caspian Sea, with a Journal of Travels from London into Persia and back, with an Account of the Revolution of Persia, containing the Reign of Shah Sultan Hussein, the Invasion of the Afghans, the Reigns of Sultans Mir Maghmud and Ashreff, the History of the celebrated Nadir Shah, and of Adil Shah, and a Chronological abridgement of the Persian Monarchy from its foundations. Maps, plates and vignettes. 2 vols. 4to. London.

1787 PUGH, JOHN. Remarkable Occurrences in the Life of Jonas Hanway, comprehending his Travels in Russia and Persia, with several Anecdotes. 8vo. London.

1754 (In German.) Beschreibung seines Reisen von London durch Russland und Persien und wieder zurück durch Russland, Deutschland und Holland, 1742-1750. Worinnen die Gross brittanische Handlung über die Caspische See und überhaupt das Handlungenswesen von Russland, Persien, von Tartarey, Turkey, von Armenien, China, . . . beschrieben. 2 Teile in I Band. 8 maps, 5 plates, and 9 vignettes. 4to. Hamburg.

1763 BELL, JOHN (of Auchtermony). Travels from St. Petersburg in Russia, to divers Parts of Asia. Folding map. 2 vols. 4to. Glasgow.

Later editions: 2 vols., 8vo, London, 1764; 2 vols., 4to, Glasgow, 1788; reprinted in Pinkerton VII, 271-516. Translated into French, Paris, 1766; into German, Hamburg, 1787. See below.
This work contains a Journey to Ispahan in 1715-18, in the suite of Artemy Petrovich Valaisky, Russian Ambassador to the Shah Hussein; to Pekin in 1719, with the Ambassador sent by Peter the Great to Kang-Hi, emperor of China; to Derbent in Persia in 1722 with the Russian army, commanded by the Czar in person; and to Constantinople in 1737-38, at the order of the Chancellor of Russia and the English Ambassador at the Court of Russia. The 1788 edition includes the Journal of De Lange in 1721-22 at Pekin.—"This work is the best model for travel-writing in the English Language."—Quarterly Review, quoted by Lowndes.

1766 (In French.) Voyages depuis St. Petersbourg en Russie dans diverses contrées de l'Asie. On y a joint une description de la Sibérie. Traduit de l'anglais par M . . . 3 vols. 12mo. Paris.

1787 (In German.) Reisen von Petersburg in verschiedene Gegenden Asiens. Aus dem Englischen. Hamburg.

1770 COOK, JOHN (M.D., of Hamilton). Voyage and Travels through the Russian Empire, Tartary and Persia. 2 vols. 8vo. Edinburgh.

1772 BRUCE, PETER HENRY. For an account of his travels in Tartary, see *Memoirs of Peter Henry Bruce,* under GENERAL TRAVELS AND DESCRIPTIONS.

1773 IVES, EDWARD. For his journey from Persia to England see his *A Voyage from England to India,* under EAST INDIES.

1787 HAMILTON, C. Historical Relation of the Rohillas, the Afghans, and Persia. London.

1790 FRANKLIN, WILLIAM. Observations made on a Tour from Bengal to Persia; with a short Account of the Remains of the celebrated Palace of Persepolis, in the years 1786-87. London.

> Extracts from this work relating to the northern part of Persia in Pinkerton VIII, 279-309.

1792 NIEBUHR, CARSTEN. For his travels in Persia and Hindustan see his *Travels through Arabia,* under NEAR EAST.

1798 FORSTER, GEORGE. For his travels through Afghanistan, Persia, and into Russia by the Caspian Sea, see his *A Journey from Bengal to England,* under EAST INDIES.

1799 Concise Account of some natural Curiosities of Malham (in Persia). London.

1800 EBN HAUKAL. The Oriental Geography of Ebn Haukal, an Arabian Traveller of the tenth Century. Translated by Sir William Ouseley. 4to. London.

> The translator, an orientalist, was secretary to his brother, Sir Gore Ouseley, Bart., Ambassador Extraordinary to the Court of Persia.

ADDENDA

1808-1814 An Account of the Government and Constitution of Persia from various sources. In Pinkerton VII, 212-236.

The Disposition and Temper of the Persians, . . . from various sources and Memoirs. In Pinkerton VIII, 199-211.

A General Description of Persia from various writings, "their several Remarks and Observations being all digested into a regular and easy Method." In Pinkerton VIII, 168-198.

1860 CLAVIJO, RUY GONZALEZ DE. Narrative of the Embassy of Ruy Gonzalez de Clavijo to the Court of Timour, at Samarkand, A.D. 1403-06. Translated for the first time with Notes, a Preface and an Introductory Life of Timour Beg, by Sir Clements R. Markham, K.C.B., F.R.S., ex-Pres. R.G.S. Map. Hak. Soc., ser. I, vol. 26. London.

> A modern edition, London, 1928. Spanish original, Seville, 1582. See below.
> The account of the journey of Ruy Gonzalez de Clavijo, in his embassy to the court of Timour, at Samarkand, is the oldest Spanish narrative of travels of any value . . . It is interesting as the first of a long series of chronicles of Spanish voyages and travels in every quarter of the globe, when Spain was at the height of her glory.—Sir C. R. Markham, Preface to the Hakluyt Society edition.

1928 CLAVIJO, RUY GONZALEZ DE. Embassy to Tamerlane, 1403-06.
       Translated from the Spanish by G. Le Strange, with an Introduction,
       Maps. Broadway Travellers. London.

1582 CLAVIJO, RUY GONCALEZ DE. Historia del Gran Tamorlan e Itin-
       rario y Enarracion del Viage y relacion de la Embaxada que Ruy
       Goncalez de Clavijo le hizo, por mandado del muy poderoso Señor
       Rey Don Henrique el Tercero de Castilla. Y un breve discurso fecho
       por Goncalo Argato de Molina, . . . Fol. Seville.

1870 SALIL-IBN-RAZIK. History of the Imams and Seyyids of 'Oman, by
       Salil-Ibn-Razik, from A.D. 661-1856. Translated from the original
       Arabic, and edited, with a continuation of the History down to 1870,
       by the Rev. George Percy Badger, F.R.G.S. Map. Bibliography.
       Hak. Soc., ser. I, vol. 44. London.

1873 BARBARO, JOSAFA, and CONTARINI, AMBROGIO. Travels to
       Tana and Persia. By Josafa Barbaro and Ambrogio Contarini. Trans-
       lated from the Italian by William Thomas, Clerk of the Council to Ed-
       ward VI, and by E. A. Roy, and Edited with Introduction by Lord
       Stanley Alderley . . . A Narrative of Italian Travels in Persia, in the
       Fifteenth and Sixteenth centuries. Translated and edited by Charles
       Grey. Hak. Soc., ser. I, vol. 49. London.

> According to D. N. B. Thomas's translation of Barbaro, dedicated to Edward VI, was published in 1551. There is an Italian edition put out at Venice in 1543. See below.

1543 BARBARO, JOSAFA, and CONTARINI, AMBROGIO. Viaggi fatti in
       Tana in Persia, in India, et in Constantinopoli, con la descrizione par-
       ticulare di citta, luoghi, siti, costumi, e della Porta del Gransuo, e della
       ultima impresa contra Portughesi. In Vinegia, nell' anno M.D. XLIII
       nella Casa di Aldo. 8vo. Venice.

> According to Pinkerton, this small collection is very scarce. It was subsequently inserted in the large collection of Ramusio, and trans-lated into Latin in the *Scriptores Rerum Persicarum*, Frankfort, 1607, by Antonio Minutio. The work contains the travels of Gasparo Con-tarino, who in 1473 visited Mingrelia, Georgia, Persia, Tartary, and Russia; two journies of Giuseppe Barbaro, two of Alevigi, and two anonymous travels.

1902 HAMD-ALLAH MUSTAWFI. Description of Persia and Mesopotamia
       in the year 1340 A.D. from the Nuzhat-al-Kulub of Hamd-Allah Mus-
       tawfi. By G. Le Strange. 8vo. London.

1924 WESSELS, C. Early Jesuit Travellers in Central Asia (1603-1721). Folding map and 5 plates. 8vo. The Hague.

1926 DON JUAN OF PERSIA (a Shi'ah Catholic, 1560-1604). Translated and edited, with an Introduction, by G. Le Strange. 3 maps. 8vo. Broadway Travellers. London.

> An edition in Spanish in 3 vols., 4to, Valladolid, 1604.
> A translation of the *Relaciones* of Don Juan, formerly Uruch Beg, a Shi'ah Moslem. He was one of the secretaries to the Persian Ambassador whom Shah Abbas sent to the princes of Europe under the guidance and personal conduct of Sir Anthony Sherley. The book described Persia and its Government, the wars between Persians and Turks, and the Journey from Ispahan into the countries of the west.—Bookseller's Note.

1929 ANDRADA, RUY FREYRE DE. For the coast of Persia and Arabia see under 1664, EAST INDIES.

X
East Indies

1499 MANDEVILLE, SIR JOHN. For his asserted description of the "marveyles of Inde," see under FAR EAST.

> In his *Travels and Travellers in India A.D. 1400-1700,* Oaten quotes Sir George Birwood: "He speaks of 'the marvyles of Inde,' but it is certain he was never there. He may be described as the father of English sensation writers," and is not to be trusted even when he may be telling the truth."

1577 EDEN, RICHARD. For a description of the "Countreys lying eyther way towardes the fruitfull and ryche Moluccaes," see his *The History of Travayle in the VVest and East Indies,* under COLLECTIONS.

VARTHEMA, LUDOVICO DI. The Navigation and Vyages of Lewes Vertomannus Gentleman of the Citie of Rome, to the Regions of Arabia, Egypte, Persia, Syria, Ethiopia, and East Indies, both within and without the River Ganges, . . . in the Yeere 1503. Conteyning many notable and straunge thinges, both hystoricall and naturall. Translated out of Latine into Englyshe by Richard Eden in the Yeere 1576. 4to. London.

> This translation is included in the *History of Travayle* of Eden's listed above as finished by Richard Willes. An abridged version appeared in Purchas, 1625. Modern reprints: Hakluyt Society, London, 1863; Aungervyle Society, London, 1884; Argonaut Press, London, 1928. Italian original, Rome, 1510, and many later translations in Spanish, French, German, and Italian, besides being included in various collections. See below.
>
> Varthema was a real traveller whose driving purpose was to see the sights. His reports on the social and political conditions of the various lands he visited are reliable as being gathered from personal contact with places and peoples, and are rich in the personal adventures of the author. His account of the overland trade is of great value in that we are made to see it before it had begun to give way to the all-seas route. He left Europe in 1502 and India in 1507. He returned home in a Portuguese ship commanded by Tristan d'Acunha. Among the places he visited in his East Indian voyage were Cambay, Calicut, Vijayanagar, Ceylon, Pegu, Malacca, Sumatra, and Borneo. He even heard of a southern continent and of a region of intense cold and very short days, being the first European probably after Marco Polo to bring back the rumor of Terra Australis. See Oaten, *Early Travels and Travellers in India.*

1863 VARTHEMA, LUDOVICO DI. The Travels of Ludovico de Varthema in Egypt, Syria, Arabia, Persia, India, and Ethiopia, A.D. 1503 to 1508. Translated from the original Italian edition of 1510, with a Preface by John Winter Jones, Esq., F.S.A., and edited, with notes and introduction, by George Percy Badger, late Government Chaplain in the Presidency of Bombay. Map. Hak. Soc., ser. I, vol. 32. London.

1884 VARTHEMA, LUDOVICO DI. Reprint of Eden's Edition, privately printed for the Aungervyle Society. 8vo. London.

1928 VARTHEMA, LUDOVICO DI. The Itinerary of Ludovico di Varthema of Bologna, from 1502 to 1508, as translated from the original Italian Edition of 1510, by John Winter Jones, F.S.A., in 1863, for the Hakluyt Society, with a Discourse on Varthema and his Travels in Southern Asia by Sir Richard Carnac Temple, Bt. 4to. Argonaut Press. London.

1510 VARTHEMA, LUDOVICO DI. Itinerario de Ludovico di Varthema nello Egypto, nella Suria, nella Arabia Deserta et Felice, nella Persia, nella India et nella Ethiopia . . . 4to. Rome.

1579 POLO, MARCO. Polo has something to say on India. See his Travels under FAR EAST.

1582 CASTANHEDA, FERNANDO LOPEZ DE. The First Booke of the Historie of the Discouerie and Conquest of the East Indies, enterprised by the Portingales, in their daungerous Nauigations, in the Time of King Don John the Second . . . Set foorth in the Portingale language by Hernan Lopes de Castanheda. And Now Translated into English by N(icholas) L(ichfield), Gentleman. 4to. London.

> Portuguese original, Coimbra, 1552-54. See below.
> Castanheda, unlike Varthema, was an historian rather than a traveller. He states in his prologue that he had been in the Indies, and while there had taken pains to inform himself of everything relating to the new discoveries. He also declares that there were no more than four persons living (among them himself) who had any knowledge thereof; and that had those persons died, the memory of those great achievements might have been buried in oblivion.—The above is the first book only of Castanheda's History, but it is the only part published in England. Lichfield, who dedicates his translation to Sir Francis Drake, professes to have translated it from the Portuguese, which he certainly did not do. As the text of the first volume existed already in a Spanish and a French version, he may have used either. The author's prologue as given in the Spanish is an abridgement of the Portuguese prologue, and it agrees closely with Lichfield's English.—Quaritch. Although relating principally to the East Indies, it contains interesting particulars of the Portuguese conquests in Brazil.—Maggs, No. 479.

> 1552-54 CASTANHEDA, FERNANDO LOPEZ DE. Historia do descobrimento e conquista da India, pelos Portuguezes, feyta por Fernando Lopez de Castanheda, e approvada pelos senhores deputados da sancta Inquisicao. 4to. Coimbra.

1588 FREDERICI, CESARE. The Voyage and Travaile of M. C. Frederici, Merchant of Venys into the Easte India and Indyes and beyond the Indyes, . . . Translated by T. Hickok from the Italian original of 1587. 4to. London.

> Reprinted in Hakluyt and in Purchas. Italian original, Venice, 1587. See below.
> Caesar de Federici, as his name is rightly spelled, set out from Venice for the East Indies in 1563 and arrived home again in 1581. He visited the chief trading cities of the Portuguese as well as the established centers of Hindu power and commerce. The great capital of the southern Hindus, long a bulwark against the Moslem invasions, namely, Vijiyanagar, which he called "Bezeneger," had been practically destroyed by the Mohammedans on their last assault two years before. After touching at Ceylon, he went up the east coast of India and on to

other places outside of India. His description of the practice of suttee is one of the best of the early accounts.—From Oaten, *Early Travels and Travellers in India.*

1587 FEDERICI, CAESAR DE. Viaggio nell' India Orientale. Venice.

1598 An addition to the Sea Journall; or Navigation of the Hollanders into Java, with a Vocabulary of Words used at St. Laurence (i. e., Madagascar). 4to. London.

An information of the Kingdomme and State of the great King of Mogor, . . . London.

> Entered in the *Stationers' Register* under date of 1597.

HOUTMAN, CORNELIUS. The Description of a Voyage made by certaine Ships of Holland into the East Indies. With their Adventures and Successe: Together with the Description of the Countries, Townes, and Inhabitants of the same. Who set forth on the second of April 1595, and returned on the 14 of August 1597. Translated out of Dutch into English by W. P(hillip). Woodcut maps and illus. 4to. London.

> There is a date of 1597 cited in the *Stationers' Register* for this item. Reprinted in Hakluyt and Purchas; in Osborne II, 393-431 (with some errors in pagination), whose account differs from that printed by Purchas and Harris; in Harris I, 925-926. A Dutch version, Amsterdam, 1598, is listed by Pinkerton XVII under the name of Houtman. See below and also the Introduction to the Hak. Soc., ser. I, vol. 54.
> Sometimes this work is cited under the name of Bernardt Langhenez, the Dutch publisher. Lowndes calls him the writer of the work. Langhenez, who at any rate was not the voyager, states that as this description fell into his hands "wherein is contained the first voyage of the Low-countrymen into the East-Indies, with the adventures happened unto them . . . I thought it good to put it into print, with many pictures and cards," etc.—From the Osborne version. This is one of the rarest of the Elizabethan travel books, containing the account of the first Dutch voyage to the East, which, as the author states on his second page, was undertaken in emulation of the famous English navigators Sir Fraunces Drake and Mr. Candish. Visits were made to the Cape of Good Hope, Madagascar, Sumatra, Java, and the Moluccas. Only a few copies of this work are now known to exist.—Maggs, No. 519. The failure of the Barents expedition to open up a route to the East by way of the North East Passage led the Dutch to attempt reaching the East by way of the Cape Route. The expedition consisting of four ships under the command of Cornelis Houtman arrived at Bantam in Java in 1596, where they tried to get a cargo of spices. But hostilities with the Portuguese arose and the fleet was compelled to sail on. The circumnavigation of Java was the first recorded attempt of this kind by any European vessel. Much knowledge of the regions later to become the exclusive territory of the Dutch resulted from the voyage.

1598 HOUTMANN, CORNELIUS. De erste Schep-vaert gedaen van de Hollanders naar Oost-Indien. 4to. Amsterdam.

LINSCHOTEN, JOHN HUYGHEN VAN. His Discours of Voyages into ye Easte and West Indies. Deuided into Foure Bookes. Engraved title and 12 folding maps with English inscriptions. 4to. London.

Reprinted by the Hakluyt Society, London, 1884; a portion in Beazley's *Voyages and Travels,* vol. II, London, 1903. Dutch original, Amsterdam, 1595-96. See below. There was a German translation in 1598, two Latin versions in 1599, and one in French in 1610, with numerous subsequent editions in various languages.

The title-page was designed and engraved by William Rogers, of London, the first Englishman known to have practiced the art of engraving on copper.—John Carter Brown. It is extremely difficult to get perfect copies of this work. It was of such great value to navigators at the time of its publication that it was used on many vessels as a log-book, with the consequence that maps became missing, and the work soiled and torn.—Quaritch.

The comprehensive and useful nature of the work can best be judged from a detailed description of its contents. The first book gives Linschoten's relation of his starting for the peninsula in 1579, his taking service in 1580 with a German nobleman travelling through Spain, his joining the Portuguese service for India in April, 1585, and his voyage to India, where he arrived in September of the same year. The second book gives The True and perfect Description of the whole coast of Guinea, Manicongo, Angola, Monomotapa, and right ouer against them the Cape of S. Augustin in Brasilia, with the compasse of the whole Ocean Seas, together with the Ilands, as S. Thomas, S. Helena, and the Ascention, with all their hauenes, channels, depths, shallows, sands and grounds. Together with diuers strange voyages made by the Hollanders: also the description of the inward partes of the same landes. Likewise a further Description of the Cards of Madagascar; otherwise called the Iland of St. Laurence, . . . also the voiages that the Portingall Pilots haue made into all places of the Indies. Extracted out of their Sea Cardes, bookes, and notes of great experience. And translated into Dutch by I. Hughen van Linschoten. And now translated out of Dutch into English by W(illiam) P(hillip). The Thirde Booke. The Nauigation of the Portingales into the East Indies, and from the East Indies into Portingall, also from the Portingall Indies to Malacca, China, Iapon, the Ilands of Iaua and Sunda, both to and fro, and from China to the Spanish Indies, . . . as also of all the coast of Brasilia, and the Hauens thereof. With a Description of the Firme land and the Ilands of the Spanish Indies lying before it, called Antillas, together with the Nauigation of Cabo de Lopo Gonsalues to Angola, in the coast of Ethiopia, with all the courses, Hauens, Ilands, Depthes, Shallowes, . . . also the times of the yeares when the winds blow, with the true tokens and knowledge of the tides and the weather, water, and streames, in all the Orientall coasts and Hauens as they are obserued and set downe by the Kings Pilots, in their continuall and dayly Viages. . . . The Fourth Booke. A most true and certaine Extract and Summarie of all the Rents, Demaines, Tolles, Taxes, Impostes, Tributes, . . . of the King of Spaine, throughout all his kingdoms, lands, Prouinces, and Lordships, as they are collected out of the originall Registers of his Chamber of accompts. Together with a briefe and cleere description of the gouernment, power and pedegree of the Kings of Portingall. Translated out of Spanish into Low Dutch by Iohn Hughen of Linschoten. And out of Dutch into English by W. P.

These surveys of commerce and trade routes, along with the translations of original Spanish and Portuguese documents on geography, statistics, navigation, etc., made this work of supreme importance to other nations. By showing the rottenness and inner weakness of the Portuguese administration of the East Indies, the work also stimulated the Dutch and English to attempt to gain advantages for themselves.

1884 LINSCHOTEN, JOHN HUYGHEN VAN. The Voyage of John Huyghen van Linschoten to the East Indies. From the English translation of 1598. The First Book containing his Description of the East. In Two Volumes, edited, the First Volume, by the late Arthur Coke Burnell, Ph.D., C.I.E.; the Second Volume, by Pieter Anton Tiele. Hak. Soc., ser. I, vols. 70-71. London.

1903 LINSCHOTEN, JOHN HUYGHEN VAN. Voyage to Goa and back, 1583-1592, with his Account of the East Indies. In Beazley, *Voyages and Travels,* vol. II. London.

1595-96 LINSCHOTEN, JOHN HUYGHEN VAN. Itinerario. Voyage ofte
schipvaert van J. H. van Linschoten naer Oost- ofte Portugaels In-
diën, inh. een beschryvinghe der landen ende zee-custen. Met aanw.
van de voorn. havens, revieren, enz. tot noch toe van de Portugesen ont-
dekt, waer bij ghevoecht conterfeytsels van de habyten, drachten, tem-
pels . . . boomen, vruchten, . . . verhalinge van de coophandelingen enz.—
Reysegeschrift vande navigatiën der Portugaloysers in Orienten.—
Beschrijvinghe van de gantsche custe Cuinea, Manicongo, . . . ende
tegenover de Cabo S. Augustijn in Brasilien. . . . Mitsg. de beschrijvinge op de caerte van Madagascar, . . . Portrait, maps, etc. 3 vols. in
1. Amsterdam.

1599 A True Report of the gainefull, prosperous and speedy voiage to Java in
the East Indies, performed by a fleete of eight Ships of Amsterdam,
. . . 4to. London.

An edition with another title, London, 1601. See below.
This work describes the second voyage of the Dutch East India Company to
the East Indies, made in 1598-99, under the command of Jacob van Neck, Wybrand
van Warwijck, and Jacob Heemskerck.—Maggs, No. 519. In 1598 a number of
expeditions were fitted out by the merchants of various cities to secure the profits
of the East India trade. This one under van Neck was financed by the merchants
of Amsterdam. It reached Banda, Amboina, and the Moluccas, besides circumnav-
igating Java. On the return trip some of the ships touched at the Island of
Mauritius, which received its name on that occasion. A garden was planted there
and fenced in for the benefit of future voyagers.—From Heawood, *Geographical
Discovery in the Seventeenth and Eighteenth Centuries.*

1601 NECK, JACOB VAN. The Iovrnall, or dayly Register, contayning a
trve Manifestation and historicall Declaration of the Voyage, accomplished by eight Shippes of Amsterdam, vnder the Conduct of Jacob
Corneliszen Neck Admirall, and Wybrandt van Warwick Vice-Admirall,
which sayled from Amsterdam the first day of March, 1598. Shewing
the Covrse they kept, and what other notable Matters happened vnto
them in the sayd Voyage. 4to. London.

This was translated at the instance of Hakluyt by William Walker
from the Dutch account of van Neck to the East, 1598. Reprinted in
vol. V of the 1809-1812 edition of Hakluyt's Voyages.—Parks.

1603 A True and large Discourse of the Voyage of the whole Fleete of Ships
set forth the 29th of April, 1601, by the Governor and Assistants of
the East Indian Merchants of London, to the East Indies. Wherein
is set down the order and manner of their Trafficke, the Description of
the Cuntrey, the Nature of the People and their Language, with the
Names of suche men as Died in the Voiage. 4to. London.

This must be the first expedition sent out by the newly incorporated English
East India Company under the command of Captain James Lancaster. Its object
was to secure pepper by direct trading and thus circumvent the rise in price of
this article which the Dutch had arbitrarily doubled. Only an indifferent amount
was secured, but agents were left at Bantam and others dispatched to the Moluccas to establish a factory against the arrival of the next fleet from England.—
From Heawood, *Geographical Discovery.*

1604 ACOSTA, JOSEPH DE. The Natural and Morall Historie of the East and West Indies. See same under SOUTH AMERICA.

SCOTT, EDMUND (Traveller). An Exact Discourse of the Subtilties, Fashi-shions, Pollicies, Religion, and Ceremonies of the East Indians, as well Chyneses as Javans, there abyding and dweling, Together with the manner of trading with those people, as well by us English as by the Hollanders: as also what happened to the English Nation at Bantam in the East Indies, since the 2. of February, 1602 untill the 6. of October, 1605. Whereunto is added a briefe Description of Java Major. Written by Edmund Scott, resident there, and in other places neere adjoyning, the space of three years and a halfe. 4to. London.

1606 MIDDLETON, SIR HENRY. The Last East-Indian Voyage. Containing mvch varietie of the State of the seuerall Kingdomes where they haue traded: with the Letters of three seuerall Kings to the Kings Maiestie of England, begun by one of the Voyage: since continued out of the faithfull obseruations of them that are come home. 4to. London, printed for Walter Burre.

> The early East India voyages made their first and only appearance in *Purchas His Pilgrimes,* with the exception of this one, which is misplaced and mutilated. This edition of 1606 is practically the sole unmutilated specimen of Early East India voyages.—Editor Hakluyt Society edition. Reprinted by the Hakluyt Society, London, 1856. See below.
> This is the original edition of Sir Henry Middleton's voyage to Bantam and the Molucca Islands. It is an account of the second voyage set forth by the Governor and Company of Merchants of London trading into the East Indies. . . . It includes letters from the Kings of Ternate, Tydore and Bantam. Walter Burre, for whom the book was printed, may be regarded as the writer of the book, as he seems to have taken the imperfect MS. of the original author, whose name he withholds, and to have completed it by means of information supplied to him by other members of the voyage.—Robinson, No. 19. The same vessels took part as were used in the first voyage of 1601-03. . . . "The returns nearly doubled the capital, a result which was rather due to successful privateering than to honest trading."—From Maggs, No. 519.

> 1856 MIDDLETON, SIR HENRY. The Voyage of Sir Henry Middleton to Bantam and the Maluco Islands, Being the Second Voyage set forth by the Governor and Company of Merchants of London trading into the East Indies. From the edition of 1606. Annotated and edited by Bolton Corney, M.R.S.L. 3 maps and 3 illus. Hak. Soc., ser. I, vol. 19. London.

1608 MATELIFF, CORNELIS. An Historicall Description of the Voiage of the Admirall Cornelis Mateliff the yonger toward the East Indyes who Departed in May 1605. Item of the Siege before Malacca and the Sea Battell against the Portuguese Armada and other Discoveries. Translated out of the Dutch copie printed at Roterdam by John Johnson Anno 1608. 4to. London.

> Dutch original, Rotterdam, 1608. See below.

1608 MATELIEF, CORNELIS. Historiale ende ware Beschrijvinge vande Reyse des Admiraels Cornelis Matelief . . . naer de Oost-Indien; uytghetrocken in Mayo 1605. Mitsgaders de belagheringhe voor Malacca, . . . 4to. Rotterdam.

1612 COVERTE, ROBERT (Captain). A True and Almost Incredible Report of an Englishman, that being cast away in the good Ship called the Ascension, in Cambaye, travelled by Land through many unknown Kingdoms, and great Cities. With a particular Description of all those Kingdoms, Cities and People; As also a Relation of their Commodities, and Manner of Traffique; and what Seasons of the Year they are most in use; Faithfully related. With the Discovery of a great Emperor called the Great Mogul, a Prince not until now known to our English Nation. 4to. London.

> Reprinted in Osborne II, 237-266; in Astley I, 336-344. Translated into Latin, Dutch, and German. For a Dutch version, Leyden, 1706, see below.
> Coverte, who was steward on the *Ascension* and apparently had no right to the title of Captain, sailed from Plymouth March 31, 1607. His ship struck the bar going into Surat and foundered, but the crew escaped ashore in boats. When they arrived at Surat an English merchant assisted them to travel to the court of the Great Mogul at Agra. Coverte started for home from Agra in January, 1610, in company with several other Englishmen. Travelling by way of Candahar, Ispahan, and Bagdad (where one of them quitted the party), they reached Aleppo in December, and thence got by sea to England, arriving there in April, 1611. A long journey forsooth. There is another account of the voyage of the *Ascension*— the fourth expedition sent out by the East India Company—written by Thomas Jones and printed in Purchas. This voyage of Coverte's lays claim to two discoveries, one of the Great Mogul's country, the other of the Red Sea; it is full of mistakes, but contains some interesting details. See Introd. to *John Jourdain's Journal*, Hakluyt Society, under 1905 below.

> 1706 (In Dutch.) Gedenkwaardige reys te lande door Indostan of Opper-Indien, Persien, Arabien, Asiatisch Turckyen, . . . Uyt het Engels. 1 map and 2 plates. 8vo. Leyden.

1615 MONFART, HENRY DE. An exact and curious Survey of all the East Indies, even to Canton, all duly performed by Land. Wherein also are described the huge Dominions of the great Mogor. 4to. London.

> Reprinted in Somer's *Collection of Tracts*, vol. III.—Lowndes. This work is also listed under the name of Henri de Feynes.

1616 CORYATE, THOMAS. Thomas Coriate. Traueller for the English VVits: Greeting. From the Court of the Great Mogvl, Resident at the Town of Asmere (Ajmir), in Eastern India. Woodcuts. 4to. London.

> This work has another title: Mr. T. Coriat to his Friends in England sendeth Greeting: from Agra. October, 1616. The book is extremely rare.
> This oddest of travellers is better known for his journies through Europe called *Coryat's Crudities*, published in 1611. See WEST EUROPE under that date. His presence in India was extremely embarrassing to Sir Thomas Roe, the English representative in India, who feared that his countryman would injure the prestige of the English by some unconventional performance. Roe's fears were well

founded, for it was not long before Coryat delivered an oration to the Great Mogul, who threw him a hundred rupees. Another time he nearly met death at hte hands of a native mob by proclaiming, when the muezzin called to prayers, that Mohammed was an impostor. He in turn was greatly vexed when he heard that King James had remarked, on learning that Coryat was in India, "Is that fool yet living?" Coryat died in Surat in 1617 from an over-indulgence in sack. As he performed most of his journies in Europe on foot, so he proceeded in the same manner from Aleppo to Ajmir. His prodigious quantity of notes, which Roe tells us were too great "for portage," were lost and only some letters make up this account.—From Oaten, *Early Travellers and Travels in India.*

1622   A Covrante of Newes from the East Indies: A True Relation of the taking of the Islands of Lantore and Polaroone in the parts of Banda in the East Indies by the Hollanders, which Islands had yeelded themselues subject vnto the King of England. Written to the East India Company from their Factors there.

No place or printer cited. Extremely rare.—Robinson, No. 19.

The Hollanders Declaration of the Affaires in the East Indies, or A True Relation of that which passed in the Ilands of Banda, in the East Indies, faithfully translated according to the Dutch Copie. 4to. London.

This may be the same item as that listed just above. For a reply see the following item.

An Answer to the Hollanders Declaration, concerning the Occurrents of the East-India. The First Part. Written by Certaine Marriners lately returned from thence into England. (Followed by) The Examination of Thomas Hackwell the 25. of January, 1621 (upon certain Articles relative to the English Merchants trading to the East Indies). The Coppie of a Letter sent unto the Dutch . . . from Monoboca . . . and delivered unto Captayne William Johnson (Commander of the *Angell*). An Answer to Objections . . . the cause of the first breach in the East Indies. 4to. London.

A true Relation of the Kingdom of the great Magor or Mogul. 4to. London.

1624   A True Relation of the Vniust, Cruell, and Barbarous Proceedings against the English at Amboyna In the East-Indies, by the Netherlandis Gouernour and Councel there. Also the coppie of a Pamphlet, set forth first in Dutch and then in English, by some Neatherlander; falsely entituled, A True Declaration Of The Newes that came out of the East-Indies, with the Pinace called the Hare, which arriued at Texel in Iune, 1624.

Together with an Answer to the same Pamphlet. By the English East-India Companie. 2nd impression. 3 parts. 4to. London.

3rd impression, London, 1632. Another edition of Part 2, London, 1624.

The authorship of this Relation has been attributed to Sir Dudley Digges, who had been sent to Holland in 1620 to endeavor to effect a settlement of the points in dispute between the English East India Company and the Dutch.—Quaritch. The massacre of the English on trumped-up charges by the Dutch authorities at Amboyna was typical of the ruthlessness of the Dutch East India Company when it deemed its monopoly of the Archipelago was encroached on. The event called forth many tracts. In Osborne are six such pamphlets. Dryden based a play upon the incident. See below.

1673   DRYDEN, JOHN. Amboyna: a Tragedy as it is enacted at the Theatre-Royale. 4to. London.

1745   A True Relation of the Unjust, Cruel, and Barbarous Proceedings against the English at Amboyna, in the East-Indies, by the Netherlandish Governor and Council there. 4th edit. in Osborne II, 278-292. London.

A True Declaration of the News that came out of the East-Indies With the Pinnace called the Hare, which arrived in the Texel in June, 1624. Concerning a Conspiracy discovered in the Island of Amboyna, and the Punishment following thereupon, according to the Course of Justice, in March, 1624. Comprehended in a Letter-Missive; And sent from a Friend in the Low-Countries, to a Friend of Note in England, for Information of him in the Truth of those Passages. In Osborne II, 293-300. London.

An Answer unto the Dutch Pamphlet, made in Defence of the Unjust and Barbarous Proceedings against the English, at Amboyna, in the East-Indies, by the Hollanders there. In Osborne II, 301-312. London.

A Remonstrance of the Directors of the Netherlands East-India Company, Presented to the Lords States-General of the United Provinces; in Defence of the said Company, Touching the Bloody Proceedings against the English Merchants, Executed at Amboyna. Together with the Acts of the Process against the said English. And the Reply of the English East-India Company, to the said Remonstrance and Defence. Published by Authority. In Osborne II, 313-324. London.

An authentick Copy of the Confessions and Sentences against Mr. Towerson and Accomplices, concerning the bloody Conspiracy enterprised against the Castle of Amboyna: The which, by the manifest Grace and Providence of God was discovered the 23rd Day of February, in the Year 1623. As also the Resolutions of the Governor Van Speult, and of the Council, taken in the Business. Translated out of the Copy delivered to the English East-India Company, from the Dutch. In Osborne II, 325-336. London.

A Reply to the Remonstrance of the Bewintherbers or Directors of the Netherlandis East-India Company, lately exhibited to the Lords States-General, in Justification of the Proceedings of their Officers at Amboyna, against the English there. In Osborne II, 337-352. London.

1625   ROE, SIR THOMAS. The Embassy of Sir Thomas Roe to the Court
       of the Great Mogul 1615-1619. In Purchas *His Pilgrimes,* vol. I. Lon-
       don.

           Purchas did a poor piece of editing, cutting the work down to a third and
       carelessly mutilating important passages. He included in his account some notes
       by Edward Terry, Roe's chaplain in India, which were later expanded into a
       small volume published in 1655 (see Terry this date below). This work has fre-
       quently been confused with Roe's own Journal. Purchas's version appeared in
       Dutch, Amsterdam, 1656. In Harris's Collection of 1705 is printed an inaccurate
       and much compressed paraphrase of Roe's Journal derived from Purchas. But
       in the 1744-48 edition the narrative is suppressed and a short account of its con-
       tents is substituted with a general history of the Company's trade. In Churchill's
       Collection of 1704 is printed the first volume of Roe's own manuscript; but this
       account is really inferior to that of Purchas's, being a piece of hackwork with
       much omission and mishandling of Roe's own words. Versions were published in
       Knox's New Collection VI, 1767, and in other later English collections, such as
       Pinkerton's, VIII, 1-56. It appeared in French in Thevenot (see under 1687,
       NEAR EAST), with additions from his original manuscripts and some extracts
       from his letters. It was included in Pietro della Valle's *Travels into East India*
       (see under 1665 below). It was edited for the Hakluyt Society, 1899, and a revised
       edition, 1926. Translated into Dutch, Amsterdam, 1656. See below.
           The complete victory of Captain Best, of the "tenth voyage," over an im-
       mensely superior Portuguese fleet at Swally, the harbor of Surat, in 1612, opened
       this port again to English traders. In consequence an attempt was made to es-
       tablish a factory at this city, but the representatives sent there failed to make
       sufficient impression, and Sir Thomas Roe, an experienced traveller, a polished
       courtier, and an excellent debater, was despatched to the court of Jehangir, the
       Great Mogul, to rehabilitate the dignity and respect of the English nation. A bet-
       ter man apparently could not have been chosen. His three years' stay was one
       prolonged combat with oriental cunning and treachery, but in the main he suc-
       ceeded by dint of an unswerving integrity in winning concessions for English
       trading rights. His journal concerns itself more with details of court life than
       with the manners of the people, but even so it is a valuable commentary on the
       administration of the Mogul Empire during the reign of its effeminate, debauched
       ruler, Jehangir. More than any one else he prepared the way for the future British
       empire in India. See Oaten, *Early Travellers and Travels in India.*

       1732   ROE, SIR THOMAS. The Journal of Sir Thomas Roe, Embassador
               from his Majesty King James the First of England, to Ichan Guire
               (Jehangir), the Mighty Emperor of India Commonly called the Great
               Mogul. Containing an Account of his Voyage to that Country, and his
               Observations there. Taken from his own Original Manuscript. In
               Churchill I, 687-737. London.

       1899   ROE, SIR THOMAS. The Embassy of Sir Thomas Roe to the Court
               of the Great Mogul, 1615-19. Edited from Contemporary Records by
               William Foster. Portrait and 2 illus. 2 vols. Hak. Soc. ser. II, vols.
               1-2. London.

       1926   ROE, SIR THOMAS. Embassy to India, 1615-19, from his Journal and
               Correspondence. Edited by Sir William Foster. Revised edition. 11
               illus. 8vo. London.

       1656   (In Dutch.) Journael van de Reysen, ghedaen door den Ed. Heeren Rid-
               der Sr. Thomas Roe . . . Afgevaerdicht naer Oostindien een den
               Grooten Mogol, ende andere ghewesten in Indien. Newen Verscheyde
               Aenmerckens en ghedenckwaerdighe gheschiedenissen, en een be-
               schrijvinghe van de volckeren, Steden, Landen, ende Druchten. Uyt het
               Engels vertaalt. 4to. Amsterdam.

1630 LORD, HENRY. A Discoverie of the Sect of the Banians, containing
their History, Law, Liturgie, Casts, Customes and Ceremonies, as the
particulars were comprized in the Booke of their Law, called Shaster;
also (separate title-page) The Religion of the Persees as it was compiled from a Book of theirs called their Zundavastaw. 4to. London.

> Reprinted in Churchill VI, 299-342; in Pinkerton VIII, 523-572. Translated
> into French, 1667. See below.
> Lord was sometime resident in India at Surat and Preacher to the Honourable
> Company of Merchants trading to East India.

> 1732 LORD, HENRY. A Description of Two Forreigne Sects in the East-
> Indies, viz., The Sect of the Banians, the Antient Natives of India, and
> the Sect of the Persees, the Ancient Inhabitants of Persia; together
> with the Religion and Manners of each Sect. In two parts. In Church-
> ill VI, 299-342. London.

> 1667 (In French.) Histoire de la Religion des Banians. 12mo. (Place?).

1633 FAREWELL, CHRISTOPHER. An East India Collation, or a Discourse of Travels in a Voyage to the East Indies. 16mo. London.

1634 HERBERT, SIR THOMAS. For his travels into India see his *Description of the Persian Monarchy,* under CENTRAL ASIA.

> Herbert paid a short visit to Surat and the regions adjacent. His book
> gives a very fair account of the closing years of Jahangir's reign and the sub-
> sequent events.—Oaten, *Early Travellers and Travels in India.*

1638 BRUTON, WILLIAM. Newes from the East-Indies: Or, A Voyage
to Bengalia, one of the greatest Kingdomes under the High and Mighty
Prince Pedesha Shassallem, usually called the Great Mogul, with the
State of the Court of Malcandy. Written by William Bruton, now
resident in the parish of S. Saviours, Southwark, who was an eye and
eare witnesse of these following Descriptions . . . 4to. London.

> Reprinted in Osborne II, 267-279.
> Bruton and another Englishman were sent from the Coromandel Coast to Ben-
> gala to negotiate trade agreements. They reached the court of the Nabob at
> Cuttack, who was so impressed by the independent attitude of his English guests
> that he granted them perfect freedom of trade and even leave to coin money.
> Bruton's experiences in Bengal were very pleasant and he has good words to say
> for the ingenuity and intelligence of the Bengalese.—From Oaten, *Early Travellers
> and Travels in India.*

1651 DARELL, JOHN. East India Trade first discovered by the English.
4to. London.

1652 DARELL, JOHN. Strange News from th'Indies; or, East-India Passages ·further discovered . . . some peradventure may apprehend from this briefe, uncouth, and unpolished Discourse, . . . the Regulation of the hitherto much abused East-India Trade, so vast, spacious, necessary, . . . to enrich and advance Kingdomes and Commonwealths, being the Trade of trades, the Magazeen of Merchandizers, the honour of Nations, the Glory of this world. . . . 4to. London.

> An account of the losses of William Courten, whose two ships, the *Bona Esperanza* and the *Henry Bonaventura,* had been seized by the Dutch. Courten's father, Sir William, was the founder of the East India Trade.

1655 TERRY, EDWARD (Reverend). Voyage to the East Indies; wherein some things are taken Notice of in our Passage thither, but many more in our Abode there, within that rich and most spacious Empire of the Great Mogul. Folding map and plates. 12mo. London.

> Reprinted slightly condensed without Terry's name in folio, London, 1665; reprinted in full, London, 1777. See Sir Thomas Roe under 1625 above. Translated into Dutch, Leyden, 1706. See below.
> Terry became chaplain to Sir Thomas Roe in 1616, remaining in this office until 1619, and accompanied the latter home. His journal is a valuable complement to Roe's and despite its constant sermonising is entertaining reading. Being a tent-fellow for a while with Coryat, he records some interesting anecdotes concerning that eccentric traveller. Terry's "requiescat" on the occasion of Coryat's death is worth quoting. "Sic exit Coryatus. Hence he went off the stage, and so must all after him, how long soever their parts seem to be: For if one should go to the extreme part of the world, East, another West, another North, and another South, they must all meet at last together in the Field of Bones, wherein our traveller hath now taken up his Lodging, and where I now leave him."—From Oaten, *Early Travellers and Travels in India.*

> 1706 (In Dutch.) Scheeps-togt van Edward Terry, Capellaan van den Ambassadeur Thomas Roe, na Oost-Indien, 1615. Map and 2 folding plates. 12mo. Leyden.

1662 MANDELSLO, JOHANN ALBRECHT VON. The Voyage and Travels of J. Albert de Mandelslo into the East Indies, 1638 to 1640, containing a particular Description of the Great Mogul's Empire, the kingdoms of Deccan . . . Zeilon, Coromandel, Pegu, . . . Japan . . . China . . . Rendered into English by John Davies of Kidwelly. Fol. London.

> 2nd edit., fol., London, 1669. Printed with Adam Olearius' *Voyages and Travels of the Ambassadors.* See this date under CENTRAL ASIA. The English version and the French translation of 1719 contain material not found in the original German. For the German edition of 1658, see below. Modern edition, Bombay, 1931.
> Mandelslo was a friend of Olearius and a former page to the Duke of Holstein, who sent in 1633 an embassy to the Persians to negotiate trade. The ambassadors remained in Persia but Mandelslo having obtained permission to proceed to India, sailed from Ormuz in 1638 and landed at Surat, whence he journied on to Agra, Goa, and Ceylon, coming back home by way of the sea route. His letters were edited by Olearius and published in 1647 as a supplement to the latter's own description of the East. His account gives a vivid picture of the

luxury, vice, cruelty, and utter disregard of life obtaining under the despotic tyr-
annies of the Mogul empire. See Heawood, *Geographical Discovery,* and Oaten,
Early Travellers and Travels in India.

1931 MANDELSLO, JOHANN ALBRECHT VON. Mandelslo's Travels in
      Western India, 1639. By M. S. Commisseriat. 6 plates. 8vo. Bombay.

1658 MANDELSLO, JOHANN ALBRECHT VON. Des Johan Albrechts von
      Mandelslo Morgenländische Reyse-Beschreibung. Herausgegeben durch
      Adam Olearium. Mit desselben unterschiedlichen Notis oder Anmerck-
      ungen wie auch mit vielen Kupffer Platen geziert. Fol. Schleszwig.

1663 PINTO, FERDINAND MENDEZ. For a description of part of India
      and the Archipelago see his *Voyages and Adventures,* under FAR
      EAST.

1664 ANDRADA, JACINTO FREYRE DE. The Life of Dom John de Cas-
      tro, the Fourth Vice-Roy of India. Wherein are seen the Portuguese's
      Voyages to the East-Indies; Their Discoveries and Conquests there,
      the Form of Government, Commerce, and Discipline of War in the
      East, and the Topography of all India and China; containing also a
      particular Relation of the most famous Siege of Diu. Translated by
      Sir Peter Wyche. Engraved portrait by W. Faithorne and 2 plates.
      Fol. London.

          First issue of the 1st edition; 2nd edit., fol., London, 1693. Modern edition,
      Broadway Travellers, London, 1929. Portuguese original, Lisbon, 1651 See below.
          Dom John de Castro (1500-1548), the great Portuguese leader in India and
      Ceylon overthrew Mahmoud, King of Cambodia, relieved Diu, defeated the great
      army under Adhel Khan, captured Broach, subdued Malacca, and invaded Ceylon.
      He was the friend of St. Francis Xavier, and died in his arms.—Maggs, No. 519.

      1929 ANDRADA, RUY FREYRE DE. Commentaries of Ruy Freyre de An-
            drada, in which are related his exploits from the year 1619, in which
            he left this Kingdom of Portugal as General of the Sea of Ormuz, and
            Coast of Persia, and Arabia until his Death. Edited, with an introduc-
            tion, by C. R. Boxer. Illus. and maps. 8vo. Broadway Travellers.
            London.

                Andrada was a brave, hot-headed, and chivalrous Portuguese Com-
            mander who saw much service at the beginning of the seventeenth cen-
            tury in the Persian Gulf at a time when his countrymen controlled
            those waters. The main interest of this most vivacious chronicle lies
            in the account it gives of the siege and capture of the island-fortress of
            Ormuz, which was the Portuguese Gibraltar.—Spectator, quoted by Pub-
            lishers.

      1651 ANDRADA, FREYRE DE. Vida de don Joanno de Castro quarto viso-
            rey da India. Lisbon.

A Treatise touching the East-Indian Trade: or, A Discourse (turned out
of French into English) concerning the Establishment of a French
Company for the Commerce of the East-Indies; to which are annexed
the Articles, and Conditions, whereupon the said Company for the
Commerce of the East-Indies is Established. 4to. London.

1665 GALATA PALLADIUS. De Gentibus Indiae et Brakmanibus, ex Grae-
co Latine vertit et Notis illustravit; adjectis Ambrosio de Moribus
Brakmanorum, et Anonymo de Brakmanibus; Edwardus Bissoens editit. London.

So cited by Pinkerton XVII.

VALLE, PIETRO DELLA. The Travels of Signor Pietro della Valle,
a Noble Roman, into East India and Arabia Deserta. In which the
several Countries, together with the Customs, Manners, Traffique, and
Rites both Religious and Civil, of those Oriental Princes and Nations
are faithfully described (translated by G. Havers from the original
Italian). Whereunto is added, A Relation of Sir Thomas Roe's Voyage into the East Indies. Fol. London.

Extracts from this work in Pinkerton IX, 1-137; reprinted by the Hakluyt
Society, 2 vols., London, 1891. Translated into French, German, and Dutch. Italian original, Rome, 1650-58. See below.
This work is divided into three parts, Turkey, Persia, and India. Only the
first part was published during the author's life time. The whole is made up of 54
letters addressed to a Neapolitan physician, M. Schipano, written in the years
1614-1626. Della Valle's travels were limited in extent as far as India was concerned, but the record of his wanderings is of the utmost value, for they were the
product of a mind well trained in observation and well stored with general knowledge. Sir Henry Yule, the editor of the Hakluyt Society reprint, remarks of him,
"The Prince of all such travellers (i. e., of those who travel for curiosity's sake
alone) is Pietro della Valle, the most insatiate in curiosity, the most intelligent in
apprehension, the fullest and most accurate in description." He embarked for Constantinople in 1614, visited Egypt, Palestine, and Bagdad, where he met an Armenian woman of the Christian faith whom he married and took with him. She
died near the Gulf of Ormuz but he carried her body with him until he returned
to Rome in 1624, where he gave her burial. The fact that foreigners could travel
in India with their womenfolk points to a comparatively high state of civilization.
Della Valle also bears witness to the tolerance in some of the states of India of
different religions. For acuteness of observation and interest of narrative this account is hardly surpassed. Gibbon pays him high tribute.

1891 VALLE, PIETRO DELLA. The Travels of Pietro della Valle to India.
From the English Translation of 1664, by G. Havers. Edited, with a
Life of the Author, by Edward Grey. 2 maps and 2 illus. 2 vols.
Hak. Soc., ser. I, vols. 84-85 London.

1650-58 VALLE, PIETRO DELLA. Viaggi di Pietro della Valle il Pellegrino
con minuto ragguaglio di tutte le cosi notabili ossueruate in essi, des-
critto da lui medesimo in 54 Lettere familiari da diversi luoghi della
intrapresa peregrinatione, mandati in Napoli all' erudito e fra piu cari,
di molti anni suo amico Mario Schipano, diuisi in tre parti, cioe la
Tvrchia, la Persia e l'India. 4 vols. 4to Rome.

1671 BERNIER, FRANCOIS. The History of the Late Revolution of the
Empire of the Great Mogol, with the most considerable Passages for
five Years following in that Empire, with a Letter to the Lord Col-
bert, touching the Extent of Indostan; the Circulation of the Gold and
Silver of the World, to discharge itself there; as also the Riches,
Forces, and Justice of the same: and the principal Cause of the Decay

of the States of Asia, English'd out of the French. Map. 12mo. London.

A Continuation appeared the same year. 2nd edit., London, 1676; both parts reprinted in Osborne II, 103-236; in Pinkerton VIII, 57-234; translated by Irving Brock, London, 1826; Brock's edition revised, London, 1891; an edition, Calcutta, 1909. French original, 2 vols., Amsterdam, 1659. See below.

A more curious and entertaining work than Bernier's Travels can hardly be imagined; the lively style of the author, combined with his intelligence, and the extraordinary nature of the scenes he witnessed render his work altogether more like a glowing romance than a detail of real events.—Lowndes. Bernier, a French physician, was one of those travellers like della Valle who was lured abroad for the sake of gratifying curiosity. Of much learning, especially in the philosophy of Gassendi, whose opinions and discoveries he inherited, capable of penetrating to the ultimate causes of an event, he proved to be a political and social historian of the first magnitude. His work is particularly valuable for its record of the struggle of the four sons of Shah Jahan to secure the throne, which finally fell to the fourth, Aurangzib. At the court of this Mogul, with whom he was a favorite, he spent twelve years. He notes in detail the weakness inherent in the Mogul system of inheritance, whereby the most vigorous and unscrupulous son succeeded to the rule; the rapacity of the governors; the corruption of its military leaders; and the rottenness of the land system, together with the miserable state of the lower classes. "The ancestors of Aurungzeb," says Sir William Hunter, "were ruddy men in boots. The courtiers among whom Aurungzeb grew up were pale persons in petticoats."—Quoted by Oaten, *Early Travellers and Travels in India*, to whom the above comment is indebted.

1891 BERNIER, FRANCOIS. Travels in the Mogul Empire, 1656-68, edited by A. Constable. Revised and Improved Edition, based on Brock's Translation (1826). Frontispiece and plates. 8vo. London.

1909 BERNIER, FRANCOIS. Bernier's Voyage to the East Indies, containing the History of the late Revolution of the Empire of the Great Mogul. 8vo. Calcutta.

1670 BERNIER, FRANCOIS. Voyages de Francois Bernier, contenant la description des états du Grand Mogol de l'Indoustan, du royaume de Cachemire, . . . où il est traité, des richesses, des forces, de la justice et des causes principales de la décadence des Etats de l'Asie, et de plusieurs événemens considérables, et où l'on voit comment l'or et l'argent après avoir circulé dans le monde, passent dans l'Indoustan d'où ils ne reviennent plus. 2 vols. 12mo. Amsterdam.

A Continuation of the Memoirs of Monsieur Bernier concerning the History of the Great Mogul. Wherein is contained, 1. An exact Description of Delhi and Agra, the Capital Cities of the Empire of the great Mogul: together with some particulars making known the Court and Genius of the Mogols and Indians; as also the Doctrine of Extravagant Superstitions and Customs of the Heathen of Indostan. 2. The Emperour of Mogol's Voyage to the Kingdom of Kachemire in the Year 1664. 3. A Letter written by the Author to Mr. Chappelle, touching his design of returning, after all his peregrinations, to his Studies. English by H. O. 2 vols. 8vo. London.

1673 OGILBY, JOHN. Asia: the First Part, being an Accurate Description of Persia, and the several Provinces thereof, the Vast Empire of Great Mogol, and other Parts of India; the Cities, Customs, Religions, Languages, Government . . . also the Plants and Animals peculiar to each Country. Maps, many folding and other copperplates of views, portraits of natives, depicting their manners and customs. Fol. London.

>Although the title page reads "First Part," this volume is complete in itself. The Second Part treats of China and is listed separately. See under FAR EAST.

1675 The Empire of the Great Mogul; with the rest of the East Indies, Palestine or the Holy Land, the Empire of Russia. London.

1678 TAVERNIER, JEAN BAPTISTE. The Six Voyages of Jean Baptiste Tavernier, Baron of Aubonne, through Turkey into Persia and the East Indies, for the space of forty years; giving an Account of the Present State of those Countries, viz., of the Religion, Government, Customs and Commerce, of every Country; and the Figures, Weight, and Value of the Money currant all over Asia. To which is added, A new Description of the Seraglio; made English by J(ohn) P(hillips). With a Description of the Kingdoms which encompass the Euxine and Caspian Seas, . . . by an English Traveller: never before Printed. Fol. London.

>Other editions: London, 1680, 1684, 1688, 1690 (with translation of the Supplement); extracts in Harris I, 810-852; and in Pinkerton VIII, 235-257. The 1684 edition in 2 vols. gives the first volume to Tavernier and the second to Bernier. Modern editions, London, 1889, reedited, London, 1925. French original, Paris, 1676-77, and its supplement in 1679. See below.
>
>Tavernier, though not equal to Chardin and Bernier, will always continue among the most valuable travellers in the East. His account of Turkey, which he did not visit himself, is formed on the memoirs of his brother, and is full of errors.—Pinkerton. But see Harris: He is more copious, and at the same time no less exact, than any of the authors who have attempted to point out the advantages derived from our commerce in the East. . . . We discover in his writings a greater compass of thought and a more masterly turn in his observations than in almost any other book of the kind, which is owing to his having considered these things over and over in consequence of the several voyages he made to the Indies.—The interest in Tavernier's travels lies in the personal experiences and adventures he relates. Though he was unfairly treated by his fellow travellers, such as Bernier and Thevenot, both of whom he met in India, he does not return ill for ill. He successfully combined his business as jeweler with his travels. Towards the end of 1663, on his sixth and last voyage, he took with him £30,000 worth of stuff, the most of which he sold at Ispahan to the Shah of Persia. He also disposed of some jewels to the Great Mogul Aurangzib. His financial transactions on the whole must have been very profitable, for when he returned to Paris in 1668 he was a man of wealth, and like a wise fellow proceeded to stay home and enjoy it. Some of his fellow travellers charged him with being a dupe, but modern scholars agree that in the main he was accurate in his statements of facts. His work is especially valuable at the time for its information on trade and trade routes, diamonds and mines. See Oaten, *Early Travellers and Travels in India.*

1680 TAVERNIER, JEAN BAPTISTE. A Collection of several Relations and Treatises Singular and Curious, not Printed among his first Six Voyages. I. A New and singular Relation of the Kingdom of Tunquin. II. How the Hollanders manage their Affairs in Asia. III. A Relation of Japon, and the Cause of the Persecutions of the Christians in those Islands. IV. A Relation of what passed in the Negotiation of the Deputies which were at Persia and the Indies, as well on the French King's as the Company's behalf, for the Establishment of Trade. V. Observations upon the East India Trade, and the Frauds there subject to be committed. Large folding map of Japan with inset map of Tonquin and 7 copperplates. Fol. London.

> This is the Supplement to Tavernier's Six Voyages. Concerning the persecutions of the Christians in Japan, he says that "from 1613 to 1629 the Christians were so multiply'd, that they were above 400,000, but in the year 1649 . . . Christianity was utterly extirpated out of the Island." His information on the Far East was derived from reading and reports, not from actual observation.

1684 TAVERNIER, JEAN BAPTISTE. Collections of Travels through Turkey into Persia and the East Indies; giving an Account of the Present State of those Countries: as also a full Relation of the five years War between Aureng-Zebby and his Brothers. And a Voyage made by the Great Mogull with his Army from Denly to Lahor, from Lahor to Dember, and from thence to Kachemire called The Paradise of the Indies. Together with a Relation of the Kingdom of Japan, Tunkin, their Manners and Trade. To which is added, A New Description of the Grand Signior's Seraglio, and the Kingdoms encompassing the Euxine and Caspian Seas. Being the Travels of Monsieur Tavernier, Bernier, and other great men. Numerous copperplates. 2 vols. in 1. Fol. London.

1889 TAVERNIER, J. B. Travels in India. Translated from the original French edition of 1676, with a Biographical Sketch of the Author, Notes, Appendices, etc., by V. Ball. Maps, portraits, and plates. 2 vols. 8vo. London.

1925 TAVERNIER, J. B. Travels in India. Translated by V. Ball. New edition, by W. Crooke. Illus. 2 vols. 8vo. London.

1676 TAVERNIER, JEAN BAPTISTE. Six Voyages de Jean Tavernier en Turquie, en Persie, et aux Indes, pendant l'espace de quarante ans par toutes les routes qu'on peut y tenir, accompagnés des observations particulières sur les qualités, la religion, le gouvernement, et le commerce du chaque pays, avec les figures, les poids, et la valeur des monnoies. Enrichis des cartes, plans, et figures. 3 vols. 4to. Paris.

1679 TAVERNIER, JEAN BAPTISTE. Recueil de plusieurs relations et traitéz singuliers et curieux qui n'ont point été mis dans les six premiers voyages. Divisé en 5 parties: 1. Une relation du Japon et de la cause de la persécution des Chrétiens dans ses Isles. 2. Une relation de ce qui s'est passé dans la Négociation des députés qui ont été en Perse et aux Indes. 3. Observations sur le Commerce des Indes Orientales. 4. Une relation singulière du Royaume de Tunquin. 5. Histoire de la conduite des Hollandais en Asie avec la relation de l'intérieur du Sérail. 5 cartes et de 15 grandes planches. 4to. Paris.

1681 KNOX, ROBERT. Historical Relation of the Island of Ceylon, in the East Indies: together with an Account of the Detaining in Captivity the Author and divers other Englishmen now living there, and of the

Author's Miraculous Escape. Folding map and 15 plates, and portrait. Fol. London.

A new edition, 12mo, London, 1818; reprinted in Beazley, *Voyages and Travels,* vol. II, London, 1903. Reprinted, 8vo, Glasgow, 1911. Translated into French, Lyons, 1684, again, Amsterdam, 1693; into Dutch, 1692; into German, 1747. See below.

Knox was a Scotch commander in the service of the East India Company. In 1657 he sailed with his father to Fort George, and on the return journey was forced by a storm into the harbor of Cottiar Bay, Ceylon, where he and his father and fourteen others were made prisoners and carried into the interior. He remained a prisoner at large for nearly twenty years, travelling about as a hawker. When the opportunity offered he escaped to the Dutch settlement of Aripo on the N. W. Coast. From there he was sent to Batavia and thence to England, where he wrote an account of his adventures. He afterwards had a very successful career with the East India Company. "His book, which is both delightful and trustworthy, is the first account of Ceylon in the English language."—Maggs, No. 521.

1818 KNOX, ROBERT. Relation of the Island of Ceylon . . . New Edition, with Sketch of the Geography, Civil and Natural History, Commerce, . . . of Ceylon, brought down to 1815 (by Robert Fellowes). 12mo. London.

1911 KNOX, ROBERT. An Historical Relation of Ceylon, together with somewhat concerning severall Remarkable Passages of my Life that hath hapned since my Deliverance out of my Captivity. Portrait and 21 engravings and map. Reprint of the rare edition of 1681. 8vo. Glasgow.

1684 (In French.) Description de l'Ile de Ceylon, traduit de l'Anglois (de 1681). Lyons.

1682 GLANIUS, ——. Relation of an unfortunate Voyage to the Kingdom of Bengal; describing the deplorable Condition and Accidents of those who undertook it; how, after the Loss of their Ship, they were forced to reside in a Desert and Barren Island . . . 8vo. London.

GLANIUS, ——. A New Voyage to the East Indies; containing an Account of several of those Rich Countries, and more particularly of the Kingdom of Bantam. Giving an Exact Relation of the Extent of that Monarch's Dominions, the Religion, Manners and Customs of the Inhabitants; their Commerce, and the Product of the Country, and likewise a faithful Narrative of the Kingdom of Siam, of the Isles of Japan and Madagascar, and of several other Parts, with such New Discoveries as were never yet made by any other Traveller. To which is added, the Effigies of the Bantam Ambassador at length. 12mo.

2nd edit., 16mo, 1682.

The work gives a very full account of Bantam, which did not get incorporated with the Dutch possessions in Java until 1808, and a description of Formosa. If this had been read the forgeries of Psalmanazaar would not have met with the success they did.—Sotheran.

A True Account of the Burning and Sad Condition of Bantam in the East-Indies; in the War begun by the Young King against his Father and of the great and imminent Danger of the English Factory there in a Letter from a Member of the Factory, to a Friend in London by the last ship; which arrived on Saturday the 23rd of this instant September, 1682. (2 pp.). Fol. London.

> A British factory or trading station was established at Bantam by Captain Lancaster in 1603, but the English were driven from their factories by the Dutch in 1683.—Maggs, No. 521.

1684 STRUYS, JEAN. For his travels through India see his *Voyages and Travels through Moscovia, Tartary, India,* under GENERAL TRAVELS AND DESCRIPTIONS.

1685 B., R. (Robert Burton ?). A View of the English Acquisitions in Guiana and the East-Indies; with an Account of the Religion, Government, Wars, Customs, Beasts, Serpents, Monsters, and other Observables in those Countries. With a Description of the Island of St. Helena, the Bay of Soldania; intermixt with pleasant Relations, and enlivened with Pictures. 12mo. London.

1687 THEVENOT, JEAN. The Travels of Monsieur Thevenot into the Levant. In Three Parts. Viz., into, I. Turkey. II. Persia. III. The East-Indies. Newly done out of French . . . 3 vols. in 1. Portrait and plates. Fol. London.

> For the Near East portion of these travels see under NEAR EAST. French original of the East India volume, Paris, 1684. See below.
> "Tavernier, Bernier, Thevenot," says Mr. S. Lane-Poole, "were all in India in the year 1666. . . . Of the three Thevenot is much the slightest. . . . His 'Travels' are necessarily more or less hurried first impressions, but he had access to some important native authorities, and his statistics are peculiarly valuable."—Quoted by Oaten, *Early Travellers and Travels in India.* But according to Oaten, if we were writing a history of India we should prefer the aid of Thevenot; if we were seeking a combination of pleasant and instructive reading, we should turn to Tavernier.

> 1684 THEVENOT, JEAN. Voyages de M. Thévenot. Contenant la relation de l'Indostan des nouveaux Mogols et des autres peuples et Pays des Indies. 4to. Paris.

1692 An Account of the famous Prince Giolo, son of the King of Gilolo, now in England, with an Account of his Life, Parentage, . . . with a Description of the Island of Gilolo, and the adjacent Isle of Celebes, their Religion and Manners, written from his own Mouth. Portrait. 4to. London.

1694 GEDDES, MICHAEL. The History of the Church of Malabar, from the Time of its being first discover'd by the Portuguezes in 1501, giving an Account of the Persecutions and Violent Methods of the Roman Prelates, to Reduce them to the Subjection of the Church of Rome, together with the Synod of Diamper in.1599. 8vo. London.

1695 FARIA Y SOUSA, MANUEL DE. The Portuguese Asia: or, the History of the Discovery and Conquest of India by the Portuguese: containing all their Discoveries from the Coast of Africk, to the farthest Parts of China and Japan; all their Battles by Sea and Land, Sieges and other Memorable Actions; a Description of those Countries, and many Particulars of the Religion, Government and Customs of the Natives. Translated by Capt. John Stevens. 3 vols. 8vo. London.

> This version is somewhat compressed. Portuguese original, Lisbon, 1666. See below.
> At the end is a list of authorities used, which comprises some 21 books and 13 MSS. The author was a celebrated Castillian poet and historian. The account, which is esteemed for its veracity and impartiality, extends down to 1628.—From Maggs, No. 479.

> 1666 FARIA Y SOUSA, MANUEL DE. Asia Portugueza. 3 vols., Lisbon.

>> He also wrote on Portugal in Europe, 3 vols., and Portuguese Africa.

1696 DUQUESNE, ——. A New Voyage to the East Indies in the Years 1690 and 1691. Being a full Description of the Isles of Maldives, Cocos, Andamants; and all the Forts and Garrisons now in possession of the French, with an Account of the Customs, Manners and Habits of the Indians. To which is added, a New Description of the Canary Islands, Cape Verd, Senegal, and Gambia, . . . Illus. and maps. Done into English from the Paris edition. 8vo. London.

> French original, Brussels, 1692. See below.
> Of the French factories in those parts we have no such account; and few better for the bulk, of all other places the author undertakes to speak of.—Churchill, *Introduction*. The second part comprises the Voyages of Le Maire to the Canary Isles, etc.

> 1692 DUQUESNE, ——. Journal du Voyage de Duquesne aux Indes Orientales, par un Gard-Marine de son Escadre. 12mo. Brussels.

A Letter to a Friend, Concerning the East India Trade. 4to. London.

OVINGTON, JOHN. A Voyage to Suratt, 1689, giving a large Account of that City, and its Inhabitants, and of the English Factory there; likewise a Description of Madeira, St. Jago, St. Helena, Johanna, Bombay, the Cape of Good Hope, . . . with Appendix, containing the History of a Late Revolution in the Kingdom of Golconda, . . . and Observations concerning the Nature of Silk-Worms. Numerous folding plates and a table of currency. 8vo. London.

A modern edition, London, 1929. Translated into French, Paris, 1725. See below.

The author was an English clergyman, who sought exile at the same time as his Royal Master, James II. He embarked for the Indies in 1689. After reaching Surat, he was interned for three years by the Great Mogul Aurangzib. According to Oaten, *Early Travellers and Travels in India,* Ovington makes claims to have described far more of India than he could have visited, seeing that he hardly went beyond Bombay and Surat. Most of his information came from other sources, which, however, were reliable. His remarks on the methods and results of Mogul administration are not to be neglected.

1929   OVINGTON, JOHN. A Voyage to Surat in the Year 1689, edited by H. G. Rawlinson. Illus. 8vo. London.

1725   (In French.) Voyages de Jean Ovington, faits à Surate, et en d'autres lieux de l'Asie et de l'Afrique, avec l'histoire de la Révolution du Royaume de Golconde; et des observations sur les vers à soye. Traduit de l'anglois. 12mo. Paris.

The translator was N. Barnabite. The work was noticed in the *Journal des Scavans,* 1726, I, 55.

1698   FRYER, JOHN. A New Account of East-India and Persia, in eight Letters, Being Nine Years' Travels, Begun 1672, and Finished 1681. Containing Observations made of the Moral, Natural and Artificial Estate of those Countries, namely, of their Government, Religion, Laws, Customs, of the Soil, Climates, Seasons, Health, Diseases, of the Animals, Vegetables and Minerals, Jewels, Housing, Cloathing, Manufactures, Trades, . . . of the Coins, Weights and Measures used in the Principal Places of Trade in those Parts. Portraits, maps, and geographical and botanical plates by Sturt. Fol. London.

Reprinted with Sir Thomas Roe's travels, London, 1873; published by the Hakluyt Society, London, 1909-1915. Translated into Dutch, 's Gravehage, 1700. See below.

Fryer was a surgeon in the service of the East India Company for nine years and travelled extensively on the Coromandel and Malabar coasts. He describes well the cities of Surat and Bombay, the life and trade there as well as at Madras. Nearly sixteen years elapsed before he could be persuaded to publish the story of his wanderings. At length piqued at the frequent appearance of translations of foreign, especially French, books of travel, in which English industry and enterprise were decried, he issued a handsome folio.—From D. N. B. His book is of great value in its account of the struggle of the Mahrattas under Sivaji to resist absorption into Aurangzib's empire, and in its analysis of the political state of the kingdom of Bijapur.—From Oaten, *Early Travellers and Travels in India.* He was well versed in the learning of the day and very curious in all questions connected with natural science.

1909-1915   FRYER, JOHN (M.D.). A New Account of East India and Persia. In eight Letters, being Nine Years' Travels, begun 1672, and finished 1681. By John Fryer, M.D., Cantabrig., and Fellow of the Royal Society. Edited with Notes and an Introduction, by William Crooke, B.A., Bengal Civil Service. 3 vols. Hak. Soc., ser. II, vol. 19, 1909; vol. 20, 1912; vol. 39, 1915. London.

1700 (In Dutch.) Negenjaarige Reyse door Oost-Indien en Persien . . . In agt Brieven beschreven door d'Heer Johan Freyer, M. P. 's Gravehage.

1699 DELLON, CHARLES (M. D.). A Voyage to the East Indies: giving an Account of the Isles of Madagascar, and Mascareigne, of Suratte, the Coast of Malabar, of Goa, Gameron, Ormus, and the Coast of Brazil, with the Religion, Customs, Trade, . . . of the Inhabitants, as also a Treatise of the Distempers peculiar to the Eastern Countries. To which is Annexed an Abstract of Monsieur de Rennefort's History of the East Indies, with his Propositions for the Improvement of the East-India Company (translated by Jodocus Crull, M. D.). 8vo. London.

> A French edition, Amsterdam, 1699. See below. The Appendix contains Rennefort's proposals for a French settlement in Madagascar. This latter work was printed at Leyden, 1688.
> While on his travels the author was denounced to the Inquisition at Goa, where he was imprisoned for two years and frequently tortured to extract a confession of heresy. As he would not confess, he was condemned to the galleys for five years and had his property confiscated. The work contains a realistic description of suttee as well as of tropical diseases.—Sotheran. The author travelled in southern India from 1669 to 1676.

> 1699 DELLON, CHARLES (M.D.). Nouvelle Relation d'un voyage faits aux Indes-Orientales; contenant la description des Iles de Bourbon et de Madagascar, de Surate, de Malabar, de Calicut, de Timor, de Goa, . . . 12mo. Amsterdam.

1699 MARIANO, JOHN DE. For Spanish and Portuguese affairs in India and the East, see his *General History of Spain,* under WEST EUROPE.

ZIEGENBALG, BARTHOLOMEW. An Account of the Religion, Manners and Learning of the People of Malabar, in the East Indies; in several Letters written by some of the most learned Men of that Country to the Danish Missionaries. Translated from the German of Bartholomew Ziegenbalg by J. T. Phillips. Map. 8vo. London.

> Another edition, London, 1717. There are several accounts of the activities of these Danish missionaries under slightly different titles. The date of the above translation is the one listed by Pinkerton XVII. See below for the later accounts.
> The Danish missionaries seem to have been quite zealous in the East Indies, for by 1805 sixty-one volumes of their Acts had appeared. Ziegenbalg founded the missionary enterprise for Frederick IV of Denmark. He died in the Indies in 1719.

> 1711 Propagation of the Gospel in the East. Being an account of the Success of two Danish Missionaries, lately sent to the East-Indies for the Conversion of the Heathens in Malabar. In several Letters to their Correspondents in Europe. Containing a Narrative of their Voyage. 2nd edit. 8vo. London.

1715 A Brief Account of the Measures taken in Denmark for the Conversion of the Heathen in the East-Indies. 12mo. London.

1719 Thirty-Four Conferences between the Danish Missionaries and the Malabarian Bramans in the East Indies, translated out of the High Dutch by Mr. Philipps. 8vo. London.

1700 FRYKE, CHRISTOPHER, and SCHWEITZER, CHRISTOPHER. A Relation of Two several Voyages Made in to the East Indies. The whole containing an exact Account of the Customs, Dispositions, Manners, Religions, . . . of the several Kingdoms and Dominions in those Parts in general; but, in particular, describing those Countrys which are under the Government of the Dutch. Done out of the Dutch by S. L. 8vo. London.

> Separate German versions are given in Pinkerton XVII. Modern editions in English, London, 1929, and in German, the Hague, 1931. See below.
> There is nothing extraordinary in them.—Churchill, *Introduction*. A most interesting work relating to the Cape of Good Hope, Mauritius, Java, Formosa, Japan, and Ceylon.—Maggs, No. 521.

1929 FRYKE, C., and SCHWEITZER, C. Voyages to the East Indies. With Introduction and Notes by C. E. Fayle. 8 plates. 8vo. London.

1688 SCHWEITZER, CHRISTOPHER. Journal und Tagebuch seiner sechs jähringen Ostindianischen Reise (from Dec. 1, 1675 to Sept. 7, 1681). 4to. Tübingen.

1692 FRIKEN, CHRISTOPHER. Ostindianische Reisen und Kriegsdienste (from 1680 to 1685). 8vo. Ulm.

1931 SCHWEITZER, CHRISTOPHER. Reise nach Java und Ceylon 1675-1682. Neu herausgegeben nach der zu Tübingen im Verlag von J. G. Cotta im Jahre 1680 erschienenen Originalausgabe. 8vo. The Hague.

1701 An Historical Description of the Kingdom of Macassar in the East Indies, in Three Books; giving a particular Account, 1. Of the Scituations of the Country, the Product and Principal Towns in it. 2. The Manners and Customs of the Inhabitants; their Government, Trade, Recreations, Habits, and Marriages. 3. The ancient Idolatry of the Macassarians; the Progress of the Christian Religion among them, and the Establishment of the Mohametan; with the Circumcision of Women, particular to those People. Together with a particular Account of the Acts and Cruelties used by the Batavians to establish themselves in, and exclude all other European Nations from that Country. 8vo. London.

1702 DANIEL, WILLIAM. A Journal or Account of William Daniel, his late Expedition from London to Surat in India, giving a short, but impartial Relation of the Dangers, Distresses, Fatigues, and Hindrances, happening to him during the said Expedition till his Return to England. 8vo. London.

> The author got no farther than Mocha. He gives accounts of the various places he visited on the Red Sea and Egypt.—Maggs, No. 521. Only a few copies of this work were printed.

1703 BALDAEUS, PHILIP. A True and Exact Description of the most celebrated East India Coasts of Malabar and Coromandel, as also of the Island of Ceylon, with all the adjacent Kingdoms, Principalities, Provinces, Cities, Chief Harbours, Structures, Pagan Temples, Products and Living Creatures, and the Manners, Habits, . . . of the Inhabitants. Maps and plates. Fol. London.

> Apparently the only edition of the only English translation. Reprinted in Churchill III, 501-822. Dutch original, Amsterdam, 1672. See below.
> The author was a Dutch missionary in the Malabar and Coromandel districts. His narrative gives considerable information on the Dutch settlements in Southern India. He bears witness to the ravages of the dreaded Malabar pirates who still infested the western coasts of India.—Oaten, *Early Travellers and Travels in India*.

> 1672 BALDAEUS, PHILIP. Beschryving der Oostindischen Landscapen Malabar, Coromandel, Ceylon, . . . 4to. Amsterdam.

1705 TOLAND, JOHN. The Agreement of the Customs of the East Indians with those of the Jews. To which are added, Instructions to Young Gentlemen that intend to Travel. 4 plates. 8vo. London.

> This is the celebrated Deist, author of *Christianity Not Mysterious*, which precipitated the Deist controversy.

1706 FINCH, WILLIAM. Travels in India in 1605. Bound up with Hawkins' Voyagie door Oost-Indien, 1608. 12mo. Leyden.

> This account first appeared in Purchas, 1625. This Leyden version is probably the Dutch account published in Pieter van der Aa's collection. Reprinted in Kerr, VIII. See under 1921 below.
> Finch was a merchant and agent to an expedition sent out in the reign of James 1 to obtain trading privileges from the Great Mogul Jahangir for the East India Company's factory at Surat. He gives interesting information about Jahangir's method of holding daily levees and confirms other travellers' stories of the Mogul's delight in bloody spectacles.—From Oaten, *Early Travellers and Travels in India*. Finch died at Babylon on his way back, from drinking poisoned water.

1708 ARGENSOLA, BARTOLOME LEONARDO DE. The Discovery and Conquest of the Molucco and Philippine Islands, containing their History, Laws, Customs, . . . with an Account of many other adjacent Islands, and several Remarkable Voyages through the Streights of Magellan, translated by Capt. John Stevens. Map and 2 plates. 4to. London.

Spanish original, Madrid, 1609. See below.

Few narratives are written with so much judgment and elegance as Argensola's History of the Conquest of the Moluccas.—Quoted by Maggs, No. 519. One of the most important works for the history of the Philippine Islands.—Robinson, No. 26. The book also contains matter relating to Sir Francis Drake and American voyages, and to the history of Spanish and Portuguese exploration in the Indies.

1609   ARGENSOLA, BARTOLOME LEONARDO DE.   Conqvista de las Islas Malvcas al Rey Felipe III. Escrita por el Licendo Bartolome Leonardo de Argensola capellan de la Magestad de las Emperatriz y Retor de Villahermosa. Fol. Madrid.

The English Acquisitions in Guinea and the East Indies.   London.

So cited in Pinkerton XVII.

LEGUAT, FRANCOIS.   A New Voyage to the East-Indies by Francis Leguat and his Companions. Containing their Adventures in Two Desert Islands, Accounts of remarkable things at the Cape of Good Hope, the Island of Mauritius, at Batavia, the Island of St. Helena and other places on their Route . . . Numerous plates and maps. 8vo. London.

Republished by the Hakluyt Society, London, 1890. It appeared in French, London and Amsterdam, 1708; also in Dutch, Utrecht, 1708. See below.

The adventures of this person and his companions in the two desert isles are rather suspicious, but there is no reason to impeach his accounts of the Cape, the Isles of St. Helena and Mauritius, and the East-Indies.—Pinkerton XVII. The claims of this work to be a genuine voyage, as it has been so accepted by critics, bibliographers, and editors, including the editor of the Hakluyt Society edition, have been completely disproved by Geoffroy Atkinson in his *Extraordinary Voyage in French Literature, 1700-1720,* (Paris, 1922). Here he demonstrates that this work is neither a story of personal adventure, true and original in all its essential details, nor a story of personal experience, embroidered somewhat by an ingenious editor or collaborator, but a fiction in which the element of first-hand experience is negligible. In short, it is "an Extraordinary Voyage, a desert island novel, written in 1707 upon sources which are exclusively French. . . . After excluding the incidents and descriptions evidently borrowed from earlier writers, not even the shell of a story is left." And furthermore the author is not Francois Leguat, but Francois Maximilien Misson. For details of the story and its subject matter and their relation to social theories of the day, see Atkinson, *op. cit.*

1890   LEGUAT, FRANCOIS.   The Voyage of Francois Leguat, of Bresse, 1690-98, To Rodriguez, Mauritius, Java, and the Cape of Good Hope. Transcribed from the First English Edition, 1708. Edited and Annotated by Capt. Samuel Pasfield Oliver, (late) R.A. Maps and illus. 2 vols. Hak. Soc., ser. I, vols. 82-83. London.

1708   LEGUAT, FRANCOIS.   Voyages et aventures de Francois Leguat et de ses compagnons en deux isles désertes des Indes Orientales. Avec la relation des choses les plus remarquables qu'ils ont observées dans l'Isle Maurice, à Batavia, au Cap de Bon Espérance, dans l'Isle de Sainte Hélène, et en d'autre endroits de leur route. Le tout enrichi de cartes et de figures. 2 vols. in 1. 12mo. Londres et Amsterdam.

1708-1710   TEIXEIRA, PEDRO.   The Travels of Pedro Teixeira with his Account of the Origin, Descent, and Succession of the Kings of Persia and Hormuz, . . . Translated by Capt. John Stevens. London.

Stevens published at first only the author's account of his two journies in 1600-01 and 1603-05, which was included in *A New Collection of Voyages and Travels*, issued in monthly parts, 4to, London, 1708-1710. The whole was reissued in 2 vols., with a new general title page in 1711. Stevens translated the rest of Teixeira in 1715 under the title, *The History of Persia*, . . . See under 1715, CENTRAL ASIA. Edited by the Hakluyt Society, London, 1901. Spanish original, Amberes, 1610. See below.

Teixeira was a careful observer and a valuable witness —Editor Hakluyt Society edition. Capt. Stevens was an antiquary and translator of wide range. Among his other translations was Bede's *Ecclesiastical History*.

1901 TEIXEIRA, PEDRO. The Journey of Pedro Teixeira from India to Italy by Land, 1604-05, With his Chronicle of the Kings of Ormus. Translated and edited by William Frederic Sinclair, with additional Notes by Donald William Ferguson. Hak. Soc., ser. II, vol. 9. London.

1610 TEIXEIRA, PEDRO. Relaciones de Pedro Teoxea (*sic*) d'el Origen Descendencia y Succession de los Reyes de Persia, y de Harmuz, y de vn Viage hecho por elmismo Avtor desde la India Oriental hasta Italia por tierro. 8vo. Amberes.

1709 CATROU, FRANCOIS. The General History of the Mogul Empire, from its Foundation by Tamerlane, to the Late Emperor of Orangzeb. Extracted from the Memoirs of M. Manouchi, a Venetian, and Chief Physician to Orangzeb for above Forty Years. Folding map of Northern India. 8vo. London.

French original, Paris, 1705. See below.

Niccolao Manucci's book, from which Catrou drew much of his material, was not printed until 1907, when it was translated by William Irvine (the Indian Text Society), of the Bengal Civil Service, for the reason that it had disappeared from view until it turned up in Berlin a few years ago. Its title was *Storia do Mogor,* and it was written partly in Italian, partly in French, and partly in Portuguese. Historians have long bewailed its disappearance, for hitherto they have been unable to check the statements of Catrou. Manucci practically spent his life in India and witnessed so many things and records them so fully and delightfully that he is almost second to none as an historian of Aurangzib's reign. For its political and social information, this Venetian's book is "destined to be of more ultimate value to the historian of India."—From Oaten, *Early Travellers and Travels in India.* For a modern edition of Manucci's book see below.

1705 CATROU, FRANCOIS. Histoire générale de l'Empire du Mogol, depuis sa Fondation, sur les Mémoires de M. Manouchi, Vénétien, par le P. Catrou, Jésuite. 4to. Paris.

1907 MANUCCI, NICCOLAO. Storia do Mogor or Mogul India, 1653-1708. Translated with Introduction and Notes by Wm. Irvine. Numerous plates. 4 vols. 8vo. Indian Texts. London.

1711 LOCKYER, CHARLES. An Account of the Trade in India, containing Rules for good Government in Trade, Price, Courants and Tables, with Descriptions of Fort St. George, Acheen, Malacca, Condore, Canton, Aujengo, Muskat, Cape of Good Hope, St. Helena, . . . their Inhabitants, Customs, Religion, Animals, Fruits, . . . with an Account of the Dutch Affairs. 8vo. London.

1712 HALL, R. The History of the Barbarous Cruelties and Massacres, committed by the Dutch in the East Indies; to which is added the Proceedings of the Council of Amboyna. Frontispiece depicting horrible tortures. 8vo. London.

> For the Amboyna Massacre see above under 1624.

1714 VAUGHAN, WALTER. The Adventures of Five Englishmen ·from Pulo Condoro, a Factory of the New Company in the East-Indies. Who were shipwreckt upon the little Kingdom of Jehore, not far distant, and being seized on by the Inhabitants, were brought before the King, and detain'd for some Months; with the many Accidents that befel them during their Abode in that Island. . . . Written by Mr. Vaughan, one of the Adventurers. 12mo. London.

1715 SYMSON, WILLIAM (Captain). A New Voyage to the East-Indies, viz., To Suratte and the Coast of Arabia, containing a Compleat Description of the Maldivy Islands, their Product, Trade, . . . To which is added, a Particular Account of the French Factories. . . . 3 plates and 1 folding map. 18mo. London.

> 2nd edit., 12mo, London, 1720. See below.

> 1720 SYMSON, WILLIAM (Captain). A New Voyage to the East-Indies (in the *Macklesfield* Frigate, 1701), to Suratte and the Coast of Arabia . . . Maldivy Islands, . . . with a Voyage to the East Indies, by the Sieur Luillier. Engravings. 12mo. London.

1719 BEECKMAN, DANIEL (Captain). A Voyage to and From the Island of Borneo, in the East-Indies. 7 engraved plates and maps. 8vo. London.

> Reprinted in Pinkerton XI, 96-158.
> An unusually interesting and well-written volume of travels. On the way from Borneo the author visited the Cape of Good Hope, and gives a lengthy account of the country and the Hottentots. In his description of Borneo he speaks of the "Oran-Ootan," the most remarkable animal there: "These grow up to be six foot high; they walk upright, having longer arms than men, tolerable good faces, handsomer, I am sure than some Hottentots I have seen."—Maggs, No. 580. An interesting work, even at this distance of time.—Lowndes.

1720 CORNWALL, HENRY (Captain). Observations upon several Voyages to India, out and home. Fol. London.

LE BRUN, CORNEILLE. For his travels in East India see his *Voyage to the Levant* under 1702, NEAR EAST.

1727 HAMILTON, ALEXANDER (Captain). A New Account of the East
Indies; being Observations and Remarks of Capt. Alexander Hamilton
who spent his time there from 1688 to 1723, Trading and Travelling
by Sea and Land, . . . between the Cape of Good-Hope and the Island
of Japan. Maps and plans. 2 vols. 8vo. Edinburgh.

> Another edition, London, 1737; Edinburgh, 1739; London (?), 1744. Re-
> printed in Pinkerton VIII, 258-522. Edited for the Argonaut Press, London, 1930.
> See below.
> Hamilton's adventures are told in a most interesting manner. His work, in
> the charm of its naive simplicity, perfect honesty, with some similarity of subject
> in its account of people little known, offers a closer parallel to Herodotus than
> perhaps any other in modern literature.—From D.N.B., quoted by Robinson,
> No. 19. Being both trader and traveller, Hamilton had occasion to visit "most of
> the countries and islands of Commerce and Navigation between the Cape of Good
> Hope and the Island of Japon."—Quoted by Oaten, *Early Travellers and Travels
> in India.*

> 1930 HAMILTON, ALEXANDER (Captain). A New Account of the East
> Indies. Now edited with Introduction and Notes by Sir William Fos-
> ter. Numerous maps, illus. Facsimile of the only known letter of Alex-
> ander Hamilton. 2 vols. 4to. Argonaut Press. London.

1728 SALMON, THOMAS. Modern History of the Present State of all Nations, Vols. 1-4 (China, Japan, Philippine Islands, Amboyna, Moluccas,
Borneo, Java, Sumatra, India, Ceylon, Persia, and Turkey). Folding
maps. 8vo. London.

> Reprinted, London, 1739.
> The author travelled many years abroad and was with Anson on his voyage
> around the world in 1740-45. He published many historical and geographical works.

1729 ARRIAN. Arrian's History of Alexander's Expedition, translated from
the Greek, with Notes historical, geographical and critical, by Mr.
Rooke. 2 vols. 8vo. London.

> See also McCrindle under 1896 below.

1731 FORBIN, COUNT DE. Memoirs, containing his pleasant Narrative of
the Voyages he made to the East Indies, his particular Account of the
Battle at La Hogue and other Fights, and his Secret History of Chevalier de St. Georges Expedition from Dunkirk to Scotland in 1708,
translated from the French. 2 vols. 8vo. London.

1732 An Historical Relation of the Island of Ceylon in the East-Indies, . . . Illustrated with cuts and a map of the Island. Fol.

> Mentioned in Churchill with no place and no date.
> The author who lived long in that country gives a general description of it,
> referring the reader to the map; and then the whole natural history.—Churchill,
> *Introduction.*

The Idolatry of the East India Pagans. A true and full Account of the Religious Worship of the Indostans, the Inhabitants of Coromandel, the Malabars, and Ceylon, with a Description of their Idols. In Churchill III, 753-821.

NIEUHOFF, JOHN. The Voyages and Travels into Brasil and the East Indies (two separate voyages). Containing an exact Description of Dutch Brasil and divers Parts of the East Indies: their Provinces, Cities, Living Creatures, and Products; the Manners, Customs, Habits and Religion of the Inhabitants; with a particular Account of all the Remarkable Passages that happened during the Author's Stay of Nine Years in Brasil; especially in Relation to the Revolt of the Portuguese and the Intestine Wars carried on from 1640, to 1649. As also a most ample Description of the most famous City of Batavia in the East Indies. In Churchill II, 1-326.

> Dutch original, Amsterdam, 1682. See below. See also Nieuhoff under 1669, FAR EAST.
> Nieuhoff, who was in the service of the Dutch East India Company, gives detailed and explicit news of the unsettled condition of the districts on the Malabar coast. He characterises the inhabitants of that region as "either Merchants or Pirates." The lower castes inhabiting the Malabar towns he shows to have been living under horrible conditions.—Oaten, *Early Travellers and Travels in India.*

1682 NIEUHOFF, J. Gedenkweerdige Brasiliaense zee- en lantreize benefens een beschrijving van gantsch Neerlandts Brasil, zoo van lantschappen, steden, gewassen, enz. en inzonderheit een verhael der merkwaardigste voorvallen die zich van 1640 tot 49 hebben toegedragen.—Zee- en lantreize door verscheide gewesten van Oost-Indien . . . benefens een beschrijving van lantschappen, steden, dieren, gewassen, draghten, zeden, enz., een verhael van Batavia. 4 maps and 45 plates, etc. Fol. Amsterdam.

Some Reasons for the Unhealthfulness of the Island of Bombay. In Churchill VI, 358.

1733 RENAUDOT, EUSEBIUS (Abbé). For an account of India in the 9th century see his *Ancient Accounts of India and China,* under FAR EAST.

1737 DOWNING, CLEMENT. A History of the Indian Wars, 1715-1723, with an Account of the Life and Actions of John Plantain, a notorious Pyrate at Madagascar, his Wars with the Natives on that Island, where having continued eight years he joined Angria and was made his chief Admiral. London.

> Reprinted, with Introduction and Notes by William Foster, 8vo, Oxford, 1924.
> A rare volume of adventures by one of the sailors on the early 18th century "East Indiamen" whose career included also a captaincy of artillery in the Mogul empire; work in fighting Marathas; and help in a famous expedition under Commodore Matthews, hunting for European pirates, at Madagascar.—Bookseller's Note.

1740 WITHINGTON, NICHOLAS. Travels of Nicholas Withington, a Factor in the East Indies. See Cockburn, John: *A Faithful Account of the Distresses and Adventures with Five other Englishmen on an Uninhabited Island,* under CENTRAL AMERICA.

1744-48 BEAULIEU, COMMODORE. The Expedition of Commodore Beaulieu to the East Indies; containing a curious and accurate Description of the Sea Coasts . . . as also Abundance of curious Observations on the Manners of the People, the Nature of their Governments, and the Means of establishing Colonies amongst them. Written by himself and published by Thevenot in his large Collection of Voyages. In Harris I, 717-749.

> Beaulieu left Honfleur Oct. 2, 1619, and returned Dec. 1, 1622.

A Compleat History of the Rise and Progress of the Portuguese Empire in the East-Indies; their Discoveries set forth in their natural Order, the Form of their Government in those Parts explained; the Causes of the Declension of their Power examined, and the present Posture of their Affairs, in those Parts of the World, truly stated. Collected chiefly from their Writings. In Harris I, 662-700.

A Generalized Account of the Discovery, Settlement, and Voyages, Zoology, Animals, Commerce, . . . of the East Indies from earliest Times down. In Harris I, 370-520.

> An account treating, in true eighteenth century style of generalised summaries, of Egyptian, Greek, Persian, Roman, Byzantine, Portuguese, English, Dutch, and French discoveries.

An Historical Account of the Intercourse between the Inhabitants of Great Britain and the People in the East-Indies; containing likewise a compleat History of the East India Company, from its Erection under Queen Elizabeth, of glorious Memory, and of the several Alterations that have been made down to the present Reign. In Harris, 873-924.

> A long account of the affair at Amboyna.

The History of the Danish Commerce to the East Indies, and their Establishment there, the Decay of their Old Company, and the Motives which induced them to set up a new One. Interspersed with Original Papers and Memoirs. In Harris I, 976-980.

PYRARD DE LAVAL, FRANCOIS.   The Voyage of Pirard de Laval to the East Indies; his Shipwreck among the Maldives, and his copious Account of that Archipelago, translated from the Original Voyage published by himself in French. In Harris I, 701-707.

> Edited for the Hakluyt Society, London, 1887-89. French original, Paris, 1611; another edition, Paris, 1613. See below.
> Pyrard's travels covered the years between 1601 and 1611, and have crowded into them a welter of shipwrecks, imprisonments, and other adventures such as seldom falls to a man without leaving him permanently scarred. He sailed out on the *Corbin,* one of the two ships fitted out by some French merchants in a belated endeavor to open up trade relations with the East. The ship was wrecked on one of the Maldive Islands and the crew imprisoned. Pyrard, who quickly learned the language of the natives, was taken into favor by the king, who kept the Frenchman by him until five years later when the place was raided by a hostile group from Chittagong, India, and Pyrard, with his three companions, were carried off to the latter place. He then travelled to the Malabar Coast, where he was for a time a prisoner to the Portuguese, who sent him on some expeditions to the Moluccas. Along with other foreign residents he was shipped to Europe on some Portuguese vessels and was wrecked again, this time on the coast of Brazil. But Europe saw him safe at home at last. His first-hand experiences and acquaintance with various parts of the mainland of India and the islands of the Archipelago make his record a valuable repository of geographical and historical knowledge of the East. Especially has it been commended for his account of the Maldive Islands, which almost up to the present day have been a Terra Incognita.—See Heawood, *Geographical Discoveries.*

1887-89   PYRARD, FRANCOIS (of Laval). The Voyage of Francois Pyrard, of Laval, To the East Indies, the Maldives, the Moluccas and Brazil. Translated from the third French edition of 1619, and edited by Albert Gray, assisted by Harry Charles Purvis Bell. Maps and illus. 2 vols. Hak. Soc., ser. I, vols. 76, 77, 80 (part II of vol. 76). London.

1611   PYRARD DE LAVAL, FRANCOIS. Discours du voyages des Francois Pyrard de Laval aux Indes Orientales, Maldives, Moluques, et au Brasil depuis 1601 jusqu'en 1611. 2 vols. 12mo. Paris.

A Succinct History of the Empire of the Great Mogul, from its Foundation by the Great Tartar Conqueror Timur Bec, or Tamerlane, to the present Time. Taken chiefly from Oriental Writers. In Harris I, 629-662.

A Succinct History of the Rise, Progress and Establishment of the Dutch East India Company, with a View of the Immense Profits arising from that Commerce, and a Prospect of their Affairs, and the Manner in which they are conducted as well at Home, as on their extensive Settlement Abroad. Collected chiefly from their Writings. In Harris I, 924-975.

> A very competent historical view of the growth of the Company.

A Succinct History of the Swedish East India Company. Including an Extract of the Royal Charter. In Harris I, 980-983.

1745 GALVANO, ANTONIO. The Discoveries of the World from their
      Original, unto the Year of our Lord 1555. Briefly written in the
      Portugal Tongue . . . Corrected, quoted, and now published in English
      by Richard Hakluyt, Sometime Student of Christ-Church, Oxford. In
      Obsorne II, 352-402.

> Hakluyt's translation was made in 1601 (or according to Parks in 1603).
> Edited for the Hakluyt Society, 1862. Portuguese original, Lisbon, 1563. See below.
> Galvano was Governor of Ternate in the Moluccas. Hakluyt, in his dedication
> to Sir Robert Cecil (dated Oct. 29, 1601), takes occasion to give high praise to
> Galvano both for his intrinsic worth and for his "restoring and settling the
> decayed state of the Isles of Moluccas." He also states that this work had been
> translated by some unknown person many years back, and that he had the work
> by him for twelve years, but he was unable to obtain the original copy. The book
> gives a good summary of the geographical exploits of the Portuguese.

> 1862 GALVANO, ANTONIO. The Discoveries of the World, From their first
>   original unto the year of our Lord 1555. By Antonio Galvano, Gov-
>   ernor of Ternate. (Edited by F. de Sousa Tavares.) Published in Eng-
>   land by Richard Hakluyt, 1601. Now reprinted, with the original Por-
>   tuguese text (1563), and edited by Vice-Admiral Charles R. Drink-
>   water Bethune, C.B. Hak. Soc., ser. I, vol. 30. London.

> 1563 GALVANO, ANTONIO. Tratado que compos o nobre notauel capitano
>   Antonio Galvano, dos diversos e desuayrados caminhos por onde nos
>   tempos passados a pimenta e especaria veto da India. . . . 8vo. Lisbon.

1745-47 An Account of the Portuguese Possessions from the Cape of Good
         Hope to China. In Astley I, 85-88.

ALBOQUERQUE, AFONSO DE. Exploits of Alboquerque, while Vice-
      Roy of India from 1510-16. Abstract in Astley I, 71-76.

> Taken from his Commentaries, which were collected from his own letters to
> King Don Manuel. The Commentaries were printed in Lisbon, 1557, with later
> reprints. An edition was published by the Hakluyt Society, 4 vols., 1875-1883. See
> below.
> In 1709 the great Viceroy Alboquerque assumed charge of Portuguese affairs
> in the East Indies and by his practical genius greatly extended the power and trade
> as well as the territorial possessions of the Portuguese.

> 1875-1883 DALBOQUERQUE, AFONSO. The Commentaries of the Great
>   Afonso Dalboquerque, Second Viceroy of India. Translated from the
>   Portuguese edition of 1774, and edited by Walter de Gray Birch, F.R.S.
>   L. Maps and illus. 4 vols. Hak. Soc., ser. I, vols. 53, 55, 62, 69.
>   London.

> 1557 ALBOQUERQUE, AFONSO DE. Commentarios do Grande Afonso d'-
>   Alboquerque, capitan general que foy das Indias Orientales, em tempo
>   do muito poderoso Rey dom Manuel, o primeiro deste nome. 4to.
>   Lisbon.

ALMEYDA, DON FRANCISCO DE. Exploits of the Portuguese in the
      year 1507 under Don Francisco de Almeyda, first vice-roy of India
      Generalized account in Astley I, 58-70.

CABRAL, PEDRO ALVAREZ. Voyage in 1500, being the second voyage of the Portuguese to the East Indies. Chiefly from Castanheda, in Grynaeus' Latin Collection. Generalized account in Astley I, 40-48.

In sailing to the East Indies Cabral avoided the perils of the Guinea Coast of Africa and headed far to the westward. In so doing he reached the coast of Brazil and so paved the way for the Portuguese colonization in South America.

CASTRO, DON JUAN DE. The Voyage of Don Stefano da Gama, from Goa to Suez, in 1540, with Intent to burn the Turkish Galleys in that Port. Written by Juan de Castro, then a Captain in the Fleet, afterwards Governor and Vice-Roy of India. Translated from the Portuguese and abbreviated. In Astley I, 107-130.

Castro was one of the great viceroys in the Portuguese East Indies.

CASTRO, DON JUAN DE. The Second Siege of Diu by Mahmud King of Cambaya, in 1545, under the government of Don Juan de Castro. Abstract in Astley I, 132-137.

DA GAMA, VASCO. Voyage to India in 1497, being the first performed by the Portuguese round Africa. Generalized Account in Astley I, 21-40. Second Voyage in 1502, being the fourth made by the Portuguese to the East Indies. Generalized Account in Astley I, 50-54.

Da Gama's famous voyage to India was related by several authorities, such as Juan de Barras, Ramusio, Massi, Faria y Sousa, and Castanheda, and others. It also formed the subject of Camoens' famous epic poem *Os Lusiads,* which was published at Lisbon, 1572, and translated into English in 1655 by Sir Richard Fanshawe. This version was superseded by William J. Mickle's translation of 1778. Edited for the Hakluyt Society, 1898. See below and also under 1869. In making for the tip end of Africa Da Gama sailed a middle course and eventually succeeded in rounding the Cape of Good Hope. Progressing up the east coast of Africa he encountered the favorable monsoon wind and reached Calicut, May 23, 1498. The famous greeting with which the Portuguese were received has often been quoted: "May the devil take thee. What brought you hither?" Well might these Moorish traders from Tunis be dismayed. And well might the voyagers be surprised on hearing themselves addressed in Castilian. After loading up with spices they set out for the return voyage, and with fleet and crew reduced in numbers and strength, they arrived at the Tagus on July 10, 1499. The effect of this discovery on the history of Europe is too well known to be recounted. What is generally overlooked is the tragic consequences to the East when "the Portuguese burst into the Indian Ocean like a pack of hungry wolves upon a well-stocked sheep-walk." The Portuguese Empire in Asia has been referred to as a tragedy; it was also a satire on human nature.—From Oaten, *Early Travellers and Travels in India.*

1898 DA GAMA, VASCO. A Journal of the First Voyage of Vasco da Gama, 1497-99. By an unknown Writer. Translated from the Portuguese, with an Introduction and Notes, by Ernest George Ravenstein, F.R. G.S. Maps and illus. Hak. Soc., ser. I, vol. 99. London.

NUEVA, JUAN DE. Voyage to India, being the third performed by the Portuguese to the East Indies. Chiefly from Castanheda. Brief abstract in Astley I, 49-50.

SOAREZ, LOPE. A brief Account of the Portuguese Transactions in India, from 1516-1521, under the government of Lope Soarez. Abstract in Astley I, 76-79.

SOLEYMAN, BASHA. The Voyage of Soleyman Basha, from Suez to India, in his Expedition against the Portuguese at Diu, in 1537. Written by an Officer of the Venetian Galleys (who was pressed into the Turkish service), and now first translated from the Italian. Together with the Siege of Diu by Soleyman Basha of Egypt. In Astley I, 88-107.

Transactions and Discoveries of the Portuguese in India from 1521-1537 and from 1537-1542. In Astley I, 79-85.

Voyages and Transactions of the Portuguese in India from 1503-1507, with the Exploits of Pachuco, from various sources. In Astley I, 54-58.

(See Astley, Vol. I, Bk. III, for abstracts of the following English Voyagers taken from Purchas.)

The Voyage of Captain James Lancaster, in the Year 1600, being the first made on Account of the East India Company. 262-279.

See *A True and Large Discourse* under 1603 above.

The Voyage of Captain (afterwards Sir) Henry Middleton, in 1604, being the second set forth by the East India Company. 279-283.

See Middleton under 1606 above.

An Account of Java, and the first Settlement of the English at Bantam. With a Journal of Occurrences there; particularly in Regard to what passed between them and the Dutch, as well as the Natives, from 1602, to 1605 inclusively. Extracted from the larger Relation, written by Edmund Scot, chief Factor. 284-305.

The Voyage of Sir Edward Michelburne, to Bantam, in 1604. 306-312.

The Voyage of Captain William Keeling, in 1607, to Bantam and Banda; being the third set out by the India Company. Written by the Captain himself, and abbreviated. 312-332.

The Voyage of Captain David Middleton to Bantam, and the Molukkos, in 1607. 332-335.

The Voyage of Captain Alexander Sharpey, in 1608; being the fourth set out by the East India Company. Written by Captain Robert Coverte. 336-344.

    See Coverte under 1612 above.

A brief Account of the same Voyage of the Ascension. Written by Thomas Jones. 344-348.

The Voyage of Captain Richard Rowles to Priaman, in the Union; being a Continuation of the fourth Voyage. 348-351.

The Voyage of Captain David Middleton to Java and Banda, 1609; being the fifth Voyage set out by the Company. Extracted from a Letter written by himself to the Merchants. 351-360.

The Voyage of Sir Henry Middleton to the Red-Sea, and Surat, in 1610; being the sixth Voyage set out by the East India Company. Written by himself. 360-389.

The Journal of Captain Nicholas Dounton, Lieutenant-General, in the same Voyage of Sir Henry Middleton. 390-429.

The Voyage of Captain Anthony Hippon to the Coast of Koromandel, Bantam, and Siam, in 1611; being the seventh set forth by the East India Company. Written by Nathaniel Marten, Master's Mate. 429-435.

The Journal of Mr. Peter Williamson Floris, Cape-Merchant in the same Voyage of Captain Hippon. Translated from the Dutch, and contracted. 435-446.

The Voyage of Captain Samuel Castleton to Priaman, in 1612. Written by John Tatten, Master. 446-451.

The Voyage of Captain John Saris to the Red-Sea, the Molukkos, and Japan, in 1611; being the eighth Voyage set forth by the East India Company. Collected out of the Captain's own Journal. 451-496.

Occurrences at Bantam, and other Parts of the East Indies, from October 1605, till October 1609; with an Account of the Marts and Commodities of those Parts. By Captain John Saris. 496-508.

1746 CEREAU, J. A. DU. For his description of Indostan and an account of the Great Moguls, see his *Nadir-Shah,* under CENTRAL ASIA.

1750 BOSCAWEN, EDWARD (Admiral). Journal, or Narrative of the Boscawen's Voyage to Bombay in the East-Indies, Benjamin Braund, Commander, with Remarks on her Remarkable Quick Passage thither, and some Surprising Events that occurr'd during the same anno 1749, by a Young Gentleman; also Thoughts on Trade, Duties, Smuggling, Shipwrecks, . . . 8vo. London.

> Another edition, 4to, Edinburgh, 1756.
> This naval expedition was sent against the French at Pondicherry. It was unsuccessful, owing to bad weather and the incapacity of the engineers, and cost the lives of 1965 British and about 200 French soldiers. In these operations Ensign Clive, afterwards Lord Clive, gained his first military distinction.—Maggs, No. 534.

1754 Explanation of the Map of the Seat of War on the Coast of Choromandel; with an Account of the War. Folding map. 4to. London.

1757 GROSE, JOHN HENRY. Voyage to the East Indies. 2 vols. London.

> Later editions, 2 vols., London, 1766; 2 vols., London, 1772 (said to be the best one). Translated into French, London and Paris, 1758. See below.
> The author was the brother of the more celebrated antiquarian, Francis Grose, author of the *Antiquities of England and Wales,* immortalised by Burns as the "chiel amang you takin' notes."

> 1766 GROSE, JOHN HENRY. Voyage to the East Indies, 1750-1764: Observations on the Deccan and Bengal Viceroyalties, Religion, Trade, European Settlements, . . . Revised edition. Six etched views. 2 vols. 8vo. London.

> 1758 (In French.) Voyage aux Indes Orientales, traduit de l'anglois par M. Hernandez. 12mo. London and Paris.

> Noticed in the *Journal des Scavans,* 1758, IV, 401; VI, 39.

A New History of the East Indies, Ancient and Modern, containing the Chorography, Natural History, Religion, Government, Manners and Customs, Revolutions, Commerce, . . . of those Countries. Folding maps. 2 vols. 8vo. London.

> This work is composed of a translation of the Abbé Guyon's History and of a supplement taken chiefly from other writers.—Bookseller's Note.

PLAISTED, BARTHOLOMEW. A Journal from Calcutta in Bengal by Sea, to Busserah, from thence through the Great Dessert to Aleppo; and from thence to Marseilles, and through France to England, in the Year 1750. 12mo. London.

> 2nd edit., with additional chapters, London, 1758. See below. Translated into French in 1758.
> A useful, entertaining, sensible little work.—Lowndes.

> 1758 PLAISTED, BARTHOLOMEW. A Journal from Calcutta, by Sea, to Busserah, from thence across the Great Desert to Aleppo, and from thence to Marseilles, and thro' France to England, in the year 1750, to which are added, Capt. Elliot's Directions for passing over the Little Desert, from Busserah, by the way of Bagdad, Orsa and Aleppo. Folding map. 8vo. London.

1760-61 CAMPBELL, JOHN. Memoirs of the Revolution in Bengal, 1757. Complete History of the War in India, 1749-1761. Reflections on the Government of Indostan. 3 vols. in 1. 8vo. London.

1762 A Voyage to the East Indies in 1747 and 1748: Java, Batavia, the Dutch Government, Canton and China. . . . Interspersed with many useful and curious Observations and Anecdotes. 11 engraved plates, including a view of St. Helena, and a folding view of Batavia. 8vo. London.

> This work is ascribed rather doubtfully to a C. F. Noble.

WYNNE, JOHN HUDDLESTONE. History of the East Indies, antient and modern. 2 vols. London.

> Wynne was a miscellaneous writer in the employ of the East India Company from 1759 to 1761.

1763 SCRAFTON, LUKE. Reflections on the Government of Indostan, with a short Sketch of the History of Bengal, from the year 1739 to 1756; and an Account of the English Affairs in 1758. 12mo. London.

> Another edition, 8vo, London, 1770.

1763-1778 ORME, ROBERT. A History of the Military Transactions of the British Nation in Indostan, from the Year 1745. To which is prefixed a Dissertation on the Establishments made by Mahomedan Conquerors in Indostan. 34 large engraved maps and views, including the large view of Calcutta, and plans of Calcutta, Madras, Pondicherry, etc. 3 vols. 4to. London.

> A portion of this work was translated into French, Amsterdam, 1765. See below. See also Orme under 1782 below.
> This valuable historical work occupies so vast a field that every future historian of India must unavoidably trench in a greater or less degree upon his premises. The large engraved view of Calcutta should alone be worth the value of the entire work.—Quoted by Maggs, No. 521. Orme was for many years connected with the affairs of the East India Company, and was the historiographer of the Company.

> 1765 (In French.) Histoire des guerres de l'Inde ou des événemens militaires arrivés dans l'Indoustan depuis l'année 1745, traduit de l'anglois de Robert Orme par J.-B. Targe. 2 vols. 12mo. Amsterdam.

1764 HOLWELL, JOHN ZEPHANIAH. Indian Tracts; including the Narrative of the Black Hole at Calcutta, Defense of Vansittart, East India Company Affairs, 1752-1760. 4to. London.

> The Narrative of the Black Hole was first published in 1758. Holwell was surgeon to the East India Company, 1732-1749, and one of the survivors of the Black Hole. He later became temporary Governor of Bengal but was dismissed for protesting Vansittart's appointment. He was also the first European to study Hindu antiquities. See Holwell under 1766-1771 below.

1766 VANSITTART, HENRY. A Narrative of the Transactions in Bengal during the Government of Vansittart, 1760-64, by Himself. 3 vols. 8vo. London.

> The work includes manners and customs of the Hindus and other odd matters. The author took service with the East India Company in 1746. In the years 1760-64 he was Governor of Bengal. His efforts to weed out corruption in the affairs of the East India Company only made him enemies. On his return to England he was coldly received by the Company and by Lord Clive. However, in 1769 he became one of the directors of the Company. On his return voyage to India his ship, after touching at the Cape of Good Hope, disappeared from all knowledge.—From D. N. B.

1766-1771 HOLWELL, JOHN ZEPHANIAH. Interesting historical Events relating to the Provinces of Bengal, and the Empire of Indostan, with a seasonable hint and perswasive to the Honourable the Court of Directors of the East India Company as also the Mythology and Cosmogony, Fasts and Festivals of the Gentoos, followers of the Shastah. 3 parts in 1 vol. 9 plates. 8vo. London.

> Translated into French, Amsterdam, 1768. See below.

> 1768 (In French.) Evénemens Historiques et intéressants Relatifs aux Provinces de Bengale et Indostan par J. Z. Holwell. Traduit de l'Anglois. 4to. Amsterdam.

> Noticed in the *Journal des Scavans,* 1768, VI, 300.

1768 DOW, ALEXANDER. The History of Indostan: translated from the Persian. 3 vols. London.

> 2nd edit., London, 1770; again, London, 1792.
> The dissertation on the religion and philosophy of the Bramahs contains many particulars relative to India and the inhabitants in their present state.—Pinkerton XVII. This history is chiefly made up from Bernier's Travels, without acknowledgement.—Lowndes. As a matter of fact this work is a translation, according to later pronouncements, of Ferishta's History of Hindustan. Dow was an historian and dramatist who served in the British military forces in India.

1770 ELLIS, JOHN. Directions for bringing over Seeds and Plants from the East Indies. London.

The Importance of the British Dominion in India, compared with that in America. 16mo. London.

1771 OSBECK, PETRUS. Voyage to China and the East Indies, with a Voyage to Suratte by Olof Toreen, and Account of the Chinese Husbandry by Capt. C. G. Eckeberg, translated by J. R. Forster; to which is added, a Faunula and Flora Sinensis. Plates. 2 vols. 8vo. London.

> Swedish original of Osbeck's voyage, Stockholm, 1756. See below. See also this date under FAR EAST.

> 1756 OSBECK, PETRUS. Dagbok oeswer en Ostindisk Resa, med Anmerkninger af Naturkundigheten, med Torene's Resa til Surate och Ostindien. 8vo. Stockholm.

TOREEN, OLOF. For his Voyage to Surat see under Osbeck this date above.

1772 BOLTS, WILLIAM. Considerations on India Affairs; particularly respecting the Present State of Bengal and its Dependencies. 2nd edition, with Additions. Map. 4to. London.

> Bolts was a Dutch adventurer who entered the Bengal civil service, and got into trouble for private trading in the name of the East India Company. After being deported to England in 1768, he published this work attacking the government in Bengal.—From D. N. B.

PATULLO, ——. Essay on the Cultivation of the Lands and Improvement of the Revenues of Bengal. London.

VERELST, HARRY. View of the Rise, Progress and Present State of the English Government in Bengal; including a Reply to the Misrepresentations of Mr. Bolts, and other Writers. 4to. London.

1773 BOLTS, WILLIAM. Civil, political, and commercial State of Bengal.
2 vols. London.

> Translated into French, the Hague, 1775. See below.

> 1775 (In French.) Etat-civil, politique et commercant du Bengale, ou histoire
> des conquêtes et de l'administration de la Compagnie Angloise dans ce
> pays. Traduit de l'Anglois (par M. Demeunier) de M. Bolts, juge de
> la Cour du Maire de Calcutta. 2 vols. 8vo. The Hague.

IVES, EDWARD. A Voyage from England to India, in the year 1754;
interspersed with some interesting Passages relative to the Manners,
Customs, . . . of several Nations in Indostan; also a Journey from
Persia to England by an unusual Route. . . . An Historical Narrative
of the Operations of the Squadron and Army in India, under the Command of Vice-Admiral Watson and Col. Clive, in the years 1755, 1756,
and 1757; including the Correspondence between the Admiral and the
Nabob Seraja Dowla. Chart, map, and 13 plates. 4to. London.

> Ive's presence at many of the transactions which he describes and his per-
> sonal intimacy with Watson give his historical narrative an unusual importance,
> and his account of the manners and customs of the countries he visited, are those
> of an enlightened and acute observer.—Sir J. K. Laughton, quoted. The appen-
> dix contains an "Account of the Diseases prevalent in Adml. Watson's squadron,
> a description of most of the Trees, Shrubs, and Plants of India, with their medi-
> cinal virtues." Ive's interest in the medicinal qualities of plants was professional
> as he was a surgeon.

The State of the British Empire in Bengal. London.

1776 RAYNAL, GUILLAUME THOMAS FRANCOIS (Abbé). Philosophical and Political History of the Settlements and Trade of the Europeans in the East and West Indies. See under WEST INDIES.

1777 KINDERSLEY, (Mrs.). For an account of India see her *Letters from
Teneriffe*, under AFRICA.

1779 DALRYMPLE, ALEXANDER. Journal of a Voyage to the East Indies
in the Grenville, 1775. 4to. London.

> Dalrymple will be remembered for his association with the project sponsored
> by the Royal Society in 1769 to send out expeditions to observe the transit of
> Venus. See Dalrymple, under 1770-71, COLLECTIONS. In 1795 he was made
> Hydrographer to the Admiralty.

FORREST, THOMAS (Captain). Voyage to New Guinea and the Moluccas, including an Account of the Magindano, Sooloo, and other Islands, during the years 1774-76. Vocabulary of the Magindano Tongue. Portrait and plates. 4to. London.

An edition, 8vo, Dublin, 1779.
See Forrest under 1779, SOUTH SEAS. This work supplies what is wanting in Sonnerat, as it is full of the physical and moral character of the inhabitants, and of their language, mode of life and trade.—Lowndes. Was this valuable work of Sonnerat's never translated into English?

SULLIVAN, SIR RICHARD JOSEPH. An Analysis of the Political History of India. London.

1781 MACKINTOSH, WILLIAM. For remarks on the British settlements in India see his *Travels in Europe, Asia, and Africa,* under GENERAL TRAVELS AND DESCRIPTIONS.

PECHEL, SAMUEL. An Historical Account of the Settlement and Possession of Bombay by the East India Company, and of the Rise and Progress of the War with the Mahratta Nation. 8vo. London.

> Never published: only a few copies given away by the author.—Halkett and Laing.

1782 MARSDEN, WILLIAM. The History of Sumatra; containing an Account of the Government, Laws, Customs and Manners of the Native Inhabitants, with a Description of the natural Productions, and a Relation of the ancient political State of the Island. Map. 4to. London.

> 2nd edit., London, 1784; 3rd edit., with roy. fol. Atlas containing 19 plates, London, 1811.
> This book gave Marsden a reputation that still holds today. He was an orientalist, in the service of the East India Company, and resided in Sumatra in 1771-79. He studied everything that came under his notice, including the difficult Sumatran tongue. He was one of the coterie of scientists that gathered around Sir Joseph Banks, President of the Royal Society.

ORME, ROBERT. Historical Fragments on the Mogul Empire and the Marattas. 2 vols. London.

> See Orme, 1763-1778, above.

1783 CAPPER, JAMES (Colonel). Observations on the Passage to India through Egypt and across the Great-Desert. Map. 4to. London.

> Later editions, London, 1785 and 1788.
> Capper was the author of several works on meteorology, such as Observations on the Winds and Monsoons, etc.

FORREST, THOMAS (Captain). Journal of the Esther Brig . . . from Bengal to Quedah. London.

1785   FORSTER, GEORGE. Sketches of the Mythology and Customs of the Hindoos. 8vo. London.

GOUGH, RICHARD. Comparative View of the Ancient Monuments of India, chiefly those in the Island of Salset, described by different Writers. Plates. 4to. London.

> Gough was the best known antiquary in Great Britain. He was never in India himself.

HUNTER, WILLIAM. Concise Account of . . . Pegu. London.

> Translated into French, Paris, 1793. See below.
> Hunter was a surgeon as well as an orientalist, who went to India in 1781 and settled at Agra. He accompanied Palmer's expedition in 1792-93 to Oujein, of which he published an account in *Asiatic Researches*. He also got out a Hindustani-English Dictionary in 1808. According to Pinkerton the information of Hunter respecting the Birman Empire was the best till the appearance of Symes' valuable work.

> 1793   (In French.) Description de Pégu et de l'Ile Ceylon; renfermant des détails exacts et neufs sur le climat, le productions, le commerce, le gouvernment, les moeurs et usages de ces contrées, par W. Hunter, Jean Christophe Losef, et Eschelskroon; traduit de l'Anglais et de l'Allemand. 8vo. Paris.

WOLF, JOHANN CHRISTOPHER. Journey to Ceylon, with an Account of the Dutch Rule at Jafnapatam. Translated from the German by Erkelskrom. London.

> German original, Berlin, 1785. See below.
> It is a question whether Erkelskrom or Eschelskroon is the correct spelling of this name. The former is given by Pinkerton XVII.

> 1785   WOLF, JOHANN CHRISTOPHER. Reise nach Zeylon, nebst Bericht von der Holländischen Regierung zu Jafnapatam. Berlin.

1786   ERADUT KHAN. Memoirs of Eradut Khan; with Anecdotes of Aurungzebe, Shaw Aulum and Jehaunder Shaw, translated by Jonathan Scott. (Included with Capper's Observations on the Passage to India, in a volume whose leading work is Rennell's Memoir of a Map of Hindoostan; see Rennell under 1788 below.)

HASTINGS, WARREN. Memoirs relative to the State of Bengal in India. London.

> An enlarged edition in 8vo, London, 1787.

1787 ROBSON, FR. Vie d'Haïder-Aly-Khan précédée de l'histoire de l'usurpation en pays de Maïssour, et autres pays voisins, par ce prince suivie
d'un récit authentique des mauvais traitements qu'ont éprouvés les anglais qui furent faits prisonniers de guerre par son fils Tippon Khan.
Traduit de l'anglais. 12mo. Paris.

> The English original of this translation has not come to the notice of the
> editor.

1788 An Account of the Prince of Wales' Island, or Pulo Peenang in the East
Indies. (From a Collection of Tracts.) London.

FULLARTON, W. A View of the English Interests in India; and an
Account of the Military Operations in the Southern Parts of the Peninsula during the Campaigns of 1782-84. With a plan. London.

HOWEL, THOMAS. Journal of the Passage from India by a Route
partly unfrequented through Armenia and Natolia or Asia Minor.
Map. 8vo. London.

> See the same under NEAR EAST.

RENNELL, JAMES (Major). Memoirs of a Map of Hindoostan or the
Mogul Empire, with Introduction on the Geography and Present Divi-
sion of the Country, and Account of the Ganges and Burrampooter
Rivers. 4 maps and plans. 4to. London.

> 2nd edit., with considerable additions and a supplementary map, 5 maps in all,
> 4to, London, 1792; 3rd edit., enlarged with a second supplementary map, London,
> 1793. To this edition was added, Memoir of the Map of the Peninsula, with a
> new title for the whole. Maggs, No. 521, cites an edition, with a slightly different
> title, under the date 1783. Translated into French, Leipzig, 1800. See below.
> James Rennell, the famous geographer, spent a great part of his life in India,
> or occupied in Indian affairs. His maps were of the greatest importance. His
> survey of Bengal, commenced in 1764, when he was only 22, was the first ever
> prepared. His second great work was the construction of the first approximately
> correct map of India.—Maggs, No. 521. He was a close friend of Sir Joseph
> Banks, the eminent naturalist. Admiral Markham remarks of him that he was the
> greatest geographer that Great Britain has yet produced. His maps of Africa and
> especially those prepared for Mungo Parks' *Travels* were the first to put the
> geography of that continent into intelligible shape.—From Smith's *Life of Sir
> Joseph Banks*.

> 1800 (In French.) Description historique et géographique de l'Indostan traduite
> de l'anglais par J.-B. Boncheseiche sur la septième et dernière édition,
> à laquelle on a joint des mélanges d'histoire et de statistique sur l'Inde,
> traduits par J. Castéra. 3 vols. 8vo. Leipzic.

> An Atlas in 4to with 11 maps is added.

1789 A Description of several artificial Caverns in the Neighborhood of Bombay. (Calcutta, 1788.) London.

A Letter from a Gentleman on board an Indiaman, giving an Account of the Island of Joanna, in 1784. From a Collection of Tracts. London.

MUNRO, INNES. A Narrative of the Military Operations on the Coromandel Coast, against the combined Forces of the French, Dutch, and Hyder Ally Cawn, from 1780 to the Peace in 1784; in a Series of Letters, in which are included many useful Cautions to young Gentlemen destined for India; A Description of· the most remarkable Manners of the East Indians; and an Account of the Isle of France, illustrated with a view of Port Louis in the Isle of France, and correct plans, upon a large scale, of the Fortifications at Trinquamallee, and of all the Battles fought by the Army under Lieut.-Gen. Sir Eyre Coote, and other Commanders, during that War. 4to. London.

1790 CRAUFORD, QUINTON. Sketches chiefly relating to the History, Religion, Learning, and Manners of the Hindoos; with the present State of the Native Powers of Hindostan. 8vo. London.

> 2nd edit., enlarged, 2 vols., 8vo, London, 1792. Translated into French, Dresden, 1791. See below.
> The author states that his intention was to draw the attention of the public, for a moment, from the exploits of Mahomedans and Europeans, and direct it to the original inhabitants of the country. He was in the service of the East India Company until 1780. He afterwards settled in France.

> 1791 (In French.) Esquisses de l'histoire, de la religion, des sciences et des moeurs des Indiens. Avec un exposé très court, de l'état politique actuel des puissances de l'Inde. Traduit de l'anglais (par le Citoyen de Montesquiou-Fesenzac). Plates. 2 vols. Dresden.

FRANCKLIN, WILLIAM (Captain). Observations made on a Tour from Bengal to Persia, in the Years 1786-87. 8vo. London.

> Original edition published in 4to at Calcutta, 1788. See under CENTRAL ASIA.

LE COUTER, JOHN. Letters chiefly from India, translated from the French. 8vo. London.

> An impartial account of the military transactions on the coast of Malabar during the late war; together with short descriptions of the religion, manners, and customs of the inhabitants of Hindostan.—Lowndes.

PENNANT, THOMAS. Indian Zoology. 16 plates, chiefly ornithological. 4to. London.

1791 RENNELL, JAMES (Major). A Bengal Atlas; containing Maps of the Theatre of War and Commerce on that Side of Hindostan. Folio map. 4to. London.

ROBERTSON, WILLIAM. An Historical Disquisition concerning the Knowledge which the Ancients had of India; and the Progress and Trade with that Country, . . . With Appendix. 2 maps. 4to. London.

> Another edition, 8vo, London, 1799. Translated into French, Paris, 1792. See below.

> 1792 (In French.) Remarques historiques sur la connoissance que les anciens avoient de l'Inde, et sur les progrès de commerce avec cette partie du monde avant la découverte du passage par le cap de Bonne Espérance. Traduit de l'anglais. 8vo. Paris.

1792 FORREST, THOMAS (Captain). Voyage from Calcutta to the Merguy Archipelago, on the Coast of the Bay of Bengal; also an Account of the Islands of Junk-Seylan, Poulo-Pinang, and the Port of Quedas; the present State of Achem, and Account of the Island of Celebes, and a Treatise on the Monsoon of the East-Indies. 2 vols. 4to. London.

> See Forrest under 1783 above.—This work is justly of great authority, for its details in maritime geography.—Lowndes.

RENNELL, JOHN (Major). The Marches of the British Armies in the Peninsula of India, during the campaigns of 1790-91; illustrated and explained by reference to a map, compiled from authentic Documents, transmitted by Earl Cornwallis from India. Folding map. 8vo. London.

STAHL, WILLIAM (Dr.). The Authentic Memoirs and Sufferings of Dr. William Stahl, a German Physician, containing his Travels, Observations, and Interesting Narrative, during four years' Imprisonment at Goa. 12mo. London.

1792-93 JONES, SIR WILLIAM (and Others). Dissertations and Miscellaneous Pieces relating to the History and Antiquities, Arts, Sciences, and Literature of Asia, by Sir William Jones, W. Chambers, Gen. Carnac, and others. Vols. I-IV. Plates. 8vo. London.

> This contains: On the Coins of Mavalipurum; Journey to Tibet; On the Indian Festivals and the Sphinx; Short Account of the Maratta State; On the Mystical Poetry of the Persians and Hindus, etc.

1793 British India Analysed. 3 vols. London.

HODGES, WILLIAM. Travels in India, during the years 1780-83. Map and plates. 4to. London.

> See also below under 1794.

ROCHON, ALEXIS (Abbé). Voyage to Madagascar and the East Indies.

> See under AFRICA.

1793-1814 BARTON, SIR E. (General). A Collection of 92 water-colour and pencil Drawings, of India Views, mostly round Delhi, Benares and Lucknow, executed by General Sir E. Barton, or presented to and collected by him. 2 vols. Oblong Fol.

1794 HODGES, WILLIAM. Choice Views in India, after designs executed on the spot, and engraved in aqua-tint, with a French and English description, and forty engravings. London.

HOME, ROBERT. Select Views in Mysore, the Country of Tippoo Sultan; from Drawings taken on the Spot by Mr. Home; with historical Descriptions. 5 maps and 29 engraved plates. 4to. London.

> See Home under 1796 below.

JOHANSEN, ANDREW. A geographical and historical Account of the Island of Bulam, with Observations on its Climate, Productions, . . . 8vo. London.

SCOTT, JONATHAN. Ferishta's History of the Dekkan from the first Mahummedan Conquests, with a Continuation to the present Day: and the History of Bengal from the Accession of Aliverdee Khan to the Year 1780. 2 vols. 4to. Shrewsbury.

> Another edition, 2 vols., 4to, London, 1800.
> Scott was an orientalist, who served as secretary to Warren Hastings; he did considerable other work in oriental fields, especially translations, among which was a revised translation of Galland's French version of the Arabian Nights, which he published in 1811. See also Dow under 1768 above.

1794-1800 MAURICE, THOMAS. Indian Antiquities: Dissertations on the Geography, Laws, Government, Literature, . . . of Hindostan. 30 engravings of views, idols, gods, etc. 7 vols. 8vo. London.

> Maurice was an orientalist who was one of the first to popularise Eastern history and religions.—D. N. B. See also under 1795-1803 below.

1795   CAMPBELL, DONALD (of Barbreck). A Journey overland to India, partly by a Route never gone before by any European, in a Series of Letters to his Son, comprehending his Shipwreck and Imprisonment with Hyder Ali and Transactions in the East. 4to. London.

> Also dated 1796. An abridgement in 12mo, London, 1796; an edition, 12mo, with slightly different title, London, 1798. Translated into German, Altona, 1796. See below.

> 1796   (In German.) Landreise nach Indien. Altona.

SULLIVAN, JAMES. Tracts upon India; written in the years 1779, 1780, and 1788. With subsequent Observations by him. 8vo. London.

1795-1803   MAURICE, THOMAS. The History of Hindostan, its Arts and Sciences during the most Ancient Periods. 2 vols.; The History of Modern Hindostan. 2 vols. Maps and engravings. 4 vols. in all. 4to. London.

1795-1808   DANIELL, THOMAS and WILLIAM. Oriental Scenery. 144 colored plates. 6 vols. Fol. London.

> These consist of views of landscape, antiquities, excavations in India, done in aqua-tint and colored in imitation of drawings. Lowndes calls them the finest specimens of their kind ever published in England. William was the nephew of Thomas Daniell.

1796   HAMILTON, ELIZA. Translation of the Letters of a Hindoo Rajah written previous to and during his Residence in England, with a Dissertation on the History, Religion, and Manners of the Hindoos. 2 vols. 8vo. London.

HOME, ROBERT. Description of Seringapatam, the capital of Tippoo Sultan, intended to accompany the six following Views drawn by Mr. Home, and engraved by M. Stadler. 4 pp. and 6 plates. Fol. London.

1796-1801   RUSSELL, PATRICK. An Account of Indian Serpents, collected on the Coast of Coromandel; containing Descriptions and Drawings of each Species; together with Experiments and Remarks on their several Poisons. 3 plain and 43 colored plates. 1796. A Continuation of an Account of Indian Serpents. Portrait, 3 plain and 42 colored plates. 2 vols. in 1. Fol. London.

> This is said to be one of the rarest books on the fauna of India.

1797   JAMES, SILAS. Narrative of a Voyage to Arabia, India, . . . in the
       years 1781-1784. 8vo. London.

       VINCENT, WILLIAM. The Voyage of Nearchus from the Indus to
       the Euphrates, collected from the original Journal preserved by Arrian,
       and illustrated by authorities ancient and modern. Maps. 4to. London.

           Alexander the Great in his retreat from India sent a detachment by sea under
           command of Nearchus, with instructions to observe closely the details of the
           route. So carefully were the instructions carried out by Nearchus that many of
           the places can still be identified. The voyage started from somewhere near modern
           Karachi and took five months to reach the Tigris. The fact that a native pilot was
           employed showed that the trip had been made before.—From Baker, *History of
           Geographical Discovery*. See also McCrindle, 1879, below.

1798   CAMPBELL, ——. An Account of the Island of Ceylon. London.

       FORSTER, GEORGE. A Journey from Bengal to England through the
       northern Parts of India, Kashmire, Afghanistan and Persia, and into
       Russia by the Caspian Sea. 2 vols. 4to. London.

           An edition of the first volume was published at Calcutta, 4to, 1790. The
           work was translated into French, with additions, by M. Langles, 3 vols., 8vo,
           Paris, 1802.

       FRANCKLIN, WILLIAM. The History of the Reign of Shah Aulum,
       the present Emperor of Hindostaun, containing the Transactions of the
       Court of Delhi, and the neighboring States, during a period of thirty-
       six years. Large folding map. 4to. London.

       PENNANT, THOMAS. View of Western and Eastern Hindoostan:
       History, Natural History, Antiquities, People, . . . 23 full-page and
       head piece engravings. 2 vols. 4to. London.

           This tireless naturalist and antiquary reached out to the ends of the world
           to gather in knowledge.

       STAVORINUS, J. SPLINTER (Admiral). Voyages to the East Indies,
       translated from the Dutch by P. H. Wilcocke; comprising a full Ac-
       count of the Possessions of the Dutch in India and at the Cape. Maps.
       3 vols. 8vo. London.

           In Pinkerton XI, 159-215; 216-287. Dutch original, Leyden, 1793. See below.

       1793   STAVORINUS, J. SPLINTER (Admiral). Reise van Seeland, over de
              Raap de Goede-Hoop, naer Batavia, Bantam, Bengalem, enz. dedaen in
              de jaaren 1768 bis 1771. 2 vols. 8vo. Leyden.

1798-1801   Asiatick Researches, or Transactions of the Society instituted in Bengal for inquiring into the History and Antiquities, Literature, . . . of Asia. Vols. I-VI. 8vo. London.

> Among some of the articles are: Narrative of a Journey from Agra to Oujein, by W. Hunter; Account of the Inhabitants of the Poggy or Nassau Islands, off Sumatra, by John Crisp; On the Religion and Literature of the Burmas, by Francis Buchanan; Description of the Caves at Ellora; Antiquities on the West and South Coasts of Ceylon.

1799   ANBUREY, THOMAS. Hindostan Scenery, consisting of 12 Select Views in India, drawn during the Campaign of the Marquis of Cornwallis, showing the difficulty of a March through the Gundecotta Pass. Collection of 12 aquatints, engraved by Francis Jukes. London.

JACKSON, JOHN. A Journey from India towards England, 1797; by a Route commonly called Over-Land. Map and engravings. 8vo. London.

> Jackson, in addition to travelling, was also interested in antiquarian researches. He did some excavating at Carthage and Udena. See under NEAR EAST.

TAYLOR, JOHN (Major). Travels to India in 1789 by way of Scanderoon, Aleppo, and the Great Desert to Bussora. 2 maps. 2 vols. 8vo. London. (With Instructions for Travellers.)

TOWNE, WILLIAM. Illustrations of some Institutions of the Maratta People. London.

1799-1804   JONES, SIR WILLIAM. Memoirs of the Life, Writings and Correspondence of Sir William Jones. By Lord Teignmouth. 2 vols. 8vo. London.

> This celebrated jurist and oriental scholar was a many-sided man, but his chief fame rests upon his editing and translations of Persian poetry and other oriental texts. He deserves especial commendation for his unravelling the intricacies of Hindu law, which he published under the title of *Institutes of Hindu Law.* His letters contain many descriptions of the country, life, and manners of the Hindus.

1800   PAOLINO DA SAN BARTOLOMEO, (Fra). Voyage to the East Indies: Manners, Customs, . . . of the Natives, 1776-89. Notes by J. Reinhold Forster. Plate. 8vo. London.

> Italian original, 4to, Rome, 1796. See below.

> 1796   PAOLINO DA SAN BARTOLOMEO (Fra). Viaggio alle Indie Orientali (1776-1789). Plates and portraits. 4to. Rome.

A Journal of an Embassy from the Government of Madras to the King
of Candy, in Ceylon, in the Year 1782. In vol. II of the *Miscellaneous
Works of Hugh Boyd*. London.

LECKIE, DANIEL ROBINSON. Journal of a Route to Nagpore, by
the way of Cuttac, Borosumbher, and the Southern Bunjare Ghaut, in
the year 1790; with an Account of Nagpur, and a Journal from that
Place to Benares, by the Suhaji Pass. Map. 4to. London.

MAURICE, THOMAS. India Antiquities; or, Dissertations relative to
the Geography, Civil Laws, Government, Commerce and Literature of
Hindustan, compared with Persia, Egypt and Greece. Large folding
maps and plates. 7 vols. 8vo. London.

SYMES, MICHAEL (Lieut.-Col.). Account of an Embassy to the Kingdom of Ava from the Governor-General of India, in 1795. Maps,
views, and plates of costumes, natural history, etc. 4to. London.

> 2nd edit., 3 vols., 8vo, with volume of plates in 4to, 4 vols. in all, London,
> 1800. In Pinkerton IX, 426-572, with some chapters omitted. Translated into
> French, Paris, 1800; into German, Hamburg, 1800. See below.
> According to Pinkerton this is the only satisfactory account of Burma till
> then published. Symes's embassy resulted in leave being given by the "Emperor of
> Ava" for 'a British Resident to reside at Rangoon to protect British subjects.—
> Sotheran.

> 1800   (In French.) Relation de l'ambassade anglaise envoyée en 1795 dans le
>   royaume d'Ava ou l'empire des Birmans. Suivi d'un voyage fait en
>   1798 à Colombo, dans l'Ile de Ceylan et à la Baie de Da Nagoa, sur la
>   côte orientale de l'Afrique, de la description de l'Ile de Carnicobas et
>   des ruines de Mevalipouram. Traduit de l'anglais avec des notes par
>   J. Castéra. 3 vols. in 8vo and an atlas in 4to. Paris.

> 1800   (In German.) Gesandtschaftsreise nach der Königreich Ava, 1795. Trans-
>   lated by Hager. 1 map and 8 plates. Hamburg.

WHITE, WILLIAM. Journal of a Voyage from Madras to Columbo,
and Da Lagoa Bay, on the East Coast of Africa, 1798. With Account
of the Manners and Customs of the Inhabitants of Da Lagoa Bay,
and a Vocabulary of the Language. 2 illus. 4to. London.

> For French translation see French version of Symes above.

ADDENDA

1801   Voyage dans l'Inde, en Perse, . . . Avec la description de l'île Poulo-Pinang, nouvel établissement des Anglais, près de la côte de Coromandel. Par différents officiers au service de la Compagnie anglaise des Indes Orientales. Traduit de l'anglais par les C * * * (L.-M. Langles et F.-J. Noel). 8vo. Paris.

> This work contains: Voyage de l'Inde à la Mekke; Voyage du Bengal à Chyraz (Dans cette partie, on trouve de nombreux détails sur la Perse) ; La 3e partie renferme la description de Poulo Pinang avec plusieurs détails tirés de voyages de Farrets et de Le Gentil.—Bookseller's Note.

1806   GOLD, CHARLES (Captain). Oriental Drawings. Sketched between the years 1791 and 1798. 49 colored plates and 1 woodcut. 4to. London.

> The subjects are expressive of the usual dress and appearance of the different Castes, and portray the general costume of India.—Bookseller's Note.

1807   BUCHANAN, FRANCIS (M. D.). A Journey from Madras through the Countries of Mysore, Canara, and Malabar. 3 vols. 4to. London.

> In Pinkerton VIII, 573-776, with omission of agricultural and commercial details.

CORDINER, JAMES. A Description of Ceylon, with the Narrative of a Tour round the Island in 1800, the Campaign in Kandy in 1803, and Journey to Ramisseram in 1804. Map, plan, and 23 aquatints and other engravings by Madlard and others. 2 vols. London.

1808-1814   BALBI, GASPARO. Voyage to Pegu. Reprinted from Purchas in Pinkerton VIII, 395-405.

> Italian original, Venice, 1590. See below.
> Balbi travelled to Pegu by way of Aleppo, Babylon, Ormuz, Diu, and Goa, following the orthodox route to India. Anna and Sion are his names for Ava and Siam.

> 1590   BALBI, GASPARO. Viaggio dell' Indie-Orientali, nel quali si contiene quanto egli in detto Viaggio ha veduto per lo spatio di IX anni consumato in esso del 1579 fin' as 1588: con la relazione di dazzu, pesi e mesure di tutti le citta: con suo viaggio, e del governo del re del Pegu, e della guerra fatta da lui con altri re d'Anna e de Sion, con tavola delle cose piu notabili. 8vo. Venice.

DE CHASTE, —— (Commander). Voyage to Tercera, Undertaken by the Commander De Chaste, Gentleman in Ordinary for the King's Bed

Chamber and Governor for his Majesty of the Towns and Castle of Dieppe and Arquis. Translated from the French of Thevenot's Collection, Vol. IV. In Pinkerton I, 833-851.

FITCH, RALPH. Voyage of Ralph Fitch (merchant of London) to Ormuz, and so to Goa in the East Indies. Begun in the Year 1583 and ended in 1591. In Pinkerton IX, 406-425.

> Modern edition, London, 1889. See also under Foster, 1921, below. A Dutch translation, Leyden, 1706. See below.
> Fitch was practically the first Englishman to follow in the footsteps of Portuguese and Italian travellers and see with his own eyes the state of India—the glory of Akbar's court, the commercial possibilities of trade, the practice of suttee, the worship of cows, the marriage ceremonies of the Bengalese, and other customs peculiar to India. He roamed far and wide, from Diu to Goa, where he and his two companions were imprisoned by the Portuguese on the charge of being spies. Agra, Fatepur, Benares, Hugli, Pegu, Macao, Malacca, Ceylon were among many other places visited. His observations, as recorded in Purchas, are not of great worth, but his adventure was of consequence to Englishmen.—Oaten, *Early Travellers and Travels in India*.

> 1899 FITCH, RALPH. Ralph Fitch, England's Pioneer to India and Burma, his companions and contemporaries, with his remarkable narrative told in his own words. By J. H. Ryley. 8vo. London.

> 1706 (In Dutch.) Aanmerklyke Reys, 1583-1591, na Ormus, Goa, Cambaya, Bacola, Chonderi, Pégu, Siam, Malacca, Ceylon, Cochin, . . . Map and 10 plates. 12mo. Leyden.

1811 KIRKPATRICK, WILLIAM (Colonel). An Account of the Kingdom of Nepaul, being the substance of Observations made during a Mission in that Country in 1793. London.

1817 FAY, ELIZA. Original Letters from India, 1779-1815. Calcutta.

> Edited by E. M. Forster, London, 1925.

1858 India in the Fifteenth Century, Being a Collection of Narratives of Voyages to India in the century preceding the Portuguese discovery of the Cape of Good Hope; from Latin, Persian, Russian, and Italian Sources. Now first translated into English. Edited with an Introduction by Richard Henry Major, F.S.A., Keeper of Maps, Brit. Mus. Hak. Soc., ser. I, vol. 22. London.

1863 JORDANUS, FRIAR. Miribilia Descriptio. The Wonders of the East. By Friar Jordanus, of the Order of Preachers and Bishop of Columbum in India the Greater, *circa* 1330. Translated from the Latin Original, as published at Paris in 1839, in the Recueil de Voyages et de Memoirs, of the Société de Geographie. With the addition of a Commentary, by Col. Sir Henry Yule, K.C.S.I., R.E., C.B. Hak. Soc., ser. I, vol. 31. London.

1865 BARBOSA, DUARTE. A Description of the Coasts of East Africa and Malabar In the Beginning of the Sixteenth Century, by Duarte Barbosa, a Portuguese. Translated from an early Spanish manuscript in the Barcelona Library, with Notes and a Preface, by Lord Stanley of Alderley. 2 illus. Hak. Soc., ser. I, vol. 35. London.

> This account appeared in Ramusio I. The choice of authorship seems to lie between Barbosa and Magellan. The latter returned to Europe from India in 1512 and the former in 1517. The editor of the Hakluyt Society edition is inclined to favor Magellan and thinks that the work may be a compilation from several sources, as it was impossible for one person to visit all the places he mentions. Even if the book is not a record of personal observation, it is valuable for the information it supplies. See Oaten, *Early Travellers and Travels in India.* See also Barbosa, 1918-1921 below and under 1873, CENTRAL ASIA.

1869 DA GAMA, VASCO. The Three Voyages of Vasco da Gama, And his Vice-royalty, from the *Lendas da India* of Gaspar Correa; accompanied by original documents. Translated from the Portuguese, with Notes and an Introduction, by Lord Stanley of Alderley. 3 illus. Hak. Soc., ser. I, vol. 42. London.

> See Da Gama, 1745-47 above, and 1898 below.

1871 CUNNINGHAM, A. The Ancient Geography of India. I. The Buddhist Period, including the Campaigns of Alexander, and the Travels of Hwen Thsang. 13 maps. 8vo. London.

> See also Watters 1904-5 below.

1877 The Hawkins' Voyage During the reigns of Henry VIII, Queen Elizabeth, and James I. Second edition. Edited by Clements R. Markham, C.B., F.R.S. Hak. Soc., ser. I, vol. 57. London.

> The portion that concerns India is the Relation of the Occurents . . . in India, 1608-1613. In 1606 the East India Company "set forth" their third voyage, which was the first to have dealings with the Mogul's dominions. In command of one of the ships was William Hawkins, who landed at Surat, whence, after countless difficulties with the Portuguese and risks of assassination, he proceeded to Agra. Here he was presented to the Great Mogul Jahangir, to whom he handed the letter from James I. Learning that Hawkins spoke Turkish, Jahangir gave him a private audience which Hawkins used to further his complaints against the extortions of the Portuguese and the natives and to plead for permission to erect an English factory at Surat. Two years he stayed there, even marrying an Armenian woman to please Jahangir, but finding the promised trading privileges not forthcoming, he left Agra in 1611 for England and on the way home died. He gives a good account of many things—the system of "life-peers," military state, and especially of the nightly debauches of Jahangir, as well he might, for being able to take his grog along with the best, he sat up as companion with the Mogul many a night. See Oaten, *Early Travellers and Travels in India.* His place as ambassador was taken by Sir Thomas Roe, who was furnished with more pretentious credentials.

LANCASTER, SIR JAMES. The Voyage of Sir James Lancaster, Knt., to the East Indies, with Abstracts of Journals of Voyages to the East Indies, during the Seventeenth century, preserved in the India Office, and the Voyage of Captain John Knight, 1606, to seek the North-West Passage. Edited by Sir Clements R. Markham, K.C.B., F.R.S., ex-Pres. R.G.S. Hak. Soc., ser. I, vol. 56. London.

This expedition of 1591 was a complete failure.

McCRINDLE, J. W. Ancient India as described by Megasthenes and Arrian, being a translation of the fragments of the Indika of Megasthenes collected by Dr. Schwanbeck, and of the first part of the Indika of Arrian. 8vo. London.

See also McCrindle under dates 1879, 1882, 1896, 1901, and 1927 below.

1879   McCRINDLE, J. W. The Commerce and Navigation of the Erythraean Sea, being a translation of the Periplus Maris Erythraei, by an anonymous writer, and of Arrian's Account of the Voyage of Nearkhos, from the mouth of the Indus to the head of the Persian Gulf, with Introduction, Commentary, Notes and Index. 8vo. London.

The famous *Periplus* was apparently written about the year A. D. 60 for the use of merchants. It displays considerable knowledge of the coast of Africa beyond Cape Guardafui and to a less degree of the west coast of India. The author seems to have known also of Ceylon, the Malay Peninsula, and China. His reference to the overland trade to and from China suggests that the Roman merchants did not yet know of the route by sea.—From Baker, *Geographical Discovery*. See also Schoff under 1912 below.

1882   McCRINDLE, J. W. Ancient India as described by Ktesias the Knidean. 8vo. London.

1886   The Dawn of British Trade to the East Indies as recorded in the Court Minutes of the East India Company, 1599-1603, containing an account of the formation of the Company, the first Adventure, and Waymouth's Voyage in search of the North-West Passage, now first printed from the original manuscript by Henry Stevens of Vermont, with an Introduction by Sir George Birdwood. 4to. London.

1886-88   HEDGES, WILLIAM. The Diary of William Hedges, Esq., Afterwards Sir William Hedges, during his Agency in Bengal; as well as on his Voyage out and Return Overland (1681-1687). Transcribed for the Press, with Introductory Notes, etc., by R. Barlow, and Illustrated by copious Extracts from Unpublished Records, etc., by Col. Sir Henry Yule, K.C.S.I., C.B., LL.D. Vol. 1. The Diary, with Index. Vol. 2. Notices regarding Sir William Hedges, Documentary Memoirs of Job Charnock, and other Biographical and Miscellaneous Illustrations of the time in India. 18 illus. (1886.) Vol. 3. Documentary Contributions to a Biography of Thomas Pitt, Governor of Ft. George, with Collections on the Early History of the Company's Settlement in Bengal, and on Early Charts and Topography of the Hugli River. Map, illus., Index to Vols. 2, 3. (1888.) Hak. Soc., ser. I, vols. 74, 75, and 78. London.

Selections from the Letters, Despatches, and other State Papers preserved in the Foreign Department of the Government of India, 1772-1785, edited by Geo. W. Forrest. 3 vols. Fol. Calcutta.

1893   TWINING, THOMAS.   Travels in India a Hundred Years Ago with A Visit to the United States. Portrait and map. 8vo. London.

1894   VESPUCCIUS, ALBERICUS.   The Voyage from Lisbon to India, 1505-06; being an Account and Journal of Albericus Vespuccius, translated from the Contemporary Flemish and edited with Prologue and Notes, by C. H. Coote. 8vo. London.

1896   McCRINDLE, J. W.   The Invasion of India by Alexander the Great as described by Arrian, Q. Curtius, Diodorus, Plutarch and Justin, being translations of such portions of the works of these and other Classical Authors as described Alexander's Campaigns in Afghanistan, the Punjab, Sindh, Gedrosia and Karmania, with an introduction containing the Life of Alexander, copious notes and indices. New edition bringing the Work up to date. Maps and illus. 8vo. London.

1896-1902   FOSTER, W.   Letters received from the East India Company from its Servants in the East. Transcribed from the "Original Correspondence" Series of India Office Records. Edited by W. Foster, with Introduction by F. C. Danvers, 1602-1617. Complete set, 6 vols. 8vo. London.

1898   DA GAMA, VASCO.   A Journal of the First Voyage of Vasco de Gama, 1497-99, by an unknown writer. Translated from the Portuguese, with an Introduction and Notes, by Ernest George Ravenstein, F.R.G.S. 8 maps and 23 illus. Hak. Soc., ser. I, vol. 99.   London.

See Da Gama under 1745-47 above.

1901   McCRINDLE, J. W.   Ancient India as described in Classical Literature, being a collection of Greek and Latin texts relating to India, extracted from Herodotus, Strabo, Diodorus Siculus, Pliny, Aelian, Philostratus,

Dion Chrysostum, Porphyry, Stobaeus, the Itinerary of Alexander the Great, the Periegesis of Dionysius, the Dionysiaka of Nonnus, the Romance History of Alexander and other works, translated and copiously annotated, with Introduction and Index. 8vo. London.

1903 BOWREY, THOMAS. The Countries round the Bay of Bengal. Edited, from an unpublished MS., 1669-1679, by Thomas Bowrey, by Col. Sir Richard Carnac Temple, Bart., C.I.E. 19 illus. and 1 chart. Bibliography. Hak. Soc., ser. II, vol. 12. London.

ELDRED, JOHN, and Others. The First Englishman who reached India overland, 1583-89. In Beazley, *Voyages and Travels,* vol. I. London.

Taken from Hakluyt, 1598-1600.

STEVENS, THOMAS. His Voyage to India by the Cape Route. In Beazley, *Voyages and Travels,* vol. I. London.

Taken from Hakluyt, 1589.
This is a letter written by Stevens from Goa to his father. The Jesuit Thomas Stevens is the first known Englishman to have visited India. He went to Goa in 1579 and became Rector of the Jesuits' College in Salsette. His own accounts are contained in letters and concern themselves with Goa alone. He was instrumental in getting Ralph Fitch and his companions released from prison.—From Oaten, *Early Travellers and Travels in India.*

1904-05 WATTERS, T. On Yuan Chwang's Travels in India, 629-645 A. D. Edited by T. W. Rhys Davids and S. W. Bushell. Reprint. 2 vols. 8vo. London.

This is one of the publications of the Royal Asiatic Society.

1905 JOURDAIN, JOHN. John Jourdain's Journal of a Voyage to the East Indies, 1608-1617. (Sloane MS. 858, Brit. Mus.) Edited by William Foster, B.A., of the India Office. With Appendices A-F, and a Bibliography, by Basil H. Soulsby. 4 maps. Hak. Soc., ser. II, vol. 16. London.

MUNDY, PETER. For his travels in India see under GENERAL TRAVELS AND DESCRIPTIONS.

Mundy made his first visit to India as a servant of the East India Company in 1628 and his third and last in 1655. Vol. V of his travels is being prepared for the press by the Hakluyt Society. Vols. II and III deal with his travels in Asia.

1909 MALLESON, ——. History of the French in India from the founding of Pondicherry 1674 to the Capture of that Place in 1761. 2 maps. London.

1910 ALBIRUNI, ———. Tarikhu'l-Hind. Alberuni's India. An Account of
the Religion, Philosophy, Literature, Chronology, Astronomy, Customs, Laws and Astrology of India about A. D. 1030. English Translation by E. Sachau. 2 vols. 8vo. London.

1912 SCHOFF, W. H. The Periplus of the Erythraean Sea. Travel and Trade
in the Indian Ocean by a Merchant of the First Century. Translated from the Greek and annotated. 8vo. London.

See McCrindle, 1879, above.

1918-1921 BARBOSA, DUARTE. The Book of Duarte Barbosa. An Account
of Countries bordering on the Indian Ocean. . . . 1518 A. D. A New Translation by Mr. Longworth Dames. 2 vols. Hak. Soc., ser. II, vols. 44, 49. London.

See Barbosa, 1865, above.

1921 FOSTER, W. Early Travels in India, 1583-1619, edited by W. Foster.
Map and illus. 8vo. London.

Contains the travels of Ralph Fitch, John Mildenhall, William Hawkins, W. Finch, N. Withington, Thos. Coryat, etc.

1923-1931 OLAFSSON, JON. The Life of the Icelander, Jon Olafsson. Vol.
1, translated and edited by Dame Bertha Phillpotts, D.B.E., Litt. D. 2 maps and 4 illus. Vol. 2. edited by the late Sir Richard Temple, Bart., C.B., C.I.E., and Lavinia Mary Anstey. 1 map and 2 illus. Hak. Soc., ser. II, vols. 53, 68. London.

These are the memoirs of an Icelandic farmer's son, who took service under Christian IV of Denmark. After voyages to the White Sea and to Spitsbergen (see vol. 1), he volunteered for service in India (see vol. 2), and in 1623-24 made a stay at the Danish fortress Dansborg on the Coromandel Coast.—From Book Notice. The above translation was made from the Icelandic edition of Sigfus Blondal of 1908-09.

1926-27 MANRIQUE, SEBASTIEN. Travels of Fray Sebastien Manrique,
1629-1643. A translation of the *Itinerario de las Missiones Orientales*, with introduction and notes by Lieut.-Col. C. Eckford Luard, C.I.E., M.A., assisted by Father H. Hosten, S.J. 2 vols. Maps and illus. Hak. Soc. ser. II, vols. 59, 61. London.

1927 McCRINDLE, J. W. Ancient India as described by Ptolemy; being a
translation of the chapters which describe India and Central and Eastern Asia in the treatise on Geography, written by Klaudios Ptolemaios.

Edited with an Introduction and Notes by Surendranath Majumdar Sastri, M.A. 2 maps. 8vo. London.

> A word for word reprint of the rare original edition with the addition of notes designed to bring the work up-to-date and to prove that the peoples of Central Asia were known to Sanskrit writers.—Heffer.

1928 For the Desert Route to India see this date under NEAR EAST.

DE LAET, J. The Empire of the Great Mogol. Translated by J. S. Hoyland. With critical Notes and Introduction by Professor S. N. Banerjee. 8vo. London.

> Latin original, Leyden, 1631. See below.
> This is the only translation of De Laet's *De Imperio Magni Mogolis,* 1631. The work long ranked as the best general account of India and is a valuable authority for the history of Akbar's reign. The first part is a good compilation from the works of Sir Thos. Roe, Purchas, Peter Teixeira and others. The second is a genuine chronicle of the Empire.—Heffer.

> 1631 DE LAET, J. De Imperio Magni Mogolis sive India Vera Commentarius e variis auctoribus congestus. 16mo. Leyden.

1929 BONTEKOE, WILLEM Y. Memorable description of the East-Indian voyage, 1618-1625. Translated from the Dutch by C. B. Bodde-Hodgkinson and P. Geyl. 10 plates. 8vo. Broadway Travellers. London.

.930 GUERREIRO, F. Jahangir and the Jesuits with the Travels of Benedict Goes and the Mission to Pegu. Translated from the original of Fernav Guerreiro, S. J., with an Introduction and Notes by C. H. Payne. 4 plates. 8vo. Broadway Travellers. London.

LOCKE, J. COURTENAY. The First Englishmen in India. Letters and Narratives of sundry Elizabethans written by themselves and edited with an Introduction and Notes by J. Courtenay Locke. 8vo. Broadway Travellers. London.

> Contains letters and relations of Newberry, Stevens, Eldred, Queen Elizabeth.— In this book the stories of the first Englishmen in India are told in their own simple but dramatic words.—Book Notice.

Relations of Golconda in the early Seventeenth Century. Edited by W. H. Moreland, C.S.I., C.I.E. Maps. Hak. Soc., ser. II, vol. 66. London.

1931 HALL, BASIL (Captain). Travels in India. Edited and selected, with an Introduction, by Professor H. G. Rawlinson, Indian Educational Service. Illus. 8vo. Broadway Travellers. London.

> Selections from Hall's best and most abiding work, *Fragments of Voyages and Travels* (1831-33). In these selections the reader will find graphic and entertaining pictures of life in the Royal Navy, a wonderful panorama of India and Ceylon, including Elephants' Caves, the jungles, and, above all, events at a rajah's court.—Book Notice.

1933 BURNELL, JOHN, Bombay in the Days of Queen Anne, Being an Account of the Settlement, written by John Burnell. With an Introduction and Notes by S. T. Sheppard, to which is added Burnell's Narrative of his Adventures in Bengal, with an Introduction by Sir W. Foster and Notes by Sir E. Cotton. Maps. Hak. Soc., ser. II, vol. 72. London.

XI

1499 MANDEVILLE, SIR JOHN. Here begynneth a lytell treatyse or book named Johan Mandevyll, Knight, born in Englonde in the towne of Saynt Albone, and speketh of the wayes of the Holy Londe towarde Jherusalem and of marveyles of Ynde and of other dyverse countrees. Woodcuts. 8vo. Emprinted at Westmynster by Wynken de Worde. London.

Many subsequent editions with some variations in title, and many versions abroad. In English: 4to, 1503; 4to, 1568; 4to, 1618; 4to, 1657; 4to, 1670; 4to, 1677; 4to, 1684; 4to, 1692; 4to, 1722; 8vo, 1725; 8vo, 1727; and among more recent editions—in Wright, 1848; fol., 1889; 8vo, 1900; 8vo, 1923; 8vo, 1928. In French, Lyons, 1480; in Italian, Mediolani, 1480; in German, Augsburg, 1492; in Dutch, Amsterdam, 1650, etc. For a bibliography of editions and translations up to 1840, see Schornborn, De C., *Bibliographische Untersuchungen über J. Mandeville*, Breslau, 1840. There is an undated edition in the Grenville Library printed by Pynson in 4to, which Grenville and Dibdin believe to be earlier than that of Wynken de Worde's. Pynson was appointed King's printer on the accession of Henry VIII. See below.

This was a very popular book in its day and illustrated the general equipment of geographical ideas of the late fourteenth century. Long accepted as an authentic and valuable record of travel, we know now that it was a spurious relation compiled from various sources by one Jehan d'Outremeuse, a citizen of Liege, and laid on the doorstep of a fictitious knight, "Sire Jehan de Mandeville." The stories which filled his work were such as appealed to the credulity and love of the marvellous dear to the Middle Ages.—From Professor A. P. Newton, *Travel in the Middle Ages*, chap. VIII, "Travellers' Tales." Mandeville is said to have set out on his travels in 1322, and after visiting Egypt, Palestine, Tartary, India, the Indian isles, etc., returned home in 1355. His death is set at 1371.

1677 MANDEVILLE, SIR JOHN. The Voyages and Travels of Sir John Mandeville, Knight; wherein is set down the way to the Holy Land and to Jerusalem, as also to the lands of the Great Cham and of Prester John, to India, and divers other Countries. Together with many and strange marvels therein. 4to. London.

1725 MANDEVILLE, SIR JOHN. The Voiage and Travaile of Sir John Mandeville, Kt., which Treateth of the Way to Hierusalem; and of Marvayles of Inde, with other Ilands and Countreys. Now publish'd entire from an original MS. in the Cotton Library. 8vo. London.

This is the completest edition up to date.

1889 MANDEVILLE, SIR JOHN. The Buke of John Maundeuill, being the Travels of Sir John Mandeville, 1322-1357; a hitherto unpublished English version from the unique copy (Egerton MS. 1982) in the British Museum. Edited, together with the French text, Notes, and Introduction, by George F. Warner. Colored frontispiece and 28 plates. Fol. Roxburghe Club. London.

1923 MANDEVILLE, SIR JOHN. The Travels of Sir John Mandeville. The Version of the Cotton Manuscript in modern spelling. With three Narratives, in illustration of it, from Hakluyt's Navigations, Voyages and Discoveries. 8vo. London.

The three narratives are the Voyage of Johannes de Carpini, the Journal of Friar William de Rubruquis, and the Journal of Friar Odoric, from the 1598-1600 edition of Hakluyt.

1480 MANDEVILLE, SIR JOHN. Ce livre est appellé Mandeville, et fut fait et composé par Jehan de Mandeville, Chevalier, natif d'Angleteere, de la ville de St. Alain, et parle de terre de promission, c'est à scavoir, de Jerusalem, et de plusieurs autres isles de la mer; et les diverses et stranges choses qui sont en dite isles. Fol. Lyons.

1480 (In Italian.) Tractato delle piu maravigliose cosse e piu notabili, che si trovano in le parte del mondo vedute . . . del cavaler J. da Mandavilla. 4to. Mediolani.

(In Latin.) Itinerarius a terra Angliae in partes Jherosolimiyanas et in ulteriores transmarinas . . . translatus in hanc formam latinam. (No place or date, but according to Ibrahim-Hilmy, at Venice.)

1650 (In Dutch.) De wonderlijke Reize van Jan Mandevyl beschrijvende de Reize en Geschied, van den Lande van Egypten, Syrien, Arabien, enz. 4to. Amsterdam.

1577 Newes lately come from the great Kingdome of Chyna. (Translation by Thomas Nicholas of a letter in Spanish from Mexico to Spain.) London.

1579 BERNARDINO DE ESCALANTE. A Discourse of the Nauigation which the Portugales doe make to the Realms and Prouinces of the East partes of the Worlde, and of the Knowledge that growes by them of the great thinges which are in the Dominions of China. Written by Barnadine of Escalanta, of the Realme of Galicia Priest. Translated out of Spanish into English, by Iohn Frampton. 4to. London.

   The dedication of Frampton to the Right Worshipful Edward Dyer, Esq., is dated Oct. 1, 1579.—Parks. Reprinted in Osborne II, 25-91. Spanish original, Seville, 1577. See below.

1745 BARNADINE, FATHER. An Account of the Empire of China: Wherein is Describ'd The Country of China, with the Provinces and States subject to that Extensive Empire. Also an Account of the Climate, Product, Navigation, Cities, Temples, Buildings, Letters, Figures, Genius . . . and of the Complexion, Apparel and Conditions of the People. To which is prefix'd, A Discourse of the Navigation which the Portuguese do make to the Realms and Provinces of the East Parts of the World. Written by Barnadine of Escalanta, of the Realm of Galicia, Priest. Translated out of Spanish into English, by John Frampton. With several Appendixes. In Osborne II, 25-91.

1577 BERNARDINO DE ESCALANTE. Discorso de la Navigacion que los Portugueses hacen à nos reinos y provincias de del Reino de China. Seville.

POLO, MARCO. The most noble and famous Travels of Marcus Paulus. Translated by John Frampton from Rodrigo de Santaelle's Spanish version, Seville, 1503. 4to. London.

   Following is the list of English editions down to 1871, as outlined by Parks (Introduction to his edition of 1927), with the exception of the versions in Harris and Pinkerton: 1579, Frampton's from a Spanish translation of an Italian translation, corrupt and incorrect; 1625, *Purchas His Pilgrimes,* an abridged and incorrect paraphrase of Ramusio's account; 1744-48, Harris I, 592-629, "taken chiefly from Ramusio, compared with an anonymous manuscript in his Prussian Majesty's Library, and with most of the translations hitherto published"; 1808-14, Pinkerton VII, 101-178, apparently a reprint of Harris; 1818, Marsden's, a full translation of Ramusio done before the original texts were edited; 1844, Murray's, well translated with some collation of texts; 1871, Yule's, the classic translation, with the best commentary on the book in any language. Of this last work there was a second edition in 1875, and a third in 1903, revised in the light of recent discoveries, by Henry Cordier, who also issued in 1920 his *Ser Marco Polo,* with Notes and Addenda to Henry Yule's edition, containing the "Results of Recent Research and Discovery." Yule's third edition was reprinted in 1926, 2 vols. In 1926, the Broadway Travellers edition, an authorized English translation of the text of L. F. Benedetto; and in 1929, the Argonaut Press edition, a reissue of Frampton's version, together with the Travels of Nicolo de' Conti, done in the light of the most recent researches in Polian history. This list does not exhaust the nineteenth century editions.

The early bibliography of Marco Polo is full of nice questions which can well be left to experts. It is curious that so few editions appeared in English before the nineteenth century. The history of the work, as sketched by George B. Parks (see above), seems to be this: After the defeat of the Venetian fleet by the Genoese, Polo, who was taken prisoner in the battle, spent about a year in jail at Genoa. While thus lodged, he dictated his story to a fellow prisoner, one Rustician by name, who wrote it down in French as the one language common to them both. After his release Polo took the manuscript with him and later gave it to the French ambassador. What the latter did with it is not known, but copies of it were made with or without Polo's knowledge. It was translated into Italian and then into Latin much corrupted. The first printed edition appeared in German in 1477, followed by versions in Italian, Latin, French, Spanish, Portuguese, and finally English. Ramusio included it in an enlarged form in his Collection. "This is the last stage of the book."

Nicholas and Maffeo, of the Polo family, made their first journey to the Far East in 1250 and returned to Venice in 1269, when Nicholas found his wife dead and a son nineteen years old. They set out again in 1271/2, this time accompanied by young Marco, and were received with high honors, especially Marco, at the court of Kubla Khan. They returned to Venice in 1295, looking more like Tartars than Italians. No one knew them. The famous dinner they gave on their return is a well known story. Polo and Rubruquis give us the most complete and remarkable accounts of all early travels into Tartary and Mongolia. The latter made known Northern Tartary and the former the Southern. Furthermore Polo travelled by sea from China to India, being the first known traveller, ancient or medieval, to use such a route. Travelling by the Khan's orders and with his armies, he had advantages accorded no one else. The territory he reported on covered Turkey in Asia, Persia, Tartary, India, China, Japan, the Asiatic islands, Siberia, and parts of Africa.

1903 POLO, MARCO. The Book of Ser Marco Polo, the Venetian, concerning the Kingdoms and Marvels of the East. Translated and Edited, with Notes by Colonel Sir Henry Yule. With a Memoir of H. Yule by his Daughter. 3rd edit. revised in the light of recent discoveries, by Henri Cordier. Portraits and a large number of maps and illus. 2 vols. 8vo. London.

1926 POLO, MARCO. The Book of Ser Marco Polo. Translated into English from the text of L. F. Benedetto by Professor Aldo Ricci. With an Introduction by Sir Denison Ross. 8vo. Broadway Travellers. London.

> In 1924 Professor Benedetto of Florence, having discovered a MS. hitherto unknown, brought out a new version containing much new and exceedingly interesting material.

1929 POLO, MARCO. The Most Famous and Noble Travels of Marco Polo. Together with the Travels of Nicolo de' Conti. Edited from the Elizabethan Translation of John Frampton. With Introduction, Notes and Appendices by N. M. Penzer, M.A. With 11 new maps and a colored frontispiece from a MS. in the Bodleian, Oxford. 4to. Argonaut Press. London.

1588 MENDOZA, JUAN GONZALEZ DE. The Historie of the great and
mightie Kingdome of China, and the situation thereof, togither with
the great riches, huge Citties, politicke gouernement and rare inuentions
in the same. Translated out of Spanish by R. Parke. 4to. London.

> Edited for the Hakluyt Society, London, 1854. Spanish original, Rome, 1585.
> See below.
> This work is mainly a compilation from the narratives of Gaspar da Cruz,
> Martin de Rada (Herrada), and Pedro de Alforo, missionaries, to which is added
> the Itinerary of Father Martin Ignaxio.—Library of Congress. In his dedication
> to Thomas Candish (Cavendish), who had just returned from his first voyage to
> the Philippines and China, Parke states that he undertook the translation "at the
> earnest request of his worshipfull friend, Master Richard Hakluyt," and urges
> Cavendish to make further attempts to find a North-West Passage . . . Ortelius,
> in his Atlas, says that he received more information from Ignacio's Itinerary than
> from any other single book.—Robinson, No. 26. The *History* is the earliest de-
> tailed account of China published in English. Eden's account in his *History of
> Travayle in the West and East Indies* is interesting but shorter.

> 1854 MENDOZA, FATHER JUAN GONZALEZ DE. The History of the
> Great and Mighty Kingdom of China and the Situation thereof. Com-
> piled by Padre Juan Gonzalez de Mendoza, and now reprinted from
> the Early Translation of R. Parke. Edited by Sir George Thomas
> Staunton, Bart., M.P., F.R.S. With an Introduction by Richard
> Henry Major, F.S.A., Keeper of Maps, Brit. Mus., Sec. R.G.S. 2 vols.
> Hak. Soc., ser. I, vols. 14-15. London.

> 1585 MENDOZA, JUAN GONZALEZ DE. Historia de las cosas mas notables
> y costumbres del gran reyno de la China . . . Con vn itinerario del Nuevo-
> Mundo. Rome.

1609 LINTON, ANTHONY. Newes of the Complement of the Art of Navigation and of the mightie Empire of Cataia, together with the Straits
of Anian. 4to. London.

1612 Relation of an Englishman shipwrecked on the Coast of Camboya. 4to.
London.

> So cited by Pinkerton XVII.

1619 A Briefe Relation of the Persecvtion lately made against the Catholike
Christians in the Kingdome of Iaponia, deuided into Two Bookes.
Taken out of the Annuall Letters of the Fathers of the Society of Iesvs,
and other Authenticall Informations. Written in Spanish, and printed
first at Mexico in the West Indies, the yeare of Christ 1616, and newly
translated into English by W(illiam) W(right) Gent. The First Part
(all published). 12mo. London.

> This book was secretly printed and is extremely rare. It was probably printed
> abroad for import into England. A second part was promised containing the events
> which succeeded the departure of the Jesuits from Japan, but there is little doubt
> that this never appeared. The translator in a note to the reader says that he had
> not yet seen the second part himself.—Quoted from Bookseller's Note.

1633 BORRI, CHRISTOFORO. Cochin-China; Containing many admirable Rarities and Singularities of that Countrey. Extracted out of an Italian Relation lately presented to the Pope, by Christoforo Borri, that liued certaine yeeres there. 8vo. London.

> Reprinted in Churchill II, 721-765; in Pinkerton IX, 771-828. Italian original, Rome, 1631. See below.
> Father Borri or Burrus was one of the earliest missionaries to Cochin China, and after his return to Europe taught mathematics at Coimbra and Lisbon, and made various improvements in the compass. His work is most important for the early history of Cochin China, as he gives much information concerning that country apart from the usual account of the progress of the missions. His account is in two parts, first, on the temporal state of the country—its boundaries, climate, soil, manners and customs of its inhabitants, elephants, etc., government, commerce, and wars. Secondly, its spiritual state.—Maggs, No. 519.

> 1631 BORRI, CHRISTOFORO. Relatione della Nuova Missione delli PP. della Compagnia di Giesu, al Regno della Cocincina. 12mo. Rome.

1635 BAUDIER, MICHEL. The History of the Court of the King of China. Written in French by the Seigneur Michael Baudier of Languedoc. Translated by E(dward) G(rimstone). 4to. London.

> See this date under NEAR EAST. Reprinted in Osborne II, 1-24.
> The author finds here a government where virtue is rewarded, bribery unknown, flattery punished, and royal favor constant. Swift should have sent Gulliver on a voyage to China.

1655 SAMEDO, ALVAREZ. The History of that Great and Renowned Monarchy of China, wherein the particular Provinces are accurately described, as also the Dispositions, Manners, Learning, Laws, Militia, Government, and Religion of that Country, by Father Alvarez Samedo, a Portuguese, of late Resident twenty-two years at the Court and other famous Citties of the Kingdom. Now put into English by a Person of Quality. To which is added, The History of the late Invasion by the Tartars. Portrait of the author, 2 maps and 2 plates. Fol. London.

> Another edition, London, 1670. Whether the original of this translation is the Spanish edition, Madrid, 1642, or the Italian edition, Rome, 1643, is not known to the editor. See below.
> This work gives a long account of China, its various provinces, inhabitants and their manners and customs, Government and Military Art, the propagation of the Gospel, and more particularly an account of the labours of the Jesuits there, written by the Procurador General of China and Japan.—Maggs, No. 519.

> 1642 SEMEDO, FR. ALVARO (Jesuit). Imperio de la China, i cultura evangelica en èl, por los Religios de la Compañia de Jesus. 4to. Madrid.

> 1643 SEMEDO, ALVARO. Relatione della Grande Monarchia della Cina. Engraved portrait of Semedo. 8vo. Rome.

1662 MANDELSLO, JOHANN ALBRECHT VON. For his description of Japan and China, see his *Voyage and Travels into the East Indies,* under EAST INDIES.

1663 CARON, FRANCIS, and SCHOUTEN, JOOST. Description of the Kingdoms of Japan and Siam, translated from the Dutch by Sir Roger Manley. 12mo. London.

> Another edition, with map, London, 1671. Given in substance in Pinkerton VII, 607-641, to which is added an Extract from Hagenaar's Voyage to and in the East Indies; modern edition, London, 1925. See below. The Dutch original is as early as 1636 at least, for in that year appeared the edition listed below.

> 1925 CARON, FRANCOIS, and SCHOUTEN, JOOST. A True Description of the Mighty Kingdoms of Japan and Siam, written originally in Dutch by Francois Caron and Joost Schouten, and now rendered into English by Capt. Roger Manley, London, 1663. Edited with an Introduction, Notes, Bibliography and Index by C. R. Boxer. 11 plates and 7 maps. 4to. London.

> 1636 CARON, FRANCIS. Beschryving van het Konikryke van Japon, bestaende in verscheydene vragen beantwort in den jare 1636, . . . 4to. The Hague.

PINTO, FERDINAND MENDEZ. The Voyages and Adventures of Ferdinand Mendez Pinto, a Portugal, during his Travels, for the Space of one and twenty years, in the Kingdoms of Ethiopia, China, Tartaria, Cauchinchina, Calaminham, Siam, Pegu, Japan and a great Part of the East-Indies, with a Relation and Description of the most of the places thereof, their Religion, Laws, Riches, Customs, and Government in the time of Peace and War, where he five times suffered shipwreck, was sixteen times sold, and thirteen times made a slave. Done into English by H(enry) C(ogan). Fol. London.

> 2nd edit., corrected and amended, London, 1663; 3rd edit., London, 1692. Modern edition in the Adventure Series, London, 1891. Portuguese original, Lisbon, 1614. See below.
> This work contains an "apologetical defence" of Pinto, consisting of references to every Portuguese work, and many Latin ones, confirmatory of those circumstances mentioned by him. And well was this needed, for poor Pinto has been stigmatised by Cervantes as the "Prince of Liars," and by another (but constantly misquoted as Shakespeare) as a "Liar of the first Magnitude." Modern travel, however, has done much to recover for Pinto and other early travellers their long-forfeited reputation.—Lowndes. (It may be mentioned here that the epithet "Liar of the first Magnitude" is used in Congreve's *Love for Love.*) The original was regarded as one of the finest books of travels that had ever been written, and prompted translators to render it in various foreign languages. It is, moreover, a classic record of the experiences and observations of one of the earliest Europeans to penetrate into the interior of oriental countries, which, in that era, were practically unknown. He was indeed the first European to enter Japan (in 1542), seven years before Saint Francis Xavier, the Apostle of the Indies.—Maggs, No. 519. Pinto's account of the Portuguese cruelties in the East Indies and their inhuman lust for blood is too horrible to believe.—Oaten, *Early Travellers and Travels in India.* His travels covered the years 1537-1558.

> 1891 PINTO, F. MENDEZ. Voyages and Adventures of F. Mendez Pinto, Done into English by Henry Cogan, with an Introduction by M. Vambéry. Adventure Series. London.

> 1614 PINTO, FERNAO MENDEZ. Peregrinacam, em que da conta de muytas y muyto estranhas chosas, que vio e ovvio no reyno da China, no da Tartaria, no da Sornam, que vulgarmente se chama Siam, no da Cal-

aminham, no da Pegu, no da Martavan, e em outros muytos reynos e senhorios das partes orientales. Lisbon.

The first account of his travels is to be found in a collection of Jesuit letters published in Venice in 1565, but the best is his own Peregrinacao.—Catholic Encyclopedia, quoted by Maggs, No. 519.

1669-1671 NIEUHOFF, JOHN. The Embassy (of Peter de Goyer and Jacob de Keyzer) from the (Dutch) East-India Company (1655) to the Grand Tartar Cham Emperour of China. Englished from the Dutch of John Nieuhoff. Also Atlas Chinensis: Second Part of a Relation of Remarkable Passages in Two Embassies from the Dutch East-India Company. Translated from A. Montanus. Portrait, 2 maps, and 58 large engravings . . . and hundreds of copperplates in the text. 2 vols. Fol. London.

The full title of the Atlas Chinensis of Montanus follows under 1671 below. Both works were translated by John Ogilby. In 1671-73 appeared a second edition of Nieuhoff's work, 1 vol., together with that of the 1671 edition of Montanus's in 2 vols., in all 3 vols., fol., London. An abstract of the first embassy in Astley III, 399-431; of the second in Astley III, 431-483; in Pinkerton VII, 231-270. Dutch original, Amsterdam, 1665. See below. Astley says that Ogilby's translation agrees in title more with the Leyden edition than with the Amsterdam. He states further that the general description seems to have been taken from Martini's *Atlas Chinensis*, and the account of the manners and customs of the Chinese from a variety of authors.
The Dutch being at the height of their power, having supplanted the Portuguese, desired to gain access to China and a portion of the Chinese trade. After much opposition the Government succeeded in sending certain merchants to try the pulse of the Chinese at Canton. Upon their report it was determined to despatch ambassadors from Batavia to the Court of Peking to solicit liberty to trade. This is the embassy written up by Nieuhoff, who was steward to the ambassadors. Its failure led the Dutch to send other embassies. These are the ones written by Montanus.

1665 NIEWHOF, JAN. Gesandshap der Neederlandische Oost-Indische Compagnie aen den grooten Tartarischen Cham, den Keyzer von China. Fol. Amsterdam.

1670 MONTANUS, ARNOLDUS. Atlas Japanensis: being Remarkable Addresses by way of Embassy from the East India Company of the United Provinces to the Emperor of Japan. Containing a Description of their Territories, Cities, Temples, and Fortresses; their Religion, Laws, and Customs; their Prodigious Wealth, and Gorgeous Habits; the Nature of their Soil, Plants, Beasts, Hills, Rivers, and Fountains. With the Character of the Ancient and Modern Japanners. Collected out of their several Writings and Journals by A. Montanus. Englished by J. Ogilby. Map, plates, folding and full page. Fol. London.

Combined with the Atlas Chinensis, 2 vols., fol., London, 1670-73. An abstract of part of this work in Astley III, 483-491. Dutch original, Amsterdam, 1669. See below.
Exceedingly rare. The plates to this work represent a high-water mark in book illustrations of the 17th century. Apart from these, this book remains one of the most curious of the numerous works of travel in the Orient during the 17th century. Among the subjects discussed are the following: Murder in Japan,

Japanese wrestlers, Japanese baths, jugglers and necromancers, burning of widows, women-raping by baboons, blood-baths, Japanese tortures, boiling waters of Sin-gok, gardens, Japanese wines, whaling in Japan, etc.—From Booksellers' Note.

> 1669 MONTANUS, ARNOLDUS. Gedenkwaerdige Gesantschappen der Oost-indische Maetschappy in't Vereenigde Nederland, aen de Kaisaren van Japan: Vervaetende Wonderlijke voorvallen op te Togt der Neder-landsche Gesanten: Beschryving van de Dorpen, Sterkten, Steden, Landschappen, Tempels, Godsdiensten, Dragten, Gebouwen, Dieren, Gewasschen, Bergen, Fonteinen, vereeuwde en nieuwe Oorlogs-daden der Japanders. Map, 24 folding plates, and many illustrations in the text. Fol. Amsterdam.

1671 MONTANUS, ARNOLDUS. Atlas Chinensis, being a Second Part of a Relation of remarkable Passages in two Embassies from the East-India Company of the United Provinces to the Vice Roy Sing La Mong, and General Taysing Lipovi; and to Ka-Konchi, Emperor of China and East Tartary. With a Relation of the Netherlanders assist-ing the Tartars against Koxinga and the Chinese Fleet, who till then were Masters of the Seas. And a more exact geographical Descrip-tion than formerly both of the whole Empire in general, and in par-ticular of every one of the fifteen Provinces. Collected out of their several Writings and Journals by Arnoldus Montanus. Englished and adorned with several Sculptures by John Ogilby. Fol. London.

PALAFOX Y MENDOZA, JUAN DE. The History of the Conquest of China by the Tartars; together with several remarkable things concern-ing the Religion, Manners and Customs of both Nations, but especially the latter. First written in Spanish by Seignior Palafox (y Mendoza), Bishop of Osma and Viceroy of Mexico, and now rendered into Eng-lish. 8vo. London.

> A Spanish edition, Paris, 1670. See below.

> 1670 PALAFOX Y MENDOZA, JUAN DE. Historia de la conquista de la China por el tártaro. Paris.

1673 VARENIUS, BERNARD. Descriptio Regni Japoniae et Siam. Item, De Japoniorum Religione et Siamensium. De diversis omnium Gen-tium Religionibus. Quibus, Praemissa Dissertatione de variis Rerum publicarum generibus, adduntur quaedam de Priscarum Afrorum fide excerpta ex Leone Africano. 8vo. Cantab. (*i. e.,* Cambridge).

> Latin original, with same title, Amsterdam, 1629.
> This work is divided into three parts. The first contains a general description of Japan, and reviews its products, climate, minerals, commerce, war, finance, man-ners and customs. The second is a translation from the Dutch of Schouten and contains a general account of Siam. The third is an account of the Religions of the Japanese, their Gods and Priests, and the introduction of Christianity.—Robin-son, No. 20.

1675 China and France, or Two Treatises, The One of the present State of
      China, as to the Government, Customs and Manners of the Inhabi-
      tants thereof; never yet known to us before in Europe. Written and
      published by the French King's Cosmographer; and now Englished.
      The other containing the most remarkable Passages of the Reign and
      Life of the present French King, Lewis the XIV; and of the Valour
      of our English in his Armies. 8vo. London.

1680 TAVERNIER, JEAN BAPTISTE. A Collection of several Relations
      and Treatises Singular and Curious, not printed among his first Six
      Voyages. I. A new and singular Relation of the Kingdom of Tun-
      quin. II. How the Hollanders manage their Affairs in Asia. III. A
      Relation of Japan, and the Cause of the Persecution of the Christians
      in those Islands. IV. A Relation of what passed in the Negotiation
      of the Deputies which were at Persia and the Indies, as well on the
      French King's as the Company's Behalf, for the Establishment of
      Trade. V. Observations upon the East India Trade, and the Frauds
      there subject to be committed. Published by Edmund Everard. Plates
      and folding map of Japan, with inset map of Tonquin. Fol. London.

      French original, Paris, 1679. For title and observations see Tavernier under
      1678, EAST INDIES.

1682 GLANIUS, ——. For an account of Siam and the Isles of Japan see
      his *A New Voyage to the East-Indies,* under EAST INDIES.

      The History of the Court of China. Done out of French (by A. G.). Lon-
      don.

1686 CHAUMONT, MONSIEUR DE (Knight). A Relation of the late Em-
      bassy of Monsieur de Chaumont, Knight, to the Court of the King
      of Siam. With an Account of the Government, State, Manners, Re-
      ligion, and Commerce, of the Kingdom. 12mo. London.

      A French version, Paris, 1687, cited by Pinkerton XVII. See below.

      1687 (In French.) Relation de l'Ambassade du Chevalier de Chaumont à la
            Cour à Siam. 12mo. Paris.
            This presumably is the original edition.

      DE SOTO, HERNANDO. Two Journies of the present Emperour of
      China into Tartary in the years 1682 and 1683. (In his *Relation of
      the Invasion of Florida,* to which it is subjoined. See the same under
      NORTH AMERICA.)

1688 MAGAILLANS, GABRIEL. A New History of China, containing a
Description of the most considerable particulars of that Vast Empire:
Language, Government, Manufactures, . . . done out of French (by
W. Ogilby). Folding plan of Pekin. 8vo. London.

>   Lowndes attributes the translation to John Ogilby, but that King's Cosmog-
> rapher is ruled out by the fact that he died in 1676. A "French translation," Paris,
> 1688 (Pinkerton XVII), 1690 (Maggs, No. 521). See below.
>   The above work, written by Magaillans, was never printed in Portuguese;
> nevertheless, there exists this French translation of it. The work was the fruit
> of his residence in China for 29 years. Gabriel de Magalhaes, a Jesuit, was born
> in Pedrogao in 1609. He left Portugal for the East in 1634, penetrated into the
> Chinese Empire, and died in Pekin May 6, 1677. There is a curious description of
> his funeral, towards which the Emperor contributed, with a donation of 800 frs.
> and ten bales of damask.—Maggs, No. 521.

>   1688 MAGELLANS, GABRIEL DE. Relation nouvelle de la Chine, contenant
>   la description des parties les plus remarquables de cet empire; composé
>   en l'année 1668 par le R. P. Gabriel de Magellans, de la Compagnie de
>   Jésus, et traduite du Portugais par le Sr. B. 4to. Paris.

TACHARD, GUY (Father). A Relation of the Voyage to Siam, Performed by six Jesuits, sent by the French King to the Indies and China,
in the Year 1685. With their Astrological Observations, and their Remarks of Natural Philosophy, Geography, Hydrography, and History.
Published in the Original by the express Order of His most Christian
Majesty; and now made English and illustrated with Sculptures. 8vo.
London.

>   The French original of this voyage, together with that of the second, was pub-
> lished in 2 vols., Paris, 1686 and 1689. See below.
>   A large part of the above work relates to the kindly reception given the
> Jesuit Fathers by the Dutch at the Cape of Good Hope. Java, Sumatra, and Ban-
> tam were also visited and described.—Maggs, No. 521. Pinkerton, who in com-
> mon with most of the editors of English collections, had a keen eye for Jesuit
> failings, describes the account as a pretty accurate work as to geography, but dis-
> figured with the author's credulity.

>   1686-89 TACHARD, GUY (Father). Premier Voyage de Siam des PP. Jésu-
>   ites, envoyées par le Roi aux Indes et à la Chine avec leurs observa-
>   tions astronomiques, et leurs remarques de physique, de géographie, d'-
>   hydrographie, et d'histoire (redigé par le P. Tachard). Second voyage
>   du P. Tachard et des Jésuites, envoyées par le Roi au Royaume de
>   Siam; contenant diverses remarques d'histoire, de physique, de géog-
>   raphie, et d'astronomie. Avec figures. 2 vols. 12mo. Paris.

1689 A New History of the Empire of China; containing a description of the
Politick, Government, Towns, Manners and Customs of the People,
. . . newly done out of French. 8vo. London.

1690   A Relation of the Revolution of Siam. Being the Substance of several
       Letters writ in October 1688, and February 1689, from Siam and the
       Coast of Coromandel. Never before published in any Language and
       now translated into English. 4to. London.

> Reprinted in Osborne II, 95-102. See below. There was a French account of
> this Revolution published in 2 vols., 16mo, Lyons, 1692, by Father Marcel Le Blanc.

> 1745   A Full and True Relation of the Great and Wonderful Revolution that
> happened lately in the Kingdom of Siam in the East-Indies. Giving a
> particular Account of the Seizing and Death of the late King, and of
> the Setting up of a new One. As also of the putting to Death of the
> King's only Daughter; his adopted Son who was a Christian; his two
> Brothers; and of Monsieur Constance, his great Minister of State, and
> Favourer of the French. And of the Expulsion of the Jesuits, Mission-
> ary Priests, Officers and Soldiers of the French Nation out of that
> Kingdom, that endeavoured to bring it under the French Domination.
> Being the Substance of several Letters writ in October 1688, and of
> February 1689, from Siam, and the Coast of Coromandel. Never be-
> fore published in any Language, and now translated into English. In
> Osborne II, 95-102.

> > This Constance was originally a Greek Christian, who after spend-
> > ing some time in England went out to the East Indies, where he was
> > employed by the English as their factor in Siam. His business abilities
> > and talents brought him into favor with the court. He used his influence
> > to bring the country under the domination of the French and the king
> > to the Catholic faith with the aid of the Jesuits. The revolution related
> > above frustrated these designs.

1693   LOUBERE, SIMON DE LA.   A New Historical Relation of the King-
       dom of Siam, by M. de la Loubère, envoy extraordinaire from the
       French King to King of Siam in the years 1687, 1688, . . . wherein
       a full and curious account is given of the Chinese Way of Arithmetick
       and Mathematick Learning. Done out of the French, by A. P., F.R.S.
       Numerous maps and plates. 2 vols. in 1. Fol. London.

> French original, Amsterdam, 1691. See below.
> In addition to the interesting account of Siam and the Siamese, this work con-
> tains many curious matters of information: The Life of Thevetat, Siamese Alpha-
> bet, Smoaking Instrument, Chess-Play of the Chinese, Relation of the Cape
> of Good Hope, with four cuts, Siamese Astronomy, Problem of Magical
> Squares according to the Indians, Manners of the Chinese.—From Maggs, No.
> 521. This embassy was one of the several sent from Louis XIV to Siam, all of
> which were accompanied by priests of the Jesuit orders. Tachard made his sec-
> ond voyage (see 1688 above) with La Loubère. French interest in Siam seems
> to have declined after this embassy. La Loubère must have been busy with his eyes
> to note so much in a three months' stay.

> 1691   LOUBERE, SIMON DE LA. Description du Royaume de Siam, par M.
> de la Loubère, Envoyé extraordinaire du Roi auprès du Roi de Siam,
> où l'on voit quelles sont les opinions, les moeurs, et la religion des
> Siamois; avec plusieurs remarques de physique touchant les plantes et
> les animaux du pays. Amsterdam. 2 vols.

1697   LE COMTE, LOUIS.   Memoirs and Observations Topographical, Phys-
       ical, Mathematical, Mechanical, Natural, Civil, Ecclesiastical, Made
       in a late Journey through the Empire of China; and published in sev-

eral Letters. Particularly upon the Chinese Pottery and Varnishing, the Silk and other Manufactures, the Pearl Fishing, the History of Plants and Animals. Description of their Cities and publick Works; number of People, their Language, Manners, and Commerce; their Habits, Oeconomy, and Government; the Phylosophy of Confusius; the state of Christianity; with many other curious Remarks . . . Translated from the Paris edition; and illustrated with Figures. 8vo. London.

> 2nd edit., London, 1699; 3rd, corrected, London, 1699; again, London, 1737, and this one reprinted, London, 1738; abstract in Astley III, 514-545. French original, Paris, 1696. See below.
> The author was a Jesuit, confessor to the Duchess of Burgundy, one of the Royal Mathematicians, and later missionary to the Far East. This work, according to the *Biographie Générale,* is "reprehensible pour les paradoxes qu'il renferme; c'est un panégyrique outre de la civilisation chinoise."—Quoted by Sotheran.

1696 LE COMTE, LOUIS. Nouveaux Mémoires sur l'Etat de la Chine. Avec figures. 2 vols. 12mo. Paris.

> This work was burnt by order of the Parliament of Paris.

1698 BRAND, ADAM. Journal of the Embassy from their Majesties John and Peter Alexievitz, Emperors of Muscovy, . . . over Land into China, through the Provinces of Ustiugha, Siberia, Dauri, and the Great Tartary, to Peking . . . By Everard Isbrand (Ides), their Ambassador in the Years 1693, 1694, and 1695. Written by Adam Brand, Secretary of the Embassy. Translated from the Original in High-Dutch, Printed at Hamburgh, 1698. To which is added, Curious Observations concerning the Products of Russia. By H. W. Ludolf. Portrait and 2 plates. 12mo. London.

> German original, Frankfort, 1697. See below.
> The relation of Brand's anticipated that of Ides' (see 1706 below.) On the appearance of the latter's account, this one showed itself to be full of inconsistencies and improbabilities.

> 1697 BRAND, ADAM. Beschreibung seiner grossen Chinesischen Reise, welche er anno 1693, 1694, 1695, in der suite des Herrn Everharrd Isbrand Ides, von Moscou über Siberien, Daurien, und durch die Grosse-Tartarey, bis in China gethan. Frankfort.

1706 IDES, EVERARD YSBRANTS. Three Years' Travels from Moscow overland to China; through Great Ustiga, Siriana, Permia, Daour, Great Tartary, . . . to Peking . . . to which is annexed an Accurate Description of China by a Chinese Author (Dionysius Kao) . . . and now faithfully done into English from the Dutch of Witzen. Map and numerous plates. 4to. London.

> Abridged extracts from the description of his reception at the court of Peking in Astley III, 566-575; reprinted more fully in Harris II. 918-961, in three sections. See also Le Brun. *Voyage to the Levant and Travels into Moscovey, Persia and the East-Indies,* under 1720, CENTRAL ASIA.

This was no easy journey in those days. Ides, who was a Dane in the service of Peter the Great, set out from Moscow March 14, 1692. Travelling as a public character, he had leisure to observe anything of note. The entire trip took two years and ten months. He composed his journal for the information and satisfaction of Peter the Great who was well pleased with the results and rewarded the author with the post of Privy Councillor. The Russian embassy had less trouble with the enormous self-esteem of the Chinese than many earlier and later embassies. Before the Tartars became masters of China, it was almost impossible for foreigners to find admittance to the Imperial Court. Under the emperor then ruling, Kang-hi, ministers were courteously received and enabled to transact their business as at any other court. This accommodation was contrary to the temper and traditions of the old Chinese, who opposed it as much as they dared. Kang-hi was desirous of preventing Russian encroachments upon his territories and the Czar was anxious to establish a regular commerce with China. The expedition added considerable geographical knowledge to the little that was known about northern Manchuria and China.

1744-48 IDES, EVERARD YSBRANTS. The Travels of his Excellency E. Ysbrants Ides, Ambassador from Peter the Great to the Emperor of China; through Great Ustiga, Siriana, Permia, Siberia, Daour, . . . to the Frontiers of China, containing an exact Description of the Extent and Limits of those Countries, the Nations by which they are inhabited; with a curious and copious Account of their Religion, Government, Marriages, Dwellings, Diet, daily Occupations, . . . Faithfully translated from the Author's Original Journal, printed under the Direction of the Burgomaster Witzen, the greatest Critick of his Time in Holland, and dedicated to the late Czar Peter the Great. In Harris II, 918-944.

The Author's Reception at the Court of the Imperial Palace, the Ceremonies of a Publick Audience; the Person and Manners of the Emperor described. An Account of the Curiosities of the City of Peking; the grand Establishment of the Jesuits there; . . . his Return from China by Land; the Accidents attending his Journey; the many and great Hardships, he sustained therein notwithstanding his Interests in both Empires, and his safe Arrival, after so many Hazards, and enduring so great Fatigues, at Moscow. In Harris II, 944-951.

A very copious and no less curious Account of the North-East Part of Asia; comprehending a distinct, particular, and authentick Description of all that hitherto passed under the general Name of Siberia, Shewing the Extent, and Situation of the several Districts thereof, their Climate, Soil and Produce, the Rise and Course of the principal Rivers, Description of all the great Cities upon their Banks, of the several Barbarous Nations that inhabit near these Rivers . . . To which is added, a succinct Recapitulation of the State of the Chinese Empire towards the Close of the last Century. In Harris II, 951-961.

1715 TEIXEIRA, PEDRO. For an account of China see his *The History of Persia* under 1715, CENTRAL ASIA.

1722 LA CROIX, P. DE. History of Genghizcan the Great, First Emperor of the Antient Moguls and Tartars; with the Manners, Customs and Laws of the Moguls. 8vo. London.

1722-23 LANGE, LAURENCE. Travels through Russia to China and Siberia. London.

> Abstract in Astley III, 575-581. Another translation, based probably on a corrected original, London, 1763. A French version, Leyden, 1726. See below.
>
> In August, 1717, Czar Peter I of Russia sent Lange, accompanied by one Garwin, an English physician, as envoy to Kang-hi, Emperor of China. His journal, which he wrote on the road, he communicated, on his return, to F. C. Weber, the author of *The Present State of Russia* (see under 1723, EAST EUROPE), who published it at the beginning of the second volume of his own work printed in German. This, the English translator informs us, Lange was not pleased with, because the journal was an imperfect piece which he intended to improve and publish himself. So after his second return from China, where he had been in 1723, he sent to the press a more complete relation. This second piece is presumably the one translated and published by John Bell, 1763, Glasgow. See below.
>
> > 1745-47 LANGE, LAURENCE. The Travels of Laurence Lange, the Russian Envoy in China, in 1717. Translated from the High Dutch. In Astley III, 575-581.
>
> > 1763 LANGE, M. DE. Journal of M. de Lange, Resident of Russia at Pekin, 1721-22. Translated by John Bell. Glasgow.

1727 KAEMPFER, ENGELBERT. The History of Japan, giving an Account of the ancient and present State and Government of that Empire, of its Temples, Palaces, Castles and other Buildings, of its Metals, Minerals, Trees, Animals, Birds and Fishes, of the Chronology and Succession of the Emperors, of the original Descent, Religions, Customs and Manufactures, . . . and of their Trade and Commerce with the Dutch and Chinese, together with a Description of Siam, translated by J. G. Scheuchzer, with a Life of the Author. Numerous copperplates and maps. 2 vols. in 1. Fol. London.

> In some copies will be found at the end of the second volume a second Appendix containing an account of a Voyage to Japan, by an English Vessel in 1673, consisting, with Scheuchzer's preface, of seven leaves. This was issued in 1728 and added to the work by Woodward, with mention made of it in the new titles printed by him in 1728. Scheuchzer's translation was apparently made from the manuscript. According to Lowndes, the Lemgo edition of 1777-79 in 2 vols. contains several things not to be found in the English translation. Extracts reprinted in Pinkerton VII, 652-821. A modern reprint, Glasgow, 1906. A French translation published at the Hague, 1729. See below.
>
> Kaempfer was a well known German physician and naturalist with a passion for travelling. Before his arrival in Japan, he had accompanied the Swedish embassy under Louis Fabricius to Persia (see under 1736, CENTRAL ASIA), then engaging as surgeon with the Dutch fleet, visited India and Batavia, and at length reached Japan, where he stayed three years collecting material for his work. Here he secured the good will of the authorities so completely that he was allowed to travel where and as he pleased. He returned to Europe in 1693 and published an account of his travels under the title of *Amoenitates Exoticae.* His *History of Japan* has long been recognized as the most authoritative account of that country published at that time.
>
> > 1906 KAEMPFER, ENGELBERT. The History of Japan, together with a Description of the Kingdom of Siam, 1690-92. Translated by J. G. Scheuchzer. Portrait of Sir Hans Sloane and reproductions of the original plates of the 1727 edition. 3 vols. 8vo. Glasgow (MacLehose).

1729 (In French.) Histoire naturelle, civile et ecclésiastique de l'Empire du Japon, composée en allemand. Et traduite en francois sur la version angloise de Jean-Gaspard Scheuchzer. 2 vols. Fol. The Hague.

SALMON, THOMAS. For accounts of China and Japan see his *Modern History of all Nations,* under GENERAL TRAVELS AND DE-SCRIPTIONS.

1732 BACKHOFF, FEODOR ISKOWSKY. An Account of Two Voyages. The first of Feodor Iskowsky Backhoff, the Muscovite Envoy into China. The second of Mr. Zachary Wagener, a Native of Dresden, in Misnia, through a great Part of the World. As also into China. Translated from the High Dutch. In Churchill II, 489-500.

> An abstract of the latter item was communicated to the editors by the author's brother-in-law. The original was printed at Berlin. Wagener left Dresden in 1633.

BARON, SAMUEL. A Description of Tonqueen by S. Baron, a Native thereof. In Churchill VI, 1-40.

> Reprinted in Pinkerton IX, 636-707.
> Dated at Fort George at Madras-Patain, on the coast of Coromandel, Aug. 25, 1685. The design of the author was at first to correct the mistakes of Tavernier (see under 1678, EAST INDIA), but the work passed beyond that intention to a full description of the region. Illustrated by a native "Tonqueener of eminent ability."

BREWER, HENRY. For a description of Formosa and China see his *Voyage to the Kingdom of Chili in America,* under SOUTH AMERICA.

CANDIDIUS, GEORGE. A Short Account of the Island of Formosa in the Indies, situated near the Coast of China; and of the Manners, Customs, and Religions of its Inhabitants. In Churchill I, 472-479.

> The writer was a minister of the Gospel in Formosa.

CANDIDIUS, GEORGE. Some Curious Remarks upon the Potent Empire of Japan. In Churchill I, 480-485.

CARERI, JOHN FRANCIS GEMELLI (Dr.). Travels in China in 1695, being the Fourth Part of his Voyage round the World (see under CIRCUMNAVIGATIONS). In Churchill IV.

> Abstract of this portion in Astley III, 546-566.
> The author was a Neapolitan Doctor of Civil Law, who set out on a voyage of Europe in 1683, of which he published the first volume. As a result of the unjust persecutions and undeserved outrages put upon him, he started out on

his travels round the world. He observed that the whole course of his life was interwoven with such strange accidents that the very remembrance of them terrified him. His book (Venice, 1719) went through several editions in Italian and was translated into other languages.

HAMEL, HENRY.   An Account of the Shipwreck of a Dutch Vessel on the Coast of the Isle of Quelpaert. Together with the Description of the Kingdom of Corea. Translated out of French. In Churchill IV, 573-595.

> Reprinted in Astley IV, 329-347; in Pinkerton VII, 517-540. A French version, 12mo, Paris, 1670. Dutch original, Rotterdam, 1668. See below.
> The author of this account, who calls himself the secretary of the ship, was one of the survivors of the wreck. After a captivity of thirteen years in Corea, he managed to get back to Holland (July, 1668). Though probably more educated than the ordinary seaman, as a writer he has no sense of style, and a long residence in Corea should have furnished him with more matter.—Churchill.

> 1668   HAMEL, HENRY.   Journal van de ongelukige Voyagie von t' Jacht de Sperwer, gedestineert na Fayovan in t'jaar 1653; hoc t'selve Jacht, op t'Quilpaarts Eyland is gestrant: als mede een pertinente beschryvinge der Landen, Provintien, Steten, ende Forten leggende in t'Coningryk Corée. 4to. Rotterdam.

NAVARETTE, DOMINGO FERNANDEZ.   An Account of the Empire of China, Historical, Political, Moral and Religious. A short Description of that Empire, and Notable Examples of its Emperors and Ministers. Also an ample Relation of many Remarkable Passages, and Things worth observing in other Kingdoms, and Several Voyages, . . . In Churchill I, 1-380.

> Abstract from the 6th Book in Astley III, 498-512. Spanish original, Madrid, 1676. See below.
> The author was a Spanish Dominican friar, who was sent out by his Order to the Philippine Islands in 1646 and became divinity professor in the College of St. Thomas, Manila and procurator-general at the Court of Madrid for the province of the Rosary in the Philippines. He was in Manila probably from 1648 to 1656. Finding no great encouragement to remain in the Philippines, he ventured over to China, where he spent several years in the Mission. Having learned the language, he read the histories of that country, and studied the manners and customs of the natives. In all he was twenty-six years travelling in Asia and America. On his arrival in Europe in 1673 he went to Rome, where he was treated with due regard and after returning to Spain, he was promoted to the archbishopric of Hispaniola. Pressure was brought to bear on the Inquisition at Rome to suppress part of the book as it apparently reflected on the conduct of the Spanish missions in China.

> 1676   NAVARETTE, DOMINGO FERNANDEZ.   Tratados Historicos, Politicos, Ethicos y Religiosos de la Monarchia de China . . . y cosas singvlares de otras Reynos y Diferentes Navegaciones que hizo el Autor a la Nueua España, a Mexico, las Philipines, Macasar, Golocondar, . . . Fol. Madrid.

1733 RENAUDOT, EUSEBIUS. Ancient Accounts of India and China, by
two Mohammedan Travellers, Who went to those Parts in the 9th
century. Translated from the Arabic by the late learned Eusebius Renaudot. 8vo. London.

> Reprinted in Harris I, 521-530; in Pinkerton VII, 179-230. French original,
> Paris, 1718. See below.
> This is a translation of a portion of Masudi's *Moruj uz Zahab*.—Doubts have
> been expressed of the authenticity of these travels; but M. de Guignes has dis-
> covered the original Arabic MS. in the Imperial Library. They contain many
> absurdities, but much of what relates to China was confirmed by Marco Polo, and
> by more modern travellers.—Pinkerton XVII. Besides the extensive remarks
> elucidating the "Ancient Accounts" the following essays are included: An Inquiry
> into the Origin of the Christian Religion in China; An Inquiry into the Time
> when the Mohammedans first entered China; An Inquiry concerning the Jews
> discovered in China; A Dissertation on the Chinese Learning.—Heffer.

> 1718 RENAUDOT, EUSEBIUS. Anciennes Relations des Indes et de la Chine
> de deux voyageurs Mahometans qui y allerent dans le neuvième siècle;
> traduites d'Arabe, avec des remarques sur les principaux endroits de ces
> Relations. 8vo. Paris.

1736 DU HALDE, JEAN BAPTISTE. General History of China, Chinese-
Tartary, Corea, and Thibet, including an exact Account of their Customs, Manners, Ceremonies, Religion, Arts, and Sciences (translated
by R. Brookes). Numerous copperplates by Van der Gucht, and maps.
4 vols. 8vo. London.

> Another edition, 2 vols., fol., London, 1738-1741; a brief abstract in Astley
> III, 513-514. French original, Paris, 1735. See below.
> This work was first published in English by Edward Cave in weekly num-
> bers. From this account Samuel Johnson was to make selections "for the embel-
> lishment of the *Gentleman's Magazine*." Johnson, in writing to Cave about them
> said, "The Chinese Stories may be folded down when you please to send, in which,
> I do not recollect that you desired any alterations to be made." Boswell asked
> Johnson if he should read this work. "Why, yes, as one reads such a book; that
> is to say, consult it." All of the first volume of 678 pages and more than half
> of the second relates to China. The whole is, for the most part, a collection of
> pieces on several subjects, transmitted by the Jesuits residing in China to those
> of their order at home in France, and is reduced into one body by Du Halde, who
> added what he saw fit from other Relations and printed works. Lowndes asserts
> that Du Halde failed to exercise a sound judgment and a scrupulous examination
> into the truth of many facts and opinions which he admitted into the work. Others
> have regarded it as the completest and most valuable history of the Chinese Em-
> pire which had appeared up to the time of its publication.

> 1735 DU HALDE, JEAN BAPTISTE. Description géographique, historique,
> chronologique, politique, et physique de l'Empire de la Chine et de la
> Tartarie Chinoise; enrichie des cartes générales et particulières de ce
> pays, de la carte générale et particulière du Thibet et de la Coréa, et or-
> née d'un grand nombre de figures et de vignettes. 4 vols. Fol. Paris.

1741 A General History of China, Chinese Tartary, Corea and Thibet, drawn
from the celebrated work of Du Halde, in which are comprised all the
authentic Accounts formerly published by Louis Lecomte. 4 vols.
8vo. London.

1743 LOCKMAN, JOHN. Travels of the Jesuits into various Parts of the World, particularly China and the East Indies (see under COLLECTIONS).

1744-48 ADAMS, WILLIAM. A succinct Account of the Adventures of Mr. William Adams, an Englishman who resided many years in the Empire of Japan, and was the Person who introduced both the English and Dutch to trade thither. Collected, as well from his own Letters as Portugueze and Dutch Writers. In Harris I, 856-873.

> His Letters reprinted by the Hakluyt Society, London, 1850. A Dutch edition of two Letters, Leyden, 1706. See below. Adams is the subject of an historical novel called *The Needle Watcher,* by Richard Blaker, London, 1932.
> Adams had one of the most remarkable careers that ever befell a shipwrecked mariner. As navigator for the Dutch East India Company he was wrecked with his ship in 1600 on the coast of Japan. After a short imprisonment he was released and taken into high favor by the Shogun, who made him a two-sworded *Daimio.* He rose to a high position in Japanese affairs and married a Japanese woman by whom he had a son and a daughter. He was an invaluable go-between in the negotiations carried on with the English and Dutch in matters of trade. He was never allowed to leave Japan, and died there about 1620.

> 1850 Memorials of the Empire of Japonia In the Sixteenth and Seventeenth Centuries. (The Kingdome of Japonia, Harl. MSS. 6249.)—The Letters of Wm. Adams, 1611 to 1617. With a Commentary by Thomas Rundall. 1 map and 5 illus. Hak. Soc., ser. I, vol. 8. London.

> 1706 ADAMS, WILLIAM. Twee Brieven van William Adams; wagens sijn Reys uyt Holland na Oost-Indien, 1598, en wat ontmoetingen hem in Japan overgekomen zijn. Map and plate. 12mo. Leyden.

BENJAMIN OF TUDELA (Rabbi). His travels are more concerned with the Near East and Central Asia, but he did reach the borders of China. See under this date, GENERAL TRAVELS AND DESCRIPTIONS.

CUNNINGHAM, JAMES (Dr.). Observations and Remarks made during his Residence on the Island of Chusan, on the Coast of China, by Doctor James Cunningham, Physician to the English Factory of that Place. From his own Accounts. In Harris I, 852-855.

> The author was in the service of the East India Company. His account was written in Sept., 1701, to a member of the Royal Society. The Factory established at Chusan broke up in 1701. He was then removed to another settlement at Pulo-Condore, near the River Cambodia. This was destroyed by the natives because of broken contracts on the part of the Director.

A Curious and Concise Description of the Country, History of the Inhabitants, and Account of the Present State of the Kingdom of Corea, together with some Hints of the Ease with which Commerce might be established in its Ports, the Benefits that might be expected from thence, the great Likelihood of gaining an Entrance from thence into Japan, or at least an Intercourse with the Japonese; and many other entertaining and instructive Particulars relative to this Subject, and the Trade that is or might be carried on in the Dominions and Dependencies of the Empire of China. Collected chiefly from the Memoirs hitherto published, and compared with all the printed Histories and Travels, in which any Mention is made of this Country, its Commerce or Inhabitants. In Harris II, 1000-1015.

By this time hope of discovering a North-East Passage had been laid aside, but speculation was not yet dead.

KAO, DIONYSIUS. A Geographical Description of the extensive Empire of China, and of the sixteen Provinces into which it is divided. In which is contained a succinct View of the Situation, Bounds, Produce, remarkable Curiosities, and whatever else is worthy of Notice in each Province, taken entirely from the Writings of the Chinese themselves, and more especially from their authentick Records and natural Histories penned by Direction of the State; with such incidental Accounts of their Antiquities and of the personal Histories of most of the famous Emperours, Heroes, Statesmen, and Philosophers, as have been born or flourished in any of those Provinces through the Course of many Ages. By Dionysius Kao, a Native of China. Illustrated with many curious Observations and Remarks drawn from the best Authors who have treated of the Affairs of the Empire both ancient and modern. In Harris II, 961-975.

This work was penned about 1694. It was translated into Latin, German, and Dutch, with remarks by Witzen. What the language of the original was and how the account got to western Europe is not known to the editor. The author had studied "physick," practiced as a surgeon, and had travelled from province to province for many years among the Christians, and so had had ample opportunity to collect material for his work. Ides judged his descriptions to be among the best he had seen. The following item is a continuation of the above.

KAO, DIONYSIUS. A Copious, accurate, and authentick Account of whatever is most remarkable in regard to Persons or Things throughout the whole Empire of China; more especially the number of Inhabitants in general; the Rivers, Shipping, Lakes, Bridges, . . . The different Religions that prevail, and have prevailed amongst the People; their Manners, Ceremonies, and extraordinary Politeness. Of the remarkable Trees, rich Fruits and valuable Drugs in this Country, together with a succinct Account of those Kingdoms, that either now depend, or formerly depended upon it. In Harris II, 976-999.

1745 SA, PEDRO DE. A Description of Siam, translated from the Portuguese Original MS. By Pedro de Sa. In Osborne II, 92-94.

1745-47 CARPINI, JOHN DE PLANO DE (Friar). The Journey of Friar
John de Plano de Carpini to the Court of Kuyuk Khan, 1245-47, as
narrated by himself. Abstract in Astley IV, 544-550.

> First printed in English by Hakluyt in 1589, together with the abstract taken
> from the 32nd book of the *Speculum Historiale* of Vincent de Beauvais. It has
> received several editings in the 19th century, viz., by the Hakluyt Society, Lon-
> don, 1900, and again in 1903; and by Manuel Komroff in his *Contemporaries of
> Marco Polo,* London, 1928. See below.
> What would have become of Europe had not Ogotay Khan died when he
> did in 1241 is a real speculation, for his death recalled to Asia the conquering
> Batu and his hordes just as they were about to descend on Hungary. In the
> respite that followed Pope Innocent IV sent two missions to the Mongols to
> acquaint them with the wrath of God and to find out what they intended to do
> to Europe. Carpini, a monk of the Dominican order, was a member of one of
> these missions. He arrived at the court of the Mongols in time to witness the
> elevation of Kuyuk Khan as the supreme ruler of the vast domains of Ghengis
> Khan. He presented his letters from the Pope and received one in return to take
> back. This last was recently uncovered in the archives of the Vatican. It sug-
> gested that the Pope go to him and offer him service and submission. In Car-
> pini's account, which is accurate and trustworthy, we have a most interesting
> story of incredible hardships and a first-hand description of the Mongol way of
> life at the height of their power.

> 1900 The Journies of William de Rubruquis and John de Plano Carpini To
>   Tartary in the 13th century. Translated and edited by the Hon. Wm.
>   Woodville Rockhill. Hak. Soc., ser. II, vol. 4. London.

> 1903 The Texts and Versions of John de Plano Carpini and William de Rubru-
>   quis. As printed for the first time by Hakluyt in 1598, together with
>   some shorter pieces. Edited by Charles Raymond Beazley, M.A., F.R.
>   G.S. Hak. Soc., Extra ser., vol. 13. Cambridge.

A Description of China: Containing the Geography, with the civil and
natural History. In Astley IV, 1-318.

> A generalised account drawn from many sources.

DESIDERI, HYPOLITO. Travels into Tibet in 1714. Now first translated from the French. Abstract in Astley IV, 655-658.

> Modern edition, London, 1932. See below.
> This account was originally written in Italian for the perusal of Ildebrand
> Grassi, another Italian missionary in India. It is dated Lhasa, April 10, 1716.
> In company with Manoel Freyre, a brother Jesuit, Desideri made the difficult
> journey from India to Tibet by way of Kashmir and the high passes of Leh to
> Lhasa, where they remained from 1716 to 1729. He gave a lively account of the
> terrors of the journey, the recollection of which, he said, still made him shudder.
> —From Heawood, *Geographical Discovery.*

> 1932 DESIDERI, IPPOLITO. An Account of Tibet. The Travels of Ippolito
>   Desideri of Pistoia, S. J., 1712-1727. Edited by Filippo de Fillipi.
>   With an Introduction by C. Wessels, S. J. Map and 16 plates. 8vo.
>   London.

A Generalised Account of Tibet from various Sources. In Astley IV,
449-476.

> See also Pinkerton VII, 541-576.

GAUBIL, ANTHONY. The Journey of Anthony Gaubil, Jesuit, from Kanton to Peking, in 1722. Translated from the French. Abstract in Astley III, 581-584.

This journal is included in a collection of Tracts and Observations, published by Souciet, a Jesuit. French original, Paris, 1729. See below.

1729 GAUBIL, ANTHONY. Observations mathematiques, astronomiques, géographiques, chronologiques, et physiques, tirées des Anciennes Livres Chinoises, au Faites nouvellement, aux Indes et à la Chine, par les Pères de la Compagnie de Jésus. 4to. Paris.

GERBILLON, JOHN. Travels into Western Tartary, by Order of the Emperor of China, or in his Retinue, between the Years 1688 and 1698. Abstract in Astley IV, 664-751.

The author, a Jesuit, made eight journies from Peking into different parts of Manchuria and Western Tartary by order of the emperor Kang-hi or in his retinue. Like most of his brother Jesuits, who had been selected for missionary enterprise on the basis of their skill in mathematics, astronomy, etc., he was a good mathematician, and so set down with care the exact bearing of every place he visited. He gave copious accounts of the inhabitants, produce of the soil, etc. These journies were published by Du Halde (see under 1736 above) in his *Description of China and Tartary*. The above extract is taken from this work.

GOEZ, BENEDICT. The Travels of Benedict Goez from Lahore in the Mogol's Empire to China in 1602. Abstract in Astley IV, 642-649, taken chiefly from the original.

Reprinted in Pinkerton VII, 577-587. A Latin version, Lyons, 1700. See below.
Goes was a lay Jesuit and coadjutor to Jerom Xavier, superior to the Mission in Akbar's realms. He spoke Persian, was acquainted with Mohammedan customs, and had the good will of the Great Mogul Akbar. He was sent on a newly conceived mission to the "Kathayans," as a result of a rumor that the Empire of Cathay and that of China might be the same and that the Kathayans were Christians who might be in error or in danger of conversion to Mohammedanism. He travelled disguised as an Armenian merchant, accompanied by an Armenian servant named Isaac, who wrote the account of the journey. A further object of the journey was the discovery of a road to China through Bokhara. He passed through countries not traversed for the last two centuries and a half by Europeans, and not to be visited again by westerners until the nineteenth century. He left Agra in 1602 or 1603 and reached Souchou in 1607, where he died of an illness. His journal was unfortunately lost in the seizure of his goods by the Mohammedans. The account we have was published in Ricci's Commentaries, book V, ch. xi-xiii, which Nicholas Trigautius or Trigault, a Dutchman, translated out of Italian into Latin and published at Rome in 1618. For an account of the labors of the learned Father Ricci see Fülop-Miller, *The Power and Secret of the Jesuits,* translated by F. S. Flint and D. F. Tait, Garden City, N. Y., 1930.

1700 GOES, BENEDICT. Itinerario ex India in Sinarum Regnum. 4to. Lyons.

GRÜBER, JOHN. Travels from China to Europe in 1661. Abstract in Astley IV, 651-655.

In Pinkerton VII, 587-606.
What relates to his travels is contained in five letters, all written in Latin by the author except the first one, which was written in Italian by one anonymous virtuoso to another setting forth the substance of a conversation which he had

had with Grüber. The fifth one by Grüber to Athanasius Kircher, the famous Dutch Jesuit scholar, furnishes the particulars of his journey from China to India. These letters were published by Thevenot in his Collection (see under 1666-1672, COLLECTIONS—ADDENDA FOREIGN); by Kircher in his *China Illustrata*, Amsterdam, 1667. Others of his letters were published in a small volume at Florence in 1687, but all are included in Thevenot. This journey of Father Grüber and his companion Dorville by the overland route from Peking through Tibet to India was a remarkable feat. They left Peking in 1661 and reached Agra eleven months after their departure from China. See Heawood, *Geographical Discovery*.

HORACE DE PENNA. An Account of the Commencement and present State of the Capuchin Mission in Tibet, and two other neighboring Kingdoms, in the year 1741. Abstract in Astley IV, 658-664.

Italian original published at Rome in 1742, apparently doctored up by the Procurator-General from an oral account by Penna. This priest had been sent to Tibet by Pope Clement XI with eleven others to inquire into the state of that kingdom and to see how a mission might be introduced there. See below.

1742 HORACE DE PENNA, FRANCISCO. Relazione del Principio e Stato presente della Missione del vasto Regno del Tibet, ed altri due Regni Consinanti, raccommandata alla Vigilanza, e zelo de Padri Cappucini, della Provincia della Marca nello Stato della Chiesa. 4to. Rome.

MESSA-BARBA, J. AMBROZIO. The Legation of Kz—, titular Patriarch of Alexandria, from the Pope to the Emperor Kang Hi, in 1720. Written in Italian by P. Viani. And now first rendered into English. Abstract in Astley III, 584-605.

An Italian edition published at Paris, 1739. See below.
Besides the Italian narrative of this memorable embassy which preceded the expulsion of the Missionaries and the complete ruin of the ecclesiastical structure in China, there is an abstract of it in the *Bibliothèque Raissonnée,* which is the source of Astley's account, Tom 25, 1st and 2nd Parts (*des Ouvrages des Savans de l'Europe*), Amsterdam, 1740.

1739 MESSA-BARBA, J. AMBROZIO. Istoria delle Cose operate in China. 4to. Paris.

REGIS, JEAN-BAPTISTE. Geographical Observations and History of Korea. Abstract in Astley IV, 319-329.

Few ships ever touched on this coast and scarcely any western man ever landed to get information from the natives. Regis never set foot in Corea; he merely traversed the northern borders. His knowledge of the inland parts of the country was derived from a Tartar lord.

RUBRUQUIS, WILLIAM DE. Travels into Tartary and China. Abstract in Astley IV, 552-580.

Hakluyt published a part of Rubruck's Journal from the MS. of Lord Lumleys. This Purchas republished complete, 1625, from the MS. in Corpus Christi College, Cambridge, which, according to him, had never appeared before in any language. Bergeron translated it from the English towards the middle of the 17th century, after comparing it with two Latin MSS. copies, and the same was inserted in Thevenot's Collection, 1666-1672. It was reprinted in Harris I, 556-

592. Astley's abstract was reprinted by Pinkerton VII, 22-100. It was edited for the Hakluyt Society, 1900 and again 1903. Both of these editions contain Carpini's Journal. It was included in Komroff's *Contemporaries of Marco Polo*, London, 1928. The latter editor draws upon Hakluyt and upon *Guillaume de Rubrouck* by Louis de Backer, Paris, 1877, to complete his version. Roger Bacon first gave notice of this work in his *Opus Major* (see the edition by John Henry Bridges, Oxford, 1897).

Rubruquis, a Frenchman of the Order of the Minor Friars, was sent in 1253 by St. Louis, of France, to the Far East on hearing that Sartach, son of Batu Khan, the conqueror of Russia, was a Christian, with the idea of establishing communication with the prince. Rubruquis had to travel on to the court of Mangu Khan in Mongolia, a journey of some five thousand miles. He returned in 1255, after experiencing some extraordinary adventures. He wrote his report in Latin at Acre and sent it on to St. Louis, who had just got home from his pilgrimage to the Holy Land. It is an amazing record and added much to the geographical knowledge of the day. Komroff regards it as important an historical record as Marco Polo's.

SHAH RUKH. The Embassy of Shah Rukh, son of Tamerlan, and other Princes, to the Emperor of Katay, or China. Translated from the Persian into French, and now first done into English. Abstract in Astley IV, 621-632.

Given by Thevenot in French, vol. 4 of his Collection. He says it was written in Persian but does not tell by whom it was translated. The embassy took place in 1419.

VAN RECHTEREN, SEYGER. The Voyages of Seyger van Rechteren to the East Indies. Abstract dealing with the first Attempts of the Dutch to trade in China, . . . Now first translated from the French. In Astley III, 492-498.

Dutch original published in 4to at Zwolle in Overyssel, 1639. Translated into French and included in vol. V of the Dutch Collection of *Voyages to the East Indies* (probably Commelin's Collection; see under 1703, COLLECTIONS). A French version, Amsterdam, 1705. See below.

The author spent the years from 1628 to 1633 in this part of the world. On board his ship were some officers who had been taken prisoners at the unfortunate attempt of the Dutch to capture Macao in 1622. From them he received his account of China and of the posture of Dutch affairs there, which he has inserted in his *Voyage*.

1705 VAN RECHTEREN, SEYGER. Voyage de Van Rechteren aux Indes-Orientales, avec le Voyage de Langes à la Chine. 12mo. Amsterdam.

VERBIEST, FERDINAND. A Journey into Eastern Tartary, in 1682. Abstract in Astley IV, 362-366.

Verbiest later made a journey into Western Tartary. These two journies to Manchuria and Mongolia were both made in the train of the Emperor Kang-hi, and were written up in two letters and sent to Europe, where they were translated from Latin into French and thence into English. They were printed at London in 1686/7 and added to De Soto's account of Florida in the 1686 edition (see De Soto under 1609, NORTH AMERICA). They were included by Du Halde in his *General History of China* (see under 1736 above). Reprinted by the Hakluyt Society, 1855. A French version, Paris, 1683, is cited by Pinkerton XVII. See below.

Verbiest was another Jesuit missionary who had won favor with the Chinese court because of his knowledge of mathematics. He it was who persuaded the

Emperor to recall the Jesuit missionaries to Peking, whence they had been banished during the minority of Kang-Hi. See Heawood, *Geographical Discovery.* His account of his journey to Manchuria is short but interesting, and, according to Astley, is the only piece of travel extant performed expressly into the heart of Eastern Tartary, as Ides had only passed by the western skirts of that country.

1855   The History of the Two Tartar Conquerors of China, Including the two Journeys into Tartary of Father Ferdinand Verbiest, in the suite of the Emperor Kang-Hi. From the French of Père Pierre Joseph d'Orleans, 1688. To which is added Father Pereira's Journey into Tartary. From the Dutch of Nicolaas Witsen. Translated and edited by the Earl of Ellesmere, with an Introduction by Richard Henry Major, F.S.A. Hak. Soc., ser. I, vol. 17. London.

1683   VERBIEST, FERDINAND. Relation d'un Voyage de l'Empereur de la Chine, en 1682 et 1683, dans la Tartarie, par le P. Verbiest. 12mo. Paris.

> Also in Bernard's *Recueil de Voyages au Nord,* 1715. (See under 1715, COLLECTIONS.)

1752   SPENCE, JOSEPH (Rev.). A particular Account of the Emperor of China's Gardens near Pekin, in a Letter from F. Attiret, a French Missionary now employed by that Emperor to paint the Apartments in those Gardens, to his Friend at Paris. 8vo. London.

> Reprinted in Dodsley's *Fugitive Pieces.* This piece may be one of those fictions to which the century was well accustomed.

1762   NOBLE, C. F. For an account of China see his *Voyage to the East Indies in 1747-48,* under EAST INDIES.

1763   BELL, JOHN. For his journey from Russia to Peking (1719) see his *Travels from St. Petersburg in Russia to Diverse Parts of Asia,* under CENTRAL ASIA.

LANGE, LAURENCE. Journal at Pekin, 1721-22. Included in the above work of Bell's.

> Lange was Resident of Russia at Peking during 1721-22. See Lange under 1722-23 above.

1771   OSBECK, PETER. For his voyage to China see his *Voyage to China and the East Indies,* under EAST INDIES.

> Osbeck was a Swede, rector of Hasloef and Wextorf, Member of the Academy of Stockholm, and chaplain to a Swedish East-Indiaman.

ECKEBERG, CHARLES AUGUSTUS (Captain). An Account of Chinese Husbandry. Included in the above work of Osbeck's.

1772 The Chinese Traveller; to which is prefixed, the Life of Confucius. Maps and plates. 12mo. London.

> 2nd edit., 2 vols., 12mo, with large additions, London, 1775.
> Collected from Du Halde, Le Comte, and other later travellers.—Lowndes.

1788 GROSIER, J. G. B. (Abbé). A General Description of China, containing the Topography of the Fifteen Provinces, of Tartary, the Isles, and other Tributary Countries, with an Account of the Natural History, Government, Religion, Customs, Arts, . . . of the Chinese. Translated from the French. Map and plates. 2 vols. 8vo. London.

> Another edition, 2 vols., 8vo, London, 1795. French original, Paris, 1785. See below.

> 1785 GROSIER, J. G. B. (Abbé). Description générale de la Chine; contenant, 1mo, La description géographique des quinze provinces qui composent cet empire, celles de la Tartarie, des Iles et autres pays tributaires qui en dependent, la nombre et la situation de ses villes, l'état, de sa population, les productions variées de son sol et les principaux détails de son histoire naturelle; 2do, Un précis des connoissances le plus récemment parvenues en Europe, sur le gouvernement, la religion, les moeurs et les usages, les arts et les sciences des Chinois. Avec cartes et figures. 2 vols. 8vo. Paris.

1789 GILBERT, THOMAS (Commander). Voyage from New South Wales to Canton in 1788, with Views of the Islands discovered. 4 folding plates. 4to. London.

> This voyage was made through a track many degrees more to the eastward than was pursued by any of the circumnavigators on their return to Europe, by way of the Indian seas; as, during it several islands, hitherto unknown, were fallen in with; and as it may become in time an established passage between our new settlements in that part of the world and the eastern coast of Asia, I trust I shall stand excused for thus laying the particulars of it before the public.— From the Preface, quoted.

1793 DONOVAN, E. Epitome of the Natural History of the Insects of China; comprising Figures and Descriptions, . . . Colored plates. 4to. London.

1794 THUNBERG, C. P. Travels in Europe, Africa, and Asia. Performed between the years 1770 and 1779. 6 plates. 4 vols. 8vo. London.

> So cited by Pinkerton XVII. Swedish original, Upsala, 1788. See below. His account of the Cape of Good Hope in Pinkerton, XVI, 1-147. See also under GENERAL TRAVELS AND DESCRIPTIONS.
> These travels, relating principally to Japan, are exceedingly valuable with respect to the natural history.—Pinkerton XVII.

> 1788 THUNBERG, K. P. Resa uti Europa, Asia, Africa, forroetad i aaren 1770 a 1779. 4 vols. 8vo. Upsala.

1795   ANDERSON, AENEAS.   A Narrative of the British Embassy in China, in 1792-94; containing the various Circumstances of the Embassy, with an Account of the Customs and Manners of the Chinese.   8vo. London.

> This narrative of Earl Macartney's embassy is of little value in comparison with that of Sir G. L. Staunton (see Staunton under 1797 below). An abridgement also appeared in 1795.—Lowndes.

WINTERBOTHAM, WILLIAM.   An historical, geographical, and philosophical View of the Empire of China; to which is added, a Copious Account of Lord Macartney's Embassy: compiled from original communications.   London.

1797   ALEXANDER, WILLIAM.   Sketches from Nature, made in China.   8vo. London.

> This ingenious artist was draftsman to Earl Macartney, during his embassy to China.—Lowndes.

CHAPMAN, WILLIAM.   Observations on the various Systems of Canal Navigation, with Inferences Practical and Mathematical; in which Mr. Fulton's Plan of Wheel-Boats, and the Utility of Subterraneous and of Small Canals are particularly investigated.   Including an Account of the Canals and Inclined Planes of China.   4 engraved plates. 4to.   London.

> Largely based on the suggestions and proposals of the great American inventor, Robt. Fulton.—Maggs, No. 521.

STAUNTON, SIR GEORGE LEONARD.   An Authentic Account of an Embassy to China, chiefly from the Papers of Lord Macartney and Sir E. Gower.   Portraits of Macartney and the Emperor Tchien Lung, and atlas of 44 large plates.   2 vols.   4to and atlas fol.   London.

> 2nd edit., corrected, 3 vols., 8vo, London, 1798. See also Anderson, 1795 above; Holme, 1798; A Complete View of the Chinese Empire, 1798; Barrow, 1804; Helen Robbins' account, 1908. Translated into French, Paris, 1798; into German, Halle, 1798, and Zurich, 1798-99. See below.
> The account of this famous embassy was prepared at Government expense. Apart from its Chinese importance, it is of considerable interest owing to the descriptions of the various places en route which were visited, including Madeira, Teneriff, Rio de Janeiro, St. Helena, Tristan d'Acunha, Amsterdam Island, Java, Sumatra, Cochin-China, etc.—Maggs, No. 521. Great Britain was anxious to establish formal diplomatic relations with China and thus open the way for unimpeded trade relations. But the pall of Chinese reserve and self-sufficiency, which for many centuries seldom admitted penetration, still hung over this empire and effectually resisted Lord Macartney's arguments and gifts. In 1793 China was as thoroughly China as it was before the days of Kang-hi. His visit was not in vain, however, for it gave us a most interesting account of Chinese manners and customs at the close of the eighteenth century.

1798 STAUNTON, SIR GEORGE LEONARD. Authentic Account of an Embassy to the Emperor of China, with Travels through that Ancient Empire and a Relation of the Voyage to the Yellow Sea and the Return via South America and St. Helena, selected from the Earl of Macartney's Papers. 3 vols. 8vo. London.

1908 MACARTNEY, GEORGE (Earl of). Our First Ambassador to China. An Account of the Life of George Earl of Macartney. With Extracts from his Letters, and the Narrative of his Experiences in China, as told by himself, 1737-1806. From hitherto unpublished Correspondence and Documents by Helen Robbins. Illus. 8vo. London.

1798 (In French.) Voyage dans l'intérieur de la Chine et en Tartarie fait dans les années 1792, 1793 et 1794. Redigé sur les papiers de Lord Macartney, sur ceux du Commodore Erasme Gower et des autres personnes attachés à l'Ambassade, par sir Georges Staunton. Traduit de l'anglais avec des notes par S. Castéra. Sec. éd. aug. d'un précis de l'histoire de la Chine, par le traducteur du voyage en Chine, et en Tartarie de J.-C. Huttner, traduit de l'allemand par même traducteur. Plates and maps. 5 vols. 8vo. Paris.

1798 (In German.) Reise der Englischen Gesandtschaft an dem Kaiser von China, 1792-93. Übersetzt von M. C. Sprengel. 2 parts in 1 vol. Halle.

The same translated by J. C. Huttner. 2 vols. Zurich.

1798 A Complete View of the Chinese Empire, exhibited in a Geographical Description of that Country, a Dissertation on its Antiquity, and a genuine and copious Account of Earl Macartney's Embassy. Portrait of Kien Long, Emperor of China. 8vo. London.

In this work will be found an account of Lord Macartney's Embassy, patched up in London from the meagre journal kept by a menial servant of the Ambassador.—Lowndes.

HOLME, SAMUEL. A Journal during his Attendance as one of the Guard on Lord Macartney's Embassy to China and Tartary. 8vo. London.

Holme may be the "menial servant" contemptuously referred to by Lowndes in the note to the preceding item.

VAN BRAAM, ANDRE EVERARD. An Authentic Account of the Embassy of the Dutch East-India Company, to the Court of the Emperor of China, in the years 1794 and 1795, containing a Description of several parts of the Chinese Empire, unknown to Europeans. Chart of the route. 2 vols. 8vo. London.

Pinkerton cites an edition in French published at Philadelphia, 1797. The author was a member of the embassy. Lowndes describes it as a clumsy production, containing, however, some valuable facts.

1800 TURNER, SAMUEL, (Captain). An Account of an Embassy to the Court of the Teshoo Lama in Tibet, describing a Journey through Bootan, and Part of Tibet; with Views taken on the Spot by Lt. Samuel Davis; and Observations, Botanical, Mineralogical, and Medical, by Robert Saunders. Folding map and 13 plates of scenery, buildings, etc. 4to. London.

> Translated into French, Paris, 1800; also into German. See below.
> This is without comparison the most valuable work that has yet appeared on Thibet; but it is to be regretted that the author could not advance further into the country.—Pinkerton XVII. Turner was a captain in the East India service. He led an expedition into Tibet in 1783-85, of which the above is an account.

> 1800 (In French.) Ambassade au Thibet et au Boutan, contenant des détails très curieux sur les moeurs, la religion, les productions et le commerce du Thibet, du Boutan et des états voisins, et une notice sur les événements qui s'y sont passés jusqu'en 1793, traduit de l'anglais avec des notes par J. Castéra. 2 vols. in 8vo, and 1 of views in 4to. Paris.

ADDENDA

1800-01 MASON, GEORGE HENRY (Major). The Costume and Punishments of China, 82 colored plates after the drawings of Pu-Qua of Canton, with Descriptions in English and French. 2 vols. Fol. London.

1804 BARROW, JOHN (F.R.S.). Travels in China, containing Descriptions, Observations, and Comparisons, made and collected in the Course of a short Residence at the Imperial Palace of Yuen-min-yuen, and on a subsequent Journey through the Country from Pekin to Canton. Illus. with several engravings. 4to. London.

> 2nd edit., with added matter, London, 1806.
> The author was private secretary to Lord Macartney, and was in China with the embassy under the latter.

1806 BARROW, JOHN. A Voyage to Cochin-China, in the years 1792 and 1793; containing a general view of the valuable Products and political importance of this flourishing Kingdom, and also of such European Settlements as were visited on the voyage, . . . to which is annexed, An Account of a Journey made in 1801 and 1802, to the Residence of the Chief of the Boesjesmans Nation in Southern Africa. Plates. 8vo. London.

1808 DE GUIGNES, ——. Voyages à Peking, Manille, et l'Ile de France, faits dans l'intervalle de 1784 à 1801. 3 vols. 8vo and fol. atlas. Paris.

> According to Pinkerton XVII this work was translated into English, 4to, London, 1809.

1808-1814   RICHARD, —— (Abbé).   The Natural and Civil History of Tonquin. In Pinkerton IX, 708-771.

> French original, 2 vols., 12mo, Paris, 1788. See below.

> 1788 RICHARD, —— (Abbé).   Histoire naturelle et civile du Tunkin. 2 vols.
> 12mo. Paris.

TURPIN, ——.   History of Siam. Translated from the French. In Pinkerton IX, 573-655.

> French original, 2 vols., 12mo, Paris, 1771. See below.
> This work was based on some MSS. which were communicated by the bishop
> of Tavolca, the apostolic vicar of Siam, and by other missionaries of that kingdom.

> 1771 TURPIN, ——.   Histoire civile et naturelle du Royaume de Siam, et des
> Révolutions qui ont bouleversé cet Empire jusqu'en 1770, publiée par
> M. Turpin, sur les manuscrits qui lui ont été communiqués par M.
> l'Evêque de Travolca, Vicare-apostolique de Siam, et d'autres mission-
> aires de ce royaume. 2 vols. 12mo. Paris.

1821   COX, H. (Captain).   Journal of a Residence in the Burhman Empire,
more particularly at the Court of Amarapoorah (in 1796). Edited by
C. M. Cox. Colored plates. 8vo. London.

1855   PEREIRA, —— (Father).   Journey into Tartary, in the suite of the
Emperor Kang-Hi. Hak. Soc., ser. I, vol. 17. London. See the full
title of this item under Verbiest, 1745-47, above.

1866   Cathay and the Way Thither. Being a Collection of medieval notices of
China, previous to the Sixteenth Century. Translated and Edited by
Colonel Sir Henry Yule, K.C.S.I., R.E., C.B. With a preliminary
Essay on the intercourse between China and the Western Nations pre-
vious to the discovery of the Cape Route. 3 maps and 8 illus. 2 vols.
Hak. Soc., ser. I, vols. 36-37. London.   (See under 1913-16 below.)

1869   BEAL, S.   Travels of 'Fah-Hian and Sung Yun, Buddhist Pilgrims, from
China to India (400 A. D. to 518). Translated from the Chinese. Map.
8vo. London..

1882   COCKS, RICHARD.   The Diary of Richard Cocks, Cape-Merchant in
the English Factory in Japan, 1615-1622, with Correspondence (Add.
MSS. 31,300-1. Brit. Mus.). Edited by Edward Maunde Thompson.
2 vols. Hak. Soc., ser. I, vol. 66-67. London.

1900   SARIS, JOHN (Captain).   The Voyage of Capt. John Saris to Japan in 1613. Edited by H. E. Sir Ernest Mason Satow, G.C.M.G. Map and illus. Hak. Soc., ser. II, vol. 5. London.

1913-16   Cathay and the Way Thither. Being a Collection of Medieval Notices of China. Translated and Edited by Col. Sir Henry Yule, K.C.S.I., R.E., C.B. New Edition revised throughout by Professor Henri Cordier, de l'Institute de France. Maps and illus. 4 vols. Hak. Soc., ser. II, vols. 33, 37, 38, 41. (1st vol. is 38; 2nd vol. 33; 3rd vol. 37; 4th vol. 41.) London.

1919   BADDELEY, JOHN F.   Russia, Mongolia, China: some Record of the Relations between them from the Beginning of the XVIth Century to the Death of the Tsar Mikhailovich, A. D. 1602-1676; rendered mainly in the form of Narratives dictated or written by the Envoys sent by the Russian Tsars, or their Voevodas in Siberia to the Kalmuck and Mongol Khans and Princes, and to the Emperors of China, with Introductions, historical and geographical, also a Series of Maps showing the Progress of Geographical Knowledge in regard to Northern Asia during the XVIth, XVIIth, and early XVIIIth Centuries; the Text taken more especially from MSS. in the Moscow Foreign Office Archives, with extensive Indexes. 27 maps, numerous illustrations in the text, facsimiles, and tables of pedigrees. 2 vols. Fol. London.

   This is regarded as one of the most remarkable books of its kind in existence and of immense historical worth.

1923   FA-HSIEN.   Travels of Fa-hsien, 399-414 A.D., or Records of the Buddhistic Kingdoms. Retranslated by H. A. Giles. 8vo. London.

1928   BOXER, C. R.   A Portuguese Embassy to Japan (1664-1667). 8vo. London.

1929   ODORIC (Friar).   The Journal of Friar Odoric, 1318-1330. In Komroff, *Contemporaries of Marco Polo*. London.

   His relation was drawn up from his own mouth by Friar William of Solanga in 1330. Ramusio has inserted it in Italian in vol. II of his Collection; Hakluyt included it in vol. II of his work, in Latin and English.
   In about the year 1318 Odoric was sent on a missionary journey to the Far East. He reached western India in about 1321, and from there proceeded to China, where he stayed three years. He visited Sumatra and Java and coasted Borneo, and travelled overland to Peking. He came back by way of Tibet, Persia and the country of the Assassins, and finally reached his home in Udine, where he died in 1331. After Marco Polo he was the first traveller to describe the lands mentioned. —From Komroff's Introduction to this text.

1931 CH'ANG-CH'UN. The Journey of the Taoist Ch'ang Ch'un from China to the Hindukush at the summons of Chingiz Khan. Translated (from the Chinese), with an Introduction, by Arthur Waley. Map. 8vo. Broadway Travellers. London.

> Chingiz (or Ghengis) Khan seems to have been particularly interested in the religions of the world. Perhaps, as Mr. Waley suggests in his extremely interesting introduction to this book, he believed that a great monarch should be able to count upon the support of a great sage. At any rate, at the beginning of the thirteenth century, when he was at the height of his power, he summoned to his court Ch'ang Ch'un, the head of a Taoist sect, whose travels are here related.— From the Publisher's Note.

XII

Siberia

1706   IDES, EVERARD YSBRANTS. For an account of Siberia see his *Three Years' Travels from Moscow overland to China*, under FAR EAST.

     The portion dealing with Siberia reprinted in Harris II, 951-961.

1722-23   LANGE, LAURENCE. For an account of Siberia see his *Travels through Russia to China and Siberia*, under FAR EAST; and F. C. Weber, *Present State of Russia*, under EAST EUROPE.

1736-38   STRAHLENBURG, PHILIP JOHANN VON. For his travels in Siberia see his *Historico-Geographical Description of the North and Eastern Parts of Europe and Asia*, under EAST EUROPE.

1744-48   A distinct Account of that Part of the North-east Frontier of the Russian Empire, commonly called the Country of Kamschatka or Kamschatska, including the Voyage of Captain Behring, for Discovery towards the East with many curious and entertaining Circumstances relating to those distant Countries and their Inhabitants; as also an Enquiry into the Probability of the Country which he described being connected with North America, with a Variety of other Points of great Consequence in Relation to designs now on foot in various Parts of Europe for making a thorough Discovery of the Superior Parts of the Northern Hemisphere, which would be of utmost Consequence to Trade and Navigation . . . Collected from the best Authorities both Printed and Manuscript. In Harris II, 1016-1041.

     For an account of Bering's voyages, with those of his predecessors and followers, and a history of the conquest of Siberia by the Russians, see William Coxe, under 1780, NORTH PACIFIC. A modern edition of Bering's voyages, New York, 1922. See below. See also the section NORTH PACIFIC for a number of works relating to discoveries on the east coast of Siberia.

     By 1697 the Russians had arrived in Kamchatka; ten years later they reached the southern end of this region and sighted the nearest islands of the Kuriles chain. Various later expeditions brought to light new regions for mapping. In 1728 Vitus Bering sailed from Kamchatka north to discover whether the shores of Asia joined with those of North America. This voyage and that of 1741, which gave him a sight of Mount St. Elias in Alaska, belong to the section NORTH PACIFIC.

     1922 BERING, VITUS. Bering's Voyages (vol. I). An Account of the Efforts of the Russians to determine the Relation of Asia and America (vol. II). By F. A. Golder. 2 vols. Amer. Geog. Research Series, No. 2. New York.

1752-57 GMELIN, JOHANNES G. Travels through Siberia, between the years 1733-1743; containing a Description of the Manners and Customs of the People; the principal Rivers, . . . Plates. 4 vols. Harlem.

> German original, Göttingen, 1751-52. See below.
> When the eighteenth century opened the Russians had become acquainted with the main geographical features of Northern Asia. The next forty years were to see many of the gaps filled in, particularly on the east and north coasts of Siberia as well as in the interior. Assisting in this work was the Academy of Sciences, (of St. Petersburg) among whose members participating in the actual work of discovery were Gmelin the naturalist, De la Croyère the astronomer, and Müller the historian. This widely planned series of land and sea journies took form in 1733 and was practically completed by 1745. Gmelin and Müller explored the region east of Lake Baikal in 1735 and in 1736 the upper reaches of the Lena basin. They returned to St. Peterburg in 1743. See Heawood, *Geographical Discovery*.

1752-57 GMELIN, JOHANNES GEORG. Reise durch Sibirien, von den Jahren 1733-1743. 4 theile. 4 Karten. Göttingen.

1763 KRASHENINNIKOF, H. The History of Kamtschatka and the Kurilsky Islands, with the Countries adjacent, illustrated with maps: published at St. Petersburgh by order of His Imperial Majesty; and translated into English, by James Grieve. London.

> Another edition, Gloucester, 1764. Russian original, St. Petersburg (Leningrad), 1754. See below.
> It is to the student Krasheninikof that we owe the first scientific account of the country.—Heawood, *Geographical Discovery*. The work deals with details of the morals, customs, religion of the inhabitants of this peninsula, as well as the power exercised by the magicians or shamans. It also treats of the differences between the dialects of the Kamchatkans and of those of the Korsacs and of the Kuriles islanders.

1754 KRASHENINIKOF, H. Opisanie Zemli Kamtschatki sotschenennoja. 2 vols. St. Petersburg.

1770 CHAPPE D'AUTEROCHE, JEAN (Abbé). A Journey into Siberia, made by order of the King of France. By M. l'Abbé Chappe d'Auteroche, of the Royal Academy of Sciences at Paris in 1761. Containing an Account of the Manners and Customs of the Russians, the present State of their Empire; with the Natural History, and Geographical Description of their Country, and Level of the Road from Paris to Tobolsky. Illus. with cuts. Translated from the French with a Preface by the Translator. 4to. London.

> French original, 3 vols., (4 with atlas), Paris, 1768. See below.
> The last volume of the French edition contains the Description of Kamtschatka by Krasheninikof, translated from the Russian. See preceding item. Some of the unfavorable remarks on the Russians drew forth some lively criticisms from the Empress Catherine II and the Count Chouvalof. These appeared first in 1771 at Amsterdam under the title, *Antidote, ou examen du mauvais livre entitulés: Voyage de l'Abbé Chappe.*—Quoted by Sotheran. For this *Antidote* see below. Dr. Johnson used this author to correct Lord Kames's *Sketches of the History of Man*, who took the incident in question from Chappe d'Auteroche.

1768 CHAPPE D'AUTEROCHE, JEAN (Abbé). Voyage en Sibérie fait par ordre du Roi en 1761; contenant les moeurs, les usages des Russes, et l'état actuel de cette puissance; la Description géographique et le Nivellement de la route de Paris à Tobolsk; l'Histoire naturelle de la même route; des Observations astronomiques et des Expériences sur l'Electricité naturelle; enrichi de Cartes Géographiques, de Plans de Profils, de Terrain; de Gravures qui representent les usages des Russes, leurs moeurs, leurs habillements, les Divinités des Calmouks, et plusieurs, morceaux d'histoire naturelle. 3 vols. and atlas, together 4 vols. Fol. Paris.

> Lowndes says that the French edition deserves attention for its splendid and accurate engravings and its powerful description of manners and character.

1772 The Antidote, or an Enquiry into the merits of a Book, entitled a Journey into Siberia, 1770. Translated into English by a Lady. London.

> This translation was made by a Lady at St. Petersburgh, and dedicated to the Empress Catherine, who was generally reported to have taken an active share in the original "Antidote."—Pinkerton XVII.

1780 COXE, WILLIAM. For an account of the Russian conquests of Siberia see under this date, NORTH PACIFIC.

1790 BENYOWSKY, MAURITIUS AUGUSTUS, COUNT DE. The Memoirs and Travels of Mauritius Augustus, Count de Benyowsky, in Siberia, Kamchatka, Japan, the Liukiu Islands and Formosa. Translated from the original Manuscript (by W. Nicholson). 2 vols. 4to. London.

> An edition, Dublin, 1790. See below. Pinkerton cites an edition, 2 vols., 4to, London, 1794. Modern reprints, edited by Capt. Pasfield Oliver, 8vo, London, 1893; edited with Introduction and Notes, by Capt. Oliver, Dryden House Memoirs, London, 1904, from the text of the 1790 Dublin edition. Translated into German, Tübingen, 1790; into French, Paris, 1791; into Dutch, Haarlem, 1793. See below.
> Pinkerton observes very rightly that some portions of the journal of this adventurer are of very doubtful authority. How far the falsification of dates and facts, voyages and adventures was carried by the writer has been set forth by Capt. Oliver in the Introduction to his 1904 edition. The journal ends with his departure from Madagascar in 1776, but his adventures continued until his death on his return to that island in 1784.

1790 BENYOWSKY, MAURITIUS AUGUSTUS, COUNT DE. The Memoirs and Travels of Mauritius Augustus, Count de Benyowsky, Magnate of the Kingdoms of Hungary and Poland, one of the Chiefs of the Confederation of Poland, . . . consisting of his Military Operations in Poland, his Exile into Kamchatka, his Escape and Voyage from that Peninsula through the Northern Pacific Ocean, touching at Japan and Formosa, to Canton in China, with an Account of the French Settlement he was appointed to form upon the Island of Madagascar. Written by himself. Translated from the original manuscript. In 2 vols. 8vo. Dublin.

1790 (In German.) Reise durch Siberien und Kamtschatka, über Japan und China nach Europa, nebst einem Auszug seiner übrigen Lebensbeschreibung. Aus dem Englischen übersetzt von Dr. Mary Liebeskind. Mit Anmerkungen von J. R. Forster. Tübingen.

1791　(In French.)　Voyages et Mémoires du comte Benjowsky contenant ses
　　　　opérations en Pologne, son exile au Kamtschatka et son Voyage à
　　　　travers l'Océan Pacifique au Japon, à Formosa, . . . Traduit de l'ang-
　　　　lais. 2 vols. Paris.

1793　(In Dutch.)　Gedenkschrifter en reizen. Naar het Englisch. Haarlem.

LESSEPS, J. B. B. DE.　Travels in Kamtschatka, 1787-1788, translated from the French. 2 vols. 8vo. London.

　　　French original, Paris, 1790. See below.
　　　This narrative gives a lively picture of the inhabitants of the northern parts
of Asiatic and European Russia.—Lowndes. De Lesseps was a member of the
expedition sent out by Louis XVI to explore more accurately the north-eastern
coast of Siberia under command of La Perouse. He was left at Petropavlovsk to
carry despatches overland across Siberia to France, a journey he successfully accomplished.

1790　LESSEPS, G. B. B. DE.　Journal historique du Voyage de M. de Les-
　　　　seps, Consul de France, employé dans l'Expédition de M. de la Peyrouse
　　　　en qualité d'Interpréte du Roi, depuis l'instant où il a quitté les frég-
　　　　ates Française au Port Saint Pierre et St. Paul en Kamtschatka. Maps
　　　　and plates. 2 vols. Paris.

1800　BILLINGS, JOSEPH (Commodore).　An Account of a geographical and
astronomical Expedition to the Northern Parts of Russia for ascer-
taining the degree of latitude and longitude of the Mouth of the River
Lena; of the whole Coast of the Tshutski to East Cape; and of the
Islands of the Eastern Ocean, stretching to the American Coast.
Performed by Command of her Imperial Majesty Catherine II, by J.
Billings in the years 1785-1794. The whole narrated from the original
Papers (by Martin Sauer). 4to. Chart. London.

　　　This date is given by Chavanne. 1802 is the date usually cited with this work.
Translated into French, Paris, 1802; into German, Berlin, 1802. See below.
　　　A valuable work, although deficient in natural history . . . Another account
was published in Russian by Captain Saretschewya.—Lowndes. This expedition
was the outcome of a suggestion made by Dr. William Coxe, the English historian
of many voyages and travels. Billings was an officer in the Russian navy, and
Sauer, under whose name the above work is sometimes listed, was his secretary.
He it was who wrote up the fullest account of the voyage. Billings left Lenin-
grad (St. Petersburg) in 1785, but he did not actually sail until 1789. He visited
Kodiak, Montague Island, Prince William Sound, and caught sight of Mt. St.
Elias. Scarcity of food caused him to return the same year to Petrapavlovsk. The
expedition accomplished little and marks the close of the Russian surveys on
the eastern coast of Siberia.

1802　(In French.)　Voyage fait par Ordre de l'impératrice de Russie Catherina
　　　　II, dans le Nord de la Russie asiatique, dans la mer glaciale . . . depuis
　　　　1785-1794 par le Commandeur Billings. Traduit de l'anglais avec des
　　　　notes par Castéra. 2 vols. avec 1 atlas. 8vo. Paris.

1803　(In German.)　Reise zur Untersuchung der Küsten des Eismeeres, oder
　　　　geographisch-astronomische Reise nach den nördlichen Gegenden Russ-
　　　　lands 1785-1794. Herausgegeben von Martin Sauer. Aus dem Englisch-
　　　　en. Maps and plates. 8vo. Berlin.

XIII

Africa

1554 BOEMUS, JOHANNES. The Description of the Contrey of Aphrique. Translated by Wyllyam Prat of London from the French. London.

> The original of Boemus's work is *Omnium gentium mores* (1520). See Boemus, 1555, under GENERAL TRAVELS AND DESCRIPTIONS.

1577 VARTHEMA, LUDOVICOS DI. For an account of Egypt see his *The Navigation and Vyageʂ of Lewes Vertomannus,* under EAST INDIES.

1583 A Pleasant Description of the Fortunate Ilandes, called the Ilandes of Canaria, with their straunge Fruits and Commodities, verie delectable to read, to the Praise of God. Composed by the poor Pilgrime. 12mo. London.

> In Hakluyt, *Principal Navigations* (1599), it is stated that this work was "composed by Thomas Nicols, English man, who remained there the space of seven yeares together."

1586 SAUNDERS, THOMAS (Captain). A True Description and breefe Discourse of a most lamentable Voyage made lately to Tripolie in Barbarie; with the barbarous Vsage of our Men there. 4to. London.

1590 WEBBE, EDWARD. For an account of his adventures in Egypt see his *Rare and most vvonderfull Thinges,* under NEAR EAST.

1591 HORTOP, JOB. The Rare Trauales of an Englishman, who was not heard of in three and twentie Yeeres Space. 4to. London.

> "Wherein is declared the dangers he escaped in his voyage to Gynnie, where after he was set ashore in a wilderness neere Panico, he endured much slauerie and bondage in the Spanish Galley."—Lowndes. See also under WEST INDIES this date.

1597 LOPEZ, DUARTE. A Report of the Kingdome of Congo, a Region of Africa. And of the Countries that border rounde about the same. 1. Wherein is also shewed, that the two Zones Torrida and Frigida, are not onely habitable, but inhabited, and very temperate, contrary to the opinion of the old Philosophers. 2. That the blacke colour which is in the skinnes of the Ethiopians and Negroes, etc., proceedeth not from the Sunne. 3. And that the River Nilus springeth not out of the mountains of the Moone, as hath been heretofore beleeved:

Together with the true cause of the rising and increasing thereof. 4. Besides the description of divers Plants, Fishes and Beastes, that are found in those Countries. Drawen out of the writinges and discourses of Odoardo Lopez a Portingall, by Philippo Pigafetta. Translated out of Italian by Abraham Hartwell. 4 engraved folding maps of Southern Africa, the Congo Basin, and the Nile Basin; ten full page woodcuts of the inhabitants, the animals, and trees of Africa. The two title pages before and after the introductory matter. 4to. London.

> Reprinted in Osborne II, 519-583; an abstract in Astley III, 132-135. A modern translation by Margarite Hutchinson, London, 1881. Italian original, Rome, 1591. See below.
> Lopez left Portugal for the Congo in April, 1578. After a stay of some years he was appointed the King of Congo's ambassador to the Pope and to Philip II of Spain, to tell them of the Congo's need for missionaries, to show various specimens of minerals, and to offer the Portuguese the advantages of free trade. On his return he was shipwrecked on the American coast (of Venezuela) and spent a year there before reaching home. He got no help from either the Pope or King Philip. In the meantime one Philip Pigafetta had orders to collect all the information he could from Lopez concerning the Congo and other parts of Africa. The result was this work, which up to the middle of the nineteenth century was one of the chief sources for authentic information concerning central Africa. As was usual with travellers, Lopez spoke more of the things he had heard than of the things he had seen. In 1589 he returned to the Congo, and nothing more was heard of him.—From Maggs, No. 519. The "Epistle to the Reader" tells that this translation was undertaken at the request of R. Hakluyt. It was afterwards translated into Latin by Augustin Cassiadore Reinius and placed by the De Brys at the head of their *Collection of Voyages to the East*. It has been pointed out that this narrative was used by Defoe for his *Captain Singleton*.

1591 PIGAFETTA, FILIPPO. Relatione del reame di Congo et delle circonvicine contrade tratta dalli scritti & ragionamenti di Odoardo Lopez Portoghese. Con dissegni vari di Geografia, di plante, d'habiti, d'animali, & altro. Maps and plates. 4to. Rome.

1598 LINSCHOTEN, JAN HUYGENS VAN. For descriptions of the west coast of Africa see *His Discours of Voyages into ye Easte and West Indies,* under EAST INDIES.

1600 LEO AFRICANUS. A Geographical Historie of Africa, written in Arabicke and Italian by John Leo a More, born in Granada, and brought up in Barbarie. Wherein he hath at large described, not onely the Qualities, Situations, and true Distances of the Regions, Townes, Mountaines, Riuers, and other places throughout all the north and principal Partes of Africa; but also of the Descents and Families of their Kings, the Causes and Euents of their Warres, with their Manners, Customes, Religions, and ciuile Government, and many other memorable Matters. . . . Before which, out of the best ancient and moderne Writers, is prefixed a generall Description of Africa, and also a particular Treatise of all the maine Lands and Isles ondescribed by John Leo. And after the same is annexed a Relation of the great

Princes, and the manifold Religions in that Part of the World. Translated and collected by John Pory, lately of Goneuill and Caius College in Cambridge. Folding map of Africa. Fol. London.

Included in great part in *Purchas His Pilgrimes,* 1625. Edited for the Hakluyt Society, 1895. See below.

Leo Africanus, whose real name was Alhassan ibn Mohammed Alwazzan, was carried off to Rome by Venetian corsairs and converted to Christianity under Leo X, but escaping to Africa after twenty years at the Papal court, naturally reverted to Islam. For a long time his work was the chief authority on the geography of Africa, and the main source of information on the Sudan.—Sotheran. It was probably first written in Arabic. After having learned Italian he seems to have rewritten it in that language. Ramusio obtained the MS. (dated Rome, 1526) in 1550 and published it that year in his *Collection of Voyages and Travels.* The Latin edition of Florianus was published at Antwerp, 1556. John Pory, the translator, used the Latin version (with perhaps some reference to the French edition). See the Introduction to the edition published by the Hakluyt Society for further details. The map shows the Nile, the Congo, and the Zambesi all originating from the same source, a lake that is situated in what is now called the Belgian Congo. Pory's translation was well esteemed by his contemporaries; though it is said to be wanting in literal accuracy, it is more faithful than that of Florianus. His translation is set after an account of the part of Africa not described by Leo compiled from various authorities and of value as a fair view of the knowledge of that continent possessed by the English in the closing years of Queen Elizabeth's reign. Nearly the whole of Leo was retranslated as an Appendix to Francis Moore's *Travels into the Inland Parts of Africa.* This version pretends to have been made from the original Italian, though it may have utilized the Latin version frequently. See Moore under 1738 below.

1895 LEO AFRICANUS. The History and Description of Africa, And of the Notable Things Therein Contained. Written by Al-Hassan Ibn-Mohammed Al-Wezaz Al-Fasi, a Moor, baptized as Giovanni Leone, but better known as Leo Africanus. Done into English in the year 1600 by John Pory, and now edited, with an Introduction and Notes, by Dr. Robert Brown. 4 maps. 3 vols. Hak. Soc. ser. I, vols. 92, 93 and 94. London.

1603 TIMBERLAKE, HENRY. For his visits to Alexandria and the Grand Cairo see his *A True and Straunge Discourse of the Trauailes of two English Pilgrimes,* under NEAR EAST.

1608 WILKINS, GEORGE. Three Miseries of Barbary: Plague, Famine, and Civill Warre. With a Relation of the Death of Mahomet the late Emperour; and a briefe Report of the now present Wars betweene the three Brothers. 4to. London.

1609 BIDDULPH, WILLIAM. For his travels in Africa see *The Travels of certaine Englishmen,* under NEAR EAST.

C., RO. A True Historicall discourse of Muley Hamets rising to the three Kingdomes of Moruccos, Fes, and Sus. The disvnion of the three Kingdomes . . . The Religion and Policie of the More. . . . The aduentures of Sir Anthony Sherley . . . in those Countries. With other Nouelties. 4to. London.

The dedication is signed Ro. C. (possibly Robert Coverte?). For Sir Anthony Sherley see *A New and large Discourse of the Travels of* under 1601, CENTRAL ASIA.

1613 Late Newes out of Barbary. In a Letter written from a Merchant there, to a Gentleman not long since imployed into that Countrie from his Maiestie, containing some strange Particulars of this new Saintish Kings Proceedings: as they have been credibly related from such as were eye-witnesses. 4to. London. (22 pp.)

1615 SANDYS, GEORGE. For some descriptions of Egypt see his *Relation of a Journey begun An. Dom. 1610,* under NEAR EAST.

1623 JOBSON, RICHARD. The Golden Trade, or a Discovery of the River Gambia and the Golden Trade of the Aethiopians; also the Commerce with a Great Blacke Merchant, called Buckor Sano, and his report of the houses covered with gold, and other strange observations for the good of our own Countrey. 4to. London.

An abstract of the Captain's Journal, which was never published before, and an Abridgement of the Narrative are to be found in *Purchas His Pilgrimes.* The above work is given in abstract in Astley II, 174-189; a modern reprint, edited by C. G. Kingsley in 4to, London, 1904; and another, Penguin Press, London, 1932. There are two works extant relating to this voyage—one, a Journal containing an account of Jobson's Passage from England to the Gambia and up that river to Tenda, with descriptions of the places he visited, is the one cited above. The other is a narrative of his transactions during his stay on the Gambia, and includes an account of the inhabitants and the natural history of that country. This is the Abridgement included in Purchas. Jobson was appointed in 1620 to command an expedition to explore the river Gambia, in the interests of "the gentlemen adventurers for the countries of Guinea and Benin." Former attempts in 1618 and 1619 had failed, in consequence of the hostility of the Portuguese and the unhealthful climate. Sailing from England Oct. 25, 1620, he arrived at the mouth of the Gambia Nov. 17, and succeeded in ascending the river as high as Tenda, though he did not meet with the gold for which he was mainly looking. He gives interesting accounts of the natives, till then unvisited by Europeans, though they had already an overland trade with the Moors of the North coast.— D.N.B., quoted by Maggs, No. 519.

1634 HERBERT, SIR THOMAS. For an account of parts of Africa see his *Some Yeares Travaile into Africk and the Greater Asia,* under CENTRAL ASIA.

1637 The Arrivall and Intertainements of the Embassador, Alkaid Jaurar Ben Abdella, with his Associate, Mr. Robert Blake. From the High and Mighty Prince, Mulley Mahamed Sheque, Emperor of Morocco, King of Fesse and Suss. With the Ambassadors good and applauded com-

mendations of his royall and noble entertainments in the Court and
the City. Also a Description of some Rites, Customes, and Lawes of
those Affrican Nations . . . 4to. London.

> This concerns the release also of 302 British subjects from Sallee, the
> stronghold of the Moorish pirates and sea-rovers.—Maggs, No. 580.

1640 HAMMOND, W. A Paradox, proving that the Inhabitants of the Isle
called Madagascar or Saint Laurence (in Temporall Things) are
the Happiest People in the World . . . with most Probable Arguments
of a Hopeful and Fit Plantation of a Colony there in respect of the
fruitfulnesse of the Soyle, the benignity of the ayre, and the Relieving
of our English Ships, both to and from the East Indies. London.

> For a similar argument see Boothby under 1646 below.

KNIGHT, FRANCIS. A Relation of seaven Years Slaverie under the
Turkes of Argeire, whereunto is added, a Second Booke containing a
Description of Argeire, its originall, . . . Frontispiece and plates. Lon-
don.

> Reprinted in Osborne II, 466-489. See below.
> Knight arrived in Algiers, Jan. 16, 1631. He had to serve in the Algerine
> galleys and relates many interesting passages at sea with the ships of the Euro-
> peans. He effected his escape after the battle of Vollonia where the Venetians
> defeated the Turkish fleet.

> 1745 KNIGHT, FRANCIS. A Relation of Seven Years' Slavery under the
> Turks of Algier, Suffered by an English Captive Merchant. Wherein
> is also contained All memorable Passages, Fights, and Accidents, which
> happened in that City, and at Sea with their Ships and Gallies during
> that Time. Together with a Description of the Sufferings of the mis-
> erable Captives under that merciless Tyranny. Whereunto is added, A
> Second Book, containing a Description of Algier, with its Original,
> Manner of Government, Increase, and present flourishing Estate. In
> Osborne II, 466-489. London. (Paging is wrong in some copies.)

1642 ROBINS, J. Relief to the English Captives in Algiers. 4to. London.

1646 BOOTHBY, RICHARD. A Briefe Discovery or Description of the
most Famous Island of Madagascar or St. Lavrence in Asia neare
unto East-India. With Relations of the Healthfulnesse, Pleasure and
Wealth of that Country . . . a very Earthly Paradise: a most fitting
and desirable place to settle an English Colony and Plantation there,
rather than in any other part of the knowne world, . . . it being the
fittest place for a Magazine or Storehouse of Trade between Europe
and Asia, farre exceeding all other Plantations in America or elsewhere. . . . London.

> Reprinted in Osborne II, 625-663, London. See Hammond, 1640, above.
> The author suggests the plantation of an English colony in Madagascar with

Prince Rupert as Viceroy. The work also treats of the cruelty of the Dutch (a frequent complaint) against some English traders at Amboyna in the Dutch East Indies (see under 1624, EAST INDIES); the loss of Ormus in Persia by the Portuguese, and the importance of that port; various matters of Indian trade; Invention, Guns, and Printing in China, etc.—Robinson, No. 19. The author was an English merchant interested in the East India trade, who had spent some months on the island and was moved to writing this work by the fact that some Englishmen had gone to Madagascar. He comments in his preface to the reader on the fact that some had objected to his placing the island in Asia instead of Africa, but he remained "unresolved, some mariners accounting it in Asia." He admits into his text "Remarks by Francis Lloyd," an East India merchant.

GREAVES, JOHN   Pyramidographia, or, a Description of the Pyramids in Egypt. Folding plate. 8vo. London.

> Reprinted in Churchill II, 625-674.
> Greaves was professor of astronomy at Oxford. He went to Egypt in 1637. Here he spent some time visiting and measuring the objects he describes. He published, with a Latin translation, the tables of latitude and longitude of the Red Sea by the Arabian geographer Abu 'lfeda, in 1650 (see Abu 'lfeda under 1745-47, NEAR EAST).

1650   HUNT, ROBERT (Lieut.-Col.)   The Island of Assada, near Madagascar Impartially defined; being a Succinct, yet Plenary Description of the Scituation, Fertility, and People therein Inhabiting. Cleerly demonstrating to the Adventurer or Planter the right way for disposing his Adventure to his most commodious advantage; Advising People of all degrees, from the highest to the lowest, how suddenly to raise their Estate and Fortunes. 4to. London. (8 pp.)

> A curious and scarce little work. Hunt refers to his having been Governor of Providence Island (i.e., New Providence Island in the Bahamas which had been settled in 1629, although Spain retook it in 1641), since when he had been waiting for an opportunity of making a similar settlement elsewhere, for the glory of God and his native country. He had decided on the Island of Assada, near Madagascar, which he compared with Barbadoes as to situation, but considers the cost of planting to be only about a tenth of what it would be at the latter. Assada was situated near the northern extremity of Madagascar, about nine miles off the western coast. He considered it a much more favorable position than the settlement which had previously been attempted at St. Augustin's Bay in the southwest of the Island, and a good point of call for English shipping between England and India.—Maggs, No. 580.

1663   THORNHILL, ——.   Account of Upper and Lower Egypt. London.

> So cited by Pinkerton XVII.

1664   A Brief Relation of the Present State of Tangier, And of the Advantages which . . . the Earle of Tiveot Has Obteyned against Gayland. . . . 4to. London. (8 pp.)

1665   The Golden Coast; or, A Description of Guinney. 1. In its Air and Situation. 2. In the Commodities imported thither, and exported thence. 3. In their Way of Traffick, their Laws and Customes, . . . In Four

Rich Voyages to that Coast, with a Relation of such Persons as got Wonderful Estates by their Trade thither. 4to. London.

A very scarce and interesting volume, mentioning America, Peru and Brazil; also referring to Sir Thomas More's *Utopia,* and Sir Francis Bacon's *New Atlantis.*—Maggs, No. 572.

1666   D'ARANDA, EMANUEL. The History of Algiers, and its Slavery, with many remarkable Particularities of Africk. Written by the Sieur Emanuel D'Aranda, Sometime a Slave there. English'd by John Davies of Kidwelly. 8vo. London.

A Latin version, the Hague, 1657. See below.

1657   D'ARANDA, EMANUELIS. Historia Captivitatis Algeriensis, Hispanice conscripta. 12mo. The Hague.

1669   TAFILETTA. A Short and Strange Relation Of some part of the Life of Tafiletta, the Great Conqueror and Emperor of Barbary. By one that hath lately been in His Majesties Service in that Country. Engraved portrait. 4to. London.

A Short Relation of the River Nile, of its Source and Current, of its overflowing the Campagnia of Egypt, and of other Curiosities (Reason why the Abyssine Emperour is called Prester John, etc.). Written by an Eye-Witnesse, who lived many years in the Chief Kingdoms of the Abyssine Empire. Translated out of a Portuguese Manuscript, at the desire of the Royal Society (by Sir Peter Wyche). 12mo. London.

Other editions: 12mo, London, 1673; with a new preface, 8vo, London, 1791; London, 1798. A French version made from the English, Paris (?), 1674. A Latin version, London, 1669, cited by Pinkerton XVII. See below.
James Bruce was greatly indebted to this work evidently.—Lowndes. According to Churchill, *Introduction,* this is only a translation of an account by a Portuguese Jesuit who lived for some years in Ethiopia, being the same as that which is given by F. Alvarez, and others of the Society of Jesus, who lived there, and no doubt is very authentic as coming from an eye-witness, who was a person of probity.

1669   WINNE, ——. Brevis Relatio de Origine, Natura, Cursu et Incremento Nili. Per Winne. London.

So cited by Pinkerton XVII, Pinkerton's general inaccuracy leads one to suspect that WINNE should be WYCHE, and that this work may be a Latin version written at the same time or perhaps first.

1674   (In French.) Relation de la rivière Nil de sa source; . . . traduit de l'original Anglois. In *Recueil de divers voyages faits en Afrique et en l'Amérique.* 4to. Paris (?).

1670   BARATTI, GIACOMO. The Late Travels of S. Giacomo Baratti, an Italian Gentleman, into the remote Countries of the Abissins, or of Ethiopia Interior. Wherein you shall find an exact account of the

Laws, Government, Religion, Discipline, Customs, . . . of the Christian people that do Inhabit there. . . . Translated by G. D. 12mo. London.

In the *Enciclopedia Italiana* (1930) there is cited an English translation of the date 1650. No Italian original is given.

DAPPER, OLFERT. Africa, being an Accurate Description of the Regions of Egypt, Barbary, Lybia and Billedulgoria, etc. London.

This draws much on Leo Africanus. It is valuable historically for its plans of Tangier which was then occupied by the English. See Hak. Soc. ser. I, vol. 92. A German version, whether original or translation not indicated by the title, appeared at Amsterdam, 1670. See also Ogilby this date below.

1670 DAPPER, OLFERT. Beschreibung von Africa und denen dazu gehörigen Königreich und Landschaften als Egypten, etc. Fol. Amsterdam.

A Letter from a Gentleman of the Lord Ambassador Howard's Retinue to his Friend in London dated at Fez, Nov. 1, 1669, wherein he gives a full Relation of the most Remarkable Passages in their Voyage thither, and of the present State of the Countries under the Power of Taffaletta, Emperor of Morocco, with brief Account of the Merchandizing Commodities of Africa, and the Manners and Customs of the People there. 4to. London.

This letter is signed S. L.—Robinson, No. 19.

1670 OGILBY, JOHN. Africa: being an Accurate Description of the Regions of Aegypt, Barbary, Lybia and Billedulgerid, the Land of the Negroes, Guinee, Aethiopia, and the Abyssines, with all the adjacent Islands, either in the Mediterranean, Atlantick, Southern or Oriental Sea, belonging thereunto, with the several denominations of their Coasts, Harbours, Creeks, Rivers, Lakes, Cities, Towns, Castles and Villages, their Customs, Modes and Manners, Languages, Religions, and inexhaustible Treasure; with their Governments and Policy, Variety of Trade and Barter, and also of their wonderful Plants, Beasts, Birds and Serpents, collected and translated from most authentick authors, with notes and maps. Fol. London.

Probably this was in the main translated from Dapper (cited above this date). Ogilby, the author of many geographical works, was "Cosmographer" to King Charles II. He also set up a printing establishment and published many works. He became the butt of ridicule on the part of Dryden and Pope, though the latter found him useful. He is said to have lost books to the value of £3,000 in the London Fire. In the preface to the above work he gives an entertaining account of his own writings.

ROBERTS, A. For his description of Algiers see the following work.

SMITH, T.   The Adventures of (Mr. T. S.), an English Merchant, taken Prisoner by the Turks of Argiers, and carried into the Inland Countries of Africa, with a Description of the Kingdom of Argiers, of all the Towns and Places of Note thereabouts; whereunto is added, a Relation of the Chief Commodities of the Countrey, and of the Actions and Manners of the People, written first by the Author, and fitted for the Publick View by A. Roberts; whereunto is annex'd an Observation of the Tide, and how to turn a Ship out of the Straights Mouth, the Wind being Westerly, by Richard Norris.   12mo.   London.

> Churchill, *Introduction,* adds more detail to the title: "Containing a short account of Argier in the year 1648 . . . and more particularly of the city Tremizen, where the author resided three years, going abroad with several parties which his master commanded, and relates some love intrigues he had with Moorish women, as also very strange metamorphoses of men and other creatures turned into stone."

VILLAULT, SIEUR DE BELLEFOND.   A Relation of the Coasts of Africk Called Guinee; with A Description of the Countreys, Manners and Customs of the Inhabitants. . . . Being Collected in a Voyage By the Sieur Villault . . . in the years 1666, and 1667. . . . 2nd edit.   12mo. London.

> Translated from the French original which was published in the preceding year. Another edition of the above, London, 1709.

1671   ADDISON, LANCELOT.   West Barbary, or a Short Narrative of the Revolutions of the Kingdoms of Fez and Morocco. With an account of the present Customs, Sacred, Civil and Domestick.   8vo.   London.

> Reprinted in Pinkerton XV, 403-441.
> The author was the father of Joseph Addison, the essayist. He was chaplain to his Majesty in Ordinary at Tangier in 1662. See also Addison under 1685.

1671   FREJUS, ROLAND.   The Relation of a Voyage made into Mauritania, in Africk . . . in the Year 1666. To Muley Arxid, King of Tafiletta, etc. For the Establishment of a Commerce in all the Kingdom of Fez. . . . Englished out of French.   8vo.   London.

> French original, Paris, 1670. See below.
> Bound up in the same volume is: "A Letter, in answer to divers Curious Questions Concerning the Religion, Manners, and Customs, of the Countrys Of Muley Arxid . . . Also their Trading to Tombotum for Gold. . . . by Mons. A**** who lived 25 years in . . . Morocco. Englished out of French. London, 1671.

> 1670   FREJUS, ROLAND.   Histoire de Muley Arxid, Roy de Tafilete, Fez, Maroc, et Tarudent. Avec la Relation d'un Voyage fait en 1666 vers ce Prince, pour l'éstablissement du Commerce en ces Estats. Et une Lettre en reponse de diverses Questions curieuses faites sur la Religion, Moeurs, et Coûtumes de son Païs; avec diverses particularitez remarquables. . . . Ecrite par Monsieur ***** 2 vols. 12mo. Paris.

1672 MURTADI IBN GAPHIPHUS. The Egyptian History treating of the Pyramids, the Inundation of the Nile, and other Prodigies of Egypt, according to the Opinions and Traditions of the Arabians. Written originally in the Arabian tongue by Murtadi the son of Gaphiphus, rendered into French by Monsieur Vattier, Arabic Professor to the King of France, and thence faithfully done into English by J. Davies of Kidwelly. 8vo. London.

> French original, Paris, 1666. See below.
> This work treats of the history, legends, antiquities, places, monuments, etc., of Egypt.

> 1666 MURTADI IBN GAPHIPHUS. L'Egypte de Murtadi de Gaphiphie, où il est traité des Pyramides, du débordement du Nil, et des autres meruilles de cette prouince, selon les opinions et traditions des Arabes, traduite de l'Arabique par Pierre Vattier, sur un manuscrit arabe tiré de la bibliothèque de feu Mgr. le Cardinal Mazarin. 12mo. Paris.

A True Relation of the Murders of Negroes or Moors, committed on three Englishmen in Old Calabar in Guinny. 4to. London.

1675 ADDISON, LANCELOT. The Present State of the Jews, more particularly relating to those in Barbary; wherein is contain'd an exact account of their Customs, secular Religion; to which is annexed, A summary Discourse of the 'Misna,' 'Talmud,' and 'Genmara.' 8vo. London.

> Reprinted 12mo, London, 1675; 3rd edit., 12mo, London, 1682.

OKELEY, WILLIAM. Eben-ezer: or, a small Monument of Great Mercy, appearing in the Miraculous Deliverance of William Okeley, William Adams, John Anthony, John Jephs, John ——, Carpenter, from the Miserable Slavery of Algiers, with the wonderful Means of their Escape in a Boat of Canvas; the great Distress, and utmost Extremeties which they endured at Sea for Six Days and Nights; their safe Arrival at Mayork: With several Matters of Remarque during their long Captivity, and the following Providences of God which brought them safe to England. By me William Okeley. Frontispiece in compartments, showing various modes of punishment and execution. 16mo. London.

> This is one of the earliest accounts of victims of the Algiers pirates, then unusually active. There are commendatory verses at the beginning and the end.— Sotheran.

1676 ALCAFARADO, FRANCISCO. An Historical Relation of the First Discovery of the Isle of Madera. Translated out of French. 4to. London.

> Another edition, London, 1680.
> This is a discovery before it was peopled, and it continued lost again for several years, and has little of certainty.—Churchill, *Introduction*. This is a little known work, which is not in Lowndes or Rich.

The Present State of Tangier. In a Letter to his Grace the Lord Chancellor of Ireland, and one of the Lords Justices there. To which is added, The Present State of Algiers. 12mo. London.

Another edition, London, 1680.

1678 BLOME, RICHARD. For an account of Algiers see his *Description of the Island of Jamaica,* 2nd edition of the 1672 issue, under WEST INDIES.

1678 VANSLEB, JOHN MICHAEL. The Present State of Egypt; or, a New Relation of a Voyage into that Kingdom in 1672-3. Wherein you have an exact and true Account of many Rare and Wonderful Particulars of that Ancient Kingdom. Englished by M. D. 12mo. London.

French original, Paris, 1677. See below.
This relates to his second voyage. The first one was performed in 1663, and was published in Italian at Paris, 1671. The real name of the author was Wansleben. This work, according to *Allg. Deutsche Biographie,* contains not only an excellent description of Egypt, its inhabitants and most important animals and plants, all based on original observations, but also valuable information concerning its Christian antiquities.—Sotheran.

1677 VANSLEB-EN, JOHANN MICHAEL. Nouvelle relation en forme de Journal, d'un (Second) Voyage fait en Egypte, en 1672 et 1673. 12mo. Paris.

1680 A Discourse Touching Tanger: In a Letter to a Person of Quality. To which is added, The Interest of Tanger: By another Hand. 4to. London.

An Exact Journal of the Siege of Tangier, from the first sitting down of the Moors before it on March 25, 1680, to the late Truce, May 19, following: in three Letters written by three Eye Witnesses of the whole Transaction. Fol. London.

A Letter from the King of Morocco to His Majesty the King of England Charles I. For the reducing of the Sally, Algiers, etc. The first of which was taken, by the assistance of the English Forces, with an account of the execution of the Pyrats and the Number of Christian Captives sent to His Majesty. London.

The Moors baffled: being a discourse concerning Tangier, especially when it was under the Earl of Teviot; by which you may find what methods and Government is fittest to secure that place against the Moors. Written by a learned person long resident in that place. London.

1682 GLANIUS, ——. For an account of Madagascar see his *A New Voyage to the East Indies,* under EAST INDIES.

LUDOLPHUS, JOB. A New History of Ethiopia; being a Full and Accurate Description of the Kingdom of Abessinia, Vulgarly though Erroneously called the Empire of Prester John. Made English by J. P. Gent. In Four Books. Many large engraved plates of animals, plants, etc. Fol. London.

> 2nd edit., fol., London, 1684, to which is added a map of the country. A version in Latin, Frankfort on the Main, 1681. See below.
> Still a valuable work, and of especial interest for its account of Ethiopic literature. The English translation Lowndes characterizes as "a work full of recondite and important information on the origin of the Abyssinians, the climate, soil, productions, etc."—Quoted by Sotheran.

> 1681 LUDOLFUS, HIOB. Historia Aethiopica, sive brevis et succincta Descriptio Regni Habessinorum, quod vulgo male Presbyteri Johannis vocatur; cum Indicibus. Large engraved map, and copperplates, including the fat-tailed sheep. Fol. Francofurti ad Maenum.

1685 ADDISON, LANCELOT. A Discourse of Tangier under the Government of the Earl of Teviot; written by Dr. Addison, Dean of Lichfield; who was Minister of the English at Tangier till the Death of the said Earl. 2nd edit. 4to. London.

> See under 1680 above.

B., R. (BURTON, ROBERT?). For an account of St. Helena see his *A View of the English Acquisitions in Guiania and the East-Indies,* under EAST INDIES.

1690 WILKINSON, WILLIAM. Systema Africanum: or, A Treatise, Discovering the Intrigues and Arbitrary Proceedings of the Guiney Company. And also how prejudicial they are to the American Planters. Together with a True Account of their Fortifications. 4to. London.

1691 BARONET, E. S. The History of the Jacobites of Aegypt, Lybia, and Nubia; their Origins, Religion, Ceremonies, Laws and Customs; to which is added, Some Account of the Jacobites in England. 8vo. London.

1693 BELON DU MANS, PIERRE. For his travels in Egypt see his *Travels in Greece, Asia Minor,* etc., under NEAR EAST.

BROOKS, FRANCIS. Barbarian Cruelty, being a true History of the distressed Condition of the Christian Captives under the Tyranny of Muly Ishmael, Emperor of Morocco. 12mo. London.

> In Dutch, Leyden, 1708. Pinkerton XVII gives a French version, Utrecht, 1637, a date that is obviously wrong. See below.

> 1637 (?) (In French.) Navigations faites en Barbarie, par F. Brooke. Traduites de l'Anglais. Utrecht.

> 1708 (In Dutch.) Ongelukkige Scheeps-togt van Francoys Brooks, na Barbaryen, 1681. Map and plates. 12mo. Leyden.

LOUBERE, SIMON DE LA. For an account of the Cape of Good Hope see his *A New Historical Relation of the Kingdom of Siam,* under FAR EAST.

1695 SAINT OLON, FRANCOIS PIDOU DE. The Present State of the Empire of Morocco; wherein the Scituation of the Country; the Manners, Customs, Government, and Religion of that People; are fully described. To which is added, Audiences given by the Emperor; with the Answers. Done into English; and adorned with Sculptures. 8vo. London.

> The author was the French King's Ambassador at the Court of Morocco.

1696 DUQUESNE, ——. For a description of the Canary Islands, Cape Verde, Senegal, and Gambia, see his *A New Voyage to the East Indies,* under EAST INDIES.

GEDDES, M. Church History of Ethiopia. London.

> So cited by Pinkerton XVII. This may be Michael Geddes, a divine who was chaplain to the English Factory at Lisbon, 1678-1688, and translator of Spanish and Portuguese works. See D.N.B.

LE MAIRE, JACQUES JOSEPH. A Voyage of the Sieur Le Maire to the Canary Islands, Cape-Verd, Senegal and Gamby, under Monsieur Dancourt, Director-General of the Royal Affrican Company. Printed at Paris this Present Year 1695. And now faithfully done into English. 12mo. London.

> Reprinted in Osborne II, 597-623; an abstract in Astley II, 248-254. French original, Paris, 1695. See below.
> The author was a physician. He embarked at Brest, April 9, 1682. He describes in some detail the inhabitants, manners, customs, and places he visited.

> 1695 LE MAIRE, JACQUES JOSEPH. Les Voyages du Sieur Le Maire aux Isles Canaries, Cap-Verd, Sénégal, et Gambie, sous Monsieur Dancourt, Directeur Général de la Compagnie Roiale d'Affrique. Map and 5 plates. 12mo. Paris.

OVINGTON, JOHN. For a description of St. Helena, Johanna, Cape of Good Hope see his *A Voyage to Suratt,* under EAST INDIES.

1698 DELLON, CHARLES. For a description of Madagascar see his *A Voyage to the East Indies,* under EAST INDIES.

FROGER, FRANCOIS. A Relation of a Voyage made in the Years 1695, 1696, 1697, on the Coasts of Africa, by a Squadron of French Men of War, under the Command of M. de Gennes. 8vo. London.

> Reprinted in Osborne II, 585-596. French original, Paris, 1698. See below. See also under SOUTH AMERICA.
> Froger was a volunteer engineer on board the ship *English Falcon.* He was a traveller obsessed by the desire to be useful to his country and to mankind by observing and recording information on all subjects connected with other lands.

> 1698 FROGER, FRANCOIS. Relation du'n voyage fait en 1695, 1696, et 1697, aux côtes d'Afrique, détroit de Magellan, . . . par en escadre des vaisseaux du roi, sous le commandement de M. de Gennes. 12mo. Paris.

MONTAUBAN, SIEUR DE. For an account of his adventures on the coast of Guinea see La Salle's *An Account of De La Salle's last Expedition,* etc., under NORTH AMERICA.

1699 DAMPIER, WILLIAM. For descriptions of parts of Africa visited see his *A Continuation of a Voyage to New Holland,* under AUSTRALIA.

1700 FRYKE, CHRISTOPHER. For a description of the Cape of Good Hope and the Island of Mauritius see his *Relation of Two Several Voyages to the East Indies,* under EAST INDIES.

1701 M., B. A Letter from a Gentleman (B. M.) to the Right Reverend Father in God, Henry, Lord Bishop of London. 4to. London. (9 pp.)

> This concerns English captives in Morocco.—Bookseller's Note.

VERYARD, ELLIS (M. D.). For travels in Egypt see his *Account of divers choice Remarks, as well Geographical, as Historical,* under NEAR EAST.

1704 PITTS, JOSEPH. A faithful Account of the Religion and Manners of the Mahometans, in which is a particular Relation of their Pilgrimage to Mecca, the place of Mahomet's birth; and a Description of Medina and of his tomb there: as likewise of Algiers and of the Country Ad-

jacent, and of Alexandria, Grand Cairo, etc. With an account of the
Author's being taken captive; the Turk's cruelty to him; and of his
Escape. In which are many things never published by any Historian
before. 8vo. Oxford.

> 3rd edit., 12mo, London, 1731.
> In 1676 Pitts sailed as apprentice on a merchantman bound for the West
> Indies, Newfoundland, Bolboa, the Canaries, and so home. On her return voyage
> the vessel was captured off the Spanish coast by an Algerian pirate, and Pitts was
> sold into slavery. The unfortunate man was tortured until he repeated the re-
> quired formula of submission to Mahomet, and in attendance on his master he
> made the pilgrimage to Mecca. He eventually escaped and reached his home in
> Exeter in 1694. His work (of which Gibbon seems to have been ignorant) is the
> first authentic record by an Englishman of the pilgrimage to Mecca. It gives a
> brief but sensible and consistent account of what the writer saw.—D.N.B., quoted
> by Robinson, No. 35.

1705 BOSMAN, WILLIAM. A New and Accurate Description of the Coast
of Guinea, divided into the Gold, the Slave, and the Ivory Coasts, containing a Geographical, Political and Natural History of the Kingdoms
and Countries . . . and the Just Measures for improving the several
Branches of the Guinea Trade, written originally in Dutch by William
Bosman . . . and now faithfully done into English. Folding map and
7 plates. 8vo. London.

> 2nd edit., 8vo, London, 1721; reprinted in Pinkerton XVI, 337-547. A modern
> edition, London, 1907. Dutch original, Utrecht, 1704. See below.
> Bosman was the chief factor for the Dutch at the Castle of St. George
> d'Elmina. He gives an omnibus type of description.

> 1704 BOSMAN, WILLIAM. Nauwkeurige beschrijving van de Guinese Goud-
> Tand- en Slavekust, nevens alle desselfs landen, Koningryken, en gemene
> besten; van de zeeden der inwoonders, hun godsdienst, . . . mitsg. de
> gesteldheid der lands, veld- en boomgewassen, dieren, . . . 2 tom. 1 vol.
> 29 plates. 4to. Utrecht.

1706 KEELING, WILLIAM. Derde Reys, gedaan voor de Engelsch Maat-
schappy na Oost-Indien, 1607-1610. Plates. 12mo. Leyden.

> Whether this is a translation or an original work is not known to the editor.
> This volume also includes David Middleton's East India voyage of 1607.
> Keeling was naval commander and the East India Company's agent; he made
> several voyages to India in the service of his Company.

1708 LEGUAT, FRANCOIS. For an account of the Island of Mauritius,
Cape of Good Hope, and the Island of St. Helena see his *A New
Voyage to the East Indies,* under EAST INDIES.

1709 PONCET, CH. JACQUES. A Voyage to Aethiopia, made in the Years
1698-1700, describing particularly that famous Empire, as also the
Kingdoms of Dongola, Sennar, part of Egypt, . . . with the Natural
History of those Parts. 12mo. London.

Reprinted in Pinkerton XV, 61-107, taken from Lockman's *Travels of the Jesuits,* London, 1743. See Lockman under date of 1743, COLLECTIONS.

Poncet was a French physician who had become favorably known for having cured an Abyssinian officer at Cairo of the distemper. He was prevailed upon to make a like attempt on the Emperor himself. Accompanied by a Jesuit missionary in the disguise of a servant, for Jesuits were not welcome in Abyssinia at this time, he followed in general the route of the Nile valley and succeeded in reaching his destination. On the way the missionary baptised a child under the pretence of giving it medicine. "The child was so fortunate as to die, after having been received into Christ's kingdom." Poncet is said to have been more successful with the Emperor. His descriptions of the route followed are believed to be faithful, but doubt has been cast on his account of his stay in Abyssinia.

1709　A View of the State of the Trade to Africa; Wherein is laid down the present Condition of the English Settlement there; their Use, Value, Strength, and to whom the Property belongs, demonstrated from Matter of Fact, and confirmed by divers Extracts from a Report made on this Subject, laid before the Queen and Council in Feb., 1707/8: in a Letter to a New Subscriber. London.

1711　GAUCHE, FRANCIS. A Voyage to Madagascar. In Stevens (see under COLLECTIONS).

MOUETTE, SIEUR. The Travels of Sieur Mouette in Fez and Morocco. In Stevens (see under COLLECTIONS).

A Dutch version, probably not the original, Leyden, 1706. See below.

1706　MOUETTE, ——. (Sieur). De Scheeps-togt van den Heere Mouette uit Vrankryk na Amerika ondernoomen; aan de Kust van Barbaryen ongelukkig voleind. Verhalende niet allen desselfs Elf-jarige Slaavernye en wedervaren in de Koninkryken van Fez en Marocco, zederd het Zaar 1670. Map and 4 folding plates. 12mo. Leyden.

The Travels of the Jesuits in Ethiopia. In Stevens (see under COLLECTIONS).

These are "digested by Balthazar Tellez." They contain an account of the Kingdom and provinces of the Empire of Abyssinia, the manners and customs of the people, etc.

1713　OCKLEY, SIMON. Account of South West Barbary: What is most Remarkable in the Territories of the King of Fez and Morocco. Written by a Person who had been a Slave there a considerable Time; and Published from his Authentick Manuscript. Folding map. 8vo. London.

Another edit., 8vo, London, 1713. In French, Paris, 1726. See below.

Ockley was professor of Arabic at Cambridge. He published some translations from the Arabic and wrote a *History of the Saracens.* See under 1708-1718, NEAR EAST. His books were the main source of the average notion of Mohammedan history for generations.—Robinson, No. 20.

1726   (In French.) Relation des Etats de Fez et de Moroc écrite par un An-
        glois . . . publiée par M. Simon Ockley, Professeur en Langue Arabe,
        dans l'Université de Cambridge. 12mo. Paris.

    Noticed in the *Journal des Scavans*, 1727, I, 86.

1718   BEECKMAN, DANIEL. For an account of the Cape of Good Hope
        see his *Voyage to and from the Island of Borneo*, under EAST IN-
        DIES.

1725   HOUSTON, ——. Voyage to Guinea. London.

    So cited by Pinkerton XVII.

    WINDUS, JOHN. A Journey to Mequinez: the Residence of the Pres-
    ent Emperor of Morocco on the Occasion of Stewart's Embassy for
    the Redemption of British Captives in 1721. 6 large folding plates.
    8vo. London.

        Reprinted 12mo, Dublin, 1725; in Pinkerton XV, 442-498.
        No work on Morocco had hitherto appeared in English, with the exception
    of the meagre *West Barbary* (1671) of L. Addison. The description of the man-
    ners of the people renders the book "a curiosity," as it was pronounced by Bos-
    well.—D.N.B.

1726   ROBERTS, GEORGE (Captain). The Four Years' Voyages of Cap-
        tain George Roberts; being a Series of Uncommon Events which be-
        fell him in a Voyage to the Islands of the Canaries, Cape de Verde,
        and Barbadoes, from whence he was bound to the Coast of Guiney.
        4 plates and a draught of all the Cape de Verde Islands. 8vo. Lon-
        don.

        The author declares that this was written by himself, and that his relation is
    true in every respect, except what he derives from others, which he has no reason
    to doubt, yet mentions them with more caution. The first 368 pages are taken
    up chiefly with his adventures on his voyage, the remaining 68 comprise his de-
    scription of the Cape de Verde Islands. He met with a series of accidents in
    consequence of his having fallen into the hands of pirates. The work may be
    one of Defoe's as it is very much in the Defoe vein, both with respect to protes-
    tation and with respect to detail.

1727   HAMILTON, ALEXANDER. For remarks on the maritime countries
        and islands between the Cape of Good Hope and Guarda Fuy see his
        A New Account of the East Indies, under EAST INDIES.

        An abstract of this in Astley III, 387-392. This part of the coast was less
    frequented and consequently less known than the west coast.

1729   BRAITHWAITE, JOHN (Captain). The History of the Revolution in
        the Empire of Morocco, upon the death of the late Emperor Muley

Ishmael, being the most exact Journal of what happen'd in those Parts in the last and part of the present Year, . . . Map. 8vo. London.

In French, Amsterdam, 1731. See below.
This contains valuable information on the physical and moral state of the people, written by one who was an eye witness of the events he describes.— Lowndes. The author, who accompanied John Russell, consul general of England, witnessed with his own eyes the remarkable events that took place during the years 1727 and 1728 in Morocco.

1731 (In French.) Historie des révolutions de l'Empire de Maroc depuis la mort du dernier Empereur Mulet Ismael. Traduit du journal anglois du Capitaine Braithwaite. 12mo. Amsterdam.

DRURY, ROBERT. Madagascar: or, Robert Drury's Journal, during Fifteen Years Captivity on that Island. Containing 1. His Voyage. 2. An Account of the Shipwreck of the *Degrave* on the Island of Madagascar; the Murder of Captain Younge and his Ship's Company, except Admiral Bembo's Son, and some few others, who escap'd the Hands of the barbarous Natives. 3. His being taken into Captivity, hard Usage, Marriage, and Variety of Fortune. . . . 6. His Redemption from thence by Capt. Mackett, Commander of the *Prince of Wales*. Large engraved map of Madagascar and several engraved plates. 8vo. London.

Another edit. 2 vols., 8vo, London, 1743. Reprinted, London, 1890. See below.
A most interesting and well written account of the author's shipwreck and subsequent adventures in Madagascar, in 1701. . . . Benbow had written some account of that island, the manuscript of which was accidentally burnt in 1714. It had been seen by several, however, and the hazy recollections of it, together with Drury's story, who had just returned to England, were worked up, not improbably by Daniel Defoe, and published under Drury's name. After his return, Drury spent the remainder of his life as a porter in a London warehouse.—Maggs, No. 508.

1890 DRURY, ROBERT. Madagascar, or Robert Drury's Journal during fifteen Years' Captivity on that Island, and further description of Madagascar by the Abbé Alexis Rochon. Edited with notes and introduction by Capt. Pasfield Oliver. Adventure Series, London.

The introduction gives a critical account of the relation of this work to its editor, who is supposed to be Defoe.

1729-1730 MORGAN, JOHN. A Complete History of Algiers. To which is prefixed, an Epitome of the General History of Barbary, from the Earliest Times. Interspersed with many curious passages and Remarks, not touched on by any Writer whatever. 2 vols. 4to. London.

Another edition, with slightly different wording of the title, 8vo, London, 1750. See below and also Morgan under 1736 below.
This work is much indebted to Leo Africanus. See Introd. Hak. Soc. ser. I, vol. 92.

1750 MORGAN, JOHN. A Compleat History of the Piratical States of Barbary—viz., Algiers, Tunis, Tripoli and Morocco, containing the Origin, Revolutions and Present State of these Kingdoms, their Forces, Revenues, Policy and Commerce, Plan of Algiers and a map of Barbary, by a Gentleman. 8vo. London.

1731 KOLBEN, PETER. The present State of the Cape of Good Hope: or, a Particular Account of the Several Nations of the Hottentots, written originally in High German by P. Kolben, done into English from the original by M. Medley. 18 engraved plates. 8vo. London.

The complete English edition was issued in 2 vols., London, the same year; the 2nd edit., 2 vols., London, 1738. See below. The original German edition, Nuremberg, 1719. Afterwards a second volume, containing the natural history of the Cape, with a map of the country possessed there by the Dutch was published by Kolben.

The author was secretary to Baron Van Krosick, privy councellor to Frederick, King of Prussia. That Lord sent Kolben to the Cape to make observations on the stars for the advancement of astronomy. Armed with the proper letters to and from the Dutch East India Company, and provided with instruments he made the trip to the settlement, where he stayed eight years. His stay was not a happy one, however, as he had to undergo many disappointments and vexations both on the voyage and during his residence at the Cape. According to Lowndes, his reputation for accuracy which he enjoyed for a while was destroyed by subsequent travellers. He started in 1704-5 and returned in 1713.

1738 KOLBEN, PETER. The Present State of the Cape of Good Hope; containing a particular account of the several Nations of the Hottentots; their Religion, Government, Laws, Customs, Ceremonies and Opinions; their Art of War, Professions, Language, Genius, . . . Together with a short Account of the Dutch Settlement at the Cape. . . . Done into English by Mr. Medley. 2 vols. 8vo. London.

1732 ANGELO, MICHAEL (the R. R. F. F. of Gattina), and DENIS DE CARPI (of Viacenza). A Curious and Exact Account of a Voyage to Congo in the Years 1666, and 1667. In Churchill I, 553-589.

Abstract in Astley III, 143-166; in Pinkerton XVI, 148-193. This was first published in Italian, then translated into French at Lyons, 1680, and turned into English in the first edition of Churchill, 1704.

The authors were Apostolic Missioners to the Congo, of the order of Capuchins. To qualify them for their arduous undertaking they were invested with some extraordinary powers, such as giving plenary indulgence, delivering a soul out of purgatory, wearing secular clothes in case of necessity, and of reading prohibited books, except Macchiavelli. The first part of the account was made out of the letters of Angelo, who died in the Congo region, and the rest composed by Denis who returned home. The account tells of Brazil as well.

BARBOT, JOHN. A Description of the Coasts of North and South Guinea. Divided into several Parts. A Description of the Coasts of Nigritia vulgarly called North Guinea, 1-95. A Description of the Coasts of South Guinea, or Guinea properly so called: Commencing at Sierra Leone river ending at Rio de Fernan Vaz, to the Southward of Cape Lope Gonzalez. With an Account of the several islands in the gulph of Guinea, by the English commonly called the Bight, 96-470. A Sup-

plement to the Description of the Coasts of North and South Guinea:
An Abstract of the most remarkable occurrences and transactions happening in North and South Guinea since the year 1682 to bring the account up to the present time (1698?), 422-455. A Voyage to New Calabar or Rio Real in 1699 by James Barbot (the author's brother), 455-466. A Description of the Lower Ethiopia (gathered from other writers), 467-496. Abstract of a Voyage to Congo River or the Zair, and to Cabinde in the year 1700. By James Barbot (the author's nephew), 497-522. Supplement: Various descriptions and observations, an appendix to the preceding Memoir of North and South Guinea, containing General Observations and an Account of the first discoveries of America by the Europeans, the Description of the Caribean Islands of America, . . . Their Products, Trade, Wars, . . . A Fragment of a Letter from Sir Thomas Roe. . . . A Table of Courses on the long Voyage by the Same, 523-668. In Churchill V, 1-668.

> Abstracts of portions of the above are given in Astley II, 310-316; III, 105-112, 200-211.
> A very full generalized account is given of those portions of Africa mentioned. The author does not relate much personal experience. Rather he was an assiduous collector of information of the useful kind. He was agent-general of the Royal Company of Africa and Islands at Paris. James Barbot, the brother, was supercargo and part owner, with his brother John and other adventurers, of a frigate.

BAUMGARTEN, MARTIN. For a description of Egypt see his *Travels through Egypt, Arabia, Palestine and Syria,* under NEAR EAST.

EVERARD, ROBERT. A Relation of Three Years' Sufferings of Robert Everard upon the Coast of Assada near Madagascar, in a Voyage to India in the Year 1686, and of his wonderful Preservation and Deliverance, and Arrival at London Anno 1693. In Churchill VI, 257-282.

> The author was an apprentice bound to Capt. John Crib, in the Ship *Bauden,* sailing to Bombay for "blacks" to take to Achin.

MEROLLA, JEROM DA SORRENTO. A Voyage to Congo and several other Countries, chiefly in Southern-Africk. Made English from the Italian. In Churchill I, 593-686.

> Abstract in Astley III, 166-199; in Pinkerton XVI, 193-316. Italian original, Naples, 1692. See below.
> Merolla was an Italian Capuchin priest and missionary, who went to Africa in 1682 to preach the Gospel. His book, which comments upon the influence of the Portuguese in the Congo, describes in detail the life of the people and the natural resources of the region.—Maggs, No. 521. Merolla was far from being an enlightened traveller, being equal to any of his apostolic predecessors in superstition and credulity. But his narrative contains some interesting pictures of life there and presents a good account of the superstitions of the natives.

1692 MEROLLA, GIROLAMO. Breve e succinta Relatione del viaggio nel regno di Congo nell' Africa Meridionale, fatto dal P. Girolamo Merolla da Sorrento, scritto e ridotto al presente stile istorico e narrativo dal P. Angelo Picardo da Napoli. 19 engraved plates, in which are depicted the inhabitants, the customs and products of the Congo. 8vo. Napoli.

PHILLIPS, THOMAS. A Journal of a Voyage made in the *Hannibal* of London, 1693, 1694, from England, to Cape Monseradoc, in Africa and thence along the Coast of Guiney to Whidaw, the Island of St. Thomas, and so forward to Barbadoes, with a cursory Account of the Country, the People, their Manners, Forts, Trade, . . . In Churchill VI, 171-239.

> Abstract in Astley (taken from Churchill) II, 387-416.
> The author was commander of a ship in the service of the Royal African Company trading for ivory, gold, and slaves. The personal adventures narrated are of unusual interest, as is also his description of the manner of stowing slaves aboard ship in transit.

TEN RHYNE, WILLIAM. An Account of the Cape of Good Hope and the Hottentotes, the Natives of that Country . . . with some Animadversions upon the Same by Henry Secreta of Zavorvit. Translated from the Latin Original. In Churchill IV, 768-782.

> Brief abstract in Astley III, 322-323. Pinkerton XVII cites a Latin version, 8vo, Basel, 1616; but it is more likely that the Latin edition published at Schaffhausen, 1686, is the original. See below.
> Ten Rhyne was a physician and a member of the Council of Justice to the Dutch East India Company. He made the voyage in 1673, and communicated his remarks to Secreta, who published them in Latin with remarks of his own. His description of the Hottentots makes them out to be at the very bottom of the scale in brutishness and bestiality.

1686 TEN RHYNE, WILLIAM. V. Cl. Whilhelmi Ten Rhyne, Daventr. Ampliss. Soc. Indiae Or. Medici & a Conciliis Justitiae, Schediasma de Promontorio Bonae spei; ijusque tractus incolis Hottentottis. Accurante, brevesque Notae addente, Henr. Screta S. a Zavorziz. 12mo. Schaffhausen.

1734 BLUET, THOMAS. Some Memoirs of the Life of Job, the Son of Solomon, the High Priest of Boonda in Affica (i.e., Bunda, near the Gambia). 8vo. London.

> Abstract in Astley II, 234-240. Job is mentioned in Moore several times. See Moore under 1738.
> The story of his captivity and deliverance made quite a stir in England. Bluet was intimate with Job, both in America and England, and drew up this account at the request of Job himself. Job was a native of Futa Jallon, who had been enslaved and sent to Maryland, but had been redeemed and returned to his own country.

SNELGRAVE, WILLIAM (Captain). A New Account of some Parts of Guinea, and the Slave Trade, containing I. The History of the late Conquest of the Kingdom of Whidaw by the King of Dahomé. The

Author's Journey to the Conqueror's Camp; where he saw several Captives sacrificed, etc. II. The manner how the Negroes become Slaves. The Numbers of them yearly exported from Guinea to America. The Lawfullness of that Trade. The Mutinies among them on board the Ships where the Author has been, etc. III. A Relation of the Author's being taken by Pirates in 1719, and the many Dangers he underwent. Map of Guinea. 8vo. London.

Another edition, 8vo, London, 1754; an abstract in Astley II, 485-519.
This is an interesting work by one of the old slave traders. The author gives a vivid picture of the capture of his vessel the *Bird Galley* by the pirates under Capt. Cocklyn and Capt. Davis off the river Sierra Leone on April 1, 1719.—Maggs, No. 508. Being mainly concerned with defending the slave trade he neglects to give a description of Guinea itself, but contents himself with referring the reader to Bosman's account of the country. See Bosman under 1705.

1735 ATKINS, JOHN. For a description of the Guinea coast see his *Voyage to Guinea, Brazil, and the West Indies*, under GENERAL TRAVELS AND DESCRIPTIONS. Abstract in Astley II, 316-321; 445-457, of description of Sierra Leone.

LOBO, JERONYMO. A Voyage to Abyssinia . . . With a Continuation of the History of Abyssinia down to the Beginning of the Eighteenth Century. From the French (by Samuel Johnson). 8vo. London.

Another edition, with additions, London, 1789. A portion in Pinkerton XV, 1-60. Pinkerton XVII cites an edition, presumably in Portuguese, Coimbra, 1659, but this must be an error, for the original manuscript never appeared in print. French original, Paris, 1728. See below.
Johnson read this work—the French version by Le Grand—at Pembroke College, and thought "that an abridgement and translation of it from the French into English might be a useful and profitable publication."—Boswell. This was his first published prose work; later he considered it as unworthy of him. Johnson took great liberties with the text as a translator, giving more of an epitome than a literal rendering. In the account of Abyssinia and the Continuation he was more faithful. Lobo, a Jesuit missionary, went to Abyssinia in 1625 with eight or nine companions. There he remained for a decade as Superior of the Jesuit mission, noting down valuable facts on the land, the people, the Nile, etc. When the reigning emperor died he had to flee the country. After many disastrous adventures and hardships he finally reached Lisbon, where he wrote his memoirs. The original Portuguese text has never been published, but as noted above, Le Grand translated it into French, adding fifteen dissertations of his own on various subjects connected with the country.

1789 LOBO, JEROME. A Voyage to Abyssinia, containing its History, natural, civil, and ecclesiastical, with a Continuation by M. Le Grand, translated from the French by Samuel Johnson, LL.D., with Other Tracts by the same Author, not published by Sir John Hawkins or Mr. Stockdale. 8vo. London.

The editor's preface is not devoid of interest. In it he condemns the "uncommonly numerous" blunders of the printer in the 1735 version, and girds at the edition of the works of Dr. Johnson of 1787.—Courtney and Smith, quoted by Sotheran.

1728 LOBO, LE PERE JEROME. Voyage historique d'Abissinie. Traduite *(sic)* du Portugais, continuée et augmentée *(sic)* de plusieurs dissertations, lettres et mémoires par M. Le Grand. 4to. Paris and the Hague.

> This contains dissertations on Prester John, the Queen of Sheba, etc. Le Grand was secretary to the Abbé d'Estrees, ambassador of the French King to Lisbon.

A Voyage to Barbary for the Redemption of Captives. Performed (in 1720) by the Mathurin-Trinitarian Fathers, Fran. Comelin, Philemon de la Motte and Jos. Bernard. Now first Englished from the French Original. With lists of more than 400 Slaves ransomed (by the Royal Bounty of their late and present Majesties) from Mequinez. To which is subjoined, The History Ancient and Modern of Oran, . . . 3 maps, 2 folding views and 2 smaller plates. 8vo. London.

> The French text of 140 pp. was written by Francis C. de la Philemon and Joseph Bernard. The translator (unknown) has added a list of Masters' and Ships' names as well as the History of Oran, with a Journal of the Spaniard's African Conquests.—Bookseller's Note.

1736 MORGAN, JOHN. Several Voyages to Barbary. Containing an Historical and Geographical Account of the Country. With the Hardships, Sufferings, and manner of redeeming Christian Slaves . . . (With Appendix, being the History, Ancient and Modern, of Oran, with a Journal of the Spaniards' Procedure in their African Conquests). 5 large folding maps and plans. 8vo. London.

> This work is sometimes attributed to Captain Henry Boyde, but it appears that he only designed the plates. See Morgan under 1729-1730 above.

1738 MOORE, FRANCIS. Travels into the Inland Parts of Africa: containing a Description of the several Nations for the space of six hundred miles up the river Gambia; and their Trade, Habits, Customs, Languages, Manners, Religions, and Government. . . . With a particular Account of Job Ben Solomon, a Pholez, who was in England in the year 1733 and known by the name of the African. To which is added, Capt. Stibbs' Voyage up the Gambia in the year 1723 to make Discoveries; with an accurate Map of that River taken on the Spot; And many other Copper-Plates. Also Extracts from the Nubian's Geography (Edrisi's), Leo the African, and other authors ancient and modern, concerning the Niger, Nil and Gambia, etc. And a Mundingo Vocabulary. Map and 10 engravings. 8vo. London.

> An abstract in Astley II, 209-233, and references to his work in the following pages dealing with this part of Africa.
> This a valuable work, introducing the reader to many parts and tribes of Africa, even yet but little known, partly drawn from the accounts of the African Prince, who came to England.—Lowndes. (For an account of this prince Job see under Bluet, 1734 above.) This is Leo's work much plagiarized.—Hak. Soc., ser. I, vol. 92. Moore was an unusually learned factor serving under the Royal African Company. He went out to this region in 1730.

RUTHERFORD, LORD GEORGE. The Moors Baffled, being a Discourse concerning Tangier; Especially while under the Government of the Renowned General Andrew Earl of Teviot, Lord Rutherford, etc. Edinburgh.

See L. Addison under 1685 above.

SHAW, THOMAS. Travels, or Observations relating to several parts of Barbary and the Levant. With a Collection of such Papers as serve to illustrate the foregoing Observations, and a Specimen Phytogtaphiae Africanae, of Coralls, of the rarest Fishes, Shells, etc. Copperplates. Fol. Oxford.

2nd edit. with figures, 4to, Oxford, 1757; 3rd edit. corrected, with some account of the author, 2 vols., Edinburgh, 1808. Reprinted in Pinkerton XV, 499-680, from the 2nd edit., but "corrected in several respects." Translated into French, the Hague, 1743; into German, Leipzig, 1765; into Dutch, Utrecht, 1773. See below. A Supplement replying to attacks, Oxford, 1746; a further vindication, Oxford, 1747. See below.
The author was chaplain for several years to the English Factory at Algiers. Later he became Regius Professor of Greek at Oxford. Dr. Pococke attacked these Travels in his Description of the East. (See Pococke 1743-45, under NEAR EAST.) The Supplements cited below are Shaw's replies.

1743 (In French.) Voyages dans plusieurs provinces de la Barbarie et du Levant, contenant des Observations géographique, physiques, philologiques et melées sur les royaumes d'Alger et de Tunis, sur la Syrie, l'Egypte et l'Arabie Pétrée, avec des figures et des cartes, traduites de l'Anglois. 2 vols. 4to. The Hague.

Noticed in the Journal des Scavans, 1746, I, 327.

1765 (In German.) Reisen, oder Bemerkungen über verschiedene Theile der Barbarie und Levante betreffend. Nach der zweiten Englischen Ausgabe, übersetzt von J. H. Merk. Mit Küpfern und Karten. 4to. Leipzig.

1773 (In Dutch.) Reizen en aanmerkingen door en over Barbaryen en het Ooste, uit het Engelsch vertaald door P. Boddaert. 2 Deelen. 4to. Utrecht.

1746 SHAW, THOMAS. A Supplement to a Book entitled: Travels, or Observations, etc., wherein some Objections lately made against it are fully considered and answered; with several additional Remarks and Dissertations. 1 plate. Fol. Oxford.

1747 SHAW, THOMAS. A further Vindication of the Book of Travels and the Supplement to it. Fol. Oxford.

1739 BROWN, EDWARD. For his travels in Egypt and Abyssinia see his *The Travels and Adventures of Edward Brown*, under GENERAL TRAVELS AND DESCRIPTIONS.

PELLOW, THOMAS.   The History of the Long Captivity and Adventures of Thomas Pellow in South Barbary; giving an Account of his having been taken by two Sallee Rovers and carry'd to Mequinez, his various Adventures for twenty-three years, his Escape and Return home. 8vo. London.

> 2nd edition, London, 17—. Apparently the 1st edit. carries no date, but it is assigned to 1739.
> Pellow was captured in 1715 off Finisterre by two Sallee pirates, was converted to Islam, and remained in captivity in the Sultan's service till 1738, when he escaped and returned to Cornwall, his native country. The details are regarded as more interesting than authentic.—Bookseller's Note.

THOMSON, WILLIAM.   Mammuth, or Human Nature Displayed on a Grand Scale in a Tour with the Thinkers into the Inland Parts of Africa. 2 vols. London.

1741 NORDEN, FREDERICK LEWIS.   Drawings of some Ruins and Colossal Statues at Thebes in Egypt; with an Account of the same, in a Letter to the Royal Society. 4to. London.

> Another edition, London, 1792. See below, and also under 1744 and 1754.

> 1792 NORDEN, FREDERICK LEWIS. The Antiquities, Natural History, Ruins, and other Curiosities of Egypt, Nubia, and Thebes, exemplified in near 200 drawings taken on the spot, . . . The whole engraved on 164 plates, by Martin Teuscher, of Nuremberg. Fol. London.

1742 LEACH, JOHN.   Travels on the Nile. Plates. 4to. London.

1743 PERRY, CHARLES.   For a view of Egypt see his *A View of the Levant*, under NEAR EAST.

1743-45 POCOCKE, RICHARD.   For his description of Egypt see his *Description of the East,* under NEAR EAST.

1744 NORDEN, FREDERICK LEWIS, and TEUSCHER, MARTIN.   Alexandria. Plan and 15 Views of Alexandria and other Places in Egypt. London.

SMITH, WILLIAM.   A New Voyage to Guinea, describing the Customs, Manners, Soil, Climate, Buildings, Marriages, . . . and Natural History. 5 copperplates of natural history. 8vo. London.

> 2nd edit., London, 1745. Abstract in Astley II, 464-481. In French, Paris, 1751. See below.
> A work containing much information in a small compass.—Lowndes. The editor of the original gives no information concerning either the author or the copy

further than that the MS. had been deposited in a certain library, from whence it was taken to be published. The work seems to be made up from imperfect materials left by Smith and some stuff from other quarters. The customs and manners of the Gold Coast, e.g., and the whole account of Benin are taken from Bosman. The object of the voyage was to make surveys and drawings of all the English settlements and forts in Guinea. This he performed with a great deal of labor and on his return published the whole in 30 folio plates. But the editor supplies only four or five plates, poorly drawn, of figures of birds and beasts. Towards the end of the work there is an account of Guinea, said to have been given by one Mr. Wheeler, in dialogue, comparing the customs of that country with those of England. It seems to be a work of the fancy rather than of actuality.—From Astley. The author was surveyor to the Royal African Company. The voyage was made in 1726.

1751. (In French.) Nouveau voyage de Guinée: coûtumes, habillements, bâtiments, commerce, languages, divertissements, marriages, etc. 16 figures and 5 plates. 2 vols. 8vo. Paris.

1744 THOMPSON, CHARLES. For his account of Egypt see his *Travels, containing his Observations on France, Italy, Turkey*, etc., under GENERAL TRAVELS AND DESCRIPTIONS.

1745 WATTS, JOHN. A True Relation of the Inhuman and Unparalleled Actions and Barbarous Murders, of Negroes or Moors: Committed on three Englishmen in old Calabar in Guiney. Of the wonderful Deliverance of the fourth Person, after he had endured horrid Cruelties and Sufferings: Who lately arrived in England and is now in his Majesty's Fleet. Together with a short but true Account of the Customs, Manners, and Growth of the Country, which is very pleasant. In Osborne II, 511-517.

This relation purports to have been taken from the mouth of one of the sufferers, John Watts, who as a youth of eighteen had shipped on board the *Peach Tree* (in 1668) bound for Guiney in the slave trade. The party was seized in revenge for some action done to one of the natives a year before. After a period of slavery he was sold to the captain of an English vessel and thus was released. See *A True Relation of the Murders of Negroes* under 1672 above.

1745-47 BATTEL, ANDREW. The Strange Adventures of Andrew Battel of Leigh, in Essex, sent by the Portuguese a Prisoner to Angola, who lived there and in the adjoining regions, near 18 Years. Abstract in Astley III, 136-142.

In Pinkerton XVI, 317-336. Taken from *Purchas His Pilgrimes*.
This voyage was made in 1589. Purchas seems to have improved Battel's Relation with particulars he received in conversation with Battel, and has inserted many remarks into his description of Angola and Congo. Battel had been taken prisoner by the Portuguese on the coast of Brazil and sent over to the Congo, in which and the neighboring countries he lived many years. He became sergeant of a company of the Portuguese.

BRUE, ANDRE. Voyages and Travels along the Western Coast of Africa, on Account of the French Commerce. Now first translated from the French. Abstract in Astley II, 27-144.

> Brue was for many years Director-general of the French Sanaga (Senegal) Company at Fort St. Louis. His voyages and travels were published by Labat in his *Nouvelle Relation de l'Afrique Occidentale,* or rather that work consists almost wholly of the Memoirs furnished by Brue.—From Astley. Brue made several voyages to this region and resided altogether about 11 years in Africa.

COMPAGNON, ——. An Account of the Discovery of the Kingdom of Bambuk, and its Gold Mines, in 1716. With a Description of the Country and its Inhabitants. Abstract in Astley II, 145-156.

> The French Senegal Company were desirous of finding out where the gold came from which was brought down the Senegal and carried to the English at Gambia, that is, the country of Bambuk—an enterprize very dangerous because of the unwillingness of the natives to allow Europeans to share the trade with Bambuk. The Sieur Compagnon alone was daring enough to adventure it and he succeeded, being the first white man to penetrate to those parts. This took place while Brue was Director-general of the Company.

ELBEE, SIEUR D'. A Voyage to Ardrah, and Travels to the Capital Assem, in 1669 and 1670. First translated from the French. Abstract in Astley III, 65-73.

> The original was inserted in Chevalier de Marchais' *Voyage to Guinea,* 2 vols. Elbée was sent out by the French West India Company to get slaves. The account gives a good description of Assem, and the state of the King of Ardrah. —From Astley.

JANNEQUIN, CLAUDE, SIEUR DE ROCHEFORT. Abstract of a Voyage to Lybia, particularly to the Kingdom of Sanaga, on the River Niger. Now first done from the French. In Astley II, 20-27.

> French original, 12mo, Paris, 1643. The author makes the Senegal identical with the Niger. While inexact he gives the reader a tolerable notion of the customs of the Negroes. It is the first account of a voyage made by the French up the Senegal. His return to France was somewhere in 1639.—From Astley.

LAMBE, BULLFINCH. A Letter to Governor Tinker, concerning the King of Dahomey. Dated from the great King Truro Audati's Palace of Abomey, in the Kingdom of Dahomey, 27 Nov., 1724. In Astley II, 482-485.

A Letter concerning the Discovery of the Gold Mines, in a Voyage up the Gambia. In Astley II, 189-193.

> This was found among Dr. Hook's papers after his death, and published in his posthumous works. It appears to be a fictitious letter, pretending to have found the gold sought for in the interior. It may have been intended to spur others on to the exploration of the Gambia.—Astley. It may be noted here that what the Gambia was to the English the Senegal was to the French.

LOPEZ, MATTEO. Embassy of Matteo Lopez to the King of France. In Astley III, 73-79.

> This embassy was from the King of Ardrah to Louis XIV in 1670. The original appeared in Chevalier des Marchais' *Voyage to Guinea,* vol. 2. Its purpose was to settle a dispute between the priority rights of the Dutch and of the French. It is unique in that it reverses the usual order in history, for here we have an embassy from a savage people to the proudest nation in Europe.

LOYER, GODFREY. A Voyage to Issini on the Gold Coast, in 1701. With a Description of the Country and its Inhabitants. Now first done from the French. Abstract in Astley II, 417-445.

> French original, 8vo, Paris, 1714. See below.
> The author was Apostolic Prefect of the Missions of Preaching Friars to the coasts of Guinea. "He has given the best account of any to be met with concerning the country about Issini and its inhabitants, which he has delivered in that plain, unaffected manner, which generally accompanies sincerity."

> 1714 LOYER, GODFREY. Relation du Voyage du Royaume d'Issyny, Côte d'Or, Païs de Guinée, en Afrique. La description du Païs, les inclinations, les moeurs, et la Religion des habitants: avec ce qui s'y est passé de plus remarquable dans l'établissement que les Francois y ont fait. 8 plates. 12mo. Paris.

MARCHAIS, CHEVALIER DES. A Voyage to Guinea, and the Adjacent Islands. Now first translated from the French. Abstract in Astley II, 457-463.

> The author made several voyages to Africa and America. He gave an exact account of everything he saw, for which he was well qualified, "being a person of great understanding and curiosity, an able draughtsman, a good geometer, and an excellent navigator." Besides he spoke most of the numerous languages to be encountered on the west coast, and he had an engaging behaviour that made him welcome wherever he went. This voyage Labat has given in 4 vols., Amsterdam, 1731.—From Astley.

MORTO, ALUISE DA CADA. The Voyage of Aluise da Cada Morto in 1455, along the Coast of Africa as far as the Rio Grande. Written by himself. Translated from the Italian. In Astley I, 572-596.

> There are two such Voyages extant, both of which are in Ramusio and Grynaeus. One was to the River Senega Gambra (Gambia), and the other to the same coast of Africa and the Cape Verde Islands. The editor says Morto was the first to discover Cape Verde, but the Portuguese give that honor to Dennis Fernandez, a Portuguese, 12 years earlier.—From Astley.

STIBBS, BARTHOLOMEW. A Voyage up the Gambra (Gambia) in 1724, for making Discoveries, and Improving the Trade of that River. Abstract in Astley II, 193-208.

> This voyage is also included by Francis Moore in his *Travels.* See above, 1738. Capt. Stibbs was sent by the Royal African Company to discover how far the Gambia was navigable, and whether there were any gold mines upon that river. But as he set out in the dry season he got only as far as the Falls of Barrakonda. He gives several reasons why he thought the Gambia was not the Niger. That question was settled finally by Mungo Park in 1798.

VAN DER BROECK, PETER. Voyage to Cape Verde and Rusisco. Now first translated from the French. Abstract in Astley II, 247-248.

> The original of this work is found in the Collection of Dutch Voyages to the East Indies, 2nd edit., (in French), Amsterdam, 1725.
> This is the first of several voyages made by the author as far as the East Indies between 1606 and 1630.

1750 LAUGIER DE TUSSY. A Complete History of the Piratical States of Barbary, etc. London.

> French original, Amsterdam, 1725. The English version of 1750 was given as an original and was retranslated into French. Paris, 1757. See below.

> 1725 LAUGIER DE TUSSY. Histoire du Royaume d'Alger; ou état présent de son gouvernement, de ses forces de terre et de mer, de ses revenues, police, politique et commerce. Amsterdam.

> 1757 LAUGIER DE TUSSY. Histoire des Etats Barbaresques qui exercent la Piraterie contenant l'origine, les révolutions et l'état présent des royaumes d'Alger, de Tunis, de Tripolie et de Maroc, etc. Par un Auteur qui y a résidé plusieurs années avec caractere public. Traduite de l'Anglois. 2 vols. 12mo. Paris.

1751 TROUGHTON, THOMAS (and Others). Barbarian Cruelty; or, An Accurate and Impartial Narrative of the Unparallel'd Sufferings and almost incredible Hardships of the British Captives, belonging to the *Inspector* Privateer, Capt. Richard Veale, Commander, during their Slavery under the arbitrary and despotic Government of Muley Abdallah, Emperor of Fez and Morocco, 1745-1750, . . . Together with: A Supplement to the Barbarian Cruelty, . . . 5 folding plates. 2 vols. in 1. 8vo. London.

> A scarce account of the adventures of the survivors of the Privateer *Inspector*, which was wrecked on the coast of Morocco. The sailors were made slaves by their captors and remained in slavery for five years until redeemed by George II.—Maggs, No. 534.

1754 The History of the States of Algiers, Tunis, Tripoli and Morocco. Translated from the English (into Italian). London (Venice).

> So cited by Pinkerton XVII.

1757 NORDEN, FREDERICK LEWIS. Travels in Egypt and Nubia. Translated from the Original published by Command of His Majesty the King of Denmark, and enlarged with Observations from ancient and modern Authors, that have written on the Antiquities of Egypt, by Dr. Peter Templeman. 159 large copper engravings of Alexandria, Cairo, Carnac, temples, plants, monuments, etc. 2 vols. in 1. Fol. London.

A Compendium of this work was published in 8vo, Dublin, 1757; other editions, London, 1780 and 1792. The English version was translated into German, Breslau, 1779. The French original, Copenhagen, 1750-55. See below.

Norden was an excellent draughtsman, especially in shipbuilding, and in order to further his progress in this field he went abroad to study, under commission from King Christian VII of Denmark. While in Florence he received orders to proceed to Egypt and examine the monuments and wonders of that land. The results are embodied in the above work. After his return he was selected to accompany one of the English expeditions in the war with Spain. In this capacity he went out with the fleet sent to reinforce Admiral Vernon in the West Indies. He received many honors in London as well as at home in Denmark. He died in Paris in 1742.

1750-55 NORDEN, FREDERICK LEWIS. Voyage d'Egypte et de Nubie. 159 plates. 2 vols. Fol. Copenhagen.

> This was a translation from Norden's various MSS., written in Danish, made by Des Roches de Parthenay. The original plates were used by Templeman in his English version.

1779 (In German.) Beschreibung einer Reise durch Aegypten und Nubien, mit Anmerkungen Dr. Templeman's, nach der Englische Ausgabe übersetzt und mit Vorbericht versehen von Joh. Esaias Steffens. 2 vols. Plates and map. Breslau.

1758 THOMPSON, THOMAS. An Account of Two Missionary Voyages. The one to New Jersey, the other from North America to Guiney. 8vo. London.

For some travels in Egypt see *Travels in Egypt, Turkey, Syria,* under NEAR EAST.

1759 ADANSON, MICHEL. A Voyage to Senegal, the Isle of Goree and River Gambia. Translated from the French. With notes by an English Gentleman, who resided some Time in that Country. Folding map. 8vo. London.

> An edition at Dublin, 1759. Reprinted in Pinkerton XVI, 598-674; French original, Paris, 1757. See below.
> The author was a French botanist who entered the service of the French East India Company in order to study the natural history round about the French settlement in Senegambia.

1757 ADANSON, MICHEL. Histoire naturelle du Sénégal: Coquillages. Avec la relation d'un voyage fait en ce pays pendant les années 1749-1757. 4to. Paris.

LINDSEY, JOHN (Rev.). A Voyage to the Western Coast of Africa; containing an Account of the Expedition commanded by Keppel. 4to. London.

EGMONT, AEGIDIUS VAN, and HEYMAN, JOHN. For their account of Egypt see their *Travels through Part of Europe, Asia Minor,* etc., under NEAR EAST.

1764   ABREU DE GALINDO, JUAN DE.   The History of the Discovery and
       Conquest of the Canary Islands.   Translated from a Spanish Manu-
       script, lately found in the Island of Palma.   With an Enquiry into the
       Origin of the ancient Inhabitants.   To which is added, A Description
       of the Canary Islands, including the Modern History of the Inhabi-
       tants, and an Account of their Manners, Customs, Trade, . . . By
       George Glas.   Folding and other maps.   4to.   London.

> Another edit, 2 vols., 8vo, London, 1767; 2 vols., Dublin, 1767; in Pinkerton
> XVI. 808-826.   Noticed in the *Monthly Review*, 1764, V, 232.   See below.
> The manuscript translated by Glas was written by Abreu de Galindo. Glas
> was educated for a physician but he followed the sea as a profession instead.
> He was an intelligent observer, with some literary and scientific attainments. His
> translation of the Spanish account is considered fairly good, and his own de-
> scriptions of the Canary Islands have considerable merit. He attempted to make
> a settlement on the coast of Africa between Cape Verde and Senegal. Later he
> was imprisoned by the Spaniards at Teneriffe for contraband trading, and to cap
> the series of misfortunes he was killed in a mutiny on board ship while returning
> home. See Hak. Soc., ser. II, vol. 21, *The Guanches of Teneriffe.*

> 1767   ABREU DE GALINDO, JUAN DE.   The History of the Discovery and
>   Conquest of the Canary Islands.   Translated from a Spanish Manuscript
>   . . . by Capt. George Glas.   With his Life and Tragical End, on board
>   the *Sandwich,* of London; and an Account of the Apprehending of the
>   four Assassins, Perpetrators of that horrid Crime.   2 vols.   12mo.
>   Dublin.

A Short Account of that part of Africa, inhabited by the Negroes . . . ex-
       tracted from divers Authors, in order to shew the iniquity of that
       Trade, and the falsity of the Arguments usually advanced in its Vin-
       dication.   3rd edit.   8vo.   London.

> This work is a reprint of the 1762 edition published at Philadelphia.

1768   DREW, RICHARD.   Copy of a Letter from Richard Drew, Esq., Late
       Governor of Annamaboe Fort, to Messrs. Richard Farr and Sons,
       Eminent Merchants in the City of Bristol, touching the State of the
       Trade to the Gold Coast of Africa, . . . Fol.   London.

1773   RIEDESEL, JOHANN HERMANN VON, BARON.   For his tour
       through Egypt see his *Travels through Sicily,* etc., under WEST
       EUROPE.

TOURTECHOT DE GRANGER, SIEUR.   A Journey through Egypt,
       made in the year 1730, in which there are to be found the most re-
       markable particulars on Natural History.   Translated from the French
       by John Reinhold Forster.   8vo.   London.

> French original, Paris, 1745.   See below.

1745 TOURTECHOT DE GRANGER, SIEUR. Relation du Voyage fait en Egypte en l'année 1730, où l'on voit ce qu'il y a de plus remarquable, particulièrement sur l'Histoire Naturelle. 12mo. Paris.

1775 SAINT-PIERRE, J. H. BERNARDIN DE. A Voyage to the Island of Mauritius (or, Isle of France), the Isle of Bourbon, the Cape of Good Hope, . . . With Observations and Reflections upon Nature and Mankind. By a French Officer. Translated from the French by John Parish. 8vo. London.

> Another edit., 8vo, London, 1800. French original, Paris, 1772. See below.
> This is the author of the celebrated novel *Paul and Virginia*. While the above work provides interesting information on the manners and customs of not only the natives but the white population as well, and on the natural history of the places he visited, it is rather to be remembered for its affirmation of the virtues of the simple life and the reality of the noble savage, so much in vogue with European romanticists.

1772 SAINT-PIERRE, J. H. BERNARDIN DE. Voyage a l'ile de France, Bourbon, la Cap de Bonne Espérance, etc. 8vo. Paris.

1777 KINDERSLEY, MRS. Letters from the Island of Teneriffe, Brazil, the Cape of Good Hope, and the East Indies, 1777. 8vo. London.

1780 IRWIN, EYLES. For some description of the coasts of Egypt and the deserts of Thebes see his *Series of Adventures in a Voyage up the Coasts of Arabia*, under NEAR EAST.

1781 DALTON, RICHARD. A Series of Prints relative to the Manners, Customs, etc., of the present Inhabitants of Egypt, from Drawings made on the Spot, A.D. 1749, with Explanations in English and French. 21 plates and 5 of costumes. Fol. London.

> See below also under 1790, and under 1751, NEAR EAST.

1783 ROOKE, HENRY. For an account of travels by the Red Sea, Egypt, and the islands of the West Coast of Africa see his *Travels to the Coast of Arabia Felix*, under NEAR EAST.

LUSIGNAN, S. History of the Revolt of Ali Bey against the Ottoman Porte, including an Account of the form of Government of Egypt; together with a Description of Grand Cairo, and of several celebrated places in Egypt, Palestine, and Syria; also the Journal of a Gentleman who travelled from Aleppo to Bassora, by S. L. 8vo. London.

> See Lusignan, under date 1788, NEAR EAST.

1785 SPARRMAN, ANDRE. A Voyage to the Cape of Good Hope, towards the Antarctic Polar Circle, and round the World; but chiefly into the Country of the Hottentots and Caffres, 1772-1776. Translated from the Swedish (by George Forster). Map and 10 plates. London.

> An edit. in Dublin, 1785; 2nd edit. corrected, 2 vols. 4to, London, 1786; 2 vols., 12mo, Perth, 1789. Translated from the English into French, London and Paris, 1786; another French version, Paris, 1787. Swedish original, 1783. See below.
> Sparrman, a Swedish naturalist, sailed round the world with Captain Cook on his second voyage, of which voyage he gives a description. Most of the work is devoted to various travels in South Africa.—Maggs No. 521. Though he did little actual exploration, being more concerned with matters of natural history, he adds considerably to the knowledge of South Africa at this period.

> 1786 (In French.) Voyage au Cap de Bonne Espérance, au pole méridional depuis les années 1772-76. Traduit de l'anglois par J. P. Brissot. 2 vols. Londres et Paris.

> 1787 SPARRMAN, ANDRE. Voyage au Cap de Bonne Espérance et autour du monde avec le Capitaine Cook, et principalement dans le Pays des Hottentots et des Caffres. Traduit par M. Le Tourneur. Maps and plates. 2 vols. 4to. Paris.

> 1783 SPARRMAN, ANDRE. Resa til Goda Hoppsudden, södra polkretsen och omkring jordklottet samt till Hottentott—och Cafferlanden aaren 1772-76. Stockholm (?).

1786 SAVARY, CLAUDE (called NICHOLAS). Letters on Egypt, containing a Parallel between the Manners of its Ancient and Modern Inhabitants, its Commerce, Agriculture, Government, and Religion, with the Descent of St. Lewis at Damietta, extracted from Joinville and Arabian Authors. Translated from the French of Nicholas Savary. Maps. 2 vols. 8vo. London.

> 2nd edit., London, 1787; another in 2 vols., Dublin, 1788; and again, 2 vols., London, 1799. French original, 3 vols., 8vo, Paris, 1785-87. See below.
> The merit of this work consists in its curious notions respecting ancient and modern Egypt, drawn from scarce and almost unknown Arabic writers. Savary describes Upper Egypt as if he had visited it, whereas he never did. The reputation of the work was cut to pieces by Michaelis in a foreign journal of oriental literature.—Lowndes.

> 1785-87 SAVARY, NICHOLAS. Lettres sur l'Egypte, où l'on offre le parallele des moeurs anciennes et modernes des ses habitants; où l'on décrit l'état, le commerce, l'agriculture, le gouvernement, l'ancienne religion du pays, et la descente de Saint Louis à Damiette, tirée de Joinville et des auteurs arabes, etc. Maps. 3 vols., 8vo. Paris.

STANLEY, EDWARD. Observations on the City of Tunis and the adjacent Country. 4to. London.

1787 VOLNEY, CONSTANTIN FRANCOIS CHASSEBOEUF, COMTE. For an account of his travels through Egypt see his *Travels through Syria and Egypt,* under NEAR EAST.

1788 BENEZET, ANTHONY. Some Historical Account of Guinea: its Situation, Produce, and the General Disposition of its Inhabitants, with an Inquiry into the Rise and Progress of the Slave Trade, its Nature and Lamentable Effects. 8vo. London.

> The author was a French philanthropist who was forced to move to England on account of religious opinions. After becoming a Quaker, he moved to America in 1731, where he took up the cause of the negro and the Indian. His writings stirred Clarkson and Wilberforce to interest themselves in the emancipation of the slaves.

1788 CHENIER, ——. The Present State of the Empire of Morocco. Its Animals, Products, Climate, Soil, Cities, Ports, Provinces, Coins, Weights and Measures, . . . Large folding map. 2 vols. London.

> A work containing much valuable information written by the Charge des Affaires from the King of France to the Emperor of Morocco.—Lowndes.

HOLLINGSWORTH, S. A Dissertation on the Manners, Governments, and Spirit, of Africa. To which is added, Observations on the present Application to Parliament for Abolishing Negro Slavery in the British West India. 8vo. Edinburgh.

> Translated into German, 1789.

MATTHEWS, JOHN. A Voyage to the River Sierra-Leone, on the Coast of Africa, containing an Account of the Country, and of the Civil and Religious Customs and Manners of the People, in a Series of Letters to a Friend in London, by John Matthews, Lieut. in the R. N., during his Residence in that Country, 1785-87, with an Additional Letter on the Subject of the African Slave Trade. A folding chart of part of the coast of Africa, from Cape St. Ann to the River Rionoonas, with a view of the Island Bananas. 8vo. London.

1789 BRISSON, M. DE. An Account of the Shipwreck and Captivity of M. de Brisson; containing a Description of the Deserts of Africa, from Senegal to Morocco. 8vo. London.

> Another edition including the *Voyage of Saugnier*, London, 1792. French original, Geneva and Paris, 1789. See below.

> 1789 BRISSON, M. DE. Histoire du Naufrage et de la Captivité de M. de Brisson avec la description des déserts d'Afrique, depuis le Sénégal jusqu'à Maroc. Geneva and Paris.

FRANCKLYN, G. An Answer to Rev. Mr. Clarkson's Essay on the Slavery and Commerce of the Human Species, in a Series of Letters from a Gentleman in Jamaica; wherein many of the Mistakes and

Misrepresentations of Mr. Clarkson are pointed out, both with regard to the Manner in which that Commerce is carried on in Africa, and the Treatment of the Slaves in the West Indies. 8vo. London.

NORRIS, ROBERT. Memoirs of the Reign of Bossa Ahadee, King of Dahomey, and Inland Country of Guiney. To which are added, the Author's Journey to Abomey, the Capital; and a short Account of the African Slave Trade. 8vo. London.

> The author states that 80,000 slaves are imported annually half of which are for the British Colonies, principally Virginia and the West Indies. They reckon, on an average, that five per cent die on the voyage.—Maggs, No. 502. Norris was an African trader who visited the King of Dahomey.

1790 AFRICAN ASSOCIATION. Proceedings of the Association for promoting the Discovery of the Interior Parts of Africa; Journeys of Ledyard and Lucas; Countries South of the Niger; Trade; Customs; . . . Folding map of Northern Africa. 4to. London.

> Another edit., 8vo, London, 1791.
> This Association was founded in 1788. Its activities mark the beginning of African exploration in a systematic way, as well as the furthering of British trade and political prestige on that continent. This Association was later merged into the Royal Geographical Society. The first concern of the African Association was the River Niger—where was its source and what was the direction of its flow, etc. The first four expeditions were unfortunate for the leaders, Ledyard, Lucas, Horneman, and Houghton, all of whom either died while enroute or were murdered by the fanatical Moors. The fifth, that of Mungo Park, was rich in geographical results, though he too died on his second expedition. See Park, 1798, below.

BENJOWSKY, COUNT MAURITIUS AUGUSTUS DE. For an account of Madagascar see his *Memoirs and Travels,* under SIBERIA.

BRUCE, JAMES. Travels (in Egypt, Arabia, Abyssinia, and Nubia), to discover the Source of the Nile, in the Years 1768-1773. Portrait, maps, and numerous plates of scenery, ethnography, antiquities, natural history, etc., by Heath and others. 5 vols. 4to. London.

> Also in 5 vols., 4to, Edinburgh, 1790 (sometimes called the best edition); an edition, with Life and Notes by A. Murray, 8 vols., with atlas, Edinburgh, 1790. The same abridged by Samuel Shaw, 8vo, London; 2nd edit. (official), enlarged with Life and Appendixes, 7 vols., 8vo, Edinburgh, 1804. Translated into French, Paris, 1790; into German, Leipzig, 1790-91. For these and related works see below; likewise Wharton, under 1800.
> Bruce especially prepared himself for this arduous task by acquainting himself with conditions in Africa, with instruments for taking bearings, and with some skill in medicine. This latter accomplishment proved to be very valuable, as, by saving some members of the royal family of Abyssinia from the smallpox, he gained needed favors. Besides he was of magnificent proportions physically and a superb horseman, both of which factors assisted him to the good graces of the Abyssinians. He might have spared himself some attacks on his veracity had he bettered his information on what had been accomplished by the Jesuits in their expeditions and explorations for the source of the Blue Nile. Probably

he really believed at the time when he stood barefooted by the little fountain whence flows out the beginnings of the Blue Nile, that he was the first white man to gaze on and identify these waters. As it was, the doubts of the truthfulness of his narrative were numerous, occasioning several parodies, best known of which are the *Travels of Baron Munchausen.* They also caused him to delay for many years the publication of his journals. The result of his travels was a very great enrichment of the knowledge of geography and ethnography. His return home was thus noticed by that arch scoffer, Horace Walpole, in a letter to Mann, July 10, 1774: ". . . has lived in the Court of Abyssinia, and breakfasted every morning with the maids of honour on live oxen." Fanny Burney (*Early Diary,* Aug. 22, 1774) comments on her first meeting with Bruce: "His figure is almost gigantic . . . I cannot say that I was charmed with him; for he seems rather arrogant, and to have so large a share of good opinion of himself, as to have nothing left for the rest of the world but contempt." She later records how Bruce was mortified by the general doubt of his accuracy in his relation of his adventures, for which his "swaggering" manners were in part responsible. In a letter of Oct., 1774, Sir William Jones writing to H. A. Schultens, says of Bruce: "He is as well acquainted with the coast of the Red Sea, and the sources of the Nile, as with his own house. He has brought with him some Aethiopic manuscripts, and amongst them the Prophecies of Enoch, but to be ranked only with the Sybilline oracles." The far more remote sources of the White Nile were as yet hardly suspected. Among the satires on Bruce is Peter Pindar's "Complimentary Epistle to James Bruce, Esq."

1800 WHARTON, RICHARD. Observations on the Authenticity of Bruce's Travels, Newcastle.

1790 (In French.) Voyage aux sources du Nîl, en Nubie et en Abyssinie, pendant les années 1768, 1769, 1770, 1771 et 1772. Traduit de l'anglois par J. H. Castéra. Maps and plates. 4to. Paris.

Noticed in the *Journal des Scavans,* 1790, V, 1719; VII, 2323.

1790-91 (In German.) Reisen zur Entdeckung der Quellen des Nils, in den Jahren 1768-1773. Aus dem Englischen übersetzt von J. J. Volkmann, und mit Zusätzen und Anmerkungen begleitet von J. F. Blumenbach und J. C. Tychsen. Maps and plates. 5 vols. 8vo. Leipzig.

DALTON, RICHARD. Remarks on Prints that were published in the year 1781, relative to the Manners, Customs, etc., of the present inhabitants of Egypt, from Drawings made on the Spot, A.D. 1749. 1 plate. 8vo. London.

See Dalton under 1781 above.

LE VAILLANT, FRANCOIS. Travels into the Interior Parts of Africa, by the Way of the Cape of Good Hope, 1780-85, translated from French. 12 copperplates by James Heath, of views, negro types, and natural history. 2 vols. 8vo. London.

A rival translation by Elizabeth Helme appeared the same year. Another edition, Dublin, 1790; in 2 vols., 8vo, Perth, 1791; in 3 vols., with map of the route of his present and former travels, and 22 other copperplates, London, 1796. French original, Paris, 1790-94. See below.

This work was attacked when published, and some of the incidents related were declared to be either exaggerated or altogether invented. It is, however, interesting as an account of South Africa at a time when comparatively little was known regarding its natural history and the Dutch settlers.—Quoted from Sotheran. These travels are valuable less for their geographical information than for their addition to the knowledge of the natural history of those regions.

1790 LE VAILLANT, FRANCOIS. Travels from the Cape of Good Hope into the Interior Parts of Africa, including many interesting Anecdotes, translated by Elizabeth Helme. 12 copperplates. 2 vols. 8vo. London.

> This work is a bowdlerized version, for the translator declares in the preface that she "softened" passages which would ill accord with the delicacy of a female translator. As might be expected, one plate which is "découverte" in the other translation is here "couverte."—From Sotheran.

1790 LE VAILLANT, FRANCOIS. Voyage . . . dans l'Intérieur de l'Afrique par le Cap de Bonne-Espérance, dans les années 1780-85. 2 vols. Paris.

> A French version of a second voyage appeared in 3 vols. Paris, 1794.

PATERSON, WILLIAM (Lieut.). Narrative of Four Journeys into the Country of the Hottentots, and Caffraria, 1777-79. Map and 17 copper plates. 4to. London.

> In German, Berlin, 1790. See below.
> Paterson is credited with having brought to England the first giraffe skin ever seen there.—D.N.B. He made four expeditions into the interior from the Cape to the Orange River and Kaffir land, mainly in the interest of natural history. He collected many birds and numerous specimens of plants. In 1789 he was one of the lieutenants who were chosen to recruit and command a corps for the purpose of protecting the new convict colony at Botany Bay. Later he was appointed Governor of New South Wales.

1790 (In German.) Reisen in das Land der Hottentoter und der Kaffern während der Jahren 1777, 1778, 1779. Aus dem Englischen übersetzt und mit Anmerkungen begleitet von J. R. Forster. Map and 15 plates. Berlin.

RENNELL, JAMES. Sketch of the Northern Part of Africa, exhibiting the Geographical Information collected by the African Association: compiled by J. R. London.

1791 CLARKSON, THOMAS. Letters on the Slave Trade, and the State of the Natives in those Parts of Africa, which are contiguous to Fort St. Louis and Goree, written at Paris in Dec., 1789, and Jan., 1790. Engraved folding map of the Travels of Mr. de Villeneuve, from the River Sallum to the Senegal; 2 plates showing the method of harnessing slaves to each other; and folding plan of Portugal. London.

> Most of the information was obtained from Geoffrey de Villeneuve, aid-de-camp to the French at Gorée.—Maggs, No. 465. See also Francklyn, 1789 above.

DALTON, RICHARD. Antiquities and Views in Greece and Egypt, with the Manners and Customs of the Inhabitants, from Drawings made on the Spot, A.D. 1749. Engraved on 79 copperplates, by Chatelain and others. (The Turkish and Egyptians habits are colored.) Fol. London.

LEMPRIERE, WILLIAM (M.D.). A Tour from Gibraltar to Tangier, Sallee, Mogadore, Santa-Cruz, Tarudant, and thence over Mount Atlas, to Morocco, including a particular Account of the royal Harem, . . . 8vo. London.

> 2nd edit., London, 1793; reprinted in Pinkerton XV, 681-801; a "corrective supplement" to this Tour published at London, 1794.
> Lempriere, a surgeon at Gibraltar, was sent for by the favorite son of the Emperor of Morocco for medical attendance, in the belief that Christian physicians were able to cure any disease. He was promised every protection and a guarantee of expenses and good rewards and the release of certain Christian captives. He embarked from Gibraltar, Sept. 14, 1789, and safely reached his destination, though he was much pestered by the sick en route. His experiences in the harem were unique, as seldom was a European admitted to those precincts. The Emperor long delayed his departure for home, as he was not cognizant of the fact that Lempriere had been sent for.

1791 POIRET, —— (Abbé). Travels through Barbary, in a series of Letters written from the ancient Numidia, 1785-86, containing an Account of the Customs and Manners of the Moors and Bedouin Arabs. Translated from the French. 12mo. London.

> French original, 2 vols., Paris, 1789. See below.
> This work is of interest from the picture it presents of the Bedouin Arabs, and from the details into which it enters respecting the natural history of the country, especially its botany. The botanical parts are omitted in this translation. —Lowndes.

> 1789 POIRET, M. L'ABBE. Voyage en Barbarie, ou Lettres écrites de l'ancienne Numidie, pendant les années 1785 et 1786, sur la religion, les coûtumes et les moeurs des Maures et des Arabes-Bédouins; avec un essai sur l'histoire naturelle. 2 vols. Paris.

1792 RIOU, (Captain). Journal of a Voyage from the Cape of Good Hope by J. van Reenen and others in Search of the Wreck of the Grosvenor. London.

SAUGNIER, ——, and BRISSON, ——. Voyages to the Coast of Africa, by Saugnier and Brisson, with subsequent Slavery, an Account of the Arabs, . . . Large folding map. 8vo. London.

> French original, Paris, 1791. See below, and also Brisson, 1789 above.
> Saugnier was shipwrecked on Jan. 17, 1784, near Cape Leven, and Brisson in July, 1785, at Cape Blanco, both in the Spanish zone of Rio del Oro.—Maggs, No. 534.

> 1791 SAUGNIER, ——. Relations de plusieurs voyages à la côte d'Afrique, à Maroc, au Sénégal, à Gorée, à Galam, etc., tirées des journaux (par J. B. de la Borde). Folding map. Paris.

WILFORD, (LIEUT.). Egypt and the Nile, from the ancient Books of the Hindus. In vol. III of *Asiatic Researches*.

1793   DALZEL, ARCHIBALD.   The History of Dahomey, an Inland Kingdom of Africa, compiled from Authentic Memoirs.   Folding map and plates.   4to.   London.

> The official situation which the author held gave him opportunities of gaining much valuable information, the accuracy of which may be depended upon.— Lowndes.

ROCHON, ALEXIS (Abbé).   Voyage to Madagascar and the East Indies . . . To which is added, M. Brunel's Memoirs on the Chinese Trade. . . . Translated by Joseph Trapp.   Folding map.   8vo.   London.

> Reprinted in Pinkerton XVI, 738-807. An abridged version is given in Capt. Oliver's edition of Drury. See Drury under 1729 above. French original, Paris (?), 1791. See below.
> Rochon was a member of several learned Academies in Europe.

> 1791 ROCHON, ALEXIS (Abbé). Voyage à Madagascar et aux Indes Orientales. Map. 8vo.

1793   RYE (Lieut., R. N.).   An Excursion to the Peak of Teneriffe in 1791.   London.

1794   BRYANT, JACOB.   Observations upon the Plagues inflicted upon the Egyptians; in which is shewn the Peculiarity of those Judgments and their Correspondence with the Rites and Idolatry of that People.   To these is prefixed, a prefatory Discourse concerning the Grecian Colonies from Egypt.   8vo.   London (?).   (Privately printed.)

FALCONBRIDGE, ANNA MARIA.   Two Voyages to Sierra Leone, 1791-92.   2nd edit.   12mo.   London.

> She was the wife of Alexander Falconbridge, surgeon on slave ships, later president of the Sierra Leone Company Council. She published an Autobiographical Narrative defending the slave trade and ridiculing her dead husband.—D.N.B.

MONTEFIORE, J.   An authentic Account of the late Expedition to Bulam, on the Coast of Africa; with a Description of the present Settlement of Sierra Leone and the adjacent Country.   8vo.   London.

THUNBERG, C. P.   For a description of the Cape of Good Hope region see his *Travels in Europe, Africa, and Asia* under FAR EAST.

> In Pinkerton XVI, 1-147.

1794-95   Substance of the Report delivered by the Court of Creditors of the Sierra Leone Company, to the General Court of the Proprietors, on

Thursday, the 27th of March, 1794. Together with the Report delivered on Thursday, Feb. 26th, 1795. Folding map of Sierra Leone. 8vo. London.

These reports contain much very interesting information concerning the history of Sierra Leone. The first report relates especially to the scandal of the slave trade there, and of the means adopted to secure slaves. The second report concerns the attack of a French squadron on the colony, and of the damage sustained by the colonists.—Maggs, No. 521.

WADSTROM, C. B. An Essay on Colonization, particularly applied to the Western Coast of Africa, with some Free Thoughts on Cultivation and Commerce; also Brief Descriptions of the Colonies already formed, or attempted, in Africa, including those of Sierra Leone and Bulama. Maps and plates. 2 vols. 4to. London.

DE PAUW, CORNEILLE. Philosophical Researches on the Egyptians and Chinese. Translated from the French. 2 vols. 8vo. London.

French original, 8vo, Berlin, Lyons, and Amsterdam, 1773. See below.

1773 DE PAUW, CORNEILLE. Recherches philosophiques sur les Egyptians et les Chinois. 2 vols. 8vo. Berlin, Lyons, et Amsterdam.

1795 An Account of the Colony of Sierra Leone, from its first Establishment in 1793. Map. 8vo. London.

1797 FALCONER, THOMAS. The Voyage of Hanno, translated and accompanied with the Greek Text; explained from the Accounts of modern Travellers; defended against the Objections of Mr. Dodwell and other Writers. Maps by Ptolemy, D'Anville, and Bougainville. 8vo. London.

The Greek original is also to be found in Hudson's *Greek Geographers.* See Hudson, 1698-1712, under GEOGRAPHY. See also Vincent, 1800, below. A modern edition edited by C. H. Schoff, Philadelphia, 1913.
That Hanno's expedition with a large body of Carthaginian colonists to the west coast of Africa was genuine seems to be borne out by the descriptions of the features observed.

1798 AFRICAN ASSOCIATION. Proceedings of the African Association. . . . Containing an Abstract of Mr. Park's Account of his Travels and Discoveries, abridged from his own Minutes by B. Edwards, Esq. Also Geographical Illustrations of Mr. Park's Journey, and of North Africa at large, by Major Rennell. 4to. London.

For the full relation of Park's Discoveries see Park, under 1799 below. A French version of Park's and Houghton's Voyages, Paris, 1798, seems from its date to be a translation of the above work. See below.

1798 (In French.) HOUGHTON et MUNGO-PARK. Voyages et décou-
      verte dans l'intérieur de l'Afrique. Avec 3 cartes et des éclaircisse-
      ments sur la Géographie d'Afrique, par Major Rennel. Traduit de
      l'anglais. 8vo. (Paris.) An VI (1798).

STOUT, B. (Captain). Narrative of the Loss of the Ship Hercules,
commanded by Captain B. Stout, on the Coast of Caffraria, the 16th
of June, 1796; also, A Circumstantial Detail of his Travels through the
Southern Deserts of Africa, and the Colonies, to the Cape of Good
Hope. With an Introductory Address to the Rt. Honourable John
Adams, President of the Continental Congress of America. 8vo.
London.

> This is written by Stout in the first person. The *Hercules* was an American
> ship and Stout a "native American."—Sabin.

BROWNE, WILLIAM G. Travels in Africa, Egypt, and Syria, in the
years 1792-98. Maps and Plates. 4to. London.

> Date of publication is given as 1800 in D.N.B. A portion in Pinkerton XVI,
> 827-838; XV, 108-162. Translated into Dutch, Amsterdam, 1800; into French,
> Paris, 1800; into German, Leipzig and Gera, 1800. See below.
> The author made several trips to the Near East and was murdered near
> Tabriz, Persia, in 1813. Lowndes calls this book a model for writers of travels
> to follow.

1800 (In Dutch.) Reize naar de binnenste gedeelten van Afrika, door Egypte,
      Syrie, en le Dar-Four. Plates. 2 vols. 8vo. Amsterdam.

1800 (In French.) Nouveau Voyage dans la Haute et Basse Egypte, la Syrie,
      le Darfur, où aucun Européen n'avait pénétré, fait depuis les années
      1792 jusqu'en 1798 par W. G. Browne, contenant de détails curieux, sur
      diverses contrées de l'intérieur de l'Afrique, sur l'Anatolie, sur Con-
      stantinople et Paswas-Oglow, etc. Avec des Notes critiques sur les
      ouvrages de Savary et de Volney, traduit de l'Anglais sur le deuxième
      édition, par J. Castéra. Maps and plates. Atlas. 2 vols. 8vo. Paris.

1800 (In German.) Reisen in Afrika, Aegypten, und Syrien in den Jahren
      1792-98. Aus dem Englischen mit Anmerkungen des Übersetzers. Maps
      and plates. 8vo. Leipzig and Gera.

LEYDEN, JOHN. An Historical and Philosophical Sketch of the Discoveries and Settlements of Europeans in Northern and Western Africa, at the Close of the Eighteenth Century. 12mo. Edinburgh.

> Leyden was much fascinated by the subject of Africa and even desired to go
> there as a missionary. In his work he took Raynal for a model. The book was
> well received and was translated into German, Bremen, 8vo, 1802. It forms the
> basis of Hugh Murray's *Historical Account of Discoveries and Travels in Africa*,
> 2 vols., 8vo, Edinburgh, 1818.

PARK, MUNGO. Travels in the Interior Districts of Africa: performed
under the Direction and Patronage of the African Association in the
years 1795, 1796, and 1797. With an Appendix, containing geograph-

ical Illustrations of Africa. By Major Rennell. Maps, portrait, and plates. 4to. London.

> 2nd edit., London, 1799; reprinted in Pinkerton XVI, 839-917, in the form of an extract from the edition of 1810. Numerous reprints in the 19th century, among which may be mentioned that in the Everyman's Library. Translated into French, Paris. See above under African Association, 1798.
> Through the friendship of Sir Joseph Banks, president of the Royal Society, the author was selected by the African Association to lead an exploring expedition into the interior of Africa. He was the first of modern Europeans to reach the well-nigh fabulous waters of the Niger. After returning from his first expedition Park settled down as a physician at Peebles, Scotland. In 1805, he set out on his second Niger journey at a bad time of the year. His party of 44 Europeans died one by one, and the five survivors, in their endeavors to force their way through to the termination of the Niger, were all drowned in an attempt to escape from a party of attacking natives.—From Maggs, No. 521. His first voyage to the Gambia revealed many of the secrets of that hinterland. Both the public and the African Association were greatly gratified by his wonderful exploit, and the Royal Society gave him its warmest approbation. They insisted that his story be drawn up in narrative form and published for his own benefit. This work, along with Doughty's *Arabia Deserta*, should thoroughly dispel any romantic notions of the Arabs and Moors. It is indeed among the classics of travel literature.

1799 SONNINI DE MANONCOUR, CHARLES NICOLAS SIGISBERT. Travels in Upper and Lower Egypt, undertaken by order of the Government of France. Translated by H. Hunter. Portrait, map, and plates. 3 vols. 8vo. London.

> Reprinted in 4to., London, 1800. French original, Paris, 1799. See below.
> This work treats of matter usually excluded from circulating libraries, but here related with the utmost candor : such as Egyptian female circumcision, serpent eating, Egyptian Lesbianism, women's cosmetics and use of depilatories, sensuality and effeminacy of the baths, red leprosy, masculine beauty, Egyptian homosexuality, circumcision of boys, etc.—Bookseller's Note. The journey was undertaken, on the recommendation of Cuvier, to collect rare Egyptian birds.

> 1799 SONNINI DE MANONCOUR, CHARLES NICOLAS SIGISBERT. Voyage dans la Haute et Basse Egypte, fait par ordre de l'ancien Gouvernement (de 1777 à 1780), et contenant des Observations de tous genres ; avec une collection de 40 planches, gravées en taille-douce, par P. Tardieu, contenant de portraits, vues, plans, carte géographique, antiquités, plantes, animaux, etc. . . . dessinés sur lieux, sous les yeux de l'auteur. Atlas 3 vols. Fol. Paris.

1800 ABDOLLATIPHI. Compendium Rerum memorabilium Egypti, Arabice et Latine, cura J. White. Oxford.

> For a slightly varied title see below the edition published in Germany, 1776.

> 1776 ABDOLLATIPHI. Abulsedae, Descriptio Aegypti, Arabice et Latine, cura J. D. Michaelis. Göttingen.

ANTES, JOHN. Observations on the Manners and Customs of the Egyptians, the Overflowing of the Nile and its Effects ; with Remarks on the Plague and other subjects. Written during a Residence of twelve years in Cairo and its vicinity. Map of Egypt. 4to. London.

NORRY, CHARLES. An Account of the French Expedition to Egypt. From the French. 8vo. London.

This work contains a view of Lower Egypt, its cities, monuments, and inhabitants, with a particular description and measurement of Pompey's Pillar, illustrated by a plate.—Ibrahim Hilmy.

RENNELL, JAMES (Major). The Geographical System of Herodotus examined and explained by a comparison with those of other ancient Authors, and with modern Geography. In the course of the work are introduced Dissertations on the Itinerary State of the Greeks, the Expedition of Darius Hystaspes to Scythia, the Position and Remains of ancient Babylon, the Alluvions of the Nile, and Canals of Suez; the Oasis and Temple of Jupiter Ammon, the ancient Circumnavigation of Africa and other subjects of History and Geography. The whole explained by eleven maps adapted to the different subjects, and accompanied by a complete Index. 4to. London.

In French, Paris, 1800. See below.

1800 (In French.) L'Afrique par le Major Rennell. Maps and plates. 2 vols. 8vo. Paris.

RIPAULT, LOUIS MADALENE (Abbé). Report of the Commission of Arts to the First Consul Bonaparte on the Antiquities of Upper Egypt, and the present State of all the Temples, Palaces, Obelisks, Statues, Tombs, Pyramids, . . . From the Cataracts of the Nile to Cairo; with an accurate Description of the Pictures with which they are decorated. Translated from the French of Citizen Ripault. 8vo. London.

French original, Paris, 1800. See below.

1800 RIPAULT, LOUIS MADALENE (Abbé). Description abrégée des principaux Monuments de la Haute Egypte, accompagnée de détails sur les tableaux, qui, en les décorant, servent à faire conjecturer à quelles divinités les temples etaient consacrés. (Extrait du Moniteur, No. 300, 3 Messidor an 8.) 8vo. Paris.

VINCENT, WILLIAM (Dean of Westminster). The Periplus of the Erythrean Sea. Part I, containing an Account of the Navigation of the Ancients, from the Sea of Suez to the Coast of Zanguebar, with Dissertations. Portrait of Vasco da Gama, plate and 3 maps. 4to. London.

A second part was published in 1805.
This work was written about 60 A.D., seemingly for the use of merchants It gives a description of the East coast of Africa from Cape Guardafui to Zanzibar, as well as some details of the Arabian and the west coast of India. See McBrindle under 1879 and Schoff under 1912, EAST INDIES.

WHARTON, RICHARD. Observations on the Authenticity of Bruce's Travels in Abyssinia, in reply to some Passages in Brown's Travels through Egypt, Africa, and Syria; to which is added, a comparative View of Life and Happiness in Europe and Caffraria. 4to. Newcastle upon Tyne.

> See Bruce 1790 above.

WHITE, WILLIAM. For a description of Da Lagoda Bay on the eastern coast of Africa, see his *Journal of a Voyage from Madras to Columbo* under EAST INDIES.

ADDENDA

1801 DAMBERGER, CHRISTIAN F. Travels through the Interior of Africa, from the Cape of Good Hope to Morocco in the Kingdoms of Mataman, Angola, Muschako, Haoussa, . . . and thence through the Sahara Desert, between the years 1781 and 1797. Map and 3 coloured plates. 8vo. London.

GRANT, CHARLES (Viscount de Vaux). The History of Mauritius and Neighboring Islands, from their first Discovery to the present Time, composed principally from the Papers and Memoirs of Baron Grant, who resided Twenty Years in the Island. 2 folding maps. 4to. London.

> From his acquaintance with most of the scientific and nautical men who visited the island, he has been enabled to collect much information connected with its physical state, its harbours, climate, soil, productions, and the manners of the inhabitants.—Stevenson's *Voyages and Travels,* quoted by Sotheran.

1801-04 BARROW, JOHN. An Account of Travels into the Interior of Southern Africa in the years 1797-98. Maps and plates. 2 vols. 4to. London.

> 2nd edit., with additions and corrections, 2 vols., 4to, London, 1806. Translated into French, Paris, 1801. See below.
> Barrow travelled to the Cape of Good Hope as the private secretary of Lord Macartney. His journies, which added materially to geographical knowledge, were undertaken after the British had ousted the Dutch from the Cape. They took him as far as the Upper Orange River. No one had as yet reached the regions of the Zambesi. Barrow was officially connected with the establishment of the new government. He is better known for his work in Polar exploration.

> 1801 (In French.) Voyage dans la partie méridionale de l'Afrique, fait dans les années 1797 et 1798. Suivi de la description de l'état présent, de la population, et du produit de cette importante colonie. Traduit de l'anglais, par L. De Grandpré. Plate and map of the colony of the Cape of Good Hope, engraved by Tardieu. 2 vols. 8vo. Paris.

1802 HORNEMANN, FREDERICK. Journal of Travels from Cairo to
      Mourzouk, the Capital of the Kingdom of Fezzan in Africa, 1797-98.
      Folding map. London.

> Hornemann was one of the unlucky four sent out by the African Association
> to solve the vexatious question of the elusive Niger—where was its source, in
> what direction did it flow, and where did it empty. He set out from Egypt,
> reached Múrzuk, but ended up in Tripoli. Starting from that country he made an-
> other attempt, but died somewhere on the Niger, without being able to inform the
> world of what he accomplished. Undoubtedly the date should be 1789, instead
> of 1797-98 as given above.

1803 GOLBERRY, S. M. X. Travels in Africa, 1785-88, in the Western
      Countries between Cape Blanco and Cape Palmas. Map and 4 views.
      2 vols. London.

1804 RENSHAW, R. Voyage to the Cape of Good Hope and up the Red Sea,
      with Travels in Egypt, through the Deserts, . . . Frontispiece. 8vo.
      Manchester.

> Another edit., with additions, portrait, 12mo, Manchester, 1813.
> The author spent from 1796 to 1801 at the Cape; he describes the forts at
> Cape Town, the Hottentots, Bushmen, Kaffirs, etc. He was a native of Man-
> chester, where he was born in 1769; he died at Iowa Falls, in the United States,
> in 1859.—Bookseller's Note.

1805 BEAVER, PHILIP (Captain). African Memoranda: an Attempt to
      Establish a British Settlement on the Island of Bulama, 1792, with
      Notices of the Tribes, Soil, Productions, etc. Folding map. 4to.
      London.

1808-1814 ABD ALLATIF. Extract from the Relation respecting Egypt.
      Translated into French by Sylvestre de Sacy, Paris, 1810. In Pinker-
      ton XV, 802-839 (translation).

> This Relation was composed in 1203.

PROYART, ABBE. History of Loango, Kakongo, and other Kingdoms
      of Africa (Paris, 1776). In Pinkerton XVI, 548-597.

SANTOS, JOANO DOS (Rev. Father). History of Eastern Ethiopia.
      Written originally in Portuguese, published at Paris, 1684. In Pinker-
      ton XVI, 337 (should be 675)-737.

> Pinkerton XVII cites an edition, fol., Evora, 1607.

1841 PEPYS, SAMUEL. Life, Journals, and Correspondence of, including
a Narrative of his Voyage to Tangier, deciphered from the shorthand
MSS. in the Bodleian Library, by the Rev. John Smith, now first published from the originals. Portrait. 2 vols. 8vo. London.

1865 BARBOSA, DUARTE. For a description of the east coasts of Africa
see his *A Description of the Coasts of East Africa and Malabar,* under
EAST INDIES.

1871 BETHENCOURT, MESSIRE JEAN DE. The Canarian or Book of
the Conquest of Canarians in the year 1402, by Messire Jean de Bethencourt, Kt. Composed by Pierre Bontier and Jean le Verrier. Translated and Edited by Richard Henry Major, F.S.A., Keeper of Maps,
Brit. Mus., Sec. R.G.S.M. Map and illus. Hak. Soc., ser. I, vol. 46.
London.

1873 LACERDA, F. J. M. DE. Lacerda's Journey to Cazembe in 1798, translated and annotated by Captain R. F. Burton. Map. 8vo. London.

> Lacerda had done some exploration on the river Cunene between the Zaire
> and the Cape of Good Hope in 1787. He now proposed to attempt a practicable
> route between the east and west coast of Africa, making Mozambique the impor-
> tant trading post. He reached the country of the Cazembe but he died there. His
> journey forwarded the knowledge of the geography of the interior Africa, though
> it failed in its main purpose.

1881 ALVAREZ, FRANCISCO (Father). Narrative of the Portuguese Embassy to Abyssinia during the years 1520-27. By Father Francisco Alvarez. Translated from the Portuguese and Edited, with Notes and
an Introduction, by Lord Stanley of Alderley. Hak. Soc., ser. I, vol.
64. London.

1890 LEGUAT, FRANCOIS. The Voyage of Francois Leguat, of Bresse,
1690-98, to Rodriguez, Mauritius, and the Cape of Good Hope. Transcribed from the First English Edition, 1708. Edited and Annotated by
Capt. Samuel Pasfield Oliver, (late) R. A. Illus. and maps. 2 vols.
Hak. Soc., ser. I, vols, 82-83. London.

See under 1708, EAST INDIES.

1896-98 AZURARA, GOMES EANNES DE. The Chronicle of the Discovery and Conquest of Guinea. Written by Gomes Eannes de Azurara.
Now first done into English and edited by Charles Raymond Beazley,

M.A., F.R.G.S., and Edgar Prestage, B.A.   Maps and illus.   Hak.
Soc., ser. I, vols. 95 and 100.   London.

> Vol. 95 has an introduction on the life and writings of the Chronicler; vol.
> 100, an introduction on the early history of African exploration, cartography, etc.

1897 D(UBOIS), SIEUR.   Voyages made by the Sieur D. B. to the Islands
of Madagascar and Mascarene, 1669-1672. Translated and edited from
the French by Capt. Pasfield Oliver. Facsimiles of all the maps and
plates, views and illustrations of people and their manners and customs, natural history, etc.   8vo.   London.

1902 CASTANHOSO and BERMUDEZ.   The Portuguese Expedition to
Abyssinia in 1541, as narrated by Castanhoso and Bermudez. Edited
by Richard Stephen Whiteway, late I.C.S. With a Bibliography by
Basil H. Soulsby, F.S.A., Superintendent of the Map Dept., Brit. Mus.
Map and illus. Hak. Soc., ser. II, vol. 10.   London.

1907 ESPINOSA, ALONSO DE (Friar).   The Guanches of Tenerife, The
Holy Image of Our Lady of Candelaria. With the Spanish Conquest
and Settlement. By the Friar Alonso de Espinosa, of the Order of
Preachers, 1594. Translated and edited, with Notes and an Introduction, by Sir Clements Markham, K.C.B., President of the Hakluyt
Society. With a Bibliography of the Canary Islands, A.D. 1341-1907,
chronologically arranged . . . and an alphabetical list of authors, editors,
and titles. 2 maps and 4 illus. Hak. Soc., ser. II, vol. 21.   London.

1921-25 MENTZEL, O. F.   Geographical and Topographical Description of
the Cape of Good Hope (1785), translated by H. J. Mandelbrote.
Folding plan.   2 vols.   8vo.   London.

1924 BARNARD, LADY ANNE.   Lady Anne Barnard at the Cape of Good
Hope, 1797-1802. By D. Fairbridge. Illustrated by a series of sketches
made by Lady Anne Barnard.   8vo.   Oxford.

> When Andrew Barnard sailed for the Cape of Good Hope in 1797 as Colonial
> Secretary to that newly won and little known colony, he was accompanied by his
> wife, Lady Anne. She kept a diary which gives an accurate and unconventional
> picture of early days at the Cape. The author has woven selections from the
> diary into a readable narrative of considerable historical and general interest.—
> Bookseller's Note.

1930 OWEN, NICHOLAS.   Journal of a Slave-Dealer. "A View of some
remarkable Axcedents in the Life of Nics. Owen on the Coast of Af-

rica from the Year 1746 to the Year 1757." Edited, with an Introduction, by Eveline Martin. 2 maps and 16 plates. 8vo. London.

> This journal of an Irishman, who set out to make his fortune as a trader on the American and West African coasts, is of absorbing interest. It is now published from the original MS. Owen had many adventures of varying success which he narrates with shrewd humor. He describes the natives and their customs, and also the plants and animals of the coast. He provides us with much valuable detail about the navigation and trade of the Atlantic of his day.—Bookseller's Note.

1934   The Early Cape Hottentots described in the Writings of Olfert Dapper (1668), William Ten Rhyne (1686), and Johannes Gulielmus Grevenbrock (1695). The original Texts with Translation into English by I. Schapera and B. Farrington, edited with Introduction and Notes by I. Schapera. Plates. 8vo. London.

End of Volume I.

ERRATA ET CORRIGENDA

Page   3, line   1, *for* Cadamasto *read* Cadamosto
Page   v, line 29, *for* takes *read* take
Page   7, line 22, *for* Varleill *read* Carleill
Page   8, line   6 (from bottom), *for* Straits *read* Strait
Page 13, line 26, *for* Puttock *read* Puttick; likewise pp. 43, 45
Page 17, line   8, *before* London *insert* 20 vols.
Page 21, line 16, *for* der Loziere *read* de Lozière
Page 25, line   1, *for* 1806 *read* 1805-10; line 2, *for* 6 vols. *read* 11 vols.
Page 26, line 12 (from bottom), *for* 1902 *read* 1903
Page 29, line 25, *for* Indian *read* Indiam
Page 31, line   6 (from bottom), *for* Land-Reyen na Ooost *read* Land-Reysen na Oost
Page 33, line 14 (from bottom), *for date* 1780-06 *read* 1780-86
Page 41, line 30, *for* Straits *read* Strait; likewise in
          line 32, *for* were *read* was
          line 18 (from bottom), *for* Jounal *read* Journal
Page 52, line   9 (from bottom), *for* Novigationum *read* Navigationum
          line   6 (from bottom), *for* parelia *read* proelia
          line   3 (from bottom), *for* appararus *read* apparatus
Page 62, line   5 (from bottom), *for* and *read* und
Page 64, line 21 (from bottom), *for* Narative *read* Narrative
Page 66, line   7, *for* Mesapotamia *read* Mesopotamia
Page 69, line 14, *for* Arnold *read* ARNOLD
Page 70, line 30, *for* Lyons *read* Lyon
Page 72, line 10 (from bottom), *for* 1621 *read* 1627
Page 80, line 31, *delete* published in
Page 82, line   9 (from bottom), *for* 1772 *read* 1782; likewise pp. 196, 256
Page 99, line at bottom of page, *for* London *read* Lugduni
Page 101, line   6, *for* Mentz *read* Mainz
Page 105, line   5, *for* Winchelsea *read* Winchilsea
Page 121, line 11 (from bottom), *for* Minou *read* Misson
Page 124, line 14, *place date* 1776 *before* DRYDEN
Page 131, line   6 (from bottom), *insert* de *before* l'anglais
Page 134, line 14, *delete* item *under* Campbell
Page 135, line   8, *for* coxscomb *read* coxcomb
Page 138, line   6, *for* Tritical *read* Critical
Page 142, line   7, *for* Bolch *read* Borch
Page 145, line   2, *for* Bern *read* Born
Page 147, line 12 (from bottom), *insert* RUTLEDGE, SIR JOHN JAMES
                      as author
Page 165, line 16 (from bottom), *for* Lallemant *read* Lallemand
Page 166, line   1, *for* Oetna *read* Aetna
Page 167, line   7, *for* Robispierre *read* Robespierre
Page 174, line 14, *for* marks *read* mark
Page 177, line 25, *for* prestigation *read* prestidigitation
Page 180, line   3, *for* Shaftsbury *read* Shaftsesbury
Page 181, line   4, *insert* VRIGNY, M. DE LE, COMTE DE *after date*
Page 195, line   7 (from bottom), *for* officer *read* officier
Page 196, line 14, *for* Biog, Gén. *read* Biog. Gén.

(403)

Page 198, line 25, *delete* comma *after* opinions
Page 208, line 9 (from bottom), *for* Arabici *read* Arabice
Page 211, line 9, *for* Turcarum *read* Turcorum
      line 9 (from bottom), *for* Pathmos *read* Patmos
Page 217, line 6, *for* original *read* edition
Page 220, line 20 (from bottom), *place* comma *after* D'ARVIEUX
Page 226, line 28, *for* propoganda *read* propaganda
Page 237, line 21, *for* COBHAM, C. B. *read* COBHAM, C. D.
Page 238, line 8 (from bottom), *for* Pausanius *read* Pausanias
Page 243, line 19, *for* 1902 *read* 1903
Page 244, line 20, *for* Peregrinatium *read* Peregrinationum
Page 248, line 8, *for* 1665 *read* 1664
Page 249, line 16, *for* den König *read* dem König
Page 253, line 11, date for this and three succeeding items 1744-48
Page 255, line 16, *for* CEREAU, J. K. *read* CEREAU, J. A.
Page 258, line 21 (from bottom), *for* Stanley Alderley *read* Stanley of Alderley
Page 260, line 4, *for* Birwood *read* Birdwood
Page 267, line 3, *for* hte *read* the
Page 273, line 3, *for* editit *read* edidit
Page 278, line 13, *for* 1685 *read* 1686; *for* Guiana *read* Guinea
Page 298, line 16, *for* C. G. Eckeberg *read* C. A. Eckeberg
      line 21, *for* oeswer *read* oefwer
Page 302, line 4, *for* Tippon *read* Tippoo
Page 304, line 18, *for* JOHN *read* JAMES
Page 305, line 13 (from bottom), *for* Mahummedan *read* Muhammedan
Page 307, line 12 (from bottom), *for* Raap *read* Kaap
Page 314, line 8 (from bottom), *for* de Gama *read* da Gama
Page 317, line 5, *for* Heffer *read* Heffer & Sons; likewise line 15, and also elsewhere
Page 320, line 9 (from bottom), *delete* de *before* del Reino
Page 327, line 5 (from bottom), *for* edition *read* version
Page 345, line 15, *for* S. Castéra *read* J. Castéra
Page 378, line 10, *for* 1744 *read* 1745